COST ACCOUNTING
Principles and Practice

THE
WILLARD J. GRAHAM SERIES
IN ACCOUNTING

Consulting Editor   ROBERT N. ANTHONY
Harvard University

COST ACCOUNTING
Principles and Practice

The First Phase of Managerial Control for
Attaining and Improving the Profit Objective
of Business Operations

JOHN J. W. NEUNER, Ph.D., C.P.A.
Baruch College of the City University of New York
School of Business Administration, Iona College

EIGHTH EDITION, 1973

Richard D. Irwin, Inc.
Homewood, Illinois 60430
IRWIN-DORSEY INTERNATIONAL, London, England   WC2H 9NJ
IRWIN-DORSEY LIMITED, Georgetown, Ontario   L7G 4B3

© BUSINESS PUBLICATIONS, INC., 1938
© RICHARD D. IRWIN, INC., 1942, 1947, 1952, 1957, 1962, 1967, and 1973

Eighth Edition

First Printing, January 1973
Second Printing, August 1973
Third Printing, June 1974
Fourth Printing, June 1975

ISBN 0-256-00375-0
Library of Congress Catalog Card No. 73-180492
Printed in the United States of America

Preface

Modern management of American business firms strives constantly to improve the profit picture of its operating results. One of the most important areas in which this objective may be achieved is through cost determination and control. Profits are improved by increasing the sales volume, or decreasing the per unit costs, or through a combination of these two activities. The control and reduction of costs are achieved through prompt cost compilation, using budgets and analyses to plan and control manufacturing operations, and fixing departmental and supervisory responsibility for the results.

The purposes of this revision are to update *the cost accounting principles and procedures* in a rapidly changing business world, and to improve the teachability of one of the most popular collegiate cost accounting textbooks by reorganizing the presentation of its information. Written from the cost accountant's viewpoint, in a direct, concise manner with a minimum of verbiage, it presents the manner in which costs are compiled; details the accepted procedures to meet business, taxing, regulatory, and public objectives; and discusses how management can receive and analyze this cost information. It involves recording, communicating, and interpreting the basic cost information, and attempts to provide a complete coverage of the subjects of cost determination, planning, and control for the accountant.

To meet these objectives, the text materials have been reorganized into four sections, namely:

Part I   Cost Determination and Analysis
Part II   Planning and Control of Costs
Part III   Profit Planning by Making Special Cost Analyses
Part IV   Applied Cost Determination Procedures

In reorganizing Part I, the Cost Determination and Analysis section, process or departmental cost procedures were placed earlier in the text. This was considered desirable because, in modern industry, most firms operate a continuous production cycle on a departmental control basis, rather than on the job order system. The principles and procedures used in accumulating material, labor, and manufacturing overhead costs are discussed after the two basic systems—job order and departmental or process—are described, since the principles and practices are equally applicable to both systems. From the beginning of this text, constant emphasis has been placed on separating the costs into their fixed and variable (controllable) elements. This first section includes the discussion of the distribution cost procedures and analysis, since this phase of accounting management is part of the complete picture of making and selling a product at a profit. Due to the increasing use of electronic data processing equipment in accounting and production control, a chapter has been added in this section descriptive of the EDP principles, procedures, and application to these two phases of control.

Part II of this text emphasizes the planning and control of operating costs. This section covers the topics of budgets, estimated costs, standard costs, installing and updating the cost accounting system, and the use of direct costing as applied to the cost determination procedures.

Part III is devoted to profit planning through special analyses. The relationship of costs and volumes to profits (C-V-P) through break-even charts, special situation analyses, and nonmanufacturing cost applications is presented.

Part IV covers the application of cost accounting procedures to a few specialized continuous production industries, and to a description of standard cost procedures in actual use.

In addition to reorganizing and updating the cost accounting practices and procedures, new problem material and review questions, carefully graded for effective instruction and learning, have been provided. Most of the problems require not only an accounting solution but, in many instances, a managerial analysis or interpretation of the data thus recorded and reported. For those instructors whose course outlines and method of instruction enable its use, a revised and abbreviated practice set—Job Order Cost Set—has been provided; it may be completed after Chapter 13.

The author acknowledges his indebtedness to the professional organizations—National Association of Accountants, the American Institute of Certified Public Accountants, the Financial Executives Institute, and the Society of Industrial and Cost Accountants of Canada—for the use of material and problems which appeared in their publications. The author is especially appreciative of the help given by the many instructors and students who, over the years, have contributed suggestions and help in this and the previous editions. Particular recognition must be given to the staff members of the Baruch College of the City University of New York, namely, Professors Max Zimering, Calvin Engler, and Leopold

Schachner; and to Deans Mathew Amat and Dominick Carbone of Iona College, School of Business Administration, for their constant interest and encouragement in this publication.

Helpful criticisms and comments were made on the original and revised editions by the late Willard J. Graham of the University of North Carolina, and most recently by Robert N. Anthony of Harvard University. I am especially indebted to Professor Janet Sievers of the accounting faculty at Valparaiso University who checked all of the problems in the text and validated their efficiency and accuracy.

The preceding edition was prepared with the collaboration of Samuel Frumer. I wish to acknowledge his valuable contributions to the seventh edition as well as the reactions, comments, and criticisms from colleagues in different kinds of institutions, so useful in evaluating it and planning this new edition.

January 1973   JOHN J. W. NEUNER

Contents

counting Firm. Accounting for Two or More Products Prepared from the Same Material in Department I. Alternative Cost of Production Report for Two Products from Same Material in Department I.

Storerooms. Controlling the Investment in Materials Inventories. Managerial Problems in the Material Acquisition.

Used in Departmentalizing Indirect Factory Costs: *Bases for Allocating and Prorating Manufacturing Overhead Departmentally. Factory Survey for the Distribution of Indirect Costs to the Departments. Transfer the Service Department Overhead Costs to the Producing Departments. Computing the Departmental Predetermined Overhead Rate. Applying Manufacturing Overhead Costs Departmentally. Recording the Actual Manufacturing Overhead Costs.* Analyzing Overhead Costs into Their Fixed and Variable Elements. Absorption Costing versus Direct Costing. Controlling Costs through the Use of a Flexible Manufacturing Overhead Budget.

PART II. PLANNING AND CONTROL OF COSTS

part I

COST DETERMINATION AND ANALYSIS

Cost determination, cost accounting, and the managerial use of cost accounting data have been undergoing many changes in the past 10 years. Some of these have been due to the changes in the organization of business through conglomeration; some through the development and use of electronic data processing of cost information; and some to the managerial need of "instant cost information."

Basically all cost control is the use of an efficient method of *cost determination,* whether this is manual or electronic. This means that certain acceptable cost accounting and income tax regulations must be understood and applied.

To achieve the maximum profit potential of a business operation is the goal of management. This goal is achieved by the reduction of costs and the increase of sales. It follows then that the more reliable the costs are and the speed with which they are made available for managerial use, the more satisfactory will be the cost accountant's contribution to management.

Although minor variations may exist, there are two functional cost determination systems: (1) job order, and (2) process or departmental costs for continuous production. The latter is the more predominant in modern industry because it favors large-scale production efficiencies. In Part I of this text, the cost determination principles and practices are discussed, with greater emphasis on process or departmental costs. The discussion of the two cost determination systems is followed by the accounting principles and practices affecting material costs, labor costs, and manufacturing overhead costs, as these affect both systems. The principles and practices of distribution cost analysis and the use of the electronic data processing have been included in this cost determination section.

This section of the text is devoted not only to the methods of determining costs but also to the accounting records for such operations. It is a reorganization of the material in the previous editions with a shifting of the sequence to make it more logical and easier to study and comprehend.

The aspects of cost determination are covered in the following sequence:

Managerial and Organizational Aspects of Cost Determination
Historical Job Order Cost Determination
Segregating the Cost Accounting and Financial Accounting Records
Historical Departmental or Process Cost Determination — Part I
Historical Departmental or Process Cost Determination — Part II
Cost Accounting for Coproducts, Joint Products, and By-products
Managerial Control of Material Acquisition Costs
Cost Determination of Materials Used
Labor Cost Control
Manufacturing Overhead Costs Applied to Production
Accounting for Actual Manufacturing Overhead Costs
Distribution Cost Analyses and Control
Electronic Data Processing for Cost Determination and Control

Once the two basic cost accounting systems — job order and process — have been presented, the managerial control of the manufacturing and distribution operations and problems are discussed as these relate to material costs, labor costs, and manufacturing overhead for both systems.

Since modern business methods must take into consideration the use of high-speed mechanical and electronic data processing, a chapter has been devoted to the use of this equipment in compiling efficiently the vast amount of cost determination data required for modern managerial control.

chapter **1**

Managerial and Organizational Aspects of Cost Determination

THE NATURE OF COST ACCOUNTING

The more modern and probably the more accurate description of cost accounting is cost determination because it encompasses four managerial functions: *planning* the manufacturing operations through the use of budgetary procedures; *organizing* the administrative and manufacturing procedures and recording the necessary financial data relating thereto; *measuring and controlling* these procedures; and finally, *evaluating* management's effectiveness in producing and distributing its products.

Every successful business operates through a previously made plan of what should be manufactured based upon what can be sold. This plan may be on a monthly, quarterly, seasonal, or annual basis; and it is known as a budget. Without it only irresponsible confusion will occur in the business organization.

Organizing the manufacturing and distribution operations of a business is a continuous procedure which results in the use of the best equipment, the most efficient flow of work in the plant, and the most profitable methods of selling the products. In the manufacturing operations, three elements of costs are always present: materials used, labor costs, and a variety of manufacturing overhead costs. The costs of each of these must be constantly studied through a modern system of accumulation and recording.

Measuring and controlling manufacturing and distribution activities result from the recording of the material, labor, manufacturing overhead, and distribution costs. Management must decide how much detail should be recorded in the cost determination system to establish this measurement and control.

3

Finally, the ultimate objective of these three phases of cost determination is the evaluation of what has been done. Through the use of reports, management will make a comparison of what has been done with what the planned or budgeted data called for, to ascertain what corrective action must be taken in the future. Only through a complete, unified system of cost determination will management be able to increase profits by reducing costs.

Cost determination can thus be summarized as consisting of four phases: planning, organizing, measuring and controlling, and evaluating. Cost determination is not as simple as may be implied by the above brief statement, because operations in manufacturing firms vary greatly. Cost determination will therefore be influenced by (1) the size of the firm; (2) the number of the products being manufactured; (3) whether the products are standardized or made to specific customers' requirements; (4) the complexity of the manufacturing and distribution activities; (5) the attitude of management toward the compilation and use of cost data; and finally, (6) the expense to be incurred in compiling cost information. It should be emphasized that modern successful business management recognizes that an effective system of cost determination and control is an absolute necessity.

COST CLASSIFICATIONS AND CONCEPTS

Before proceeding to the specific cost determination methods and problems, the reader should have a clear understanding of the various cost concepts. There is no one definition of the term "cost." The term "cost" must be interpreted in accordance with the conditions and purposes for which it is used. It is a monetary measurement incurred or to be incurred for a specific purpose, that is, the planning, measuring, or controlling and evaluating of business operations. Some of these descriptions and classifications are:

1. Classification on the basis of the elements of the finished product.
2. Functional business activity classification.
3. Classification on the basis of the manufacturing operations.
4. Classification according to the time factor of cost determination.
5. Costs defined on the basis of the volume of production.
6. Costs for nonmanufacturing operations.
7. Costs used in making special-purpose analyses.

1. *Costs defined on the basis of the elements of the finished product.* The most commonly used classification of costs refers to the three elements that are totaled in computing the cost of making a salable product. These are:

a) *Direct material* — costs of the substances which can be identified with a specific unit of production or can be identified with a department or process.

b) *Direct labor* — wages paid for work done on a specific unit of production or performed in a specific department.

c) *Manufacturing overhead costs,* sometimes known as manufacturing expenses, are the variety of indirect manufacturing costs which cannot be identified and allocated, or which it is inexpedient to attempt to allocate, to specific units of production.

Diagrammatically, these may be shown as:

Direct material costs ($5,000) + Direct labor costs ($15,000) +
Manufacturing overhead costs ($4,000) = Work-in-process costs ($24,000)
less Cost of unfinished work (work-in-process inventory) ($6,000) =
Cost of production — finished goods ($18,000).

2. *Costs classified according to the function of business activity.* For example:

a) *Manufacturing costs* deal with the cost of producing or manufacturing a definite product.

b) *Distribution or marketing costs* are incurred in selling a finished product and the sale of parts and services.

c) *Administrative costs* are incurred in administering and setting policies for all the activities of a business.

3. *Costs classified according to the nature of manufacturing operations.*

a) *Job order costs* which refer to the material, labor, and manufacturing overhead necessary to complete a *specific* order or lot of finished goods. These goods may be manufactured for a specific customer or for the stock room. In this type of costs, a *definite quantity* is to be manufactured on a specific order. All material, labor, and overhead costs are accumulated and recorded on the basis of the amount used or assigned to this particular job or order. Since each job or order is given a number, the accumulations are recorded on a form known as the *job order cost sheet,* to which an identifying number has been assigned.

b) *Process* or *departmental costs* are used by firms manufacturing products on a more or less continuous or regular basis; and they include the production of such items as gas, electricity, chemicals, petroleum products, coal, minerals, etc. In such firms, costs are accumulated not on a job order basis but by *departments* or *processes,* for a *definite period of time.* Costs are recorded on *departmental cost sheets* and summarized on *cost of production reports.*

c) *Class costs* are a form of job order costs in which a number of jobs may be combined into a single production cycle, providing that they include a number of products of similar sizes or classes. The best illustration of this method is found in gray iron foundries where costs are determined by classes such as:

Group I — a number of job orders calling for castings weighing from 1 to 10 pounds.

Group II — refers to castings weighing from 11 to 25 pounds.

Group III — refers to castings from 26 to 50 pounds, etc.

To compute the cost per pound of castings, costs must be apportioned on the basis of the amount of labor involved in each group or class of products.

d) *Assembly costs* are a form of job order costs used by firms which manufacture or purchase finished parts to be used in assembling a salable product. Many firms manufacturing such products as oil burners, washing machines, or vacuum cleaners use this method of assembling parts into a salable product. Assembly costs involve primarily labor and manufacturing overhead, since the costs of materials were determined when the parts were manufactured or purchased. The summary sheets used for compiling these costs are known as *assembly* or *subassembly cost sheets.*

4. *Costs classified according to time factor of cost determination* would include the following:

a) *Postmortem* or *historical costs* which may be job order, process, assembly, or class costs determined during the manufacturing operations but not available until some time *after* the completion of the manufacturing operations.

b) *Estimated, standard,* or *predetermined costs* which also may refer to job order, process, assembly, or class costs computed or ascertained *before* manufacturing operations begin. In other words, it is frequently necessary to compute beforehand the *expected* costs of manufacturing a product — either to fix selling prices or to measure effectiveness of the historical costs.

c) *Daily, weekly,* or *monthly costs* which refer essentially to continuous process work and merely indicate the period of time for which the summaries are prepared.

5. *Costs classified on the basis of volume of production.* Costs sometimes have a definite relationship to the volume of production. As

such, they are described as *fixed* or *variable,* and sometimes further delineated as *semivariable.*

a) *Fixed costs* remain fairly constant and do not fluctuate with the volume of production, such as fire insurance on the buildings, depreciation of buildings and machinery, real estate taxes, and rent.
b) *Variable costs* fluctuate in the same manner as the volume of production. Among these are direct materials, direct labor, and such manufacturing overhead costs as supplies, electric power, compensation insurance, payroll taxes, royalties, and spoilage.

When such costs do not fluctuate consistently with production but by steps and degrees, a more precise description terms these costs as *semi-fixed* when certain costs arise because of plant expansion or *semivariable* as in the case of supervision and inspection. As volume increases, the per unit cost of the fixed costs decreases, whereas the per unit cost of the variable costs remains more or less constant.

These costs have been further characterized as *controllable* and *non-controllable.* In the long run, all costs are controllable. However, in cost accounting, management is primarily concerned with the short-run controllable costs because these offer the greatest opportunities for cost reduction. Variable costs are the controllable costs because these are under the direction of intermediate management and supervisors who will be held accountable for operating results.

6. *Costs classified according to type of business activity.* Costs may also be classified according to type of business not engaged in manufacturing. This phase of cost accounting, though simpler than that of manufacturing costs, has been receiving increased attention in recent years. In this classification are found such cost analyses as:

a) *Cost accounting for banks,* whereby it is possible to determine, for example, the cost of maintaining a checking account, rendering a trust service, or making a loan.
b) *Cost accounting for municipalities,* whereby it is possible to compute the cost of police protection, fire protection, schools and education, water and sanitation services, etc.
c) *Cost accounting for retail or department stores,* which is a form of departmentalized distribution cost analysis.
d) *Cost accounting for large service organizations,* such as insurance companies, public utility firms, etc. This type is mainly an analysis of the costs of the various types of office work.

7. *Costs for special planning and decision-making analyses.* These are costs compiled for use in making managerial decisions when there are alternatives. They are special situation costs and are sometimes termed economic costs. Such compilation of costs would provide the answers to these questions:

Should the firm buy or make all or part of its product?

Should the firm buy a new machine to replace an old one?

Should a firm take an order for a job at less than the total cost to manufacture?

What effect will raising or lowering the selling price have on the breakeven point and earnings of the firm?

THE FOUR PHASES OF COST DETERMINATION AND CONTROL

Four managerial procedures make up the important operation of cost determination and control:

1. Production planning.
2. Responsibility and functional organization.
3. Managerial control.
4. Managerial evaluation.

Production planning is the first phase of managerial control of costs. A formal approach to planning is necessary to solve such problems as outmoded products, labor and material cost increases, material price increases, unwieldy inventories, and idle time and equipment. *This formal approach is established through the preparation and use of a budget of what is to be produced, based upon what the firm expects to sell.* This budget may be on a short-term (one year or less) or a long-term basis (5 to 10 years). For cost control, the short-term budget is used to indicate the kind and quantity of material and labor required to manufacture the planned volume of production. Included in this budget must be a projection of the fixed and variable indirect manufacturing costs.

Responsibility and functional organization is the second phase of effective cost determination. Efficient production requires the use of organization charts and many printed forms to fix responsibility. The proper use of machines and equipment so that the manufacturing work will flow smoothly through the plant is under the direction of the plant superintendent. Organization charts should present the functional accounting and administrative setup so that responsibility may be fixed for the recording and accumulation of the numerical data of the manufacturing operations. In studying organization charts, it should be noted that the chief accounting officer is the *controller*. Under his supervision, in addition to the work of cost determination, are (*a*) planning or budgeting, (*b*) systems and procedures, (*c*) general and financial accounting, (*d*) data processing, (*e*) taxes and reports, and (*f*) internal auditing. Cost determination, because of volume of detail, is usually segregated from the financial accounting. The simplest method is to treat cost data as statistical data, completely independent of the usual financial accounting. The more effective method for auditing and control is to tie in the cost accounting with the financial accounting records. This can be achieved by using separate factory journals and ledgers with appropriate controlling accounts for material inventories, work-in-process, and indirect manufacturing overhead costs.

Two organization charts are given: Illustration 1–1 indicates the functional organization of a manufacturing concern in which the chief accounting officer is the controller. In Illustration 1–2, the detailed organization within the accounting department is shown, with emphasis on the makeup of the cost accounting work.

Illustration 1–1. Organization Chart of a Manufacturing Company

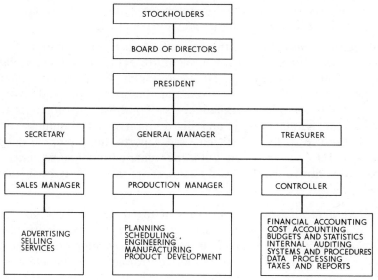

Illustration 1–2. Organization of the Controller's Department

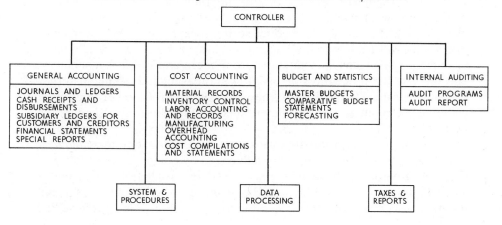

Among the forms used to record and fix responsibility in the cost accounting work, the following are basic:

1. *Production orders* instructing the superintendent what to manufacture.
2. *Material requisitions* used to authorize the release from the storeroom of the required materials and to control their use.
3. *Labor tickets* to record the labor costs used on the various jobs, operations, or in specific departments.
4. *Summary reports* known as *job order cost sheets* when the firm operates a specific job manufacturing operation, or as *cost of production reports,* when a firm operates on a more or less continuous production cycle with departmental costs indicated.

Managerial control is the third phase of cost determination. Control is not historical; it is a projection of future action based upon planned (budgeted) and historical data. The major elements of cost determination are material costs, labor costs, fixed manufacturing overhead costs, and variable manufacturing overhead costs. To these manufacturing cost elements, the administration and distribution costs should be added. Through the use of forms, entries, and reports, the historical data will be compiled for comparison with the planned budgetary data. This managerial control for successful business operations may be further described as:

1. *The determination of the costs* of the material, labor, and manufacturing overhead incurred on a specific job — or in a specific manufacturing department or for a specific process — in the manufacture of a single unit or a group of units for managerial control and reports. This work is known as cost finding or *cost keeping* and is essentially a routine bookkeeping or clerical operation.

2. Having determined these unit costs, management is able to study and analyze them *with the view of reducing them.* Reductions in cost may be effected by managerial decisions such as using substitute materials, changing the design of the product so that less material or fewer labor operations will be required, changing wage systems to reduce idle labor or overtime labor costs, installing more modern and efficient machinery, and revising the procedures involved in purchasing and issuing materials to reduce waste. This analysis is known as *cost control* and becomes more effective when budgets and predetermined costs are used for comparative purposes.

3. Unit costs of production provide a guide for *testing the adequacy of selling prices.* selling prices are influenced by competition, supply and demand, governmental regulations, and trade association practices, as well as by the costs of production. By means of a cost accounting system, the unit costs can be ascertained promptly so that any changes in selling

prices may be made without delay, provided that competition and other outside influences permit it. Furthermore, a comparative study of unit costs of the same product over a long period of time may enable a manufacturer to decide whether the economies of production can be passed along to the buyers to increase the volume of sales.

4. An effective cost accounting system facilitates the preparation of a series of reports for *managerial decisions*. The essential purposes of some of these reports are:

a) Periodic comparisons of materials, labor, and manufacturing overhead costs by products or departments will enable management to exercise more specific and more prompt cost reduction control to eliminate inefficiencies. These comparisons may enable management to decide whether *to manufacture certain units* or *to purchase them*, and also, whether *to add new products* or *to drop unprofitable items now being produced*.

b) Specific reports on spoilage, scrap, defective work, idle time, efficiency of specific workmen, and inefficient or idle equipment help to localize specific areas of cost reduction and to place responsibility for inefficiencies.

c) Reports on the cost of plant and equipment operations will indicate whether to increase plant capacity or to use several shifts, or whether there is too much idle equipment which might be sold or used in producing new products. Sometimes this report will result in the acceptance of orders at less than full cost (but in excess of variable costs) so that some of the fixed manufacturing overhead costs can be absorbed by the additional production.

d) Reports on distribution costs may be used to determine what products should be emphasized by the sales force because of their larger margin of profit, what products are unprofitable and might be eliminated, what territories are not producing a sufficient volume of business and should either be further developed or eliminated, and finally what methods of distribution are most profitable for the firm.

Evaluation of management's effectiveness in manufacturing and selling the firm's product is the fourth phase of cost determination and analysis. Using the reports indicated in the previous phase of cost determination, top management can approve or disapprove past operating results and make plans and adjustments for the future.

TYPES OF COST DETERMINATION SYSTEMS

Cost determination may be on a *historical* or a *predetermined basis*. Under a historical system costs are accumulated as they occur. On a predetermined, budgeted, or standard system, costs are determined in advance of production. Variations from the predetermined costs are accumulated in separate accounts so that management may be able to make plans and adjustments in the operations when the causes of the variations are identified, especially if they are unfavorable. Both historical and predetermined costs may be accumulated on a specific job basis, or

Illustration 1–3

Material costs	$10,000		
+			
Labor costs	15,000	*by jobs* = Work-in-process by jobs....................	$28,000
+			
Indirect manu-facturing costs	3,000		

Less unfinished work by jobs, (work-in-process inventory)....................	8,000
Cost of completed work (finished goods)	$20,000
Less finished goods on hand......................	4,000
Cost of goods sold and shipped.................	$16,000

Illustration 1–4

DEPARTMENT I:	Material costs.................................$25,000		
	Labor costs.................................... 15,000		
	Indirect manufacturing overhead costs... 12,000		
	Total work-in-process, Dept. I	$ 52,000	
	Transferred to Dept. II	40,000	
	Work-in-process, Dept. I....................		$12,000
DEPARTMENT II:	Cost received from Dept. I.................$40,000		
	Additional materials used 10,000		
	Labor costs in Dept. II 30,000		
	Indirect overhead costs 12,000		
	Total work-in-process, Dept. II	$ 92,000	
	Transferred to Dept. III....................	80,000	
	Work-in-process, Dept. II..................		$12,000
DEPARTMENT III:	Cost received from Dept. II...............$80,000		
	Additional materials used 18,000		
	Labor costs in Dept. III.................... 12,000		
	Indirect overhead costs 10,000		
	Total work-in-process, Dept. III.........	$120,000	
	Transferred to finished goods stock room...................................	100,000	
	Work-in-process, Dept. III		$20,000
FINISHED GOODS STOCK ROOM:	Finished goods, completed.................	$100,000	
	Finished goods inventory..................	25,000	
	Cost of sales		$75,000

departmentally if production is on a more or less continuous basis. The former are known as *job order costs;* the latter as *process or departmental costs.*

An example of the flow of costs under the job order system is shown in Illustration 1–3.

The flow of costs under the *continuous process system* differs since the work completed in one department usually is transferred to a second department, where additional work is performed before it is transferred to a third department, and so on, until the work is completed and placed in the finished goods stock room, preparatory to shipment on customers' orders. This process costing procedure is shown in Illustration 1–4.

GOVERNMENTAL INFLUENCE ON COST ACCOUNTING

At the present time, government interest in cost accounting operates through a number of regulatory agencies. The Internal Revenue Service is interested in cost accounting because the methods of computing costs have an effect on the income of a business concern and hence on the income tax report prepared for the government. The Federal Trade Commission is interested in cost accounting because the cost of manufacture and the cost of distribution are factors in determining compliance with the Robinson-Patman Act. The operation and enforcement of the Social Security Act comes under the control of the Internal Revenue Service. The Wages and Hours Law operates through the Labor Department. Either directly or indirectly, all of these agencies affect cost accounting.

For income tax purposes the government is particularly interested in the following four items because of their effect on cost and profits:

1. The valuation of inventories.
2. Rates of depreciation of plant equipment.
3. Valuation bases on which depreciation is computed.
4. Treatment of interest on investment as an element of cost.

The government's position on inventory valuation as reflected by the Internal Revenue Service is that the method used must conform, as nearly as possible, to the best accounting practice in the trade or industry in which the concern operates; and that, in addition, the inventory valuation practice must be consistent from year to year.

Items to be included in the cost of goods manufactured are specified by the Internal Revenue Service. Such regulations are necessary because the items used in the computation of costs affect the final figure on which income taxes are calculated. The general regulations require the inclusion of:

1. The cost of materials and supplies entering into or consumed in producing the article.

2. The cost of the direct labor used in manufacturing the article.
3. Indirect costs incident to and necessary for the production of the article. However, these indirect costs do *not* include the cost of selling, interest on capital, or estimated profit.

Depreciation of plant and equipment is included in the indirect costs. This item has given governmental tax bureaus a great deal of difficulty. Differences in the depreciation allowance may increase or decrease the cost of goods manufactured and, ultimately, the inventories and net income. The desire for correct operating statements, therefore, has caused governmental authorities, through the Internal Revenue Service, to specify methods and tentative depreciation rates to be used in preparing income tax returns.

The Robinson-Patman Act, enforced through the agency of the Federal Trade Commission, has stimulated and extended the interest of government in cost accounting. The purpose of the act is to prohibit price discrimination by the seller between purchasers of large and small quantities of the same goods. Unless a manufacturer can prove that the cost of selling (*distribution* or *marketing cost*) is less when sales are made in large quantities, he is prohibited from setting different unit prices for large and for small quantity orders.

The present defense program of the United States has brought the government into the market as a purchaser of huge quantities of naval and military materials. Most of these supplies are purchased through agreements with private contractors to manufacture according to government specifications. For these contracts the price is set in relation to the cost of production. In some instances, the price paid by the government is *cost plus a fixed fee*. Therefore, the government agents in making price agreements and the government accountants in examining a manufacturer's records to determine prices to be paid on contracts must be thoroughly familiar with cost accounting practices and procedures. These government officials must be able to distinguish between legitimate and incorrect charges to the cost of manufacturing; they need to know what items are to be omitted and what items included. They must be able to protect the interests of the government and yet allow the manufacturers fair prices. This interest of the government in cost accounting is of primary importance.

Because of laws such as the Federal Insurance Contribution Act, the federal and state unemployment insurance laws, and the Fair Employment and the wages and hours laws, accounting requirements for labor costs have been materially increased. Complete records must be kept of the time spent in employment, the hourly wages, and the total earnings. These governmental requirements for financial accounting have aided cost accounting in that the keeping of such records makes easier the task of compiling labor costs.

THE COST ACCOUNTING STANDARDS BOARD[1]

One action of the government which may have an important effect not only on cost accounting but later on the entire public accounting work is the passage of a law by Congress which established a Cost Accounting Standards Board to set up *standards of cost accounting* in connection with defense procurement contracts. By the word "standards" is meant uniform accounting procedures by firms involved in defense procurement contracts on a cost-plus basis. Although defense contractors claim that uniform accounting standards are not practical because of varying conditions, nevertheless it seems that this act will no doubt provide the beginning of more responsible accounting and legislation to this effect. The American Institute of Certified Public Accountants has been interested in this legislation and had contributed a feasibility study before the legislation was actually adopted.

This action by Congress presumably is an outgrowth of the Armed Services Procurement Regulations which contained cost principles and rules. It is hoped that adoption of these standards will save money for the government on its procurement contracts. The need for cost accounting standards was based upon the analysis of more than 450 cases involving cost problems encountered by the auditors from the Defense Contract Audit Agency of the General Accounting Office.

The function of the CASB will probably become a permanent part of the federal government, to be expanded to other than defense cost type contracts to include negotiated procurement contracts at fixed prices. It is hoped that the CASB will begin with the pronouncements of the Accounting Principles Board of the AICPA to provide a coordination of generally accepted accounting principles with the suggested cost principles and practices.

It must be realized that as time goes on, the government will become more and more interested in accounting procedures and practices — in more uniformity of principles applicable to income tax, cost accounting, and investor accounting to avoid deception and manipulation.

QUESTIONS FOR REVIEW

1. What are the elements of manufacturing cost determination? Which of these are variable?
2. Are the fixed or variable costs more important for cost determination and control?
3. What are the four phases of cost determination and control? Which of these do you consider more important from top management's viewpoint?

---

[1] For excellent discussion of this CASB, see Leonard Savoie. "Achieving Cost Accounting Standards," *NYS CPA*, May, 1971, p. 353.

4. Costs may be calculated on the basis of special jobs or by departments where there is a continuous flow of production. Which type of manufacturing operations is more common today?

5. What is meant by the term "manufacturing overhead costs"? What are some illustrations of fixed manufacturing overhead costs?

6. What are the variable costs of manufacturing? Why are variable costs more important than fixed costs for managerial control?

7. What effect does the volume of production have on the *unit* cost when related to fixed overhead costs?

8. Budgetary plans may cover a short or immediate period of time such as six months or a year; or they may cover a 5- or 10-year period. What items should be considered in a 5- or 10-year budgetary plan?

9. What elements make up an integrated cost accounting system?

10. Under modern business management, the profit motive is basic to all other considerations. How does modern cost determination affect this philosophy?

11. How does the federal government influence cost determination practices in modern industry?

PROBLEMS – GROUP A

Problem 1-1.   Purpose: *Simple Cost Computations and Income Statement*

The Albert Manufacturing Company produces a patented electronic calculating machine which sells for $3,000. During the coming year, it is expected that 1,200 of these machines will be manufactured and sold, with an expected profit before taxes of 20 percent on sales.

All materials used are purchased from outside suppliers. These materials are made to Albert's specifications. Direct labor used in assembling these machines is on the piece rate basis which is high enough to meet the minimum wage and hour law requirements. Both the material costs and the labor costs are known on a machine cost basis. The main controllable cost of manufacturing to insure a net income of 20 percent is the manufacturing overhead.

The cost of the material parts used in producing *one* of these machines is $600; the piece rate costs per machine is $1,000.

Fifteen hundred machines were manufactured; 1,200 sold. The total selling expenses for the year were $360,000, and the administrative expenses were $120,000.

In order to complete the requirements of this problem, it will be necessary to compute what the maximum overhead cost would be to realize the 20 percent profit.

Required:

From this information, you are asked to prepare for the year ending December 31, 19 –, (a) the cost of manufacturing a single machine; and (b) an income statement assuming that the 20 percent net income before taxes was realized on the sales.

Problem 1–2. Purpose: *Cost Computations*

In June, 1972, the Arden Manufacturing Company sold the Cooperative Apartments Company 5,000 air-conditioning units for $300 each. The costs of producing each of these units were:

> Materials $90
> Direct labor.. 60
> Manufacturing overhead (50% of labor)................. 30

On the bank loans to finance manufacturing operations, it was estimated that $1.50 was the interest cost of funds used for each unit.

Effective July 1, 1972, material costs increased 10 percent, while direct labor costs increased 25 percent.

Required:

a) Assuming no change in the rate of manufacturing overhead in relation to the direct labor costs, compute the sales price per unit to produce the same ratio of *gross profit*.

b) Assuming that $12 of the manufacturing overhead consists of fixed expenses, based upon production of 5,000 units, and will not change if the labor rates and volume change, compute the gross profit if 7,000 units are sold at the price of $300.

(Adapted from AICPA Uniform Examination)

Problem 1–3. Purpose: *Cost Computations and Income Statement*

The Ancient Manufacturing Company produces colored television sets which it markets under its own name but which it also supplies under special trade names to a national marketing association of a large chain of appliance stores. During the coming year, it plans to produce 50,000 of these sets for the national marketing association and 10,000 for its own distribution under the name of *Magnacolor*. It plans to earn a profit of $150 a set on the chain special-label sets and a profit of $200 a set on its own labeled receivers.

All parts are purchased on Ancient's specifications, and the company has contracted with outside suppliers for the parts to produce 48,000 units for sales and 3,000 units for inventory. The total material parts costs for each receiver is $180 per set.

The manufacturing overhead is estimated to be $50 per set. Selling expenses per set for each set under its own trade name *Magnacolor* is $50. None applies to the chain store sales. Administrative expense costs for all sets manufactured including those for the chain are $60 per set.

The selling price of the chain stores is $650 per machine, and for those under the trade name *Magnacolor* it is $750.

Required:

a) Compute the maximum cost that can be paid per set for the direct labor if the workers are to be paid on a piece rate for assembling each machine.

b) Prepare a cost sheet detailing the costs to make and sell a set for the chain and for Ancient's own trade name.

c) Prepare an income statement for the year if 45,000 sets are made and sold to the chain, 4,000 sets of *Magnacolor* are sold, and an inventory of *Magnacolor* of 2,000 sets is on hand at the end of the year.

Problem 1–4. Purpose: *Relationship between Production Costs and Profits*

The Allen Chemical Company produces an antipollution chemical under the trade name of *Airpur* at the following costs:

> Materials.....................................$8 per cwt.
> Labor costs .... 5 per cwt.
> Variable overhead costs.................. 3 per cwt.

The monthly fixed overhead costs for operating the plant are $100,000.

During the month of March, 50,000 cwt. are produced and 40,000 cwt. are sold at $50 per cwt.

Required:

a) Compute the gross profit and the ending inventory for the Allen Chemical Company for the month of March.
b) Compute the unit cost per cwt. of the product.
c) Compute the gross profit and the ending inventory for March on the assumption that 45,000 cwt. had been produced and 30,000 cwt. sold. Compute the unit cost per cwt.
d) Explain the differences between (b) and (c).

Problem 1–5. Purpose: *Statements: Cost of Goods Sold and Income*

The following information was taken from the books of the Applied Manufacturing Company for the year ending June 30, 19 – :

1. Fifteen hundred units of their single product were completed, of which 1,200 were sold at a unit price of $500 each.
2. Material costs showed:

> Inventory, at beginning, July 1..................$ 10,000
> Purchases during year............................ 100,000
> Inventory at end, June 30........................ 20,000

3. Direct labor costs totaled $45,000, and manufacturing overhead incurred was $39,000.
4. There was no work-in-process inventory at the beginning of the year. At the end of the year, June 30, the work-in-process costs were material costs, $6,000; direct labor costs, $4,000; and manufacturing overhead, $3,200.
5. There were 300 units on hand at the end of the year, June 30.
6. Selling and administrative expenses were 25 and 10 percent, respectively, of the selling price.

Required:

a) A schedule of the cost of goods manufactured and sold.
b) A condensed income statement.

PROBLEMS – GROUP B

Problem 1–6.   Purpose: *Simple Cost Computations*

In September, 1972, the Zarden Manufacturing Company sold the Acme Builders, Inc., 1,000 refrigerators at $250 each. These were to be manufactured and delivered in November and December.

When this sale was consummated, the manufacturing costs were:

Materials	$60.00
Direct labor	30.00
Applied manufacturing overhead costs	
(25% of direct labor)	7.50
Total	$97.50

In October, due to a wildcat strike, a new labor contract was made which increased the labor costs per refrigerator by 40 percent. There was no change in the percentage rate of applied manufacturing overhead.

Bank loans to finance the sales resulted in an interest cost of $2.50 per refrigerator and was considered an added manufacturing cost.

Required:

a) Compute the new sales price per unit which will result in the same rate of gross profit.

b) Assuming that $4 of the manufacturing overhead cost is a fixed cost, that the bank interest cost is part of manufacturing overhead, and the budgeted production is 4,000 units for the year, what will the gross profit be if 3,200 units are produced and sold at $260 each?

Problem 1–7.   Purpose: *Cost Computations and Income Statement*

The Zawie Stove Company manufactures an infrared electric range which it sells under its own registered brand name of *Electromagic*. It also supplies this range to large retail chain stores under their own private labels.

During the coming year, the company plans to produce 26,000 of these for the chain organizations and 5,200 under its own brand name. On the special-label chain units, it plans to make a profit (net) of $100, and on those of its own label, $150.

All parts required in manufacturing are purchased from outside suppliers with whom the firm has contracts for the parts required for 32,000 units. Material costs total $80 per range. The manufacturing overhead is estimated to be $40 per unit.

The selling expenses for the firm's own brand ranges is $20 per unit. No selling expenses are applicable to the chain store purchases. For all units sold, however, the estimated administrative expense cost is $10 per unit.

The sales price to chain stores is $300 per unit and that of the *Electromagic* label is $370.

Required:

a) Compute the maximum direct labor piece rate costs that can be allowed to meet the profit and cost projections for assembling these ranges.

b) Prepare a *comparative* cost sheet per unit to make and sell the ranges to the chains and directly to the public.

c) Prepare an income statement if 20,000 sets are made and sold to the chains and 5,000 are manufactured and sold directly to the public.

Problem 1–8.   Purpose: *Various Manufacturing Cost Computations*

The Yarrow Chemical Company manufactures a patented detergent cleaning powder known as *Sudsy*. The costs of manufacturing 1 cwt. of this product are:

> Materials..$5
> Labor 3
> Variable manufacturing overhead.................. 2

In addition, the monthly *fixed* overhead for the plant operations is $30,000. During the month of May, 100,000 cwt. were produced, of which 90,000 cwt. were sold at $25 per cwt.

Packaging and selling costs average $2 per cwt.

Required:

a) Compute the *gross profit* for the month of May.

b) What is the cost to manufacture 1 cwt. of *Sudsy?*

c) What is the amount of the *finished goods inventory*, May 31?

chapter 2

Historical Job Order
Cost Determination

The job order cost determination system on a historical basis requires a series of forms, accounting entries, and reports, all related to the manufacturing cycle of a specific lot of goods either for a customer or for the replenishment of the finished goods inventory. Manufacturing operations start with the issuance of a *production order* authorizing the factory foreman to proceed with the manufacturing. When this order has been issued, the cost accounting department prepares a cost summary form known as the *job order cost sheet*. For control purposes each job is assigned an identification number. Once the production order has been issued and the job order cost sheet prepared, costs are accumulated by jobs for the materials and direct labor used in the manufacturing. This accumulation is made through the use of a number of supplementary printed forms.

FORMS USED IN JOB ORDER COST DETERMINATION

The *job order cost sheet* is the summary form on which is recorded the job number and other specifications and descriptive information as given on the production order. Separate columns are provided in which to record the material costs, the direct labor charges, and the amount of estimated manufacturing overhead applied to specific jobs. The design of this form and the number of columns to be used must be adapted to the departmental and manufacturing characteristics of the business operations. Basically, the recorded cost determination information will be grouped under the three major headings: material costs, direct labor costs, and applied manufacturing overhead costs.

Two illustrations of these job order cost sheets are given, and they can be adapted to meet the needs of most business firms: Illustration 2–1 gives a job order cost sheet of a factorywide, nondepartmentalized organization; and Illustration 2–2 gives a job order cost sheet in which materials are used in only the initial department but direct labor and manufacturing overhead costs are recorded on a departmental basis.

Illustration 2–1. Nondepartmentalized Job Order Cost Sheet

FOR F. & M. Supply Co.   JOB ORDER NO.: 136
DESCRIPTION: Five Maple Kitchen Cabinets
                      From Blueprint Supplied
DATE STARTED: 3/3/—   DATE COMPLETED: 3/15/—

MATERIAL COSTS		LABOR COSTS		FACTORY OVERHEAD COSTS	
19— 3/3 3/10 3/12	$60.00 15.00 10.00	19— 3/10 3/15	$130.00 200.00	19— 3/10 3/15	$195.00 300.00
Total	$85.00		$330.00		$495.00

COST ANALYSIS

	ESTIMATED COST	ACTUAL COSTS	DIFFERENCE
Materials..........................	$ 95.00	$ 85.00	
Labor.............................	300.00	330.00	
Factory overhead..................	450.00	495.00	
	$ 845.00	$ 910.00	+$65.00
Selling price......................	$1,250.00	$1,250.00	
Manufacturing cost................	845.00	910.00	
Selling and administrative expenses, estimated 10% of sales price.......	125.00	125.00	
Profit............................	$ 280.00	$ 215.00	−$65.00

MATERIALS USED FORMS

Materials used in manufacturing are classified as *direct materials* — those which become part of the finished product — and *indirect materials* or *factory supplies*. The former are charged directly to the job on which they are used; the latter are part of the manufacturing overhead and are allocated to the various jobs in a manner which will be described later.

Illustration 2–2. Departmentalized Job Order Cost Sheet

PRODUCTION ORDER & JOB ORDER COST SHEET

FOR *Ward & Co.*   JOB NUMBER *178*

ADDRESS *Toledo, Ohio*   DATE *December 22, 19—*

DESCRIPTION *20 Special Machines*   CUSTOMER'S NUMBER

DATE COMPLETED *1/10/--*   SELLING PRICE $*20,000.00*   TOTAL COST $*13,979.60*   UNIT COST $*698.98*

DATE	DIRECT LABOR COSTS								MATERIAL COSTS		
	MACH. DEPT. #1		MACH. DEPT. #2		ASSEMBLING		FINISHING				
	Mach. Hrs.	Amount	Mach. Hrs.	Amount	Labor Hrs.	Amount	Amount		Date	Req. No.	Amount
Jan 2		2,000.00		1,400.00		1,000.00	400.00		Jan 2		3,200.00
10	206	328.60	38	68.40					10	605	110.00
Totals		2,328.60		1,468.40		1,000.00	400.00				3,310.00

DATE	APPLIED MANUFACTURING OVERHEAD COSTS											SUMMARY	
	MACH. DEPT. #1			MACH. DEPT. #2			ASSEMBLING			FINISHING				
	Hrs.	R.	Amt.	Hrs.	R.	Amount	Hrs.	R.	Amount	Cost	%	Amt.	Cost Element	Amount
Jan 2			2,400.00			1,120.00			850.00			600.00	MATERIAL	3,310.00
10	206	2.20	453.20	38	1.30	49.40							LABOR #1	2,328.60
													LABOR #2	1,468.40
													LABOR #3	1,000.00
													LABOR #4	400.00
													O.H. #1	2,853.20
													O.H. #2	1,169.40
													O.H. #3	850.00
													O.H. #4	600.00
Total			2,853.20			1,169.40			850.00			600.00	TOTAL COST	13,979.60

As part of the manufacturing control cycle, most firms have what is known as a *planning, routing, scheduling department.* It is the function of this group of employees to plan, route, and schedule what is to be manufactured, and to schedule the issuance of materials used in manufacturing so that a smooth manufacturing procedure will result. Usually this department will be responsible for the issuance of forms to authorize the release of materials from the storeroom at the proper time and to indicate the job to be charged for the cost.

In a job order cost system, two types of forms may be used: (1) an *individual material requisition* which is used to account for a single issuance of materials; and (2) a *standard bill of materials* which is used to cover all the materials to be issued for a job. Usually a minimum of *three* copies of each of these is used: one is kept by the department authorizing the issuance; one is sent to the stores department to support its records of materials issued; and one is sent to the cost accounting department for accumulation and recording on the summary cost accounting sheet. These two forms are shown in Illustrations 2–3 and 2–4.

Illustration 2–3. Individual Material Requisition for Job Order Cost System for Job No. 782

WALLACE MANUFACTURING CO.

DATE 3/2/——	MATERIAL REQUISITION	

WHERE USED
Stamping Department

ACCOUNT CHARGED
Work-in-Process Job UCS 782

No. B 154

QUANTITY	DESCRIPTION	PRICE	TOTAL	
800 lbs	Tempered Blade Steel			
	Spec. 482	12	96	00

RECEIVED ABOVE	APPROVED	DELIVERED BY			
F. Mascari	*J. Farber*	*C. C. Rye*			

ENTERED COST LEDGER	ENTERED IN CAT.	PRICED	EXTENDED	CHECKED	POSTED	PUNCHED
√KC	√KC	ℒ 7	ℒ.7.	VC	✓	✓

Original to Stores Dept.
   Duplicate to Cost Department
      Triplicate to Planning or Originating Dept.

Illustration 2-4. Standard Bill of Materials

BILL OF MATERIALS

For Job No. _128 XB_   Date __7/2/--__
Authorized by_ J.M. K----_
Per 100   Stock No.__ 3841 __

Del. By Dept. No.	Quan.	Description	Stock No.	Del. By Dept. No.	Quan.	Description	Stock No.
12	20	Sheets 18 ga. steel 36x120					
	20	Sheets 16 ga. steel 36x120					
	52	Sheets 18 ga. steel 46x 16					
	300	20 ga. end pieces					
17	100	Drawer fronts	53369				
	100	Drawer bodies	51699				
	100	Drawer liners	55572				
18	200	Case strips supports	59464				
	200	Case strips	13787				
	400	Corner sockets	58217				
	200	Braces	51503				
	100	Drawer strips	58216				
	200	Splice plates	57176				
	400	Legs	58218				
	800	Clamp plates	52211				
	200	Bronze bindings	4471				
	400	¼ x ¼ R.H. screws					
	400	⅜ x16x2 Hex. head screws					
	400	⅜ " Lock washers					

Original—To Stores Dept.

Duplicate—To Cost Dept.

Triplicate—To Planning or Originating Dept.

*Column 1 indicates to what departments the various materials are to be issued.

When the forms are received in the storeroom, the stores ledger clerk will enter on the appropriate inventory cards the quantity and cost of materials issued.

It is the job of the cost accounting department to accumulate the requisitions and, usually weekly, enter the cost of the materials used on the appropriate job order cost sheets.

FORMS USED TO ACCUMULATE THE LABOR COSTS BY JOBS

As in the case of materials, labor costs under a variety of terms are either *direct labor,* which refers to wages paid to those actually doing the manufacturing work, or *indirect labor,* which represents all other factory labor costs. Among the latter are such costs as superintendence, auxiliary helpers, idle time, and overtime bonuses.

The cost of the direct labor used on a specific job is accumulated by using job time tickets. Each factory worker who is directly associated with working on a particular job uses an individual job time ticket on which is recorded his name, department, the job number for which the

Illustration 2–5. Individual Job Time Ticket

Hours	Pieces	Hourly Rate	Piecework Rate
4		$2.60	
JOB TIME TICKET			
Employee's Name J. Robinson		Date April 2	
Clock No. 547		Department Bending	
Operation Bending		Time Finished 12:00	
Job No. 762		Time Started 8:00	
Hours	Pieces	Hourly Work	Piecework
4		$10.40	
		Approved Y. Lorde	

Adding Machine Tape

```
        Job #762
            *
        10.40
         8.20
        11.60
        15.00
        24.00
         8.30
        16.20
        93.70 *
```

work was performed, the time started, the time work was completed, the rate of pay, and the total pay thus earned. If an employee works on more than one job on any given day, he must have separate job time tickets for each job. Daily these are sent to the cost accounting department where the tickets are sorted by jobs and the totals accumulated and entered on the respective job order cost sheets. Illustration 2–5 shows one of these job time tickets for Job 762 for J. Robinson, supplemented by the adding machine tape for all the direct labor costs for a single day for this job.

To reduce the volume of paper work, some firms use a *daily job time ticket* — one for each day for each employee. On this ticket (see Illustration 2–6) provision is made for indicating the starting and stopping time for as many as six different jobs in one day. These will be tabulated by jobs each day before posting to the job order cost sheets.

MANUFACTURING OVERHEAD JOB COST PROCEDURE

Since the indirect factory costs applicable to a specific job cannot be determined in the same manner as the costs for direct materials and direct labor, a different procedure must be devised. Some of these costs, such as depreciation, may not be recorded until the end of the fiscal accounting period. Business firms have therefore used an estimated cost procedure. At the beginning of each accounting period, the manufacturing firm will prepare a budget or an estimate of what the firm expects these indirect manufacturing costs to be. This budget will show the expected indirect material costs, the expected indirect labor costs including supervision, and the other factory expenses such as rent, real estate taxes, insurance, depreciation, and repairs. This budget of course will have to take into consideration the estimated production for this period. The firm thus will also have to estimate its production volume which may be expressed in terms of units (for a single product company), direct labor hours, direct machine-hours, or direct labor costs. Dividing the budgeted manufacturing overhead total by the estimated volume of production will produce a predetermined manufacturing overhead rate which is used in charging the various jobs for their share of these indirect costs. It is known as the *applied manufacturing overhead.* For example, if the total budgeted manufacturing overhead for the year is $24,000 and the estimated or budgeted production for this same period expressed in terms of direct labor hours is 8,000, then the predetermined manufacturing overhead rate to be used on the various job order sheets is $3 per direct labor hour. If Job No. 546 used 60 direct labor hours in its manufacturing operations, it would be charged with $180 for its share of the indirect factory costs. When this figure is added to the direct material and direct labor costs for this job, the manufacturer is able to compute the cost of completing this job.

Illustration 2–6. Daily Job Time Ticket

WORKMAN'S	TIME TICKET AND				RECORD	
CUSTOMER NAME	ABC COMPANY				QUIT	12:00
JOB NO. 762	OPERATION	REG.	OVT.			
DATE Apr. 2-	BENDING	4			BEGAN	8:00
WORK NO. 547						
CUSTOMER NAME	M-N Corporation				QUIT	5:00
JOB NO. 780	OPERATION	REG.	OVT.			
DATE Apr. 2	Bending	4			BEGAN	1:00
WORK NO. 547						
CUSTOMER NAME					QUIT	
JOB NO.	OPERATION	REG.	OVT.			
DATE					BEGAN	
WORK NO.						
CUSTOMER NAME					QUIT	
JOB NO.	OPERATION	REG.	OVT.			
DATE					BEGAN	
WORK NO.						
CUSTOMER NAME					QUIT	
JOB NO.	OPERATION	REG.	OVT.			
DATE					BEGAN	
WORK NO.						
CUSTOMER NAME					QUIT	
JOB NO.	OPERATION	REG.	OVT.			
DATE					BEGAN	
WORK NO.						

CUSTOMER WORK		COMPANY WORK			FOREMAN AND CLERKS	COME BACK	SHOP & UNAS-SIGNED	TRNG. PROG.		TOTAL	
		TRADE &REPOS	A & H	ALL OTHER						REG.	OVT.
REG.	OVT.										
8										8	

APPROVED   *C J Collins*   SIGNED   *J Robinson*

WORKMAN NO.

Moore's Business Forms

ACCOUNTING ENTRIES FOR JOB ORDER COST DETERMINATION

Entries for Material Costs. In a manufacturing firm, the accounting records must indicate the cost of materials purchased and the cost of materials used. Materials used may become part of the finished product in which case they are known as direct materials; or they may be used to facilitate the manufacturing operations, such as factory supplies, in which case they are known as indirect materials and become part of the manufacturing overhead costs. Most firms use a single control account— Stores—to record all manufacturing materials purchased. For managerial inventory control, some form of detailed inventory record is maintained for each important type of materials purchased and used. This is known as the perpetual or book inventory and may be maintained on cards, punched card records, and more recently on computerized records. A separate card or record is kept for each kind of material showing the quantity and cost of materials purchased; the quantity and cost of materials issued for the various jobs; and the quantity and cost of the balance on hand. These perpetual or book inventory records are in reality the subsidiary records for a Stores *Control* account and must therefore agree in total with the balance in the control account.

Entries to record the purchase of materials placed in the storeroom and/or returned to the vendors would be:

(1)

Stores Control..20,000
    Accounts Payable..   20,000
    To record the purchases for the month.

(2)

Accounts Payable...   650
    Stores Control..   650
    To record stores returned to vendors.

Posting to the Stores Control account will also require an entry in the received section of the subsidiary ledger accounts. This simple procedure is followed by most firms and is illustrated diagrammatically in Illustration 2–7.

In recording the cost of materials used, the requisitions must be separated and accumulated according to (1) the materials used which become part of the finished product (direct materials) and which are charged directly to various jobs by making entries on the appropriate job order cost sheets; and (2) materials used in facilitating the manufacturing operations, such as maintenance supplies, which do not become part of the finished product. This last group of materials is charged to the Manufacturing Overhead Control account. The cost of the direct materials used on the various jobs is summarized in an entry charging the cost of the work-in-process. For better control and for correlation with the job

Illustration 2–7. Materials Purchased

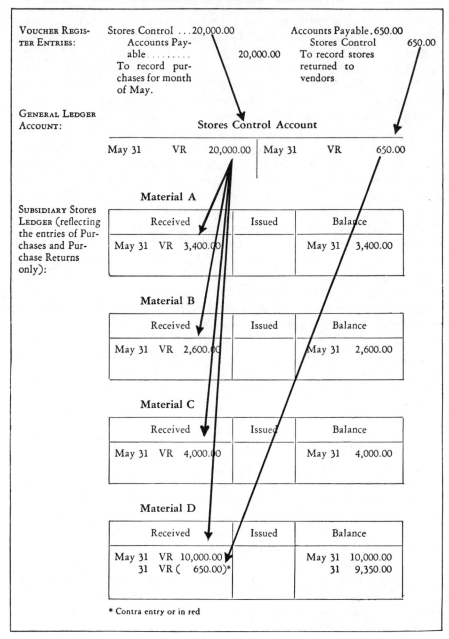

VOUCHER REGIS-TER ENTRIES:

Stores Control ...20,000.00
    Accounts Pay-
    able 20,000.00
    To record pur-
    chases for month
    of May.

Accounts Payable . 650.00
    Stores Control   650.00
    To record stores
    returned to
    vendors.

GENERAL LEDGER ACCOUNT:

Stores Control Account

| May 31 | VR | 20,000.00 | May 31 | VR | 650.00 |

SUBSIDIARY Stores LEDGER (reflecting the entries of Purchases and Purchase Returns only):

Material A

Received	Issued	Balance
May 31 VR 3,400.00		May 31 3,400.00

Material B

Received	Issued	Balance
May 31 VR 2,600.00		May 31 2,600.00

Material C

Received	Issued	Balance
May 31 VR 4,000.00		May 31 4,000.00

Material D

Received	Issued	Balance
May 31 VR 10,000.00		May 31 10,000.00
31 VR (650.00)*		31 9,350.00

* Contra entry or in red

order sheet entries, the work-in-process account is subdivided into three accounts: Work-in-Process — Materials, Work-in-Process — Labor, and Work-in-Process — Manufacturing Overhead.

Since the materials issued to the factory may be either direct or indirect, the summary entry made periodically (usually weekly) would be:

```
Work-in-Process — Materials.....................................................6,200
Manufacturing Overhead Control (Indirect Materials Used)............  160
    Stores Control................................................................          6,360
```

On the subsidiary perpetual inventory records, entries must be made in the Issued section for the materials thus requisitioned. The procedure is shown diagrammatically in Illustration 2–8.

Accounting for Labor Costs. Two types of entries are made in a job order cost system to record the labor costs: (1) the financial accounting entries representing the computation of the earnings less deductions required by law or authorized by the employees; and (2) entries for the allocation or distribution of these labor costs to the various jobs or to the Manufacturing Overhead Control account.

1. Following are the financial accounting entries for gross earnings and deductions which are made in the payroll journal and then in the voucher register, and the check register when payment is made:

```
Payroll ...........................................................................12,000
    FICA Tax Payable (5.2%)...............................................        624
    Federal Withholding Taxes Payable...................................      1,576
    State Withholding Taxes Payable......................................        350
    Life Insurance Premiums Payable.....................................         40
    Payroll Accrued..........................................................      9,410
Payroll journal entry.

Payroll Accrued.................................................... 9,410
    Accounts Payable.......................................................      9,410
Entry in voucher register for weekly payroll.

Accounts Payable................................................. 9,410
    Cash ....................................................................      9,410
Entry in the check register.
```

The journal entry for the *employer's* liability for the various payroll taxes is:

```
Manufacturing Overhead Control (Payroll Taxes) ...........................1,100
    FICA Taxes Payable (5.2%) ...............................................       624
    Federal Unemployment Taxes Payable ...................................        96
    State Unemployment Taxes Payable......................................       380
```

When these payroll taxes are paid, the entries would clear through the voucher and check registers.

2. Gross factory payroll costs must periodically be summarized. The direct labor costs entered on the various cost sheets are summarized in the Work-in-Process — Labor account. All other factory payroll costs

Illustration 2–8. Materials Issued

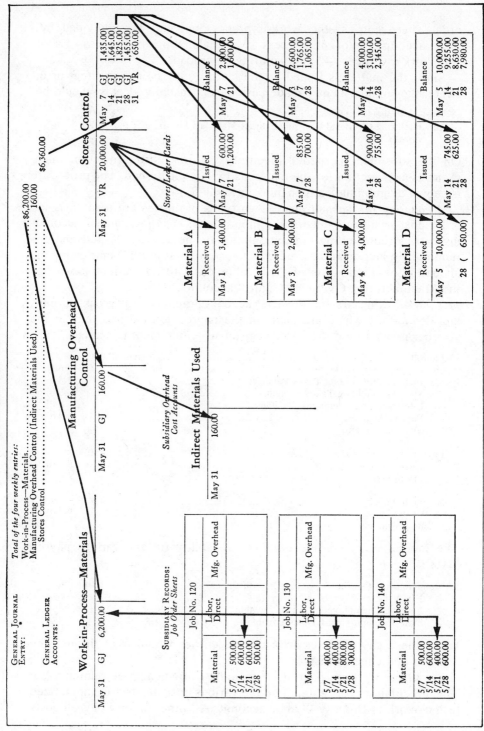

* Although the illustration shows the entry on a monthly basis, it would be practical to make these entries weekly or even daily.

are summarized in the Manufacturing Overhead Control account. This entry, made weekly or monthly, is:

```
Work-in-Process — Labor.....................................................10,000
Manufacturing Overhead Control (Indirect Labor) ..................... 2,000
    Payroll...................................................................          12,000
    To distribute the payroll costs.
```

Illustrations 2-9 and 2-10 show the financial and the cost accounting procedures and entries for payrolls in a firm using the job order costing.

Accounting for Manufacturing Overhead. As previously indicated, manufacturing overhead refers to those manufacturing costs which cannot be identified with a specific job or lot of production. Many of these are not known until the end of the accounting period. It is therefore necessary at the beginning of the accounting period to estimate or budget these costs and also estimate the volume of production in order to compute a predetermined overhead rate. Meanwhile, during the accounting period, the actual manufacturing overhead costs are being accumulated in a summary controlling account known as Manufacturing Overhead Control and the details are recorded in the individual overhead cost accounts in a subsidiary ledger. The difference between the total of the actual manufacturing overhead costs and the total applied to the various jobs during the accounting period represents the over- or underapplied manufacturing overhead costs. This over- or underapplied manufacturing overhead is due to errors in estimating the overhead costs or the volume of the production at the beginning of the accounting period — in other words, it is due to a mistake in the rates. This difference is usually closed out to the *Cost of Goods Sold account.* To record the total amount entered on the job order cost sheets, using the predetermined rate, a summary entry is made, weekly or monthly, as follows:

```
Work-in-Process — Manufacturing Overhead ............................ 2,100
    Applied Manufacturing Overhead ......................................          2,100
    To summarize the overhead charged to the various jobs at the
    predetermined rate of $1.50 per direct labor hour.
```

To record the actual manufacturing overhead incurred during the period, four types of entries are made:

a) For indirect materials used:

```
Work-in-Process — Materials ............................................. 6,200
Manufacturing Overhead Control (Indirect Materials)...........   340
    Stores Control........................................................          6,540
    To record the materials used.
```

b) For indirect labor costs:

```
Work-in-Process — Labor...............................................10,000
Manufacturing Overhead Control (Indirect Labor) ..............   300
    Payroll.................................................................          10,300
    To close the factory payroll account.
```

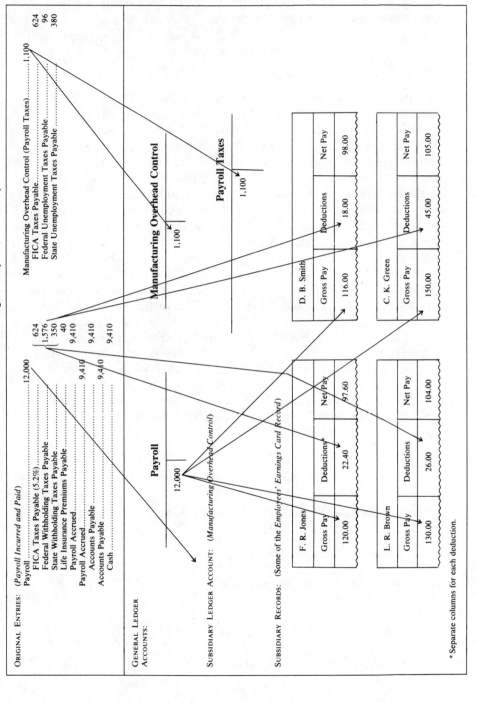

Illustration 2–9. Financial Accounting for Payrolls in Factory

ORIGINAL ENTRIES: *(Payroll Incurred and Paid)*

Payroll..12,000
   FICA Taxes Payable (5.2%).. 624
   Federal Withholding Taxes Payable.................................. 1,576
   State Withholding Taxes Payable................................... 350
   Life Insurance Premiums Payable................................... 40
   Payroll Accrued.. 9,410

Payroll Accrued...9,410
   Accounts Payable.. 9,410

Accounts Payable..9,410
   Cash.. 9,410

Manufacturing Overhead Control (Payroll Taxes)............1,100
   FICA Taxes Payable.. 624
   Federal Unemployment Taxes Payable................................ 96
   State Unemployment Taxes Payable.................................. 380

GENERAL LEDGER ACCOUNTS:

Payroll

12,000

Manufacturing Overhead Control

1,100

Payroll Taxes

1,100

SUBSIDIARY LEDGER ACCOUNT: *(Manufacturing Overhead Control)*

SUBSIDIARY RECORDS: *(Some of the Employees' Earnings Card Record)*

F. R. Jones

Gross Pay	Deductions*	Net Pay
120.00	22.40	97.60

L. R. Brown

Gross Pay	Deductions	Net Pay
130.00	26.00	104.00

D. B. Smith

Gross Pay	Deductions	Net Pay
116.00	18.00	98.00

C. K. Green

Gross Pay	Deductions	Net Pay
150.00	45.00	105.00

*Separate columns for each deduction.

Illustration 2–10. Distribution of Payroll Costs in Job Order Cost Accounting Cycle

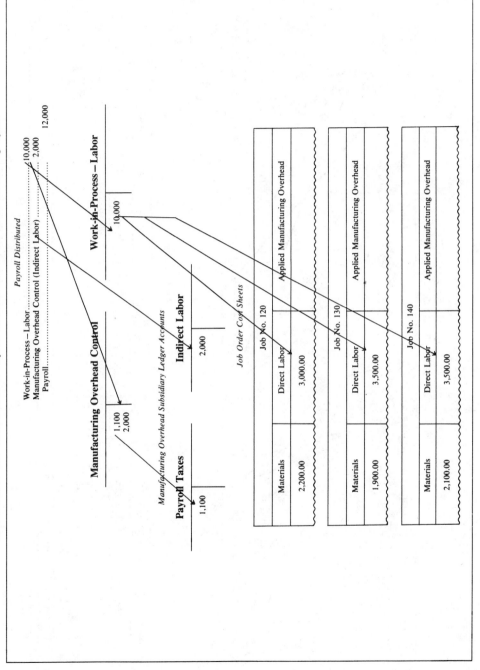

Illustration 2–11. Manufacturing Overhead Accounting in Job Order Cost Cycle

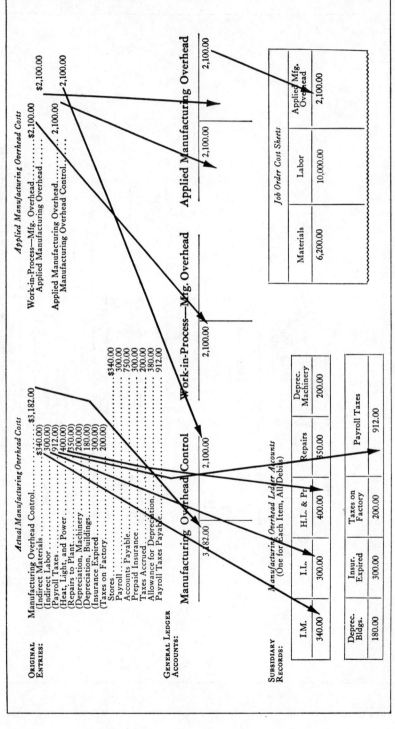

ORIGINAL ENTRIES:

Actual Manufacturing Overhead Costs

Manufacturing Overhead Control........$3,182.00
(Indirect Materials.................$340.00)
(Indirect Labor....................300.00)
(Payroll Taxes.....................912.00)
(Heat, Light, and Power............400.00)
(Repairs to Plant..................350.00)
(Depreciation, Machinery...........200.00)
(Depreciation, Buildings...........180.00)
(Insurance Expired.................300.00)
(Taxes on Factory..................200.00)
    Stores.........................$340.00
    Payroll........................300.00
    Accounts Payable...............750.00
    Prepaid Insurance..............300.00
    Taxes Accrued..................200.00
    Allowance for Depreciation.....380.00
    Payroll Taxes Payable..........912.00

Applied Manufacturing Overhead Costs

Work-in-Process—Mfg. Overhead......$2,100.00
    Applied Manufacturing Overhead.......$2,100.00
Applied Manufacturing Overhead.........2,100.00
    Manufacturing Overhead Control.......2,100.00

GENERAL LEDGER ACCOUNTS:

Manufacturing Overhead Control

3,182.00 | 2,100.00

Work-in-Process—Mfg. Overhead

2,100.00 |

Applied Manufacturing Overhead

| 2,100.00

Job Order Cost Sheets

Materials	Labor	Applied Mfg. Overhead
6,200.00	10,000.00	2,100.00

SUBSIDIARY RECORDS:

Manufacturing Overhead Ledger Accounts
(One for Each Item, All Debits)

I.M.	I.L.	H.L. & Pr	Repairs	Deprec. Machinery
340.00	300.00	400.00	350.00	200.00

Deprec. Bldgs.	Insur. Expired	Taxes on Factory	Payroll Taxes
180.00	300.00	200.00	912.00

c) For items involving a cash disbursement:

> Manufacturing Overhead Control (Taxes).......................... 200
>   Accounts Payable... 200
>   To record voucher for taxes.

d) For valuation costs:

> Manufacturing Overhead Control (Depreciation of
>   Equipment)... 200
>   Allowance for Depreciation—Machinery........................ 200
>   To record equipment depreciation.

Illustration 2–11 diagrammatically presents the accounting for the actual and applied manufacturing overhead costs in a job order cost determination system.

Accounting for Completed Jobs and the Cost of Sales. Entries to summarize the cost of jobs completed when placed in the storeroom and the cost of goods shipped are as follows:

(1)

> Finished Goods..16,500
>   Work-in-Process—Materials 6,000
>   Work-in-Process—Labor... 8,800
>   Work-in-Process—Manufacturing Overhead 1,700
>   To record the cost of jobs completed.

(2)

> Cost of Sales 12,000
>   Finished Goods.. 12,000
>   To record the cost of goods shipped during the month.

Illustration 2–12 diagrams the complete accounting and procedure cycle of a job order cost determination system.

Illustration 2–12. Diagrammatic Summary of the Job Order Cost Cycle

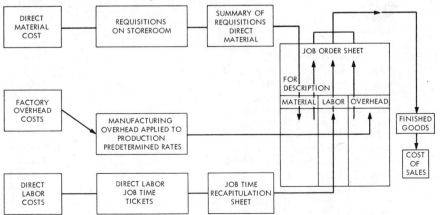

Illustration 2–13. Condensed Statement of Income

Exhibit B

BRENNER MANUFACTURING COMPANY
New York, New York

CONDENSED STATEMENT OF INCOME
For Year Ended December 31, 19—

Sales		$295,000.00
Sales Returns		2,000.00
Net Sales		$293,000.00
Cost of Sales (Schedule B-1)		190,000.00
Gross Profit on Sales		$103,000.00
Selling Expenses (Schedule B-2)	$46,000.00	
Administrative Expenses (Schedule B-3)	14,000.00	
Total Selling and Administrative Expenses		60,000.00
Net Operating Profit		$ 43,000.00
Financial Management Income	$ 4,200.00	
Financial Management Expense	3,000.00	
Net Financial Management Income		1,200.00
Net Income		$ 44,200.00

Illustration 2–14. Cost of Goods Sold Statement Starting with the Initial Work-in-Process Inventory – One Work-in-Process Account

Schedule B-1

BRENNER MANUFACTURING COMPANY
New York, New York

STATEMENT OF COST OF GOODS MANUFACTURED AND SOLD
For the Year Ended December 31, 19—

Work-in-Process Inventory, 1/1/—		$ 10,000.00
Direct Materials: *		
Inventory, 1/1/—	$ 75,000.00	
Purchases	100,000.00	
Freight-In	3,000.00	
Total	$178,000.00	
Less: Inventory, 12/31/—	85,000.00	93,000.00
Direct Labor		98,000.00
Applied Manufacturing Overhead		60,000.00
Total		$261,000.00
Less: Work-in-Process Inventory, 12/31/—		72,000.00
Cost of Goods Manufactured at Normal		$189,000.00
Deduct: Increase in Finished Goods Inventory:		
Finished Goods Inventory, 12/31/—	$102,000.00	
Finished Goods Inventory, 1/1/—	100,000.00	2,000.00
Cost of Goods Sold at Normal		$187,000.00
Add: Underapplied Manufacturing Overhead		3,000.00
Cost of Goods Sold at Actual to Exhibit B		$190,000.00

*In many statements, instead of showing the purchases, inventories, and resulting figure of materials used, only one figure is shown for the materials used. (See Illustration 2-17.)

FINANCIAL STATEMENTS FOR THE JOB ORDER COST DETERMINATION SYSTEM

A review of the procedures and entries given in this chapter indicates that the cost of goods sold is summarized in an account with this title. Many accountants use this account when preparing the income statement without presenting the details of the material, labor, manufacturing overhead, and work-in-process and finished goods inventories. Such a statement would appear as follows:

Sales...		$450,000
Less: Cost of sales............................		300,000
Gross profit on sales..........................		$150,000
Less operating expenses:		
Selling expenses.............................	$20,000	
Administrative expenses..................	6,000	
Financial expenses	1,000	
Total.......................................	$27,000	
Deduct other income	2,000	25,000
Net Income		$125,000

Illustration 2–15. Cost of Goods Sold Statement Starting with the Initial Work-in-Process Inventories When Three Work-in-Process Accounts Are Used

Schedule B-1

BRENNER MANUFACTURING COMPANY
New York, New York

STATEMENT OF THE COST OF GOODS MANUFACTURED AND SOLD
For the Year Ended December 31, 19—

Direct Material Costs:		
Work-in-Process, 1/1/—..................................	$ 3,500.00	
Applied during the Year.................................	93,000.00	
Total...	$ 96,500.00	
Less: Work-in-Process, 12/31/—.......................	20,000.00	$ 76,500.00
Direct Labor Costs:		
Work-in-Process, 1/1/—..................................	$ 4,000.00	
Applied during the Year.................................	98,000.00	
Total...	$102,000.00	
Less: Work-in-Process, 12/31/—.......................	35,000.00	67,000.00
Manufacturing Overhead Costs:		
Work-in-Process, 1/1/—..................................	$ 2,500.00	
Applied during Year......................................	60,000.00	
Total...	$ 62,500.00	
Less: Work-in-Process, 12/31/—.......................	17,000.00	45,500.00
Cost of Goods Manufactured at Normal......................		$189,000.00
Less: Increase in Finished Goods Inventory:		
Finished Goods, 12/31/—................................	$102,000.00	
Finished Goods, 1/1/—..................................	100,000.00	2,000.00
Cost of Goods Sold at Normal..............................		$187,000.00
Add: Underapplied Manufacturing Overhead Costs............		3,000.00
Cost of Goods Sold at Actual to Exhibit B..................		$190,000.00

Illustration 2–16. Cost of Goods Sold Statement Starting with the Initial Finished Goods Inventory

Schedule B-1

BRENNER MANUFACTURING COMPANY
New York, New York

STATEMENT OF COST OF GOODS MANUFACTURED AND SOLD
For Year Ended December 31, 19—

Finished Goods Inventory, 1/1/—............			$100,000.00
Work-in-Process Inventory, 1/1/—............		$ 10,000.00	
Direct Materials:*			
Inventory, 1/1/—........................$ 75,000.00			
Purchases.............................. 100,000.00			
Freight-In.............................. 3,000.00			
Total..............................$178,000.00			
Less: Inventory, 12/31/—.................. 85,000.00		93,000.00	
Direct Labor.............................		98,000.00	
Applied Manufacturing Overhead.............		60,000.00	
Total...............................		$261,000.00	
Less: Work-in-Process Inventory, 12/31/—......		72,000.00	
Cost of Goods Manufactured at Normal.......			189,000.00
Total...............................			$289,000.00
Less: Finished Goods Inventory, 12/31/—.......			102,000.00
Cost of Goods Sold at Normal................			$187,000.00
Add: Underapplied Manufacturing Overhead.....			3,000.00
Cost of Goods Sold at Actual to Exhibit B......			$190,000.00

*In many statements, instead of showing the purchases, inventories, and resulting figure for materials used, only one figure is shown for the *materials used.*

Illustration 2–17. Cost of Goods Sold Statement Starting with the Material Costs without the Details of the Materials Inventory and Purchases

Schedule B-1

BRENNER MANUFACTURING CCMPANY
New York, New York

STATEMENT OF COST OF GOODS MANUFACTURED AND SOLD
For Year Ended December 31, 19—

Direct Materials Used......................................		$ 93,000.00
Direct Labor Costs...		98,000.00
Applied Manufacturing Overhead Costs.......................		60,000.00
Total Costs of Manufacturing...........................		$251,000.00
Deduct: Increase in Work-in-Process Inventories:		
Work-in-Process Inventory, 12/31/—......................$ 72,000.00		
Work-in-Process Inventory, 1/1/—....................... 10,000.00		62,000.00
Cost of Goods Manufactured at Normal......................		$189,000.00
Deduct: Increase in Finished Goods Inventories:		
Finished Goods Inventory, 12/31/—......................$102,000.00		
Finished Goods Inventory, 1/1/—....................... 100,000.00		2,000.00
Cost of Goods Sold at Normal..............................		$187,000.00
Add: Underapplied Manufacturing Overhead...................		3,000.00
Cost of Goods Sold at Actual to Exhibit B...................		$190,000.00

However, for internal managerial use, most firms need and use a detailed statement showing the elements which make up the cost of sales. This will require an analysis of the various accounts in order to obtain the details necessary for such a statement. For these firms, a separate schedule is prepared showing the cost of goods sold, and this is followed by a condensed income statement as shown above. This schedule may be presented in different forms, depending upon the placement of the initial and final stores, work-in-process and finished goods inventories. The final cost of the goods sold will be the same no matter which form is used.

Illustration 2–13 shows a condensed statement of income which is supported by a statement of cost of goods manufactured and sold (Schedule B–1) as shown in Illustrations 2–14, 2–15, 2–16, and 2–17.

QUESTIONS FOR REVIEW

1. The cost accounting cycle may be expressed in three different ways. Which of these is the more comprehensive picture of the cost accounting system?

2. What are the three elements of the cost of goods manufactured? How does the accounting for these differ in a job order and a departmental cost accounting system?

3. Manufacturing overhead costs may be classified as fixed and variable. What is the managerial significance of this classification?

4. Why is the use of business forms an important phase of managerial control of cost determination?

5. Why has the use of the daily job ticket been more effective for control than the use of the individual job time ticket?

6. When using a Stores Control account, two charges are made to this account when materials are used. What are these and why is the separation necessary in a job order cost system?

7. What are the offsetting credits for the charge to the Manufacturing Overhead Control account for payroll taxes?

8. Four types of entries are usually involved in accumulating the Manufacturing Overhead Control. What are these?

9. Which type of cost of goods manufactured statement is more practical when the cost accounting records are integrated with the financial accounting entries?

10. What are the various forms of cost of goods manufactured statement? Which of these seems to be the more logical presentation?

PROBLEMS—GROUP A

Problem 2–1.   Purpose: *Job Order Cost Computations*

The Batman Manufacturing Company makes machines as per customer orders. The manufacturing operations go through three departments.

The operating cost for completing Job 733 for 20 special designed machines for the Downing Company were as follows:

Cost Information	Dept. A	Dept. B	Dept. C
Materials used	$6,000	$3,000	0
Labor hours worked................	400	500	300
Labor cost per hour	$4.50	$5.00	$4.80
Machine-hours used................	100	0	300
Estimated overhead			
costs	$5.00 per machine-hour	$2.00 per labor hour	$4.00 per machine-hour

The customer has agreed to pay for these machines on the basis of cost to manufacture plus a gross profit of 60 percent of the cost.

Required:

a) A cost sheet for the completion of this job.
b) The selling price of each of these machines.

Problem 2–2. Purpose: *Journal Entries for the Cost Accounting Cycle Prepared from Cost of Goods Manufactured and Sold Statement*

The following schedule represents the cost of goods manufactured and sold for three months ended March 31, 19—, for the Burly Manufacturing Company:

BURLY MANUFACTURING COMPANY
Cost of Goods Manufactured and Sold
For Three Months Ended March 31, 19—

Cost of Manufacturing:

Stores Purchased...		...$25,000	
Less: Stores Inventory, 3/31	$ 5,000		
Indirect Materials Used	1,200	6,200	
Direct Materials Used			$18,800
Direct Labor...			30,200
Manufacturing Overhead Applied (30% of Direct			
Labor Cost)..			9,060
Total			$58,060

Less: Increase in Work-in-Process Inventory:

	January 2	March 31	
Materials in Process $12,000		$14,850	
Labor in Process... 10,700		10,000	
Overhead in Process....................................... 3,210		3,000	
Total..$25,910		$27,850	1,940
Cost of Goods Manufactured at Normal...............................			$56,120

Add: Decrease in Finished Goods Inventory:

Finished Goods, January 2, 19— ....$ 8,600			
Finished Goods, March 31, 19— 6,000			2,600
Cost of Goods Sold at Normal...			$58,720
Less: Overapplied Manufacturing Overhead			2,120
Cost of Goods Sold Adjusted to Actual Cost			$56,600

Required:

Prepare entries in journal form to record the data shown in this statement. The overapplied manufacturing overhead cost is to be closed out to the Cost of Sales account. Use three work-in-process accounts.

Problem 2–3. Purpose: *Journal Entries for the Cost Accounting Cycle Using Job Order Cost Sheet Data*

The Barton Manufacturing Company had in production during the month of February the following three jobs, all of which were completed: Job F201, Job F202, and Job F203. Job F202 is a special order for a customer and is to be shipped as soon as completed without being entered in the Finished Goods account. The other two jobs are completed and are to be placed in the stockroom.

The cost accounting data for these three jobs for the month of February were:

	Job F201	Job F202	Job F203
Work-in-process, February 1:			
Materials	$ 800	$1,200	$1,000
Labor	2,500	2,000	1,500
Applied manufacturing overhead (30% of			
direct labor costs)	750	600	450
Operating costs for February:			
Materials used	1,000	1,800	1,000
Labor costs	1,600	2,000	1,200
Overhead applied 30% of labor costs	?	?	?

Required:

From this information, prepare (*a*) job order cost sheet for Job F201, and (*b*) journal entries in logical order to summarize the month's transactions including the shipment of Job F202.

Problem 2–4. Purpose: *Profit Change Analysis*

The Benson Manufacturing Company has been concerned over the decline in profit during the past six months, even though sales prices were increased over the preceding six-month period. You are asked to prepare an analysis of the causes for the decline and suggest corrective action.

	January–June	July–December
Sales	$1,000,000	$1,100,000
Cost of goods sold	500,000	800,000
Gross profit	$ 500,000	$ 300,000
Selling and administrative costs	100,000	120,000
Net Income	$ 400,000	$ 180,000

PROBLEMS—GROUP B

Problem 2–5.   Purpose: *Preparation of the Cost of Goods Manufactured and Sold Statement, Supported by a Separate Schedule of the Manufacturing Overhead*

The Bordwell Manufacturing Company's books for the year ended December 31, 19—, produced the following cost data:

Inventories	January 1, 19—	December 31, 19—
Stores	$100,000	$85,000
Work-in-process	60,000	73,000
Finished goods	96,000	90,000

Stores purchased	$360,000
Direct labor costs	480,000
Manufacturing overhead applied to production at a rate of 25% of direct labor costs	?
Indirect materials used (part of the Stores account)	12,000
Indirect labor costs	15,000
Power, heat, and light costs	8,000
Compensation insurance	13,000
Other factory property insurance	9,000
Superintendence	25,000
Depreciation of factory equipment	10,000
Rent of factory	12,000
Miscellaneous factory expenses	6,000

Required:

a)   Prepare a statement of the cost of goods manufactured and sold, supported by—

b)   A separate schedule of the actual manufacturing overhead costs.

Problem 2–6.   Purpose: *Preparation of Income Statement and Cost of Goods Manufactured and Sold Schedule*

The following accounts represent part of the ledger of the Brennen Manufacturing Company for the month of June:

Stores Control

June 1	Balance	32,000	June 30	Return to vendors	2,000
30	Purchases	48,000	30	Requisitions	27,000
30	Return to storeroom	500			

Payroll

June 30	Factory	36,000	June 30	Into production	36,000

Manufacturing Overhead Control

June 30	Indirect materials	6,000	June 30	Applied	16,500
30	Indirect labor	3,000			
30	Taxes	350			
30	Depreciation	3,150			
30	Insurance	300			
30	Sundry	4,200			

Work-in-Process—Materials

June 1	Balance	3,000	June 30	Returns	500
30	Stores	21,000	30	Finished goods	18,000

Work-in-Process—Labor

June 1	Balance	1,700	June 30	Finished goods	28,000
30	Direct labor	33,000			

Work-in-Process—Manufacturing Overhead

June 1	Balance	850	June 30	Finished goods	14,000
30	Applied	16,500			

Finished Goods

June 1	Balance	5,000	June 30	Cost of sales	60,000
30	Jobs completed	60,000			

Cost of Goods Sold

June 30	Goods shipped	60,000	June 30	Profit and loss	60,000

Sales

June 30	Profit and loss	80,000	June 30	For the month	80,000

Selling Expense Control

June 30	Sundry charges	6,000	June 30	Profit and loss	6,000

Administrative Expense Control

June 30	Sundry charges	4,000	June 30	Profit and loss	4,000

Profit and Loss

June 30	Cost of sales	60,000	June 30	Sales	80,000
30	Selling expenses	6,000			
30	Administrative expenses	4,000			

Required:

From these ledger accounts you are to reconstruct the following:

a) Condensed income statement for the month of June, supported by—
b) Statement of cost of goods manufactured and sold.
c) Schedule of manufacturing overhead costs.

Problem 2-7.   Purpose: *Journal Entries for Cost Accounting Cycle Prepared from Cost of Goods Sold Statement*

The following statement of the cost of goods sold for the month of July has been prepared by the controller of the Yinkan Manufacturing Company.

YINKAN MANUFACTURING COMPANY
COST OF GOODS SOLD STATEMENT
For Month Ended July 31, 19—

Finished Goods Inventory, 7/1/—			$150,000
Work-in-Process Inventory, 7/1/—		$ 98,000	
Stores Inventory, 7/1/—	$ 18,000		
Purchases during July	280,000		
Total	$298,000		
Less: Materials Used in Making:			
Machinery for Factory	$ 8,000		
Factory Supplies Used	6,000		
Inventory, 7/31/—	14,000	28,000	
Stores Used in Production	$270,000		
Direct Labor Costs	200,000		
Applied Manufacturing Overhead	100,000		
Current Cost of Manufacturing		570,000	
Total Manufacturing Costs		$668,000	
Less: Work-in-Process Inventory, 7/31/—		138,000	
Cost of Goods Manufactured			530,000
Cost of Goods Available for Sale			$680,000
Less: Finished Goods Inventory, 7/31/—			230,000
Cost of Goods Sold			$450,000

Required:

Assuming a single work-in-process account—

a) Prepare the entries in journal form that were made to record the information thus summarized.
b) What effect on the net income would have occurred if the materials used in making machinery had been charged to operating expenses instead of being capitalized?
c) Comment on the correctness of the accounting and income tax procedures indicated in (b).

Problem 2-8.   Purpose: *Profit Change Analysis*

The Watson Manufacturing Company has been concerned over the decline in profits during the past year, even though sales increased over the preceding period.

The comparative income statements were as follows:

	1972	1973
Sales	$1,600,000	$2,000,000
Cost of sales:		
Materials.............................$	600,000	$ 800,000
Labor	300,000	450,000
Variable manufacturing overhead...........................	100,000	150,000
Fixed manufacturing overhead..........................	60,000	60,000
Totals..............................	1,060,000	1,460,000
Less: Inventories........................	160,000	180,000
Cost of sales......................		900,000	1,280,000
Gross profit................................	$ 700,000	$ 720,000
Selling and administrative expenses.............................		200,000	300,000
Net Income for the Year		$ 500,000	$ 420,000

Required:

a)   An analysis of the causes for the decline in the net income.

b)   Possible corrective action to be taken.

chapter **3**

Segregating the Cost Accounting and Financial Accounting Records

INTRODUCTION

Since cost determination usually involves much detailed clerical and forms procedure work, many firms have separated their cost entries and records from the required financial accounting work by using separate factory ledgers with interlocking reciprocal accounts. Such a system is especially effective when a firm has a number of factory locations and wishes to establish localized or branch managerial control. Modern inter-company, instant communication and recording systems for business operating data has facilitated this type of managerial control. By means of the Teletype and similar communicating devices, a firm can maintain localized factory operating records and still have summarized managerial control data recorded in the centralized administrative offices. The ac-counts and the kinds of records maintained at the factory locations are not uniform. Basically, the minimum records must include a factory journal and a factory ledger. On the factory ledger a reciprocal control account—General Ledger Control[1]—will be set up. On the central administrative office records, a corresponding reciprocal account to control the factory operations will be used. This is the Factory Ledger Control account.[1] On the factory ledger, subsidiary ledgers are kept for stores, work-in-process, finished goods, and manufacturing overhead. Frequently, the factory payroll records are maintained at the factory office.

---

[1] These accounts are sometimes titled Factory Office Control and General Office Control.

ACCOUNTING PROCEDURES WHEN FACTORY JOURNAL IS USED

When a factory journal is used to supplement the financial accounting records, the general office will charge or credit the factory office for the following:

1. Materials sent to the factory by suppliers.
2. Materials returned to the vendors by the factory.
3. Money transferred to the factory office for payrolls.
4. Various overhead costs incurred or recorded by the main office. These include factory costs for which the main office has spent cash; depreciation charges for plant assets recorded on the general office books; and accrued or deferred factory expenses recorded on the main office books.
5. Cost of finished goods shipped to customers.

To illustrate in parallel columns the cost accounting cycle entries made on the general office and factory office books, Illustration 3–1 is given. These four entries are representative of the transactions affecting both the general office and factory office so that reciprocal entries must be made. On the basis of these entries, the Factory Office account on the general office books and the General Office account on the factory books are as shown below. It should be noted that the debit balance in the Factory Office account on the general office books is offset by the credit balance in the General Office account on the factory ledger.

Factory Office

(1) Purchases	2,500	(4) Cost of sales	3,250
(2) Payrolls	8,000		
(3) Manufacturing overhead	800		

General Office

(4) Cost of Sales	3,250	(1) Materials received	2,500
		(2) Factory payrolls	8,000
		(3) Manufacturing overhead charges incurred by general office	
			800

The balance of each of these accounts is as follows: On the general office books, the *debit* balance of the Factory Office account is $8,050; and on the factory office books, the *credit* balance of the General Office account is $8,050. When the trial balances of the general office and the factory office are combined, these debit and credit items cancel each other, making a trial balance as though it were for a single set of books.

Illustration 3–1

Nature of Entry	General Office Books	Factory Office Books

1. Materials shipped to factory.	Factory Office............2,500
	   Accounts (Vouchers) Payable........ 2,500
	To record the voucher for materials purchased.
		Stores............2,500
		   General Office........ 2,500
		Materials received.

2. Payroll remitted by the general office to factory.	Factory Office............8,000
	   FICA Taxes Payable (5.2%).......... 416
	   Federal Withholding Taxes Payable.......... 1,744
	   State Withholding Taxes Payable... 600
	   Accounts Payable.......... 5,240
	To record voucher for weekly factory payroll.
		Payroll............8,000
		   General Office........ 8,000
		To record weekly factory payroll sent to the general office.

3. Manufacturing overhead costs involving the payment of cash.	Factory Office............800
	   Insurance Expense......... 300
	   Heat, Light, and Power......... 400
	   Office Supplies, etc......... 100
	To transfer charges applicable to the factory.
		Manufacturing Overhead Control......... 800
		   General Office......... 800
		To record factory overhead costs paid for by general office.

4. Shipped to customers.	Accounts Receivable............4,600
	   Sales......... 4,600
	Selling prices of orders.
	
	Cost of Sales............3,250
	   Factory Office......... 3,250
	Cost of sales shipped.
		No entry.
		
		General Office............3,250
		   Finished Goods......... 3,250
		Cost of goods shipped to customers.

FORM OF THE FACTORY JOURNAL

Two forms of the factory journal can be used:

1. *A condensed summary type* in which entries are made less often in summary form, and
2. *The multicolumn form* in which the entries are made more frequently.

These forms are shown in Illustrations 3–2 and 3–3. In small plants entries may be made each week in summary form for the materials received, materials used, the factory payrolls, and factory overhead. For such a firm the *condensed summary* type may be used. For other firms requiring more detailed cost information, the *multicolumn* factory journal may be used. Each of these forms is illustrated.

The special features of the *condensed* summary form are:

1. The total purchases received during a week are lumped together into a single entry which summarizes the journal vouchers or duplicate invoices received from the general office or shippers.
2. A similar procedure is followed for the manufacturing overhead items charged to the factory from memoranda received from the general office.
3. Materials used, labor costs applicable to production, the applied manufacturing overhead, and the cost of work completed *during the week* are each recorded in a single summary entry.
4. The total cost of all goods shipped to customers *during the week* is entered in a single entry.

INTEROFFICE ACCOUNTING FORMS

No matter which journal form is used, there must be some method whereby the factory is informed by the general office as to what entries must be made and vice versa. Otherwise, the reciprocal accounts will not check each other. In order that each office may know what the other is doing so that each office may make corresponding entries, *interoffice* vouchers are used. These are known as *journal* or *transfer* vouchers. Sometimes these vouchers are kept in a binder and used as the book of original entry from which postings are made directly to the ledgers affected.

The main office may purchase material and have it sent directly to the factory. The invoice is sent to the main office to be recorded in the voucher register. But how does the factory bookkeeper know the cost of the goods when they are entered on perpetual inventory cards? One method is to have a duplicate invoice sent directly to the factory. Another method is to use a factory journal voucher (a specially printed form prepared by the main office) on which is recorded the data and informa-

Illustration 3-2. Factory Journal—Condensed Form

DEBIT General Ledger Control Amount	DEBIT Factory Operating Accounts — Account	DEBIT Amount	DEBIT L.F.	Date	Explanation	CREDIT L.F.	CREDIT Factory Operating Accounts — Account	CREDIT Amount	CREDIT General Ledger Control Amount
	Stores	2,300.00	11	Sept. 7	Stores Received during Week	✓			2,300.00
	Payroll	3,000.00	12	7	Payroll for Week	✓			3,000.00
	Manufacturing Overhead Control	1,260.00	13	7	Journal Voucher No. 12	✓			1,260.00
	Work-in-Process—Material	1,410.00	14	7	Requisitions for Week	✓			
	Manufacturing Overhead Control	190.00	13		Supplies Used	11	Stores Control	1,600.00	
	Work-in-Process—Labor	2,750.00	14	7	Payroll Analysis for Week	✓			
	Manufacturing Overhead Control	250.00	13		Indirect Labor Costs	12	Payroll	3,000.00	
	Work-in-Process—Manufacturing Overhead	1,375.00	14	7	Applied Manufacturing Overhead	17	Applied Manufacturing Overhead	1,375.00	
	Finished Goods	4,000.00	15	7	Job Orders Completed	14	Work-in-Process—Material	1,300.00	
						14	Work-in-Process—Labor	1,800.00	
						14	Work-in-Process—Overhead	900.00	
3,600.00	General Ledger		✓	7	Cost of Goods Shipped	15	Finished Goods	3,600.00	
37,000.00 (4)		40,000.00 (✓)						55,000.00 (✓)	22,000.00 (4)

Illustration 3-3. Multicolumn Factory Journal

Date	Explanation	General Ledger Cr.	Stores Dr.*	Pay-roll Dr.	Manu-facturing Overhead Control Dr.	Work-in-Process Dr.*†	Finished Goods Dr.*	General Ledger Dr.	Miscel-laneous Dr.	Miscel-laneous Cr.	L. F.	Miscellaneous Accounts
Sept. 1	Stores from Brown & Co.	700 00	700 00								11	
2	Stores Summary					510 00				510 00	11	Stores
3	Supplies Received	120 00	120 00									
4	Payroll for Week‡	380 00		380 00								
5	Depreciation of Machines	178 00			178 00							
6	Taxes on Factory	82 00			82 00							
8	Supplies Used				61 00					61 00	11	Stores
9	Sundry Factory Charges	102 00			102 00							
10	Labor in Process				80 00	300 00				380 00	12	Payroll
11	Overhead in Process					320 00				320 00	13	Manufacturing Overhead
12	Goods Finished						1,021 00			1,021 00	14	Work-in-Process
13	Goods Shipped							768 00		768 00	15	Finished Goods
		1,562 00	820 00	380 00	503 00	1,130 00	1,021 00	768 00		3,060 00	√	
		(4)	(11)	(12)	(13)	(14)	(15)	(4)	(√)			

*It is possible to have separate columns for Stores, Cr., Work-in-Process, Cr., and Finished Goods, Cr., thus reducing the number of entries in the Miscellaneous Accounts section.

†Often there are three work-in-process accounts — one each for Materials, Labor, and Manufacturing Overhead.

‡Payroll and withholding taxes recorded on general office books only. Payroll book is used as memorandum record.

tion to be used by the factory bookkeeper in making entries in the factory books.

When this form is used to transfer part of an account already in the general office books, it is sometimes known as a *transfer voucher* (see Illustration 3–4). For example, at the end of a fiscal period the main office opens a depreciation account for plant and equipment and credits the allowance for depreciation account. That portion of the depreciation which is a factory cost and which must be recorded on the factory books is entered on a transfer voucher which is sent to the factory office. The

Illustration 3–4. Journal and Transfer Voucher

☐ GENERAL LEDGER
☑ FACTORY LEDGER
☐ BOTH LEDGERS

JOURNAL VOUCHER

October 30. 19--

J. V. No. 7-612

PAGE 1 OF 4

DEBIT							CREDIT						
✓	DETAIL AMOUNT	DISTRIBUTION ACCT.	BRANCH	ORDER	✓	CONTROL AMOUNT	✓	DETAIL AMOUNT	DISTRIBUTION ACCT.	BRANCH	ORDER	✓	CONTROL AMOUNT
	300 –	Insurance	#3			300 –		1600 –	General Office	GO			1600 –
	1000 –	Depreciation Plant	#3			1000 –							
	300 –	Depreciation Equipment	#3			300 –							
		TOTAL DEBITS				1600 –			TOTAL CREDITS				1600 –

EXPLANATION: Monthly allocations to Factory #3

DATE PREPARED 10/28
PREPARED BY W. Collins
APPROVED BY G. Porter
POSTED BY J. Ryan
KEY PUNCHED BY Kate Brown

transfer voucher is the equivalent of a letter from the main office stating that the factory account has been charged or credited with the information, and in the amount of the voucher. The reverse procedure is used if the factory office wishes to notify the general office that the general office has been charged or credited with a certain amount.

The purposes of the factory journal voucher and the transfer voucher are identical, i.e., to provide the basis for entries in the factory journal or in the general journal.

ILLUSTRATIVE ENTRIES WHEN A FACTORY JOURNAL IS USED

On the factory books, entries must be made for the receipt and use of materials; for the incurrence of the payroll liability and its payment; for the manufacturing overhead and its application to the finished product; and for the shipment of the finished product. Although conditions in firms may differ, in order to understand the entries given in Illustration 3–5, the following assumptions are made:

1. All cash receipts and disbursements are handled and recorded through the general office. Therefore, all accounts payable, accounts receivable, purchase books (or voucher registers), cash disbursements, and cash receipts journals are kept in the general office.
2. All plant accounts, such as Factory Buildings, Machinery, Tools, and Patterns, as well as their respective valuation allowances for depreciation, are kept in the general ledger.
3. Such accounts as Prepaid Taxes and Prepaid Insurance, as well as Estimated Income Taxes Payable, are kept in the general ledger.
4. All manufacturing or cost accounts are kept in the factory ledger. By the use of carbon copies of the purchase vouchers and journal vouchers, the general office informs the factory office what entries are to be made on the factory books; by means of duplicate shipping reports, the factory informs the general office what customers are to be billed for the goods sold.

Illustrative entries made in journal form are given for the general and factory office records in Illustration 3–5.

SUBSIDIARY LEDGERS ON THE FACTORY OFFICE BOOKS

As previously indicated, in addition to the reciprocal accounts, certain subsidiary ledgers are usually maintained at the factory office. These are for stores, finished goods, manufacturing overhead, work-in-process, and sometimes for plant and equipment.

The *Stores Control* account summarizes the detailed information recorded in a large number of subsidiary inventory ledger accounts, each representing a single kind of material. The entries in the control account summarize in a few figures the details recorded in the subsidiary accounts representing the receipt of materials in the storeroom either by purchase or as a return from the factory as excess issues, and the issuance of materials for use in the factory or as a return to the vendor. In the subsidiary accounts, a running balance is usually maintained. The accounts and entries in Illustration 3–6 show the Stores Control and the subsidiary records.

The balance in the Stores Control account on March 31 is $2,050.

Illustration 3–5. Entries of the Cost Accounting Cycle

Transaction	General Office Entry	Factory Office Entry
1. Materials or supplies purchased and sent to factory.	Dr. Factory Ledger Cr. Accounts Payable This entry is made in the voucher register upon receipt of invoice from vendor and notification that goods have been received and approved by factory.	Dr. Stores Cr. General Ledger This entry is made in factory journal upon receipt of goods. The cost of the goods may be determined from duplicate invoices from vendor, duplicate copy of purchase order from general office, or by duplicate copy of voucher. When this entry has been made, detailed entries are also made on stores ledger cards.
2. Materials requisitioned from storeroom for use in factory.	No entry	Dr. Work-in-Process—Materials Dr. Mfg. Overhead Control (Indirect Materials) Cr. Stores This entry is a summary entry made in the factory journal either daily, weekly, or monthly from a summary of material requisitions. The material requisitions are also deducted on the individual perpetual inventory cards.

3. Factory payroll for the week.	(3b) Dr. Factory Ledger
	      Cr. Accounts Payable
	This entry is made in the voucher register to record voucher check for payroll.
	
	(3c) Dr. Accounts Payable
	       Cr. Cash
	To record the issuance of payroll check in check register.
	
	(3h) Dr. Factory Ledger
	       Cr. F.I.C.A. Taxes Payable
	       Cr. Federal Withholding
	            Taxes Payable
	       Cr. State Withholding
	            Taxes Payable
	To record the liability for payroll taxes and withholding taxes prior to payment.
		(3a) Dr. Payroll*
		       Cr. Payroll Accrued
		       Cr. F.I.C.A. Taxes Payable
		       Cr. Federal Withholding
		            Taxes Payable
		       Cr. State Withholding
		            Taxes Payable
		This entry is made in the factory payroll book.
		
		(3d) Dr. Payroll Fund*
		       Cr. General Ledger
		To record the receipt of check for payroll.
		
		(3e) Dr. Payroll Accrued*
		       Cr. Payroll Fund
		To record disbursement of fund.
		
		(3f) Dr. Work-in-Process—Labor
		       Dr. Mfg. Overhead Control
		            (Indirect Labor)
		       Cr. Payroll
		Summary entry in factory journal to record the analysis of job time tickets and indirect labor costs.
		
		(3g) Dr. F.I.C.A. Taxes Payable*
		       Dr. Federal Withholding
		            Taxes Payable
		       Dr. State Withholding
		            Taxes Payable
		       Cr. General Ledger
		To transfer the payroll and withholding tax liability to the general office for payment.

*If no Payroll Fund account is to be used and payroll taxes are to be shown in general office books only, then entry (3a) would be Dr. Payroll and Cr. General Ledger, and entries (3d), (3e), and (3g) are omitted.

Illustration 3–5 (continued)

Transaction	General Office Entry	Factory Office Entry
4. To record factory expenses entered in general office books originally but now being transferred to factory ledger.	Dr. Factory Ledger Cr. Allowance for Depreciation of Factory Buildings Cr. Allowance for Depreciation of Machinery To set up and charge factory with depreciation. This entry is made in general journal usually at the time of closing or summarizing of books.	Dr. Mfg. Overhead Control (Depreciation of Factory Buildings and Depreciation of Machinery) Cr. General Ledger This entry is recorded in factory journal upon receipt of a debit memorandum from general office.
5. Vouchering of taxes or any other factory expense involving the payment of cash.	Dr. Factory Ledger Cr. Accounts Payable This entry is made in voucher register.	Dr. Mfg. Overhead Control (Taxes, etc.) Cr. General Ledger This entry is made in factory journal.
6. To set up accrual for compensation insurance.	Dr. Factory Ledger Cr. Compensation Insurance Payable This entry is made in general journal.	Dr. Mfg. Overhead Control (Compensation Insurance) Cr. General Ledger This entry is made in factory journal.
7. To record overhead charged to production.	No entry	Dr. Work-in-Process—Mfg. Overhead Cr. Applied Mfg. Overhead This entry is made weekly or monthly in factory journal.
8. To close the Applied Manufacturing Overhead into the actual Manufacturing Overhead Control account.	No entry	Dr. Applied Mfg. Overhead Cr. Mfg. Overhead Control This entry is made at end of fiscal period in factory journal.
9. To record cost of work completed in factory.	No entry	Dr. Finished Goods Cr. Work-in-Process—Materials Cr. Work-in-Process—Labor Cr. Work-in-Process—Mfg. Overhead This entry is made periodically in factory journal.
10. Sale of goods.	(10a) Dr. Accounts Receivable or Cash Cr. Sales This entry is made at selling price in sales register. (10b) Dr. Cost of Goods Sold Cr. Factory Ledger This entry may be made in sales register or general journal.	No entry for sales price of goods sold (10b) Dr. General Ledger Cr. Finished Goods This entry is made in factory journal for cost price of goods shipped.
11. To close out the over- or underapplied manufacturing overhead at the end of the accounting period.	Dr. Cost of Goods Sold Cr. Factory Ledger (assuming that the applied overhead is less than the actual) This entry is made in general journal at the close of the accounting period.	Dr. General Ledger Cr. Mfg. Overhead Control This represents the balance in the account after entry 8 has been posted. It is usually not closed out until the end of the accounting period.

The sum of the balances in the accounts in the subsidiary ledger equals this amount, viz:

Material A	$ 700
Material B	600
Material C	750
Total	$2,050

Illustration 3-6

Stores Control

Mar.	1	Inventory at beginning	1,900 00	Mar.	31	Materials issued		
	31	Purchases for month	3,150 00			during the month	3,000 00	

The subsidiary ledger accounts (one for each kind of material) show the following information:

Material A

Receipts		Amounts Issued		Balance	
		Mar. 3	500.00	Mar. 1	800.00
Mar. 4	400.00			3	300.00
				4	700.00
		10	300.00	10	400.00
20	700.00			20	1,100.00
		24	400.00	24	700.00

Material B

Receipts		Amounts Issued		Balance	
		Mar. 4	350.00	Mar. 1	600.00
Mar. 5	800.00			4	250.00
				5	1,050.00
		10	450.00	10	600.00

Material C

Receipts		Amounts Issued		Balance	
		Mar. 5	250.00	Mar. 1	500.00
Mar. 12	550.00			5	250.00
		15	600.00	12	800.00
				15	200.00
26	700.00			26	900.00
		27	150.00	27	750.00

A similar arrangement of controlling accounts and the subsidiary ledger is usually established for Finished Goods. However, the debits to the Finished Goods Control account will represent the balance on hand at the beginning of the period and the *cost of the goods manufactured and placed in the stock room* during the period.

A *Manufacturing Overhead Control* account is used to summarize a variety of indirect manufacturing costs. Since there are a large number of indirect costs, it becomes a practical matter to summarize these in a controlling account. The relation of the controlling account to the individual indirect cost account parallels that of the Accounts Receivable Control account to the individual customer accounts.

Illustration 3–7

Work-in-Process—Materials

Mar.	1	Balance	1,000	00	Mar.	31	Orders completed	7,500	00
	31	Requisitions for month	8,000	00					

Work-in-Process—Labor

Mar.	1	Balance	3,000	00	Mar.	31	Orders completed	12,000	00
	31	Job time tickets for month	13,000	00					

Work-in-Process—Manufacturing Overhead

Mar.	1	Balance	900	00	Mar.	31	Orders completed	3,600	00
	31	Applied to production during month (30% of labor)	3,900	00					

The *Work-in-Process Control* is peculiar to cost accounting. It summarizes the costs incurred in manufacturing until the product is completed. The *subsidiary records* of the Work-in-Process Control account are the various job order cost sheets. For a job order cost system instead of a single account, the Work-in-Process Control is usually presented in three accounts, each representing one of the elements of costs, namely, Work-in-Process — Materials, Work-in-Process — Labor, and Work-in-Process — Manufacturing Overhead. This subdivision may be illustrated with its subsidiary cost sheets as shown in Illustration 3–7.

At the end of the month three uncompleted job orders were still in the factory; they contain the detail shown in Illustration 3–8.

At the end of the month the balances in the three control accounts for the work-in-process were:

Work-in-Process — Materials......................................$1,500
Work-in-Process — Labor 4,000
Work-in-Process — Manufacturing Overhead................. 1,200

The subsidiary records (job order sheets) showed the following balances:

	Material	Labor	Overhead
Job Order No. 172..................$	600	$1,800	$ 540
Job Order No. 178..................	400	1,000	300
Job Order No. 179.................	500	1,200	360
Total ....$	1,500	$4,000	$1,200

Illustration 3–8

Manufactured for: Stock	Job Order No. 172 Date started: March 2, 19—
30 Model XX Machines	Date completed:———————

Material Charges	Labor Charges	Manufacturing Overhead Applied
Mar. 31 600.00	Mar. 31 1,800.00	Mar. 31 540.00

Manufactured for: Mullins Mfg. Co. Detroit, Michigan	Job. Order No. 178 Date started: March 5, 19—
25 Model XBR Special Machines	

Material Charges	Labor Charges	Manufacturing Overhead Applied
Mar. 31 400.00	Mar. 31 1,000.00	Mar. 31 300.00

Manufactured for: Stock	Job Order No. 179 Date started: March 6, 19—
20 Model 2XR Machines	

Material Charges	Labor Charges	Manufacturing Overhead Applied
Mar. 31 500.00	Mar. 31 1,200.00	Mar. 31 360.00

PLANT AND EQUIPMENT CONTROL ACCOUNT

A *Plant and Equipment Control* account is used by some firms. To maintain operating plant efficiency, many firms are required to make large investments in factory buildings and equipment. The federal government through its internal revenue division is vitally interested in the amount recorded as an operating cost in the form of depreciation of these assets, because of the effect on the net income reported for tax purposes. To substantiate the amounts claimed for depreciation, and gain and loss on equipment sold or replaced, most firms are required to maintain detailed records of the costs, maintenance, current and accumulated depreciation, and the disposal of important pieces of equipment. This is accomplished through the use of a subsidiary ledger in which records for each major piece or group of equipment are made. Some firms keep the Buildings and Equipment accounts and their subsidiary ledgers on the general office books. Others maintain them on the factory office books. In either case, the records become an important phase of the cost determination, since the depreciation charges are part of the manufacturing overhead costs.

ADAPTING THE VOUCHER REGISTER TO COST ACCOUNTING WORK

In modern business, the use of the voucher register system is an accepted procedure because of the more effective internal control provided by the canceled checks, and also because this system expedites the accounting work. In studying the voucher system for a manufacturing concern, a comparison should be made of the differences in the form of the voucher register (1) when no factory ledger is in use, and (2) when a factory ledger is used.

1. When no separate factory ledger is used, the voucher register must provide columns for stores, factory payroll, and for those manufacturing overhead costs for which cash is expended. A separate payroll journal is maintained for the factory workers. In Illustration 3–9 it is assumed that the office salaries and salesmen's salaries are not included in this payroll journal but paid separately by check. This payroll journal would produce the summary entry shown in the illustration. Since the payroll journal is a book of original entry, the entry in the voucher register for the factory payroll will merely show a debit to the Payroll Accrued, whereas the entries for the office and sales salaries must record the liability for payroll taxes deducted from the workers' earnings.

2. When the voucher register in the *general office* is used in connection with a separate factory ledger, all charges for stores purchased, factory payroll, and manufacturing overhead paid for will all appear as debit charges to the Factory Ledger Control account. On the factory

Illustration 3-9. Factory Payroll Journal

Week Ended March 14, 19 —

| Name of Employee | W. H. Status | Clock No. | Regular | | | Overtime | | Gross Pay | Deductions | | | | | | Net Pay | Check No. |
			Hours	Amount	Rate Hourly	Hours	Amount		Fed. W. H.	State W. H.	FICA 5.2%	Union Dues	Total		
A. G. Brown 543-01-4509	2	44	42	$ 84.00	2.00	1	$ 2.00	$ 86.00	$ 11.00	$ 1.00	$ 4.47	$ 3.00	$ 19.47	$ 66.53	61-101
V. E. Kelly 769-07-9632	3	45	46	92.00	2.00	3	6.00	98.00	8.60	0.90	5.10	3.00	17.60	80.40	61-102
J. C. Marbery 176-03-4816	1	46	40	80.00	2.00	0	—	80.00	12.30	1.20	4.16	3.00	20.66	59.34	61-103
			2,600	$5,200.00		80	$160.00	$5,360.00	$480.00	$56.20	$278.72	$165.00	$937.04	$4,380.08	

Summary of postings made weekly from this record:

Dr. Payroll...$5,360.00
    Cr. Federal Withholding Taxes Payable................$ 480.00
    Cr. State Withholding Taxes Payable.................. 56.20
    Cr. FICA Taxes Payable, 5.2%........................ 278.72
    Cr. Union Dues Payable.............................. 165.00
    Cr. Payroll Accrued................................. 4,380.08

* At rate in effect when illustration was prepared.

Illustration 3–10. Voucher Register for Manufacturing Concern NOT Using a Factory Ledger

Date	Payable	Voucher No.	Paid Date	Check No.	Accounts Payable, Cr.	FICA Taxes Payable, Cr. 5.2%*	Federal Withholding Taxes Payable, Cr.	Stores, Dr.	Payroll† Accrued, Dr.	Mfg. O/H Control L.F.	Code	Amount	Selling Exp. L.F.	Code	Amount	Admin. Exp. L.F.	Code	Amount	Sundry Account	L.F.	Amount Dr.	Amount Cr.
Oct. 1	Service Realty Co.	815	10/2	732	400 00					✓	403	400 00										
2	Butler Harris & Co.	816			125 00					✓	401	125 00										
4	Knox Manufacturing Co.	817	10/10	736	622 52			622 52														
8	Payroll of Factory†	818	10/9	733	1,087 00				1,087 00													
8	Office Salaries	819	10/9	734	122 20	7 80	20 00									✓	602	150 00				
8	Salesmen's Salaries	820	10/9	735	164 60	10 40	25 00						✓	502	200 00							
10	A. N. Stewart & Co.	821			725 00			725 00														
12	A. C. Collins	822			200 00					✓	406	200 00										
15	Payroll of Factory	823	10/16	737	1,482 00				1,482 00													
18	Brown & Sharpe	824			3,000 00														Machinery	71	3,000 00	
24	Payroll of Factory	825	10/25	738	1,008 00				1,008 00													
25	Tower Supply Co.	826			50 00											✓	604	50 00				
27	National Fuel Co.	827			100 00					✓	405	100 00										
31	Payroll of Factory	828	10/31	739	1,531 00				1,531 00													
31	Office Salaries	829	10/31	740	386 60	23 40	40 00									✓	602	450 00				
31	Salesmen's Salaries	830	10/31	741	478 80	31 20	90 00						✓	502	600 00							
31	Internal Revenue Service	831	10/31	742	1,410 49														FICA Tax. Pay.	72	410 49	
																			Fed. W.H. Tax. Pay.	73	1,000 00	
					12,893 21	72 80	175 00	1,347 52	5,108 00	50	✓	825 00	55	✓	800 00	56	✓	650 00		✓	4,530 49	120 00
					(42)	(72)	(73)	(44)	(48)													
31	A. N. Stewart & Co.	821																	Accounts Pay.	42	120 00	
																			Stores	44		120 00

* Assumes rate in effect when text was written.
† Assumes use of payroll journal as book of original entry.

Illustration 3–11. Voucher Register for Manufacturing Concern Using Factory Ledger

Date	Payable to	Voucher No.	Paid Date	Check No.	Accounts Payable, Cr.	FICA Taxes Payable, Cr. 5.2%*	Withholding Taxes Payable, Cr.	Factory Ledger, Dr.	Selling Expense L.F.	Selling Code	Selling Amount	Admin. Expense L.F.	Admin. Code	Admin. Amount	Sundry Account	Sundry L.F.	Sundry Amount, Dr.	Sundry Amount, Cr.
Oct. 1	Service Realty Co.	815	10/2	732	400 00			400 00										
2	Butler, Harris & Co.	816	10/10	736	125 00			125 00										
4	Knox Mfg. Co	817	10/9	733	622 52			622 52										
8	Payroll for Factory†	818	10/9	734	1,087 00		{Fed. 15 00 / State 5 00}	1,087 00										
8	Office Salaries	819	10/9	735	122 20	7 80	{Fed. 20 00 / State 5 00}					✓	602	150 00				
8	Salesmen's Salaries	820			164 60	10 40			✓	502	200 00							
10	A. N. Stewart & Co.	821			725 00			725 00										
12	A. C. Collins	822			200 00			200 00										
15	Payroll for Factory†	823	10/16	737	1,482 00			1,482 00										
18	Brown & Sharpe	824			3,000 00										Machinery	71	3,000 00	
24	Payroll for Factory†	825	10/25	738	1,008 00			1,008 00										
25	Tower Supply Co.	826			50 00							✓	604	50 00				
27	National Fuel Co.	827			100 00			100 00										
31	Payroll for Factory	828	10/31	739	1,531 00			1,531 00										
31	Office Salaries	829	10/31	740	386 60	23 40	{Fed. 30 00 / State 10 00}					✓	602	450 00				
31	Salesmen's Salaries	830	10/31	741	478 80	31 20	{Fed. 75 00 / State 15 00}		✓	502	600 00							
31	Internal Revenue Service	831	10/31	742	1,410 49										FICA Taxes Payable	72	410 49	
															Federal Withholding Taxes Payable	73	1,000 00	
31	A. N. Stewart & Co.	821													Accounts Payable	42	120 00	120 00
															Factory Ledger	45	120 00	
					12,893 21	72 80	175 00	7,280 52	55	✓	800 00	56	✓	650 00		✓	4,530 49	120 00
					(42)	(72)	(73)	(45)										

* Assumes rate in effect when text was written.
† Payroll tax deductions for factory payroll are made in payroll book at factory.

journal, the debits to the Stores, Payroll, and Manufacturing Overhead will be offset by credits to the General Ledger Control account.

Illustrations of these records are given in Illustration 3–9, factory payroll journal; Illustration 3–10, voucher register when no factory ledger is used; and Illustration 3–11, voucher register when a factory ledger is used.

QUESTIONS FOR REVIEW

1. Why is it necessary and desirable to segregate the cost accounting records from the financial accounting records?
2. Under what conditions would you recommend the use of a multicolumned factory journal and also a condensed factory journal?
3. What are the differences in the columnar headings of a voucher register when a factory journal is used and when a factory journal is not used?
4. When a voucher system is used, is it more satisfactory to record the deductions from the workers' earnings in the payroll journal or in the voucher register? Explain.
5. What controlling accounts are usually associated with the factory journal and factory ledger? Why are these necessary?
6. How often are the direct labor costs usually recorded on the job order cost sheets?
7. What accounting control is created by having the job order work-in-process recorded in three separate accounts?
8. Many firms maintain their cost accounting records on a statistical basis – that is, they are not tied in with the accounting records. What serious internal control weakness results from this procedure?
9. What are reciprocal accounts? What is the purpose of their use when a separate factory journal is used?
10. Compare the check register with the cash disbursements journal.

PROBLEMS – GROUP A

Problem 3–1. Purpose: *Journal Entries for the Job Order Cost Accounting Cycle Using General Office and Factory Office Journals*

The Collin Manufacturing Company maintains its cost accounting records in a separate factory ledger. On the factory ledger, the following accounts are kept:

Stores	Work-in-Process – Materials
Factory Payroll	Work-in-Process – Labor
Manufacturing Overhead Control	Work-in-Process – Manufacturing Overhead
Applied Manufacturing Overhead	Finished Goods

For March, the following is a summary of the transactions:

1. Stores purchased, $100,000.

2. Freight on purchases, $1,200 (treat this as manufacturing overhead).
3. Materials used: direct, $22,000; indirect factory supplies, $2,500.
4. Materials returned as defective, credited by vendor, $950.
5. Summary of factory payroll: direct labor, $32,000; indirect labor, $5,000.
6. Deductions from factory payroll:

> FICA taxes $1,924
> Federal withholding tax................. 9,000
> State withholding tax.................... 2,400

7. Manufacturing overhead applied to costs at the rate of 80% of direct labor costs.
8. Vouchers received from the general office by the factory covered the following manufacturing overhead items:

> Depreciation of plant and equipment....................$7,600
> Heat, light, and power costs............................ 4,800
> Rent of factory premises................................. 3,600
> Factory insurance... 1,500

9. Employer's share of factory payroll taxes:

> FICA taxes $1,924
> State and federal unemployment taxes................. 1,200

10. Cost of jobs completed during the month:

> Materials..$19,500
> Direct labor 28,000

11. Cost of goods sold, $60,000.
12. Sales for the month, $95,000.

Required:

Use a form with the following columnar headings: Transaction No., General Office Entry, and Factory Office Entry. Record and summarize the above transactions as parallel entries in journal form.

Problem 3–2. Purpose: *CPA Problem Covering Cost Accounting Cycle*

The ledger of the Coudert Manufacturing Company contained the following balances on the general office books at December 31, 19 —:

COUDERT MANUFACTURING COMPANY
Trial Balance, December 31, 19 —

Cash	$ 35,100	
Notes Receivable	23,000	
Accounts Receivable	25,000	
Furniture and Fixtures	7,900	
Plant and Equipment	150,000	
Factory Ledger Control	180,000	
Allowance for Bad Debts		$ 800
Allowance for Depreciation — Furniture and Fixtures		1,500
Allowance for Depreciation — Plant and Equipment		15,000
Notes Payable		4,800
Salaries Payable		1,500
Accounts Payable		25,400
8% First Mortgage Payable		100,000
Capital Stock, No Par, Common		150,000
Retained Earnings		122,000
	$421,000	$421,000

On the same date, the factory ledger contained these balances:

Petty Cash Fund	$ 1,000	
Manufacturing Overhead Control	16,000	
Stores Control	45,000	
Work-in-Process — Materials	20,000	
Work-in-Process — Labor	40,000	
Finished Goods Control	60,000	
Payroll Accrued		$ 2,000
General Ledger Control		180,000
	$182,000	$182,000

During the month of January, 19 —, the following vouchers were issued:

Stores purchased	$30,000
Factory supplies purchased	8,000
Administrative expenses incurred	2,000
Selling expenses incurred	3,000

Factory payrolls prepared at the general office for the month amounted to $16,000, of which $2,000 was for nonproductive labor. Payroll taxes withheld totaled $3,800. Of the payroll checks drawn, $800 remained unclaimed, January 31.

Materials requisitioned from the storeroom during January were: direct materials, $18,000; factory supplies, $3,000.

Depreciation recorded for the month of January covered 12% a year for the furniture and fixtures (administrative expense); and plant and equipment was also recorded at the rate of 12% a year.

Sales salaries for the month were $4,000, and office salaries were $1,600. These were paid.

There were 11,200 machine-hours used in the manufacturing operations. Manufacturing overhead was applied at the rate of $1.50 per machine-hour.

The prime cost of work completed totaled $60,000 ($25,000 for materials, and $35,000 for direct labor). There were 9,000 machine-hours on the work completed and sent to the stock room.

Sales of finished goods amounted to $118,000. The cost of these sales were $82,400.

Factory overhead costs incurred during the month for which the general office made cash payments totaled $2,780.

Required:

a)   Using both general office and factory office books, record the above transactions in journal form using parallel columns to indicate the corresponding entries. Use the headings General Office Books and Factory Office Books.

b)   Prepare a condensed income statement for the month of January.

Problem 3–3.   Purpose: *Entries to Record the Cost Accounting Cycle*

The Curran Manufacturing Company operates a job order cost system. From their records for the month of October, the following data has been obtained:

Inventories	Oct. 1, 19—	Oct. 31, 19—
Stores..$50,000		$35,000
Work-in-process—materials.................................. 16,000		14,000
Work-in-process—labor 20,000		22,000
Work-in-process—manufacturing		
overhead.. 10,000		11,000
Finished goods.. 0		40,000

During the month of October, the following transactions occurred:

Materials purchased $100,000
Direct labor incurred...................................... 100,000
Factory overhead applied to production at a
rate of 50% of direct labor cost.

Of the stores used, $3,800 was attributed to factory supplies.

Required:

Using the above information, you are asked to prepare T-ledger accounts for the following:

Stores	Work-in-Process—Materials
Finished Goods	Work-in-Process—Labor
Cost of Sales	Work-in-Process—Manufacturing Overhead

Enter the October information in these accounts.

Problem 3–4.   Purpose: *Manufacturing Overhead Problems Arising in the Cost Accounting Cycle*

The Cimbal Manufacturing Company constructs specialized automatic machinery to customers' specifications. On December 31, the following inventories appeared on the company's balance sheet:

Materials and supplies (stores)................$35,000
Work-in-process.................................. 54,800
Finished goods 15,000

The work-in-process consisted of two unfinished jobs—Job MF–416 and Job MK–300—on which the following costs have been incurred:

Job No.	Materials	Labor	Mfg. Overhead	Total
MF–416........................$15,000	$12,500	$10,500	$38,000
MK–300 7,000	5,000	4,800	16,800
	$22,000	$17,500	$15,300	$54,800

Finished machines of a standard model for the trade consisted of one Model X786, at a cost of $10,600, on hand December 31, 19—.

Manufacturing overhead has been based in the past upon direct labor costs, but these have been fluctuating so much that no sound calculation has been possible. The firm has therefore switched to the labor hours basis for applying manufacturing overhead to production. For the coming year, the budgeted manufacturing overhead is $150,000 based upon 75,000 direct labor hours.

In January, two new job orders were started: JA–440 and JA–50.

Costs incurred during January were as follows:

Job No.	Materials Cost	Labor Hours	Labor Costs
MF–416 ....$ 2,000	800	$2,800
MK–300.......................... 5,000	2,000	4,800
JA–440........................... 12,000	2,500	7,000
JA–50 9,000	2,400	6,000

During January, $18,000 of materials and supplies (stores) were purchased. January 31, the inventory of stores was $15,000. Factory payroll for January was $22,000. Other manufacturing overhead costs for the month were:

Power, heat, and light......................$ 500
Depreciation................................ 1,800
Insurance 1,000
Repairs and maintenance.................. 3,000
Property taxes.............................. 400

Jobs MF–416 and MK–300 were completed and billed at $80,000 and $60,000 respectively. Jobs JA–440 and JA–50 were still incomplete January 31, 19—.

Required:

a) The manufacturing overhead rate for work in January.
b) Journal entry to record the total applied manufacturing overhead in January.
c) The over- and/or underapplied manufacturing overhead for January.
d) The total cost and gross profit on Jobs MF–416 and MK–300.
e) The work-in-process inventory, January 31, 19—.

PROBLEMS—GROUP B

Problem 3-5.   Purpose: *Journal Entries Covering Job Cost Accounting Cycle*

The following transactions represent the cost accounting for the Cranston Manufacturing Company for the month of January, 19—:

1. Materials purchased on account, $40,000.
2. Materials issued during the month totaled $28,000, of which $1,500 was for factory supplies.
3. Materials used to correct defective work, $300 (not customary).
4. Freight paid in cash for materials purchased, $750 (freight-in is treated as part of the manufacturing overhead).
5. Materials returned to vendors, $300.
6. Scrap material received in the storeroom had a sales value of $240. This was credited to the Manufacturing Overhead Control account.
7. Materials returned to the factory storeroom during the month were: direct materials, $1,000; factory supplies, $150.
8. Factory payroll for the month was as follows:

    Paid to the workers after deductions.....................$41,000
    Withholding federal income taxes......................... 8,500
    Withholding state and city income taxes............... 1,600
    FICA taxes.. 2,800

9. Employers' payroll taxes on factory wages were:

    FICA taxes $2,800
    Federal unemployment taxes.................. 560
    State unemployment taxes..................... 1,350

10. Of the total factory payroll, $52,000 was direct labor and the balance indirect labor.
11. Monthly depreciation charges were factory buildings, $4,000; machinery and equipment, $5,000.
12. Real estate taxes accrued during the month were $900; and the insurance expired, as a credit to the Prepaid Insurance account, $800.
13. Factory overhead is charged to production at the predetermined rate of 30% of the direct labor cost.
14. Cost of goods completed during the month totaled $80,000.
15. Goods costing $75,000 were sold for $90,000.
16. The over- or underapplied manufacturing overhead is closed out to the Cost of Sales account.

Required:

a) Journal entries to record the preceding transactions on the factory books, assuming the use of a separate factory journal and ledger.
b) Factory ledger accounts for:
    Work-in-Process (one account is used for all three elements)
    Finished Goods
    General Ledger Control
c) Should the over- or underapplied manufacturing overhead account have been deferred or closed out to the Cost of Sales? Explain.

Problem 3–6.   Purpose: *Cost Accounting Cycle Entries with a Factory Ledger*

The Cayuga Manufacturing Company uses a separate factory ledger in its job order cost accounting system. On December 31, 19—, the post-closing trial balances of this firm were as follows:

Ledger Accounts	General Ledger		Factory Ledger	
	Debit	Credit	Debit	Credit
Cash	$ 15,000			
Accounts Receivable	18,000			
Allowance for Bad Debts		$ 2,000		
Work-in-Process—Materials............			$ 18,000	
Work-in-Process—Labor			12,500	
Work-in-Process—Manufacturing				
Overhead.................................			2,500	
Finished Goods			16,000	
Stores...			20,000	
Machinery and Equipment..............			30,000	
Factory Petty Cash			1,000	
Allowance for Depreciation—				
Equipment				$ 15,000
Accounts Payable..........................		40,000		
Payroll Taxes Payable....................		3,000		
Capital Stock...............................		80,000		
Retained Earnings				
(debit balance)	7,000			
General Ledger Control..................				85,000
Factory Ledger Control..................	85,000			
Totals...............................	$125,000	$125,000	$100,000	$100,000

During the month of January, the following represent some of the transactions which are to be recorded in journal form with explanations on the general office and factory office books:

1. Purchases were: direct materials, $100,000; factory supplies, $8,000; factory repair parts, $2,000.
2. Materials used cost $98,000, of which $5,000 were indirect materials.
3. Factory payrolls totaled $96,000, of which $90,000 was for direct labor. On the general office books, the following deductions were recorded for this payroll: income taxes withheld, $18,000; payroll taxes, $3,000. The employer's share of payroll taxes was $4,200.
4. Office payrolls totaled $4,000, on which income taxes withheld were $850; payroll taxes, $340; sales payroll totaled $8,000 on which income taxes withheld were $1,950; and payroll taxes, $680. The employer's share of payroll taxes were for office workers, $400; for sales workers, $800.
5. Manufacturing overhead incurred for which the home office paid cash amounted to $21,000.
6. Allowance for depreciation of machinery and equipment was increased by $2,000.
7. The departmental analysis of the actual and applied manufacturing overhead costs were as follows:

Department	Actual	Applied
Department I..	$ 6,200	$ 5,300
Department II	10,000	8,700
Assembling department	12,000	14,300
Finishing department	10,000	8,600
Totals...................................	$38,200	$36,900

8. The cost of work completed and placed in the stock room totaled $225,000, made up of materials, $100,000; direct labor, $90,000; and manufacturing overhead, $35,000.

9. All but $26,000 of the finished goods on hand was sold on account for $330,500.

10. Cash received on account from customers totaled $320,000, after discounts of $6,000.

11. Total selling expenses, exclusive of payrolls and payroll taxes previously indicated, amounted to $14,880 for which cash was paid.

12. Total administrative expenses, exclusive of payrolls and payroll taxes previously indicated, totaled $10,600 for which cash was paid.

13. Total cash paid for vouchers issued, excluding payrolls and selling and administrative expenses, totaled $131,000.

Required:

a) Entries in journal form to record the above information on the general office and factory office books.

b) T-ledger accounts for the posting of the items after recording the opening balances.

c) Trial balance of each ledger, January 31, 19—.

d) Condensed income statement supported by a schedule of the cost of goods manufactured and sold.

Problem 3–7. Purpose: *Manufacturing Overhead Problem in the Job Order Cost Accounting Cycle*

The Yorty Machine Company produces special machines on customers' orders. On June 30, the following inventory appeared on the firm's balance sheet:

Stores control...................................$30,000

The work-in-process consisted of two unfinished jobs on which the following costs have been incurred:

	Job 410	Job 412
Materials costs...	$20,000	$12,000
Direct labor costs	15,000	15,000
Applied manufacturing overhead costs.................	10,500	10,500
Totals	$45,500	$37,500

One completed machine was on hand ready for shipment. This machine cost to produce, $14,600.

Manufacturing overhead has been applied in the past on the basis of direct labor costs, but this has been proven unsatisfactory because of the wide fluctuations in labor costs on similar jobs. It has been decided that in the coming six-month period, ending December 31, to use the *labor hours* basis. The budgeted manufacturing overhead costs for this period based upon 40,000 direct labor hours would be $100,000.

In July, two new jobs were started: 701 and 702. Costs incurred during this period were:

	Job 410	Job 412	Job 701	Job 702
Material costs	$1,500	$2,500	$ 6,400	$8,600
Labor costs	2,500	8,000	10,000	9,000
Labor hours	600	1,800	2,600	2,400

During July the following transactions occurred:

1. Stores inventory, July 31, was $27,200.
2. Stores purchased during July, $21,000.
3. Factory payroll for July was $33,000.
4. Factory overhead incurred in addition to indirect labor was:

> Power, heat, and light.......................................$1,000
> Depreciation of plant and equipment.................. 3,000
> Insurance.. 1,800
> Repairs and maintenance 2,000
> Property taxes 1,200

5. Jobs 410 and 412 were completed and billed at $72,000 and $75,000 respectively. Jobs 701 and 702 are still uncompleted.

Required:

a) Manufacturing overhead rate for July.
b) Journal entry to record the applied manufacturing overhead for July.
c) The over- or underapplied manufacturing overhead for July.
d) The total cost and gross profit on Jobs 410 and 412.
e) Work-in-process inventory, July 31.

Problem 3–8. Purpose: *T-Ledger Accounts for Cost Accounting Cycle*

The Yurris Manufacturing Company uses a job order cost determination system. From the accounting records for the month of June, the following data was taken:

Inventories	June 1	June 30
Stores...	$82,100	$64,100
Work-in-process—materials.......................................	16,000	12,000
Work-in-process—labor	25,000	28,000
Work-in-process—manufacturing overhead..................	6,250	7,000
Finished goods..	4,100	9,400

During the month of June, the following transactions occurred:

Materials purchased...$48,000
Direct labor costs 84,000
Of the materials used, $6,000 was for factory supplies.

Required:

Using this information, you are asked to complete the following T-ledger accounts:

Stores	Work-in-Process — Materials
Finished Goods	Work-in-Process — Labor
Cost of Sales	Work-in-Process — Manufacturing Overhead

chapter 4

Historical Departmental
or Process Cost
Determination – Part I

DEPARTMENTAL OR PROCESS COSTS DEFINED

Process costs are best understood when they are compared with specific job order costs. Under a system of specific job order costs, the materials, labor, and manufacturing overhead are accumulated by jobs or lots. Unit costs are not available until the job or lot is completed. When the job is completed, unit costs are calculated by dividing the total cost of work done on the job by the number of completed units produced. Each job is usually independent of every other job; and costs may vary considerably from job to job, even when the same product is being manufactured.

On the other hand, process cost accounting is used by a firm manufacturing products in a more or less continuous flow, without reference to specific orders or lots. Emphasis is placed on *production for a given period* – a day, a week, or a month – and this period of time may be comparable to the job or lot in specific order cost accounting. Furthermore, the continuous nature of the production usually implies that in many concerns there will be work-in-process inventories at the beginning and at the end of the given period. This gives rise to the problem of how to treat the work-in-process in computing unit costs. Emphasis in process cost accounting is therefore placed on the *period of time* and on the *number of units* (or quantity) completed and in process. The continuous nature of the production also means that unit costs are in reality daily, weekly, or monthly *average* costs.

Furthermore, since the products are manufactured on a continuous basis, the factory production is generally for warehouse stocks, not for specific customers. The quantities to be produced will be governed to a large extent by the estimated sales or demand for the products.

Industries to which the process cost accounting system may be applied vary widely in such matters as (1) the number of products; (2) the length of the production cycle; (3) the number of operations or departments involved; (4) the number of departments in which materials must be added, and whether these materials increase the number of units being produced or merely alter the units already in production; (5) the amount of shrinkage or waste; and, finally (6), whether or not at the end of the month there is any work-in-process. These factors determine whether the continuous process cost accounting system will be a simple or a complicated procedure.

To indicate the diversity of operations to which process cost accounting procedure is applicable, the following list of types of firms which use a continuous process cost accounting system is given:

Manufacturing	Mining	Public Utilities
Textiles	Coal mining	Gas manufacturing
Sugar refineries	Copper mining	Electricity producers
Bakeries	Salt production	
Petroleum products		
All other types of chemical manufacturers		
Rubber goods producers		
Plastics		

CLASSIFICATION OF PROCESS COST MANUFACTURERS

By attempting to visualize the manufacturing conditions under which process operations may be conducted, the understanding of process cost accounting is simplified. First of all, process manufacturers may produce but a single product on a continuous basis, or they may produce a variety of products. These may be further subdivided for cost accounting purposes as follows:

1. Firms manufacturing a *single product* continuously. This single product may be produced in one department or in several consecutive departments. Single-product continuous process costs may be further classified into those in which:

    a) *Materials to be processed are placed into production only in the initial department.* All subsequent departments merely add labor and manufacturing overhead to the cost of manufacturing.

    b) Materials to be processed are placed into production, not only in the initial department but *also* in some of the subsequent departments. This additional material may either *increase the number of units being manufactured* or merely increase the unit costs but not the number of units being produced.

c) *There is no work-in-process inventory in any of the departments* at the end of the cost accounting period. The simpler the manufacturing processes and the more perishable the product, the less likely it is that there will be any work-in-process inventory at the end of the period. And if there is no work-in-process inventory at the end, the simpler becomes the computation of unit process costs.

d) *There is a work-in-process inventory in at least some of the departments* at the end of the cost accounting period. The longer the manufacturing production cycle and the more involved the manufacturing operations, the more likely it is that there will be some unfinished work in some of the departments at the end of the cost accounting period. For example, bread bakeries, ice-cream manufacturers, and food canners usually complete all work placed in process before computing unit costs. There are no work-in-process inventories for these firms. But in oil refineries, gas and electric utility firms, steel mills, and textile manufacturers, the operations invariably involve some unfinished work-in-process no matter when the costs are summarized. These work-in-process inventories complicate the computation in the cost accounting work.

2. Firms manufacturing *more than one product* on a continuous basis. There are several possible conditions which may exist here:

a) *Separate products are produced in different departments which have no relation to each other.* This is the same as a number of single-product firms. Cost accounting procedure would be the same as though each product were produced in a separate factory.

b) *Separate products are produced, but the second product uses some of the first product in its manufacturing operations.* In a fertilizer plant, acid phosphate is produced in one department. Some of this is sold, and the rest is used in manufacturing fertilizer. This does not raise very serious cost problems since the effect is the same as though each product were made in separate departments. However, it becomes necessary to determine the costs of the acid phosphate before any cost can be computed for the fertilizer.

c) *A number of products are produced.* In the course of manufacturing operations the work done in one department is transferred to several departments, after which further production results in several products. This type of continuous process manufacture is used by rubber manufacturers, oil refineries, and industrial chemical producers and involves essentially the problem of prorating costs to several coproducts.

PROCESS COST ACCOUNTING PROCEDURES

Process costs are in reality daily, weekly, or monthly *average* costs. In order to emphasize this *average* characteristic, there are certain procedures which must be stressed at this time. These are as follows:

1. Material, labor, and manufacturing overhead costs are accumulated and recorded by *departments* or *processes*. However, the cost accounting procedure differs slightly from that of specific job order cost accounting, viz:

    a) *Material Costs.* Stores ledger cards may be kept for each kind of material. Material requisitions may be used but are not necessary. In place of them, so-called *consumption reports* are kept by either the stores or the manufacturing departments. Since the same materials are used in the same departments time after time, the use of consumption reports simplifies the accounting; in effect, they take the place of recapitulation sheets in job order costs. Furthermore, in process cost accounting, no distinction is ordinarily made between direct and indirect materials. In some concerns the materials are actually stored in or near the departments in which they are to be used, thus simplifying the handling and issuing of the material and the recording of the material consumed. Since in many concerns all materials used in manufacturing are to be placed in manufacturing in the initial department, the procedure for handling material costs will be controlled by this department.

    The accounting entries to record the use of materials in production are a charge to the work-in-process account for the department in which used. Entries are made periodically, usually weekly or monthly, viz:

Work-in-Process — Department A	3,200	
Work-in-Process — Department B	1,800	
Work-in-Process — Department C	2,000	
Stores Control		7,000

    To summarize the materials used in production as indicated by the departmental (or factory) consumption reports for month.

    b) *Labor Costs.* No distinction is usually made between direct and indirect labor. Job time tickets are not necessary. Payrolls are prepared by departments or production centers and provide the labor cost for manufacturing during a certain period. Although most labor is on an hourly basis, piece-rate work may also be involved.

    The accounting entry for both direct and indirect labor costs will be a charge to the departmental work-in-process accounts, viz:

```
Work-in-Process—Department A ...............................4,000
Work-in-Process—Department B...............................3,000
Work-in-Process—Department C...............................2,000
    Payroll or Payroll Clearing Account........................          9,000
    To allocate the payroll of the factory to the depart-
    ments for the month.
```

Although not a necessary record, but for purposes of control, the simple form of labor distribution shown in Illustration 4–1 might be set up on a pegboard so that the departmental sheets may be overlapped. For control purposes, direct and indirect labor costs are herein separated.

c) *Manufacturing Overhead.* In process cost accounting, manufacturing overhead may be charged to the various departments on a predetermined basis, the same as in job order costing. However, it is not customary to do so in those process industries where the very evenness and regularity of the continuous flow of production automatically "normalizes" the amount of the *actual* manufacturing overhead. Under these circumstances, the use of a predetermined normal rate of applied manufacturing overhead is unnecessary. However, if the process work is not produced uniformly throughout an accounting period, costs may fluctuate considerably from period to period unless a predetermined overhead rate is used. This is also true if the work is on a seasonal plan. Therefore, when production varies from period to period or from season to season, such as in a canning plant or in a coal mine or meat-packing plant, the use of a predetermined rate is desirable in the interest of more "normal" costs. Another problem arises in the concurrent manufacture of several products (or various sizes, shapes, or weights of the same product) in the same departments or cost centers. Here the application of manufacturing overhead to the various products on a predetermined basis cannot be on the basis of the number of units but must be on some suitably weighted method.

It should be further noted that some process manufacturing concerns keep separate accounts for *fixed manufacturing overhead* and for *variable manufacturing overhead.* The variable overhead may then be charged *directly* into the departmental work-in-process accounts, and the fixed overhead may be prorated on a *predetermined rate* to the production for the period. Such proration would assume, as in standard costs, that idle capacity should be considered in measuring efficiency and that part of the underapplied manufacturing overhead should be charged against management as their responsibility. Proration would therefore be based upon normal production capacity.

It should be noted, however, that there is an increasing trend toward the use of a predetermined overhead rate in process cost accounting because it permits more satisfactory comparisons of unit costs from period to period.

The entry for the manufacturing overhead charged to production would be:

```
Work-in-Process — Department A .................................3,150
Work-in-Process — Department B.................................2,000
Work-in-Process — Department C.................................1,800
    Manufacturing Overhead Control ..........................         6,950
    To record the distribution of the manufacturing over-
    head to the departmental accounts and production.
```

If a predetermined overhead rate is used, the entry would be:

```
Work-in-Process — Department A .................................3,150
Work-in-Process — Department B.................................2,000
Work-in-Process — Department C.................................1,800
    Applied Manufacturing Overhead ..........................         6,950
    To record the application of overhead to work-in-
    process on predetermined departmental rates.
```

2. The second characteristic of process cost accounting has already been indicated. Costs are kept on a *time basis,* not on a job basis. That is, material, labor, and manufacturing overhead costs are summarized daily, weekly, or monthly, as required by the individual needs of any particular firm.

Illustration 4–1. Labor Distribution Sheets

LABOR DISTRIBUTION FOR MONTH ENDING *March*	DEPARTMENT A		DEPARTMENT B		DEPARTMENT C	
CLASSIFICATION	HOURS	AMOUNT	HOURS	AMOUNT	HOURS	AMOUNT
DEPARTMENTAL PAYROLL						
HOURS WORKED_____	2,800	4,000 00	2,200	3,000 00	1,700	2,000 00
REGULAR EARNINGS_____		2,800 00		2,750 00		1,700 00
OVERTIME BONUS PAY_____		900 00		150 00		100 00
VACATION PAY_____		300 00		100 00		200 00
TOTAL WAGES_____		4,000 00		3,000 00		2,000 00
PAYROLL DISTRIBUTION						
DIRECT LABOR HOURS_____	2,600		1,950		1,600	
DIRECT LABOR REGULAR EARNINGS_____		2,600 00		2,500 00		1,600 00
INDIRECT LABOR HOURS_____	200		250		100	
INDIRECT LABOR COSTS: REGULAR_____		200 00		250 00		100 00
OVERTIME BONUS_____		900 00		150 00		100 00
VACATION PAY_____		300 00		100 00		200 00
TOTALS – HOURS_____	2,800		2,200		1,700	
TOTALS – PAY_____		4,000 00		3,000 00		2,000 00

3. A third characteristic of process cost accounting relates to the summary report of costs made weekly, daily, or monthly. It is known as a *cost of production report* and covers the cost of materials, labor, and manufacturing overhead for a *definite period* of time on a *departmental* basis.

4. A fourth characteristic of process cost accounting is that the cost of production must always contain a *quantity of production report,* either as an integral part or a supplementary report. This will show the number of units started or received into production and the number completed, in process, lost, and transferred out of the department, viz:

QUANTITY OF PRODUCTION REPORT DEPARTMENT I For Month of January, 19—		
Put into Process—to Be Accounted For...................		60,000 lbs.
Accounted for as Follows:		
Completed and Transferred to Dept. II.................	45,000 lbs.	
Work-in-Process (1/31/—)...........................	15,000 lbs.	
Lost in Production.................................	0	
Total Accounted For..............................		60,000 lbs.

SUMMARY COST OF PRODUCTION REPORT

The form of the summary cost of production report for a process type of manufacturing is not standardized. The form depends upon the type and number of products being manufactured and the number of departments through which material must pass during the manufacturing cycle. However, such a report usually consists of two parts: (1) the departmental costs segregated by the elements of material, labor, and manufacturing overhead; and (2) a quantity statement showing completed production, transfers out, and work-in-process in each department. The cost of production report shown in Illustration 4–2, may be readily adapted to meet the requirements of most departmental cost accounting.[1] The characteristics of this summary cost of production report which should be noted are these:

1. For each department the costs are shown separately for each element, namely, material, labor, and manufacturing overhead. These costs are shown in total and on a *per unit* basis.

---

[1] Specialized applications of process cost accounting are given in Chapter 24.

2.   An analysis is made of the total costs of production in each department. This analysis shows: the cost of production transferred to the next department; the cost of work completed and not transferred; and the unfinished work, or work-in-process, in the department. In later reports, the problem of units lost in production will be introduced.
3.   A *quantity of production report* is necessary for the computation of unit costs. This report will show for each department the quantity received and to be accounted for and the disposition of the quantity thus received.

In the preparation of this summary cost of production report, the following three factors must be considered:

1.   The nature of the *units of production.*
2.   The computation of *unit costs* through the medium of *equivalent production,* and determination of stage of completion of the work in process.
3.   The treatment of interdepartmental transfers.

These factors will be discussed in connection with Illustration 4–2.

NATURE OF UNITS OF PRODUCTION IN PROCESS COST PROCEDURES

In a process type of industry, the costs of production are reduced not only to the *unit basis* but in most instances to *units by elements of cost,* that is, the cost for materials, labor, and manufacturing overhead in each department. The units of manufacture are variously expressed, e.g.:

1.   In the production of ice cream, *gallons* of milk and cream, *pounds* of sugar and gelatin, and *ounces* of flavoring are mixed to produce *gallons, quarts,* and *pints* of the finished product. It is evident that the *units of the materials* used in manufacturing are not the deciding factors used in computing the *unit costs* of production. It is rather the *units of the completed production in each department*—in this instance, gallons of ice cream.
2.   In the production of paint products, *pounds* of lead, zinc, and titanium are mixed with *gallons* of linseed oil, dryers, and solvents to produce *gallons* of paint. The units of production must be that of the completed units—gallons of paint.
3.   In the manufacture of cement, *tons* of rock and shale are combined with other materials to produce *bags* or *barrels* of cement. The *bags* or *barrels* are units of production used in computing unit costs, not the tons of rock and shale.

So, whenever and wherever in this discussion the quantity report is used, the figures given refer to the *units* being produced—the units of the

Illustration 4–2

ALTON MANUFACTURING COMPANY
SUMMARY COST OF PRODUCTION REPORT
For Month of January, 19—

	Department I Cost	Per Unit	Department II Cost	Per Unit	Department III Cost	Per Unit	Totals Cost	Per Unit
COST IN PRECEDING DEPARTMENT:								
Transferred in during Month..........			$22,500.00	$0.50	$24,000.00	$0.96	xxx	xxx
COST IN CURRENT DEPARTMENT:								
Material Costs........	$18,000.00	$0.30	$10,500.00	$0.30	$ 4,400.00	$0.20	$18,000.00	$0.30
Labor Costs........	7,500.00	0.15	5,600.00	0.16	3,080.00	0.14	22,400.00	0.65
Manufacturing Overhead Costs*........	2,500.00	0.05					11,180.00	0.35
Total Departmental Costs........	$28,000.00	$0.50	$16,100.00	$0.46	$ 7,480.00	$0.34	$51,580.00	$1.30
CUMULATIVE COST TOTAL........	$28,000.00	$0.50	$38,600.00	$0.96	$31,480.00	$1.30	$51,580.00	$1.30
Transferred to Next Department........	$22,500.00	$0.50	$24,000.00	$0.96	$26,000.00	$1.30		
Work-in-Process:								
Completed and on Hand, 1/31/—........	0		4,800.00	0.96	0			
Work-in-Process, 1/31/—........	5,500.00		9,800.00		5,480.00			
CUMULATIVE COST DISTRIBUTION........	$28,000.00		$38,600.00		$31,480.00			

QUANTITY OF PRODUCTION REPORT (In Pounds)

	Department I	Department II	Department III
QUANTITY TO BE ACCOUNTED FOR:			
Completed and on Hand, 1/1/—........			
Work-in-Process, 1/1/—........			
Put into Process or Received from Preceding Departments........	60,000	45,000	25,000
To Be Accounted For........	60,000	45,000	25,000
QUANTITY ACCOUNTED FOR AS FOLLOWS:			
Transferred to Next Department........	45,000	25,000	20,000
Work-in-Process:			
Completed and on Hand, 1/31/—........	0	5,000	0
Work-in-Process, 1/31/—........	15,000	15,000	5,000
(Stage of Completion			
Material Costs........	(100%)	0	0
Labor Costs........	(33⅓%)	(33⅓%)	(40%)
Mfg. Overhead Costs)........	(33⅓%)	(33⅓%)	(40%)
Lost or Spoiled Production........	0	0	0
Total Accounted For........	60,000	45,000	25,000

* Both direct and apportioned overhead costs.

finished production in each department. These may change from department to department. Therefore, in most process manufacturing firms, little attention is given to the number of units put into process unless these are expressed in the same terms as the completed units. Production for each department is usually analyzed into:

1. Units completed and transferred to a subsequent department.
2. Units completed but remaining in the department (not yet transferred).
3. Units still in process, for which an estimate must be made of the stage of completion.

From this quantitative analysis of departmental production, unit costs can be computed. In the illustration given, all production, including the materials put into process, is expressed in terms of pounds. This simplifies the computation of unit costs.

COMPUTATION OF UNIT COSTS THROUGH EQUIVALENT PRODUCTION

Because in process cost accounting many firms will have some unfinished work at the end of the accounting period, it is necessary to convert this work-in-process to *equivalent* finished units. The problem of *equivalent production* arises *only* in those plants in which there is some unfinished work (work-in-process) at the end of the period for which the cost of production report is being prepared. It is necessary to compute the equivalent production so that unit costs may be calculated. To indicate how the equivalent production is computed and used in determining the unit costs by elements, reference is made to the summary cost of production report (Illustration 4–2) and the following data:

Department I

1. Sixty thousand pounds of material costing $18,000 were put into process.
2. Payroll cost for the month was $7,500.
3. Overhead costs for month were $2,500.
4. Forty-five thousand pounds were completed and transferred to Department II.
5. Fifteen thousand pounds are still in process. On this work-in-process, all necessary material for the finished product has been used, but it was considered one-third complete as to labor and manufacturing overhead costs.
6. Since both the completed and work-in-process *units of production* already are complete as far as the material costs are concerned and since no units of production were lost or spoiled in the manufacturing, the equivalent production for the *material costs* is as follows:

Units

Completed and transferred to the next department ....45,000 lbs.
In process but complete as to material costs 15,000
Equivalent Production for Material Costs, Department I...<u>60,000</u> lbs.

Dividing these 60,000 units into the $18,000 material costs results in a *unit* cost for materials in Department I of 30 cents.

The computation of unit costs for the elements of labor and manufacturing overhead is different, viz:

Forty-five thousand units were completed and transferred to Department II. As far as labor and manufacturing overhead costs are concerned, these units are equivalent to 45,000 finished units.

Fifteen thousand units are still in the process in Department I and are *estimated* to be one-third complete in the matter of labor and manufacturing overhead costs. These 15,000 are therefore *equivalent to* 5,000 finished units for these two elements of cost.

The total equivalent production in Department I for these two cost elements is therefore 50,000 units (45,000 + 5,000). Dividing the labor costs ($7,500) and the manufacturing overhead costs ($2,500) by this equivalent production (50,000) results in unit costs of 15 cents and 5 cents for labor and manufacturing overhead, respectively.

It is obvious that without the computation of an *equivalent production* it would not be possible to calculate the unit costs for labor and manufacturing overhead.

Department II

1. Payroll costs were $10,500.
2. Overhead costs were $5,600.
3. Of the 45,000 pounds received in the department from Department I, 25,000 pounds were completed and transferred to Department III; 5,000 pounds were completed and still in Department II; 15,000 pounds are still in process, being considered one-third complete as to labor and manufacturing overhead costs in Department II.
4. Since there was no material added in Department II, equivalent production must be computed only for labor and manufacturing overhead. The equivalent production for labor and overhead is:

Units

Units finished and transferred out 25,000
Units finished and on hand 5,000
Unfinished units, $\frac{1}{3}$ complete, equivalent
   to ($\frac{1}{3} \times$ 15,000)... <u>5,000</u>
Equivalent Production for Labor and
Overhead, Department II ....<u>35,000</u>

Dividing this quantity into $10,500 and $5,600 will result in a unit cost of 30 cents for labor and 16 cents for overhead.

Department III

1. Payroll costs were $4,400.
2. Overhead costs were $3,080.
3. Of the 25,000 pounds received in this department from Department II, 20,000 pounds were completed and sent to the stock room and 5,000 pounds are still in process and are estimated to be 40% complete as to labor and manufacturing overhead costs.
4. The equivalent production in Department III for labor and overhead is computed as follows:

	Units
Units completed and transferred	20,000
Units in process, 5,000, which are 40% complete, equivalent to (40% × 5,000)	2,000
Equivalent Production for Labor and Overhead, Department III	22,000

Dividing this quantitative figure into the payroll and overhead costs of $4,400 and $3,080 will result in unit costs of 20 cents and 14 cents respectively.

DETERMINING THE STAGE OF COMPLETION OF WORK-IN-PROCESS

The methods of determining or estimating the stage of completion of the work-in-process differs with industries. For some firms, it is possible to compute quite accurately the time it would take in a given department to complete the manufacture of a product. This may be done by determining *the* number of machine operations required, the length of time for each operation, or the number of man-hours required for the complete manufacturing cycle in a given department, and by computing the number which have already been used on the work-in-process. In other firms this is not so exact, and therefore an estimate or average must be used. For example, in the textile industry, where many departments are involved, instead of computing a separate "stage of completion" for each department, it is assumed that all work-in-process at the end of any given period is either one-half or one-third complete. In the manufacture of some products which require a carefully controlled period of aging, curing, or chemical action, it is possible to have separate batches or quantities started from day to day. The progress of these quantities, separately recorded, can furnish a fairly reliable figure of the stage of completion. For example, assume that one product requires three days for completion in a given department and that each day a new lot is started. At the end of the accounting period, some of the material will be one-third complete, some will be two-thirds complete, and the remainder will be completed. The determination of a reliable "stage of completion" is an important factor in the calculation of dependable unit cost figures in process industries. However, since in many cases the applied manufacturing overhead is based upon labor hours or labor costs, the same ratio or stage of completion is used for manufacturing overhead costs as is used for labor costs.

TREATMENT OF INTERDEPARTMENTAL TRANSFERS

Some concerns have a separate cost of production report for each department on which are recorded the costs for the material, labor, and overhead for that particular department, together with the quantity of production statistics—quantity of units received into the department, quantity completed and transferred out, quantity in process at end of period, units lost or spoiled. Periodically, the cost accounting department prepares a composite summary report of the costs and quantity of production for the entire plant. This summary report will show the interdepartmental transfers.

The simplest treatment is shown in Illustration 4–2, in which the cost data is shown in *sequential flow* from one department to another, as well as the analysis in each department of work completed and transferred out; work completed and on hand; work-in-process at end of the period; together with the quantity statement for each of these costs plus the quantity lost or spoiled. Since this method is simple and logical, the entries for it will be illustrated in the subsequent discussion. The flow chart for this procedure is shown in Illustration 4–3.

ACCOUNTING ENTRIES FOR DEPARTMENTAL TRANSFERS

In job order cost accounting, there was one Work-in-Process—Materials account and one for each of the other two elements, namely, Work-in-Process—Labor and Work-in-Process—Manufacturing Overhead. In process cost accounting, the work-in-process accounts are maintained on a departmental basis, not on an element-of-cost basis. Since the number of departments is limited, fewer summary entries and postings will be necessary. In a firm making a weekly cost of production report, for four operating departments, only five summary entries each week are necessary—one each for the total costs in each department and one for the transfer to the Finished Goods account. These entries can

Illustration 4–3

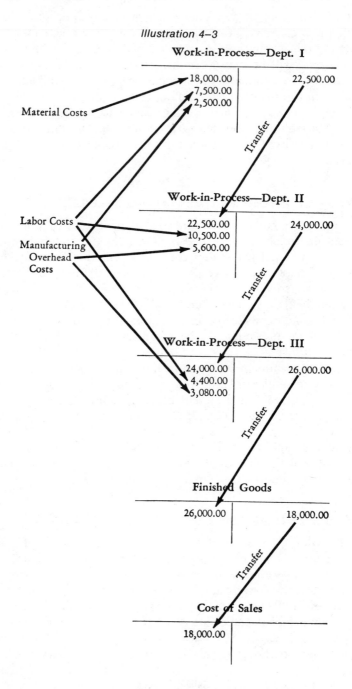

only be made after the cost of production report is completed, since the cost of the transfers from one department to the next are computed on this report.

To illustrate these entries taken from the cost of production report in Illustration 4–2, the following are given. It should be noted, however, that the amounts of *the departmental transfers are calculated by using the unit costs which have been computed and accumulated and the quantities which have been transferred.*

(1)

Work-in-Process—Department I 28,000		
Stores Control...	18,000	
Payroll...	7,500	
Manufacturing Overhead Control	2,500	

To record cost of materials, labor, and overhead used in Department I during January.

(2)[1]

Work-in-Process—Department II 22,500	
Work-in-Process—Department I	22,500

To record cost of work transferred to Department II from Department I (45,000 pounds × $0.50).

(3)

Work-in-Process—Department II 16,100	
Payroll...	10,500
Manufacturing Overhead Control	5,600

To record costs incurred in Department II during January.

(4)[2]

Work-in-Process—Department III...31,480	
Work-in-Process—Department II	24,000
Payroll...	4,400
Manufacturing Overhead Control	3,080

To record the transfer and the departmental costs for Department III during the month of January (25,000 pounds × $0.96).

(5)

Finished Goods...26,000	
Work-in-Process—Department III....................................	26,000

To record cost of work completed and sent to finished goods stock room (20,000 pounds × $1.30).

If these entries are posted to the various accounts, the balances in departmental work-in-process accounts represent the work-in-process inventories in each department. *It should be noted that work completed but not transferred out of a department is part of the work-in-process inventory of that department,* viz:

---

[1] Two separate entries are made to record costs in Department II—one for departmental transfer and one for additional costs in department during month. These two entries may be combined as illustrated in next footnote.

[2] Both the departmental transfer and the departmental costs are combined into a single entry.

Work-in-Process — Department I

(1)	28,000	(2)	22,500

Work-in-Process — Department II

(2)	22,500	(4)	24,000
(3)	16,100		

Work-in-Process — Department III

4)	31,480	(5)	26,000

Finished Goods

(5)	26,000		

It is possible to verify the accuracy of the work-in-process inventories in each department by mathematical computations, viz:

Department I

Material costs of work-in-process:
15,000 units 100% complete, at $0.30..$4,500
Labor and overhead costs in process:
15,000 units $\frac{1}{3}$ complete, at $0.15   750
15,000 units $\frac{1}{3}$ complete, at $0.05   250
     Total.. $ 5,500

Department II

15,000 units in process:
Cost in preceding department (Department I):
15,000 units 100% complete, at $0.50..$7,500
Cost in Department II (labor and overhead $\frac{1}{3}$ complete):
15,000 units $\frac{1}{3}$ complete, at $0.30 1,500
15,000 units $\frac{1}{3}$ complete, at $0.16   800
     Total cost of unfinished units... $ 9,800
5,000 units completed but not transferred out:
Cost in preceding department (Department I):
5,000 units 100% complete, at $0.50...$2,500
Cost in Department II (labor and overhead 100% complete):
5,000 units 100% complete, at $0.30.. 1,500
5,000 units 100% complete, at $0.16..   800   4,800
     Total Cost of Inventory... $14,600

Department III

5,000 units in process:
Cost in preceding departments (Departments I and II):
5,000 units 100% complete, at $0.96..$4,800
Cost in Department III (labor and overhead 40% complete):
5,000 units 40% complete, at $0.20   400
5,000 units 40% complete, at $0.14   280
     Total .... $ 5,480

SPECIAL PROBLEMS OF PROCESS COST ACCOUNTING

In view of the wide variety of conditions under which process cost accounting might operate, a number of special problems will arise. These will be discussed in detail in this and in subsequent chapters. Among these problems are:

1. *The effect of lost units* (whether due to spoilage or shrinkage) on process cost accounting. These units may be lost at the beginning, during, or at the end of the departmental manufacturing operations. This problem of lost units must be further analyzed to determine:
   a) The *effect on the unit costs* in the department in which the loss occurs, and
   b) The *effect on the cumulative unit costs.*
2. The *meaning of* and the *methods of computing the final work-in-process* inventories. Two methods can be used, and these check each other:
   a) The *account-balance* method, and
   b) The *analyzed-by-elements* method.
3. The accounting treatment of *materials added to production in any department after the first.* These materials may:
   a) *Increase* the number of the units in production, or
   b) *Not* affect the number of the units in production.
4. The treatment of the *work-in-process inventory* at the beginning of the period when computing unit costs. Two methods are used:
   a) The *average method;* and
   b) The *first-in, first-out method* (Fifo).
5. The proration of costs when *multiple products* are manufactured simultaneously in a given department and complete segregation of operations and costs is not possible. Sometimes this problem is referred to as *joint-product* or *coproduct* accounting.
6. The effect of *by-products* on process cost accounting.

EFFECT OF LOST UNITS ON PROCESS COST ACCOUNTING

Lost or spoiled units occur in some industries due to shrinkage, evaporation, or defective work. Lost or spoiled units do not affect the *total* costs of manufacturing during a given period but do increase the *unit* costs. This increase in unit costs is due to the fact that the cost of the work done on the lost units must be absorbed by the remaining good units, thus increasing the unit costs of these good units.

The problem of lost unit cost accounting involves two phases: (*a*) the cost of the work done on the lost units in the *department in which the loss or spoilage occurs,* and (*b*) the cost of the work done on the lost units in the *preceding departments.*

The cost of work done on the lost units in the department in which the loss occurs is handled quite simply. By omitting the lost unit quantity from the production in that department, a smaller equivalent production results. Dividing a smaller quantity into the material, labor, and overhead costs yields a *higher per unit cost* for each element.

The unit cost of the work done on the lost units in preceding departments is computed as follows:

a) Determine the *cost* of the work transferred into the department, including those subsequently lost or spoiled.
b) Divide this cost by the remaining good units (after deducting those spoiled or lost). This gives the corrected *cost per unit* for preceding departments.
c) Subtracting from this *corrected unit cost,* the unit cost of the units when transferred in gives the lost unit cost.

Another method, which is perhaps easier to compute, is as follows:

a) Multiply the *lost units* by the *unit cost* for the preceding departments.
b) Divide this result by the remaining good units (those received from preceding department less spoiled units) to obtain the lost unit cost.

ILLUSTRATION OF THE COMPUTATION OF LOST UNIT COSTS

The *lost unit cost* may be recorded as a separate element of cost on the cost of production report. To illustrate the computation of the lost unit costs and the effect of these lost unit costs on the cost of production report and the work-in-process inventory, the summary cost of production report of the Alton Manufacturing Company, previously given for the month of January, is again used; but the quantity of production figures has been changed to provide for the lost units. The material costs have been changed to simplify the computations.

The data relating to the summary cost of production report are shown in Illustration 4–4. The summary cost of production report for January for these data is given in Illustration 4–5. The computations for the departments are as follows:

Department I

1. Equivalent production for material costs is:

	Units
Completed and transferred to next department	45,000
In process but complete as to material costs	10,000
Equivalent Production for Material Costs, Department I	55,000

$$\frac{\$16,500}{55,000 \text{ units}} = \$0.30 \text{ unit cost for material.}$$

Illustration 4–4

ANALYSIS OF COST OF PRODUCTION DATA

For Month of January, 19—

QUANTITY OF PRODUCTION DATA (In Pounds)

	Department I	Department II	Department III
QUANTITY TO BE ACCOUNTED FOR:			
Put into Process....................	60,000		
Received in Department.............		45,000	25,000
To Be Accounted For.............	60,000	45,000	25,000
QUANTITY ACCOUNTED FOR AS FOLLOWS:			
Completed and Transferred to Next Department.......................	45,000	25,000	20,000
Completed and on Hand in Department..	.....	5,000	.....
Work-in-Process:			
Material, 100% Complete, Labor and Overhead, 50% Complete.........	10,000		
Labor and Overhead, 33⅓% Complete		15,000	
Labor and Overhead, 50% Complete.			4,000
Lost or Spoiled Production...........	5,000	0	1,000
Total Accounted For.............	60,000	45,000	25,000

DEPARTMENTAL COST OF PRODUCTION DATA

	Department I	Department II	Department III
Material Costs.........................	$16,500.00	....	....
Labor Costs..........................	7,500.00	$10,500.00	$4,400.00
Manufacturing Overhead (Direct and Apportioned).........................	2,500.00	5,600.00	3,080.00
Total Departmental Costs.........	$26,500.00	$16,100.00	$7,480.00

2. Equivalent production for labor and overhead costs is:

	Pounds
Completed and transferred	45,000
In process, ½ complete, 10,000 pounds, equal to.................	5,000
Equivalent Production for Labor and Overhead, Department I	50,000

$$\frac{\$7,500}{50,000 \text{ lbs.}} = \$0.15 \text{ unit cost for labor.}$$

$$\frac{\$2,500}{50,000 \text{ lbs.}} = \$0.05 \text{ unit cost for overhead.}$$

Illustration 4–5

ALTON MANUFACTURING COMPANY
SUMMARY COST OF PRODUCTION REPORT
For Month of January, 19—

	Department I Cost	Per Unit	Department II Cost	Per Unit	Department III Cost	Per Unit	Totals Cost	Per Unit
COST IN PRECEDING DEPARTMENT:								
Transferred in during Month...............			$22,500.00	$0.50	$24,000.00	$0.96	xxx	xxx
Additional Cost for Lost Units...........					xx	0.04		$0.04
Adjusted Unit Cost Total...............			$22,500.00	$0.50	$24,000.00	$1.00		$0.04
COST IN CURRENT DEPARTMENT:								
Material Costs...............	$16,500.00	$0.30	$10,500.00	$0.30	$4,400.00	$0.20	$16,500.00	$0.30
Labor Costs...............	7,500.00	0.15	5,600.00	0.16	3,080.00	0.14	22,400.00	0.65
Manufacturing Overhead Costs............	2,500.00	0.05					11,180.00	0.35
Total Departmental Costs.............	$26,500.00	$0.50	$16,100.00	$0.46	$7,480.00	$0.34	$50,080.00	$1.30
CUMULATIVE COST TOTAL............	$26,500.00	xx	$38,600.00	xx	$31,480.00	xx	$50,080.00	xx
Transferred to Next Department............	$22,500.00	$0.50	$24,000.00	$0.96	$26,800.00	$1.34	$26,800.00	$1.34
Work-in-Process:								
Completed and on Hand, 1/31/—............			4,800.00	0.96	4,680.00		4,800.00	xx
Work-in-Process, 1/31/—............	4,000.00		9,800.00	0.96			18,480.00	
CUMULATIVE COST DISTRIBUTION............	$26,500.00		$38,600.00		$31,480.00		$50,080.00	

QUANTITY OF PRODUCTION REPORT (In Pounds)

	Department I	Department II	Department III
QUANTITY TO BE ACCOUNTED FOR:			
Completed and on Hand, 1/1/—............			
Work-in-Process, 1/1/—............			
Put into Process or Received from Preceding Departments............	60,000	45,000	25,000
To Be Accounted For.............	60,000	45,000	25,000
QUANTITY ACCOUNTED FOR AS FOLLOWS:			
Transferred to Next Department............	45,000	25,000	20,000
Work-in-Process:			
Completed and on Hand, 1/31/—*............	0	5,000	0
Work-in-Process, 1/31/—............	10,000(⅓)	15,000(⅔)	4,000(¾)
Lost or Spoiled Production............	5,000	0	1,000
Total Accounted For............	60,000	45,000	25,000

* Figures in parentheses indicate stage of completion of work-in-process for labor and overhead.

By omitting the 5,000 pounds lost in production, the equivalent production is a smaller quantity. Dividing by a smaller quantity results in a larger unit cost.

3. Computation of work-in-process inventory, January 31, in Department I:

10,000 lbs. × 100% × $0.30 (material cost) $3,000
10,000 lbs. × 50% × $0.15 (labor cost).............................. 750
10,000 lbs. × 50% × $0.05 (overhead cost)......................... 250
Work-in-Process Inventory, Department I.................$4,000

Department II

1. Equivalent production for labor and overhead costs is:

                                                                    Pounds
Completed and transferred 25,000
Completed and on hand 5,000
In process, $\frac{1}{3}$ complete (15,000 × $\frac{1}{3}$)................. 5,000
Equivalent Production for Labor and
Overhead, Department II....................35,000

$$\frac{\$10,500}{35,000 \text{ lbs.}} = \$0.30 \text{ unit cost for labor.}$$

$$\frac{\$5,600}{35,000 \text{ lbs.}} = \$0.16 \text{ unit cost for overhead.}$$

2. Computation of work-in-process inventory, January 31, Department II:

5,000 lbs., complete as to Departments I and II @ $0.96.................$ 4,800
15,000 lbs., cost in Department I .... @   0.50................. 7,500
15,000 lbs. × $\frac{1}{3}$ × $0.30, Department II (labor cost) 1,500
15,000 lbs. × $\frac{1}{3}$ × $0.16, Department II (overhead cost)................... 800
Work-in-Process Inventory, Department II $14,600

Department III

1. Equivalent production for labor and overhead, omitting the 1,000 pounds lost in production, is 20,000 pounds plus one half of 4,000 pounds, or 22,000 pounds. The cost of the work done on the 1,000 pounds in Department III *only,* is automatically absorbed by dividing by a smaller quantity with the following resulting unit costs in Department III:

$$\frac{\$4,400}{22,000 \text{ lbs.}} = \$0.20 \text{ unit cost for labor.}$$

$$\frac{\$3,080}{22,000 \text{ lbs.}} = \$0.14 \text{ unit cost for overhead.}$$

2. Computation of the additional *unit cost* for work done in Departments I and II on the lost units is as follows:

> 1,000 pounds × the cumulative cost for Departments I and II ($0.50 plus $0.46) or $0.96 equals $960.
>
> Dividing this figure ($960) by the remaining good units that came into Department III (25,000 pounds less 1,000), 24,000 pounds, results in an additional unit cost of $0.04 for the lost units.

3. Computation of the work-in-process inventory, January 31, Department III:

4,000 lbs. × $0.96 (cost in Departments I and II)	$3,840
4,000 lbs. × $0.04 — in additional cost for first two departments for lost units	160
Total costs for Departments I and II	$4,000
4,000 lbs. × ½ × $0.20 (for labor cost in Department III)	400
4,000 lbs. × ½ × $0.14 (for overhead cost in Department III)	280
Work-in-Process Inventory, Department III	$4,680

Although in the preceding illustration, the lost unit cost was stated as a separate computation for any department after the first, such a separate unit cost statement may not be necessary. Dividing the total costs for the preceding department by the quantity received from the preceding departments *minus* the number of units lost or spoiled will produce the "corrected unit cost" for the work done in the preceding departments.

Using Illustration 4–4, Department III, dividing 24,000 units (25,000 units minus the lost 1,000 lost units) into $24,000, the cost of work done in the preceding departments, results in a *corrected unit* cost of $1.

ILLUSTRATIVE ACCOUNTING ENTRIES FOR THE PROCESS COST ACCOUNTING CYCLE

The accounting entries in journal form to record the production costs and the interdepartmental transfers for the month of January would be as follows:

(1)

Work-in-Process — Department I	26,500	
Stores		16,500
Payroll		7,500
Manufacturing Overhead Control		2,500

To record the cost of work put into process in Department I in January.

(2)

Work-in-Process — Department II	38,600	
Work-in-Process — Department I		22,500
Payroll		10,500
Manufacturing Overhead Control		5,600

To record the transfer from Department I of 45,000 units at 50 cents and the charges for payroll and manufacturing overhead during January in Department II.

(3)

Work-in-Process—Department III...31,480
    Work-in-Process—Department II 24,000
    Payroll... 4,400
    Manufacturing Overhead Control 3,080
To record the transfer from Department II of 25,000 units at
96 cents, and the charges for payroll and manufacturing
overhead during January in Department III.

(4)

Finished Goods...26,800
    Work-in-Process—Department III................................. 26,800
To record the transfer to finished goods stock room—
20,000 units at $1.34.

If a summary entry is to be made for the entire month's operation
with but a single Work-in-Process account, not on a departmental basis,
the following journal entries might be used:

(1)

Work-in-Process...50,080
    Stores.. 16,500
    Payroll... 22,400
    Manufacturing Overhead Control 11,180
To record operating costs for the month.

(2)

Finished Goods...26,800
    Work-in-Process... 26,800
To record cost of the finished work—20,000 units at $1.34.

AN ALTERNATIVE METHOD OF RECORDING FINISHED GOODS FOR A PROCESS COST ACCOUNTING FIRM

An alternative method of recording the finished goods for a firm using
a process cost accounting system eliminates the departmental transfers.
This is accomplished by computing the *final work-in-process inventory
in each department* from the individual or summary cost of production
reports and transferring the balance in the work-in-process accounts to
the Finished Goods account. The accounting effect is the same as when
there are departmental transfers. The departmental transfer method is
more desirable because it is more logical and follows the data shown on
the cost of production report. It also is probably less prone to mistakes,
since there must be detailed verification on the cost of production reports
as indicated by the details which make up the "CUMULATIVE COST
TOTAL ACCOUNTED FOR" in each departmental column. To illustrate the entry to be made when there are no departmental transfer
entries, the illustration of cost of production report (Illustration 4–5) for
the month of January is used. Exclusive of the departmental transfers,
the charges to the three departmental work-in-process accounts and the
amount of the final work-in-process inventories are given so that the

amount of the charge to the Finished Goods account may be computed, viz:

Department	Charges to Work-in-Process Account	Final Work-in-Process Inventory	Difference as Charge to Finished Goods Account
Work-in-Process — Department I $26,500		$ 4,000	$22,500
Work-in-Process — Department II.............. 16,100		14,600	1,500
Work-in-Process — Department III 7,480		4,680	2,800

The journal entry to record this without departmental transfers would then be:

```
Finished Goods.................................................................26,800
       Work-in-Process — Department I ......................................      22,500
       Work-in-Process — Department II .....................................       1,500
       Work-in-Process — Department III....................................       2,800
       To record cost of finished goods for the month.
```

ACCOUNTING FOR TWO OR MORE PRODUCTS PREPARED FROM THE SAME MATERIAL IN DEPARTMENT I

In some firms using a department or process cost accounting system, material processed in the initial department is then sent to two different departments *to prepare simultaneously two or more different products.* It is termed a "tree problem" because from one trunk, two branches or products are developed. The simplest method of solving a problem of this type is to treat the cost of production of the basic material in Department I as a separate one-department problem. Then separate cost of production reports are prepared for each of the two different products. The cost of the materials received from Department I is treated in Department II for either product as though it were purchased from an outsider. Thus it will be merged with whatever other materials are used in Department II. Hence no separate computation or unit cost figures will appear in Department II for lost units. The effect of this procedure is to make three separate problems summarized on one or two cost of production reports: one problem for costing the production in Department I; and one problem each, for Product A, covering the costing in Departments II and III; and one for Product B, covering the costing in Departments II and III. To illustrate this procedure diagrammatically, Illustration 4–6 should be studied.

To illustrate the solution of such a problem and the resulting cost of production reports (Illustration 4–7A), the data of production shown in Illustration 4–7 must be considered.

Illustration 4–6

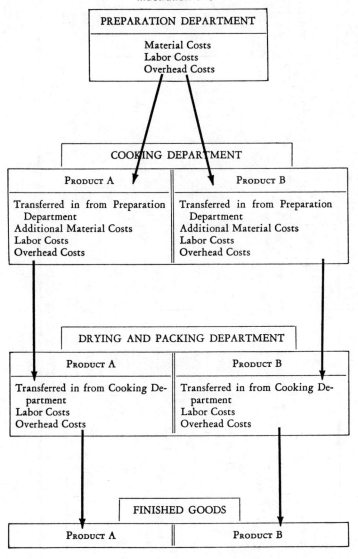

Illustration 4–7. Analysis of Cost of Production Data

For Month of March, 19—

QUANTITY OF PRODUCTION DATA (In Pounds)

	Preparation Department, Dept. I	Cooking Department, Dept. II		Drying and Packing, Dept. III	
		Product A	Product B	Product A	Product B
QUANTITY TO BE ACCOUNTED FOR:					
Put into Production	100,000	22,000	18,000	0	0
Received in dept., from preceding dept.	0	38,000	32,000	45,000	30,000
To Be Accounted For	100,000	60,000	50,000	45,000	30,000
QUANTITY ACCOUNTED FOR AS FOLLOWS:					
Finished and Transferred:					
Product A	38,000				
Product B	32,000				
Total	70,000	45,000	30,000	35,000	20,000
Work-in-Process, 3/31/—:					
All Materials, 3/5 Labor and Overhead	25,000				
All Materials, 1/2 Labor and Overhead		10,000	16,000		
All Materials, 3/4 Labor and Overhead				7,000	
5/7 Labor and Overhead					8,000
1/2 Labor and Overhead					
Lost or Spoiled Production	5,000	5,000	4,000	3,000	2,000
Total Accounted For	100,000	60,000	50,000	45,000	30,000

COSTS OF PRODUCTION

	Preparation Department, Dept. I	Cooking Department, Dept. II		Drying and Packing, Dept. III	
		Product A	Product B	Product A	Product B
Material Costs	$19,000.00	$26,500.00	$12,800.00	0	0
Labor Costs	34,000.00	24,000.00	25,200.00	$18,000.00	$ 7,680.00
Manufacturing Overhead Costs	12,750.00	10,000.00	4,200.00	4,800.00	2,400.00
Total Departmental Costs	$65,750.00	$60,500.00	$42,200.00	$22,800.00	$10,080.00

Illustration 4–7A

SUMMARY COST OF PRODUCTION REPORT—PREPARATION DEPARTMENT

For Month of March, 19—

	Total	Per Unit
COSTS IN DEPARTMENT DURING WEEK:		
Material Costs*	$19,000.00	$0.20
Labor Costs†	34,000.00	0.40
Manufacturing Overhead Costs‡	12,750.00	0.15
Total Departmental Costs	$65,750.00	$0.75
CUMULATIVE COST TOTAL ANALYSIS:		
Finished and Transferred:		
Product A	$28,500.00	
Product B	24,000.00	
Work-in-Process, 3/31/—:		
Materials (25,000 × $0.20)	5,000.00	
Labor (25,000 × $\frac{3}{5}$ × $0.40)	6,000.00	
Manufacturing Overhead (25,000 × $\frac{3}{5}$ × $0.15)	2,250.00	
Cumulative Cost Accounted For	$65,750.00	

* $19,000.00 ÷ (70,000 units + 25,000 units) = $0.20
† $34,000.00 ÷ [70,000 units + $\frac{3}{5}$ (25,000)] = $0.40
‡ $12,750.00 ÷ [70,000 units + $\frac{3}{5}$ (25,000)] = $0.15

Illustration 4–7A (continued)

SUMMARY COST OF PRODUCTION REPORT
For Month of March, 19—

	COOKING DEPARTMENT				DRYING AND PACKING DEPARTMENT			
	Product A		Product B		Product A		Product B	
	Total Cost	Unit Cost	Total Cost	Unit Cost	Total Cost	Unit	Total	Unit
COST IN PRECEDING DEPARTMENT:								
Transferred into Department during Month					$75,600.00	$1.68	$45,000.00	$1.50
Additional Costs for Lost Units					xx	0.12	xx	0.1071
Adjusted Unit Cost Total					$75,600.00	$1.80	$45,000.00	$1.6071
COST IN CURRENT DEPARTMENT:								
Material from Preparation Department	$28,500.00		$24,000.00					
Additional Materials Added in This Department	26,500.00		12,800.00					
Total Material Costs	$55,000.00	$1.00	$36,800.00	$0.80	xxx	$0.45	xxx	
Labor Costs	24,000.00	0.48	25,200.00	0.60	$18,000.00	0.12	$ 7,680.00	$0.32
Manufacturing Overhead Costs	10,000.00	0.20	4,200.00	0.10	4,800.00		2,400.00	0.10
Total Departmental Costs	$89,000.00	$1.68	$66,200.00	$1.50	$22,800.00	$0.57	$10,080.00	$0.42
CUMULATIVE COST TOTAL	$89,000.00	$1.68	$66,200.00	$1.50	$98,400.00	$2.37	$55,080.00	$2.0271
Finished and Transferred	$75,600.00		$45,000.00		$82,950.00		$40,542.00	
Finished and on Hand	0		0		0		0	
Work-in-Process, 3/31/—:								
Preceding Department Cost					11,760.00		12,000.00	
Lost Unit Cost					840.00		856.80	
Material Costs	10,000.00		12,800.00		0		0	
Labor Costs	2,400.00		7,200.00		2,250.00		1,280.00	
Manufacturing Overhead Costs	1,000.00		1,200.00		600.00		400.00	
CUMULATIVE COST TOTAL ANALYSIS	$89,000.00		$66,200.00		$98,400.00		$55,078.80*	

ALTERNATIVE COST OF PRODUCTION REPORT FOR TWO PRODUCTS FROM SAME MATERIAL IN DEPARTMENT I

Instead of using a cost of production report showing the costs of the two products on a *departmental* basis as given in this chapter previously, it is possible to prepare such a report on a *product* rather than on a *departmental* basis. In that event, the rearrangement of the columns would be as follows:

COST DESCRIPTION	PRODUCT A				PRODUCT B			
	Cooking Dept.		Drying and Packing		Cooking Dept.		Drying and Packing	
	Total	Unit	Total	Unit	Total	Unit	Total	Unit

The ultimate figures would be the same as previously given, but the emphasis in the cost of production report is on the products not on the departments.

QUESTIONS FOR REVIEW

1. What are the four characteristics of process cost accounting that distinguish it from job order cost determination?

2. What is the simplest method of determining the work-in-process inventory in any department of a firm using process cost determination? What alternative method can be used to verify this figure?

3. What is the meaning and purpose of equivalent production? Under what conditions is it necessary to compute this figure?

4. Why is it usually necessary to compute a different equivalent production for materials and for labor?

5. In Department I, the quantity of production for the month of June indicated the following:

	Units
Completed and transferred	50,000
Completed and not transferred	10,000
Work-in-process—materials, 25% complete	6,000
Work-in-process—labor and manufacturing overhead, 20% complete	6,000
Units lost or spoiled in production	4,000

How many units were started in production? What is the equivalent production for materials, labor, and manufacturing overhead?

6. In Department II, 20,000 units were received from Department I at a unit cost of $3.60. In Department II, 14,000 units were completed and transferred to Department III, 4,000 were still in process, with one half the labor and overhead applied thereon, and 2,000 units were lost or spoiled. Compute the corrected unit cost in Department II for work done in Department I. What is the lost unit cost?

7. The unit costs in Department II were as follows:

> Corrected unit cost for Department I $3 $30,000
> Labor costs in Department II 2   16,000
> Manufacturing overhead costs in Department II.................. 1   8,000

The number of units received from Department I, 12,000, of which 2,000 were lost. Work-in-process at the end of the period was 3,000 units, one-third complete as to labor and overhead. All completed work was transferred to Department III. Prepare entries in journal form to cover all the transactions affecting Department II.

8. Instead of transferring the cost of manufacturing sequentially from one department to the next, it is possible to make one compound entry charging the Finished Goods account for work completed during the period and crediting the various work-in-process accounts. Explain how the figures for this entry are obtained. Why is it more desirable to use the accounting method whereby a record is made of the transfers from one department to another, instead of making a single compound entry to the Finished Goods account at the end of the period?

9. The cost of work done on the lost units in the department in which these units are lost is not considered in process cost accounting. Explain the meaning of this statement.

10. Journal entries to record the cost of production in Department II or Department III of a plant may be made in two separate entries, or may be combined into a single entry. What are the two sets of information recorded in these entries? What is the source of the data for these entries?

PROBLEMS—GROUP A

Problem 4–1. **Purpose:** *Cost of Production Report and Journal Entries for a Three-Department Factory; Lost Units in Department I Only*

The Dartmouth Manufacturing Company produces a single product in its three-department factory. Materials are used only in the first department.

The production statistics for the month of April (in units) were as follows:

	Dept. I	Dept. II	Dept. III
Completed and transferred out......................	60,000	40,000	25,000
Completed and on hand...............................	20,000	5,000	0
Work-in-process, 100% material,			
40% of labor and overhead......................	25,000	15,000	15,000
Units lost or spoiled...................................	5,000	0	0

There was no work-in-process at the beginning of the month. During the month materials used cost $42,000.

The labor and manufacturing overhead costs for the month were:

	Dept. I	Dept. II	Dept. III
Labor costs	$54,000	$25,500	$62,000
Manufacturing overhead costs.................	36,000	15,300	12,400

Required:

From this data, you are asked to prepare:

a) Cost of production report, showing costs, quantity statement, and equivalent production for each department.
b) Journal entries to record the manufacturing operations.
c) The departmental work-in-process inventories in analyzed form.

Problem 4–2.   Purpose: *Cost of Production Report and Journal Entries; Units Lost in All Departments*

The Dolfin Manufacturing Company operates a plant on a continuous process manufacturing basis with a single product going through three successive producing departments. Materials are used in the initial department only. There is no work-in-process at the beginning of the month of May for which the following cost data were obtained:

Department I

Units put into production	85,000
Units completed and transferred	60,000
Units in process, May 31, on which	
50% of material and 40% of the labor	
and overhead had been applied...........................	20,000
Units lost...	5,000

Department II

Units completed and transferred	35,000
Units completed and not transferred yet.................	5,000
Units in process, two-thirds complete	
as to labor and overhead costs...........................	15,000
Units spoiled or lost	5,000

Department III

Units completed and sent to stock room 20,000
Units in process, one-half complete as
   to labor and overhead costs 8,000
Units lost in production....................................... 7,000

The operating costs departmentally were as follows:

	Dept. I	Dept. II	Dept. III
Material costs $73,500		0	0
Labor costs.................................... 42,500		$60,000	$72,000
Manufacturing overhead.................. 17,000		45,000	42,000

Required:

From this information you are asked to prepare:

a) Cost of production report showing the costs, quantity statement, equivalent production, and work-in-process in analyzed form for each department.
b) Journal entries to cover the manufacturing cycle.

Problem 4–3. Purpose: *Process Costing When Two Products Are Manufactured Simultaneously from Materials Produced in the Initial Department*

The Davis Manufacturing Company has three producing departments. In Department I raw materials are processed and transferred to Department II where they are used to prepare simultaneously two products known as A and B. This segregation is continued in Department III.

The production statistics for the month of June were as follows:

	Department I	Department II		Department III	
		Product A	Product B	Product A	Product B
Work-in-process June 30—:					
80% complete as to material, 60% complete as to labor and overhead.........................25,000 units		10,000	8,000	15,000	10,000
Transferred out:					
Product A 80,000		60,000		40,000	
Product B 88,000			75,000		60,000
Lost or spoiled.......................... 5,000		10,000	5,000	5,000	5,000

Costs for the month of June were:

	Department I	Department II		Department III	
		Product A	Product B	Product A	Product B
Material costs $105,280		0	0	0	0
Labor costs 58,560		$39,600	$39,900	$17,640	$26,400
Overhead costs 42,090		26,400	15,960	11,760	18,480

Required:

Using a cost of production report designed as follows, prepare a composite report:

		Department II		Department III	
	Department I	Product A	Product B	Product A	Product B
Cost in Preceding Department...					
Material costs.........................					
Labor costs............................					
Overhead costs........................					

In this report, show the quantity statement and the work-in-process in analyzed form. Using one work-in-process account for each department, prepare entries in journal form to record the cost accounting cycle. (Compute unit costs correct to six decimal places.)

Problem 4–4.   Purpose: *Problem Involving a Simple Process Cost Accounting Situation; Added Materials in Department after the First Do Not Increase Volume*

The Daley Manufacturing Company produces a single product on a continuous basis. Two manufacturing departments are involved. Materials are added in each department but do not increase the number of units in production.

Production for the month of July (in units) is:

	Machining Dept.	Assembling Dept.
Completed and transferred.............................180,000		150,000
In process, 75% of material, 50% labor and overhead.. 40,000		20,000
Lost or spoiled in production 20,000		?

The costs of manufacturing in the departments for the month of July were:

	Machining Dept.	Assembling Dept.
Material costs...$73,500		$66,000
Labor costs.. 84,000		44,800
Manufacturing overhead................................ 68,000		40,000

Required:

a) Cost of production report for month of July (correct to six decimal places).

b) Journal entries to record cost accounting cycle.

Problem 4–5.   Purpose: *Journal Entries Covering the Cost Accounting Cycle for a Three-Department Process Plant*

The following cost of production report has been submitted to you for consideration and analysis. On the basis of this statement, prepare journal entries with explanations to record the accounting information covering the cycle for the month of August.

DAWSON MANUFACTURING COMPANY
SUMMARY COST OF PRODUCTION REPORT
For Month Ending August 31, 19—

	Department I		Department II		Department III	
	Total Cost	Unit Cost	Total Cost	Unit Cost	Total Cost	Unit Cost
Cost in Preceding Dept................			$4,500		$5,200	
Unit Cost Corrected for Lost Units.............................				$0.50		$0.88
Current Costs:						
Material Costs........................	$2,500	$0.20	$1,000	$0.12	$2,000	$0.30
Labor Costs............................	1,500	0.15	1,500	0.15	1,200	0.20
Overhead Costs......................	1,000	0.10	500	0.05	300	0.05
Total Current Cost...............	$5,000	$0.45	$3,000	$0.32	$3,500	$0.55
CUMULATIVE COST TOTAL ..	$5,000	$0.45	$7,500	$0.82	$8,700	$1.43

Units completed, 5,000; units sold, 4,000.

PROBLEMS — GROUP B

Problem 4–6. Purpose: *Cost of Production Report and Journal Entries, Three Departments; Units Lost in Each Department*

The costs of production of the Dellis Manufacturing Company for the month of April were as follows:

	Material Costs	Labor Costs	Manufacturing Overhead Costs
Department I..	$127,600	$15,400	$66,000
Department II	0	22,500	15,000
Department III.....................................	0	10,500	4,500

Production statistics for the month (in units) were as follows:

	Department I	Department II	Department III
Completed and transferred 90,000		60,000	40,000
Completed and not transferred yet........10,000		0	0
In process:			
80% complete as to materials............20,000			
50% complete as to labor and overhead..................................20,000			
60% complete as to labor and overhead...................................		25,000	
66⅔% complete as to labor and overhead			15,000
Lost in production 10,000		5,000	5,000

Required:

a) From this information you are asked to prepare for the month of April, a cost of production report, showing the costs by elements, by departments, the total departmental, and the total cumulative costs, as well as the unit costs by elements and in total (correct to six decimal places).
b) In addition, prepare a statement of the work-in-process inventories in analyzed form for each department.
c) Make journal entries to cover the transactions recorded on the cost of production report.

Problem 4–7.   Purpose: *CPA Problem of Cost of Production for a Single-Product Firm, So That Inventory Values May Be Verified on the Basis of Cost or Market Whichever Is Lower*

The Denver Supply Company produces a single product in its one-department factory. Inventories of work-in-process, finished goods, and defective work are valued at cost or market whichever is lower. At December 31, the market price of the finished goods and work-in-process were considerably above the cost. However, the market price of the defective work (seconds) was $1 per unit.

Materials are put into production at the start of operations. Overhead is applied at the rate of 80% of direct labor costs.

The following information has been taken from the accounting records:

Description	Units	Material Costs	Direct Labor Costs
Inventory, January 1, 19—..........................	100,000	$100,000	$160,000
New production during year........................	500,000	550,000	997,500
Units completed during year:			
Good units...	500,000		
Defective units......................................	10,000		
Finished goods inventory, December 31, includes the 10,000 defective units			

Defective units occur at the end of the manufacturing operations.
The company records showed the following inventories as of December 31:

Finished goods inventory, 110,000 units valued at..................$504,900
Work-in-process, 90,000 units, 50% completed...................... 330,480

Required:

From this information, you are asked to prepare schedules showing:

a) Effective or equivalent production.
b) Unit costs of production of materials, labor, and manufacturing overhead.
c) Pricing of inventories of finished goods, defective units, and work-in-process.
d) Journal entries if any to correctly state the inventory valuation of finished goods and work-in-process, ignoring the income tax implication.

(Adapted from an AICPA Uniform Examination)

Problem 4–8. Purpose: *Simplified Cost of Production Report and Managerial Implications of the Operating Results; Three Departments*

The Damont Manufacturing Company operates a continuous cost accounting system. This firm produces a single rug cleaning compound, the manufacture of which goes through three successive departments.

Cost and production data for Department I for the month of July were:

	Pounds
Production in this department and transferred.............................40,000	
In process, July 31, 6,000 pounds, $\frac{5}{6}$ complete as to materials,	
$\frac{1}{3}$ complete as to labor and manufacturing overhead costs	6,000
Lost in the production process...	2,000

Manufacturing costs in Department I during July were: material costs, $22,500; direct labor costs, $84,000; and manufacturing overhead costs, $21,000.

Cost and production data for Department II for the month of July were:

Of the 40,000 pounds received into this department, 36,000 pounds were completed and transferred to Department III. Three thousand pounds were still in process with two thirds of the required labor and manufacturing overhead applied. The balance was lost in production.

Manufacturing costs in Department II were: materials, 0; labor costs, $9,500; and manufacturing overhead costs, $4,560.

Cost and production data for Department III for the month of July were:

Work completed and packed ready for shipment, 30,000 pounds; 5,000 pounds were in process, estimated to be two-fifths completed as to labor and manufacturing overhead. The costs in this department for July were labor costs, $14,720; manufacturing overhead costs, $10,880.

All units not otherwise accounted for are presumed to have been lost in the processing.

Required:

a) Summary cost of production report for the month of July (correct to seven decimal places).
b) Statement of final work-in-process inventory in each department in analyzed form.
c) Journal entries to summarize the operating costs and departmental transfers for the month of July.
d) The sales income of the total finished goods production, if the gross profit is estimated at a rate of 50% of the sales price.

chapter 5

Historical Departmental or Process Cost Determination — Part II

INTRODUCTORY REVIEW

In the preceding chapter, it was indicated that process cost accounting requires a summary cost of production report on which are shown a *quantity of production statement, for a definite period of time,* on a *departmental basis.* Two methods of computing the final work-in-process inventory in each department were given: the *account method* and the *equivalent production method.*

In this chapter, the discussion, limited to a single product firm, covers the following procedures and problems:

1. Accounting treatment and computation of unit costs when materials are added to production in a department after the first and these materials—
   a) Do not increase the number of units in production, and
   b) Do increase the number of units being produced.
2. The effect of *lost units* on the unit costs when materials added to production in a department after the first and there is an *increase in the number of units* being produced.
3. The *average cost accounting method* of treating the initial work-in-process inventory in any given accounting period.
4. Simplifying unit cost computations in a department after the first.

PROCEDURES WHEN MATERIALS ARE ADDED TO PRODUCTION IN A DEPARTMENT AFTER THE FIRST

In many process type plants the necessary materials are placed into production in the initial manufacturing department, and thereafter it is merely a matter of additional factory labor and overhead in the other de-

111

partments to complete the work. In some plants, additional materials may be required in departments after the first. When additional materials are added, two possible situations may result:

1. The additional materials may merely change the nature or character of the product being manufactured but *will not add to the number of units* being produced. This would be the case in the manufacture of toys by the continuous process method, whereby, in departments after the first, materials are added to color the toys or ornaments are added to embellish them but neither of these materials—paint and ornaments—increases the number of toys being produced.
2. The additional materials may add to the quantity being produced, thus increasing the number of units. In the manufacture of paints, the addition of oils, dryers, pigments, etc., in a department after the first will increase the number of gallons being produced.

The procedure to be followed when the additional material *does not increase* the number of units being produced is similar to that previously described, except that in the departments after the first there will be an additional element of cost (materials) for which a unit cost must be computed. If, however, the addition of materials increases the *number of units being produced,* the unit costs for the preceding departments must be adjusted when cumulative *unit* costs are being computed. For example, 25,000 gallons were received from Department I at a unit cost of 30 cents with a total cost of $7,500. In Department II, 5,000 additional gallons of material were added, making the production in Department II on the basis of 30,000 gallons. In determining the *cumulative* unit cost, the total cost for Department I ($7,500) must be spread over 30,000 units now in production, making the adjusted unit cost for Department I, 25 cents ($7,500 ÷ 30,000 gallons). In the second department, the unit costs will be computed on the basis of the actual production of 30,000 gallons. However, in computing *cumulative unit costs* for the first and second departments, the *adjusted* unit cost for the first department must be used. This same adjusted unit cost for the first department must be used in computing the *work-in-process inventory in the second department.*

ILLUSTRATION WHEN ADDED MATERIALS DO NOT INCREASE NUMBER OF UNITS IN PRODUCTION

For the sake of illustration and comparison, as well as a proper understanding of the effect that additional material has upon the number of units of production, the cost of production statement in Illustration 5–2 is for a situation in which the materials *do not increase* the number of units in production.

The data used in Illustration 5–2 are:

	Dept. I	Dept. II
Costs of production:		
Material costs	$48,000	$ 5,400
Labor costs	25,000	8,000
Manufacturing overhead costs	10,000	3,000
Totals	$83,000	$16,400
Quantity production figures in units:		
Started in production	15,000	6,000
Added materials—no increase in units	0	0
To Be Accounted For	15,000	6,000
Transferred to next department	6,000	4,000
Completed and on hand	2,000	0
Work-in-process: complete as to material, ½ complete as to labor and overhead	4,000	2,000
Lost in production	3,000	0
Total Accounted For	15,000	6,000

Illustration 5–1

COMPUTATION OF EQUIVALENT PRODUCTION AND UNIT COSTS, WHEN ADDED
MATERIALS DO NOT INCREASE NUMBER OF UNITS IN PRODUCTION

	Computation of Equivalent Production	Computation of Unit Costs
Department I:		
Material	12,000 units	$48,000 ÷ 12,000 units $4.00
Labor and overhead:		
Completed and transferred	6,000 units	
Completed and on hand	2,000	
In process, ½ complete (4,000 × ½)	2,000	
	10,000 units	
Labor costs		25,000 ÷ 10,000 units 2.50
Overhead costs		10,000 ÷ 10,000 units 1.00
Total Unit Costs		$7.50
Department II:		
Material	6,000 units	$5,400 ÷ 6,000 units $0.90
Labor and overhead:		
Completed and transferred	4,000 units	
In process, ½ complete (2,000 × ½)	1,000	
	5,000 units	
Labor costs		8,000 ÷ 5,000 units 1.60
Overhead costs		3,000 ÷ 5,000 units 0.60
Total Unit Costs		$3.10

It should be noted that the added material in Department II does not require the adjustment of the unit cost for work done in Department I, since the added material *did not increase* the number of units in production. The computation of the equivalent production and the unit costs for

Illustration 5-2

COMPANY A MANUFACTURING COMPANY
SUMMARY COST OF PRODUCTION REPORT
For the Month of January, 19—
(Additional Material in Department II Does Not Increase Quantity of Production)

	Department I		Department II	
	Cost	Per Unit	Cost	Per Unit
COSTS FOR THE MONTH OF JANUARY:				
Material Costs............................	$48,000.00	$4.00	$ 5,400.00	$ 0.90
Labor Costs...............................	25,000.00	2.50	8,000.00	1.60
Manufacturing Overhead Costs............	10,000.00	1.00	3,000.00	0.60
Total Costs in January................	$83,000.00	$7.50	$16,400.00	$ 3.10
Completed and on Hand, 1/1/—...........				
Work-in-Process, 1/1/—.................				
Transferred into Department in January....			45,000.00	7.50
CUMULATIVE TOTAL COST.............	$83,000.00	$7.50	$61,400.00	$10.60
Transferred to Next Department.............	$45,000.00	$7.50	$42,400.00	$10.60
Completed and on Hand, 1/31/—...........	15,000.00	7.50		
Work-in-Process, 1/31/—.................	23,000.00	5.75	19,000.00	9.50
CUMULATIVE COST DISTRIBUTION....	$83,000.00	xxx	$61,400.00	xxx

QUANTITY PRODUCTION REPORT (In Pounds)

QUANTITY TO BE ACCOUNTED FOR:		
Completed and on Hand, 1/1/—.................................		
Work-in-Process, 1/1/—...		
Put into Production in January...................................	15,000	
Received from Preceding Departments............................		6,000
To Be Accounted For...	15,000	6,000
QUANTITY ACCOUNTED FOR AS FOLLOWS:		
Transferred to Next Department.................................	6,000	4,000
Completed and on Hand, 1/31/—................................	2,000	
Work-in-Process, 1/31/—.....................................	4,000	2,000
Material Costs..	(100%)*	(100%)
Labor Costs..	(50%)	(50%)
Overhead Costs...	(50%)	(50%)
Lost or Spoiled in Production..................................	3,000	
Total Accounted For.....................................	15,000	6,000

* Indicates degree of completion of work-in-process.

this method is shown in Illustration 5–1. The cost of production report for this information is shown in Illustration 5–2.

ILLUSTRATION OF WHEN ADDED MATERIALS INCREASE THE NUMBER OF UNITS IN PRODUCTION

Using essentially the same data as in Illustration 5–2 except that in Department II the additional material used increases the number of units in production by 3,000, the cost of production report and the supporting tabulation of the computation of equivalent production are shown in Illustrations 5–4 and 5–3, respectively. Because the added materials in Department II do increase the number of units in production, there is required an adjustment of the *unit cost* for Department I; the *detailed computations of the work-in-process inventory* in Department II are shown, as well as the *journal entries covering* the cycle of production. Compare Illustrations 5–2 and 5–4. Because of the increase in number of units in Department II due to added materials, the total costs of units transferred to Department II must be spread over a larger number of

Illustration 5–3

COMPUTATION OF EQUIVALENT PRODUCTION AND UNIT COSTS WHEN ADDED MATERIALS INCREASE THE NUMBER OF UNITS IN PRODUCTION

	Computation of Equivalent Production	Computation of Unit Costs
Department I:		
Material.............................	12,000 units	$48,000 ÷ 12,000 units $4.00
Labor and overhead:		
Completed and transferred..............	6,000 units	
Completed and on hand...............	2,000	
In process, ½ complete (4,000 × ½)....	2,000	
	10,000 units	
Labor costs.........................		25,000 ÷ 10,000 units 2.50
Overhead costs......................		10,000 ÷ 10,000 units 1.00
Total Unit Costs..................		$7.50
Department II:		
Material.............................	9,000 units	$5,400 ÷ 9,000 units $0.60
Labor and overhead:		
Completed and transferred..............	7,000 units	
In process, ½ complete (2,000 × ½)....	1,000	
	8,000 units	
Labor costs...........................		8,000 ÷ 8,000 units 1.00
Overhead costs.......................		3,000 ÷ 8,000 units 0.375
Total Unit Costs....................		$1.975

Illustration 5–4

COMPANY B MANUFACTURING COMPANY
SUMMARY COST OF PRODUCTION REPORT

For the Month of January, 19—

(Material Added in Department II Increases the Number of Units Being Produced)

	Department I		Department II	
	Cost	Per Unit	Cost	Per Unit
COSTS FOR THE MONTH OF JANUARY:				
Material Costs..........................	$48,000.00	$4.00	$ 5,400.00	$0.60
Labor Costs.............................	25,000.00	2.50	8,000.00	1.00
Manufacturing Overhead Costs............	10,000.00	1.00	3,000.00	0.375
Total Costs in January................	$83,000.00	$7.50	$16,400.00	$1.975
Completed and on Hand, 1/1/—............				
Work-in-Process, 1/1/—.				
Transferred into Department in January......			45,000.00	5.00*
CUMULATIVE TOTAL COST..............	$83,000.00	$7.50	$61,400.00	$6.975
Transferred to Next Department.............	$45,000.00	$7.50	$48,825.00	$6.9750
Completed and on Hand, 1/31/—.............	15,000.00	7.50		
Work-in-Process, 1/31/—..................	23,000.00	5.75	12,575.00	6.2875
CUMULATIVE COST DISTRIBUTION......	$83,000.00	xxx	$61,400.00	xxx

* Adjusted for added material.

QUANTITY PRODUCTION REPORT (In Pounds)

QUANTITY TO BE ACCOUNTED FOR:		
Completed and on Hand, 1/1/—.............................		
Work-in-Process. 1/1/—..................................		
Put into Production in January.............................	15,000	3,000
Received from Preceding Departments........................		6,000
To Be Accounted For.....................................	15,000	9,000
QUANTITY ACCOUNTED FOR AS FOLLOWS:		
Transferred to Next Department.............................	6,000	7,000
Completed and on Hand, 1/31/—.............................	2,000	
Work-in-Process, 1/31/—.................................	4,000	2,000
Material Costs...	(100%)*	(100%)
Labor Costs...	(50%)	(50%)
Overhead Costs..	(50%)	(50%)
Lost or Spoiled in Production................................	3,000	
Total Accounted For.................................	15,000	9,000

* Indicates degree of completion of work-in-process.

units, thus adjusting the unit cost for Department I to a lower figure in the cumulation, e.g.:

Transferred to Department II ....$45,000.00 ÷ 6,000 units = $7.50

Increase in units due to added materials..................... 3,000

Adjusted unit cost for Department I, for work in
  Department II...$45,000.00 ÷ 9,000 units = $5.00

When this figure of $5 is added to the unit costs of $1.975 for Department II, the cumulative unit cost for the finished production is $6.975. This figure must be used when computing the work-in-process inventory in Department II at the end of January, as is illustrated in the following tabulation:

Work-in-process inventory, Department II, Company B:

2,000 units (adjusted unit cost for Department I)	@ $5.00............	$10,000
2,000 units, material costs, Department II	@ 0.60............	1,200
2,000 units, labor costs, Department II ($\frac{1}{2} \times$ $1.00)	@ 0.50............	1,000
2,000 units, overhead costs, Department II ($\frac{1}{2} \times$ $0.375) @	0.1875.........	375
Total Work-in-Process Inventory, Department II............................		$12,575

Journal entries to summarize the data presented on the cost of production report for Company B (Illustration 5–4) where added materials increase the number of units being manufactured would be:

(1)

Work-in-Process—Department I 83,000		
Stores...		48,000
Payroll...		25,000
Manufacturing Overhead..		10,000
To record costs for January in Department I.		

(2)

Work-in-Process—Department II 61,400		
Work-in-Process—Department I		45,000
Stores...		5,400
Payroll...		8,000
Manufacturing Overhead..		3,000
To record costs for January in Department II including transfer from Department I.		

(3)

Finished Goods...48,825		
Work-in-Process—Department II		48,825
To record the cost of work completed and placed in stock room.		

EFFECT OF LOST UNITS ON ADDED MATERIALS COSTS

In any department after the first, lost units require an adjustment of the unit costs for the preceding departments before calculating the cumulative unit cost. This adjustment is affected by the addition of materials which increase the number of units in production.

The basic rule to remember when computing lost unit costs in a department after the first when materials are added which increase the number of units in production is:

> *If the number of units are increased in a department after the first because of added materials, the unit cost for the preceding departments must FIRST be adjusted for the added materials before computing the lost unit cost.*

The computation of lost unit costs in the department when materials are added and the increased number of units being manufactured necessitates *first* computing the *adjusted unit cost for the preceding departments* and then using this adjusted unit cost in computing the lost unit cost is as follows:

In Department III the cost and production figures, which included the increased volume due to added material, for the month of March were:

15,000 units	Cost in preceding departments: total	$30,000	unit cost	$2
10,000 units	Material costs (100% complete) total	$ 5,000	unit cost	$0.50
	Labor costs ($\frac{1}{3}$ complete) total	2,100	unit cost	0.10
	Overhead costs ($\frac{1}{3}$ complete) total	6,300	unit cost	0.30
25,000 units	Total to Be Accounted For	$43,400		$2.90

Of the 25,000 units to be accounted for in Department III, the results showed:

	Units
Completed and transferred	20,000
In process, all material, one-third labor and overhead	3,000
Lost in production	2,000
Total Accounted For	25,000

The *adjusted unit cost* for the first two departments after giving effect to the added materials would be:

15,000 units + 10,000 units = 25,000 units, divided into $30,000 = $1.20.

The *lost unit cost* can now be computed using the $1.20 figure, e.g.:

(2,000 units × $1.20) ÷ 23,000 units = $0.1043 as the lost unit cost.

Thus the *total adjusted and corrected unit* cost for the two preceding departments, taking into consideration both the added materials and the lost units, is $1.3043 ($1.20 + $0.1043). Again, it should be emphasized that it is *first* necessary to adjust the previous department's unit cost for added material before computing the lost unit cost.

SIMPLIFYING CUMULATIVE UNIT COST CALCULATIONS WHEN MATERIALS ARE ADDED IN A DEPARTMENT AFTER THE FIRST AND UNITS ARE LOST

The completion of a cost of production report and the computation of the unit costs for the *preceding department* can be simplified somewhat by making only a single division, and thus obtaining an adjusted and corrected unit cost as a single figure. Unless the lost unit cost is necessary for administrative control, there is no need to compute it. Therefore, in Department II, if the following figures are used:

	Units			*Unit Cost*
Transferred into Department II	20,000	Costing	$44,000	$2.00
Increase in units by added materials	15,000			
Total Units to Be Accounted For	35,000			
Units lost in Department II	3,000			
Good units in production	32,000	Cost of work done in Department I	44,000	

Dividing 32,000 units into $44,000 results in a *corrected and adjusted unit* cost for work done in Department I of 1.375

A second method of simplifying the computation of units costs in a department after the first, when materials are added that increase the volume of production and units are lost, considers each department as a separate factory, whereby each subsequent department merely assumes as a purchase the materials received from the preceding department. Thus whatever is received in a department after the first is considered a part of the materials cost in the second and subsequent departments. This procedure eliminates the computation of the lost unit costs and costs in the preceding departments, and it treats each department as though it were the initial department. Since this simplified process costing has many applications to small business firms, it is given in detail here.

To properly understand this second method of simplifying process cost accounting, cost data for two months of operations are used in the following illustration. Operating data for the month of January for a firm having three departments were as follows:

Operating data for the month of January were:

	Dept. I	Dept. II	Dept. III
Costs, not including transfers:			
Material costs.......................................	$16,500		$10,000*
Labor costs..	7,500	$10,500	6,400
Manufacturing overhead....................	2,500	5,600	4,480
Production quantity statistics (pounds):			
Material put into production	60,000 lbs.		10,000 lbs. *
			(Increase in volume)
Completed and transferred out	45,000	25,000 lbs.	30,000
Completed and not transferred out......	0	5,000	0
Work-in-process..............................	10,000	15,000	4,000
Stage of completion of work-in-process:			
Materials.......................................	100%	100%	100%
Labor..	50	33⅓	50
Overhead.......................................	50	33⅓	50
Lost in production.............................	5,000 lbs.	0	1,000 lbs.

*Increase in volume.

The cost of production report prepared from these data under the simplified method is shown in Illustration 5–5. It should be noted that the transfers from one department to another become part of the material costs of the department in which they are received.

Computations for this work sheet:

Department I, Unit Costs

Equivalent production for materials: 45,000 completed
                                        10,000 in process 100% complete
                                        55,000 units

Cost of materials, $16,500, resulting in a unit cost of $0.30 ($16,500/55,000).
     Equivalent production for labor and overhead: 45,000 completed
         10,000 units × 50%............................... 5,000 in process
                                                          50,000 units

Cost of labor, $7,500, resulting in labor unit cost of $0.15 ($7,500/50,000).
Cost of overhead, $2,500, resulting in overhead unit cost of $0.05 ($2,500/50,000).
Transferred to Department II, 45,000 units × $0.50, or $22,500.
In process, January 31:
    Materials: 10,000 × 100% × $0.30 = $3,000
    Labor: 10,000 × 50% × 0.15 =   750
    Overhead: 10,000 × 50% × 0.05 =   250
                                          $4,000

Department II, Unit Costs

Equivalent production for materials: 25,000 completed and transferred
                                        5,000 completed and on hand
                                        15,000 in process, 100% complete
                                        45,000 units

Illustration 5–5

COST OF PRODUCTION REPORT

For Month of January
(First Month of Operations)

	Department I		Department II		Department III	
	Total	Unit Cost	Total	Unit Cost	Total	Unit Cost
WORK-IN-PROCESS AT BEGINNING OF MONTH, JANUARY 2, 19—:						
Material Costs	0		0		0	
Labor Costs	0		0		0	
Manufacturing Overhead Costs	0		0		0	
COSTS DURING THE MONTH:						
Material Costs	$16,500.00	$0.30	$22,500.00	$0.50	{$10,000.00*} 24,000.00	$1.00
Labor Costs	7,500.00	0.15	10,500.00	0.30	6,400.00	0.20
Manufacturing Overhead Costs	2,500.00	0.05	5,600.00	0.16	4,480.00	0.14
TOTAL COSTS TO BE ACCOUNTED FOR	$26,500.00	$0.50	$38,600.00	$0.96	$44,880.00	$1.34
Completed and Transferred Out	$22,500.00	$0.50	$24,000.00	$0.96	$40,200.00	$1.34
Completed and on Hand	0		4,800.00		0	
Work-in-Process at End of Month, January 31, 19—:						
Material	3,000.00		7,500.00		4,000.00	
Labor	750.00		1,500.00		400.00	
Manufacturing Overhead	250.00		800.00		280.00	
CUMULATIVE TOTAL COST ACCOUNTED FOR	$26,500.00		$38,600.00		$44,880.00	

QUANTITY OF PRODUCTION REPORT (In Pounds)

	Department I	Department II	Department III
Work-in-Process at Beginning of Month, January 1, 19—	0	0	0
Put into or Received in Production during Month	60,000	45,000	{10,000* / 25,000}
To Be Accounted For	60,000	45,000	35,000
Completed and Transferred Out during Month	45,000	25,000	30,000
Completed and on Hand at End of Month	0	5,000	0
Work-in-Process at End of Month:			
Materials	10,000 100%	15,000 100%	4,000 100%
Labor	50%	33⅓%	50%
Manufacturing Overhead	50%	33⅓%	50%
Lost or Spoiled in Production	5,000	0	1,000
Total Accounted For	60,000	45,000	35,000

*Added material increases volume of production.

Material costs, $22,500, resulting in unit cost of $0.50 ($22,500/45,000).
Equivalent production for labor and overhead: 25,000 completed, transferred
                                                5,000 completed, on hand
    15,000 units × 33⅓%........................... 5,000 in process
                                                35,000 units

Labor costs, $10,500, resulting in labor unit cost of $0.30 ($10,500/35,000).
Overhead costs, $5,600, resulting in overhead unit cost of $0.16 ($5,600/35,000).
Transferred to Department III, 25,000 units × $0.96, or $24,000.
In process, Department II, January 31:
  Materials: 15,000 × 100% × $0.50 = $7,500
  Labor: 15,000 × 33⅓% × $0.30 = 1,500
  Overhead: 15,000 × 33⅓% × $0.16 =   800
                                        $9,800

Department III, Unit Costs

Equivalent production for materials: 30,000 completed, transferred
                                            4,000 in process, 100% complete
                                            34,000 units

Material costs, $10,000 plus $24,000, resulting in a unit cost of $1 ($34,000/
34,000 units).
Equivalent production for labor and overhead: 30,000 completed, transferred
    4,000 units × 50%................................. 2,000 in process
                                                32,000 units

Labor costs, $6,400, resulting in unit cost of $0.20 ($6,400/32,000).
Overhead costs, $4,480, resulting in unit cost of $0.14 ($4,480/32,000).

Accounting entries for month of January:

(1)

Work-in-Process — Department I 26,500
  Stores..   16,500
  Payroll...   7,500
  Manufacturing Overhead...   2,500
  To summarize cost of production in Department I for the month
  of January.

(2)

Work-in-Process — Department II 38,600
  Work-in-Process — Department I   22,500
  Payroll...   10,500
  Manufacturing Overhead...   5,600
  To summarize the cost of production in Department II during
  January.

(3)

Work-in-Process — Department III..44,880
  Work-in-Process — Department II   24,000
  Stores..   10,000
  Payroll...   6,400
  Manufacturing Overhead...   4,480
  To summarize cost of production in Department III, including
  added materials increasing volume of production, for month
  of January.

(4)

Finished Goods...40,200		
Work-in-Process—Department III.....................................		40,200

To record the cost of work completed and sent to finished
goods stock room.

In continuing this illustration for the second month of operations
(February), the final work-in-process inventories in the respective departments, January 31, become the initial inventories for the work during
the month of February. During the month of February, the same elimination of the separate statement of the departmental transfers and separate
lost unit costs computation is followed. All transfers become part of the
material costs in the department in which received.

The operating data for the month of February are as follows (*costs not
including transfers*):

	Dept. I	Dept. II	Dept. III
Work-in-process, 2/1/19—:			
Completed and on hand...............	0	$ 4,800	0
Material costs...........................$	3,000	7,500	$ 4,000
Labor costs	750	1,500	400
Manufacturing overhead..............	250	800	280
Additional manufacturing costs:			
Material costs...........................	21,320	0	0
Labor costs	11,202	19,620	14,720
Manufacturing overhead..............	5,726	9,760	8,540
Production statistics for February:			
Units in process, 2/1/19—	10,000 units	5,000 } units 15,000 }	4,000 units
New production started...............	70,000		
Completed and transferred out......	60,000	5,000 } 60,000 }	58,000
Work-in-process, 2/28/19—	16,000	10,000	10,000
Stage of completion, work-in-process:			
Materials	100%	100%	100%
Labor......................................	40%	60%	50%
Manufacturing overhead..............	40%	60%	50%
Lost in production........................	4,000 units	5,000 units	1,000 units

The cost of production report from these data under the simplified
costing method is shown in Illustration 5–6.

Accounting entries for February: Following the entries made at the
end of January, the following entries summarize the cost accounting
work for February:

Illustration 5-6

COST OF PRODUCTION REPORT
For Month of February (Second Month)

	Department I		Department II		Department III	
	Total	Unit Cost	Total	Unit Cost	Total	Unit Cost
WORK-IN-PROCESS AT BEGINNING OF MONTH, FEBRUARY 1, 19—:						
Material Costs	$ 3,000.00		$ 7,500.00		$ 4,000.00	
Labor Costs	750.00		1,500.00		400.00	
Manufacturing Overhead Costs	250.00		800.00		280.00	
Completed and on Hand			4,800.00			
COSTS DURING THE MONTH:						
Material Costs	21,320.00	$0.32	35,400.00	$0.61286	{ 4,800.00 / 65,571.60	$1.0937
Labor Costs	11,202.00	0.18	19,620.00	0.32	14,720.00	0.24
Manufacturing Overhead Costs	5,726.00	0.09	9,760.00	0.16	8,540.00	0.14
TOTAL COSTS TO BE ACCOUNTED FOR	$42,248.00	$0.59	$79,380.00	$1.09286	$98,311.60	$1.4737
Completed and Transferred Out	$35,400.00	$0.59	{ $ 4,800.00 / 65,571.60	$0.96 / 1.09284	$85,474.60	$1.4737
Completed and on Hand	0					
Work-in-Process at End of Month, February 28, 19—:						
Material	5,120.00		6,128.60		10,937.00	
Labor	1,152.00		1,920.00		1,200.00	
Manufacturing Overhead	576.00		960.00		700.00	
CUMULATIVE TOTAL COST ACCOUNTED FOR	$42,248.00		$79,380.20*		$98,311.60	

QUANTITY OF PRODUCTION REPORT (In Pounds)

	Department I	Department II	Department III
Work-in-Process at Beginning of Month, February 1, 19—	10,000	{ 5,000 / 15,000	{ 4,000 / 5,000
Put into or Received in Production during Month	70,000	60,000	60,000
To Be Accounted For	80,000	80,000	69,000
Completed and Transferred Out during Month	60,000	{ 5,000 / 60,000	58,000
Completed and on Hand at End of Month	0		
Work-in-Process at End of Month, February 28, 19—	16,000	10,000	10,000
Materials	100%	100%	100%
Labor	40%	60%	50%
Manufacturing Overhead	40%	60%	50%
Lost or Spoiled in Production	4,000	5,000	1,000
Total Accounted For	80,000	80,000	69,000

*Error of $0.20 due to rounding

(1a)

Work-in-Process—Department I 38,248.00		
Stores...	21,320.00	
Payroll	11,202.00	
Manufacturing Overhead	5,726.00	

To summarize the cost of production in Department I
during the month of February.

(2a)

Work-in-Process—Department II 64,780.00		
Work-in-Process—Department I	35,400.00	
Payroll ....:	19,620.00	
Manufacturing Overhead	9,760.00	

To summarize the manufacturing costs in Department
I during February.

(3a)

Work-in-Process—Department III 93,631.60		
Work-in-Process—Department II	70,371.60	
Payroll	14,720.00	
Manufacturing Overhead	8,540.00	

To summarize the manufacturing costs in Department
III for the month of February.

(4a)

Finished Goods 85,474.60		
Work-in-Process—Department III	85,474.60	

To record the cost of goods completed and transferred
to finished goods stock room during February.

LEDGER ACCOUNTS

Work-in-Process—Department I

Jan. 31 (1) 26,500.00	Jan. 31 (2) 22,500.00
Feb. 28 (1a) 38,248.00	Feb. 28 (2a) 35,400.00

Balance, $6,848.00*

*W-I-P—
Mat. $5,120.00
Labor   1,152.00
O.H.   576.00
          $6,848.00

Work-in-Process—Department II

Jan. 31 (2) 38,600.00	Jan. 31 (3) 24,000.00
Feb. 28 (2a) 64,780.00	Feb. 28 (3a) 70,371.60

Balance, $9,010.00†

†W-I-P—
Mat. $6,130.00
Labor   1,920.00
O.H.   960.00
          $9,010.00

Work-in-Process—Department III

Jan. 31 (3) 44,800.00	Jan. 31 (4) 40,200.00
Feb. 28 (3a) 93,631.60	Feb. 28 (4a) 85,474.60

Balance, $12,837.00‡

‡W-I-P—
Mat. $10,937.00
Labor   1,200.00
O.H.   700.00
          $12,837.00

Finished Goods

Jan. 31 (4) 40,200.00	
Feb. 28 (4a) 85,474.60	

TREATMENT OF WORK-IN-PROCESS INVENTORY AT THE BEGINNING OF PROCESS ACCOUNTING PERIOD

The treatment of the initial work-in-process inventory is important because it affects the computation of the unit costs in a department. Two characteristics of the initial work-in-process inventory must be recognized:

1. Because of the different stage of completion of the initial work-in-process inventory as far as material, labor, and manufacturing overhead costs are concerned, this initial work-in-process inventory will be shown on the cost of production report in *analyzed form;* that is, separate figures will be shown for the work-in-process – material, work-in-process – labor, and work-in-process – manufacturing overhead.
2. In the work-in-process inventory in the first manufacturing department, these figures represent the total cost of this inventory. In the subsequent departments, the work-in-process inventory must also include a cost figure for the work done on this inventory in the *preceding departments.*

There are two accounting treatments of this beginning work-in-process inventory when computing unit costs. The first, and probably more popular because it is characteristic of the nature of the process costs (average costs), is known as the *average cost method.* This method involves the merging of the departmental costs, *by elements,* of the initial work-in-process inventory with the costs incurred in the department during the month and dividing the total cost by elements thus computed by an equivalent production based upon the sum of units in process at the beginning of the period and the units put into production during this period. *A second method,* known as *first-in; first-out* (Fifo), is predicated on the assumption that the costs for the current period will be used first to complete the initial work-in-process and then will be applied against the new production.

THE AVERAGE COST METHOD OF TREATING INITIAL WORK-IN-PROCESS INVENTORY – DEPARTMENT I

To illustrate the *average cost method,* the cost of production report for Department I of the Alton Manufacturing Company is prepared for the month of February. It is assumed that there were in process, February 1, 10,000 pounds (units) on which *all the material* and *one half of the labor and manufacturing overhead* had already been applied in January. The costs of this work-in-process inventory as taken from the January Department I cost of production report were:

Material costs $3,000
Labor costs 750
Manufacturing overhead costs................ 250

During February, 76,000 pounds (units) were started. The costs of material were $22,600; labor costs were $9,000; and manufacturing overhead amounted to $3,650. The quantity statement showed these results for the month's operation (these include the 10,000 units in process at the beginning):

	Units
Finished and transferred to Department II..................................	60,000 lbs.
In process, February 28 (all the material complete, but only $\frac{1}{4}$ complete as to labor and overhead)...	20,000
Lost in the process of manufacturing during February.................	6,000
Total to Be Accounted For	86,000 lbs.

The departmental cost statement prepared on February 28 from this information for Department I is shown in Illustration 5–7. In studying this production report the work-in-process on February 1 requires our attention first. The amount, $4,000, is in analyzed form; *that is, the cost for each element is given.* In computing the unit costs for the month of February it is, therefore, a simple matter to add the cost of materials used in production for the month to the cost of material in the in-process inventory February 1 to get the *total material cost* and then to divide this figure by the *equivalent material production* to get the unit cost for material. For example, the computations would be:

	Quantity (pounds)	Cost Value
In process, February 1	10,000	$ 3,000
Put into process during February..................	76,000	22,600
Total	86,000	$25,600
Units lost	6,000	
Equivalent Production	80,000	$25,600

Dividing the equivalent production for material in Department I for February (80,000 units) into the total cost ($3,000 + $22,600) of $25,600 results in an average unit cost for materials in Department I for the month of February of $0.32.

A similar procedure is followed in computing the unit costs in Department I for labor and overhead for the month of February, viz:

Illustration 5–7

DEPARTMENT I

COST PRODUCTION REPORT

For Month of February, 19—

	Total Cost	Unit Cost
COST IN PRECEDING DEPARTMENT:		
Work-in-Process, 2/1/—.	0	
Transferred into Department during Month.	0	
Total.	0	
Additional Cost for Lost Units.	xx	0
Adjusted and Corrected Unit Cost Total.	0	0
COST IN CURRENT DEPARTMENT:		
Work-in-Process, 2/1/—:		
Material Costs.	$ 3,000.00	
Labor Costs.	750.00	
Manufacturing Overhead Costs.	250.00	
Cost in Department during Month:		
Material Costs.	22,600.00	$0.32
Labor Costs.	9,000.00	0.15
Manufacturing Overhead Costs.	3,650.00	0.06
Total Cost in Current Department.	$39,250.00	$0.53
CUMULATIVE COST TOTAL.	$39,250.00	$0.53
Work Completed and Transferred Out:.	$31,800.00	
Work-in-Process, 2/28/—:		
Completed but Not Transferred Out.	0	
Work-in-Process—Materials.	$ 6,400.00	
Work-in-Process—Labor.	750.00	
Work-in-Process—Manufacturing Overhead.	300.00	
Total Work-in-Process.	$ 7,450.00	
CUMULATIVE COST TOTAL ACCOUNTED FOR....	$39,250.00	

QUANTITY PRODUCTION REPORT (In Pounds)*

QUANTITY TO BE ACCOUNTED FOR:	
Pounds-in-Process, 2/1/—.	10,000
Put into Process during February.	76,000
To Be Accounted For.	86,000
QUANTITY ACCOUNTED FOR AS FOLLOWS:	
Completed and Transferred to Dept. II.	60,000
Completed and on Hand.	0
Work-in-Process (All Material, ¼ Labor, ¼ Manufacturing Overhead)	20,000
Lost or Spoiled in Production.	6,000
Total Accounted For.	86,000

*For the computation of the equivalent production see pages 127 and 129.

	Actual Production (Including W-I-P at the Beginning of Month)	Equivalent Production	Total Cost, Including W-I-P at Beginning of Month	Unit Cost
Completed	60,000 units	60,000		
In process, February 28, ¹/₄ complete	20,000	5,000		
Lost in production	6,000	0		
Total	86,000 units	65,000		
Labor costs ($750 + $9,000)			$9,750	
Labor unit cost ($9,750 ÷ 65,000)				$0.15
Overhead costs ($250 + $3,650)			$3,900	
Overhead unit cost ($3,900 ÷ 65,000)				$0.06

SUMMARY OF PROCEDURE IN DEPARTMENT I USING AVERAGE COST METHOD FOR INITIAL WORK-IN-PROCESS

To summarize the procedure based upon the above, when there is a work-in-process inventory at the beginning of the accounting period, the following is given:

1. The inventory of the initial work-in-process must be stated in analyzed form — that is, separate figures for materials cost, labor cost, and manufacturing overhead cost.
2. The number of units in the initial inventory are added to the units received into the department during the period, giving the total units to be considered.
3. The cost in the initial inventory of the work-in-process for each element of cost is added to the corresponding cost for the same element for work performed during the period, thus obtaining the total cost for each element.
4. Dividing the total costs obtained in 3 by the corresponding equivalent production for each element gives the *average unit departmental cost* for that element.

AVERAGE METHOD OF TREATING THE INITIAL WORK-IN-PROCESS INVENTORY — DEPARTMENT II

Continuing the previous illustration, the data summarizing the cost of production for February in Department II are tabulated and the cost of production report for Department II is presented. See Illustrations 5–8 and 5–9.

The following explanations are necessary to understand the figures and computations relating to Illustration 5–9:

1. The 5,000 pounds on hand and complete in Department II, February 1, are not used in computing any unit costs. They represent merely the first 5,000 units to be transferred to Department III during February.
2. There were 15,000 pounds in process February 1. The cost of these in Department I for work done on them in January was ....$ 7,500
3. Received from Department I during February were 60,000 pounds which cost in Department I.. 31,800
4. The total cost for work done in Department I for those units worked on in Department II during February was $39,300 for 75,000 pounds (60,000 + 15,000).
   This resulted in an *average unit cost* of production for Department I of $0.524
5. To compute the unit costs for labor and overhead in Department II the *equivalent production* must be computed for the sum of the units in process at beginning of period and the units received into the department during February 15,000 + 60,000. This equivalent production is 65,000 units + $\frac{1}{2}$ (10,000)...   70,000 lbs.
6. To compute the *unit cost* for labor and for overhead, the equivalent production (70,000) must be divided respectively into the total labor cost and total overhead cost used on this production, e.g.:
   Labor: $1,500 + $18,100 = $19,600 ÷ 70,000 units $0.28
   Overhead: $ 800 + $11,100 = $11,900 ÷ 70,000 units 0.17
7. The *work-in-process inventory, February 28*, in Department II is 10,000 pounds, complete as far as Department I is concerned but $\frac{1}{2}$ complete as far as labor and overhead costs in Department II are involved. This is computed:
   For Department I Cost: 10,000 pounds × $0.524 ....$5,240
   For Department II Cost:
     Labor ....10,000 × $\frac{1}{2}$ × $0.28 1,400
     Overhead ....10,000 × $\frac{1}{2}$ × $0.17 .... 850 $7,490

Illustration 5–8

DEPARTMENT II

	Quantity	Cost Value	
February 1, 19—			
Completed and on hand (not transferred in January) (to be issued on first-in, first-out basis)..................	5,000 lbs.	@ $0.96	$ 4,800
In process...	15,000		
Cost in Dept. I in January.........................			7,500
Cost in Dept. II in January:			
Labor..			1,500
Overhead....................................			800
Costs during February:			
Received in dept. during February, costs for Dept. I.....	60,000	@ 0.53	31,800
Costs for labor in Dept. II............................			18,100
Costs for overhead in Dept. II........................			11,100
To Be Accounted For...........................	80,000 lbs.		$75,600
Accounted for as follows:			
Transferred to Dept. III:			
Completed and on hand at beginning (2/1/—)........	5,000 lbs.		
Completed during month..........................	65,000		
Work-in-process, 2/28/—($\frac{1}{2}$ complete)...............	10,000		
Accounted for during February...................	80,000 lbs.		

Illustration 5–9

DEPARTMENT II

COST PRODUCTION REPORT

For Month of February, 19—

	Total Cost	Unit Cost
COST IN PRECEDING DEPARTMENT:		
Work-in-Process, 2/1/—...................................	$ 7,500.00	$0.50
Transferred into Department during Month.....................	31,800.00	0.53
Total..	$39,300.00	$0.524*
Additional Cost for Lost Units.............................	xx	0
Adjusted and Corrected Unit Cost Total....................	$39,300.00	$0.524
COST IN CURRENT DEPARTMENT:		
Work-in-Process, 2/1/—:		
Material Costs..	0	
Labor Costs...	$ 1,500.00	
Manufacturing Overhead Costs.............................	800.00	
Cost in Department during Month:†		
Material Costs..	0	
Labor Costs...	18,100.00	$0.28
Manufacturing Overhead Costs.............................	11,100.00	0.17
Total Cost in Current Department........	$31,500.00	$0.45
Cost of Goods Completed in January but Not Transferred (5,000 at $0.96)..	$ 4,800.00	
CUMULATIVE COST TOTAL...............................	{$70,800.00} {4,800.00}	$0.974 0.96
Work Completed and Transferred Out:		
5,000 @ $0.96..	$ 4,800.00	
65,000 @ $0.974...	63,310.00	
Work-in-Process, 2/28/—:		
Completed but Not Transferred Out...........................	0	
Cost in Dept. I...	$ 5,240.00	
Work-in-Process—Materials................................	0	
Work-in-Process—Labor...................................	1,400.00	
Work-in-Process—Manufacturing Overhead....................	850.00	
Total Work-in-Process................................	$ 7,490.00	
CUMULATIVE COST TOTAL ACCOUNTED FOR..............	$75,600.00	

*Average unit price ($39,300.00 ÷ 75,000 pounds).
†Equivalent production of 70,000 pounds (see page 130).

Illustration 5–9 (continued)

QUANTITY PRODUCTION REPORT (In Pounds)

QUANTITY TO BE ACCOUNTED FOR:	
Pounds-in-Process, 2/1/—.	15,000
Pounds Completed but Not Transferred, 2/1/—.	5,000
Put into Process during February (from Dept. I).	60,000
To Be Accounted For.	80,000
QUANTITY ACCOUNTED FOR AS FOLLOWS:	
Pounds Completed and Transferred to Dept. III.	70,000
Completed and on Hand.	0
Work-in-Process (½ Labor, ½ Manufacturing Overhead).	10,000
Lost or Spoiled in Production.	0
Total Accounted For.	80,000

AVERAGE METHOD OF TREATING THE INITIAL WORK-IN-PROCESS INVENTORY IN DEPARTMENT III

Continuing the previous illustration, the data summarizing the cost of production for February in Department III are tabulated and the cost of production report for Department III is presented. See Illustrations 5–10 and 5–11.

Illustration 5–10

DEPARTMENT III

	Quantity	Cost Value	
February 1, 19—			
In process: Cost in Depts. I and II in January.	4,000 lbs.	@ $1.00	$ 4,000
Cost in Dept. III in January:			
Labor.			400
Overhead.			280
Costs during February:			
Received in Dept. III during February, costs for			
Depts. I and II.	{ 5,000	@ 0.96	4,800
	65,000	@ 0.974	63,310
Costs for labor in Dept. III.			14,300
Costs for overhead in Dept. III.			10,220
To Be Accounted For.	74,000 lbs.		$97,310
Accounted for as follows:			
Transferred to finished goods stock room.	69,000 lbs.		
Work-in-process, ¼ complete as to labor and overhead	4,000		
Lost in production.	1,000		
Accounted for during February.	74,000 lbs.		

The following explanations are necessary to understand the figures and computations shown on Illustration 5–11.

1. The 4,000 pounds in process *February 1*, cost per unit in the two preceding departments $0.96 plus $0.04 for lost units, total $1. (See Department III report for January, Chapter 4, page 121.)
   4,000 pounds @ $1 ....$ 4,000

Illustration 5–11

DEPARTMENT III

COST PRODUCTION REPORT

For Month of February, 19—

	Total Cost	Unit Cost
COST IN PRECEDING DEPARTMENT:		
Work-in-Process, 2/1/—(4,000 @ $1.00)...................	$ 4,000.00	
Transferred into Department during Month................	68,110.00	
Total...	$72,110.00	$0.97446
Additional Cost for Lost Units (1,000 × $0.97446 ÷ 73,000 lbs.)	xx	0.013349
Adjusted and Corrected Unit Cost Total...............	$72,110.00	$0.987809
COST IN CURRENT DEPARTMENT:		
Work-in-Process, 2/1/—:		
Material Costs.......................................	0	
Labor Costs...	$ 400.00	
Manufacturing Overhead Costs.........................	280.00	
*Cost in Department during February:**		
Material Costs.......................................	0	
Labor Costs...	14,300.00	$0.21
Manufacturing Overhead Costs.........................	10,220.00	0.15
Total Cost in Current Department...................	$25,200.00	$0.36
CUMULATIVE COST TOTAL............................	$97,310.00	$1.347809
Work Completed and Transferred Out (69,000 @ $1.347809)....	$92,998.82	
Work-in-Process, 2/28/—:		
Completed but Not Transferred Out........................	0	
Cost in Depts. I and II (4,000 @ $0.97446).................	$ 3,897.84	
Lost Unit Cost (4,000 @ $0.013349).......................	53.40	
Work-in-Process—Material, Dept. III......................	0	
Work-in-Process—Labor, Dept. III........................	210.00	
Work-in-Process—Mfg. Overhead, Dept. III................	150.00	
Total Work-in-Process.............................	$ 4,311.24	
CUMULATIVE COST TOTAL ACCOUNTED FOR..........	$97,310.06	

*Equivalent production, 70,000 pounds.
†Discrepancy of $0.06 due to decimals in unit costs.

Illustration 5–11 (continued)

QUANTITY PRODUCTION REPORT (In Pounds)

QUANTITY TO BE ACCOUNTED FOR:	
In Process, 2/1/—...	4,000
Put into Process (from Dept. II) during February..................	70,000
To Be Accounted For.......................................	74,000
QUANTITY ACCOUNTED FOR AS FOLLOWS:	
Completed and Transferred to Finished Goods Stock Room...........	69,000
In Process (¼ Labor, ¼ Manufacturing Overhead)................	4,000
Lost in Process of Manufacturing...............................	1,000
Total Accounted For.......................................	74,000

2. The cost of the *labor* and *overhead* applied in *January* to the 4,000 units in process February 1 amounted to:

Labor cost...	400
Manufacturing overhead cost....................................	280

3. Received into Department III from Department II during February:

5,000 lbs. at $0.96	$ 4,800
65,000 lbs. at $0.974..	63,310
70,000 lbs.	$68,110

4. The equivalent production for labor and overhead for work done in Department III during February was $[69,000 + \frac{1}{4} (4,000)]$ .... 70,000 lbs.

5. The unit costs for labor and overhead in Department III for work done in February was as follows:

Labor:	$14,300 + $400 = $14,700 ÷ 70,000 lbs........................	$0.21
Overhead:	$10,220 + $280 = $10,500 ÷ 70,000 lbs.......................	0.15

6. The lost unit cost is computed by multiplying 1,000 units lost by the average cost of $0.97446 for Departments I and II, and dividing the product by the remaining good units:

$(1,000 \times \$0.97446) \div (74,000$ lbs. $- 1,000$ lbs.$)$ $0.013349

A COMPLETE COST OF PRODUCTION REPORT OF AVERAGE METHOD OF COSTING INITIAL WORK-IN-PROCESS INVENTORY

A cost of production report for the entire factory for the month of February is shown in Illustration 5–12. This represents the composite report of the three individual departmental reports just discussed, and it is the result of the cost accounting department's work in consolidating the various reports submitted by each department.

ACCOUNTING ENTRIES FOR FEBRUARY COSTING CYCLE

To record the information shown on Illustration 5–12—that is, the cycle of production for the month of February where there is an *initial work-in-process inventory* treated on the *average cost method*—the following entries in journal form are given, supplemented by the three de-

Illustration 5-12

ALTON MANUFACTURING COMPANY

SUMMARY COST OF PRODUCTION STATEMENT

For Month of February, 19—

	Department I		Department II		Department III	
	Cost	Per Unit	Cost	Per Unit	Cost	Per Unit
COST TRANSFERRED FROM PRECEDING DEPARTMENTS:						
Work-in-Process, 2/1/—........	0		$ 7,500.00	$0.50	$ 4,000.00	$1.00
Transferred into Department during February................	0		31,800.00	0.53	4,800.00	0.96
Transferred into Department during February................	0		0	0	63,310.00	0.974
Total Cost of Work Done in Preceding Departments....	0		$39,300.00	$0.524*	$72,110.00	$0.97446
Additional Costs for Lost Units.....		0		0		$0.013349
						0.987809
COSTS IN DEPARTMENT:						
Work-in-Process, 2/1/—:						
Material Cost...............	$ 3,000.00		0		0	
Labor Cost.................	750.00		$ 1,500.00		$ 400.00	
Manufacturing Overhead Cost.	250.00		800.00		280.00	
Costs for the Month of February:						
Material Costs..............	22,600.00	$0.32	0		0	
Labor Costs.................	9,000.00	0.15	18,100.00	$0.28	14,300.00	$0.21
Manufacturing Overhead Costs.	3,650.00	0.06	11,100.00	0.17	10,220.00	0.15
Total Departmental Costs....	$39,250.00	$0.53	$31,500.00	$0.45	$25,200.00	$0.36
Cost of Goods Completed in January but Not Transferred......			$ 4,800.00	$0.96		
CUMULATIVE COST TOTAL....	$39,250.00	$0.53	$70,800.00 / 4,800.00	$0.974 / 0.96	$97,310.00	$1.347809
Transferred to Next Department....	$31,800.00		$68,110.00		0	
Work-in-Process, 2/28/—:						
Cost in Preceding Departments...	0		$ 5,240.00		$ 3,897.84	
Lost Unit Costs...............	0		0		53.40	
Material Cost.................	$ 6,400.00		0		0	
Labor Cost...................	750.00		1,400.00		210.00	
Manufacturing Overhead Cost....	300.00		850.00		150.00	
Total Work-in-Process......	$ 7,450.00		$ 7,490.00		$ 4,311.24	
Transferred to Finished Goods Stock Room..................	0		0		$92,998.82	
CUMULATIVE COST TOTAL....	$39,250.00		$75,600.00		$97,310.06†	

*Average unit price ($39,300.00 ÷ 75,000 pounds).
†Discrepancy of $0.06 due to decimals in unit costs.

Illustration 5–12 (continued)

QUANTITY PRODUCTION REPORT (In Pounds)

QUANTITY TO BE ACCOUNTED FOR:			
Pounds-in-Process, 2/1/—......................	10,000	20,000	4,000
Put into Process during February...............	76,000	60,000	70,000
To Be Accounted For......................	86,000	80,000	74,000
QUANTITY ACCOUNTED FOR AS FOLLOWS:			
Completed and Transferred to Next Department...	60,000	70,000	0
Completed and on Hand, 2/1/—................	0	0	0
Work-in-Process, 2/1/—......................	20,000‡	10,000§	4,000**
Lost or Spoiled in Production..................	6,000	0	1,000
Completed and Transferred to Finished Goods Stock Room..	0	0	69,000
Total Accounted For......................	86,000	80,000	74,000

‡All material, ¼ labor, ¼ manufacturing overhead.
**One-fourth labor, ¼ manufacturing overhead.
§One-half labor, ½ manufacturing overhead.

partmental work-in-process ledger accounts and the Finished Goods account:

Balances in the work-in-process accounts, February 1, 19—:
    Work-in-Process—Department I $4,000
    Work-in-Process—Department II:
        Completed but not transferred out................. 4,800⎤
        Partially completed work............................ 9,800⎦
    Work-in-Process—Department III 4,680

(1)

Work-in-Process—Department I 35,250.00
    Stores... 22,600.00
    Payroll 9,000.00
    Manufacturing Overhead 3,650.00
    To record costs in department for February.

(2)

Work-in-Process—Department II................................61,000.00
    Work-in-Process—Department I.............................. 31,800.00
    Payroll 18,100.00
    Manufacturing Overhead 11,100.00
    To record costs in Department II during February.

(3)

Work-in-Process—Department III 92,630.00
    Work-in-Process—Department II.............................. 68,110.00
    Payroll 14,300.00
    Manufacturing Overhead 10,220.00
    To record costs in Department III for February.

(4)

Finished Goods 92,998.82
    Work-in-Process — Department III 92,998.82
    To record cost of work completed during February.

Work-in-Process — Department I				Work-in-Process — Department II			

2/1 Balance	4,000.00	2/28 (2)	31,800.00	2/1 Balance:
				  Com-
				  pleted
				2/1 Uncom-
				  pleted
				2/28 (2)
					
					4,800.00
					
					9,800.00
					61,000.00
						2/28 (3)	68,110.00

2/28 (1)	35,250.00						

Work-in-Process — Department III				Finished Goods		
2/1 Balance	4,680.00	(4)	92,998.82	2/28 (4)	92,998.82	
2/28 (3)	92,630.00					

LOST UNIT COSTS WHEN THERE IS AN INITIAL WORK-IN-PROCESS INVENTORY

In any department after the first, lost unit cost computations are affected not only by the addition of materials which increase the volume of production but also by work-in-process inventory at the beginning of the period. The basic rule to follow when computing lost unit costs in a department after the first when there is an initial work-in-process inventory is:

When there is a work-in-process inventory at the beginning of the period, it is not possible to determine whether the lost units came from this inventory or from the units received into the department during the period. Therefore, all the units must be considered when calculating the *lost unit cost.* This means *computing an average unit cost* for the work done in the preceding departments, BEFORE computing the lost unit cost.

If there is a work-in-process inventory at the beginning of the period in any department after the first, an *average unit cost* must be computed for that portion of this inventory which represents the cost in the preceding departments, plus the cost of the units received into the department during the period, before computing the *lost unit cost addition.* For example:

In Department II, the work-in-process inventory at the beginning of the month was as follows:

Units

10,000	Cost in Department I	$15,000
	Labor cost in Department II......................	4,000
	Overhead cost in Department II.................	3,000
15,000	Received into Department II during the month. Cost for work done in Department I	24,000

Of the 25,000 units worked on in Department II, during the current month the production statistics were:

Units

Completed and transferred..................	20,000
In process.......................................	3,000
Lost in production.............................	2,000
Total..................................	25,000

Since it is not known whether the 2,000 units lost were part of the 10,000 or part of the 15,000 lot, it is necessary to compute an *average unit cost* for Department I *before* calculating the lost unit cost, e.g.:

Units

10,000 units	Work-in-process...	$15,000
15,000 units	Received from Department I during month.................	24,000
25,000 units	Total Cost for Department I	$39,000

Average unit cost of manufacture for Department I is:

$$\$39,000 \div 25,000 \text{ units} = \$1.56.$$
Lost unit cost $(2,000 \text{ units} \times \$1.56) \div 23,000 \text{ units} = \$0.136.$

Thus the unit cost for Department I, corrected for units lost in Department II, would be $1.696 ($1.56 + $0.136).

Should materials be added in Department II to increase the volume of production, then, as previously illustrated, it is possible to obtain the corrected (for lost units) and the adjusted (for added materials) unit cost in a single operation, by dividing the total costs for the preceding department by the sum of the units in process February 1, plus the units received from Department I during February, less the lost units in Department II during February.

	Units	
Units in process February 1	10,000	$15,000
Received from Department I during February	15,000	24,000
Added materials increasing number of units.........................	5,000	0
Total to Be Accounted For	30,000	$39,000
Less units lost in Department II during February.................	3,000	0
Remaining good units	27,000	

Dividing $39,000 by 27,000 units will result in a corrected and adjusted unit cost for work done in Department I of $1.444 in a single mathematical operation.

FIFO METHOD OF COSTING INITIAL WORK-IN-PROCESS INVENTORY

A recent study has indicated that the Fifo method of costing the initial work-in-process inventory has very limited practical application in modern industry. However, the theory supporting this method seems logical; and therefore the professional examinations include problems in this area. The underlying principle of this method is that the costs in any given period for materials, labor, and manufacturing overhead must first be considered as being used to complete the initial work-in-process before being allocated to the new production. If this principle is followed, then it must be assumed that the final work-in-process inventory in any department must be costed at the unit costs of the latest or new production.

The conditions under which it is possible to use the Fifo method of costing the initial work-in-process inventory vary from firm to firm. Three types of situations are considered as possibly practical for the use of this method, viz:

1. The lot of production represented by the initial work-in-process is kept separately throughout the manufacturing operations, not only in the costing in the department in which presently located but in the transfer from department to department. It is almost like job-lot costing applied to a process industry. Some pharmaceutical product manufacturers are known to use this method. It becomes increasingly complicated if there are many producing departments, each one having some work-in-process at the beginning. It is probably the most accurate method, but also the most expensive to operate. For example if there were three operating departments in a firm, in the final department the *finished goods produced* would show separate costs for the following:

Work-in-process, Department I, at beginning of period
New production, Department I, carried through Departments II and III
Work-in-process, Department II, at beginning of period
Work-in-process, Department III, at beginning of period

This method is practical only if there are no added materials in any departments after the first which would increase the number of units in production, and if there are no lost units in any department after the first. This method might be termed "pure Fifo" since it keeps separately the costs of production for each initial work-in-process inventory.

2. When there are *lost units* in any department after the first, it is not

possible to identify these lost units either with the initial work-in-process inventory or the new production received into the department. Therefore, where there are *lost units* in any department after the first, a *modified Fifo* procedure must be followed—that is, the costs of the preceding department, though separately stated for the initial work-in-process inventory and the new production received into the department, *must now be averaged* before *computing the lost unit cost adjustment*. Thereafter, in computing the total cost of goods transferred out of a department, the final work-in-process inventory in that department must be computed at the latest unit costs for that department, and the balance of the total costs for the department is considered the total cost of the goods transferred out. Dividing this total cost by the number of units transferred results in the unit cost of the transfer—actually it is an average cost figure.

3.   When there are *added materials* in a department after the first, which added material increases the number of units in production, it is desirable to follow a procedure similar to that used when there are lost units—using the average costs of the transfer into a department before computing the *adjusted unit cost* resulting from the added materials.

Each of these methods will be discussed and illustrated in more detail.

Method No. 1: Using the Fifo method in costing the initial work-in-process inventory when there are no lost units except in first department and no added materials in a department after the first increasing the volume of production.

This method might be termed "pure Fifo" since the work-in-process inventories at the beginning of the period and the new production are separately costed on the first-in, first-out basis; that is, the work-in-process must first be completed before considering the cost of the new production.

To explain and illustrate this method, the quantity and cost of production statistics are shown separately for Departments I and II before consolidating them into a single summary cost of production report for the month of March.

Department I

1.   *In Department I,* on March 1, there were in process, 5,000 units, 100 percent complete as to materials, 60 percent complete as to labor and overhead costs. The material, labor, and overhead costs were $10,-000, $3,000, and $1,800, respectively.
2.   During March, 45,000 additional units were started into production.
3.   Additional costs of production during March were: materials, $107,-500; payroll, $4,100; and manufacturing overhead, $8,200.
4.   During March, 40,000 units were transferred out of the department

—5,000 of the units in process at the beginning of the month and 35,000 new production. In process, March 31, 100 percent complete as to materials and 50 percent complete as to labor and overhead costs, were 8,000 units. Lost in production during March, 2,000 units.

5. From the preceding information, it is necessary to compute the equivalent production for material, labor, and overhead costs. On the Fifo basis, this equivalent production is made up of *three items:*
    a) Equivalent units to complete *initial* work-in-process.
    b) Equivalent units of other work completed during period.
    c) Equivalent units of *final* work-in-process inventory.

    For Department I *the equivalent production for the costs incurred and the unit costs* would be:

		Equivalent Production	
		Materials	*Labor and Overhead*
1.	To complete work-in-process, March 1............	0	2,000 units
2.	Units completed during March in addition to work-in-process, March 1..............................	35,000 units	35,000
3.	Work-in-process, March 31:		
	Materials, 8,000 × 100%..........................	8,000	
	Labor and manufacturing overhead, 8,000 × ½...		4,000
	Total Equivalent Production....................	43,000 units	41,000 units
4.	Costs incurred:		
	Materials...$107,500		
	Labor...		$4,100
	Manufacturing overhead		8,200
5.	Dividing by equivalent production, the unit costs would be:		
	Materials...	$2.50	
	Labor...		$0.10
	Manufacturing overhead...........................		0.20

The units transferred out of Department I totaled 40,000, of which 5,000 were in process at beginning of month and 35,000 were new production. To compute the cost of *units transferred out of Department I* during March, using the Fifo method, the following calculations are required:

Units		*Costs*
5,000	Costs on March 1	$ 14,800
	Labor costs during March, 5,000 × 40% × $0.10	200
	Manufacturing overhead costs during March, 5,000 × 40% × $0.20......	400
	Total cost to complete 5,000 units	$ 15,400
35,000	Costs during March, all new production, 35,000 × 100% × $2.80	98,000
40,000	Total Transferred Out of Department I during March..............	$113,400

To compute the work-in-process inventory on March 31, the following calculations are used:

Material-in-process: 8,000 units × 100% × $2.50......................$20,000
Labor-in-process: 8,000 units ×   50% × $0.10.......................   400
Overhead-in-process: 8,000 units ×   50% × $0.20.......................   800
                Total Work-in-Process, Department I, March 31.................$21,200

The cost of production report for Department I for the month of March, using the Fifo method of accounting for the initial work-in-process inventory, is as shown in Illustration 5–13.

Continuing the illustration given previously for Department I, the production statistics for *Department II* for the month of March were:

1. In process on March 1, 6,000 units, 30 percent complete as to labor and manufacturing overhead costs in Department II. The costs for this in-process inventory, March 1, were: costs in Department I, $17,100; labor costs in Department II, $5,400; and overhead costs in Department II, $3,000.

2. *During March, there were received into Department II:*

Units
 5,000   Costs per production report for Department I.................$ 15,400 $3.08
35,000   Costs per production report for Department I................   98,000   2.80
40,000   Total..$113,400

3. Additional costs of production in Department II during March were:

                Payroll costs...$115,020
                Manufacturing overhead costs.................   38,340

4. During March, 42,000 units were transferred out of Department II. This total was made up of:

 6,000 units in process in Department II on March 1
 5,000 units representing first lot from Department I during March
31,000 units second lot received from Department I during March
42,000 units – total completed
 4,000 units – in process in Department II, March 31, 60% complete as to labor and
               manufacturing overhead.
46,000 units – Total quantity to be accounted for in Department II during March

5. On the basis of the foregoing information, it is necessary to compute the equivalent production for labor and overhead costs in the same manner as for Department I, when the Fifo procedure was to be followed, namely:

    a)   Equivalent units to complete *initial* work-in-process in Department II.

Illustration 5–13
DEPARTMENT I
COST OF PRODUCTION REPORT
For Month of March, 19—

	Total Cost	Unit Cost
COST IN CURRENT DEPARTMENT:........................		
Work-in-Process, 3/1/—:		
Material Costs..	$ 10,000.00	$2.00
Labor Costs...	3,000.00	0.60
Manufacturing Overhead Costs............................	1,800.00	0.36
Cost in Department during Month:		
Material Costs..	107,500.00	2.50
Labor Costs...	4,100.00	0.10
Manufacturing Overhead Costs............................	8,200.00	0.20
Total Cost in Current Department........................	$134,600.00	$2.80
CUMULATIVE COST TOTAL...............................	$134,600.00	
Work Completed and Transferred Out: 5,000 @................. {	$ 15,400.00	$3.08
35,000 @................. {	98,000.00	2.80
Work-in-Process, 3/31/—:		
Completed but Not Transferred Out...........................	0	
Work-in-Process—Materials (8,000 × 100% × $2.50)............	$ 20,000.00	
Work-in-Process—Labor (8,000 × ½ × $0.10).................	400.00	
Work-in-Process—Manufacturing Overhead: (8,000 × ½ × $0.20).	800.00	
Total Work-in-Process.................................	$ 21,200.00	
CUMULATIVE COST TOTAL ACCOUNTED FOR..............	$134,600.00	

QUANTITY OF PRODUCTION REPORT (In Pounds)

QUANTITY TO BE ACCOUNTED FOR:	
Work-in-Process, 3/1/—..	5,000
Put into Production or Received from Preceding Departments................	45,000
To Be Accounted For...	50,000
QUANTITY ACCOUNTED FOR AS FOLLOWS:	
Transferred to Next Department..................................... {	5,000
	35,000
Completed but Not Transferred Out....................................	0
Uncompleted Work-in-Process...	8,000
Units Lost in Production...	2,000
Total Accounted For...	50,000
Equivalent Production:	
Material..	43,000
Labor and Manufacturing Overhead.....................................	41,000

b) Equivalent units of other work completed in Department II during March.

c) Equivalent units of *final* work-in-process inventory in Department II, March 31.

See Illustration 5–14.

For Department II the equivalent production and unit costs for the total costs incurred during March are as follows:

Labor and Manufacturing Overhead	Units
To complete *initial* work-in-process, March 1, 6,000 units × 70%..........	4,200
Units completed in addition to initial work-in-process inventory (42,000 units − 6,000 units)	36,000
Equivalent production of *final* work-in-process inventory, March 31, 4,000 units × 60%..	2,400
Equivalent Production for Labor and Manufacturing Overhead in Department II during March	42,600

The unit costs for labor and manufacturing overhead in Department II for the month of March can now be computed as follows:

$$Labor:\ \ \$115,020 \div 42,600 = \$2.70$$
$$Manufacturing\ Overhead:\ \ \$38,340 \div 42,600 = \$0.90$$

To compute the cost of units transferred out of Department II on the *pure Fifo basis, each separate lot* of production must be considered on the basis of the appropriate costs. In this instance, three separate batches or quantities must be considered in the following order, viz:

Units	Quantity in Process in Department II, March 1	
6,000	Costs in Department I during February @ $2.85	$ 17,100
	Costs in Department II during February:	
	Work-in-process—labor..	5,400
	Work-in-process—manufacturing overhead.........................	3,000
	Costs to complete in Department II during March:	
	Labor costs: 6,000 × 70% × $2.70....................................	11,340
	Manufacturing overhead costs: 6,000 × 70% × $0.90...........	3,780
		$ 40,620
	Transferred into Department II during March	
5,000	Costs in Department I during February and March @ $3.08	$ 15,400
	Costs in Department II during March:	
	Labor costs: 5,000 × $2.70..	13,500
	Manufacturing overhead costs: 5,000 × $0.90....................	4,500
		$ 33,400
31,000	Costs in Department I during March @ $2.80	$ 86,800
	Costs in Department II during March:	
	Labor costs: 31,000 × $2.70...	83,700
	Manufacturing overhead costs: 31,000 × $0.90	27,900
		$198,400
42,000	Total Transferred Out of Department II during March......	$272,420

The computation of the final (March 31) work-in-process inventory in Department II is as follows:

Units
4,000   Cost in Department I in March, 4,000 units × $2.80 .... $11,200
        Costs in Department II during March:
        Labor costs: 4,000 × 60% × $2.70 6,480
        Manufacturing overhead costs: 4,000 × 60% × $0.90 2,160
4,000   Total Work-in-Process, Department II, March 31 .... $19,840

Illustration 5–14
DEPARTMENT II
COST OF PRODUCTION REPORT
For Month of March, 19—

	Total Cost	Unit Cost
COST IN PRECEDING DEPARTMENT:		
Work-in-Process, 3/1/—, (6,000 units @ $2.85)	$ 17,100.00	$2.85
Transferred into Department during Month: { 5,000	15,400.00	3.08
{ 35,000	98,000.00	2.80
Total Cost in Preceding Department	$130,500.00	
COST IN CURRENT DEPARTMENT:		
Work-in-Process, 3/1/—:		
Material Costs	0	
Labor Costs	$ 5,400.00	
Manufacturing Overhead Costs	3,000.00	
Cost in Department during Month:		
Material Costs	0	
Labor Costs	115,020.00	$2.70
Manufacturing Overhead Costs	38,340.00	0.90
Total Cost in Current Department	$161,760.00	
CUMULATIVE COST TOTAL	$292,260.00	
Work Completed and Transferred Out: 6,000	{ $ 40,620.00	$6.77 }
5,000	33,400.00	6.68
31,000	198,400.00	6.40
Work-in-Process, 3/31/—:		
Completed but Not Transferred Out	0	
Cost in Preceding Department	$ 11,200.00	$2.80
Work-in-Process—Materials	0	
Work-in-Process—Labor (4,000 × 60% × $2.70)	6,480.00	1.62
Work-in-Process—Manufacturing Overhead (4,000 × 60% × $0.90)	2,160.00	0.54
Total Work-in-Process	$ 19,840.00	
CUMULATIVE COST TOTAL ACCOUNTED FOR	$292,260.00	

Illustration 5–14 (Continued)
QUANTITY PRODUCTION REPORT (In Pounds)

QUANTITY TO BE ACCOUNTED FOR:	
Work-in-Process, 3/1/—	6,000 units
Put into Production or Received from Preceding Departments	40,000
To Be Accounted For	46,000
QUANTITY ACCOUNTED FOR AS FOLLOWS:	
	6,000
Transferred to Next Department	5,000
	31,000
Completed but Not Transferred Out	0
Uncompleted Work-in-Process	4,000
Units Lost in Production	0
Total Accounted For	46,000
Equivalent Production:	
Material	0
Labor and Manufacturing Overhead	42,600

Illustration 5–15 shows the summary results of cost and production for the two departments for March. It must be evident that where the "pure Fifo" method is used, keeping track of the various lots of production becomes more complicated as the number of manufacturing departments increase. For example, the material transferred out of Department II is made up of three different lots; those that will be transferred out of Department III will be four different lots; and so on. This makes for cumbersome cost accounting. Therefore, the modified Fifo method, as described in the following pages, is used more frequently by those firms planning to use the Fifo method of costing the initial work-in-process inventories.

Method No. 2: Handling initial work-in-process inventory on a Fifo basis when there are lost units in a department after the first.

When there are lost units in a department after the first, it is not always possible in a process plant to ascertain definitely whether these lost units came from the initial work-in-process inventory or from the units transferred into the department during the current period. Furthermore, as indicated previously, using the pure Fifo method becomes increasingly complicated as the number of producing departments becomes larger. Therefore, a modified Fifo procedure is devised, as follows:

1. The *final* work-in-process inventory in any department will be valued at this month's or the current manufacturing costs.
2. The amount transferred from any department is determined by subtracting from the *total* costs of manufacturing, the *final* work-in-process inventory. Without separating this figure into separate lots, the transfer becomes a composite figure of the initial work-in-process inventory and the new production.

Illustration 5–15

SUMMARY COST OF PRODUCTION REPORT

For Month of March, 19—

	Department I Total Cost	Department I Unit Cost	Department II Total Cost	Department II Unit Cost
COST IN PRECEDING DEPARTMENT:				
Work-in-Process, 3/1/—, 6,000 @ $2.85...			$ 17,100.00	$2.85
Transferred into Department during				
Month 5,000......................			$ 15,400.00	$3.08
35,000......................			98,000.00	2.80
COST IN CURRENT DEPARTMENT:				
Work-in-Process, 3/1/—:				
Material Costs.....................	$ 10,000.00	$2.00	0	
Labor Costs........................	3,000.00	0.60	$ 5,400.00	
Manufacturing Overhead Costs........	1,800.00	0.36	3,000.00	
Cost in Department during Month:				
Material Costs.....................	107,500.00	2.50	0	
Labor Costs........................	4,100.00	0.10	115,020.00	$2.70
Manufacturing Overhead Costs........	8,200.00	0.20	38,340.00	0.90
Total Cost in Current Department....	$134,600.00	$2.80	$161,760.00	$3.60
CUMULATIVE COST TOTAL..........	$134,600.00		$292,260.00	
Work Completed and Transferred Out:......	$ 15,400.00	$3.08	$ 40,620.00	$6.77
	98,000.00	2.80	33,400.00	6.68
			198,400.00	6.40
Work-in-Process, 3/31/—:				
Completed but Not Transferred Out......	0		0	
Cost in Preceding Department...........	0		$ 11,200.00	$2.80
Work-in-Process—Materials.............	$ 20,000.00		0	
Work-in-Process—Labor...............	400.00		6,480.00	1.62
Work-in-Process—Manufacturing Overhead................	800.00		2,160.00	0.54
Total Work-in-Process...............	$ 21,200.00		$ 19,840.00	
CUMULATIVE COST TOTAL ACCOUNTED FOR....................	$134,600.00		$292,260.00	

QUANTITY OF PRODUCTION REPORT (In Pounds)

	Department I	Department II
QUANTITY TO BE ACCOUNTED FOR:		
Work-in-Process, 3/1/—.............................	5,000 units	6,000 units
Put into Production or Received from Preceding Departments...	45,000	40,000
To Be Accounted For..............................	50,000 units	46,000 units
QUANTITY ACCOUNTED FOR AS FOLLOWS:		
Transferred to Next Department.....................	5,000	6,000
	35,000	5,000
		31,000
Completed but Not Transferred Out...................	0	0
Uncompleted Work-in-Process........................	8,000	4,000
Units Lost in Production............................	2,000	0
Total Accounted For...........................	50,000	46,000

3. To obtain the *unit cost* of the transfer, the quantity transferred is divided into the total cost of the transfer. This actually is an *average unit cost* of the transfer.

If there are lost units in the second or a subsequent department, *the costs for the preceding departments* of the initial work-in-process inventory and the units transferred into the department during the period must be averaged before *computing the lost unit cost adjustment.*

To illustrate the procedure involved in this method of costing the *initial work-in-process inventory* and the computation of the *lost unit cost adjustment,* the following cost data for the month of February will be considered:

QUANTITY OF PRODUCTION DATA FOR MONTH OF FEBRUARY

	Department I	Department II	Department III
In Process, Feb. 1, All Materials, ½ Labor and Overhead Costs..........................	10,000 units		
In Process, Feb. 1, ⅓ Labor and Overhead Costs...		15,000 units	
In Process, Feb. 1, ½ Labor and Overhead Costs...			4,000 units
Put into Production during February............	76,000		
QUANTITY ACCOUNTED FOR AS FOLLOWS:			
Transferred to Next Department..............	60,000 units	65,000 units	64,000 units
In Process, Feb. 28, All Materials, ¼ Labor and Overhead Costs.....................	20,000		
In Process, Feb. 28, ½ Labor and Overhead Costs....................................		8,000	
In Process, Feb. 28, ¼ Labor and Overhead Costs....................................			4,000
Lost in Production.........................	6,000	2,000	1,000
Total Accounted For...................	86,000 units	75,000 units	69,000 units

The cost of production statistics for the three producing departments for the month of February were:

	Dept. I	Dept. II	Dept. III
Work-in-process, 2/1/ — :			
Cost in preceding departments........................	0	$ 7,400	$ 4,000
Material costs in department ....$	3,000	0	0
Labor costs in department	750	1,500	400
Manufacturing overhead costs in department......	250	800	280
Costs during month of February:			
Material costs..	23,100	0	0
Labor costs...	9,000	17,920	13,860
Manufacturing overhead costs	3,600	11,520	9,450

On the basis of this data, Illustration 5–16, showing the summary cost of production for the month of February is prepared. In this it must be emphasized that the Fifo principle requires *that the costs of production for the current period must first be used to complete the initial work-in-process inventory, and then be applied to the new production.*

Equivalent Production and Unit Cost Computations for Department I

Materials: *Units*

To complete initial work-in-process inventory 0
New production for month..50,000
Work-in-process inventory, February 28, 100% complete
   as to materials 20,000
     Equivalent Production for Materials for Department I....................70,000

Dividing 70,000 into $23,100 results in a unit cost for materials in
   Department I for February production of..$0.33

Labor and Overhead: *Units*

To complete initial work-in-process inventory, already $\frac{1}{2}$ complete,
   10,000 × $\frac{1}{2}$.. 5,000
New completed production for the month...50,000
In process, February 28, $\frac{1}{4}$ completed: 20,000 × $\frac{1}{4}$.............................. 5,000
     Equivalent Production for Labor and Overhead for Department I 60,000

Dividing 60,000 into $9,000 results in unit cost for labor in Department
   I for February production of $0.15
Dividing 60,000 into $3,600 results in unit cost for overhead in
   Department I for February production of.. 0.06

Equivalent Production and Unit Cost Computations for Department II

Labor and Overhead: *Units*

To complete initial work-in-process inventory, already $\frac{1}{3}$ complete,
   15,000 × $\frac{2}{3}$..10,000
New completed production for month...50,000
In process, February 28, $\frac{1}{2}$ completed: 8,000 × $\frac{1}{2}$ 4,000
     Equivalent Production for Labor and Overhead for Department
     II 64,000

Dividing 64,000 into $17,920 results in a unit cost for labor in
   Department II for February production of..$0.28
Dividing 64,000 into $11,520 results in a unit cost for overhead in
   Department II for February production of.. 0.18

Equivalent Production and Unit Cost Computations for Department III

Labor and Overhead: *Units*

To complete initial work-in-process inventory, already $\frac{1}{2}$ complete,
   4,000 × $\frac{1}{2}$ 2,000

Illustration 5–16
SUMMARY COST OF PRODUCTION REPORT
For Month of February, 19—

FIFO METHOD WITH LOST UNITS IN ALL DEPARTMENTS

	Department I		Department II		Department III	
	Total Cost	Unit Cost	Total Cost	Unit Cost	Total Cost	Unit Cost
COST IN PRECEDING DEPART-MENT:						
Work-in-Process, 2/1/—............	0		$ 7,400.00		$ 4,000.00	$1.00
Transferred into Department during Month........................	0		32,050.00		65,026.71	1.00041
Total........................	0		$39,450.00	$0.5260	$69,026.71	$1.000371
Adjusted Unit Cost for Added Materials	0		0		xx	0
Additional Cost for Lost Units........	0		x	0.014411	xx	$0.0147115
Adjusted and Corrected Unit Cost Total......................	0		$39,450.00	$0.540411	$69,026.71	$1.0150987
COST IN CURRENT DEPARTMENT:						
Work-in-Process, 2/1/—:						
Material Costs....................	$ 3,000.00	$0.30	0		$ 400.00	$0.10
Labor Costs.....................	750.00	0.075	$ 1,500.00	$0.030	280.00	0.07
Manufacturing Overhead Costs......	250.00	0.025	800.00	0.016		
Cost in Department during Month:						
Material Costs....................	23,100.00	0.33	0	0	0	0
Labor Costs.....................	9,000.00	0.15	17,920.00	0.28	13,860.00	0.22
Manufacturing Overhead Costs......	3,600.00	0.06	11,520.00	0.18	9,450.00	0.15
Total Cost in Current Department.	$39,700.00	$0.54	$31,740.00	$0.46	$23,990.00	$0.37
CUMULATIVE COST TOTAL.......	$39,700.00		$71,190.00		$93,016.71	
Work Completed and Transferred Out....	$32,050.00	$0.53416	$65,026.71	$1.00041	$88,586.32	$1.3850987*
Work-in-Process, 2/28/—:						
Completed but Not Transferred Out....	0		0		0	
Cost in Preceding Department.......			$ 4,323.29	$0.540411	$ 4,060.39	$1.0150987
Work-in-Process—Materials.........	$6.600.00		0		0	
Work-in-Process—Labor............	750.00		1,120.00		220.00	
Work-in-Process—Manufacturing Overhead.....................	300.00		720.00		150.00	
Total Work in Process...........	$ 7,650.00		$ 6,163.29		$ 4,430.39	
CUMULATIVE COST TOTAL AC-COUNTED FOR..................	$39,700.00		$71,190.00		$93,016.71	

QUANTITY OF PRODUCTION (In Pounds)

	Department I	Department II	Department III
QUANTITY TO BE ACCOUNTED FOR:			
Completed and on Hand, 2/1/—.......	0	0	0
Work-in-Process, 2/1/—.	10,000(½)	15,000(⅓)	4,000(½)
Put into Production or Received from Preceding Departments............	76,000	60,000	65,000
To Be Accounted For...........	86,000	75,000	69,000
QUANTITY ACCOUNTED FOR AS FOLLOWS:			
Transferred to Next Department......	{10,000 {50,000	{15,000 {50,000	{ 4,000 {60,000
Completed but Not Transferred Out....			
Uncompleted Work-in-Process........	20,000(¼)	8,000(½)	4,000(¼)
Units Lost in Production............	6,000	2,000	1,000
Total Accounted For............	86,000	75,000	69,000
Equivalent Production:			
Material............................	70,000	0	0
Labor and Manufacturing Overhead....	60,000	64,000	63,000

* Figures may not be exact due to rounding.

New production for the month, completed...60,000
Equivalent production for work-in-process, February 28, 4,000 × $\frac{1}{4}$ .... _1,000_

    Equivalent Production for Labor and Overhead for Department III...63,000

Dividing 63,000 into $13,860 results in a unit cost for labor in
    Department III for February production of $0.22
Dividing 63,000 into $9,450 results in a unit cost for overhead in
    Department III for February production of 0.15

Thus the unit costs within each department are computed by using the equivalent production resulting from first completing the initial work-in-process and then considering the new production. Now with further reference to the figures on Illustration 5–16, it is necessary to compute the transfers out of the department and the unit costs for lost units in departments after the first.

When the Fifo method of treating the initial work-in-process inventory is in use and there are lost units in any department after the first, the following rules or principles should govern the procedure after computing the unit costs for each element of cost in each department:

1. Compute the final work-in-process inventory, *not* including "units completed but not transferred out," in any department. Subtract this amount from the total *cumulative* costs of manufacturing. The difference represents the total costs of the *units completed.* Computing a unit cost for the completed units and multiplying by the number of units transferred out of the department will result in the cost of work transferred out of the department.

2. If there are lost units in any department after the first, it is necessary to compute the average *unit cost for the preceding departments* before attempting to compute the lost unit cost. This average is made up of the costs of the preceding department for the work-in-process at the beginning, plus the new production received into the department during the month, divided by the total units of the initial work-in-process inventory and units received into the department. When this corrected unit cost (which includes the lost unit cost) has been computed for the preceding departments, and the unit costs in the department have been calculated, it is then possible to compute the work-in-process inventory at the end of the month in any department. Deducting this amount from the total cumulative costs results in the total cost of completed units. From this it is a simple matter to compute the unit cost of the work transferred to the next department.

QUESTIONS FOR REVIEW

1. What is meant by the statement that the initial work-in-process inventory in any department must be in analyzed form? Why is this necessary? What is the source of this information when it is recorded on the current cost of production report?

2. What procedure is followed in handling the quantity figures and the cost figures of the initial work-in-process inventory when the average cost determination method is used?

3. In Department II, 20,000 units were received from Department I at a total cost of $48,000. In Department II, 12,000 units were added to the quantity of production due to added materials, at a cost of $36,000. In Department II, 2,000 units were lost in the processing. What is the adjusted and corrected unit cost in Department II for the work done in Department I?

4. Compare the effect on the unit costs for the preceding department when (a) materials are added to the production in a department after the first, but these do not increase the volume of production units; and (b) when the added materials do increase the number of units in production.

5. The initial work-in-process in Department II was composed of 30,000 units on which 80 percent of the materials and 75 percent of the labor and overhead had been applied in the preceding period. During the month, 80,000 units were completed, and 20,000 were still in process on which 60 percent of the materials and 50 percent of the labor and manufacturing overhead had been applied. When the Fifo method of accounting for the initial work-in-process inventory is used, what are the equivalent production figures for material, labor, and manufacturing overhead for this month?

6. Under the simplified process accounting, no provision is made on the cost of production report for a separate section of "cost in preceding department." Explain why this is so.

7. Under what business conditions would you recommend the use of the so-called simplified process cost accounting procedure? Explain.

8. As of June 30, the total cumulative costs for Departments I and II were $60,000. Unit costs in Department I were $0.30. In process in Department II were 6,000 units, on which all the material had been applied, and 30 percent of the labor and overhead. Unit costs in Department II during the month of June were: materials, $1; labor, $0.40; and manufacturing overhead, $0.15. What was the cost of the work transferred to Department III if the Fifo method of cost determination is used?

9. The effect on the unit costs of production when materials are added in a department after the first and these increase the volume of production is the opposite of that created when there are lost units in a department after the first. Explain why this is so.

10. What journal entry is made for the adjustment of unit costs for the preceding departments when materials added increase the volume of production? Explain.

PROBLEMS — GROUP A

Problem 5-1. Purpose: *Cost of Production Report for Firm in Which Materials Are Added in All Departments, Increasing Volume of Production; Lost Units in All Departments*

The manufacturing operations of the Everglad Manufacturing Company are based upon a continuous process cost determination system. For the month of February, the following are the cost and production data:

Department I:
  Started into production, 75,000 units, of which 40,000 were completed and transferred to Department II; 5,000 units were lost or spoiled; and the remaining 30,000 units were still in process, 80 percent complete as to material costs and 20 percent complete as to labor and overhead costs. Material costs were $115,200; labor costs, $138,000; and manufacturing overhead costs, $18,400.

Department II:
  The costs for materials were $77,000; labor costs, $50,000; and manufacturing overhead costs, $26,000. The production statistics indicated an increase in the number of units due to added materials of 20,000 units. Of the total production, 40,000 units were completed and transferred to Department III. In process were 15,000 units, with 100 percent of the material applied and 66⅔ percent of the labor and overhead costs applied. The remaining units were lost or spoiled.

Department III:
  In Department III, 50,000 units were completed and transferred to the finished stock room. In process were 12,000 units, 75 percent complete as to material and 33⅓ percent complete as to labor and manufacturing overhead costs. Lost in production were 8,000 units. Increase in the volume of production was due to the added materials in this department. The costs in this department were materials, $106,200; labor, $59,400; and manufacturing overhead, $21,600.

Required:
  On the basis of this information, you are asked to prepare —

a) Summary cost of production report for the month of February (unit costs corrected to six decimal places).
b) Journal entries to record the production, departmental transfers, and the finished goods.
c) Work-in-process inventory schedule, February 28, in analyzed form by departments.

Problem 5-2. Purpose: *Cost of Production Report for Firm Using the Average Method of Costing the Initial Work-in-Process Inventory; No Added Materials or Lost Units Except in Department I*

The Euclid Manufacturing Company has been in operation for three months. For the month of June, the production costs and statistics of the factory (in units) were as follows:

	Dept. I	Dept. II	Dept. III
Work-in-process, June 1, 19—:			
Units in process, 100% material, 20% labor			
and overhead 8,000			
Units in process, 50% labor and overhead		12,000	
Units in process, 25% labor and overhead			10,000
New production started during June..................72,000			
Completed and transferred out during June 60,000		60,000	45,000
Work-in-process, June 30, 19—:			
100% material, 50% labor and overhead.........16,000			
33⅓% labor and overhead............................		12,000	
20% labor and overhead			25,000
Units lost in production 4,000			

The production costs incurred during the month were as follows:

	Dept. I	Dept. II	Dept. III
Work-in-process, June 1, 19—:			
Cost in preceding departments......................	0	$36,000	$60,000
Material costs..$15,000		0	0
Labor costs...	20,000	9,000	2,000
Manufacturing overhead costs.......................	1,750	3,960	3,000
Operating costs during month:			
Material costs	99,000	0	0
Labor costs	61,600	80,600	62,000
Manufacturing overhead costs.......................	25,450	30,600	32,000

Required:

From this information, you are asked to prepare for the month of June:

a) Cost of production report (unit costs correct to six decimal places).
b) Journal entries to record the costs of production, departmental transfers, and finished goods.
c) Work-in-process inventory schedule, June 30, in analyzed form for each department.

Problem 5–3. Purpose: *Cost of Production Report for Firms Using the Average Method of Costing the Initial Work-in-Process Inventories; Materials Added in Each Department Increasing Number of Units in Production; Lost Units in All Departments*

The Evers Manufacturing Company has a three-department manufacturing plant. Materials are added to production in each department, thereby increasing the volume of production. The initial work-in-process inventories are costed on the average method.

For the month of October, the quantity of production statistics (in units) were:

	Dept. I	Dept. II	Dept. III
Work-in-process, October 1, 19—.....................15,000		9,000	7,000
Increase in volume due to added			
materials...57,000		12,000	14,000
Transferred to next department...................60,000		57,000	61,000
Work-in-process, October 31, 19—:			
All material, $^2/_5$ labor and overhead			
applied 10,000			
All material, $^2/_3$ labor and overhead			
applied		21,000	
80% material, $^3/_5$ labor and overhead			
applied...			15,000
Units lost in production	2,000	3,000	2,000

The cost data for these operations for the month of October were:

	Dept. I	Dept. II	Dept. III
Work-in-process, October 1, 19—:			
Cost in preceding department	0	$32,000	$40,000
Material costs...$ 30,000		13,000	3,000
Labor costs	1,500	4,000	5,000
Manufacturing overhead costs	2,000	2,000	1,200
Operating costs for month:			
Material costs...	117,000	91,520	53,240
Labor costs	62,500	92,000	83,440
Manufacturing overhead	46,640	46,000	34,980

Required:

a) Cost of production report for the month of October (unit costs correct to six decimal places).

b) Journal entries to record the production, departmental transfers, and finished goods.

c) Schedule of work-in-process inventories, October 31, on a departmental basis by elements of cost.

Problem 5–4.   Purpose: *Completion of the Cost of Production Report When There Is a Work-in-Process Inventory at the Beginning; Use of the Average Method; Lost Units in All Departments*

The following cost information was taken from the books of the Emply Manufacturing Company. From this information, you are to prepare a cost of production report, journal entries, and departmental work-in-process inventories at December 31, 19—.

	Department I		Department II	
	Total Cost	Unit Cost	Total Cost	Unit Cost
COST IN PRECEDING DE-PARTMENTS:				
Work-in-Process, 1/1/—...............			24,000	
Transferred into Department........				
Adjusted Unit Cost for Added Material................................				
Corrected and Adjusted Unit Cost.				
Totals				
COST IN CURRENT DE-PARTMENT:				
Work-in-Process, 1/1/—:				
Material Costs	60,000		15,000	
Labor Costs	30,000		12,000	
Manufacturing Overhead Costs..	10,000		4,000	
Costs during Period:				
Material Costs	122,000		150,000	
Labor Costs	66,000		30,000	
Manufacturing Overhead Costs..	26,000		10,000	
Total Current Costs..............	314,000			
CUMULATIVE COST TOTAL	314,000			
Work Completed and Transferred				
Work-in-Process, 12/31/—:				
Completed but not transferred				
Cost in Preceding Department......				
Work-in-Process — Materials				
Work-in-Process — Labor..............				
Work-in-Process — Overhead.........				
Total Work-in-Process...........				
CUMULATIVE COST TOTAL ACCOUNTED FOR				

QUANTITY OF PRODUCTION REPORT		
QUANTITY TO BE AC-COUNTED FOR:		
Work-in-Process, 1/1/—...............	50,000	10,000
Put into Production or Received from Preceding Departments	100,000	90,000
Increase in Volume Due to Added Materials.....................		60,000
Total to Be Accounted For	150,000	160,000
Transferred to Next Department......	90,000	120,000
Completed and on Hand................	10,000	0
Work-in-Process...........................	40,000 (all Mat., ½ L. & O.H.)	30,000 (all Mat., ⅔ L. & O.H.)
Lost or Spoiled Units....................	10,000	10,000
TOTAL ACCOUNTED FOR........	150,000	160,000

Problem 5-5.   Purpose: *Simplified Process Cost Accounting; Materials Added in All Departments; Lost Units in All Departments; Materials Transferred Are Treated as Part of Material by Receiving Department*

The production statistics (in units) for the month of November for the Eurom Manufacturing Company were as follows:

	Dept. I	Dept. II	Dept. III
Started into production...................................	90,000		
Increased volume due to added materials		30,000	20,000
Completed and transferred...............................	70,000	80,000	75,000
In process, 80% material, $\frac{2}{3}$ labor and overhead...	15,000		
In process, 100% material, $\frac{1}{2}$ labor and overhead...		10,000	
In process, 80% material, $\frac{1}{2}$ labor and overhead...			20,000
Lost in production...	5,000	10,000	5,000

The costs of production taken from the departmental cost sheets were as follows:

	Dept. I	Dept. II	Dept. III
Material costs...	$50,840	$45,000	$30,000
Labor costs..	32,000	17,000	28,050
Manufacturing overhead...................................	24,000	51,000	42,500

Required:

a) Prepare a cost of production report on which the costs from the preceding department are treated as material costs by the receiving department.

b) Prepare journal entries to record the manufacturing operations and the transfer to the Finished Goods account.

PROBLEMS—GROUP B

Problem 5-6.   Purpose: *CPA Problem Relating to Process Cost Accounting*

The Erie Supply Company manufactures a single product on a continuous manufacturing basis. This firm uses a process type of cost accounting.

To manufacture this product, which is known as *Klebo,* the following procedure is involved:

A special alloy metal *Nicled* is stamped to make the frame which is used with purchased parts X. One part of X is assembled with the frame after which it is machined and cleaned, and then two parts of Y are assembled to make the finished product *Klebo*.

Time and motion studies indicate that of the total time required for the manufacture of a unit: the first operation required 25% of the labor cost; the first assembly an additional 25%; machining and cleaning, 12½%; the second assembly, 25%; and the final painting, 12½%.

Manufacturing overhead cost is considered to follow the same pattern by operations as does the labor.

The following data are presented to you as of July 31, the end of the first month's operation:

Material *Nicled* purchased, 100,000 lbs.	$25,000
Part X purchased 80,000 units	16,000
Part Y purchased, 150,000 units	15,000
Primer and enamel paint used	1,072
Direct labor costs	45,415
Manufacturing overhead costs	24,905
Production statistics were:	
Units finished and sent to the finished goods warehouse	67,000 units
Units assembled but not painted	5,000 units
Units ready for the second assembly	3,000 units
Inventories, July 31, 19—:	
Finished units	7,500
Material *Nicled*	5,800 lbs.
Part X	5,000 units
Part Y	6,000 units
Klebos in process	8,000 units

Required:

a) A schedule of the equivalent labor production.
b) A schedule of the total and the unit costs incurred in the production for:
   (1) Each kind of material.
   (2) Labor cost.
   (3) Manufacturing overhead cost.
   (4) Total cost of production.
c) A schedule of detailed material, labor, and manufacturing overhead costs for the work-in-process.

(Adapted from an AICPA Uniform Examination)

Problem 5–7. Purpose: *Completion of Partial Cost of Production Report for Firm Having an Initial Work-in-Process Inventory Costed on Fifo Basis; Added Materials and Lost Units*

The following data represents the cost and production for the Elfers Manufacturing Company for the month of July. The firm uses the Fifo method of costing the initial work-in-process inventories.

Production Costs	Dept. II	Dept. III
Cost of units received from Department I during July.........$63,000		
Work-in-process, July 1, 19—:		
Cost in preceding department 27,200		$24,500
Material costs... 0		3,600
Labor costs 4,800		2,100
Manufacturing overhead costs 1,200		1,080
Costs during July:		
Material... 0		36,450
Labor costs 24,200		20,944
Manufacturing overhead costs 4,840		11,088

In Units

Volume of Production Statistics	Dept. II	Dept. III
Units in process, July 1, 60% complete as to		
labor and overhead 10,000		
Units in process, July 1, 100% complete as to		
materials, 50% complete as to labor		
and overhead		8,000
Received from preceding departments during July.............. 23,000		25,000
Increased in volume due to added materials......................		7,000
Total to Be Accounted For 33,000		40,000
Accounted for as follows:		
Units completed and transferred out 25,000		30,000
Units in process, July 31, 50% complete as		
to labor and overhead.. 6,000		
Units in process, July 31, 100% complete as		
to materials, 60% complete as to labor		
and overhead		8,000
Units lost in production... 2,000		2,000
Total Accounted For 33,000		40,000

Required:

a) Prepare a cost of production report for the month of July, using the Fifo method of costing the initial work-in-process (unit cost correct to six decimal places).
b) Journal entries to record the manufacturing operations for July.
c) Compute cost of each finished unit.

Problem 5–8. Purpose: *Completion of Partial Cost of Production Report with Added Materials Increasing Volume of Production; Entries*

The following is a partial cost of production report of the Enders Manufacturing Company for the month of February:

ENDERS MANUFACTURING COMPANY
COST OF PRODUCTION REPORT
February 28, 19—

	Department I		Department II		Department III	
	Total Cost	Unit Cost	Total Cost	Unit Cost	Total Cost	Unit Cost
COST IN PRECEDING DEPARTMENT:						
Work-in-Process, 2/1/—			40,000		90,000	
Transferred into Department..............			259,000		320,000	
Corrected and Adjusted Unit						
Totals			299,000		410,000	
COST IN CURRENT DEPARTMENT:						
Work-in-Process—Materials.................			0		9,000	
Work-in-Process—Labor			2,000		9,000	
Work-in-Process—Overhead			3,000		4,000	
Costs during Period:						
Material Costs..............................			0		200,000	
Labor Costs..................................			70,000		110,000	
Manufacturing Overhead Costs			33,000		64,000	
Total Current Costs.....................			108,000		396,000	
CUMULATIVE COST TOTAL			407,000		806,000	
Work Completed and Transferred						
Work-in-Process, 2/28/—						
Work Completed but Not Transferred ...						
Work-in-Process—Materials.................						
Work-in-Process—Labor						
Work-in-Process—Overhead						
Cost in Preceding Department..............						
Total Work-in-Process						
CUMULATIVE COST TOTAL						

QUANTITY OF PRODUCTION REPORT FOR PERIOD ENDING
February 28, 19—

	Department I	Department II	Department III
QUANTITY TO BE ACCOUNTED FOR:			
Work-in-Process, 2/1/—		20,000	30,000
Put into Production or Received from Preceding Department		120,000	100,000
Increase in Volume, Added Material		0	65,000
TOTAL TO BE ACCOUNTED FOR ..		140,000	195,000
Transferred Out of Department		100,000	150,000
Completed and on Hand......................		10,000	0
Work-in-Process 2/28/—		20,000 ($\frac{1}{2}$ L. + O.H.)	40,000 $\left(\begin{array}{c}\text{all material}\\ \frac{1}{2}\text{ L. + O.H.}\end{array}\right)$
Units Lost or Spoiled		10,000	5,000
TOTAL ACCOUNTED FOR		140,000	195,000
EQUIVALENT PRODUCTION:			
Materials			
Labor...			
Overhead...			

Required:

a) Complete the cost of production report using average method of pricing initial work-in-process inventory (unit costs correct to six decimal places).

b) Prepare journal entries for the figures given for Departments II and III.

Problem 5–9.   Purpose: *CPA Problem: Computation of Fifo and Average Costing Methods of the Initial Work-in-Process Inventories*

The Eigner Manufacturing Company manufactures a single product in its two-department factory.

For each unit in Department I output, two units of raw material X are put into production at the start of operations. For each unit in Department II, three cans of raw material Y are put in at the end of processing. Two pounds of Department I output are placed in the start of work in Department II for each unit of finished goods started.

Spoilage generally occurs in Department II when processing is approximately 50% complete.

Work-in-process accounts are maintained for materials, conversion costs, and prior department costs.

The company uses Fifo basis for inventory valuation for work-in-process—Department I and finished goods, and it uses the Average cost for inventory valuation for work-in-process—Department II.

The data for the month of April:

1. Units transferred:

> From work-in-process—Department I ....2,200 lbs.
> From work-in-process—Department II to finished goods .... 900 gals.
> From finished goods to cost of goods sold.................................. 600 gals.

2. Units spoiled in Department II: 100 gals.
3. Raw materials unit costs: X, $1.51 per unit; Y, $2 per can.
4. Conversion costs: Department I, $3,344; Department II, $4,010.
5. Spoilage recovery: $100 (treated as cost reduction).
6. Inventory data:

	Department I		Department II		Finished Goods	
	Initial	*Final*	*Initial*	*Final*	*Initial*	*Final*
Units...	200	300	200	300	700	1,000
Fraction complete conversion costs....................	$\frac{1}{2}$	$\frac{1}{3}$	$\frac{1}{2}$	$\frac{2}{3}$		
Valuation:					$13,300	
Materials	$560		0			
Conversion costs....................	$108		$390			
Prior department costs			$2,200			

Required:

a) Journalize April entries to record the transfer of costs from Department I to Department II, and from Department II to finished goods; and finished goods to the cost of goods sold.
b) Prepare schedules of computation to show computations.

(Adapted from AICPA Uniform Examination)

Problem 5–10.   Purpose: *Cost of Production Report for Process Cost Determination Using the Fifo Method of Costing the Initial Work-in-Process Inventory*

The following is the Department II figures of the cost of production report for the Eckhardt Manufacturing Company for the month of March. This firm uses the Fifo method of treating its initial work-in-process inventory.

ECKHARDT MANUFACTURING COMPANY
COST OF PRODUCTION REPORT
March 31, 19–, Fifo

	Department I		Department II		Department III	
	Total Cost	Unit Cost	Total Cost	Unit Cost	Total Cost	Unit Cost
COST IN PRECEDING DEPARTMENT:						
Work-in-Process, 3/1/–			6,300			
Transferred into Department			77,500			
Corrected and Adjusted Unit						
Totals			83,800			
COST IN CURRENT DEPARTMENT:						
Work-in-Process – Materials			3,300			
Work-in-Process – Labor			2,100			
Work-in-Process – Overhead			1,200			
Costs during Period:						
Material Costs			45,000			
Labor Costs			57,500			
Manufacturing Overhead Costs			37,500			
Total Current Costs			146,600			
CUMULATIVE COST TOTAL			230,400			
Work Completed and Transferred						
Work-in-Process, 3/31/–						
Work Completed, Not transferred						
Work-in-Process – Materials						
Work-in-Process – Labor						
Work-in-Process – Overhead						
Cost in Preceding Department						
Total Work-in-Process						
CUMULATIVE COST TOTAL						

QUANTITY OF PRODUCTION REPORT FOR PERIOD ENDING 3/31/–

	Department I	Department II	Department III
QUANTITY TO BE ACCOUNTED FOR:			
Work-in-Process, 3/1/–		3,000 $\left(\begin{array}{l}\text{all material}\\ \frac{1}{3}\text{L.}+\text{O.H.}\end{array}\right)$	
Put into Production or Received from Preceding Department		20,000	
Increase in Volume, Added Material		5,000	
TOTAL TO BE ACCOUNTED FOR		28,000	
Transferred Out of Department		22,000	
Completed and on Hand		3,000	
Work-in-Process		2,000 $\left(\begin{array}{l}\text{all material}\\ \frac{1}{2}\text{L.}+\text{O.H.}\end{array}\right)$	
Units Lost or Spoiled		1,000	
TOTAL ACCOUNTED FOR		28,000	
EQUIVALENT PRODUCTION:			
Materials			
Labor			
Overhead			

Required:

a) Complete the cost of production report for the Department II for March.

b) Compute unit cost of material transferred to Department III.

Problem 5–11. Purpose: *Cost of Production Report and Journal Entries for a Two-Department Plant Using Process Costs*

The Elegant Manufacturing Company manufactures a single product in a two-department plant. This firm uses the average method of treating the initial work-in-process inventory. Materials added in the second department increase the volume of production accordingly.

The accounting and statistical data given below were taken from the records for the month of June.

Work-in-process in Department I, June 1, was 8,000 units on which 80% of the materials had been applied and 50% of the labor and overhead. The costs for this work were materials, $12,800; labor, $5,200; and manufacturing overhead, $2,000.

During the month of June, 42,000 additional units were started into production in Department I. The costs during the month of June in Department I were materials, $71,200; labor, $19,100; and manufacturing overhead, $10,150. In this department, 36,000 units were completed and transferred, 10,000 were in process with 60 percent of the material, and 45 percent of the labor and manufacturing overhead applied.

On June 1, there were 5,000 units in process in Department II on which all the materials had been applied and only two fifths of the labor and manufacturing overhead. The costs already incurred on this work-in-process were cost in Department I, $15,200; material costs in Department II, $10,000; labor, $1,400; and manufacturing overhead, $800. During the month of June, the following costs were incurred: materials, $64,800; labor, $46,600; and manufacturing overhead, $11,200. Added materials in Department II increased the volume by 7,000 units.

The volume of production in Department II was completed and transferred to the stock room, 36,000 units; in process, June 30, 10,000 units, 80 percent complete as to material costs, and 40 percent complete as to labor and overhead costs. The balance was lost in Department II.

Required:

From this information, you are asked to:

a) Prepare a cost of production report for the month of June.
b) Journal entries to record in summary form the cost accounting from the use of the raw material until the goods are transferred to Finished Goods account.

Problem 5–12. Purpose: *Completion of Cost of Production Report for Firm Using Departmental Costs*

The firm of Etna Manufacturing Company uses a departmental cost accounting system. The following data has been presented to you on their usual summary forms and you are asked to complete them to show the unit costs for each element for each department and cumulatively as well. The firm uses the Average Method of treating the initial work-in-process inventory.

Required:

a) Prepare journal entries for month of June.
b) Prepare work-in-process in analyzed form for each department.

	Department I		Department II		Department III	
	Total Cost	Unit Cost	Total Cost	Unit Cost	Total Cost	Unit Cost
COST IN PRECEDING DEPARTMENT:						
Work-in-Process, June 1............			7,800			
Transferred during June.............						
Work-in-Process, June 1:						
Material................................	6,000		1,500			
Labor....................................	8,000		1,300			
Overhead...............................	3,000		800			
Cost during June:						
Material................................	15,000		17,500*		24,000†	
Labor....................................	48,250		12,300		15,750	
Overhead...............................	22,000		9,400		10,500	
CUMULATIVE COST TOTAL...						

QUANTITY STATEMENT

	Department I		Department II		Department III	
TO BE ACCOUNTED FOR						
Units in Process, June 1............	4,000		2,000			
Received from Preceding Department..........................	–		18,000		14,000	
Put into Process......................	26,000		–		6,000	
TO BE ACCOUNTED FOR	30,000		20,000		20,000	
Accounted for as Follows:						
Completed and Transferred........	18,000		14,000		15,000	
Completed and On Hand...........	4,000		1,000		–	
Work-in-Process—All Material, ½ Labor and Overhead...........	6,000		4,000		5,000	
Lost in Production During Month	2,000		1,000		–	
	30,000		20,000		20,000	

* Does not increase number of units being produced.
† Increases number of units being produced.

chapter **6**

Cost Accounting for Coproducts, Joint Products, and By-products

NATURE OF COPRODUCTS, JOINT PRODUCTS, AND BY-PRODUCTS

Coproducts, joint products, and by-products are associated primarily with a process or departmental type of manufacturing operation. Chemical companies, lumber mills, oil refineries, flour mills, and meat-packers, are representative firms involved in cost accounting problems affecting these three products. The main accounting problems involved are those of apportioning manufacturing costs on some reasonable or acceptable basis so that the net income for the firm and the inventory valuations meet acceptable accounting and income tax standards. Since the manufacturing operations of the firms having by-products or coproducts vary widely both in volume and in product sales values, as well as procedures, only generalized costing practices can be given. The costing problems for a lumbering concern vary from those of a meat-packing concern or from those of an oil refinery.

To clarify the discussion of the accounting procedures, it is necessary to define and distinguish between the various multiple products under two headings: (1) *joint* and *coproducts,* and (2) *by-products,* since the accounting principles and procedures will be developed on this basis.

Joint products are two or more products manufactured simultaneously by a common or series of processing operations. The quantity and sales value of each product are such that their production costs cannot be separated effectively, and none of them may be properly designated as the main product. Illustrations of such joint products are found in the meat-packing industry in which hams, ribs, etc., are obtained from the slaughter

165

of pigs; and in the oil refining industry in which gasoline, naphtha, kerosene, benzine, etc., are obtained from the basic crude oil.

Coproducts, if and when a distinction must be made, refer to the production of two or more products *at the same time,* but not necessarily from the same processing operations or the same raw materials. For example, in lumbering operations, it is possible to obtain oak, pine, maple, and walnut boards *at the same time* but from different stumpage (raw materials).

By-products are produced under conditions similar to those of joint or coproducts — that is, from common processing operations. However, where there are *by-products,* the distinction between the various types of products is made on the basis of the relative importance of the *quantity and value of each.* A *by-product* is essentially the *secondary* result of manufacturing operations. A rather arbitrary rule has been suggested in interpreting the meaning of "secondary" — if the value of a product is less than 10% of the total value of all products, it could be considered a *by-product,* not a *coproduct* or *joint product.* What may be considered as a by-product for one firm may be the main product of another, and vice versa. For example, in large cities where the demand for manufactured gas for cooking and heating is important, the main product is gas and the by-products, coke, tar, etc.; whereas in Connelsville, Pennsylvania, where the demand in the steel mills for coke is large, coke is the main product and gas becomes one of the by-products. *Time* as well as *location* frequently alters the by-product picture. Many years ago, gasoline was the by-product of the oil industry when kerosene was the main product; later the reverse was true; and finally after 1928, gasoline and heating oils were both important enough relatively to be considered as joint products.

CHARACTERISTICS OF JOINT OR COPRODUCTS

Sometimes in manufacturing operations multiple products result because of different sizes of the same product, or various grades, or various styles. *Joint* and *coproducts* are to be distinguished from these multiple products in several respects:

1. The joint or coproduct must be the *primary* objective of the manufacturing operations.
2. The sales value of the joint or coproduct must be *relatively high* if it is to be compared with a by-product resulting at the same time.
3. In the case of certain joint products, the manufacturer must produce *all* of the products of a certain process, if he produces any of them. For example, in meat-packing there will always be hams, sausage, and bacon every time a pig is slaughtered.

4. In certain joint products, the manufacturer has no control over the *relative* quantities of the various products that will result. From each pig that is slaughtered, there will be two hams, two shoulders, etc., no more and no less.

In spite of these definitions and limitations, expediency rather than accurate accounting often determines whether a multiple product is to be treated as a joint product or a by-product.

PROBLEMS IN COSTING JOINT AND BY-PRODUCTS

A number of problems arise in the accounting for joint and by-products, the solution of which creates a variety of different costs even for the same products. Among these problems are:

1. Some firms, either because of clerical costs or lack of sufficient volume of production, find it impractical to develop systems and accounting for apportioning the costs between the several products except on some approximate or arbitrary basis. This results in costs which vary widely for the same products with different firms.
2. The volume and selling price of the by-product do not justify spending the money to determine its cost. Therefore many by-products are treated and sold as scrap.
3. Sometimes the manufacturing operations are such that it is difficult to measure with any degree of accuracy the amount of labor and overhead applicable to the various products.
4. Management does not understand why reasonably accurate costs should be determined for the joint products and the by-products. Not only is this necessary to help fix selling prices but also to determine the advisability of extending the manufacturing operations to develop new joint products.

CLASSIFICATION OF JOINT OR MULTIPLE PRODUCT COST PROCEDURES

There are a variety of conditions under which process manufacturing firms operate when several products are being manufactured. Among these are:

a) Several different products are manufactured, each in a different department having no relation to the others.

The accounting procedures under these conditions are similar to those existing where each product is manufactured in a separate factory. The problems would be the same, therefore, as those in a firm manufacturing a single product. These have been discussed previously.

b)   Several products are manufactured, each in a different depart-ment, but part of at least one of the products is used in the manufacture of one or more of the other products.

In this situation part of, say, the first product is completed and sent to the finished goods stock room while the remainder is forwarded to one or more of the departments making the other products. Although the ac-counting procedures are similar to those for a single-product firm, the analysis of the cost of production report the quantity and cost figures for part or all of the following:

1.   Work completed and transferred to the finished goods stock room.
2.   Work completed and transferred to other manufacturing depart-ments.
3.   Work completed but still in the department.
4.   Work-in-process.
5.   Lost in production.

Work completed in one department and received in subsequent depart-ments for use in other products will be treated as though purchased from an outside firm. The costs for the second and third departments or for other products will be computed in a manner similar to the single-product firm except that the costs for these products cannot be computed until the costs for preceding departments have been determined.

c)   A number of products are being manufactured either simultane-ously in the same department or in different departments from the same materials purchased from the outside or prepared in another department.

These are sometimes known as *coproducts* or *joint products*. It is with this last phase of process cost accounting that this chapter is primarily concerned. The major problem in this type of work is the method of pro-rating or allocating the costs between the various products with some degree of accuracy.

PRORATING COSTS WHEN SEVERAL PRODUCTS ARE BEING MANUFACTURED

This is one of the major problems of multiple product process costing. Different methods of proration will produce different costs. The important principle to keep in mind is that the method be reasonable and reliable and result in fairly accurate costs for each product. Otherwise the manu-facturer is not in a position to measure accurately the profitableness of the various products being made and sold.

Since the *materials* used in manufacturing usually have a direct rela-tionship to the volume of production of the various products, materials are therefore a basic influence on the method of prorating costs equitably among the various products. Firms using *multiple product* cost procedures may be grouped accordingly, viz:

1. Firms in which the use of a *single raw material* may result in several finished products, such as the chemical industries, lumber producers, and meat-packing plants.
2. Firms in which *several raw materials* are used in the production of *two or more products*.

ONE RAW MATERIAL IS USED TO PRODUCE SEVERAL PRODUCTS

There are three methods of prorating the costs for multiple products: (1) on a quantity basis, (2) on a weighted average or market value basis, and (3) by formula. If the *units of production* (such as gallons, pounds, tons, etc.) are the same for all products, it is possible to prorate the material costs and labor costs, and also the overhead costs of their *joint production,* on a *unit or quantity* basis.

In the production of several products from a single source, such as crude oil in the refining business, the quantity of each product extracted can be used as the basis of cost proration of the material costs, or labor costs, or both. To illustrate this proration, it is assumed that 10,000 barrels of crude oil were run through the refinery, from which the quantity of each product resulting from the refining after deducting the loss of 200 barrels from the manufacturing operations was:

Product	Quantity (barrels)	Percent
Gasoline	2,600	26.52
Benzine	200	2.04
Kerosene	1,000	10.21
Lubricating oil	300	3.06
Fuel oil	5,000	51.03
Gas oil	300	3.06
Miscellaneous	400	4.08
Total	9,800	100.00
Loss	200	
	10,000	

If these percentages are fairly uniform, they may be used regularly in apportioning the cost of materials used. Labor may be apportioned similarly, unless a more specific and accurate method can be developed.

A schedule of the cost allocation for this particular run for materials is illustrated, assuming the total cost of $26,000 ($2.60 per barrel):

Product	Quantity after Loss (barrels)	Percent of Total	Cost of Material Allocated
Gasoline.....................................2,600		26.52	$ 6,895.20
Benzine...................................... 200		2.04	530.40
Kerosene....................................1,000		10.21	2,654.60
Lubricating oil 300		3.06	795.60
Fuel oil 5,000		51.03	13,267.80
Gas oil 300		3.06	795.60
Miscellaneous............................ 400		4.08	1,060.80
Total..............................9,800		100.00	$26,000.00

But since this method of proration is not always useful, that is, since some products may be more valuable than others, and also because in some concerns the *units* of the manufacturing products are not always the same, some firms use the *weighted average* (sometimes known as the *market value*) method. The quantity of production is weighted (multiplied) by the *average sales price* or assumed market price before computing the proportion of the total cost for material and/or labor applicable to each product.

For example, in extensive copper mining, it may be assumed that the gold, silver, and other valuable metals being produced are coproducts (as contrasted with the term "by-product") of the mining operations. Copper production is expressed in pounds or tons, whereas the silver and gold are in ounces. Furthermore, the great disparity in the sales prices of the products would indicate that some method which gave some consideration to the sales prices as well as the quantities would be more equitable. Copper sells for 55 cents per pound; gold, $35 an ounce; and silver, $1.80 an ounce.

To illustrate this method, it is assumed that the costs of mining for the period amounted to $7,825,000, for which 18,000,000 pounds of copper, 3,000,000 ounces of silver, and 10,000 ounces of gold were produced. Taking into consideration the market prices of each of these products, the apportionment of costs on the basis of a weighted average (sales price) would be as follows:

```
Copper............18,000,000 lbs. at $ 0.55............$ 9,900,000
Silver.............. 3,000,000 oz. at    1.80............  5,400,000
Gold..............     10,000 oz. at  35.00............    350,000
                                                       $15,650,000
```

It will be noted that the cost of production, $7,825,000, is 50% of the weighted average or hypothetical sales price allocation of the finished products ($15,650,000). Therefore in allocating the costs of production of the various coproducts, 50 percent of the sales value of the respective products provides the cost figures, e.g.:

50% of $9,900,000...................$4,950,000	Cost of copper produced
50 of 5,400,000.................. 2,700,000	Cost of silver produced
50 of 350,000.................. 175,000	Cost of gold produced
Total Cost of Production $7,825,000	

In other words, when this method is used, the first step is to compute the total costs of production of all the products. Then compute the estimated sales income to be derived from the total sales of this production. Determine the ratio of the total *cost of production to the total sales income.* This ratio multiplied by the sales income for the various products gives the cost allocation for the respective products. The cost allocation for the respective products divided by the volume of production for the respective products results in the *unit cost* or production for each product: e.g., 18,000,000 pounds of copper produced at an allocated *cost* of $4,950,000 results in a unit cost of $27\frac{1}{2}$ cents per pound.

It should be noted that no matter what cost allocation is made, the total income for the firm when the entire output has been sold will be the same. In other words, only the unit profit is affected, not the total profit. If all the production is not sold, it will have an interim effect on the valuing of the work-in-process or finished goods inventories.

A third method is to prorate the costs in any department on a theoretical or formula basis. For example, it is agreed that during a given period, for every 5,000 pounds of production of certain material there will be 3,000 pounds of Product A and 1,800 pounds of Product B, with 200 pounds lost. This would establish a ratio of 18/48 for Product B and 30/48 for Product A, to be used in prorating the material costs and, if necessary, the labor and overhead costs of all joint production of Products A and B.

SEVERAL RAW MATERIALS ARE USED TO PRODUCE SEVERAL PRODUCTS

Where several raw materials are used to produce several products, the situation may be one in which (1) all the materials are used in one department, with the production of the several products in that department being sent to the finished stock room or to other departments for additional processing; or (2) some of the material is used in one department to manufacture several products, and then in the next department additional material is used to continue the production of one or more of the products of the first department. In either case, it is a problem of adapting the methods previously discussed to the multiproduction. This may be accomplished by using an *average quantity basis* in each department if the relative value of each product does not differ too greatly and the unit of production is the same for each product. Otherwise, a *weighted average* or *formula basis* might be used. Most of these calculations and apportionments will be shown on the cost of production reports. Only the totals will appear in the ledger accounts for work-in-process and finished goods. Wherever possible, the costs should be allocated directly to the products. The chemical industries, in particular, are subject to a great deal of criticism for the methods used in the allocation of costs to several products. Because of the complexity of the operations, it is frequently difficult to obtain reasonably accurate costs. The best that can be hoped for is an honest statement or interpretation of the relation existing between the various products being manufactured. For example, one of the large manufacturers of photographic film devoted part of its activities to the manufacture of educational films. Because of an incorrect allocation of costs to the educational film division, this firm could not meet competitive prices, with the result that it had on several occasions planned to discontinue a necessary phase of its industrial work. Any good cost accountant could have discovered this situation in a few hours of work and perhaps expanded a profitable activity so that the firm's total profit would have been increased.

BY-PRODUCTS COST ACCOUNTING

By-products present an accounting problem in many continuous process manufacturing plants. The main feature distinguishing a by-product from the main product and from scrap is one of relative value, the by-product being a secondary result of operations. Usually, if the value of the product is less than 10% of the total value of all products, it may be considered a by-product. By-products in some industries become the main products of others.

Illustrations of by-products are:

Industry	Main Product	By-products
1. Gas	Gas	Coke, tar, and ammonia
2. Coke	Coke	Gas, tar, and ammonia
3. Copper mining, smelting	Copper	Silver and gold
4. Meat-packing	Dressed meats	Hides and trimmings
5. Milling	Flour	Feed, bran, and cereals
6. Soap	Soap	Glycerine
7. Leather tanning	Tanned leather	Split leather

By-products are sometimes classified as (1) those requiring no further processing after separation from the main product, and (2) those requiring additional processing after separation from the main product.

By-products vary greatly in importance in the various industries. In some concerns the sales value of the by-product is so small relatively that the by-product becomes practically synonymous with scrap. In others, the sales value becomes so important that it may be questionable whether the product is a by-product or a joint product. Such wide variations in the nature of by-products result in equally divergent accounting treatments.

There are five methods of by-product accounting:

1. Treat sales of by-product as other income.
2. Treat sales of by-product as reduction in cost of main product.
3. Treat by-product as having no cost at time of separation but charge by-product with all costs after separation.
4. Record cost of by-product before and after separation from main product.
5. Reversal cost method (sales price method).

1. Treat Sales of By-product as Other Income. If the value of the by-product is comparatively small, many manufacturers treat the by-product as though it were scrap material, and a *quantity* inventory may be set up as the by-products are recovered. When the by-product is sold, an entry is made, which in journalized form is:

```
Accounts Receivable.................................................................xxxx
    By-product Sales ...............................................................          xxxx
    To record sale of by-products.
```

On the income statement, by-product sales are treated as an item in the *Other Income* section. Although this method is not very accurate, it is inexpensive and simple and is used in instances where the market value of the by-product is *small* and does not, therefore, warrant setting up inventory and sales accounts for by-products.

2. Treat Sales of By-product as a Reduction of the Cost of the Main Product. There are a variety of conditions under which this procedure may be followed, viz:

a) Reduce the cost of the main product by the total estimated income from by-product.
b) Reduce the cost of the main product by the total estimated income from by-product less the selling expenses to be incurred therefrom.
c) Reduce the cost of the main product by the total estimated income from by-product less the selling expenses and an estimated amount for profit.

In each of these situations, it is assumed that the by-product has a small but readily ascertainable sales value. In the first of these situations, the by-product recoveries are set up in the Stores account at the estimated sales value, with a credit to the work-in-process account of the department in which the by-product was created, e.g.:

```
By-product Stores ................................................................1,200
    Work-in-Process — Department B.........................................    1,200
    To record the by-product at the estimated sales value.
```

This situation develops a complication if the subsequent sales price of the by-product is different from the inventory value. A simple treatment under such conditions is to credit or charge the difference to *Profit and Loss on Sale of By-product*. This method is not usable when the by-product requires further processing after separation. In the second situation, where allowance is to be made for selling expenses incurred with the disposition of the by-product, the credit to the work-in-process account will be reduced accordingly, e.g.:

```
Sales value of the by-product recoveries .......................................$1,200
Less: Selling expenses to be incurred .............................................   120
Amount to be credited to the work-in-process of the main product .....$1,080
```

In the third situation, where an allowance will also be made for an estimated profit on the sale of by-product, the credit will be further reduced before making the entry, e.g.:

```
Sales price of by-product.................................................    $1,200
Selling expenses............................................................$120
Estimated profit ..........................................................   60      180
Amount to be credited to the cost of main product.................           $1,020
```

3.   Treat By-product as Having No Cost at Time of Separation but Charge By-product with All Costs after Separation.   This method should be used when the by-product requires further processing after separation and when the by-product has no salable value at time of separation. This method overstates the cost of the main product and understates the cost of the by-product, but it is used for practical reasons rather than for theoretical accuracy.

The journal entry to record this is:

```
By-product Costs.................................................................xxxx
    Direct Labor...............................................................    xxxx
    Materials..................................................................    xxxx
    Overhead ..................................................................    xxxx
    To charge by-products with cost for processing after separation.
```

Sales of by-products may be recorded as:

(1)

```
Accounts Receivable...........................................................xxxx
    Sale of By-product.........................................................    xxxx
```

or

(2)

```
Accounts Receivable...........................................................xxxx
    By-product Costs...........................................................    xxxx
    Profit and Loss on Sale of By-products ...................................    xxxx
```

4. Recording Cost of By-product or Joint Product before and after Separation from Main Product. This method is used when the by-product has a relatively high value—equivalent to a coproduct or joint product—and requires additional processing after separation from the main product. By some this method is called *joint* product cost accounting.

It is the most accurate method but also more costly. Therefore, the value of the by-product must warrant the expenditure incurred. It is considered as a method of by-product accounting only when the nature of product or its value *obviously* makes the product a by-product. Otherwise, it is a method of the previously discussed joint product accounting.

Apportioning the costs before separation between the main product and the by-product is one problem of this method. The bases of this apportionment are similar to those of joint products, namely:

a) The value of the by-product and main product.
b) A standard of quantity—such as gallons, bushels, or pounds—common to both.
c) A weighted average of the quantity weighted by the sales price. This is necessary when the sales values vary widely or when the main product and by-product do not have a common unit of measurement.
d) Approximation.

Journal entries at time of separation are:

```
By-product Costs.......................................................................xxxx
Main Product Costs ....................................................................xxxx
      Work-in-Process—Department B...........................................    xxxx
      To record costs at time of separation.
```

Thereafter, individual cost reports are used for each product containing charges for the materials, labor, and overhead necessary for their completion.

5. Reversal Cost Method (Sales Price Method). The purpose of this method is *to compute the amount of the costs before separation* that should be charged to a by-product or a coproduct. The procedure is to work back from the selling price, making allowance for a fixed percentage for profit, selling, and administrative expenses, and then to deduct the costs applicable to the by-product or coproduct after separation from the main product. The resulting balance is the amount of the costs before separation which should be applied to the by-product or coproduct.

To illustrate more specifically, it is assumed that the costs of manufacturing before the separation of the products were $25,600. The main product is known as Alpha. Two by-products are manufactured, known as *Creatna* and *Pyrota*. The sales prices of the by-products per ton are $50 and $80, respectively; selling and administrative expenses are estimated at 25 percent of the selling price; net profit, 10 percent of selling price. After separation from the main product the costs of manufacturing each ton are $9.50 and $14, respectively. You are asked to compute the amount of the cost per ton before separation that should be allocated to each by-product and thus credited to the main product.

The following illustrations indicate the method of computing this amount:

	By-product Creatna	By-product Pyrota
Sales price per ton	$50.00	$80.00
Net profit, 10%; selling and administrative expenses, 25%	17.50	28.00
Cost to manufacture	$32.50	$52.00
Costs after separation	9.50	14.00
Amount of costs before separation for which main product should be credited, per ton basis	$23.00	$38.00

The final per ton costs can be multiplied by the production for the given period to determine the total credit to the main product for costs before separation which should be applicable to the by-products.

This reversal cost method can be used not only in by-product cost accounting but also with coproducts.

FEDERAL INCOME TAX REGULATIONS AFFECTING JOINT AND BY-PRODUCT COSTS

Federal income tax laws affecting joint products are quite broad and general. The tax laws affect multiple product cost accounting because the unsold product becomes part of the final inventory. Therefore it is necessary to compute its value in determining the net profit for the period. The following is a statement of accepted practice in inventorying joint or by-product costs:

A taxpayer engaged in mining or manufacturing who by a single process or uniform series of processes derives a product of two or more kinds, sizes, or grades, the unit cost of which is substantially alike, and who in conformity to a recognized trade practice allocates an amount of cost to each kind, size or grade of product, which in the aggregate will absorb the total cost of production, may use such allocated cost as a basis for pricing inventories, provided such allocation bears a reasonable relation to the respective selling values of the different kinds of product.

This seems to indicate that the government will accept any of the methods discussed in this chapter if they represent accepted trade practices and if the manufacturer and his accountant can justify his method as being reasonably accurate.

SUMMARY OF COPRODUCT AND BY-PRODUCT ACCOUNTING

Except for costs after separation, it cannot be said that in the case of coproducts there is profit on one product and a loss on the other. Tracing costs before separation does not seem to accomplish very much because it cannot be said that one product is made independently of the other. Both from the viewpoint of cost and inventory valuation, costs are apportioned on the basis of their market value. The theory back of this is that neither product could be made without the other, and it is assumed that, except for special competitive conditions, the same rate of profit should be maintained on each product.

By-products, on the other hand, arise under such a variety of conditions that no one method will fit all situations. The importance, dollarwise, of the by-products will determine the treatment as a separate source of income, or a reduction in the cost of the main product.

MANAGERIAL DECISION ASPECTS OF JOINT AND BY-PRODUCT COSTING

The preceding discussion has covered the accounting aspects of joint and by-product costing. The decision of which method to use in allocating the costs before separation of one product from the other is somewhat varied and even arbitrary. Management is faced with two main problems in joint and by-product costing—namely, the cost basis to use in pricing the salable product and the extent to which the firm should expand its manufacturing operations after separation to make a better or a new salable product.

How much costs before separation should be allocated to each product will no doubt involve (1) the volume of each product, (2) the competitive price situation for each product, and (3) price differential if one or both of the products were to be processed further. Since each of these factors differs with each type of business activity, no fixed rules can be promulgated. However, in Chapter 21, a study of the cost-volume-price relationship of various manufactured products is given. These same principles will apply not only to joint products but also to by-products. Management may however take into consideration the income tax impact of the various methods of cost allocation. If one of the products is not readily marketable and has a high profit rate but a long storage life before being sold, it might be wise to allocate a greater proportion of the cost before separation to the other product which is more readily salable, assuming of course that the allocation method is reasonable. Sometimes the decision to process a product further after separation from a common source may be determined by (1) plant facilities available for further processing; (2) additional investment, if any, in equipment or factory space, to process further; and (3) whether the additional profit from further processing warrants the above investment. If not, then the product can be sold at the time of separation either as a joint product or as a by-product. The determining factor is the *profit impact*.

QUESTIONS FOR REVIEW

1. Distinguish between coproducts and joint products. How important is this distinction in cost determination? What are some of the objections or difficulties which make some manufacturers avoid joint or by-product accounting?

2. What is the attitude of the federal income tax authorities toward multiple product cost accounting procedures?

3. The Farnsworth Chemical Company manufactures two chemical insecticides jointly. For the month of July, the production data was:

    Joint manufacturing costs.....................................$70,000
    Production BDM, 20,000 lbs., sales value.............. 40,000
    Production of AKFM 15,000 lbs., sales value......... 75,000

    The company can extend the processing of AKFM at an additional cost for materials and labor of $30,000 and produce 24,000 pounds of a *Multikill* product which can be sold for $96,000. Should the company change its manufacturing to eliminate the sale of AKFM and promote *Multikill?* Explain.

4. A manufacturer produces several products, one of which is of small volume but a comparatively high sales value. The income from this product is about 10 percent of the sales for the firm. The manufacturer feels that these sales should be recorded as *Other income*. Explain your reaction to this procedure.

5. What three methods of cost proration among multiple products can be used? When would you recommend the use of the quantitative method?

6. What is the purpose of the "reversal sales" method of cost determination of by-products and coproducts? What are the difficulties of using this method?

7. What methods of cost allocation can be used in by-product cost determination? Under what conditions should each be used?

8. The Fresh Manufacturing Company produces three types of detergents: powder, liquid, and solid cake. During the month of April, the costs of the simultaneous production of these products were $400,000. Production data and sales values were:

Product	Production Units (pounds)	Sales Units	Sales Income
Powder 120,000		100,000	$150,000
Liquid (pints) 200,000		180,000	126,000
Solid cakes 80,000		50,000	100,000

Using the quantity method and also the sales price (weighted average) method of cost proration, compute the gross profit for each product. Which method would you recommend? Why?

9. By-products may not require additional processing after separation from the main product. What method of accounting could be used in such a case? How would you change this if it did require additional processing?

10. What should determine whether management should adopt a particular method of accounting for coproducts and by-products?

PROBLEMS—GROUP A

Problem 6–1.   Purpose: *Comparison of Cost of Goods Manufactured, Sold, and Inventories, Using Average and Weighted Average Method of Costing Coproducts*

The Faraway Manufacturing Company processed 2,200 tons of raw material for which it paid $180 a ton. For every 110 tons of materials, 99 tons of output were obtained. From the materials thus used, the following three products were obtained, all of the same consistency but different in thickness and widths, in the following proportions:

> Product A..................50% of production, salable at $400 per ton
> Product B..................30% of production, salable at $300 per ton
> Product C..................20% of production, salable at $200 per ton

The labor and overhead costs were $60,000.

During this period, sales were 900 tons of Product A, 400 tons of Product B, and 300 tons of Product C.

There were no work-in-process inventories at the beginning or end of the accounting period, and no finished goods inventory at the beginning of the period.

Required:

Compute the cost of goods manufactured, the cost of goods sold, and the final inventories when—

a) The average method of apportioning costs is used, and
b) The weighted averaged method is used.
c) Which method is preferable?

Problem 6–2.   Purpose: *Cost of Production Report for Coproducts; Statement of Operations for Coproducts*

The Feeny Chemical Company manufactures two products from the same ingredients, viz: every 3,000 pounds of raw material produces 1,500 pounds of Product A and 1,200 pounds of Product B. Of the latter product one third is waste and unsalable.

The plant is divided into three departments. Raw materials are used only in the first department.

The raw materials consumed in the initial department amounted to 3,000,000 pounds at a cost of $0.10 per pound. The other manufacturing costs were as follows:

Manufacturing Costs	Department I	Conversion Department Product A	Conversion Department Product B
Labor costs..................................	$ 70,000	$ 75,000	$ 25,000
Heat, light, and power	15,000	18,000	9,000
Depreciation...............................	6,000	27,000	29,000
Equipment maintenance	4,000	12,000	12,000
Rent	16,000	20,000	10,000
Insurance	3,000	5,000	8,000
Departmental expense	6,000	3,000	7,000
	$120,000	$160,000	$100,000

The selling and administrative expenses applicable to both products amounted to 25 percent of the cost to manufacture. Product A sells for $1 less discounts of 30 percent and 10 percent; Product B sells for $0.90 less a discount of 10 percent.

Required:

a) Prepare a production report showing the unit costs for each product.
b) Prepare a statement indicating to management the profitableness of each product.

(Adapted from NYS CPA Examination)

Problem 6–3. Purpose: *Income Statements for By-product Accounting under Different Methods*

The Ellenwild Manufacturing Company manufactures a product known as ELL–400. In its operations, a by-product known as BYPO–100 results.

The sales and production data for the first year's operation ending June 30, 19–, were:

    Sales of Ell–400.....................90,000 lbs. at $6.00
    Sales of Bypo–100..................50,000 lbs. at 0.60

    Costs of production:
      Before separation of the products.................$320,000
      After separation:
        Ell–400   80,000
        Bypo–100   6,000
    Inventories, June 30, 19–:
        Ell–400 .... 10,000 lbs.
        Bypo–100 .... 10,000 lbs.
    Selling and administrative expenses were ....$ 88,000

Required:

On the basis of this information, you are asked to prepare income statements, when—

a) By-product has no cost before separation, and by-product recoveries are treated as other income.
b) By-product costs both before and after separation.
c) Which method of accounting is preferred? Why?

Problem 6–4. Purpose: *By-product Costing When All Costs Except Materials Are Prorated*

The Eureka Chemical Company manufactures a product used as a roofing coating and known as *Roofex*. It sells for $1,200 a ton. In its manufacture, a by-product known as *Wallset* is also produced.

Selling and administrative expenses for both products are 20% of the cost of manufacturing.

Materials used in producing *Roofex,* all of which are used in the initial department:

Material A...................45 percent, costing $160 per ton
Material B...................30 percent, costing   80 per ton
Material C...................25 percent, costing   50 per ton

Four operating departments are involved in the manufacturing, for which the labor and manufacturing overhead costs are:

Department	D. L. per Ton	Applied Overhead as Percent of D. L. Costs
Mixing	$32	80%
Cooking	18	250
Drying	25	100
Grinding and packing.........................	80	50

General factory overhead, not departmentalized but applied as a supplemental rate, is 20 percent of direct labor costs.

In the cooking department, 20 percent of volume is transferred to the by-product operations, where 25 percent in volume is lost.

The net profit on *Wallset* is $60 per ton, after all manufacturing costs except materials are prorated to it. Income from the by-product does not affect the profit computation of the main product of *Roofex.*

Required:

a) From the foregoing, prepare a statement showing the net profit on each ton of *Roofex* sold.

b) What is selling price per ton of *Wallset?*

Problem 6–5. Purpose: *By-product Cost Accounting: (a) When By-product Is a Reduction of Cost of Main Product, and (b) Cost Both before and after Separation from Main Product*

The Eckland Manufacturing Company manufactures a special chemical compound known as *Soiltex* which sells for $1,600 per ton. The four successive departments covering the manufacturing cycle are: mixing, grinding and reduction, extraction, and refining and finishing. Materials are used in the first two departments and increase the volume of production.

Costs and production statistics for the month of October were:

Mixing Department:

Materials used: 300 tons of Material A at $190 a ton and 900 tons of Material

B at $110 a ton. Labor and overhead applied to production were $45 and $40 a ton respectively.

Grinding and Reduction Department:

Two hundred fifty tons of Material C at a cost of $80 per ton; 300 tons of Material D at $100; and 120 tons of Material E at $200 per ton. Labor and overhead costs were $30 and $60 per ton respectively.

Extraction Department:

In this department, materials received from the preceding department are processed, 60% of the volume being used to manufacture *Soiltex,* the balance being applied to produce a by-product known as *Polyseal.* Both of these semifinished products are sent to the refining and finishing department to be separately processed. Labor and overhead costs in this department were $40 and $50 per ton respectively.

Refining and Finishing Department:

In this department, 40 percent of the material used in making *Polyseal* is lost, the balance becoming the by-product. Furthermore, four times as much labor is used in completing *Soiltex* as in making a ton of *Polyseal.* Labor costs in this department are at the rate of $80 per ton of the finished product, and overhead also at the rate of $80 per ton of finished product.

Selling and administrative expenses are estimated to be 25% of the sales price of the main product. No selling and administrative expenses are allocated to the by-product.

Polyseal sells for $200 per ton.

Required:

From this information, you are asked to prepare statements of the cost of production and income statement for the month of October, assuming that the entire production is completed and sold

a)   when the by-product income is treated as a reduction of the cost of the main product, *Soiltex;* and

b)   when costs both before and after separation are computed for both products.

c)   Which method of accounting seems preferable? Why?

PROBLEMS—GROUP B

Problem 6–6.   Purpose: *Reversal Sales Method of Prorating Costs before Separation for Coproducts and By-product*

The Fardue Manufacturing Company makes three products: A and B which are considered coproducts; and X, a by-product. Raw materials are processed in the initial department, primarily for the making of Product A. However, some of this material is then used in the manufacture of Products B and X in the subsequent departments.

On the basis of the previous method of cost accounting, Products B and X have shown a high profit return based upon the selling price, and Product A has shown a lower rate because all costs before separation of the production in the initial department were charged to Product A.

Management feels a more reliable picture of operations would be obtained if the costs in the initial department were allocated on more equitable basis to Products B and X. Therefore, management has decided to use the reversal sales method of prorating the costs before separation.

Production and sales for the year were:

> 220,000 lbs. of Product A, salable at $6.00
> 180,000 lbs. of Product B, salable at 3.00
> 50,000 lbs. of Product X, salable at 0.90

Production costs for the year:

Costs before separation into various products.................$276,600	
Costs after separation:	
Product A	320,000
Product B	190,000
Product X	6,900

Estimated, desired NET profit for each product based upon selling prices:

> Product A...................20%
> Product B..................15
> Product X..................10

Selling and administrative expenses are estimated at 40 percent of the selling price.

Required:

a) Using the above information, you are asked to prepare comparative income statements for the year ended November 30, 19—, (*a*) when such costs are prorated, and (*b*) when they are not. It is assumed that all production for the year has been sold.

b) Comment on these two methods of cost computations.

Problem 6–7. Purpose: *Coproduct Cost Accounting after Split-Off in First Department*

Farco Inc., has perfected a process for manufacturing from three raw materials, A, B, and C, two chemical detergents. The raw materials used in manufacturing are in the following proportions by weight:

> *Parts*
> A 3
> B 5
> C .... _2_
>   10

All the raw materials are put into production in the mixing and blending department and are then transferred to the cooking department where they are separated. The first product *Fresh* then goes to the drying and packaging department; product *Cleco* goes through an electrolysis and is filtered into drums for commercial use.

One hundred thousand (100,000) pounds of raw materials will be processed. The costs of these materials are: A at $2 per pound; B at $50 per ton; and C at $4 per gallon.

Other costs of production are estimated to be:

Mixing, blending, and cooking $16,090
Additional costs for *Fresh* (drying and packaging).................. 4,660
Additional costs for *Cleco* (electrolysis and
    filtering into drums) 6,920

The cooking department reduces the weight of the combined raw materials by 40 percent. Of the 100,000 pounds of original raw materials, 20,000 pounds of pre-*Cleco* are obtained. Of the *Cleco* electrolyzed, 75 percent becomes a marketable liquid being filtered into 50-gallon drums without further attention. The cost of returnable drums is not to be included either in the cost or sales price of *Cleco*.

Each product is to be sold on the basis of list price less 35 percent and 10 percent. Of the net selling price of each product, 25 percent is to be allowed for selling and general administrative expenses, including provision for income tax, and a 20 percent profit after provision for all costs and expenses.

It is estimated that one gallon of *Cleco* weighs 7.5 pounds and 1 gallon of raw material weighs 8 pounds.

Required:

From the above information, prepare the following statements supported by whatever explanatory schedules may seem necessary:

a)   Statement to show at what list price and at what net price per pound of *Fresh* should be sold.
b)   Statement to show at what list price and at what net price per gallon of *Cleco* should be sold.
c)   Condensed income statement to show separately and combined the results of operations in manufacturing *Fresh* and *Cleco* on the assumption that the entire quantity of each product manufactured will be sold at the respective prices indicated in (a) and (b) above, and that selling and administrative expenses are to be included in the same estimate as allowed in setting selling prices.

(Adapted from AICPA Uniform Examination)

Problem 6–8.   Purpose: *Coproduct Cost Allocations*

The Vertrax Company's operations involves the manufacture of three joint products from the same raw materials in Department I. During the month of August, the manufacturing costs in Department I totaled $110,000. This cost resulted in the subsequent production of—

1,000 units of Product A
800 units of Product B
600 units of Product C

The additional costs in the departments after the first in which these products were completed ready for sale, were on a per unit basis: $8 for Product A; $12 for Product B; and $5 for Product C.

The inventory of each product on August 31 was Product A, 150 units; Product B, 100 units; and Product C, 60 units.

The sales prices of the various products on a per unit basis are Product A, $40; Product B, $120; and Product C, $250.

Selling and administrative expenses for each product are estimated at 20% of the selling price.

Required:

a) Prepare an income statement by products and in total if the costs before separation are allocated on a quantitative basis.

b) Prepare an income statement by products and in total if the costs before separation are allocated on a sales-price basis.

c) Which method would you prefer on a financial statement basis? Why?

d) Which method would you prefer on a managerial decision basis assuming (1) that the products are salable at the time of completion in department; and (2) if they should be processed further, if the sale at the time of separation could be made at a markup of 80% above the cost of production.

Problem 6–9. Purpose: *Coproduct Cost Allocations and Managerial Decision of Sell or Process Further*

The Ventura Chemical Company produces three chemical products which are used as oil and gas additives from the same raw materials processed in Department I. Each of the products AO, CO, and XO require further processing if these are to be sold at higher prices for specialized uses. However, the material produced in Department I can be sold without further processing as raw materials to be used by the purchasers.

The production of Department I was 150,000 gallons at a cost of $450,000. This could be sold for $600,000 with an additional cost for selling and administration of $30,000.

If, however, further processing was incurred, the production of these products and the additional processing costs would result:

Product and Quantity Allocation	Additional Costs	Sales Price per Gallon
Product AO...80,000 gallons	$280,000	$ 5
Product CO...30,000 gallons	90,000	6
Product XO...40,000 gallons of which		
(10,000 gallons would be		
lost in processing)	150,000	15

Selling and administrative costs for these products would be 20% of the sales price.

Required:

a) Assuming that the entire production could be sold at the end of Department I's operation, what would be the net profit?

b) Assuming additional processing and the sales of the entire output at prices indicated, what would be net profit?

c) What managerial decision would you make as to sale of product at Department I's completion, or the further processing of product?

chapter 7

Managerial Control of Material Acquisition Costs

NATURE OF MATERIAL COST CONTROL

There are two phases of material cost control: (1) the problems of the purchase, receipt, and storage of materials; and (2) the problems of issuing and pricing materials and the internal control of inventories. The same problems arise, whether the firm operates a job order or a process cost accounting system.

The managerial objectives of the purchase, receipt, and storage of materials are:

1. *Procurement* of a sufficient quantity of the required materials at the lowest prices so that manufacturing operations will be performed smoothly and uninterruptedly.
2. *Storage* of the materials in the plant so that the material handling costs, both receiving and issuing, will be kept at a minimum, and at the same time the materials will be properly protected against loss by theft, damage, or deterioration.
3. *Elimination* of all inactive, obsolete, and defective materials from the regular storeroom areas.
4. *Investment* in inventories at a minimum, consistent with smooth factory operations, the delivery time of purchases, storage facilities, and market-price forecasts.

To achieve the maximum managerial control over material costs in a manufacturing firm, the following organizational and operating procedures should be followed:

1. *Budgeting* of the sales, finished goods inventory, and production schedules on both a long- and short-term basis so that a *centralized* purchasing department will have guidelines for its operations.

2. *Routinizing and systematizing* the ordering, purchasing, receiving, storing, and issuing of all materials.
3. Using a well-integrated series of *printed forms* to prevent errors and fix responsibility.
4. Protecting the inventory investment by an adequate *system of internal checks* to insure accurate accounting and the prevention of fraud and theft.
5. *Maintaining* efficient inventory records of the quantities received, issued, and balance on hand of all materials, together with the costs thereof. In many large business firms these records are maintained mechanically by the use of punched cards, punched tapes, and magnetic tapes used with computers.
6. *Pricing* all requisitions and inventories on a basis to insure reliable costs of manufacturing and effective income tax planning.
7. *Controlling* and *summarizing* the accounting for the acquisition and use of materials by means of control accounts, subsidiary ledgers, and reports of material usage, returns, and spoilage.
8. *Organizing* the administrative and supervisory staff of the material cost control so that decisions can be made promptly and effectively.

FUNCTIONAL CYCLE OF MATERIALS CONTROL

There are five activities associated with materials procedures:

1. Engineering, planning, and routing of factory production.
2. Purchase of materials.
3. Receipt and inspection of materials.
4. Storage and issuance of materials.
5. Accounting for materials transactions, including book inventory records.

The *engineering, planning, and routing departments* of an organization have an important role in business management, in addition to that of controlling the flow of production through the plant. First, they must design the product and prepare material specifications before much of the materials can be purchased. They must further study the effects of the use of various materials and their substitutes and make recommendations. In addition, these departments must make up bills of materials to be issued for the various kinds of production orders. The work of these departments will be discussed in detail later in the chapter. Here it serves as an introduction to materials control.

The *purchasing department* performs the following business activities: (1) receives or prepares purchase requisitions for all materials and equipment to be used in the factory; (2) requests price quotations from the vendors; (3) prepares and places purchase orders; (4) approves ven-

Illustration 7–1. Organization Chart of the Materials Control Function

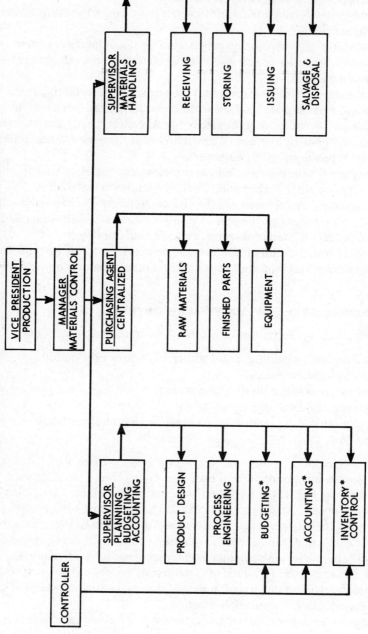

*These functions must be coordinated by the manager – materials control and the controller.

dors' invoices; and (5) sends approved invoices to the general accounting department for entry. The purchasing department may operate either as a service department of the factory organization or as a part of the central administrative staff of the business, whereas the receiving and storeroom departments are essentially factory service departments.

The *receiving department* performs the following functions: (1) receives the goods from truckmen, railroads, or other carriers and signs the authorized receipts; (2) counts, weighs, or otherwise verifies the quantity of goods received; (3) inspects quality of goods and reports breakage; (4) moves the goods to the storeroom; and (5) sends copies of the receiving report to the purchasing department and to the storeroom department.

The *storeroom department* (1) receives and acknowledges the goods from the receiving department; (2) verifies the quantity received; (3) places the goods in the proper bins, shelves, or yards; (4) issues materials on properly authorized requisitions; (5) enters receipts and issuances on the bin cards; and (6) sometimes summarizes the requisitions for the *cost accounting department*.

Entries must be made to record the purchase of materials, the return of materials purchased to the vendors, the use of materials, the return of excess materials to the storeroom, and spoilage or defective production. Subsidiary inventory records must also be maintained. Each of these operations will be described later in the chapter.

FUNCTIONAL ORGANIZATION AND PERSONNEL OF MATERIALS CONTROL

The organization and personnel of materials control varies somewhat with the size of the organization and the extent to which materials costs are a part of the total cost of a product. In the larger firms, the huge investment in inventories necessitates more detailed control and greater supervision. As previously indicated, the three functional activities for adequate materials control are (1) planning, budgeting, and accounting; (2) purchasing; and (3) receiving, storing, and issuing. These must be properly coordinated into a single management function responsible to the top management, as shown in Illustration 7–1.

FORMS AND REPORTS USED IN MATERIAL ACQUISITIONS

Printed forms are used to fix responsibility for business activities, reduce the possibility of error, and are essential for internal control. One copy of the form is always retained in the department in which it is prepared.

The forms most frequently found in controlling the purchase and the receipt of materials are:

1. Purchase requisition.
2. Purchase order.
3. Receiving report.

4. Returned purchases report.
5. Stores ledger card.

   1. The *purchase requisition* (see Illustration 7–2) is a request to the purchasing department to buy certain materials, either to replenish present stocks on hand or to acquire original stock. If it is a replenishment of stock, the requisition is prepared by the storeroom clerk; if it is for new

Illustration 7–2. Purchase Requisition

PURCHASE REQUISITION		
No. 24		Date Jan. 15, 19—
Quantity	*Description*	*Ordered from*
5 tons	Tempered Blade Steel	*Name* United States Steel Corp.
		Address Gary, Indiana
		Price $200.00
		Terms 2/10/N/30
		Delivery—How Railroad, F.O.B.
		Delivery—When Jan. 20, 19—.
		Remarks

Above Quantity Will Last for Three months			
Present Stock Will Last for Six months			
Quot. from Loraine	*Quot. from Duluth*	*Quot. from Joliet*	*Quot. from Gary*
Price $197.00	*Price* $198.00	*Price* $210.00	*Price* $200.00
Terms 2/10/N/30 F.O.B.	*Terms* 2/10/N/30 F.O.B.	*Terms* 2/10/N/30 F.O.B.	*Terms* 2/10/N/30 F.O.B.
Delivery RR.	*Delivery* RR.	*Delivery* RR.	*Delivery* RR.
Original—to Purchasing Dept.			

File Copy

or experimental stock, the requisition is made or authorized by a member of the engineering or factory staff. Two copies of the requisition are prepared—one kept as a memorandum in the storeroom department and the other sent to the purchasing department.

   2. The *purchase order* (see Illustration 7–3) is prepared by the purchasing department authorizing the shipment of the goods by the vendor.

Illustration 7–3. Purchase Order

COUTRALDS,
INC.

SHIP TO THIS ADDRESS UNLESS
OTHERWISE INDICATED IN BODY
OF PURCHASE ORDER.

COUTRALDS, INC.
1300 Airport Road
Harlan, Iowa 50010
Phone 515-232-3700

VENDOR NOTE:
SHOW THIS P. O. NUMBER ███████
███████ ON ALL INVOICES.
PACKING SLIPS AND CERTIFICATIONS.

PURCHASE ORDER

INSPECTION REQUIRED:	VENDOR SUBMIT FIRST ARTICLE FOR APPROVAL

No. 27239

[x] VENDOR CERTIFICATION	GOVERNMENT SOURCE INSPECTION	Q.C.	REQ'NR.

VENDOR'S NAME AND ADDRESS

REQUISITION NO.	R.R.	P.O. DATE
ALC 4651		October 27, 19--

ALLEGHANY LUDLUM CO.
Chicago, Illinois   60607

REQUISITIONED BY   JC. Kolin   CONFIRMING WITH

DELIVER TO   Harlan, Iowa   F.O.B. POINT   Harlan, Iowa

DELIVERY REQUIRED	SHIP VIA	CHARGE JOB/ACCT. NO.	TERMS
Nov. 15, 19--	N.Y.C. RR		3/10 eom n/60x

DELIVERY PROMISED	RESALE PERMIT	RENEGOTIABLE	BUYER	PRIORITY	GOVT. CONTRACT NO.
	[ ] YES [ ] NO	[ ] YES [ ] NO			

ITEM	QUANTITY	UNIT		UNIT PRICE	EXTENDED COST
	5	Tons	Tempered Blade Steel per Specifications attached	$200.00	$1,000.00

THIS PURCHASE ORDER IS NOT BINDING ███████ UNTIL YOUR COMPANY
HAS RETURNED THE ACKNOWLEDGMENT COPY PROPERLY COMPLETED AND SIGNED.

NOTE: THE TERMS AND CONDITIONS SHOWN ON THE REVERSE SIDE HEREOF ARE APPLICABLE TO THIS ORDER AND SELLER AGREES THERETO BY ACKNOWLEDGMENT OR PERFORMANCE.

GENERAL INSTRUCTIONS TO VENDOR

1. ACKNOWLEDGMENT COPY OF THIS ORDER MUST BE SIGNED AND RETURNED, ADVISING DEFINITE SHIPPING DATE.
2. PACKING LISTS MUST ACCOMPANY EACH CASE OR PARCEL, SHOWING OUR ORDER NUMBER AND OUR COMPLETE DESCRIPTION AND PART NUMBER FOR EACH ITEM.
3. ALL ITEMS ARE SUBJECT TO INSPECTION AND ACCEPTANCE AT OUR PLANT. WHEN REQUIRED, **CERTIFICATIONS MUST ACCOMPANY EACH SHIPMENT.**
4. SEND INVOICES IN TRIPLICATE PROMPTLY FOR EACH SHIPMENT, SHOWING OUR ORDER NUMBER.

5. INVOICE EACH PURCHASE ORDER SEPARATELY.
6. INVOICES CANNOT BE HONORED UNLESS ACKNOWLEDGMENT COPY IS RETURNED PROPERLY COMPLETED AND SIGNED.
7. RENDER COMPLETE ITEMIZED STATEMENT MONTHLY.
8. C.O.D. SHIPMENTS WILL NOT BE ACCEPTED.
9. OVER SHIPMENTS, UNLESS SPECIFICALLY AUTHORIZED, WILL NOT BE ACCEPTED.

BY *George Jacobson*
PURCHASING AGENT

MAIL TO:
COUTRALDS, Inc.
Harlan, Iowa 50010

VENDOR'S ACKNOWLEDGMENT

THIS ORDER IS ACCEPTED SUBJECT TO ALL THE TERMS AND CONDITIONS STATED ON THE FACE AND ON THE REVERSE SIDE HEREOF.

[ ] THE "DELIVERY REQUIRED" DATE SHOWN ABOVE IS THE ACKNOWLEDGED DELIVERY DATE FOR THIS ORDER.
[ ] WE CANNOT MEET THE "DELIVERY REQUIRED" DATE, BUT WE DO PROMISE DELIVERY ON OR BEFORE_____
[ ] PRICE DATA SHOWN ABOVE IS CORRECT, EXCEPT FOR:_____

FOR THE VENDOR (By)_____ Date_____

ACKNOWLEDGMENT—SIGN AND RETURN

8128G (6-66) $

ORIGINAL -- TO VENDOR
ACKNOWLEDGMENT COPY
PURCHASING DEPT. COPY
RECEIVING DEPT. COPY
ACCOUNTING DEPT. COPY
STORES LEDGER CLERK COPY

In addition to the original, which is sent to the vendor, sufficient copies are made to meet the requirements of the departments interested. Usually, one copy is for the receiving department so that it may know what goods to expect. If the quantities are omitted from this copy and only the items are stated, the copy is called a *blind receiving report;* the receiving department must fill in the quantities received and return it to the purchasing department.

A third copy of the purchase order is sent to the department requisitioning the material, and one copy is retained by the purchasing department. However, variations from this procedure are not uncommon. For example, one large machine company finds it convenient to prepare six copies of the purchase order; three are sent to the receiving department. The receiving department uses these three extra copies in lieu of receiving reports mentioned later.

3.   The *receiving report* (see Illustration 7–4) is prepared to show the quantity and kind of material received on specific purchase orders. The procedure followed in preparing this report might be:

a)   An examination by receiving clerk or his assistants who weigh or count material received and prepare a report indicating Date, Received from, Via, Charges, Purchase Order No., Packages, Quantity, Description, and identification by name or initial of the receiver and checker. Preparation of the report is in triplicate; the original is sent to the purchasing department so that it may be compared with the purchase order; the duplicate is sent with the material to the stores department; and the triplicate is filed by the receiving department.

Sometimes the system of control varies the number of copies of the receiving report that must be prepared; but three, as indicated above, is the *minimum.* In some firms, additional copies of the receiving report are sent to the accounting department for comparison with the invoice received and to the planning department for use in planning and scheduling production.

b)   Some firms send three to five additional copies of the purchase order to the receiving department when the order is placed with the vendor. The receiving department uses these copies in place of a separate receiving report. This method saves time and expense in operating the receiving department, but it is deficient in the matter of internal control and internal check.

4.   *Returned purchases report* is similar in form and content to the *receiving report.* The original goes to the purchasing department which forwards it to the accounting department for entry in the voucher register and on the voucher if it has not already been paid; one copy is for the storeroom for entry in the stores ledger subsidiary record; and one copy is retained by the shipping department, which has prepared the report and taken care of the shipment.

Illustration 7–4. Receiving Report

OREGON METAL PRODUCTS CO.

AUTOMOTIVE DIVISION

RECEIVING REPORT

OMP

RECEIVING REPORT NUMBER	▷ B 12013

AMP 65-145-1

RECEIVED FROM: *U.S. Steel Corpn*   VENDOR CODE NO.:   DATE RECEIVED: *7-23- ~*

PURCHASED FROM: *U.S. Steel Corpn*   PURCHASE ORDER NO.: *J-6-7100*   REQUISITION NO.: *4800-7*

RECEIVED VIA: *Penna R.R.*   P.P.:   EXPRESS: REQUISITIONED BY OR DEPT.: *Milling*

| BOXES: | CARTONS: | BUNDLES: *40* | PACKAGES: | BAGS: | SKIDS: | CRATES: | CAR INITIAL AND NO.: *482-1200* | DEL. OR PRO. NO.: |

SHIPMENT COMPLETE ☑ CHECK | OVER-UNDER ORDER QUAN. ◁ CHECK | RECEIVED BY: | PPD. ▷ ✔ | COL. ▷

QUANTITY	MATERIAL CODE	SIZE - PART NUMBER - DESCRIPTION	CARRIER WEIGHT	OUR WEIGHT GROSS	NET
40	S-4162	Tempered Blade Steel — per our Specification		10040	10040	10,000

ORIGINAL--PURCHASING DEPARTMENT

STORES DEPARTMENT-COPY-2

ACCOUNTING DEPARTMENT-COPY 3

RECEIVING DEPARTMENT FILE-COPY-4

5.   The *stores ledger card* (often referred to as the perpetual inventory record) is one of the basic records for material accounting in a cost system. (See Illustration 7–5.) There are several forms of this record in common use today, but basically there are three sections or divisions on this inventory card record, each with appropriate subdivisions in which to record information as to date, requisition number, purchase order number, job order number, quantity, unit price, and total cost. The three divisions are *Receipts, Issues,* and *Balance.*

When goods are received in the storeroom, entries are made in the *Receipt section.* The goods are checked against the receiving report for quantities and against a purchase order for the unit price and description before making the entries. A separate card is used, not only for each kind of material but also for each different size of the same material.

Illustration 7-5. Stores Ledger Card, Using Average Price Method

STORES LEDGER

NAME OF COMMODITY: Copper Rods	CODE NO.	CLASS S-W-4
DESCRIPTION: Solid Copper Rods		SIZE 3/4"
MAXIMUM QUANTITY 1500	MINIMUM QUANTITY 200	SHEET NO. 48 — UNIT Pounds

PURCHASE ORDERS

No.	Date	Quantity	Purchased From	Pur Ord	Inv. Date
~~401~~	~~5/3~~	~~800~~	~~Brown & Co.~~		
~~401~~	~~5/4~~	~~300~~	~~Brown & Co.~~	401	5/3
~~402~~	~~5/7~~	~~1000~~	~~Butler & Co.~~	401	
				402	5/7
~~403~~	~~5/15~~	~~1200~~	~~Brown & Co.~~		
403	5/16	200	Brown & Co.	403	5/15

RECEIVED

Date Rec'd	Quantity	Unit Del. Price	Value
5/4	500	$.11	$ 55 00
5/8	300	11.08	33 24
5/10	1000	.09775	97 75
5/16	1000	.1065	106 50

ON RESERVE

Date	Prod. Order No.	Quantity
5/6	6151	200
5/13	6501	200
5/14	6151	100

ISSUED

Date	Job No. or Dept.	Req. No.	Quantity	Unit Del. Price	Value
5/5	6150	301	600	$.105	$ 63 00
5/9	6152	302	400	.1075	43 00
5/11	6462	303	300	.10	30 00
5/12	6471	304	600	.10	60 00
5/14	6151	305	100	.10	10 00
5/17	6483	306	600	.105	63 00

BALANCE

Quantity	Value	Unit Cost
500	$ 50 00	$.10
1000	105 00	.105
400	42 00	.105
700	75 25	.1075
300	32 25	.1075
1300	130 00	.10
1000	100 00	.10
400	40 00	.10
300	30 00	.10
1300	136 50	.105
700	73 50	.105

When goods are issued for use in the factory, a materials requisition form is used indicating the quantity and kind of material and the job or department in which it is to be used. This information is entered in the *Issued section* of the stores ledger card.

If material is returned to the vendor, encircled entries (contra entries) are made in the Received section; if material is returned from the factory the encircled entry is made in the Issued section.

For the larger manufacturing firms in which greater managerial control of the inventory is necessary, two sections are added to this inventory card: *Material on order* and *Material reserved.* The former is used to avoid duplicating the purchase orders when some time elapses between the placement of the order and the receipt of the goods. When the goods are received, the On Order item is canceled by drawing a line through it.

The Reserve section is used to indicate the material to be required for the work-in-process. Using this section enables the stores department to know the quantity available for issuance and prevents holding up production in process because the required material is not available when needed. Two methods of handling this Reserve section are in use: (1) When materials are reserved, they are immediately subtracted from the balance on hand. This is not a satisfactory method, since the inventory balance is incorrect, until such time as the materials are actually issued. (2) Add an additional balance column in which is indicated the "balance available for issue." Thus the Reserve section will in no way affect the Balance on Hand until the materials are actually issued. Illustration 7–5 shows the five-section stores ledger card.

PROCEDURAL ANALYSIS OF MATERIAL ACQUISITIONS

The complete picture of the managerial and accounting procedure involved in material acquisitions may be illustrated by (1) a descriptive flow of work tabulation (Illustration 7–6), and (2) by a diagrammatic chart (Illustration 7–7).

ACCOUNTING FOR THE PURCHASE AND RECEIPT OF MATERIALS

Materials purchased for a manufacturing concern may be *direct materials* which become part of the manufactured product; *indirect materials* or *factory supplies;* and *packaging and shipping supplies.* In many firms these are all stored in a single storeroom for control purposes. Therefore, it has been convenient to record all materials thus purchased in a single account, known as the *Stores Control account,* and maintain the classification of the materials in the subsidiary stores ledger cards.

Entries for the purchase of materials are usually made in a voucher register:

Stores Control..xxxxxx
    Accounts Payable   xxxxxx
To summarize the purchases for the month.

Any material returned to the vendors will be recorded as contra entries.

Illustration 7–6

FORM PROCEDURE FOR MATERIALS CONTROL—PURCHASING, RECEIVING, AND STORING

Purchase Requisitions: Usually *two* copies are prepared in the *stores* department, and these are used as follows:
1. Copy is filed in department originating request.
2. Copy is sent to the purchasing agent for his action.

Purchase Order: Four copies, more or less, may be prepared in the *purchasing* department and used as follows:
1. Copy is filed in department originating request.
2. Copy is sent to the *receiving* department to enable the clerks to anticipate the arrival of the material and to make arrangements for the work in connection therewith.
3. Copy is sent to the *stores ledger clerk* so that he may know his request received favorable action.
4. Copy is filed in the *purchasing* department as its record.

Receiving Report: Usually *three* copies may be prepared by the receiving clerks, and these are used as follows:
1. Copy is sent to the *purchasing* department for comparison with purchase order and invoice.
2. Copy is sent with goods to the *stores* department as a means of internal check and as an aid in making entries on stores ledger cards.
3. Copy is kept on file in the *receiving* department.

Stores Ledger Cards: One copy of this record is maintained in the stores department. Entries for the receipts are made in the *Receipts section,* showing quantity, unit cost, total cost, and these figures are added to those in the *Balance section.*

CODING ACCOUNTS FOR MATERIALS CONTROL

Every modern up-to-date accounting system uses letters, numbers, or a combination of these to characterize its accounts. Since the number of material accounts kept in the subsidiary records is very large, codes for these accounts are usually in numerical form. For example, if a firm has one hundred different material items in its storeroom, the code numbers 400 to 500 could be assigned to this group. Further subdivisions might be made as follows: 400 to 420 might refer to the lumber products used in manufacturing; 420 to 450 to the metal products; 450 to 475 to the

Illustration 7–7. Materials Control—Purchasing, Receiving, and Storing

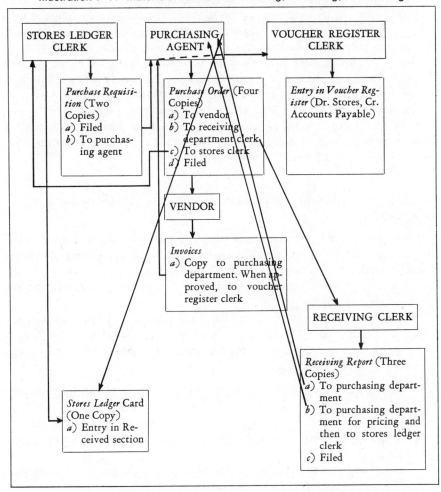

finished parts used; and the remaining numbers to the miscellaneous items. Sometimes by use of a decimal it is possible not only to classify the material but to indicate its location. For example, 480 might be the code number for a certain type of sponge rubber used in the upholstering department of a factory. The code 480.47 could then be used to refer to this material in storeroom number 4, bin number 7.

The use of location numbers in the codes expedites the location of the material when it is to be issued and also expedites the placing of the material into the proper bins and storerooms. In one factory, for example, there are 15,000 different items in the storeroom. Without the use of a numerical code, which not only classifies the material but also indicates its location, serious delays in issuing the material would result. There is a second reason for using codes. Numerous references must be made to the various material accounts or ledger cards. By using code numbers instead of account titles, much time can be saved. For instance, less time is needed to write "Charge Account 6–3" than to write "Charge Stores Control, Lumber." Such a saving in time, repeated many times a day, becomes a worthwhile factor in reducing the cost of accounting.

The increased use of punched card accounting, punched tape transmission and recording (integrated data processing), and electronic data processing makes the use of numerical codes for material accounting and inventory control an absolute necessity.

SPECIAL ACCOUNTING PROBLEMS AFFECTING MATERIALS PURCHASED

There are several problems affecting the purchase of materials to be used in manufacturing on which there is no uniform accounting practice. These include (a) treatment of freight-in, (b) accounting for material handling charges, (c) accounting for containers, and (d) treatment of purchase discounts.

Freight-In. Freight-in on materials purchased to be used in manufacturing is actually part of the cost of the materials. However, this may cause some clerical and accounting difficulties. Freight-in may be treated in one of three ways. It may be—

1. Immediately charged to the Stores Control account and also to the respective inventory cards.
2. Set up as a Freight-In account and allocated to the individual inventory cards. Subsequently the total is closed to the Stores Control account.
3. Treated as a manufacturing overhead cost; that is, it is not distributed to the Stores Control account or the inventory cards.

If freight-in is charged immediately to the Stores Control account by debiting stores in the voucher register, the total amount must be prorated and added proportionately on the perpetual inventory cards affected. This entry is made in the *Received* section of the inventory card, with a notation "Freight" if a separate column is not provided for freight in this section. The total cost of goods plus freight is extended to the Total Amount column in the *Balance* section. The addition of freight may result in the determination of unit prices of a fractional cent. This procedure involves additional clerical labor in the computation of the cost of material requisitions and may result in more clerical errors. For example, if 300 units were purchased at 12 cents each and the freight amounted to $1.75, an additional unit cost of 0.5833 cents is necessary, making the unit price 12.5833 cents. Many concerns find it more practical, therefore, to treat freight-in as an overhead cost item even though such treatment is not accurate.

Some concerns carry all freight-in charges to a Freight-In account. At the end of each month an entry is made closing this account into the Stores Control account and distributing the amount, on some equitable basis, to the various book inventory cards. A freight debit memorandum is sent to the stores ledger clerk informing him which accounts to charge. This method raises the same difficulties as the direct charge to the stores ledger cards at the time the goods are received.

Because of these practical difficulties, some concerns include the freight-in as one of the material handling costs. As such it may be included with other indirect costs — that is, as part of the manufacturing overhead — or treated as one of the special material handling indirect costs and charged to jobs or production on the basis of the weight or cost of the material used.

Accounting for Material Handling Charges. The term *material handling costs* refers to the expense involved in receiving, storing, issuing, and handling materials. It might be extended to include part of the cost of operating the purchasing department. Logically, such costs are part of the cost of materials to the same extent as freight-in. But the practical difficulty arises as to how to allocate this cost to the various materials. For this reason, many companies include these costs with those of manufacturing overhead and apply them to production as such. A few companies, however, have resorted to the practice of establishing *a material handling overhead rate,* similar in computation and application as the general predetermined manufacturing overhead rate, and of charging the handling cost to the material cost of production on a *weight* basis. In some firms, such as the manufacturers of rubber goods, the weight basis is used to apportion the handling charges for some of the material, and the cost basis for other materials.

Accounting for Containers. In accounting for containers, two phases of the subject must be considered. First, in the purchase of material such as acids, special containers, such as carboys, are used. These are returnable. Care must be taken to segregate from the material costs the deposit required for such containers and included in the invoice. The entry in the voucher register would be:

```
Stores ...................................................................................800
Deposit for Containers................................................... 40
    Accounts Payable ...................................................         840
```

When the containers are returned for credit or cash, the entry would be:

```
Cash, or Accounts Payable or Accounts Receivable...............................40
    Deposit for Containers...............................................         40
```

If, however, an expensive, nonreturnable container is used for stores purchased, the cost must be merged with the cost of the material, and an average unit price ascertained for the stores thus purchased.

Second, there is the question of special containers required to market such products as perfumes or candy. Should the cost of these containers be considered as part of the cost of the article being manufactured (perfume or candy), or should these items be treated as selling and marketing costs? This raises the question of whether perfumes, on the one hand, or perfumes and containers, on the other, are being manufactured. The principle usually accepted is that when a container is necessary for the sale of the product, the container is part of the manufacturing cost. When the container is used primarily for shipment of the goods, the container is treated as a shipping and selling expense.

Purchase Discount Accounting.   Purchase discounts in this discussion refer to cash discounts allowed on the purchase of direct materials and of supplies to be used in manufacturing. There are several methods for handling purchase discounts.

1.   In sound accounting theory, there is but one method: The amount of the discount should be deducted from the invoice price and the materials recorded at net cost:

```
Stores ................................................................................9,900
      Accounts Payable ...........................................................        9,900
      Goods invoiced at $10,000 less 1 percent.
```

There cannot be any real justification for recording materials at an amount greater than their cash price. The uncertainty as to whether or not the invoice will be paid promptly and the discount taken should have no effect on the cost of the materials. When payments are not made within the discount period, the cost of deferring payment should be:

```
Purchase Discounts Lost................................................................100
      Accounts Payable ................................................................        100
      To voucher additional cost.
```

2.   Despite the desirability of recording invoices at net price, stores purchased are still often entered in the voucher register at invoice price ($10,000 in the above illustration), and the discount is recorded on the date of payment in the check register:

```
Accounts Payable................................................................10,000
      Purchase Discount ..........................................................        100
      Cash ...........................................................................        9,900
      For payment.
```

In the income statement, the purchase discount may be shown as an offset to gross purchases or as financial management or other income.

Treating purchase discounts on stores as a reduction of the cost of purchases raises the same problems in maintaining the book inventories of stores as were indicated in the treatment of freight-in. Purchase discounts on stores, therefore, may be treated as a credit to the Manufacturing Overhead Control account.

At least in theory, materials purchased for manufacturing should be priced at net cost. This is an accurate figure and prevents the statement of work-in-process and finished goods inventories at a price inflated by the amount of the purchase discounts. Many governmental agencies require that the *cost of materials* on their contracts be net after deduction of benefits of any kind arising from such purchases. Such benefits are to be considered whether taken or not, as long as they are available; and they included cash discounts on purchases in excess of 1 percent.

INTERNAL CONTROL THROUGH LOCATION OF STOREROOMS

A well-recognized rule of management is that at least two persons should be involved in all transactions affecting materials: one should handle or be responsible for the handling of the materials; the other should be responsible for the records of materials. The purpose of this rule is to reduce and prevent errors, fraud, and thefts except by collusion.

The location of the book inventory records will influence the effectiveness of the division of these two activities. Where but a single storeroom is required, it is possible to have the inventory records located in the storeroom, but entries are made thereon by a stores ledger clerk as distinguished from the storekeeper. When the materials have been issued against a properly authorized requisition, a copy of this requisition is given to the stores ledger clerk for entry.

In very large plants provision is usually made for substorerooms. These are placed throughout the factory in convenient locations to permit prompt delivery of the materials needed. Although it is possible to have a separate stores ledger for each location, a single book inventory kept in the cost accounting department is usually more practical. Copies of all receiving reports and stores requisitions are sent to this department for entry. The segregation of the handling and the record-keeping activities reduces the possibility of fraud except by collusion.

CONTROLLING THE INVESTMENT IN MATERIALS INVENTORIES

Management is faced with a problem in material acquisition of keeping the investment in inventory as low as possible without imperiling the smooth flow of manufacturing operations. This problem is solved by determining *how much* to buy at a time, *how often* to purchase, and the *minimum amount* to have on hand as a safety measure. Basic in controlling the investment and the purchasing and inventory practices is the firm's budget and forecast of sales and production for the coming year. Management must then consider —

a) Quantity of material now on hand.
b) Expected requirements during the budgeted period—on a monthly, quarterly, semiannual, and annual basis.
c) Length of time required for delivery of any newly ordered material.
d) Material presently on order.
e) Amount of material to be maintained as a safety or base-stock requirement.
f) Forecasted conditions which might require higher or lower commitments.
g) Most economic quantity that should be purchased.

Management realizes that investment in large inventory not only is expensive because of the interest lost on such an investment of funds but also because of the cost of carrying such an inventory—storage, warehousing, insurance, and personnel costs. The carrying cost of an inventory has been variously estimated at from 5 to 30 percent of the inventory cost.

A large industrial firm which usually carried an inventory of $30,000,-000 to maintain its production schedules, realized that some savings might be achieved by reorganizing its materials procurement and storage procedures. It made a study of these factors. By changing its delivery methods, purchasing from suppliers nearer its plants, and altering the quantities to be purchased, it was able to reduce its average inventory investment to $20,000,000 without affecting the manufacturing efficiency. Thus $10,000,000 which was tied up in inventories was released for other operations.

No fixed rules can be set up for inventory control because some firms operate on a seasonal basis and others have a uniform schedule of production throughout the year. Some firms use materials whose prices fluctuate frequently; others use materials, the price of which is more or less stabilized. For firms using materials with fluctuating prices, long-term purchase commitments may be made at fixed prices but with staggered deliveries. For those firms having a stabilized price for materials, management has given increased attention in materials inventory control to the most economical quantity (EOQ) to purchase to keep the inventory investment at a minimum. Two methods may be used in determining the necessary basic inventory and the quantity to purchase: (a) the inventory turnover rates, and (b) the cost of maintaining and carrying the inventory.

To ascertain the inventory turnover, the total inventory on hand, $40,000, divided into the amount used during the year, $120,000, would result in an inventory turnover of three and an inventory of four months' supply on hand. This, however, ignores the economy resulting from the carrying costs of the inventory. If it is assumed that this figure is 30 percent of the average inventory, then a charge of $12,000 should be taken into account in determining whether or not to order more frequently or having speedier deliveries by such means as airfreight, thus reducing the average inventory on hand.

By preparing a table showing the number of orders, the average inventory, and the carrying charges, it will be possible to determine the most economic quantity to be ordered. For example, in the following table it becomes quite evident because of the high carrying costs that the more frequent the order the lower the inventory cost, provided it does not interfere with the smoothly functioning manufacturing operations:

No. of Orders	Units per Order	Average Inventory (One-half Purchases)	Average Inventory Investment @$10 per Unit	Inventory Carrying Charge (30%)	Clerical Cost per Purchasing Order ($15 per Order)	Total Cost of Inventory and Purchasing
1..............	1,200	600	$6,000	$1,800	$ 15	$1,815
2..............	600	300	3,000	900	30	930
3..............	400	200	2,000	600	45	645
4..............	300	150	1,500	450	60	510
5..............	240	120	1,200	360	75	435
6..............	200	100	1,000	300	90	390
7..............	172	86	860	258	105	363

Assuming that the total units to be ordered in a given period such as a year, with an average inventory of one half the purchase, an inventory carrying charge of 30 percent and clerical costs per order of $15, it is evident that ordering a smaller quantity more often (in this instance seven times a year) results in an inventory carrying cost of $363 compared with a carrying cost when only a single order is placed for the entire year's supply.

A somewhat simpler formula has been developed for determining the most economical quantity to purchase on a single order by using the following formula:

$$\text{Economical quantity to order} = \sqrt{\frac{2GS}{Ci + B}}$$

in which the following data are used:

G = Cost of placing and following up an order (assumed).......$16.00
S = Number of units required in a year (assumed)............... 900
C = Purchase price net, plus freight and receiving (assumed) ...$25.00
i = Interest rate per annum (assumed)............................. 6%
B = Annual cost of storage per unit of material (assumed) $15.50

Solving this equation results in the following:

$$\text{Quantity} = \sqrt{\frac{2 \times \$16 \times 900 \text{ units}}{\$25 \times 6\% + \$15.50}}$$

This will result in the most economical quantity to order of 41 units. For some of the smaller manufacturing firms, a "rule-of-thumb" arrangement may be practical such as the following:

Projected Annual Requirements	Order Quantity
$ 0–$1,000	1 year's supply
1,001– 2,500	6 months' supply
2,501– 5,000	4 months' supply
5,001–10,000	3 months' supply
10,001–25,000	2 months' supply
Over $25,000	1 month's supply

To illustrate the need for inventory control, a hypothetical situation is used. Assume that the cost of each unit of material is $10. The annual requirements are 12,000 units. What effect on costs, other factors such as market conditions, manufacturing cycle, etc., being equal, would a monthly purchase rather than an annual purchase have?

	Monthly Purchase Basis	Annual Purchase Basis
Quantity order on each order	1,000 units	12,000 units
Inventory investment at beginning of the year	$10,000	$120,000
Inventory investment at end of year	0	0
Average inventory (divided by two)	$ 5,000	$ 60,000
Annual carrying cost—20% of average inventory	$ 1,000	$ 12,000
Clerical cost of placing an order— $30 each order	360	30
Carrying cost of inventory	$ 1,360	$ 12,030

This extreme illustration could be modified by purchasing every two, three, four, or six months; and the savings would be affected accordingly.

The question is also raised about how much to have on hand as a safety stock. One firm which used 50 items per month and had to wait two months for delivery feels that for a margin of safety there should be one-half month's supply on hand. This means that there should be a reorder whenever the inventory falls below 150 items. Another firm feels that there should be a safety supply of one month's usage for each month (lead time) required for delivery. In this illustration since it takes two months for delivery, the margin of safety should be 200 items. Whenever the stock falls below 200 items, there should be a reorder. This is the reorder point (ROP).

Another factor to be considered is the relative cost of the items in the inventory. In one instance, 10 percent of the items make up 70 percent of the investment in inventory. These should be studied on an individual basis; and they are known as the A items; a second group of items covers 20 percent of the inventory list and makes up 18 percent of the usage. These should be analyzed individually. The remaining items could be ordered when needed since they cover 70 percent of the items and only about 6 percent of the usage.

Turnover computations are also useful not only in analyzing the investment in the stores inventory but also the investment in the work-in-process and finished goods. These turnover measures are:

Turnover of all inventories as a single figure =

$$\frac{\text{Cost of sales}}{\text{Average total inventories}}$$

$$\text{Turnover of finished goods} = \frac{\text{Cost of sales}}{\text{Average finished goods inventory}}$$

$$\text{Turnover of work-in-process} = \frac{\text{Cost of goods manufactured}}{\text{Average work-in-process inventory}}$$

$$\text{Turnover of raw materials} = \frac{\text{Cost of materials used}}{\text{Average raw materials inventory}}$$

MANAGERIAL PROBLEMS IN THE MATERIAL ACQUISITION

A review of the preceding discussion of material acquisition costs points up that to be effective management must—

1. Coordinate the sales and production through a budgetary system planning purchases, inspecting materials when received, storing materials in the most accessible and most controllable locations.
2. Maintain adequate internal control over the material acquired by means of reliable book and physical inventories.
3. Establish a clearly outlined organization chart for fixing responsibility for the acquisition of materials.
4. Establish procedures for regularly reviewing the different kinds of materials which are or may be used.
5. Regularly study and revise the most economical quantity to order— determining *when* and *how much* to acquire on any given order.

6. Simplify, combine, and eliminate the forms and paper work used in material acquisition procedures.

7. Select well-trained, responsible personnel to supervise the material acquisitions and pay them a salary commensurate with the responsibilities involved in supervising materials, oftentimes involving millions of dollars.

QUESTIONS FOR REVIEW

1. For management to have effective control of the material costs in manufacturing, four procedures must be followed. Explain the significance of these.

2. How does budgeting used properly influence effective material cost control?

3. How does an effective planning, routing, and scheduling department aid in proper material cost control?

4. Stores ledger cards may be used with three main sections or with five sections. Which is the more practical under modern business systems?

5. Outline the forms, routines, and procedures involved in the usual materials acquisition accounting and control.

6. The location of storerooms in the plant affects production efficiency. Explain how this affects the material acquisition procedure.

7. Coding of accounts used in material cost control is more important today than ever before. Explain the procedure involved and the benefits derived by a good system of coding.

8. Investment in inventory is receiving increasing attention of modern management. What information does management need and how is it obtained so that the investment is most satisfactory?

9. Internal control is an important managerial responsibility in the matter of material cost control. Explain how this may be achieved most effectively.

10. Explain the procedure in the receiving department when copies of the purchase order are used in lieu of a separate receiving report. What practices may interfere with the successful use of this procedure?

PROBLEMS—GROUP A

Problem 7–1. **Purpose:** *Journal Entries Recording Material Control Transactions; General Office and Factory Office Journals*

The Grosse Center Manufacturing Company uses a factory journal and ledger to segregate its cost accounting. Using three vertical columns, headed respectively, Transaction, General Office Entry, and Factory Office Entry, prepare entries in journal form to record the following:

1. Stores purchased on account, $22,500.

2. Stores used in manufacturing: direct materials, $9,800; indirect factory supplies, $800; shipping and packing supplies, $1,200.

3. Materials returned to vendors, $750.
4. Paid vendors on account: $18,000 from which purchase discounts of $2,400 were deducted. Net payment, $15,600.
5. Purchased stores on account, $8,000. Paid the Burlington Northern Railroad Company freight on this purchase, $460.
6. Returned to factory storeroom excess materials: direct materials, $380; factory supplies, $150.
7. Materials issued for factory roof repairs, $325.
8. Scrap material placed in storeroom has an estimated sales value of $735. An inventory card is maintained for scrap at estimated sales value.
9. Materials issued for use in constructing a special machine for use in the factory cost, $1,350. The Machinery and Equipment Control account is maintained on the general office books.
10. All the scrap material on hand has been sold for $820.
11. Materials issued for making machine repairs, $420.
12. Shipping supplies purchased and received at the factory, $1,000.

Problem 7–2. **Purpose:** *Summarizing the Materials Requisition Journal; Analysis of Forms and Procedures of Materials Cost Control*

Among the books of record used by the Georgia Manufacturing Company at its factory is a materials requisition journal in which the following entries have been recorded for the month of March:

MATERIALS REQUISITION JOURNAL

Date	Req. No.	Description	Direct Materials	Indirect Materials	Shipping Supplies	Total
Mar. 1	301	Material X, Job 42	$ 820			
3	302	Material Y, Job 46	430			
8	303	Shipping supplies			$425	
12	304	Department I, supplies		$300		
15	305	Material X, Job 43	400			
19	306	Material Z, Job 42	280			
22	307	Material Y, Job 46	135			
24	308	Department II, supplies		128		
24	309	Material Z, Job 43	155			
30	310	Department III, supplies		262		
30	311	Material Y, Job 45	100			
30	312	Shipping supplies			275	
		Totals for month	$2,320	$690	$700	$3,710

Required:

a) Prepare entries in journal form on the general office and factory office books to summarize the materials requisitions journal.
b) Using the following columnar headings, prepare a tabulation for the transactions recorded in the materials requisitions journal: Transaction Dates, Name of Forms Used, Number of Copies, and Disposition of the Copies.

Problem 7-3. Purpose: *Review of Cost Accounting Cycle through Entries in T-Ledger Accounts; Cost of Good Sold; and Condensed Income Statement*

The Garrison Manufacturing Company produces small color printing machines. No factory ledger is used.

Work-in-process inventories, March 1, 19—, were materials, $9,000; labor, $10,000; manufacturing overhead, $6,000. Stores inventory, March 1, was $54,-000; finished goods inventory, March 1, was $25,000.

The transactions for the month of March were:

1. Stores purchased, $150,000. Returned to vendors, $10,000.
2. Stores requisitions: direct materials, $120,000; indirect materials, $11,000; shipping supplies, $2,500.
3. Direct materials returned from the factory to the storeroom as excess, $2,400.
4. Payrolls for the month of March were:

	Gross Amount	FICA Tax	Federal Withholding Tax	State Withholding Tax
Direct labor	$150,000	$8,700	$34,500	$9,500
Indirect labor	12,000	620	2,100	1,000
Superintendence	2,500	150	750	300
Sales salaries............	14,000	680	2,200	1,200
Office salaries............	4,000	210	800	720

5. Payroll tax liabilities in addition to the employer's share of the FICA tax were:

	Factory	Selling	Office
Federal unemployment tax	$ 656	$ 56	$ 16
State unemployment tax......................	4,650	390	114

6. Manufacturing overhead is applied to production at the rate of 60% of direct labor costs.
7. In addition to the indirect materials and indirect labor and payroll taxes, manufacturing overhead costs incurred totaled $50,000.
8. Sales for the month were as follows:

Gross sales..$450,000
Sales returns and allowances.................. 10,000
Sales discounts.................................. 4,000

9. The cost of the sales returns were $3,500.
10. Sundry selling expenses were $36,000; sundry administrative expenses, $48,000.
11. Inventories on hand, March 31, 19—, were: work-in-process—materials, $15,000; work-in-process—labor, $32,000; work-in-process—overhead, __?__ ; finished goods, $60,000.

Required:

From the above information, you are asked to prepare:
a) Entries in the following T-ledger accounts: Stores, Work-in-Process (three accounts), Manufacturing Overhead, Finished Goods, Cost of Sales, Selling Expense Control, Administrative Expense Control (no Applied Manufacturing Overhead account is used), Sales.
b) Condensed income statement.
c) Statement of cost of goods sold for the month of March, 19—.

Problem 7–4.   Purpose: *CPA Problem on Materials Control*

In anticipation of the annual audit of the Greatline Manufacturing Company for the year ended December 31, 19—, the firm took its annual physical inventory on November 30, 19—.

The firm's inventory account which includes the raw material and work-in-process is supported by a book inventory on the first-in, first-out basis. There is no finished goods inventory.

The company's physical inventory revealed that the book inventory of $60,570 was understated by $3,000. To avoid distorting the interim financial statements, the firm decided not to adjust the book inventory until year-end, except for obsolete items.

Your examination revealed the following information relative to the inventory on November 30:

1. Pricing tests showed that the physical inventory was overpriced by $2,200.
2. Footing and extension errors resulted in a $150 understatement of the physical inventory.
3. Direct labor included in the physical inventory amounted to $10,000. Overhead was included at the rate of 200 percent of direct labor. You determined that the amount of direct labor was correct and the overhead rate was proper.
4. The physical inventory included obsolete materials recorded at $250. During December these obsolete materials were removed from the inventory account by a charge to the Cost of Sales.

Your investigation also disclosed the following information about the December 31, inventory:

1. Total debits to certain accounts during December were:

> Purchases in December $24,700
> Direct labor................................. 12,100
> Manufacturing overhead................. 25,200
> Cost of sales............................... 68,600

2. The cost of sales of $68,600 included direct labor of $13,800.
3. Normal scrap loss on established product lines is negligible. However, a special order started and completed during December had excessive scrap loss of $800 which was charged to manufacturing overhead.

Required:

a) Computation of the corrected physical inventory on November 30, 19—.
b) Computation of the inventory on December 31, 19—.
c) Computation of direct labor in inventory.
d) Computation of the underabsorbed manufacturing overhead.

(Adapted from AICPA Uniform Examination)

Problem 7-5. Purpose: *Entries Affecting Materials Control*

The Grossett Manufacturing Company incurred the following transactions during the month of February. This firm does not use a factory journal. You are asked to prepare entries in journal form to record these transactions.

1. Materials costing $18,500 were purchased on account.
2. Material requisitions for the first two weeks of the month were for direct materials, $6,800; shipping supplies, $850; factory supplies, $1,000; repair of machinery, $350.
3. Invoices for materials purchased were paid: gross amount, $10,000 less discounts of 3 percent.
4. Materials costing $680 were returned to vendors for credit. These were found to be defective.
5. Freight on materials purchased amounted to $630. Freight-in is part of the manufacturing overhead.
6. The factory returned to the storeroom, materials costing $400. Of this, $50 was for factory supplies not necessary.
7. Materials issued for the repair of the factory roof cost $168.
8. Production Department A returned to the storeroom scrap material which had a sales value of $146. The company maintains an inventory record for scrap materials at the estimated sales value.
9. Shipping supplies costing $210 were returned to the vendor as being the wrong size. The invoice for these had already been paid.
10. Scrap material in entry 8 was sold for $180 cash.
11. Indirect materials purchased on account, $2,500.
12. A physical inventory at the end of the month showed:
     a) 100 pounds of Material X in excess of the inventory card record. The inventory price is $1.24 per pound.
     b) The price of Material Y, of which 300 pounds were on hand, costing 85 cents per pound, now had a market value of $1 per pound.

PROBLEMS—GROUP B

Problem 7-6. Purpose: *Summarizing the Materials Requisitions Journal; Analysis of Forms and Procedures for Materials Cost Control*

The Grimex Manufacturing Company uses a separate set of factory books to record its cost accounting data. Among these records is the materials requisitions journal in which are recorded the transactions for the month of May, viz:

MATERIALS REQUISITIONS JOURNAL

Date	Req. No.	Description	Direct Materials	Indirect Materials	Shipping Supplies
May 1	701	Material X, Job 75	$ 750		
3	702	Material Y, Job 76	350		
8	703	Shipping supplies			$250
12	704	Factory supplies		$130	
15	705	Material X, Job 77	400		
19	706	Material Z, Job 75	200		
22	707	Material Y, Job 78	180		
23	708	Factory supplies		70	
23	709	Material Y, Job 78	120		
31	710	Material X, Job 76	100		
31	711	Factory supplies		160	
31	712	Shipping supplies			140
		Totals for month	$2,100	$360	$390

Required:

a) Prepare in journal form the accounting entries on the general office and factory office books to summarize the materials requisition journal.

b) Using a columnar arrangement as given, prepare a tabulation for the transactions recorded in the materials requisition journal: Transaction Dates, Name of Forms Used, Number of Copies, and Disposition of the Copies.

Problem 7–7.   Purpose: *Economic Order Quantity (EOQ)*

The Xerxes Manufacturing Company is a small firm which is studying its purchasing and inventory procedures to reduce operating costs. The production manager feels that the purchasing procedure might result in a small cost saving and more efficient production procedure if the purchasing was rescheduled.

The main raw material used in manufacturing is a liquid chemical known as XPO and is purchased in barrel containers. The firm uses 1,560 barrels a year, about 30 a week. To process the purchase order costs about $14 each. The carrying costs of the inventory (interest, taxes, insurance, warehousing, etc.) is estimated at 10 percent of the cost of the average inventory. The average inventory is figured at one half of the order size.

Purchase discounts are allowed by the main supplier of this raw material depending upon the size of the quantity ordered. The basic price is $5 per barrel, and discounts are as follows:

Quantity Ordered (Barrels)	Discount
1 to 99	0
99 to 499	2%
500 to 999	5
Over 1,000	10

Required:

On the basis of this information, you are asked to compute —

a) The most economic order quantity.
b) Indicate the limitations of this computation from the managerial viewpoint.

Problem 7–8. Purpose: *CPA Problem on Materials Control*

The Xenophan Supply Company maintains its inventory on the *first-in, first-out* basis of pricing. The physical inventory showed by actual count, a value of $28,785. The book inventory records of stores and work-in-process indicated that the inventory should be $30,285. There was no finished goods inventory. The above discrepancy was noted on February 28, one month before the close of the fiscal year. To avoid distorting the interim financial statements, the controller of the firm decided not to adjust the book inventory until year-end, except for obsolete items.

Further investigation of the inventory records showed that there was a footing error that resulted in a $75 understatement of the physical inventory. The physical inventory was "priced," and it was found to be overpriced by $1,100.

Manufacturing overhead was applied to the inventory at the rate of 200 percent of direct labor costs. The amount of direct labor which was included in the inventory was $5,000. This amount was found to be correct.

Obsolete material in the physical inventory was recorded at $125. During March, these obsolete materials were removed from the inventory and charged to the Cost of Goods Sold.

Certain amounts were charged to the following accounts during the month of March: Purchases, $12,350; Direct Labor, $6,050; Manufacturing Expense, $12,600; Cost of Goods Sold, $34,300.

The $34,300 of cost of goods sold included $6,900 of direct labor.

The manufacturing operations are such that excessive scrap loss is rare. However, on a special order completed during March, $400 of excessive scrap was charged to manufacturing expense. The amount was considered correct.

Required:

a) Determine the correct physical inventory, February 28.
b) Determine the correct physical inventory March 31 if the February 28 inventory was $28,850. Do not let this answer prejudice your answer to (a) above.
c) Compute the over- or underapplied manufacturing expense, if any, March 31.

(Adapted from AICPA Uniform Examination)

Chapter 8

Cost Determination
of Materials Used

MANAGERIAL PLANNING, ROUTING, AND ISSUING MATERIALS

In the larger industrial plants, production must be carefully planned, scheduled, and routed through the factory to avoid production confusion and delays. This activity is the responsibility of the production manager. He is one of the most important executives in the plant. The staff in this department produces descriptions of all production or jobs in the form of *production orders,* informing the factory superintendent what is to be done. Definite time schedules must be arranged so that the required materials will be delivered to the various departments when needed—not too long beforehand nor after they are required. This department determines the issuance of materials, as well as scheduling the machines and tools to be used.

In one large industrial plant, the production planning and engineering department performs the following functions:

1. Prepares master production orders.
2. Prepares necessary subproduction orders.
3. Prepares blueprint orders.
4. Acknowledges and checks blueprint receipts.
5. Prepares bills of material.
6. Prepares tool orders.
7. Prepares and checks laboratory records.

COST ACCOUNTING FOR MATERIALS USED

Managerial control of the issuance of materials consists of the use of forms, procedure analyses, journal entries, subsidiary inventory records, and proper costing of the materials issued. Special problems arise in budgeting long-term material requirements, storing the materials, taking physical inventories, and accounting for scrap, spoiled, and defective work. Each of these affect the determination of *reliable unit costs*.

Budgeting material requirements has been discussed previously. The internal control may be achieved by having a well-staffed and supervised storeroom, or having several storerooms to facilitate the delivery of the material when needed.

FORMS USED IN CONTROLLING THE ISSUANCE OF MATERIAL

Forms are necessary for fixing responsibility, providing reliable cost information, and especially for internal control of material inventories. Computerizing the procedures has expedited the use of forms for this purpose, but the following must still be considered in studying this phase of cost determination:

1. Material requisitions or standard bills of materials.
2. Returned materials report.
3. Scrap report.
4. Spoiled material report.
5. Stores inventory records.

1. *Material requisitions or standard bills of materials* are forms used to authorize the issuance of materials from the storeroom. If the same material is used on practically all jobs, it is possible to have a printed standardized form so that only the quantity to be issued must be inserted. Otherwise, an individual type of form is used to indicate the particular material to be issued. These are prepared by the planning and routing department in large firms, by the foremen's department in medium-sized firms, and by the individual worker in the small firms. Copies of these forms are distributed as follows to provide internal control and reliable cost records: (1) copy to storeroom to authorize the issuance of material, (2) copy retained for verification and control, and (3) copy to the cost accounting department for cost accumulation. Both forms are illustrated. Because of the speed in sorting and accumulating the requisitions, many firms use punched cards for the requisitions; others use telegraphic handwriting, and even common language punched adding machine tape for use with computers, thus expediting the cost accounting procedure. See Chapter 2, Illustrations 2–3 and 2–4, for these requisition forms.

2. *Returned materials report* reverses the procedure indicated previously so that the proper job or department may be credited for materials not used.

3. *Scrap report* is a form used to maintain a record of the quantity of scrap received. This is mainly a control report.

4. *Spoiled or defective material report* is primarily a managerial

Illustration 8–1. Punched Card Requisition

Illustration 8–2. Returned Materials Report

DATE 4/7/--	STORES AND SUPPLIES RETURNED CREDIT MEMO.		No A 4107	
WHERE USED Stamping Department				
ACCOUNT CHARGED Work-in-Process, Job #UCS782				
QUANTITY	DESCRIPTION		PRICE	TOTAL
56 lbs.	Tempered Blade Steel			
	Spec. 482		12	6 72

RECEIVED ABOVE C. C. Rye	APPROVED J. Farber	DELIVERED BY F. Mascari		
ENTERED COST LEDGER JKC	ENTERED IN CAT. JKC	PRICED 8.7.	EXTENDED 27	CHECKED KC	POSTED ✓	PUNCHED ✓

Original--Dept. Returning material

Duplicate--Cost Dept.

Triplicate--Stores Department

report which indicates the type and causes of spoiled or defective material and the probable cost of making this salable.

5. *Stores inventory records* have been illustrated previously. Where necessary, the *on order* and the *on reserve* sections should be used; otherwise, the three sections—Received, Issued, and Balance—are satisfactory.

Two additional illustrations are given: (1) Illustration 8–1, which shows the punched card individual requisition form; and (2) Illustration 8–2, a returned materials report.

DESCRIPTIVE PROCEDURAL ANALYSIS OF MATERIAL ISSUED

The following flow of work description summarizes the forms procedure involved in the issuance of materials:

FORMS PROCEDURE FOR MATERIALS CONTROL—ISSUANCE OF MATERIALS

Materials Requisitions: At least three copies are prepared either in the planning and routing department or in the department requiring the material. These are used as follows:
  1. Copy sent to the stores department to authorize the issuance of the material.
  2. Copy sent to the cost department for both direct and indirect materials.
  3. Copy is retained in department requesting the material.

Returned Materials Report: At least three copies are prepared in the stores department, and these are used as follows:
  1. Copy is sent to department returning the material.
  2. Copy is sent to the cost accounting department for deductions in the *Material Costs* section of the job order sheets.
  3. Copy is kept by the stores department for entry in red or encircled in the *Issued* section of the stores ledger cards affected, and for addition to the *Balance* section.

Returned Purchases Report: At least three copies are prepared in the shipping department, and these are used as follows:
  1. Copy is sent to the purchasing department which forwards it to the accounting department for entry in the voucher register, debiting Accounts Payable and crediting Stores Control.
  2. Copy is sent to the stores department for entry in red or encircled in the *Received* section of the respective stores ledger cards, and for deduction from the *Balance* section of these cards.
  3. Copy is retained by the shipping department for its record.

ACCOUNTING FOR MATERIALS ISSUED

Costs of materials issued must be classified before these are recorded as *direct materials, indirect materials,* and *packing and shipping supplies.* This classification is accomplished by sorting the stores requisitions. Accounting entries must then be made (1) on the stores inventory cards, (2) the cost summary sheets, and (3) on the general accounting records.

Entries on the stores inventory record are made from the requisitions in the issued section and the balance extended, both as to quantity and total costs, as illustrated:

Received			Issued			Balance		
Units	Price	Total	Units	Price	Total	Units	Price	Total
						500	1.00	500.00
300	1.00	300.00				800	1.00	800.00
			250	1.00	250.00	550	1.00	550.00

Entries on the cost summary sheets are also made from copies of the requisitions. For direct materials used, a total entry is made periodically on the job order sheets if job order cost system is used, and on the cost of production report for a process type of industry. The indirect materials used costs and the packing and shipping supplies costs are totaled and recorded in the general accounting records — the indirect material being charged to the Manufacturing Overhead Control account and the shipping supplies charged as a selling expense.

Entries on the general accounting records are usually made weekly. For direct and indirect materials used the entries would be:

For a job order system:

```
Work-in-Process — Materials.....................................................3,690
Manufacturing Overhead Control (Indirect Materials) ....................  310
    Stores Control................................................................              4,000
```

For a process type of industry:

```
Work-in-Process — Department I.................................................3,690
Manufacturing Overhead Control.............................................  310
    Stores Control................................................................              4,000
```

MATERIAL REQUISITIONS JOURNAL

In some firms, use is made of a running or continuous record of the requisitions. If desirable, this may be in the form of a book of original entry. Such use is limited to firms in which the number of requisitions is small and the amounts involved are large; otherwise it is an unnecessary duplication of clerical effort. The rulings of such a requisition journal as a book of original entry would be:

Date	Requisition Number	Job Order Number	Work-in-Process— Materials Dr.	Manufacturing Overhead Dr.	Shipping Supplies Dr.	Stores Cr.
	Totals					

This requisition journal may be primarily a memorandum record whereby the foremen or superintendent use it like a work sheet to maintain operating records and accumulate the totals.

DIAGRAMMATICALLY SUMMARIZING THE MATERIALS ISSUED PROCEDURES

Illustration 8–3 reviews the procedures and accounting for materials used by a manufacturing firm.

COSTING MATERIALS USED IN PRODUCTION

There are a number of accepted methods of costing the materials used in manufacturing. The method used will affect the cost of the completed product and the inventory values of the work-in-process and finished goods. These in turn affect the profit on sales and the income tax for the firm. Management must determine the practice to be followed. Some of the more commonly used methods of costing materials used are:

1. Fifo—first-in, first-out method.
2. Lifo—last-in, first-out method.
3. Moving average method.
4. Average price at the close of the preceding period.
5. Miscellaneous methods.

First-In, First-Out (Fifo) Inventory Pricing. The first-in, first-out method of inventory pricing is based upon the principle that materials should be issued in the order and at the price of their original purchase. For example, if 500 pounds of copper were purchased at 80 cents a pound

Illustration 8–3. Materials Control—Issuance of Materials

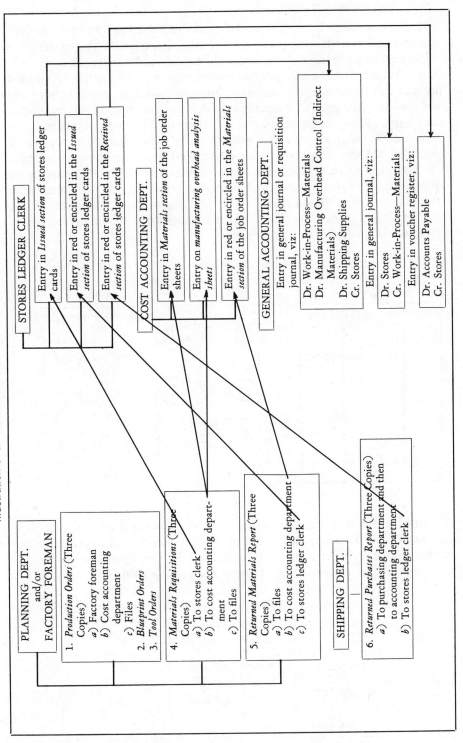

and, later, another lot of 750 pounds was purchased at 89 cents a pound, the first 500 pounds to be used will be charged into production at the price of 80 cents and thereafter charges will be made at 89 cents. Theoretically it is assumed that the 500 pounds will be segregated from the 750-pound lot and will be issued first. Actually, however, since the goods in both lots are identical, the goods are not separated. A careful study of this method of inventory pricing emphasizes the fact that the Balance column must be extended in such a way as to indicate clearly the quantity and price of each lot. If three or more lots are on hand at one time, the balance must be extended on three lines. This procedure is awkward if there are many such items. But, from a practical angle, few concerns will have more than two lots of materials on hand at one time unless they anticipate a rising market. The balance, therefore, normally ought not to contain more than two quantities or prices at a given date.

Illustration 8—4. Inventory Card—First-In, First-Out Pricing Method

RECEIPTS			ISSUES			BALANCE		
Nov. 1	600 @ 12¢	$72.00				Nov. 1	600 @ 12¢	$72.00
			Nov. 3	300 @ 12¢	$36.00	3	300 @ 12¢	36.00
			5	125 @ 12¢	15.00	5	175 @ 12¢	21.00
12	500 @ 14¢	70.00				12	175 @ 12¢	21.00
							500 @ 14¢	70.00
			14	50 @ 12¢	6.00	14	225 @ 12¢	27.00
							500 @ 14¢	70.00
			15	225 @ 12¢	27.00			
				25 @ 14¢	3.50	15	475 @ 14¢	66.50
			18	300 @ 14¢	42.00	18	175 @ 14¢	24.50
21	300 @ 13¢	39.00				21	175 @ 14¢	24.50
							300 @ 13¢	39.00

Illustration 8—4 represents the *first-in, first-out* method of costing requisitions. The same data, used in this illustration and in those for the other inventory pricing methods which follow, cover the following transactions so that comparisons between the pricing methods can be made:

Purchases		Issues		Returns to Store-room from Factory	
Nov. 1	600 units				
		Nov. 3	300 units		
		5	125 units		
12	500 units			Nov. 14	50 units
		15	250 units		
		18	300 units		
21	300 units				

For the *first-in, first-out* method, it is claimed that since the materials are charged into production at actual cost in the order of receipt, the method is more accurate. This is one of the reasons the Internal Revenue Service favors this method. However, the Internal Revenue Service also favors this method because in a market of rising prices, income calculations include closing inventories of raw materials at more recent, higher prices and the cost of goods sold, thereby, at a lower figure. The net effect taxwise is a larger income tax to be paid currently on higher net income. (The opposite income tax effect is involved in the last-in, first-out method of costing the closing raw materials inventories.) The main disadvantage from the point of view of business is in the amount of clerical work involved in extending balances on the inventory cards if these inventory balances include materials at several different prices.

Two other problems arise in the use of this method of inventory pricing. The first is the question of returns to the vendor of merchandise found unsatisfactory some time after purchase. The vendor will always be charged with the goods *at the price at which purchased.* However, if the Balance column no longer contains goods at the price of the original purchase because all subsequent purchases were either at a higher or lower price, the entry in the stores ledger card for the return will use the price of the next available lot; the entry will be made in the *Receipts* section, circled. However, the entry in the voucher register for the return must account for the difference through an inventory adjustment entry. For example, the goods being returned are 200 units at 14 cents, but only 10-cent units are on hand according to the inventory card. The vendor must be charged with the 14-cent price, although on the inventory card, it will be at 10 cents. Therefore the adjustment entry would be:

Accounts Payable	28	
Stores		20
Manufacturing Overhead—Materials Adjustment		8

A second problem arises in the treatment of returns from the factory to the storeroom of excess materials. Assume that in the foregoing illustration all the 12-cent material and some of the 14-cent material had been issued. Thereafter, some of the material issued at 12 cents is returned to the storeroom as excess. Should it be treated as old material and placed before the remaining 14-cent material, or treated as though it were a new purchase and placed after the 14-cent material? *Theoretically,* at least, either treatment would state the previous issue of 14-cent material incorrectly, since there are still some 12-cent materials on hand which according to the first-in, first-out rule should have been allocated to this order. No fixed rule has been determined for handling such transactions because the small amounts involved in such situations do not cause much concern in business.

This rule, however, might be used: If goods are returned to the storeroom, the price used is the same as that at time of issue. If no goods have since been issued at a different price, the returned goods would be placed first in the Balance column: if goods have been issued at a different price, the returned goods are treated as though they were a new purchase and placed last.

The Fifo method of inventory pricing can be used satisfactorily where the following three conditions exist:

a) Inventories turn over rapidly.

b) Inventory is not a major factor in the profit or current asset situation.

c) The nature and type of goods used in the inventory changes frequently.

Last-In, First-Out (Lifo) Inventory Pricing. The last-in, first-out method is predicated upon the principle that in a rising market, inventory or speculative inventory profits should not be recognized since the inventory used in production must be replaced at higher costs. Under this method the cost of current purchases of materials used in production is applied as the cost of current production. In other words, the cost of current production is charged with the cost of materials at prices which most nearly correspond in point of time with those which are being paid to replace the materials consumed.

During recent years, the last-in, first-out method of inventory pricing has come to be more widely used than ever before. This is due primarily to the steady rise in the cost of practically all materials and the rather widely held opinion that prices will probably not return to lower levels under present economic conditions and practices. To illustrate this method, the same figures used in the first-in, first-out method are used. When materials are requisitioned, the assumption is that the prices are taken from the last additions to the inventory (see Illustration 8–5).

A distinction must be made between Lifo applied as a *continuous pricing method* under a book inventory procedure (as in Illustration 8–5) and Lifo applied as a *periodic* inventory method. For example, if there had been only a *periodic* inventory of the item in the foregoing illustration, all of the 475 units in the final inventory would be priced at 12 cents under the Lifo method since the number of units in the final inventory is not greater than in the first purchase at 12 cents. The *elective* method, which may be used in computing taxable income (under certain conditions), is a periodic inventory Lifo method. Under the elective method, the units in the final inventory not in excess of those in the initial inventory are priced the same as in the initial inventory. Excess units may be priced (consistently from year to year) at earliest purchase price (or prices), at latest purchase price (or prices), or at average purchase prices.

The last-in, first-out method of inventory pricing can be used whenever it would be possible to use the first-in, first-out method or the moving-average pricing method. The practical aspects of the problem, however, suggest that some or all of the following conditions should be present:

a)   That there is a continued need for substantial quantities of materials, the price of which may be subject to considerable price fluctuations.
b)   That the relative value of the materials used in production is large in comparison to the total cost of the finished product.
c)   That the selling prices of the finished product react rather sharply and quickly to the fluctuations in the replacement cost of the materials used.

During a period of inflation or in a rising price market, the last-in, first-out method of inventory pricing tends to reduce the amount of the

Illustration 8–5.   Inventory Card – Last-In, First-Out Pricing Method

RECEIPTS			ISSUES			BALANCE		
Nov. 1	600 @ 12¢	$72.00				Nov. 1	600 @ 12¢	$72.00
			Nov. 3	300 @ 12¢	$36.00	3	300 @ 12¢	36.00
			5	125 @ 12¢	15.00	5	175 @ 12¢	21.00
12	500 @ 14¢	70.00				12	175 @ 12¢	21.00
							500 @ 14¢	70.00
			14	50 @ 12¢	6.00	14	225 @ 12¢	27.00
							500 @ 14¢	70.00
			15	250 @ 14¢	35.00	15	225 @ 12¢	27.00
							250 @ 14¢	35.00
			16	250 @ 14¢	35.00			
				50 @ 12¢	6.00	18	175 @ 12¢	21.00
21	300 @ 13¢	39.00				21	175 @ 12¢	21.00
							300 @ 13¢	39.00

stated profit and consequently decreases any taxes based on the calculation of profits. This effect is created because the so-called "inventory profits," that is, profits which have not been transformed into cash or receivables are minimized. The costs of production and, consequently, the cost of goods sold are based upon the cost of materials most recently purchased, which is at higher prices than on the first-in, first-out basis. It results in higher cost of sales, smaller profits, and unrealistic, underpriced stores inventory on the balance sheet.

Moving-Average Method of Inventory Pricing.   This method is used by firms desiring the *average cost* of units of materials rather than the actual costs. If the prices of stores fluctuate frequently, more satisfactory costs are secured by the use of the average method than by the first-in, first-out method.

The procedure for pricing on the inventory cards is as follows: Entries for the receipt and issue of materials are the same as those described for the first-in, first-out method. When materials are received, the quantity is added to the quantity in the Balance column; the cost of the material received is added to the amount of cost already shown in the Balance column. This total is divided by the total quantity to determine the new average price. Because the average price is determined after the total of quantity and cost are obtained, it is suggested that the unit price column in the *Balance* section be placed last. One rule to remember in using this method is *that no new average price is computed unless a new purchase is made.* For example, if the Balance column contains 1,200 units at an average price at 12 cents and 100 units previously issued at 11½ cents are returned as excess issue, the quantity in the Balance column becomes 1,300 and the total price $155.50, but the unit price for future issues remains 12 cents until a new purchase is made. After the purchase a new average is computed—an average which will absorb the discrepancy created by the returns.

To illustrate the moving-average price method and to facilitate comparison, the same figures are used as were used for the first-in, first-out method (see Illustration 8–6).

*Illustration 8–6. Perpetual Inventory Card
Moving-Average (after Each Purchase) Price Method*

Receipts				Issues				Balance			
Nov 1	600 @ 12¢	$72.00						Nov. 1	600	$72.00 @ 12¢	
				Nov. 3	300 @ 12¢	$36.00		3	300	36.00	
				5	125	12¢	15.00	5	175	21.00	
12	500	14¢	70.00	14	⟨50⟩	12¢	⟨6.00⟩	12	675	91.00	13.5¢
								14	725	97.00	
				15	250	13.5¢	33.75	15	475	63.25	
				18	300	13.5¢	40.50	18	175	22.75	
21	300	13¢	39.00					21	475	61.75	13¢

Method of Average Price at the Close of the Preceding Month.[1] Some concerns find it expedient to ascertain the average price of each kind of material on hand at the close of each month and to use this price in costing all requisitions for the following month. For such a system to function without extreme variations, the price of materials must not fluctuate too widely from month to month. Furthermore, the company must make most of its purchases on a month-to-month basis, *buying a sufficient quantity*

---

[1] Sometimes called "weighted average method."

near the end of each month to carry operations for the following month.
The requisitions may be priced by the cost accounting department before
they are entered on the cost sheets. This is possible because at the end of
each month a list can be prepared giving the prices to be used during the
following month. The stores ledger clerk records the quantities and costs
of all stores received. All requisitions are entered and computed at the
determined price. It is unnecessary to extend the balance of quantity or
amount after each entry. At the end of the month the total receipts are
added to, and the total issues are subtracted from, the opening balance to
ascertain the figures to be used in computing the unit price for the next
month. The accompanying inventory card (see Illustration 8–7) shows the
calculations when this method is used. The figures are the same as those
used in Illustration 8–6. The computations are:

Balance at beginning of November	600	$ 72
Puchases during month.......................................	800	109
Total	1,400	$181
Issues during month...	925	111
New balance, end of November...........................	475	$ 70

Illustration 8–7. *Perpetual Inventory Card—Average Price at Close of the Month*

Receipts			Issues			Balance		
						Nov. 1	600 @ 12¢	$72.00
			Nov. 3	300 @ 12¢	$ 36.00			
			5	125 12¢	15.00			
Nov. 12	500 @ 14¢	$ 70.00	14	(50) 12¢	(6.00)			
			15	250 12¢	30.00			
			18	300 12¢	36.00			
21	300 @ 13¢	39.00						
	800	$109.00		925	$111.00	Dec. 1	475 @ 14.7¢	$70.00

The price to be used during December will be 14.7 cents per unit
($70 ÷ 475 units).

If the prices of materials fluctuate widely, especially in a rising market,
the resulting price figures may disrupt the accounting for the cost of materials. To illustrate an extreme case, let us assume that 1,000 pounds of
materials, valued at 20 cents per pound, are on hand at the end of the
month. During the following month, purchases are: 8,000 pounds at 24
cents, 7,500 pounds at 26 cents, and 10,000 pounds at 28 cents. Total
requisitions for the month amount to 25,000 pounds. The resulting figures
would be:

		Pounds	
Balance on hand	at beginning	1,000	$ 200
Purchases	at 24 cents	8,000	1,920
	at 26 cents	7,500	1,950
	at 28 cents	10,000	2,800
	Total	26,500	$6,870
Requisitions	at 20-cent average price at end of preceding month	25,000	5,000
	Balance at end of month	1,500	$1,870
	Average price to be used next month		$1.246

It is evident that under such wide fluctuations it would be illogical to use $1.246 as the price for the next month. Therefore, to be practical, this method must presume that the purchasing department will buy near the end of each month sufficient material to carry on the production for the coming month.

Miscellaneous Pricing Methods.   Three other methods of inventory pricing and material requisition costing used infrequently are:

a)   *Market price at time of issue* regardless of purchase price. The stores clerk maintains the book inventory on a quantity basis only. Requisitions are priced in the cost accounting department either at the price of the *last purchase* or the *current market price*. The use of this method is restricted to cost accounting operated as statistical compilations since it is not generally approved by the Internal Revenue Service, nor by professional accounting societies.

b)   *Standard* or *predetermined* costs for each item of material. This simplifies the accounting procedure. It is discussed in more detail in Chapter 16. Where inventories are maintained at standard costs, these must be adjusted to the actual cost basis (Lifo or Fifo) for balance sheet presentation.

c)   *Base stock inventory pricing* method is similar in effect to the Lifo method. A basic quantity of material is assumed to be on hand at all times to keep production facilities operating. This basic stock is costed at the prevailing cost when the material was first acquired and is assumed it will never be used up. All purchases above this basic stock are presumed to be for current operations, not for replenishment of base stock. These purchases may be costed on any of the pricing methods previously discussed.

OBSOLETE INVENTORY VALUATION

Obsolete inventory valuation refers to finished stock and sometimes raw materials which have become obsolete under current business operations. Changing the production models in the automotive industry obsoletes many of the finished parts or raw materials on hand; electronic improvements such as transistors have obsoleted the vacuum tubes; the lower cost of competitive production (on a cost or market basis) or newer materials might make the value of the materials in stock at less than cost; and finally the discontinuance of a product might make finished goods and even raw materials an obsolescence-valuation problem. The loss of a special customer for whom a certain product was manufactured may also result in the obsolescence-valuation of inventory. All of these situations present rare but peculiar inventory valuation problems for a manufacturing concern which must be recognized.

For management to take into consideration the obsolescent factor in inventory valuations, be it raw materials or finished parts, certain procedures may be necessary: (a) parts inventories should be on a comparative basis, from year to year, to ascertain the slow-moving items, and the causes therefor; (b) comparison should be made of items used in current production and those which cannot be used, thus indicating obsolescence; (c) where designs or models change regularly, parts relative to the older production should be aged on an obsolescent schedule, such as one—two years old, 80 percent; two—three years old, 60 percent of cost; three—four years old, at 40 percent of cost; and over four years, at 30 percent. This aging schedule may be determined at the time of manufacture or purchase. The adjustment in value should be taken into consideration in the period in which the obsolescence is established and recognized in the statements prepared for the Internal Revenue Service.

COMPARATIVE RESULTS OF MATERIAL INVENTORY PRICING METHODS

A comparison of the effect of the various inventory pricing methods on business operations is a difficult matter because conditions vary so much from one manufacturing firm to another. However, it is apparent from the illustrations given of the four most common methods that inventory values at the end of the accounting period—and therefore income for the period—will vary under these methods:

Inventory balance—Fifo..$63.50
Inventory balance—Moving average after each purchase............ 61.75
Inventory balance—Moving average at end of month 70.00
Inventory balance—Lifo... 60.00

Since this discrepancy is the result of but one item in the inventory, and since many inventories consist of thousands of different materials, it is evident that the choice of inventory pricing methods may have a significant effect on periodic profits. Even though over a period of years the differences in annual profits for a firm may tend to "average out" as the result of price fluctuations in one direction and then the other, yet the *periodic* costs of work-in-process, finished goods, and cost of sales and the *periodic* net profits are important items of information and must be computed as accurately as possible. Taxable income should be computed on the basis most favorable to the taxpayer—but within the bounds of the law. To illustrate the effect of various market conditions on the results shown by different inventory pricing methods over a period longer than one month, the table in Illustration 8–8 shows the effect over a period of two years, during which prices increased the first year and decreased in the second.

If these figures were used in the final inventories of the income state-

Illustration 8–8

COMPARATIVE TABLE SHOWING INVENTORY EFFECT OF VARIOUS METHODS OF INVENTORY PRICING OVER TWO-YEAR PERIOD*

	Quantity	FIFO	Average Cost	LIFO
FIRST YEAR—PRICE TREND UPWARD				
Initial Inventory: 200 @ $1.00..........	200	$ 200.00	$ 200.00	$ 200.00
Purchases—One Contract, Installment				
Deliveries: 900 @ $1.40..............	900	1,260.00	1,260.00	1,260.00
Total Charges to Stores..........	1,100	$1,460.00	$1,460.00	$1,460.00
Issued to Production:	500			
FIFO: 200 @ $1.00.................		200.00		
300 @ 1.40.................		420.00		
Average Cost: 500 @ $1.327..........			663.50	
LIFO: 500 @ $1.40.................				700.00
Final Inventory at Cost at End of Year..	600	$ 840.00	$ 796.50	$ 760.00
SECOND YEAR—PRICE TREND DOWNWARD				
Initial Inventory:				
FIFO: 600 @ $1.40...........	600	$ 840.00		
AVERAGE: 600 @ 1.327...........			$ 796.50	
LIFO: 200 @ 1.40...........				$ 200.00
400 @ 1.00...........				560.00
Purchases: 800 @ 1.05...........	800	840.00	840.00	840.00
Total Charges to Stores..........	1,400	$1,680.00	$1,636.50	$1,600.00
Issued to Production:				
FIFO: 600 @ $1.40...........		840.00		
150 @ 1.05...........	750	157.50		
AVERAGE: 750 @ 1.169..........			876.75	
LIFO: 750 @ 1.05...........				787.50
Final Inventory at Cost at End of Second Year.............................	650	$ 682.50	$ 759.75	$ 812.50

* Adapted from J. H. March, *Cost Accounting* (New York: McGraw-Hill Book Co.).

ment, then the net income for the first year under the *average cost* method would be $43.50 *less,* and under the Lifo method $80 *less,* than under the Fifo method. However, at the end of the second year much of this effect is offset since the net income for the second year will be $78 *more* under the *average cost* method, and $130 *more* under the Lifo method, than under the Fifo method. Other items in the stores inventory would be similarly affected.

However, it should be noted that in the long-continued price increase, price declines have *not* offset price increases. As a result, the selection of one inventory pricing method as against another has had a *cumulative* effect on reported profits. Firms which chose the elective method (Lifo) early in the last two decades have consistently reported lower profits (and have paid less income tax) than similar firms using Fifo. Even now, it appears doubtful that in the foreseeable future, price declines will cancel out any important part of this tax saving. In anticipation of continued price increases (inflation, perhaps), an increasing number of firms in the manufacturing field have been changing to the Lifo method.

FACTORS TO BE CONSIDERED IN SELECTING A MATERIAL PRICING METHOD

The factors which should be taken into consideration when choosing a materials-used costing method are as follows:

1. Methods most commonly used by the industry in which engaged; this produces a sounder competition and more comparable figures.
2. Frequency of price fluctuations and frequency of material purchases.
3. Relative value of material cost to total cost of products manufactured.
4. Frequency of raw material purchases.
5. Quantities of materials to be purchased at any one time.
6. The effect of the different pricing methods on income taxes.
7. Trend of prices and income taxes over a long period of time.
8. The possibility of using different methods for various classes of items in the inventory.

PHYSICAL INVENTORY AS PART OF MATERIALS COST CONTROL

To account properly for *materials used in manufacturing,* a perpetual or book inventory is desirable. Such an inventory enables management to prepare financial statements without the delays and expense of taking a physical inventory. Such an inventory, however, must be checked against a physical inventory to eliminate the errors that might occur where such a large amount of detailed work is involved. The physical inventory checkup may be *continuous* or *periodic.*

Under the *continuous method* (more recently called the *cycle* or *rotating method*), the counting is spread throughout the fiscal year, following a pattern used in cycle billing. Each inventory card is checked against a physical count at least once a year, sometimes three or four times. This is accomplished by counting part of the inventory each day, each week, or each month, under a systematic plan, thus avoiding the overtime and use of untrained personnel required in the annual inventory. One concern, with a book inventory of four hundred items, checks three items each day by physical count. Thus each year, every item is verified at least twice. Some firms count the *bin stock* at the time of reordering or at the time the purchase requisition is issued. Through the use of this continuous or cycle method of verifying the physical inventory, errors are quickly detected and are not carried on the books until an annual checkup is made. An early detection of errors permits a possible elimination of their cause. *The trend today is away from the annual all-at-one-time physical inventory and toward the continuous count.*

Under the *periodic* method, the entire book inventory is verified at a given date by an actual count of materials on hand. This physical inventory is usually taken near the end of the fiscal period. Some firms even suspend plant operations when this is done.

The following procedure is recommended to facilitate prompt and accurate results in taking a complete physical inventory at a given date:

The date of inventory should be set to conform with the date of financial records. An inventory may take several days; therefore, if the inventory is taken December 20–24 and the book inventory adjusted, the book inventory may then be accepted as correct for a balance sheet dated December 31. When the date of inventory taking has been set, every effort should be made to reduce the stocks as of that date.

A method for taking inventory in a large plant in a *single day* developed over a period of years for a number of large and small companies in the automotive, aircraft, electrical appliance, and farm equipment industries, involves a few simple steps, viz:[2]

1. Draw an easily understood diagram of each floor area in the plant to be inventoried, with sufficient copies so that each counting team will have a copy for the floor for which they are responsible.
2. Divide the manpower available for actual counting into two-man teams and prepare an assignment sheet indicating areas each team is to count. (Each area must be counted twice.)
3. List all classes of items to be counted in each area indicating whether recording is to be in pounds, barrels, dozens, etc.
4. Organize two-man teams to supervise counting in each area or group of areas, with a foreman or accountant to supervise the teams.
5. Prepare the patched (two-part) system tags for recording on a separate tag

---

[2] With permission, the Tag Manufacturers Institute. System devised by G. H. Kline, General Foods Corporation.

the quantity of each different class of materials found in each separate area to be inventoried. These tags must be *prenumbered* in sequence. (See Illustration 8–9.)

Illustration 8–9. Inventory Tag

INVENTORY TAG

O   NO. 701

SECOND COUNT

NO. 701

LOCATION ___ 42-613 ___
QUANTITY ___ 310 ___
UNIT OF COUNT ___ Feet ___
COUNTED BY ___ *ZOZ* ___

FIRST COUNT

NO. 701

LOCATION ___ 42-613 ___
ARTICLE ___ Cable Wire Br. Lg ___
DESCRIPTION ___ Brass Long ___
QUANTITY ___ 310 ___
UNIT OF COUNT ___ Feet ___
COUNTED BY ___ *CJK* ___
DATE ___ 12/23/-- ___

REVERSE SIDE OF INVENTORY TAG

O

DATE	RECEIVED AFTER COUNT	ISSUED AFTER COUNT
12/27	300 ft.	
12/29		220 ft.

6. Each supervisory team is given a sufficient quantity of tags for counting the material in its area. To control these tags, an Inventory Tag Control Schedule should be prepared, viz:

INVENTORY TAG CONTROL SCHEDULE							
Prepared By					Date:		
Building	Inventory Location Number	Assigned Foreman	Assigned Accountant	Prenumbered Inventory Tags Charged Out	Number of Tags Charged Out	Tags Ret'd Spoiled or Voided	Signature of Accountant Receiving Tags
C&C Basement	B-1	Smith	Fletcher	001–075	75		
	B-2	Black	Fletcher	076–150	75		
C&C 1st Floor	PR	Parker	Martin	151–300	150		
C&C Warehouse	W-1	Burns	Hogan	801–900	100		
No. 2 Warehouse	A-1	Mapes	Long	901–1050	150		
Yard (Skids & Drums)		White	Long	1051–1100	50		

7. Prepare and issue lists of counting instructions for the guidance of each supervisory team and counting team.
8. Have a meeting to review all typed and mimeographed instructions.
9. As early as possible on day selected, start the actual count. If tags assigned are insufficient, do not allow one team to borrow from another. Additional tags must be obtained from central control.
10. *First counting team* counts an area and attaches tags to each pile, unit, or bin counted, filling out lower section of tag, and giving it to supervisor. *A second counting team* records its figures on second section of tag, tears this off and turns it in to the supervisor, who matches these with those of the first team.
11. The accountant classifies the inventory from these tags after they have been checked — as stores, work-in-process, or finished goods.
12. The inventory sheets are prepared; the items and quantities are listed on the sheets (Illustration 8–10), priced, and extended by expert calculating ma-

Illustration 8–10. Inventory Sheet

Tag No.	Code No. of Material	Description	Quantity	Unit Price	Extended Total	Checking Total
\multicolumn{7}{l}{Listed By B.J.N. Extended By N.C.B. Sheet No. 14 | 14}						
\multicolumn{7}{l}{Priced By C.O'Brien Checked By N.B.S.}						
701	a-42	Cable Wire	310 ft.	.30		93--
702	C-1	Brass Caps	400	.02		8--
703	c-4	Brass Studs	200	.08		16--
		(other items not listed)				
750	D-3	Hand Screws	600	.01		6--
				Total		543--

chine operators. Since the possibility of mathematical error exists, a second detachable extension column is used. The first calculating machine operator places the extensions in the column at extreme right. These are totaled and detached from inventory sheets. Later, a second operator repeats the extension work and places the results in the second column from the right on the original inventory sheets. A comparison is made of the totals of each set of extension columns, and all errors are corrected.

ADJUSTMENT OF PHYSICAL AND BOOK INVENTORIES

Certain problems of inventory valuation must be considered at the time physical inventorying is being completed.

1. If book inventory records of stores have been maintained, *quantity* differences between physical count and the clerical stock record must be reconciled. Ordinarily, these differences are shortages in stock due to such factors as breakage, spoilage, and evaporation, and to clerical errors in storeskeeping. Management must, at this point, consider the nature of these shortages to discover weaknesses in its internal control of inventories, and even to consider theft as a possible reason for unusually large shortages.

The clerical records must be corrected to agree with the physical count, and the verified differences, usually due to normal loss in handling or to the physical nature of the stores themselves, must be recorded:

Manufacturing Overhead Control (Inventory Shortage) xxxx
   Stores   xxxx
   To account for difference in quantity (units lost × unit price).

When shortages in stores inventories are unusually large, due to some unusual cause, then the difference may be considered a nonmanufacturing loss and charged to some special loss account and finally closed out to the Profit and Loss account.

The balance sheet valuation of *stores* inventories is usually at cost on the assumption that any differences between market price and cost price will ultimately find their way into the cost of goods completed in the normal course of manufacturing.

2. The method of accounting for losses in *finished goods* inventory values should be contrasted here with the accounting for losses in *stores* inventory. Two problems arise in handling losses in finished goods inventory values. One results, as in the case of stores inventories, from differences in quantity between physical count and book inventory records if such records have been maintained. The other arises from the balance sheet valuation of the finished goods inventory if the inventory is reported at the lower of cost or market.

The clerical records for finished goods inventories must be corrected to agree with physical count of stock, and the verified differences, usually shortages, must be recorded:

Inventory Shortages (to Profit and Loss) xxxx
   Finished Goods   xxxx
   To record losses due to shortages in stock.

It would be a tedious and expensive task to adjust finished goods inventory records, if they exist, to the lower of cost or market, as each inventory card might possibly call for adjustment. Such a procedure is not the practical solution. To adjust to the lower of cost or market price and so reconcile the inventory ledger cards and the physical inventory at cost with the balance sheet figure, the following journal entry would be recorded:

Loss Due to Fluctuation in Inventory Value (to Profit and Loss).......xxxx
    Allowance for Decline in Inventory Values (valuation allowance)...   xxxx

The allowance would be deducted from the inventory figure at cost to report the inventory at the lower figure.

ACCOUNTING FOR SCRAP MATERIAL

Scrap is salable material resulting from the primary manufacturing operations. If scrap has little value, no entry is usually made for the quantity or value until it is sold. At that time Cash or Accounts Receivable is debited and the income account, Sale of Scrap, is credited. If the value and quantity are relatively important and the scrap is to be sold, an inventory card may be set up showing the quantity and the market value. Because of the difficulty of valuation and perhaps the delay in selling the material, scrap is usually recorded as to quantity only. When the scrap material is received in the storeroom, a scrap report similar to the receiving report is made out. From this report an entry is made on the book inventory card for the scrap.

There are three possible methods of accounting for scrap sold:

1. Credit the sales prices to the material cost of the job on which scrap originated.
2. Credit the sales price to Manufacturing Overhead Control.
3. Credit the sales price as miscellaneous income.

The most accurate and ideal method is to credit the material cost of the job on which the scrap originated. But in most instances this method is not practical because the difficulty of segregating the amount of scrap occurring on the various jobs and the difficulty of valuation are too great. The cost of segregating and valuing the scrap may be greater than the amount realized from its sale.

The second most desirable method is to treat the value of the scrap as a credit to manufacturing overhead. This method reduces the cost of all the jobs passing through the department. When the scrap is placed in the storeroom, an entry is made debiting Scrap Material and crediting Manufacturing Overhead Control with the expected sales value. This procedure may raise the question of the correct price to use in recording the scrap when it is placed in the storeroom. If the market price does not fluctuate very much, the sales or market price of scrap is used when recording the scrap stored. When this scrap is sold, the journal entry would be:

Cash or Accounts Receivable xxxx
    Scrap (or Stores Control if inventoried)   xxxx
    To record the sale of scrap.

If there is no fixed price for the scrap, some firms merely record the quantity on an inventory card, or they make no entry at all until the scrap is sold. If the practice of reducing the manufacturing overhead costs by the amount received for scrap is used, the entry made at the time of the sale would be:

Cash or Accounts Receivable xxxx
    Manufacturing Overhead (Sale of Scrap)..................................   xxxx

However, because the scrap may be sold in a period different from that in which it was created and because scrap has a relatively low sales value, many concerns reduce their accounting for scrap to a minimum by making only a quantity record of the scrap while it is being collected, or they make no entry at all. When the scrap is sold, the entry for the sale of scrap would be:

Cash or Accounts Receivable xxxx
    Sale of Scrap   xxxx

The Sale of Scrap account is then treated as other income on the income statement.

Scrap is not always sold. For example, scrap from the manufacture of tin and zinc is sent to the storeroom to be reissued and used on other jobs. Although referred to as *scrap,* such materials actually represent a return to the storeroom of excess materials issued and should be treated as such on the inventory records. If the manufacturing processes result in genuine scrap, a new materials account can be opened for scrap and some reasonable value assigned to it; then, when it is used in manufacturing, the job may be properly charged with the cost of the scrap.

Parts scrapped while in the process of manufacture, or finished parts scrapped during assembling operations because subsequent use results in their being defective, may be included as scrap; but a more accurate cost accounting treats them as spoiled or defective material, discussed in the following section.

NATURE OF SPOILED AND DEFECTIVE WORK

One problem facing many manufacturing concerns today is that of quality control. This problem involves not only manufacturing and production control through more effective supervision but also control through forms and reports on spoiled and defective work. Many manufacturers have found it to be more profitable to spend more on *Inspection Control* before the product leaves the plant than to pay for the correction of quality defects after the product has been sold.

ACCOUNTING FOR SPOILED AND DEFECTIVE MATERIALS

A distinction is sometimes made between *spoiled* and *defective* materials. The distinction is based on the condition of the goods as it leaves the manufacturing process. *Spoiled* materials are goods which in the process of manufacture have developed some imperfection which cannot economically be corrected, and thus the goods must be sold as seconds. *Defective* materials are goods which in the process of manufacturing have developed some imperfection but which, unlike spoiled materials, can by the expenditure of additional labor, and possibly materials, be made into perfect finished articles.

The cost of spoiled goods may be handled by either of two methods: (1) the loss due to spoilage *may be charged to the production order on which the spoilage occurred, or* (2) *the spoilage loss may be charged to manufacturing overhead control and thus spread over the cost of all jobs.* If a job is produced on special order—that is, the specifications are distinct and the spoilage is clearly traceable to the work done on that order—the loss resulting from spoiled goods should be treated as a part of the cost of the job on which it occurred. If, however, the manufacturing is being done on a mass-production basis and, owing to the nature of the manufacturing processes, spoilage is the general rule though irregular in amount on the various orders, the loss arising from the spoiled goods should be treated as a *manufacturing overhead* cost and the total prorated over all the jobs by means of the manufacturing overhead rate. In either case the spoiled goods are recorded on the books at the expected sales price.

The manufacture of shirts may be used to illustrate these methods of handling the loss on spoiled goods. A job order calling for 1,200 shirts was sent through the factory. The cost elements per shirt were:

```
Materials ................................................................32¢
Labor ...................................................................80
Predetermined manufacturing overhead ...........................28
```

When the shirts were manufactured, it was found that 100 were spoiled and would have to be sold as seconds at a price of 50 cents each.

Under the first method, where the loss is charged to the specific job, the entries are as follows:

```
Work-in-Process ..................................................1,680
    Stores ...........................................................        384
    Payroll ..........................................................        960
    Applied Manufacturing Overhead .......................        336
    To record cost of work put into process.

Spoiled Goods Inventory .......................................   50
    Work-in-Process .............................................         50
    To record the sales value of work spoiled in process.

Finished Goods ...................................................1,630
    Work-in-Process .............................................      1,630
    To record the cost of shirts finished.
```

As a result of these entries, the total cost of manufacturing 1,100 good shirts is $1,630, at a unit price of $1.482.

When the second method is used, the entries for handling the spoilage losses are as follows:

```
Work-in-Process ...................................................................1,680
    Stores ...........................................................................        384
    Payroll...........................................................................        960
    Applied Manufacturing Overhead ........................................        336
    To record the cost of the work put into process.

Spoiled Goods Inventory .........................................        50
Manufacturing Overhead Control (Loss on Spoiled Work) .............        90
    Work-in-Process ..................................................................        140
    To set up the inventory of spoiled goods and to charge the loss
    to the Manufacturing Overhead Control.

Finished Goods......................................................................1,540
    Work-in-Process ..................................................................        1,540
    To record the cost of shirts completed.
```

As a result of these entries, the total cost of manufacturing 1,100 shirts is $1,540 at a unit cost of $1.40. A comparison of the two unit costs shows that under the first method there is a loading of $0.082 per shirt because of the loss due to the spoiled goods. It should be noted that if the spoilage on this order is representative of the average loss incurred from this cause, then the predetermined manufacturing overhead rate must be higher under the second method so that $0.082 additional will be allocated to the cost of each shirt. The *total cost* of manufacturing the shirts will not be affected by the choice of a method of allocating the indirect cost arising from the spoilage.

The rules governing the accounting for *defective work* are similar to those relating to *spoiled goods*. If the job is a special order, the additional costs caused by defective work should be charged to that job. If defective work occurs on the regular manufacturing orders, the additional costs of perfecting the goods should be set up as a part of the manufacturing overhead. It should be noted that no asset account similar to Spoiled Goods is set up. Since the defective work is subsequently perfected, the cost of making the changes is either charged to Work-in-Process or set up in an account, Loss on Defective Work, a manufacturing overhead account.

The manufacture of hand saws is given as an illustration of the entries necessary to account for defective material. One hundred dozen were put into process on a certain job order. The costs for each dozen were: materials, $12.50; labor, $26; and manufacturing overhead, $19.50. Upon the completion of the order it was found that 10 dozen were defective and had to be returned for reprocessing, which required additional labor and overhead. No additional materials were necessary. The additional labor cost was $4, and the manufacturing overhead, $3 per dozen.

Under the first method, where the additional cost *is to be charged directly to the job,* the entries are:

```
Work-in-Process ..................................................................5,800
    Stores .........................................................................    1,250
    Payroll ........................................................................    2,600
    Applied Manufacturing Overhead ......................................    1,950
    To charge Work-in-Process for materials, labor, and overhead used.

Work-in-Process .................................................................    70
    Payroll ........................................................................        40
    Applied Manufacturing Overhead ......................................        30
    To record additional labor and overhead necessary to correct
    defective work.

Finished Goods ..................................................................5,870
    Work-in-Process ...........................................................        5,870
    To record the finished goods transferred from Work-in-Process.
```

The foregoing entries result in the per dozen cost of $58.70.

Under the second method *the loss due to defective work is charged to the manufacturing overhead account* and prorated over all the jobs worked on during the period. The entries for this method would be:

```
Work-in-Process .................................................................5,800
    Stores .........................................................................    1,250
    Payroll ........................................................................    2,600
    Applied Manufacturing Overhead ......................................    1,950
    To charge Work-in-Process for the materials, labor, and overhead
    used.

Manufacturing Overhead Control (Loss on Defective Work) ...........    70
    Payroll ........................................................................        40
    Applied Manufacturing Overhead ......................................        30
    To charge labor and overhead due to defective work.

Finished Goods ..................................................................5,800
    Work-in-Process ...........................................................        5,800
    To record the finished goods transferred from Work-in-Process.
```

The second method results in a unit cost of $58. Again it should be noted that under the second method the predetermined manufacturing overhead rate must have included an estimated amount for expected losses due to defective work.

CONTROLLING SCRAP AND DEFECTIVE WORK

To control scrap and defective work, many of the larger manufacturing concerns use daily or weekly defective material reports. These will show the order numbers on which the spoiled work occurred, the reason for its occurrence, why material was rejected as defective, and the cost of correcting the defects. The preparation of such reports requires time and expense and will be justified only if over a period of time the making of these reports results in the elimination of avoidable causes and expense. Illustration 8–11 shows one type of defective work report that can be used to study and control spoilage.

Illustration 8–11. Spoilage Report

						SALVAGE	
Machine Operator	Total Units Produced	Spoiled Work	Per Cent of Spoilage	Unit Cost of Spoilage	Total Cost of Spoilage	Labor Penalty 10%	Scrap Value 20¢ Each

WEEKLY REPORT ON SPOILAGE

Stitching Department No. 23   Foreman C. E. Bowman

Week Ending March 30, 19—

Machine Operator	Total Units Produced	Spoiled Work	Per Cent of Spoilage	Unit Cost of Spoilage	Total Cost of Spoilage	Labor Penalty 10%	Scrap Value 20¢ Each
401	250	13	5.2	$.36	$ 4.68	$ .46	$ 2.60
402	258	15	5.8	.36	5.40	.54	3.00
403	262	15	5.7	.36	5.40	.54	3.00
404	255	15	5.9	.36	5.40	.54	3.00
405	270	18	6.7	.36	6.48	.64	3.60
406	265	17	6.4	.36	6.12	.61	3.40
407	267	15	5.6	.36	5.40	.54	3.00
408	264	12	4.5	.36	4.32	.43	2.40
409	270	15	5.6	.36	5.40	.54	3.00
410	280	30	10.7	.36	10.80	1.08	6.00
Total	2641	165	6.2		$59.40	$5.92	$33.00

DEBATABLE MATERIAL COSTS

Certain costs that may, under given circumstances, be proper additions to the cost of inventory, receive various treatments in practice as shown in the following discussion.

Packaging Costs. If the goods are packaged before being sent to the finished goods warehouse, the cost of packaging is considered part of the cost. If they are packaged just before shipment, the cost is treated as a selling and shipping expense, not part of the inventory. But the acceptance of this rule is by no means uniform. In a survey made by the Committee of Research of the N.A.A., it was found that approximately one half of the firms packaging goods at time of shipment treated this packaging cost as part of the manufacturing costs and included it in the inventories.

Storage Costs. About one half of the firms surveyed in the N.A.A. study considered the storing of goods awaiting sale *at the factory* as a manufacturing cost and included it in the inventory of finished goods. The other half of the firms felt that the manufacturing operations were completed when the goods were placed in the warehouse and that, therefore, warehouse or storage costs were part of the selling expenses.

Administrative Salaries.   In some cases, salaries of corporate officers above the rank of factory superintendent have been included in the cost of inventories. Salaries of those officers primarily concerned with the manufacturing operations are often included as part of the manufacturing costs applicable to inventories. In a few instances, the salaries of top officials, such as president down to the controller, are prorated between the manufacturing and financial operating costs of the firm, the former thus becoming part of the inventory.

"Direct Costing."   In recent years a number of companies have been experimenting with the idea of including in manufacturing cost only direct labor and direct material and those indirect manufacturing costs which fluctuate with production, excluding all fixed costs. There have been a number of instances in which firms have considered as the cost of goods manufactured, and hence the finished goods inventory, only material and labor costs. Direct costing is discussed in detail in Chapter 20.

COST REDUCTION THROUGH PHYSICAL DISTRIBUTION CONTROL OF INVENTORIES[3]

Inventory costs of both raw materials and finished goods are running as high as 30 cents on the dollar. This refers to the cost in capital investment to store the inventory and to protect it. Offsetting this cost is the loss due to not having enough inventory, resulting in inefficient production methods and in the case of finished goods of loss in sales and damage to the firm's competitive standing.

Inventory costs and *transportation* costs are essentially *time* costs. Both of these are closely related to each other. To reduce inventory costs, it is usually necessary to increase transportation costs. Therefore, these two costs should be correlated—time can be reduced by shortening the *transportation distance.* Inventory costs can be reduced by *location*—the costs of maintenance of goods in *procurement* and/or *distribution.* Among the location cost factors are warehousing, protective packaging, plant and warehouse locations, requirements forecasting, and order processing.

Management may be able to reduce costs by the so-called "trade-off policy"—offsetting higher costs in one area by greatly reduced costs in another area such as *production planning*—large lot buying, and low-cost transportation to prevent production downtime, yet owning and ware-

---

[3] Adapted from data from United Airlines.

housing costs may be greater than the savings of large lot buying versus small lot buying more frequently delivered by airfreight. It is the *total costs* that counts.

A common and costly mistake is often made in charging the distribution costs—costs of packing, shipping room activities, and warehousing—to costs of production. Even the question of state and local personal property taxes must be considered. Closing down warehouses and resorting to direct-to-customer shipments and using higher transportation costs may result in cost reduction, provided *total costs* are studied.

The use of electronic computer techniques in modern business under a highly centralized department of purchasing and distribution might be management's answer to this cost reduction through inventory control—both of raw materials as well as finished goods, with wide-open communication among middle management personnel. An electronic computer program can be written to test all possible combinations of procurement and distribution to provide the best answer to these management problems affecting inventories.

MANAGERIAL CONTROL OF INVENTORIES

In many large industrial concerns, the materials inventories require an investment of millions of dollars. The first requisite for effective managerial control is to have this work placed under an executive who has the authority and responsibility for the investment in inventories, the use of the materials, spoilage reports, transportation and storage costs, in addition to the usual clerical and accounting records.

The primary purpose of inventory control is to maintain a *minimum of investment in inventory, consistent with smoothly operating production schedules.* First, in managerial control is the *materials budget* which will indicate *when* the materials should be purchased and *how much.* The concentration of the effort in this budget should be placed on the more important materials—those purchased in quantities sufficiently large to make them account for an important part of the cost of goods manufactured. As part of this materials control, it might be wise to standardize the kinds and size of materials or parts to be purchased. A second phase of managerial control is the *systematic procedure* to be followed in purchasing, receiving, storing, issuing, and pricing the materials to be used. A by-product of this is an effective system of internal control to reduce the possibility of losses by theft. The proper coordination of the budget and the accounting procedure will result in a minimum investment in inventories, reduction in obsolete stock, and losses from fraud or theft.

One concern accomplishes part of this control by having a simple report made for each four-week period showing the balances in various

Nature of Transaction	Forms Used	Book of Original Entry	Source of Entry	Journal Form of Entry
Ordering materials	1. Purchase requisition 2. Purchase order			
Receiving materials	1. Receiving report 2. Purchase order 3. Creditor's invoice	Voucher register	Creditor's invoice	Dr. Stores Cr. Accounts Payable
Issuing direct materials	1. Material requisition 2. Summary of stores requisitions	General journal	Summary of stores requisitions	Dr. Work-in-Process—Materials Cr. Stores
Issuing indirect materials	1. Material requisition 2. Summary of stores requisitions	General journal	Summary of stores requisitions	Dr. Manufacturing Overhead (Indirect Materials) Cr. Stores
Payment of invoice	1. Voucher check 2. Invoice	Check register	Vouchered invoice	Dr. Accounts Payable Cr. Cash
Direct materials returned to stores	1. Returned material report 2. Summary of returned materials	General journal	Summary of returned materials	Dr. Stores Cr. Work-in-Process—Materials
Indirect materials returned to stores	1. Returned material report 2. Summary of returned materials	General journal	Summary of returned materials	Dr. Stores Cr. Manufacturing Overhead (Indirect Materials)
Materials returned to vendor	1. Returned shipping report	General journal or voucher register	Returned shipping report	Dr. Accounts Payable Cr. Stores
Inventory adjustment—physical less than book	1. Stores inventory report	General journal	Stores inventory department memo	Dr. Manufacturing Overhead (Inventory Adjustment) Cr. Stores
Inventory adjustment—physical more than book	1. Stores inventory report	General journal	Stores inventory department memo	Dr. Stores Cr. Manufacturing Overhead (Inventory Adjustment)
Cost of finished parts manufactured	1. Cost memo 2. Summary of cost of finished product	General journal	Summary of cost of finished product	Dr. Finished Parts—Stores Cr. Work-in-Process—Materials Cr. Work-in-Process—Labor Cr. Work-in-Process—Manufacturing Overhead
Issuing finished parts for further use in production	1. Material requisition 2. Summary of finished parts requisitioned	General journal	Summary of material requisitions	Dr. Work-in-Process—Materials Cr. Finished Parts—Stores
Placing scrap material in storeroom	1. Scrap report 2. Summary of returned materials	None	Summary of returned materials	
Spoiled work (material cost)	1. Spoiled material report 2. Summary of spoiled work	General journal	Summary of spoiled work	Dr. Stores (scrap value) Dr. Manufacturing Overhead (Loss on Spoiled Work) Cr. Work-in-Process—Materials (original cost)

* Actual overhead work sheet.
† Subsidiary overhead ledger account.

Illustration 8–12 (Continued)

Subsidiary Accounting Record (Perpetual Inventory Control)	Entry on Subsidiary Account Record	Cost Record or Summary Form Used*	Entry on Cost Record or Cost Summary†	Source of Cost Entry
Stores ledger card	Memo in ordered section			
Stores ledger card	In Received section cross out memo in Ordered section			
Stores ledger card	Issued section	Job order sheet	Material section of job sheet	Summary of stores requisitions
Stores ledger card	Issued section	Standing order or overhead work sheet	Standing order for indirect material or subsidiary overhead ledger account	Summary of stores requisitions
Stores ledger card	Received section or in RED in Issued section	Job order sheet	Entry in RED in Material section of job sheet	Summary of returned materials
Stores ledger card	Received section or in RED in Issued section	Standing order or overhead work sheet	In RED standing order for indirect material or subsidiary overhead ledger account	Summary of returned materials
Stores ledger card	Issued section or in RED in Received section			
Stores ledger card	Issued section	Standing order or overhead work sheet	Standing order for inventory adjustment or subsidiary overhead ledger account	Stores inventory dep't. memo
Stores ledger card	Received section	Standing order or overhead work sheet	In RED, standing order for inventory adjustment or subsidiary overhead ledger account	Stores inventory dep't. memo
Stores ledger card— finished parts stores	Received section	Job order sheet	Summarize finished job orders	
Finished parts stores— stores ledger card	Issued section	Job order sheet	Material section of job sheet	Summary of material requisitions
Stores ledger card	Received section quantity only	Job order sheet	In RED—Material section of job sheet	Summary of returned materials
Stores ledger card	Received section	Job order sheet, standing order or overhead work sheet	1. Standing order for loss on spoiled work or subsidiary overhead ledger account— loss on spoiled work 2. In RED, Material section	Spoiled work report

inventory accounts, broken down into broad classes of products as to stores, work-in-process, processed parts, and finished goods. From this report, the upward or downward trend in inventories can be studied from period to period.

Another concern prepares annually an inventory showing in three groups the value of the material on hand: Group A, material of which there is a one-year supply on hand—this is the active material; Group B, material of which there is a two-year supply on hand—this is a slow-moving material; and Group C, material of which there is stock on hand for a period beyond two years—this is considered obsolete stock. Group C is written off the books completely, and for Group B an estimated loss allowance is set up. If any Group C material is later sold, it is credited directly to Miscellaneous Income. The loss for Group B is charged against current *Profit and Loss*. This policy assumes, of course, that the long-term supply indicates obsolescence and deterioration.

Many concerns use periodic spot checking on the quantities and the condition of the inventories on hand.

CURRENT TRENDS IN INVENTORY PRICING METHODS

Periodically the American Institute of Certified Public Accountants makes a study of the current trends in accounting practices. Included in this are certain interesting figures relating to inventory pricing methods. In their 1964 study, the following figures were of interest:

In pricing finished goods inventory, the most popular method was lower of "cost or market."

In costing production, no doubt due to rising inflationary costs, out of a total of about 640 firms, 190, approximately 30 percent of the firms, were using last-in, first-out method; 160, or approximately 25 percent, were using average costing methods; and approximately 188, or almost 30 percent, were using first-in, first-out method. The remaining firms were using such methods as standard costs (32), actual costs (14), and production costs (10).

Peculiar circumstances of a particular firm probably influenced the use of the methods. It is surprising, however, that so many still used the first-in, first-out method.

TABULATED SUMMARY OF THE ACCOUNTING
FOR MATERIAL COSTS

Illustration 8–12 (pages 242–43) gives a complete summary and analysis of materials accounting under a cost system.

QUESTIONS FOR REVIEW

1. Why is it desirable to establish maximum and minimum quantities for the various inventory items used in manufacturing operations? How are these determined?

2. Modern electronic computers have made the control of the maximum and minimum quantities more efficient. More firms are using this method. Explain how this is done.

3. Materials used during the week were as follows:

Used in production	$15,000
Used as shipping supplies	3,000
Used as factory maintenance	1,000
Used in building a new machine to be used in the factory	8,000

Prepare journal entries to record these, assuming the use of a Stores account and general office and factory office journals.

4. Punched card accounting procedures have facilitated the maintenance of a perpetual or book inventory. Explain how this is done.

5. The selection of the pricing methods of the various inventories of a manufacturing concern affects the income statements of a firm. What effect will the Fifo, Lifo, and the average methods have on the work-in-process, finished goods, cost of sales, and the income tax?

6. There are usually two causes of variations between the book and the physical inventories. What are these? How are the variations recorded on the accounting records? Explain.

7. The accepted accounting theory recommends that freight-in and discount on purchases be treated as adjustments of the materials purchased. Why then do most firms treat these items differently when related to materials purchased to be used in manufacturing?

8. Accounting for spoiled and defective work in manufacturing has two different applications depending on the nature of the loss or spoilage. What are these? What reasoning underlies the use of each method?

9. A requisition journal has very limited use in modern manufacturing operations. Under what conditions do you feel such a journal could be used?

10. Distinguish between a *material requisition* and a *bill of materials*. Under what conditions should each be used?

PROBLEMS—GROUP A

Problem 8-1. Purpose: *Comparative Income Results Using Different Inventory Pricing Methods*

The Harlton Manufacturing Company manufactures a single product. During the year ended December 31, 19—, 5,000 units were started into production, 4,800 were completed, and 4,500 were sold at a price of $20 each. Work-in-process had all the materials and one half of the labor and overhead applied.

Conversion costs for the year were $14,700. Selling and administrative expenses totaled $13,500.

Federal income taxes are to be considered in determining the net income after taxes at the following rates: $27\frac{1}{2}$ percent on the first $25,000; and 52 percent on all amounts over $25,000.

The raw materials inventory records showed the following:

> Purchases:
> January 2.................... 600 units at $2.20
> March 10....................2,000 units at $2.00
> June 15 ....3,000 units at $2.50
> October 10..................2,500 units at $3.00
> Materials used:
> April 15...................... 400 units
> August 10 ....3,000 units
> November 5...............1,600 units

Required:

a) Prepare comparative income statements when each of the following inventory pricing methods are used: Fifo, Lifo, and average methods.

b) Which method would you prefer? Why?

Problem 8–2. Purpose: *Comparative Inventory Pricing Methods, Using Three-Section Inventory Cards; Journal Entries*

The Harmon-Wilson Company is making a study of the comparative inventory pricing methods. The following transactions represent the transactions of its main raw material for the month of June:

June 1   Balance on hand, 400 lbs. at $2.

      6   Issued 150 lbs. for Production Order No. 701, Requisition No. 150.

      8   Received 400 lbs. on Purchase Order No. 400; price, $2.40.

      9   Issued 280 lbs. for Production Order No. 750, Requisition No. 160.

    11   Received 350 lbs. Purchase Order No. 420; price, $2.60.

    16   Returned 100 lbs. to vendor on Purchase Order No. 400, defective.

    19   Issued 250 lbs. for Production Order No. 730, Requisition No. 165.

    21   Received in storeroom as excess, 60 lbs., issued on Requisition No. 160.

    24   Issued 60 lbs. for Production Order No. 740, Requisition No. 168.

    29   Received 400 lbs. on Purchase Order No. 430 at $2.80.

    29   Returned to vendor, 60 lbs. received on Purchase Order No. 420.

    30   Received in storeroom as excess, 10 lbs. issued for Production Order No. 740.

    30   Received 220 lbs. on Purchase Order No. 436 at $2.30.

    30   Issued for Production Order No. 720, 140 lbs., Requisition No. 172.

Required:

a) Prepare three separate stores ledger cards with sections for Received, Issued, and Balance, using respectively, the Lifo, Fifo, and Moving-Average pricing methods. The heading for these cards should be:

| MATERIAL: | RUMIN METAL | CARD No.: | B-101 | LOCATION: | B-1-35 |
| MAXIMUM: | 1,200 lbs. | MINIMUM: | 200 pounds | | |

b) Entries in journal form, using the Fifo pricing method, to summarize the materials entries for the month.

c) A comparative statement of the final inventory balances under each of these methods.

d) A statement of which method you would recommend for pricing.

Problem 8–3.   Purpose: *Journal Entries and Procedures for Spoiled Work*

The Hibbard Shirt Company produces fine quality permanent press shirts. In the manufacturing process, there are from time to time, a number of rejects which are sold as seconds.

During the month of February, the firm produced on job lot orders for stock and for special customers, 48,000 shirts. The manufacturing costs for the month were:

Materials, trimmings, etc.................................$26,400
Direct labor costs... 48,000
Manufacturing overhead applied........................ 24,000

During this month, 480 shirts had to be rejected and sold as seconds for $1.50 each. The good shirts sold for $52.80 a dozen, less 10%.

Sales, in addition to the seconds, were 2,500 dozen.

The firm uses a factory journal for recording its cost accounting information. The following summarize the transactions for the month:

1. Materials purchased, $34,500.
2. Actual manufacturing overhead incurred, $26,420.
3. The spoiled shirts were sold for cash.

Required:

Prepare entries in journal form in the general office and factory office books to record the foregoing information under the following conditions:

a) When the loss on spoiled work is customary and charged to the production of the good shirts.

b) When the loss is not customary, the loss on spoiled work is treated as a manufacturing overhead cost.

Problem 8–4.   Purpose: *Review of Journal Entries for Materials Cost Control*

The Hourty Company maintains its cost accounting in a separate factory journal and ledger. The following transactions summarize the cost transactions for the material accounts for the month of March, 19—:

1. Materials purchased and placed in the storeroom, $32,000.
2. Freight paid on purchases, $360. A separate Freight-In account is used.

3. Materials requisitioned total $22,400, of which $18,000 were for direct; $2,100, factory supplies; and balance for packing and shipping.
4. Direct materials returned from factory to the storeroom, $680.
5. Materials returned to the vendors cost $1,800.
6. Estimated sales value of scrap placed in storeroom, $450.
7. Spoiled work received in the storeroom had a sales value of $100. The manufacturing cost of this was $215. It is not customary to have spoiled work in this firm.
8. Scrap inventory in 6 was sold for $350.
9. Spoiled work was sold for $135.
10. Stores inventory, March 31, was $5,300; its market value was $4,800.
11. Finished goods inventory March 31 was $18,400; market value, $15,000.
12. A reserve for possible future loss on finished goods inventory was set up on the books; amount, $3,000.

Required:

Using the three following vertical columnar headings, prepare entries in journal form for the above transactions: Transaction No., General Office Journal Entry, and Factory Office Journal Entry.

Problem 8–5. Purpose: *Journal Entries Affecting Materials Cost Control; No Factory Journal Is Used*

The following list of transactions were incurred by the Haddon Manufacturing Company for the month of April, 19—:

1. Materials purchased and placed in the stock room cost $7,000, of which $5,000 was for direct material, $1,500 for factory supplies, and the balance for packing and shipping supplies. Freight-in was $60, all applicable to the direct materials.
2. Material requisitions totaled $4,850, of which $800 was for indirect material, $150 for packing and shipping supplies.
3. Materials returned to the storeroom was $180, as excess on Job. No. 168.
4. Materials issued, costing $260, was charged to Job No. 124 and should have been charged to Job No. 142.
5. Materials charged to Job No. 140 costing $124 was used in repairing the factory roof.
6. Indirect materials returned to the storeroom as being in excess, $45.
7. Scrap materials sent to the storeroom, valued at selling prices:

> From direct materials.....................$160
> From indirect materials.................   30

8. Spoiled work received in the stock room: original cost, $100; salable value, $35. Spoiled work is customary.
9. Scrap material sold for $150. (See item 7.)
10. Finished goods returned by customers: selling price, $840; cost, $560.
11. Raw materials inventory book record showed 8,240 units at $2 each. Actual count showed 8,500 units.
12. Spoiled work was sold for $50 cash. (See item 8.)

Required:

Using only a general office set of books (no factory journal), prepare entries in journal form to record the above transactions.

PROBLEMS—GROUP B

Problem 8–6.   Purpose: *Comparison of Inventory Pricing Methods*

The Warwick Manufacturing Company started business in January 1, 1970. At the end of 1972, it wishes to make a study of the effect that the various inventory pricing methods would have had on its net income for the three years.

The figures taken from the books of the firm indicated the following:

INVENTORY

	Lifo Cost	Fifo Cost	Market	Lower of Cost or Market
December 31, 1970..................	$10,500	$10,000	$ 9,800	$ 9,000
December 31, 1971..................	9,500	9,000	8,600	8,400
December 31, 1972..................	10,400	11,000	11,800	10,000

Required:

a) On the basis of these figures, which inventory pricing method would show the highest net income for 1970?

b) Which inventory pricing method would show the highest net income for 1971?

c) Which inventory pricing method would show the lowest net income for the three years combined?

d) For the year 1971, how much higher or lower would profits be on the Fifo basis than on the *lower of cost* or *market?*

e) On the basis of the information given, what was the movement of prices for the items in the inventory in 1970 and 1972?

Problem 8–7.   Purpose: *Comparative Materials Cost Accounting Methods*

The Warren Manufacturing Company is making a comparative study of the various methods of accounting for the auxiliary material costs such as purchase discounts, freight and transportation on purchases, and material handling costs. Budgeted material costs at list price are $12,000.

The accountant has suggested two possible procedures:

1. Treat purchase discounts as other income; add 10 percent to the cost of materials for handling and storage costs; and add the transportation costs to the cost of materials purchased; or—

2. Deduct the purchase discounts, whether taken or not, as a reduction in the cost of materials; and treat transportation costs as part of manufacturing overhead. All materials handling costs, estimated at 8 percent of the cost of the materials, are included in the manufacturing overhead.

The following are some of the transactions for this firm used in making the comparative study:

1. Materials purchased, terms 3/10, n/60, $12,000. Freight-in, $840.
2. Materials used totaled $10,000 at list price. Used on Job No. 21, $4,000; Job No. 28, $5,000; and Job No. 30, $1,000.
3. Direct labor costs were Job No. 21, $7,000; Job No. 28, $6,000; and Job No. 30, $4,800.
4. Manufacturing overhead is applied on the basis of direct material costs. The budgeted manufacturing overhead, basis without adjustment for freight-in and handling costs, is for this production $8,000.
5. All jobs were completed and sold at cost plus 40 percent.
6. Selling and administrative expenses were 15 percent of the cost to manufacture.

Required:

On the basis of the information given, you are asked to—

a) Compute and show in parallel columns the cost of manufacturing each job under the two methods of accounting.
b) Compute the net profit on each job.
c) Comment on the accounting procedures involved.

Problem 8–8.   Purpose: *Comparative Study of the Various Inventory Pricing Methods*

The Wolpar Manufacturing Company had the following transactions relating to the Material account No. 4502:

April 1   Balance: 600 units; cost, $1,200.
       3   Purchase Invoice No. 831, 350 units, $735.
       7   Requisition No. 104, 300 units.
      15   Purchase Invoice No. 482; 260 units, $572.
      18   Requisition No. 116, 200 units.
      22   Requisition No. 120, 180 units.
      26   Purchase Order No. 763, 200 units, $400.
      30   Requisition No. 131, 240 units.

Required:

a) Prepare three separate materials inventory ledger cards showing date, invoice number, requisition number, unit cost, total, for the receipts, issues, and balance using the following pricing methods:
    1. Fifo costing.
    2. Lifo costing.
    3. Moving average.
b) Compute the inventory balance under each method and indicate the effect on the net income for the firm.
c) Prepare journal entries to *summarize* the above transactions.

Problem 8–9.   Purpose: *Accounting Problems for Spoiled Goods*

The Worumb Manufacturing Company manufactures a single product in which from time to time there is a certain amount of spoilage.

The unit costs of manufacturing each item are:

$$
\begin{array}{lr}
\text{Materials}\dots\dots\dots\dots\dots\dots\dots\dots\dots\dots\dots\dots\dots\dots\dots & \$12 \\
\text{Direct labor}\dots\dots\dots\dots\dots\dots\dots\dots\dots\dots\dots\dots\dots & 10 \\
\text{Manufacturing overhead}\dots\dots\dots\dots\dots\dots\dots\dots & \underline{8} \\
& \$30
\end{array}
$$

The following situations are presented to you for accounting consideration when 300 units were spoiled out of a production of 3,300.

1. Spoilage is customary and is therefore charged to the job in which it occurred. Sales price of spoiled units, $6.
2. Spoilage was due to accidental breakdown of certain machines. This is not customary. The loss is chargeable to manufacturing overhead. Sales price of units is $4.50 each.
3. Spoilage was considered defective but could be corrected. The cost of the correction was material, per unit, $2; direct labor, $4; and manufacturing overhead, $3.20. It was customary to have some defective work on each job.

Required:

a) Prepare journal entries to record each of the above. It is assumed that a factory journal is used.
b) From a managerial viewpoint, regardless of the cause of the spoilage, which method, from an income tax angle, do you consider the most conservative accounting practice?

chapter **9**

Labor Cost Control

MANAGERIAL ASPECTS OF LABOR COST CONTROL

A manufacturer is engaged primarily in converting raw materials into a finished salable product. One major element in this conversion process is the labor cost. Labor costs are variable costs and therefore must be constantly studied and reduced. There are two groups of factory workers: *productive or direct labor* and *nonproductive or indirect labor*. *Direct labor* refers to that used in producing the article in such a manner that it can be identified economically with a specific job or productive department, whereas *indirect labor costs* are all other auxiliary factory labor costs not directly restricted to a particular job. Among the latter are superintendence, repairmen, and factory clerical workers. The managerial control of factory labor costs is achieved most effectively through:

1. Production planning.
2. Use of labor standards.
3. Use of labor budget.
4. Use of labor performance reports.
5. Study of the probable effectiveness of wage incentive systems.
6. Reduction in cost of labor cost accounting.

Production planning and cost accounting are closely related. Without production planning, cost accounting becomes merely a clerical compilation of useless figures. Without a sound cost accounting system, production planning loses most of its managerial control effectiveness.

There are three phases of production planning: *product engineering; process engineering;* and *planning, scheduling, and routing.*

Product engineering has as its function the creation of new products or the improvement in the design or construction of current products. The purpose of product engineering is to increase the sales potential of the products either by a more attractive design, a more substantial product

252

at the same price, or the same product at a lower price. This increase in sales may be achieved by reducing the cost of an article by using cheaper material, or less material, or redesigning the product so that less labor will be required in its production. Product engineering for many concerns is a continuous business function. However, it may precede, parallel, or follow the work of the cost accounting department. While it is essentially an engineering function, product engineering measures the effectiveness of its work through the figures compiled by the cost accounting department.

Process engineering is closely associated with product engineering and cost accounting in aiding management to create a finished product at the lowest possible cost. Process engineering refers to the setting up of the proper machines, dies, and flow of work so that the minimum of labor will be required in the manufacture of a high-quality product. In most instances, it results in simplifying the manufacturing operations through the use of more automatic machinery and tools. Naturally, the processes of manufacturing cannot be organized until the product has been properly designed or engineered. Then the cost accounting department measures the effectiveness of the work through the presentation of the unit costs. There are many illustrations of how product engineering and process engineering have worked together to reduce the cost of labor required. For example, designing all-steel automobile bodies eliminated the labor operations of sewing or attaching waterproof tops to cars; designing cars so that the fenders and the body of the car are one continuous piece of steel eliminated the labor operations previously required in bolting the fenders to the body; and casting the entire motor block as one piece instead of two, eliminated the labor operation of bolting the two pieces together. Every industry has numerous illustrations of how product and process engineering have worked together to reduce not only the cost of materials but the labor costs as well. *But it is the task of the cost accounting department to measure the effectiveness of this work.*

Product engineering and process engineering are not always sufficient to manufacture an article at the lowest possible cost. Much confusion, idle time, and other inefficiencies may occur in the factory operations unless all work is carefully *planned, routed,* and *scheduled,* so that the work will flow uninterruptedly from one department to another. This phase of production control is usually directed by a group of engineers who are responsible for having the machines, tools, and manpower available for the work to be done. The machines must be properly set up in time so that the men will not be idle waiting for the work or the machines. Materials must be available when needed to avoid the delays and inefficiencies resulting from bottlenecks in the flow of work. Definite time schedules must be adhered to so that any interruptions or breakdowns in the schedule will be quickly located and eliminated.

Illustration 9-1. Process Sheet—Specifications and Routing

PROCESS SHEET · SPECIFICATIONS & ROUTING

| PART NO. 33018 | PART NAME GUARD | | | SUB. ASSMB. USED ON 33000 | RELEASE APPROVAL A.E.N. | ENG. RELEASE |
| WRITTEN BY NAVARRD | CHECKED BY E.J.MILLER | APPROVED H.J.D. | | DATE RELEASED TO PROD. CONTROL 5-26- | ENG. CHANGE ORDER NO. | ENG. CHANGE DATE |

MATERIAL DESCRIPTION .032 x 2 3/8 x 3 3/8 -52 S AL ALLOY (PINK-BLUE)
DATE 5-31-   MAT. SPEC. NO. 1103   MAT. CODE NO. 26333

OPER. NO.	OPERATION DESCRIPTION	DEPT.	GROUP	MACH.	EQUIPMENT DESCRIPTION—TOOL, JIG, GAGE OR FIXTURE NUMBER & DESCRIPTION	PIECES PER HR.	STD. HRS. PER 100 PIECES
1	PIERCE AND BLANK	414	6	517	#3½ TOLEDO PUNCH PRESS / PIERCING AND BLANKING P & D / T.41624 BOLSTER 1003	600	.166
2	FORM	414	6	1181	#3½ TOLEDO PUNCH PRESS / FORMING P & D 41625 / BOLSTER 1001 / CHECKING GAUGE 48695	333	.300
3	BURR AND WASH	440			POLISHING JACK / TANK	200	.500
4	INSPECT	475			BENCH / CHECKING GAUGE 48695	200	.500
5	ANODIZE AS PER SPEC. #26 (SEND OUTSIDE)						

DATE OF LAST PREVIOUS CHANGE

TIME & LABOR STANDARDS

CLASS	STD. SET-UP TIME	NORMAL MCH. HRS. PER 100 PCS.	NORMAL MAN HRS. PER 100 PCS.
T	.5	.166	.166
T	.5	.300	.300
T	-	-	.500
T	-	-	.500

Both the process engineering and the planning, scheduling, and routing of work in the factory must make use of *labor standards*. By means of time-and-motion studies for each operation, a firm is able to compute how much, under normal operating conditions, a worker should be able to produce; and on the basis of this computation, it should know how many workmen should be hired to do a certain volume of work. Without such standards management is at a loss to know whether in spite of all appearances to the contrary the workmen are actually turning out the work in the volume that is expected of them. These standards will not be set until as a result of time-and-motion studies the most efficient machines and operations have been installed and developed. Labor standards are primarily time standards. When the planning, scheduling, and routing department knows how long it will take to complete certain operations, it will be able to schedule and route the work through the factory with the minimum of delay or confusion. A simple standard time sheet for the manufacture of a guard is shown in Illustration 9–1.

Closely related to the time standards and the production schedules is

Illustration 9–2. Labor Budget

MOTOR ASSEMBLY DEPARTMENT Labor Budget For the Month of December, 19— Issued November 24, 19—			
Production Order Nos.	Units Scheduled	Direct Labor Hours per Unit	Total Direct Labor Hours for Month
D-481	2,000	2	4,000
D-482	2,100	2	4,200
D-483	2,100	2	4,200
D-484	1,800	2	3,600
			16,000

Labor Budget		
Fixed:		
Supervision.................................$ 1,800.00		640
Clerical....................................... 1,250.00		400
Total Fixed Labor Budget...............$ 3,050.00		1,040
Variable:		
Direct Labor, 16,000 Hours @ $2.50..........$40,000.00		16,000
Other Indirect Labor, 800 Hours @ $1.50...... 1,200.00		800
Total Variable Labor Budget............$41,200.00		16,800
Total Labor Budget, Based on 40-Hour Week, plus 5% for Absence:		
Fixed Labor.............................$ 3,050.00		1,040
Variable Labor........................... 41,200.00		16,800
5% for Absence.............................		892
Total....................................$44,250.00		18,732
Number of Workers, 40 Hours per Week..................		469

the *labor budget*. Production schedules must be made several weeks to a month in advance; and when the standards of producing each unit are used, it is possible to prepare and use a labor budget in controlling costs. Such a labor budget is given in Illustration 9–2.

Performance reports are a necessary part of a managerial control and cost control. To be most effective, these reports should be given to the departmental foremen for their attention and action. A good foreman will make careful use of these reports in improving the work in his department. Two illustrations are given of production reports: (1) A weekly or daily departmental *efficiency* report (Illustration 9–3), which shows

Illustration 9–3. Department Efficiency Report

DEPARTMENTAL EFFICIENCY REPORT					
Department No. 78			Week Ending April 12, 19—		
Ford A. Waters, Foreman					
No.	Name	This Week	Last Week	Previous Month	Remarks
401	J. Columbus	96%	98%	95%	O.K.
402	R. Donlon	99%	100%	100%	O.K.
403	C. Cohen	90%	92%	95%	O.K.
404	R. Burton	100%	100%	102%	Exceptional Worker
405	F. George	100%	96%	98%	O.K.
406	A. Flint	70%	76%	80%	New Worker Not Familiar with Machine
407	M. Barb	80%	85%	90%	Machine Repairs
408	S. Chensi	80%	82%	80%	Delayed Waiting For Work
	Average	89.3%	91%	92.5%	

Ninety to 100 percent operating efficiency considered good. Above or below this figure some comment should be made in Remarks column.

the efficiency of each worker; it requires a great deal of clerical work and is therefore expensive but if properly used should pay big dividends in increased production. (2) Departmental labor *cost* (Illustration 9–4), showing the weekly actual and standard labor costs, with variations from standard together with the causes therefor. Other labor reports of production may be prepared, but it is important that a checkup be made of what use the foremen make of these reports.

Illustration 9-4. Labor Cost Report

DEPARTMENTAL LABOR COST REPORT

Department No.   16   Foreman L. E. Falconer

Production 200—Model   4-F   Week Ending March 8, 19—

Operations	Actual Labor Cost	Standard Labor Cost	Variation from Standard	Remarks
Planing	$1,210.00	$1,190.00	+$20.00	Waiting for Material
Drilling	1,300.00	1,250.00	+ 50.00	Machine Repairs
Cutting	1,120.00	1,120.00	—	O.K.
Bolting	1,150.00	1,175.00	− 25.00	Use of Special Tools —Revise Standards
Spraying	150.00	150.00	—	O.K.
Total	$4,930.00	$4,885.00	+$45.00	

INCENTIVE WAGE SYSTEMS AS A PHASE OF MANAGERIAL CONTROL OF LABOR COSTS

Management can reduce the per unit cost for the *fixed overhead* charges if it can increase the number of units produced in a given period of time. To offer the workers some inducement to increase production, a variety of incentive wage systems have been introduced—from the simple straight piece rate to the more complicated graduated bonus system. All incentive systems are a variation of the straight piece-rate system—payment of wages for *output* rather than for time alone. Because of the minimum wage and hour laws, and also to offer encouragement to the use of an incentive system, most incentive plans guarantee the worker a minimum hourly wage even if his production does not justify it. A good incentive system in times of high production will help create wholesome labor relations through increased earnings. However, in many industries, unions oppose the use of these systems. In others, such as the garment and shoe industries, the unions work out the piece rates in cooperation with the manufacturer. One large shoe manufacturing corporation has had as many as 250,000 different piece rates in its agreement with the union.

An incentive system to be successful must have these characteristics:

1. It must be easy for the workman to understand.
2. Rates must be set fairly so that the exceptional worker can increase his earnings accordingly.

Illustration 9–5. Comparative Table of Five Common Incentive Wage Systems

System	Production per Hour	Rate per Piece	Total Pay per Hour	Pay per Piece	Overhead per Hour	Overhead per Piece	Total Overhead and Labor per Piece
TAYLOR DIFFERENTIAL PIECE-RATE system uses two piece rates—a low rate for the poorer worker, and a higher rate for better production. Although no minimum is guaranteed, the wage and hour laws require a $1.40 minimum payment per hour.	30 pcs.	$0.015	$1.40*	$0.0466	$1.50	$0.05	$0.0966
	50	0.015	1.40	0.028	1.50	0.03	0.058
	59	0.015	1.40	0.0237	1.50	0.0254	0.0491
	60	0.03	1.80	0.03	1.50	0.025	0.055
	80	0.03	2.40	0.03	1.50	0.01875	0.04875
	100	0.03	3.00	0.03	1.50	0.015	0.045

* Minimum per hour when illustration was prepared.

	Production per Hour	Hourly Wage	Total Pay	Pay per Piece	Overhead per Hour	Overhead per Piece	Total Overhead and Labor per Piece
HALSEY PREMIUM WAGE system guarantees a minimum wage per hour. The worker is paid for a percentage of time saved in producing more than the standard quantity. In this illustration, the payment is for 50% of time saved.	30 pcs.	$1.80	$1.80	$0.06	$1.50	$0.05	$0.11
	50	1.80	1.80	0.036	1.50	0.03	0.066
	59	1.80	1.80	0.0305	1.50	0.0254	0.0559
	60	1.80	1.80	0.03	1.50	0.025	0.055
	80	1.80	2.10	0.02625	1.50	0.01875	0.045
	100	1.80	2.40	0.024	1.50	0.015	0.039

	Production per Hour	No. of B's Credit	Pay per B Unit	Total Pay	Pay per Piece	Overhead per Hour	Overhead per Piece	Total Overhead and Labor per Piece
POINT SYSTEMS of wage payment such as Bedaux, Mannit, Kim, etc. Production is converted in "B's," Mannits, etc., which represent amount of work that should be done in one minute. Worker should earn 60 B's an hour. Excess production is paid for at ¾ usual piece rate, the other ¼ going to supervisor or foreman. Minimum guaranteed is $1.80.	30 pcs.	30	$0.03	$1.80	$0.06	$1.50	$0.05	$0.11
	50	50	0.03	1.80	0.036	1.50	0.03	0.066
	59	59	0.03	1.80	0.0305	1.50	0.0254	0.0559
	60	60	0.03	1.80	0.030	1.50	0.025	0.055
	80	80	60 X $0.03	2.25	{0.028125*	1.50	0.01875	0.04875
			20 X $0.02¼	0.15	0.001875*}			
			20 X $0.003¾*					
	100	100	60 X $0.03	2.70	{0.027*	1.50	0.015	0.045
			40 X $0.02¼	0.30	0.003*}			
			40 X $0.003¾*					

* Bonus shared by indirect workers.

Production per Hour	Hourly Wage	Total Pay per Hour	Pay per Piece	Bonus Rate	Overhead per Hour	Overhead per Piece	Total Overhead & Labor per Piece
30 pcs.	$1.80	$1.80	$0.06		$1.50	$0.05	$0.11
50	1.80	1.80	0.036		1.50	0.03	0.066
59	1.80	1.80	0.0305		1.50	0.0254	0.0559
60	1.80	2.16	0.036	20%	1.50	0.025	0.061
80	1.80	2.88	0.036	60%	1.50	0.01875	0.05475
100	1.80	3.60	0.036	100%	1.50	0.015	0.051

STANDARD TIME SYSTEM—Gantt task and Bonus. There is a set time for each task or job and a fairly high standard. When worker achieves this standard he gets a bonus which is a percentage of his earnings. Minimum hourly pay is guaranteed.

Efficiency Percentage	Bonus of Base Pay	Hourly Rate if Base Pay Is $1.80 per Hour	Overhead per Hour	Total Cost	Units Produced	Total Unit Cost
66⅔%	5%	$1.89	$1.50	$3.39	40	$0.08475
80	10%	1.98	1.50	3.48	48	0.0725
100	20%	2.16	1.50	3.66	60	0.061
125	50%	2.70 (75 minutes + 20%)	1.50	4.20	75	0.056
166⅔%	100%	3.60 (100 minutes + 20%)	1.50	5.10	100	0.051

GRADUATED BONUS SYSTEM—Emerson, Wennerlund, etc. Increasing bonus rate based upon pay, as production per hour increases. Minimum hourly rate is guaranteed.

3. The standards of production must be guaranteed.
4. There must be enough work to keep the workers busy.
5. There must be a guaranteed minimum and payment for holidays.

The basic principle underlying incentive wage systems is the *reduction of the fixed overhead cost per unit* by increasing the quantity of production in a given period of time. Some incentive wage systems also attempt to reduce the unit cost of labor by using a graduated incentive rate.

Four types of incentive wages systems are generally used: (*a*) straight piecework, (*b*) efficiency systems, (*c*) point systems, and (*d*) group bonus system. Illustration 9–5 on the preceding pages uses a simple example in computing the earnings under the more commonly known incentive wage systems, viz:

```
Standard production per hour ...........................................................60 pieces
Hourly rate of pay...................................................................... $1.80
Minimum hourly wage except for the Taylor System ($1.40).................  1.80
```

In a study in 1963, it was reported that only about 26% of the industrial firms were using incentive systems. This number will probably decrease in the future due to (*a*) union opposition, (*b*) the effect of the wage and hour laws, and (*c*) increased automation whereby the volume of production is controlled by the machine or conveyor systems.

GROUP BONUS PAY SYSTEM

Some firms use an incentive system under which several employees are paid a bonus collectively, and this bonus is distributed on some equitable basis. The reasons for a group bonus are: (1) it develops cooperation among the group of workers, particularly where the work of one may delay the work in some subsequent operation; (2) it reduces the amount of clerical work involved in computing bonuses—that is, a bonus is figured for group production, not for each individual's production; and (3) it reduces the amount of supervision necessary. The group bonus system has found definite application in the large automobile factories where the conveyorized organization is used, and in other assembly types of business, such as washing machine, radio, and refrigerator manufacturing.

The Wennerlund, the Bedaux, and the Halsey systems have been applied to the group plan. Bonuses are generally computed on the weekly or monthly production to avoid periods of speedup and periods of slow production. If all the workers in a group are doing the same kind of work and receiving the same basic pay, the bonus can be figured on the output and distributed equally. If the workers do not perform the same kind of work and do not receive the same rate of pay, the bonus will be distributed in proportion to the time earnings for each task, as shown in Illustration 9–6.

Illustration 9–6. Group Bonus Pay Sheet

GROUP PAY SHEET						
DEPARTMENT Assembling				WEEK ENDING SEPTEMBER 30		
Name	Clock No.	Total Hours	Hourly Base Rate	Total Base Earnings (Hrs. × Rate)	Bonus	Total Pay
Paul Brown	203	50	$1.84	$ 92.00	$11.79	$103.79
Walter Kahn	204	49	1.60	78.40	10.05	88.45
Frank Smith	205	50	1.50	75.00	9.62	84.62
John Norman	206	45	1.50	67.50	8.65	76.15
Edward Hastie	207	46	1.00	46.00	5.90	51.90
		Total		$358.90	$46.01	$404.91

PRODUCTION ORDER NO.   525   ACCOUNT NO.   62
DESCRIPTION   Assembly of C. S. PRESS   QUANTITY   10
GROUP ALLOWANCE (For completed job)..............................$404.91
GROUP BASE EARNINGS..$358.90
GROUP BONUS (To be distributed)......................................$ 46.01
PERCENT OF BONUS TO BASE EARNINGS............................. 12.82%

ACCOUNTING PROCEDURES FOR PAYROLL COSTS

The ultimate objective of all payroll accounting for a manufacturing concern is to establish (1) how much the worker must be paid weekly; and (2) how this payroll cost should be allocated to the various jobs, products, departments, and to manufacturing overhead. Accounting for payroll costs starts with a *timekeeping department* which determines the time worked by each employee and his gross earnings, and also the allocation of these earnings to the various jobs or departments. The financial accounting is handled by the *payroll department* which computes and records the gross pay for each employee, the payroll taxes and other deductions, and payment to the employee. The *cost accounting* department allocates the factory labor costs to the various jobs, departments, or to the manufacturing overhead.

TIMEKEEPING FOR PAYROLL PURPOSES

Timekeeping is an important phase of industrial accounting because it is used to prove compliance with the federal and state wage and hour laws. It is also required for the computation of the payrolls and the variety of payroll tax and income tax deductions. Timekeeping is also necessary for computing the labor costs applicable to the various jobs or operations. The timekeeping records most frequently used in industry are explained below.

Time-Clock Cards. A time-clock card is an individual card for each employee on which a time clock records the "in" and "out" time each day. These cards may also contain spaces and references for computing and recording the gross earnings, deductions, and net pay. Two forms of these cards are in use: (1) the traditional form which is based upon a clock showing the hours on a normal 12-hour basis, and (2) the continental clock which records the time on a 24-hour cycle. The latter is becoming increasingly important because of the ease with which the elapsed time may be computed. This form is shown in Illustration 9–7.

Job Time Tickets. In allocating the direct labor costs to specific jobs, the workman must record the time he started and the time he finished each job during the day. Two forms of the job time ticket have been used. One is an *individual job time ticket*, which is a small printed form on

Illustration 9–7. Time-Clock Card—Continental Time

Card of Harry Smith, social security No. 292-07-4871, with two income tax exemptions. Overtime computations are based upon regular pay for 40 hours per week and time and one half for all time over 40 hours. Mr. Smith works in a state where the employee as well as the employer contributes to the state unemployment fund (1 percent). State disability insurance deductions are at the rate of 30 cents per week. Federal and state withholding income taxes are indicated, as well as union dues of $1 per week. To compute hours worked each day on continental time, start at bottom of each column and subtract top figure. After allowing one hour for lunch, the difference represents hours worked.

which is recorded the employee's name and number, department, job number on which he is working, time he started on that job, time finished, total time spent on job and rate of pay. The final computation of the cost of labor on these cards is done in the cost accounting department. In some firms, use is made of a *daily job time ticket,* on which the daily working time, at 15-minute intervals, is printed. The worker merely marks the time he starts and finished each job and inserts the job number. This form has the advantage of showing on one form how the day's work was performed, but it has the disadvantage of requiring an analysis of the charges by jobs when they have been computed — an extra clerical task.

Several procedural improvements have been made in the use of the job time tickets. In one firm, telephones connected with a central switchboard are located throughout the plant. Whenever a worker starts a new job, he telephones the information to the clerk who records it on a punched card. When he completes the job, this information is also phoned to the operator. This saves the time of the production worker in preparing the forms and enables faster processing of the data because it is already on a punched card.

Another improvement is the use of a time clock which not only records the time the job was started and the time it was completed but also computes automatically the elapsed time. It has been estimated that use of such a clock saves the time of one cost clerk for each 200 production workers in the factory.

PAYROLL TAXES IN LABOR ACCOUNTING PROCEDURES

Management today is concerned not only with the problems and procedures of preparing the various payrolls but also with the various deductions required by state and federal laws and union contracts. Basically, the federal and state regulations apply to two types of payroll deductions: (1) FICA tax for social security and medicare (federal regulation); and (2) income tax deductions both federal and state, known as withholding taxes. In a few states, the state laws require an employee to pay part of the unemployment tax, in which case there must be a deduction for this employee's share. These payroll taxes are becoming increasingly important because the firm must pay these whether it sustains a profit or not. The taxes on payrolls are as follows:

1. *Federal Insurance Contributions Act Tax (FICA).* With few exceptions, all employees and self-employed persons are taxed on wages up to a certain statutory limit received in any one calendar year. The *employee* and *employer* contribute equal amounts, whereas the self-employed person pays a higher amount when he files his annual federal income tax report. The following are the most recent rates which include medicare:

SUMMARY OF 1970 SOCIAL SECURITY TAXES
INCLUDING MEDICARE

Years	Federal Insurance Contributions Act Rate of Tax	Federal Hospital Insurance Program Rate of Tax	Total	Self-employed Worker Rate of Tax		Total
1971–72................4.6%		0.6%	5.20%	6.9%	0.60%	7.5%
1973–75................5.0		0.65	5.65	7.0	0.65	7.65
1976–79................5.0		0.7	5.70	7.0	0.70	7.70

The above rates must be paid by both the employee and the employer on wages up to a limit of $7,800 at present, but will probably be raised in the future.

The above is paid only by the self-employed person on a limit of $7,800 income.

FEDERAL UNEMPLOYMENT TAX

Rate of Tax

State tax is 2.7% unless a merit rating is given.

Federal tax is 3.2% less credit for the state tax of 2.7%, or a net tax of 0.5%.

Present maximum earnings taxable is $3,000 but is subject to change by law. In 1972 the maximum becomes $4,200.

All employees of a covered industry — where a firm has four or more employees — are covered.

2. *State Unemployment Tax (SUT).* This tax varies with the states. In some states the *employer* must pay the entire tax; in others, the employees are also taxed but not necessarily at the same rate as the employer. The present rate for many of the states is 2.7 percent of the total wages paid any employee in one calendar year, not exceeding a wage base of $3,000. With the increase of the base wage for the federal unemployment tax to $4,200 starting in 1972, no doubt the base wage for the states will also be increased. Some states permit a merit rating which reduces this rate.

3. *Federal Unemployment Tax (FUT).* This tax is paid entirely by the employer at a rate of 0.5 percent on maximum earnings of $3,000 a year, or $15 per employee. It is expected that in 1972, the maximum base pay on which this is computed will be increased to $4,200, making the maximum tax per employee per year to become $21. To be subject to this tax, starting in 1972, any firm having one or more employees who earn more than $1,500 in any three-month period in the year must pay the tax.

4. *Federal Withholding (Income) Tax (FWHT).* This is the estimated income tax on employees which is withheld from their pay. The amount withheld depends upon the amount of the earnings and taxable status (number of exemptions) of the employee.

5. *State withholding taxes.* Increasingly the states which have income

taxes are asking employers to do some of their bookkeeping work, just as the federal government does. Since the work is parallel and similar, though the rates are different, the additional computations are not too laborious. The trend in this direction is increasing; so the problem may as well be faced in present payroll accounting.

6. *City income taxes.* The collection method is not uniform but the future indicates it will follow the federal and state procedures.

It is evident that the recording and collection of these taxes involves considerable work on the part of the employer. Furthermore, the payroll taxes, the cost of which the employer must bear (not the deductions from the employee's gross pay), constitute additional labor costs, sometimes known as *fringe labor costs,* and may be an important part of the total cost of labor in manufacturing, especially when they are added to the welfare benefits paid on the workers' account as a result of union contracts. It has been estimated by some that these indirect labor costs amount to as much as 10 to 20 percent of the regular payroll.

A calendar of the duties of the present-day business firm in the matter of the federal payroll taxes is shown in Illustration 9–8.

FINANCIAL ACCOUNTING FOR LABOR COSTS

Financial accounting for labor refers to the computation of the earnings of the worker less *deductions.* Some of these deductions are authorized by law, such as the federal insurance contribution taxes, state unemployment taxes, and withholding (income) taxes. Other deductions are authorized by the worker himself or through his representatives in labor unions, such as union dues, deductions for insurance, and for the purchase of bonds. The customary forms used in the financial accounting for labor include: (1) *timecards,* previously discussed; (2) *payroll records;* (3) *voucher register;* (4) *record of individual employees' earnings;* and (5) *deductions authorization card.*

In some concerns the *payroll record* may be in the form of a bound book or loose-leaf sheets. Posting may be made directly from the payroll records, using them as books of original record, or from summary entries prepared therefrom and entered in a journal. The payroll record should contain the following information:

1. The time-clock card number assigned to the employee.
2. Name and social security number of the worker.
3. Type of work performed—sometimes necessary for compensation insurance classification and premium calculation.
4. Total hours worked.
5. Rate of pay per hour, per day, or per week.
6. Gross earnings.

7. Deductions for FICA tax.
8. Deductions for state unemployment taxes, where such deductions are made.
9. Deductions for federal and state withholding (income) taxes.
10. Deductions for advances, insurance, and stock or bond purchases.

Illustration 9–8

CALENDAR OF EMPLOYER'S DUTIES

On Hiring New Employees

For Income Tax Withholding. Ask each new employee for a withholding exemption certificate on Form W–4.

For Social Security (Federal Insurance Contributions Act) Taxes. Record the account number and name of each new employee from his social security account number card. If he has no account number, have him file application on Form SS–5.

On Each Payment of Wages to an Employee

For Income Tax Withholding. Withhold tax from each wage payment in accordance with the employee's withholding exemption certificate and the applicable withholding rate.

For Social Security Taxes. Withhold 5.65 percent from each wage payment (1973–75).

By 15th Day of Each Month

After each of the first two months of each quarter deposit both income tax withheld and employee and employer social security taxes for such month, if the total is more than $100, in a Federal Reserve bank or other authorized bank. Tax for the third month of a quarter may be either deposited or paid with the quarterly return.

On or before Each April 30, July 31, October 31, and January 31

File a quarterly return on Form 941 with the Internal Revenue Service and pay balance amount of taxes due for the previous quarter on both income tax withheld from wages and employee and employer social security taxes.

Before December 1 of Each Year

For Income Tax Withholding. Request filing of a new certificate, Form W–4, by each employee whose withholding exemptions will be different in the next year from the exemptions shown on his last certificate.

On or before Each January 31 and at End of Employment

Give each employee a withholding statement in duplicate on Form W–2, showing (1) the total wages and the amount of income tax withheld and (2) the amount of social security employee tax withheld and the amount of wages subject to this tax. If Form W–2 is not required, give statement of social security wages and employee tax deducted.

On or before January 31 of Each Year

For Income Tax Withholding. File Form W–3, Reconciliation of Income Tax Withheld from Wages, together with all District Director's copies (Copy A) of withholding statements furnished employees on Form W–2 for the preceding calendar year.

For Federal Unemployment Tax Act (FUTA) Tax. File annual return on Form 940, before January 31.

11. Remarks.
12. Signature of employees (usually only required in small plants). (In larger plants receipts are given out with the pay envelopes, and these must be signed and returned.)

The subject of *payroll deductions* has become increasingly important in business today: first, because of the large amount of clerical work involved in computing and recording the numerous deductions and, second, because these deductions are taking an increasingly large proportion of the workers' earnings. These deductions may be of a *fixed* nature — the same amount each payday, such as bond or insurance deductions — or may fluctuate, such as the social security and withholding tax deductions. Except for those authorized by law, the worker must authorize deductions made periodically by the employer. Such authorization is usually made on a card signed by the employee, similar to that approving the purchase of government bonds by payroll deductions.

To give effect to the payroll and to these deductions, the following entry or its equivalent will be made in the *payroll record* or a summary journal each week:

(1)

Payroll 10,500.00	
FICA Taxes Payable (5.2%).....................................	546.00
Employees' Insurance Premium Payable......................	75.00
Federal Withholding Taxes Payable	800.00
State Withholding Taxes Payable...............................	100.00
Union Dues Payable	200.00
Employees' Bond Purchase Deposit...........................	150.00
Payroll Accrued..	8,629.00

Checks will be drawn to pay for the various deductions. Entries for each of these checks must first be made in the *voucher register* and then in the *check register*. For the payroll itself, the entry is given below. For the others, the same type of entry would be made.

In the *voucher register:*

(2)

Payroll Accrued 8,629.00	
Accounts Payable...	8,629.00

In the *check register:*

(3)

Accounts Payable.. 8,629.00	
Cash...	8,629.00

The voucher register has been discussed in Chapter 3. Here attention should be called to the heading of the column used to record the payroll liability. In the entry given above, the payroll record was used as a posting medium, and therefore the column in the voucher register would be headed *Payroll Accrued.* Should the payroll book be merely a memo-randum record, the column heading would be *Payroll,* and the various deductions would be recorded either in special columns (credits) or in the *Sundry General Ledger, Credits* section of the voucher register.

Periodically, the payroll must be analyzed and distributed to accounts which will indicate whether it is direct labor, indirect labor (manufacturing overhead), selling expense, or administrative expense. For this the entry would be:

```
Work-in-Process — Labor .................................................6,000.00
Manufacturing Overhead Control (Indirect Labor)..............1,000.00
Selling Expenses (Sales Salaries) .....................................1,200.00
Administrative Expenses (Officers' Salaries)......................1,000.00
Administrative Expenses (Office Salaries) .........................1,300.00
    Payroll....................................................................              10,500.00
    To close out the Payroll account to appropriate accounts.
```

At least quarterly, although some firms do it monthly, it is necessary to record the employer's share of the various payroll taxes. The entry for this would be:

(5)

```
Payroll Taxes........................................................................871.50
    FICA Taxes Payable (5.2%) ...........................................          546.00
    Federal Unemployment Taxes Payable (0.4%)....................           42.00
    State Unemployment Taxes Payable (2.7%).......................          283.50
    To record employer's liability for payroll taxes.
```

It is necessary, however, to keep a record of how much of these pay-roll taxes are selling expenses, how much administrative, and how much factory overhead costs. At the end of the fiscal accounting period, an entry is made to close the Payroll Tax account, viz:

(6)

```
Manufacturing Overhead (Payroll Taxes)................................581.00
Selling Expense (Sales Payroll Tax).......................................  99.60
Administrative Expense (Office Payroll Tax)...........................190.90
    Payroll Taxes..........................................................              871.50
    To close out the Payroll Tax account to appropriate expense
    accounts, at 8.3% of gross payroll.
```

ACCRUING THE PAYROLL AT THE END OF THE YEAR — SPLIT PAYROLLS

When the books of a firm are closed in the middle of a pay period, it may be necessary to accrue the payroll for part of the week before pre-paring the financial statements. Dividing the payroll in this form is known as *splitting payrolls.* Although there are two methods of handling this situation, it should be noted in each case that FICA taxes are not accrued at the end of the period, unless the wages are actually paid in that period. If the year ends in the middle of the week and workers are not paid until the end of the week, the FICA taxes must be computed as of the date of payment. Those who have exceeded the maximum limit in the year just ending will have to pay FICA taxes on those earnings made in the end of the preceding year but paid for in the first week of the new year.

This problem must be considered in studying the two methods. One method is to summarize the payroll book for the part of the week ending with the closing of the fiscal year, as follows:

```
Payroll ...................................................................................xxxx
        Payroll Accrued.......................................................        xxxx
        To record payroll accrued to date without FICA and withholding
        deductions.
```

No entry is made in the voucher register, but the payroll book is ruled and closed. This entry may be made in the general journal if the payroll book is not used as a book of original entry. The payroll for the remainder of the week will then be calculated and recorded, with the FICA deductions and the full weekly withholding tax liability. The entry is:

```
Payroll ...................................................................................xxxx
        FICA Taxes Payable.....................................................        xxxx
        Federal Withholding Taxes Payable.....................................        xxxx
        State Withholding Taxes Payable .......................................        xxxx
        Payroll Accrued..........................................................        xxxx
```

A single voucher is then made out for the sum of the two payroll accrued figures.

A second method is sometimes used. A voucher is prepared for the payroll up to the closing date. A second voucher is prepared for the amount of the payroll for the remainder of the week immediately following the closing date. Both voucher checks are put through the bank on the same day and thus provide the cash for the total payroll for the week.

Where the cost records are integrated with the financial accounting records, it is necessary to analyze, summarize, and record the job time tickets for the period up to the date of closing the books. The accrual for the payroll taxes to be paid by the employer must also be recorded. Since in many instances this is an impractical procedure, many firms make no attempt to reconcile the cost and the financial accounting records until the end of the fiscal accounting period.

COST ACCOUNTING FOR LABOR COSTS

The cost accounting problems involved in factory payrolls are (a) separating the payroll costs into those which are considered *direct labor* and those which are considered *indirect labor;* and (b) computing the amount of labor costs which should be charged to the specific jobs or in process costing to the various departments.

Separating the payroll costs into *direct* and *indirect* requires the use of the individual or daily job time tickets. (See Illustrations 9–9 and 9–10.) That labor which is directly applicable to the manufacturing operations of a specific product is known as direct labor. Generally speaking all other factory labor costs are *indirect;* but for managerial control, these should be classified under the headings of supervision, inspection, maintenance, idle time, and others.

When daily job time tickets are used, an analysis of these tickets must be made in the cost accounting department to compute the amount applicable to the various jobs. (See Illustration 9–11.)

When individual job time tickets are used, these can be sorted by job numbers, totaled on the adding machine and then posted to the respective cost accounting sheets.

When costs are kept on a departmental or process basis instead of by jobs, no distinction is made between the direct and indirect labor. The total departmental payroll, both direct and indirect, is charged to the departmental work-in-process cost.

Since both the materials requisitions and the labor time tickets require a great amount of sorting and tabulating and posting to the cost sheets, many of the larger firms have recorded these requisitions and time tickets on punched cards, thus facilitating and expediting the clerical work involved.

Illustration 9–9. Payroll Calculations Derived from Daily Job Time Tickets

The accounting entries made from the payroll cost analyses would be as follows:

Job Order System	*Process Cost System*[1]
Work-in-Process — Labor	Work-in-Process — Department I
Manufacturing Overhead Control	Work-in-Process — Department II
Payroll	Payroll

[1] In process cost accounting no distinction is made between direct and indirect labor: the entire departmental payroll is charged to the work-in-process, unless a predetermined overhead rate is used for each department.

Illustration 9–10.   Individual Job Time Ticket

HOURS	PIECES	DAY WORK RATE	PIECE WORK RATE
2		2.63	

	HOURS	PIECES	DAY WORK RATE	PIECE WORK RATE
NAME	2	61	2.63	
DEPT.				

TIME TICKET

PART NO. STOP	NAME *Geo. Stiblins*		DATE 9/7
START	DEPT. 3		BADGE NO. 070

PART NO. 418

STOP 12 0	OPERATION *Assemble* #91	
START 10 0	JOB NO. 5472	ACCOUNT NO. 301

Frank Locke

AUTHORIZED SIGNATURE

HOURS	PIECES	DAY WORK	PIECE WORK
2	61		5.26

Illustration 9–11.   Daily Job Time Recapitulation Sheet

DATE MARCH 5, 19--

DAILY JOB TIME REPORT RECAPITULATION SHEET

EMPLOYEE NO.	760	763	768	770	774	IDLE TIME	REPAIRS	TOTAL
J. JONES 201	14⁰⁰		3⁶⁰		2⁰⁰	2⁰⁰		21⁶⁰
A. SMITH 202		15⁰⁰		7⁰⁰				22⁰⁰
C. BROWN 203	8⁰⁰		4⁰⁰	4⁰⁰	4⁰⁰			20⁰⁰
C. BUTLER 204		10⁰⁰	11⁰⁰		6⁰	3⁶⁰	1⁸⁰	27⁰⁰
TOTALS	182⁰⁰	216⁰⁰	140⁰⁰	72⁰⁰	90⁰⁰	18⁰⁰	27⁰⁰	740⁰⁰

Diagrammatically, labor cost accounting can be summarized as shown in Illustration 9–12.

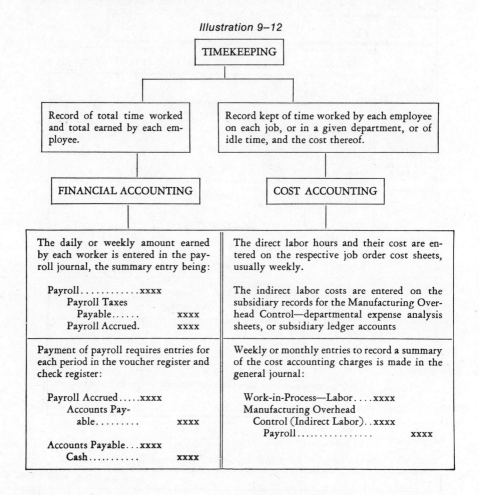

Illustration 9–12

TIMEKEEPING

| Record of total time worked and total earned by each employee. | Record kept of time worked by each employee on each job, or in a given department, or of idle time, and the cost thereof. |

FINANCIAL ACCOUNTING — **COST ACCOUNTING**

| The daily or weekly amount earned by each worker is entered in the payroll journal, the summary entry being:

Payroll............xxxx
  Payroll Taxes
    Payable......   xxxx
  Payroll Accrued.   xxxx | The direct labor hours and their cost are entered on the respective job order cost sheets, usually weekly.

The indirect labor costs are entered on the subsidiary records for the Manufacturing Overhead Control—departmental expense analysis sheets, or subsidiary ledger accounts |
| Payment of payroll requires entries for each period in the voucher register and check register:

Payroll Accrued.....xxxx
  Accounts Payable........   xxxx

Accounts Payable...xxxx
  Cash...........   xxxx | Weekly or monthly entries to record a summary of the cost accounting charges is made in the general journal:

  Work-in-Process—Labor....xxxx
  Manufacturing Overhead
    Control (Indirect Labor)..xxxx
      Payroll...............   xxxx |

PROCEDURAL ANALYSIS OF PAYROLL ACCOUNTING

A complete picture of the procedural sequence of payroll accounting is shown in Illustration 9–13 which gives the tabulation of transactions, forms, books of original entry, cost record entries and their sources.

SPECIAL PAYROLL COST ACCOUNTING PROBLEMS

Six special problems affecting payroll costs should receive attention by management. These are (1) treatment of overtime bonus or shift bonus; (2) costs of pensions for factory workers; (3) the guaranteed an-

Illustration 9–13. Summary of Labor Accounting and Procedure

Transaction	Forms Used	Book of Original Entry	Source of Entry	Entry in Journal Form	Entry on Cost Record or Summary	Source of Cost Record Entry
1. To record the payroll at end of each week	a) Time-clock cards b) Payroll record	a) Payroll book	a) Time-clock cards b) Payroll summary	(1) Dr. Payroll Cr. F.I.C.A. Taxes Payable Cr. Federal W.H. Taxes Payable Cr. State W.H. Taxes Payable Cr. Payroll Accrued		
2. To voucher and pay wages	a) Payroll sheet b) Employees' individual ledger cards	a) Voucher register b) Check register	a) Payroll sheet	(2) Dr. Payroll Accrued Cr. Accounts Payable (3) Dr. Accounts Payable Cr. Cash		
3. To record distribution of payroll	a) Job time tickets b) Payroll recapitulation sheet of job time tickets	a) General journal	a) Recapitulation of job time tickets	(4) Dr. Work-in-Process Labor Dr. Mfg. Overhead—Indirect Labor Cr. Payroll	a) Direct Labor section of job order cost sheets b) Standing order sheet for indirect labor costs.	a) Recapitulation sheet of job time ticket
4. To record employer's payroll taxes	a) Payroll sheet	a) General journal	a) Payroll sheet	(5) Dr. Mfg. Overhead (Payroll Taxes) Cr. F.I.C.A. Taxes Payable Cr. Federal U.T. Payable Cr. State U.T. Payable	a) Standing order sheet	

nual wage; (4) vacation, holiday, and bonus pay; (5) setup costs; and (6) apprenticeship and training costs.

Overtime Bonus Payments.   They are treated in various ways. Some firms treat the overtime bonus as an element of cost (manufacturing overhead), and it is therefore reflected in the inventory values of the work-in-process and finished goods. Other firms exclude all overtime premium payments from the cost of manufacturing. The obvious reason for this latter practice is that if there is overtime in one period and not in another, the costs are not comparable when used as a measure of production efficiency.

Where the overtime bonus is *included in the inventory costs,* the procedures followed vary. Two methods of accomplishing this have been used. Some firms treat the overtime bonus as part of the *direct labor costs* and thereby add it directly to the job order or department for which the work is done. This method undoubtedly distorts the direct labor costs when similar jobs are compared, especially if some incur overtime and others do not. Therefore, a more acceptable procedure is to include all overtime bonus payments for factory labor as an element of *manufacturing overhead,* prorating it equitably over all work done during a given period. Firms which exclude overtime bonus as a part of the cost of manufacturing usually record the bonus in a separate account which is closed directly into the Profit and Loss account.

Similar treatment is accorded the premium paid workers employed on the late afternoon or night shifts.

Whatever the disposition of these excess labor costs, it must be remembered that the type of product manufactured frequently determines the treatment of this cost. In a shipyard, it is a simple matter to allocate overtime costs directly to the job. On the other hand, if a variety of products are being manufactured, it is not so simple. The particular job being worked on in overtime may just be a matter of chance, and therefore distorted costs result if this job is penalized. There seems to be a growing tendency, however, to include all overtime premiums in manufacturing overhead or to spread them by including them in standard costs rather than penalizing the job "caught" in the overtime. Care should be taken in the treatment of overtime if manufacturing overhead is applied to production on the basis of a percentage of labor costs, for in such cases the bonus payment arising from overtime must not be included in the direct labor costs. Similarly, if manufacturing overhead is applied to production on a labor hour basis, care should be taken that only the regular hours are used (not the time-and-one-half hours) in applying the manufacturing overhead.

Accounting for Pension Costs.[2]   Accounting for pension costs becomes a most difficult problem because of the wide variety of conditions and plans

---

[2] See AICPA Accounting Principles Board, *Opinion No. 8,* November, 1966.

under which these are established. Through the Accounting Principles Board of the AICPA an attempt has been made to arrive at some practical and acceptable procedure from this complicated morass.

Basically, the opinion of the Accounting Principles Board indicates that the problem is one of determining the amount of the pension costs. Since there are many pension systems, this becomes a complicated problem. In some plans the company assumes direct responsibility for the payment of the benefits of the plan. If the pension is inadequate, the company is liable for the deficiency. In contrast the terms of most funded plans limit the company's legal liability to the amount in the pension fund.

There is some confusion about the amount of the pension cost and the *nature of it*. It is sometimes considered as a supplemental fringe benefit; sometimes as a means of promoting efficiency by providing for the retirement of older employees; sometimes as the fulfillment of a social obligation which constitutes a business expense which must be incurred. The problems of the nature of pension costs, the uncertainties of the future requirements, and the actuarial approaches to the problem make the accounting for pension costs a difficult problem. And as a result different viewpoints arise. And the accounting, especially the cost accounting practices, become confused. For example: (*a*) some view pension costs as relating solely to the existing employee group at the time the plan is adopted; (*b*) others consider pensions costs as pension benefits to be paid to continuing employee groups as whole—thus covering charges against income for transactions and events—past, present, and reasonably anticipated. Management decisions determine the interpretation of the pension plan and its accounting. Management no doubt wants to provide the minimum of the pension costs in its operating expenses.

But what happens to the recording of the cost of operations for payments to pension funds for past and prior service? Fortunately or unfortunately, the interest of the Internal Revenue Service helps in this decision. What may even further complicate this situation is that the federal government is seriously considering the funding of all pension plans to provide the transfer of pension values of the employees when a change of jobs occurs and to avoid loss of pension values established in previous employments.

All of these legal and accounting difficulties complicate the problem of accounting for pensions. So the Accounting Principles Board of the AICPA has attempted to set up guidelines for pension costs for the varying conditions that may arise. Among these are the following suggestions of the AICPA Principles Board:

1. The entire cost of benefit payments ultimately to be made should be charged against *Income* subsequent to the adoption or amendment of the plan and no portion of such costs should be charged directly against the *Retained Earnings*.
2. The *annual* provision for pension costs should not be less than the total of

(1) normal cost, (2) an amount equivalent to interest on any unfunded prior service cost, and (3) a provision for vested benefits should be made under certain conditions.

3. The annual provision for pension costs should not be greater than the total of (1) normal cost, (2) 10 percent of the past service cost until fully amortized, (3) 10 percent of the amounts of any increases or decrease in prior service cost arising from amendments of the plan until fully amortized.

4. The difference between the amount which has been charged against income and the amount which has been paid should be shown on the balance sheet as accrued or prepaid pension cost.

The Accounting Principles Board recommends the use of one of the various actuarial methods of computing the pension costs. The principal actuarial cost methods currently in use are given by the Accounting Principles Board *Opinion No. 8* and include (*a*) *accrued benefit method* used when the funding is under a group annuity contract and where the benefit is a stated amount per year of service (it is not frequently used where the benefit is a fixed amount); and (*b*) *projected benefit cost method* which assigns the entire cost of an employee's *projected* benefits to past, present, and future periods. There are a number of different methods of computing this cost, but in most instances it results in a level annual premium.

The application of pension costs is quite varied depending upon the management's decision. One important industrial firm involved in a union contract agreed to place in the pension fund, $20,000,000 at the start of the program. Then, all pension costs exceeding this amount would be paid into the fund and would be treated as an operating expense. The above amount was charged against Retained Earnings to cover past service costs.

A more acceptable procedure might be the actuarial computations for both past and present services reduced to an hourly basis, with a provision that any excess which would be due to miscalculated past service credit be charged to the Retained Earnings account.

To illustrate such an hourly basis computation which could be calculated by an outside specialist pension actuary, the following data is given:

Assume the following conditions (all are average figures):

Number of employees.......................... 200
Annual pension....................................$1,200
At expected age of 62 years..................Retirement
Expected period for which payments will
  be made (life expectancy) .... 15 years
Expected period for which employee will
  work for the firm............................. 30 years

On the basis of these figures, the estimated eventual cost will be:

$1,200 a year for 15 years..................$ 18,000
200 employees at $18,000.................. 3,600,000

If each employee is expected to have worked an average of 30 years before retirement, then the annual cost will be

$3,600,000 ÷ 30 years...................................$120,000
Per employee cost ($120,000 ÷ 200
    employees)...   600
Hourly cost of pension per hour, per employee,
    $600 ÷ 2,000 hours ....   30¢

On this basis it is possible to convert the pension costs to an hourly basis and treat it as additional labor cost per hour. As such, pension costs would be treated as direct labor costs, indirect labor costs, sales salaries, or administrative salaries.

There still remains the problem of how you are to treat the pension costs for past services. As suggested before, since this is a nonrecurring expense, it might be practical to charge the Retained Earnings. Accounting practice no longer is an exact science—it is one of practical adjustment of extenuating circumstances.

The Guaranteed Annual Wage (GAW). This is a recent innovation in manufacturing plants where the unions have attempted, and succeeded in part, in obtaining unemployment benefits beyond those granted by the state unemployment laws. The plans vary. Some firms have had guaranteed employment for years. Most of these are process manufacturing plants, not job order plants. For a job order plant to have a guaranteed annual wage whereby the worker is paid for any unemployment during a given year is almost a managerial impossibility. An analysis of the economic implications of such a plan will readily reveal its managerial difficulties.

Some of the recent acceptances of the GAW principle have provided that the employer pay into a fund a certain amount for each hour that an employee works in his firm, with a top limit to the size of the fund. In some instances, the firm has paid in or will pay in a lump sum at a given date. After a waiting period of one or two weeks, the employee will receive from this fund up to 60 or 65 percent of his weekly wage for a period not exceeding 26 weeks. The 60 or 65 percent of his weekly wage will be decreased by any amount that the employee will receive from any state unemployment fund.

Thus the GAW becomes a supplement to the state unemployment insurance tax laws. The legal or restrictive clauses are not important here. Until a wider adoption of the GAW plans and more uniformity is developed, the best that can be hoped for is that the cost will be limited to a fixed amount per hour, no matter how the fund is to be administered or distributed. Ultimately, the GAW will probably result in a higher state unemployment tax, so that all firms will come under the benefits presently available only to the employees of the larger firms which have signed union agreements covering the GAW. In other words, as the state unemployment insurance plans raise their taxes and benefits to the worker, there will be less need for GAW; the state will assume that responsibility to the worker.

Where a corporation must pay into the fund for the GAW benefits, the problem of accounting for these payments arises. One large corporation has merely added the hourly payment (5 cents) to the regular earnings rate for the employee, increasing the direct labor or indirect labor costs accordingly; the journal entry being as follows:

Payroll	100,000	
FICA Taxes Payable (5.2%)		5,200
Federal Withholding Taxes Payable		18,000
State Withholding Taxes Payable		1,250
GAW Fund Payable		2,500
Accounts Payable		73,050
To record the payroll for the period.		

This probably is the most accurate method, since the 5 cents per hour contribution to the fund is merely an increase in the labor costs. The Internal Revenue Service has thus far allowed the firm to deduct as a manufacturing cost the 5 cents per hour thus contributed, and the employee is not required to include in his income for income tax purposes, the 5 cents per hour paid into the fund on his account. The employee however is taxed on the supplemental payment when he receives the money.

In some firms, the agreement with the union has established a GAW fund, independent of the union and the employer, in which an amount is deposited to the credit of each individual employee in much the same fashion as a savings account. If the employee leaves the firm, he is entitled to his "deposit." If he is unemployed, the fund is used to pay unemployment wages. This arrangement is somewhat different from a fund which is trusteed and from which the employee gets nothing if he leaves his present employment or if he dies. Under the "savings" type of unemployment insurance, the amount thus contributed is, no doubt, not only a deduction for the employer but also taxable income for the employee in the year of contribution to the fund.

If the GAW goes far enough in industry, each firm will know exactly what its total labor cost for the year will be whether or not there is any production. Thus direct labor tends to become a *fixed cost* rather than a variable cost.

Vacation, Holiday, and Bonus Payments. Although there are several methods of treating these payments in a cost accounting system, probably the most satisfactory is as an element of the indirect labor costs, and thus as a charge to the manufacturing overhead costs. Along with this treatment, some firms accrue these labor costs on the basis of the labor budget estimates. An entry to illustrate this procedure would be:

Work-in-Process — Labor 600	
Manufacturing Overhead (Indirect Labor) 40	
Manufacturing Overhead (Bonus) 30	
Manufacturing Overhead (Holiday and Vacation Pay)........................ 80	
Payroll	670
Liability for Vacation and Holiday Pay......................................	80

Setup Time Costs. Oftentimes, considerable time and labor costs may be required to set up the machines, conveyor systems, and other facilities before production on a particular job can be started. The costs thus incurred are known as *setup costs.* There are several methods of treating these costs in the accounting records: (1) treat the costs as part of the *direct labor costs* on the job, since it is a direct cost but not direct labor; (2) treat it as a *direct cost of the job* but under a separate heading — *setup costs* — thus showing the cost of manufacturing under four divisions — direct material, direct labor, setup costs, and manufacturing overhead; and (3) treat the costs as part of the manufacturing overhead. This method would not be very accurate if some jobs had more and others less, proportionately, of such costs.

Apprenticeship and Trainee Costs. In some firms opening a new plant, it may be necessary to spend some time and money for unusual costs in training new employees either for the regular shifts or for a second or third shift. Since this is an unusual situation and the costs may be considerable before the plant will operate at normal efficiency, these costs may be deferred and written off over a reasonable period of time.

If the firm has a continuous apprenticeship and trainee program, that part of the wage compensation which is due to subnormal production should be treated as an indirect cost and charged to the Manufacturing Overhead Control account. Included in this overhead charge should be the cost of instruction.

REDUCING THE CLERICAL COST OF LABOR COST ACCOUNTING

Calculating the elapsed time on jobs, sorting the tickets by jobs, and preparing the cost sheets with a minimum of delay involves a great amount of clerical time and expense. Machines have been used to reduce the costs. The Calculagraph is a time recorder which computes automatically the elapsed time on any job time ticket, in hours and fractions of an hour. (See Illustration 9–14.) When used in conjunction with *time and payroll tables,* the computation of the dollars and cents cost of the time used on a job is expedited. Further, if the job time ticket is in the form of an IBM prepunched job time ticket, the sorting by jobs and subsequent tabulation of results become even more efficient and less costly. A second method of reducing the cost of job labor costing is to combine the daily "in" and "out" time-clock card with the *individual* daily job

Illustration 9–14. Job Time Ticket Prepared on Calculagraph

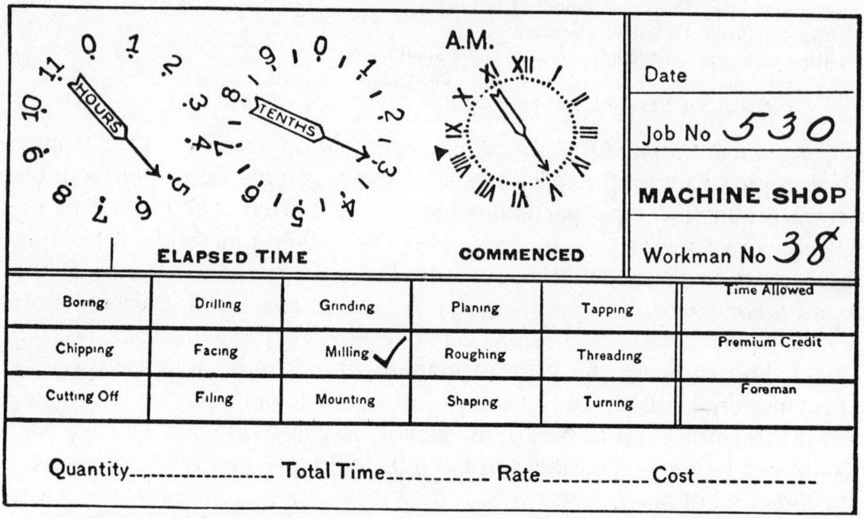

This Calculagraph record shows that workman No. 38 commenced work at 8:24 A.M., that he was performing a milling operation on Job No. 530, and that he was employed 5.3 hours.

time tickets (Illustration 9–15). The top portion of this card shows the daily "in" and "out" time record for payroll purposes. The remainder of the card shows the perforated sections to be used when time stamped for the daily job time cost computations. In this illustration, Henry Jones worked on the third shift, starting at 6:00 A.M. and ending at 2:12 P.M. The first job on which he worked was 201. He is being paid $2 per hour. On this job he worked 1.3 hours, earning $2.60.

A third method of reducing the clerical work of cost accounting requires the use of the Tel-Autograph sending and receiving machines. Each worker writes on the shop machine information regarding job work, and this information is shown on a machine in the cost accounting office, from which items are posted to individual payroll and job order cost records.

A fourth method, which is surprisingly prevalent, is the use of payroll tables which show the earnings for any number of hours or fractional hours, at almost any hourly rate. These tables range in cost from $5 to as much as $600, but they seem to justify their cost in the amount of clerical labor saved.

A fifth method has been discussed in the use of telephones in reporting the time a job was started and again when it was completed.

Punched-card accounting has long been useful in computing, sorting, and summarizing labor costs by jobs for prompt analysis. More recently, dictating machines, tape recorders, and intercom systems for central time recording have expedited the cost accounting for labor on various jobs.

By using a computer it is possible to reduce payroll accounting and job cost accounting for labor to one simple operation—turning a key in a slot. This of course is applicable only for firms large enough to be customers of a *data processing center*—about 250 workers is the break-even point for operating this system. It is a substitute for the slow manual time clocks and manual payroll accounting.

The system consists of a recording console and pairs of key transmitting stations, any number of which can be placed throughout the factory. One transmitting station of each pair is an "IN" station and the other an "OUT" station. Every worker has his own key made of plastic harder than steel. When he comes to work he inserts the key in the hole in the nearest "IN" station to his work and turns it. At the end of the day or at noon if he goes out of the building for lunch, the worker turns his key in the "OUT" station. The time signals transmitted to the console are punched on a tape along with the worker's code number. The punched tape is forwarded to the data processing center where it goes through a computer. The computer has been programmed (instructed via magnetic tape) to match the code number with the worker's name, his hourly rate, and hours worked during the week, to calculate his pay. It is programmed to figure regular time as well as overtime with proper pay rates separately for each type of time. Thus this arrangement supersedes the use of time clocks for payroll accounting.

Illustration 9–15. Combination Daily Time-Clock and Individual Job Time Ticket

For job order costs, this same arrangement has application. The time in which a job is started is similarly recorded with a code for the job number. When the work has been completed by the employee on the job, the "OUT" key is inserted. The analysis of this tape with its costs and hours by the programmed tape will serve as a basis for reporting the actual labor costs and the estimated labor costs. If standards have been set for the normal amount of hours that a job should require, the difference between the actual and standard hours can be computed and used for managerial control.

PAYROLL AND LABOR COST ACCOUNTING ILLUSTRATED

To illustrate the sequence, as well as the entries, affecting both the financial and the cost accounting for payroll, the following transactions will be recorded in general journal form, with indications of the books of original entry used and the subsidiary records affected. *Since the more common practice* is to treat payroll taxes, overtime, and other fringe benefits as *manufacturing overhead,* not as part of the direct labor costs, this procedure is followed in the illustration.

a) The payroll period is for the month of January, 19—

JANUARY, 19—						
SUN.	MON.	TUE.	WED.	THURS.	FRI.	SAT.
1	2	3	④	5	6	7
8	9	10	⑪	12	13	14
15	16	17	⑱	19	20	21
22	23	24	㉕	26	27	28
29	30	31				

b) The workers are paid on Wednesday of each week for wages earned through the preceding Saturday.

The December 31 (past) payroll amounted to $20,000 and was journalized on that date as: Dr. Payroll, $20,000; Cr. Payroll Accrued, $20,000. The workers were paid on January 4 when the other payroll liabilities (federal withholding tax, $4,000; state withholding tax, $1,000; and FICA tax withheld, $880) were recorded as deductions and accruals.

c) Payroll figures for salaries and labor costs for the month of January, 19—, were:

	For Week Ended			
	Jan. 7	Jan. 14	Jan. 21	Jan. 28
Direct labor costs...........................	$12,000.00	$11,000.00	$10,500.00	$13,000.00
Indirect labor costs.......................	6,200.00	6,300.00	5,800.00	5,900.00
Sales salaries	8,000.00	8,000.00	8,000.00	8,000.00
Office and administrative salaries	3,000.00	3,000.00	3,000.00	3,000.00
Total................................	$29,200.00	$28,300.00	$27,300.00	$29,900.00
Federal withholding taxes payable...	6,200.00	5,800.00	5,700.00	6,400.00
State withholding taxes payable	1,420.00	1,360.00	1,350.00	1,480.00
FICA taxes payable (5.2%)............	1,518.40	1,471.60	1,419.60	1,554.80

d) Payroll accrued for the period January 30 and 31 inclusive, amounted to $13,000, of which amount, direct labor costs were $6,600; indirect labor, $2,400; sales salaries, $2,600; and office salaries, $1,400.

e) The employer's payroll taxes recorded monthly at the following rates: *FICA*, 5.2 percent; *state unemployment*, 2.7 percent; *federal unemployment tax*, 0.4 percent. The employees are subject to the FICA tax deduction at the rate of 5.2 percent, recorded in the payroll journal. However, this deduction is made at the time of *payment*, that is, *only for wages actually paid*. Therefore, for accrued payroll at the end of the fiscal period, no payroll deductions are recorded. for the accrual. The FICA tax is deducted on the pay received during the first week of the new year, even though some of that pay was earned in the preceding year and exceeded the maximum limit, which for 1971 is $7,800. It is the time of payment, not the time of earning, that fixes the tax deduction date for FICA tax.

The following entries illustrate the payroll and tax accounting for the first month of the year. (At this time, no employee has yet earned the maximum amount taxable under the various payroll tax laws.)

Date	Entry		Book of Original Entry

19 —
Jan. 4
	Payroll Accrued..............................14,120.00
	     Accounts Payable*....................
	    To voucher payroll of December 31.
		14,120.00	Voucher register

4	Accounts Payable 14,120.00
	     Cash.......................................
	    Payment of December 31 payroll.
		14,120.00	Check register

4	Payroll Accrued.............................. 5,880.00
	    Federal Withholding Taxes
	       Payable ....
	    State Withholding Taxes
	       Payble.................................
	       FICA Taxes Payable.................
	    To record payroll deductions on
	    December 31 payroll in year of
	    payment.
	    (Employer's payroll taxes on above
	    payroll may be assumed to have
	    been accrued at year-end.)
		4,000.00
		
		1,000.00
		880.00
			Payroll journal

7	Payroll 29,200.00
	    Federal Withholding Taxes
	       Payable ....
	    State Withholding Taxes
	       Payable ....
	       FICA Taxes Payable (5.2%).......
	       Payroll Accrued.......................
	    Payroll liabilities, week ended 1/7.
		6,200.00
		
		1,420.00
		1,518.40
		20,061.60
			Payroll journal

*The vouchering for payment of the tax liabilities of the previous year have not been included in this illustrative problem.

Date	Entry	Book of Original Entry

19—
Jan. 7
	Work-in-Process — Labor 12,000.00
	Manufacturing Overhead (Indirect
	  Labor)....................................... 6,200.00
	Selling Expense (Sales Salaries).......... 8,000.00
	Administrative Expense (Office
	  Salaries) 3,000.00
	    Payroll 29,200.00
	Distribution of weekly payroll.†
		General journal

11	Payroll Accrued.............................20,061.60 Accounts Payable .... 20,061.60 To voucher payroll of January 7.	Voucher register
11	Accounts Payable ....20,061.60 Cash...................................... 20,061.60 Payment of January 7 payroll.	Check register

14	Payroll 28,300.00
	    Federal Withholding Taxes
	      Payable 5,800.00
	    State Withholding Taxes
	      Payable 1,360.00
	    FICA Taxes Payable (5.2%)....... 1,471.60
	    Payroll Accrued....................... 19,668.40
	Payroll liabilities.
		Payroll journal

	Work-in-Process — Labor 11,000.00
	Manufacturing Overhead (Indirect
	  Labor)....................................... 6,300.00
	Selling Expenses (Sales Salaries) 8,000.00
	Administrative Expense (Office
	  Salaries) 3,000.00
	    Payroll 28,300.00
	Distribution of payroll.
		General journal

18	Payroll Accrued.............................19,668.40 Accounts Payable .... 19,668.40 To voucher payroll of January 14.	Voucher register
	Accounts Payable ....19,668.40 Cash...................................... 19,668.40 Payment of January 14 payroll.	Check register

21	Payroll 27,300.00
	    Federal Withholding Taxes
	      Payable 5,700.00
	    State Withholding Taxes
	      Payable 1,350.00
	    FICA Taxes Payable (5.2%)....... 1,419.60
	    Payroll Accrued....................... 18,830.40
	Payroll liabilities, week ended 1/21.
		Payroll journal

†Some firms reduce the clerical work by distributing the labor costs monthly instead of weekly.

Date	Entry		Book of Original Entry
19— Jan. 21	Work-in-Process — Labor ....10,500.00 Manufacturing Overhead (Indirect Labor).. 5,800.00 Selling Expense (Sales Salaries)......... 8,000.00 Administrative Expense (Office Salaries) .... 3,000.00 Payroll .... Distribution of payroll.	27,300.00	General journal
25	Payroll Accrued...............................18,830.40 Accounts Payable .... To voucher payroll of January 21.	18,830.40	Voucher register
25	Accounts Payable ....18,830.40 Cash...................................... Payment of January 21 payroll.	18,830.40	Check register
28	Payroll ....29,900.00 Federal Withholding Taxes Payable .... State Withholding Taxes Payable .... FICA Taxes Payable (5.2%)....... Payroll Accrued........................ Payroll liabilities, week ended 1/28.	6,400.00 1,480.00 1,554.80 20,465.20	Payroll journal
28	Work-in-Process — Labor ....13,000.00 Manufacturing Overhead (Indirect Labor).. 5,900.00 Sales Expense (Sales Salaries)........... 8,000.00 Administrative Expense (Office Salaries) .... 3,000.00 Payroll .... Distribution of payroll.	29,900.00	General journal
31	Payroll ....13,000.00 Payroll Accrued...................... Accrual for January 30 and 31.	13,000.00	Payroll journal
31	Work-in-Process — Labor .... 6,600.00 Manufacturing Overhead (Indirect Labor).. 2,400.00 Selling Expense (Sales Salaries)......... 2,600.00 Administrative Expense (Office Salaries) .... 1,400.00 Payroll .... Distribution of payroll accrued, two days.	13,000.00	General journal

Date	Entry				Book of Original Entry
19 — Jan. 31	Manufacturing Overhead Control (Payroll Taxes)............................ 5,937.80 Selling Expenses (Payroll Taxes)....... 2,688.00 Administrative Expenses (Payroll Taxes).. 1,008.00				
	FICA Taxes Payable (5.2%).......			5,964.40	
	State Unemployment Tax Payable (2.7%)			3,095.90	
	Federal Unemployment Taxes Payable (0.5%)			573.50	
	Payroll taxes for payrolls, January 7, 14, 21, and 28 as follows:				General journal
		Factory	*Selling*	*Office*	
	FICA.........................$3,676.40		$1,664.00	$ 624.00	
	SUT 1,908.90		864.00	324.00	
	FUT 352.50		160.00	60.00	
	Totals.................$5,937.80		$2,688.00	$1,008.00	
31	Manufacturing Overhead (Payroll Taxes)...................................... 756.00 Selling Expenses (Payroll Taxes)....... 218.40 Administrative Expenses (Payroll Taxes)...................................... 117.60				
	FICA Taxes Payable (5.2%).......			676.00	
	SUT Tax Payable (2.7%)			351.00	
	FUT Tax Payable (0.5%)..........			65.00	
	Accruals for January 30 and 31.				General journal
Feb. 1	(Note: Month-end entries for two payrolls may be reversed and then included in the next weekly payroll.)				
15	FICA Taxes Payable.......................13,688.80 Federal Withholding Taxes Payable ...28,100.00				
	Accounts Payable*			41,788.80	
	To voucher social security and withholding tax liabilities on payrolls for January, due 2/15.				Voucher register
15	Accounts Payable 41,788.80				
	Cash.....................................			41,788.80	
	Payment to federal depository for taxes.				Check register

*The total includes liabilities for the last December payroll paid in January 4, but does not include the payroll taxes on accrual for January 30 and 31.

QUESTIONS FOR REVIEW

1. What are the three phases of accounting for labor in a manufacturing company? How may each of these be mechanized?

2. Fringe benefits for factory workers are increasing in amount at a very rapid pace. What can management do to reduce or control these?

3. Managerial control of labor involves the consideration of six factors. What are these?

4. The payroll of the Ninth Manufacturing Company for the month of April totaled $35,000. This amount included the following: superintendence, $4,000; indirect labor, $2,000; overtime bonuses, $1,500; idle time payments, $400; office salaries, $1,600; sales salaries and commissions, $3,000. Federal withholding taxes were $8,000; state withholding taxes, $2,000; FICA taxes were at the rate of 5.2 percent. Assuming the use of only one set of books, prepare all the journal entries necessary to record this data, both financial and cost accounting.

5. Pension costs for factory workers are becoming increasingly important moneywise in modern business. Explain the financial and cost accounting problems of the treatment of these costs.

6. Management needs labor cost reports to measure the efficiency of its factory operations. What are some of these reports and how can management use them?

7. Indicate the various methods that have been used to reduce the clerical labor cost accounting work.

8. What effect will increased automation of factory operations have on the practices of the cost accounting for labor?

9. An employee operating a drill press is paid $4.50 an hour for a 40-hour week, with time and one half for overtime, and double time for Sunday and holiday work. In the first week of March, he worked eight hours a day, Monday through Friday; six hours on Saturday; and four hours on Sunday. What were (1) his total earnings, and (2) his overtime premium? If all of this time was spent on Job 717, how much should be charged to the job for his work?

10. The National Company has set up a pension plan starting January 1. The end of the year showed the following: payment on account of pension costs based upon past services; payable to the Pension Insurance Company, $6,000; payment on account of the current year's contribution for costs based upon current year's factory wages, $8,000. What entries should be made to correctly state the accounting and cost accounting effects of these payments?

PROBLEMS—GROUP A

Problem 9–1. Purpose: *Payroll Accounting Records and Entries*

The Illiad Manufacturing Company maintains factory journals and ledgers at each of its five plants. At the Buffalo, N.Y., plant, the payroll is prepared for all employees, forwarded to the home office in Chicago, from which payroll checks are received. Liability for payroll taxes are kept on the home office books. Over-time premium and payroll taxes for factory employees are part of the manufacturing overhead.

For the week ending January 10, 19—, the factory payroll summary was:

Department	Labor Hours	Total Payroll	Overtime Premium	Federal Withholding Tax	State Withholding Tax	FICA Tax
Planing	300	$ 940.00	$ 85.00	$245.00	$ 35.00	$ 47.20
Machining	450	1,450.00	50.00	385.00	76.20	76.10
Stamping	210	680.00	10.00	140.00	42.10	36.20
Assembling	180	500.00	0	110.00	20.00	27.00
Storeroom	84	206.00	6.00	16.00	5.60	10.40
Toolroom	86	265.00	9.00	20.00	7.40	13.20
Finished stock room	40	100.00		15.00	1.50	5.20
Shipping	40	100.00		10.00	1.00	5.20
Total Factory	1,390	$4,241.00	$160.00	$941.00	$188.80	$220.50
Branch sales office		$1,000.00		$260.00	$ 40.00	$ 52.00
Branch office salaries		400.00		130.00	18.00	21.80

A recapitulation of the job time tickets were as follows:

Job No.	Planing Dept.	Machining Dept.	Stamping Dept.	Assembling
104	$100	$ 210	$100	$ 80
105	115	165	95	75
106	120	230	120	20
107	120	270	110	95
108	115	180	95	90
109	190	150	80	80
110	95	195	70	60
	$855	$1,400	$670	$500

Required:

Prepare all the necessary entries in journal form as they would appear on the Buffalo general office and factory journal to record:

a) Preparation of the payroll.
b) Payment of payroll.
c) Distribution of payroll.
d) Recording the employer's share of payroll taxes, using the FICA as given, federal unemployment tax at rate of 0.4 percent, state unemployment tax at 2.7 percent.

Problem 9–2.   Purpose: *Estimating Labor Costs and Fringe Benefits*

The Industrial Manufacturing Company is contemplating building a new plant in Georgia. Preparatory to making a final decision, management is interested in determining the labor costs, including the payroll taxes and fringe benefits.

At this plant, two products will be manufactured: Product A which will require 10 labor hours to complete a unit; and Product B, 20 hours. After the first six months, the time required will be reduced 10%.

The normal work period in this location is 8 hours per day, 5 days a week, 50 weeks a year.

Budgeted production for the first six months is 50,000 units of Product A and 40,000 units of Product B. A similar quantity is budgeted for the second six months of the first year's operation.

The expected wage rate in this location is $3 per hour.

Payroll taxes are: FICA, 5.2 percent on a maximum of $7,800; federal and state unemployment taxes, 3.1 percent on a maximum of $3,000.

Each employee will receive two weeks paid vacation and eight paid holidays during the year.

Employer's contributions to a pension plan are expected to be $10 per month per employee.

Required:

a) A statement with computations of how many employees should be required during the first six months and the second six months.
b) The direct labor costs for the year.
c) Other labor costs for the year.

Problem 9–3.   Purpose: *Summary and Distribution of Payroll*

The Imfret Manufacturing Company uses a job order cost system in its plant of four producing and three service departments. Payrolls are computed weekly. For the week ending March 24, the following payroll data was presented:

Department	No. of Employees	Total Hours	Total Payroll	Overtime Premium	Federal Withholding Tax
Department I..................6		260	$1,080	$120	$206
Department II 5		210	750	40	104
Department III..............3		100	360	0	58
Department IV..............2		90	300	35	42
Toolroom......................2		84	180	16	20
Storeroom.....................2		80	160	0	15
Shipping 3		120	300	0	45

The payroll for the sales and administrative offices amounted to $1,500 with federal withholding taxes of $360.

FICA taxes are at the rate of 5.2 percent. None of the employees have exceeded the maximum earnings of $7,800. Union dues deducted are $1.50 for each of the factory employees. Unemployment taxes total 3.1 percent.

Pension contributions by the employer are 3 percent of the total payroll for both factory and office employees. This is accrued weekly and paid quarterly to the trustee.

A recapitulation of the job time tickets for the week were as follows:

Job Order No.	Dept. I	Dept. II	Dept. III	Dept. IV
Ma–401..............$250	$120	$ 65	$ 25
Ma–402.............. 280	100	85	20
Ma–403.............. 195	180	70	35
Ma–404.............. 105	160	80	45
Ma–406.............. 110	140	60	25
$940	$700	$360	$150

Required:

Journal entries in logical sequence on both the factory journal and general office journal to—

a) Summarize the payrolls.
b) Payment of workers.
c) Distribution of payrolls.
d) Employer's liability for taxes and other fringe benefits.

Problem 9–4. Purpose: *Factory Payroll Entries for Job Order Cost System*

The Iriqois Manufacturing Company has prepared the following payroll and cost information for the week of February 10, 19–:

			Distribution of Hours by Jobs				
	Hourly		Job Numbers				
Employee	Rate of Pay	Total Hours Worked	210	211	220	230	240
Allen $3.00	44	15	15	10	4	
Brown 2.80	40	20	10		10	
Collins........ 3.00	40	10	10	10		10
Darwin 2.50	46	12	18	10	6	
Ellis 3.00	40	Nonproductive worker foreman.				
Farrah 5.00	40					

Assume FICA tax deduction at the rate of 5.2 percent; unemployment taxes, both federal and state, of 3.1 percent; federal withholding income taxes at the rate of 15 percent; and state withholding taxes of 6 percent. Overtime at one and one-half times for all hours over 40 per week.

Required:

a) Compute the total payroll for the week.
b) Prepare journal entries to cover the accounting and cost accounting for the week. No factory journal is used.
c) Distribute the payroll by making a journal entry.

Problem 9–5. Purpose: *Pension Plan Calculations*

The Illin Manufacturing Company has adopted a pension plan for its employees. A trial balance of the pension fund at December 31, 1973, was as follows (this plan was started January 1, 1972):

	Debit	Credit
Cash...	$ 600	
Investments at cost	4,000	
Income from investments received in 1973........		$ 500
Employee's equity:		
Allen		2,000
Brown..		1,400
Cohen..		700
	$4,600	$4,600

The following is the status of the employees of the firm:

Employee	Date of Start of Employment	Date Terminated	Salary Paid in 1973
Allen............	Dec. 8, 1968		$18,000
Brown..........	Feb. 1, 1970		14,000
Cohen	Dec. 8, 1970	Apr. 9, 1973	3,500
Dart.............	Sept. 15, 1971		8,000
Evans...........	Sept. 21, 1973	Dec. 22, 1973	2,600
Frank...........	May 6, 1973		6,900
			$53,000

The pension plan provides the following:

1. The corporation shall contribute 10 percent of its net income before taxes and pension contribution, but not in excess of 15 percent of the total wages paid to the participants in the plan, who are in the employ at the corporation year-end. Employees do not contribute to the plan.
2. An employee shall be eligible to participate in the plan on January 1, following the completion of one full year of employment.
3. The corporation's contribution shall be allocated to the participants' equities on the following point system:
   a) For each full year's employment, two points.
   b) For each $100 of salary paid in the current year, one point.
4. A participant shall have a vested interest of 10 percent of his total equity for each full year of employment. Forfeitures shall be distributed to remaining participants in proportion to their equities at the beginning of the year. Terminated employees shall receive their vested interests at year-end.
5. Income from the plan's investments shall be allocated to the equities of the remaining participants in proportion to their equities at the beginning of the year.

The Illin Manufacturing Company's net income before taxes and pension contribution for the year 1973 was $75,000.

Required:
a) A schedule computing the corporation's contribution to the plan for the year 1973.
b) Prepare a schedule computing the vested interests of the participants terminating their employment in 1973.

c) Prepare a schedule showing the allocation of the corporation's 1973 contribution to each participant.

d) Prepare a schedule showing the allocation of the plan's 1973 income on investments and forfeitures by terminated participants.

(Adapted from AICPA Uniform Examination)

PROBLEMS – GROUP B

Problem 9–6.   Purpose: *Payroll Accounting for a Manufacturing Concern Using a Factory Journal*

The following tabulation is a summary of the weekly payroll for the United Manufacturing Company as of January 24. The manufacturing operations are recorded in a separate factory journal. Payroll disbursements are made through the main office.

Payroll tax deductions not otherwise indicated are at the following rates, and it is assumed that none of the employees have reached the maximum pay subject to these taxes:

FICA tax, 5.65 percent
Federal unemployment tax (FUT), 0.5 percent (employers only)
State unemployment tax (SUT), 2.7 percent (employers only)
Disability insurance 30¢ per week per employee for both the
    employee and employer (total 60¢)
Union dues, factory workers only, $2 per week

Factory Department	No. of Workers	Total Payroll	Overtime Bonus	Withholding Income Taxes
Department No. 1 24		$ 3,920	$160	$ 720
Department No. 2 20		3,000	100	560
Cutting department 10		1,440		256
Finishing department................ 8		1,200	48	208
Toolroom 4		504	12	100
Storeroom 4		480		80
Finished stock room* 2		240		40
Shipping department* 4		512		102
Totals 76		$11,296	$320	$2,066

*Costs treated as selling expenses.

An analysis of the job order tickets for the week disclosed the following direct labor costs:

Department 1 ....$3,600
Department 2 2,800
Cutting department 1,240
Finishing department.................. 920

Administrative office payrolls were:

> Sales office expenses (12 employees) ....$3,200 (withholding, $480)
> General office expense (6 employees).............. 1,200 (withholding, $168)

Provision is made on the general office books for the accumulation of the employer's share of payroll taxes.

Required:

In two parallel columns (general office and factory office) entries in journal form to record the above payroll transactions.

Problem 9–7. Purpose: *Payroll Accounting Entries for a Manufacturing Concern Which Does Not Use a Factory Journal*

The summarized payroll for the week ended March 4 of the Urgent Machine Company was as follows:

Departments	No. of Workers	Total Payroll	Overtime Bonus	Withheld Income Taxes	Disability Insurance Deduction
Mixing department................15		$2,600.00	$180.00	$ 577.20	$ 4.50
Cooking department 12		1,880.00	120.00	377.80	3.60
Drying and packing.............. 5		800.00	80.00	155.40	1.50
Toolroom 2		280.00		48.84	0.60
Storeroom........................... 2		260.00	20.00	46.62	0.60
Finished goods storeroom....... 1		140.00		22.20	0.30
Shipping department.............. 2		280.00		48.84	0.60
Sales office......................... 9		2,600.00		480.00	2.70
General office...................... 4		1,000.00		188.70	1.20
Totals 52		$9,840.00	$400.00	$1,945.60	$15.60

A recapitulation of the job time tickets for the various departments showed:

> Mixing department $2,320
> Cooking department.................. 1,720
> Drying and packing   680
> Total............................$4,720

Provision for the payroll taxes were at the following rates:

> FICA at a rate of 5.65 percent
> Federal unemployment tax rate, 0.5 percent
> State unemployment tax rate, 2.7 percent
> Employer's disability tax is 30¢ per employee per week

None of the employee earnings have exceeded the limit for payroll taxes.

Required:

Prepare entries in journal form to record the above, assuming the use of a payroll journal, a voucher register, a check register, and general journal for the following:

a) Payroll and related liabilities.

b) Vouchering and payment of payroll.

c) Distribution of payroll costs.

d) Employer's liability for payroll taxes and disability insurance.

Problem 9–8.   Purpose: *Pension Computations for a Manufacturing Concern*

The Ultimate Manufacturing Company is planning a pension system for its employees. It is planning to fund this plan through the trust department of one of the large commercial banks by making an annual deposit of $12,000 for the next 10 years. In addition it wishes to make a lump-sum payment as of January 1, 1970, to cover the expected pension payments which will start January 1, 1980.

Estimated pension payments starting January 1, 1980, through January 1990 are expected to be as follows:

January 1, 1980	$ 6,000	January 1, 1986	$18,000
January 1, 1981	8,000	January 1, 1987	12,000
January 1, 1982	10,000	January 1, 1988	10,000
January 1, 1983	14,000	January 1, 1989	6,000
January 1, 1984	18,000	January 1, 1990	4,000
January 1, 1985	22,000		

It is expected that the funds will earn $3\frac{1}{2}\%$ compounded annually during the life of the fund.

From the various interest and annuity tables, the following figures represent the $3\frac{1}{2}$ percent computations:

Period	Amount of $1 at Compound Interest	Present Value of $1 at Compound Interest	Amount of Annuity of $1 at End of Each Period	Present Value of Annuity of $1 at End of Each Period
1	1.0350	0.9662	1.0000	0.9662
2	1.0712	0.9335	2.0350	1.8997
3	1.1087	0.9019	3.1062	2.8016
4	1.1475	0.8714	4.2149	3.6731
5	1.1877	0.8420	5.3625	4.5151
6	1.2293	0.8135	6.5502	5.3286
7	1.2723	0.7860	7.7794	6.1145
8	1.3168	0.7594	9.0517	6.8740
9	1.3629	0.7337	10.3685	7.6077
10	1.4106	0.7089	11.7314	8.3166
11	1.4600	0.6849	13.1420	9.0016
12	1.5111	0.6618	14.6020	9.6633

Required:

a) Compute the amount of payment which should be made on January 1, 1970.

b) Show all supporting computations in schedules in good form.

(Adapted from AICPA Uniform Examination)

Chapter 10

Manufacturing Overhead Costs Applied to Production

NATURE OF INDIRECT MANUFACTURING COSTS

In the conversion of direct material into a finished product, direct labor and a large number of indirect costs are incurred. These indirect costs are summarized in the *manufacturing overhead control account,* supported by a subsidiary ledger for the detailed indirect cost accounts. Manufacturing overhead is sometimes termed *factory expense, factory burden,* or *factory on-cost.* Since many of the indirect manufacturing costs will not be known and recorded until the end of the *fiscal accounting period,* it has become necessary to charge most jobs or the departmental work-in-process accounts with an *estimated* amount for the manufacturing overhead. Furthermore, the *actual* overhead fluctuates so much *from month to month* that the results from using the actual overhead rate for each month would be misleading from the standpoint of valuing inventories and measuring operating efficiency.

Because of the difficulty of tracing the amount of the various indirect manufacturing overhead costs to each job or to each department, the firm must budget the *volume* of production for the period and also the budgeted or *estimated overhead costs.* Volume of production may be expressed in terms of units, labor costs, or labor or machine-hours. Dividing the budgeted overhead costs by the budgeted volume will provide a predetermined rate at the beginning of the accounting period. This rate then is used in allocating manufacturing overhead costs to the various jobs or the departments. Periodically entries are made charging the work-in-process account and crediting an applied manufacturing overhead account. This predetermined rate can be used both for job order and for process costing.

CLASSIFICATION OF THE INDIRECT MANUFACTURING COSTS

Manufacturing overhead may be classified, according to the nature of the item, as fixed, variable, and semivariable, or as general overhead and departmental overhead. In addition, there is an underlying classification of these indirect costs under three primary headings: *indirect materials and supplies, indirect labor payroll costs,* and *other indirect costs.* The heading *other indirect costs* is too broad to be handled effectively for managerial control. It is therefore subdivided further into the following groups: (1) maintenance; (2) fixed charges; (3) power, heat, and light; (4) special service department costs; and (5) sundry indirect costs. To illustrate more specifically the various items which may appear in each group, the following lists are given:

INDIRECT MATERIALS	INDIRECT LABOR
Shop supplies	Superintendence
Factory office supplies	Foremen
Fuel	Inspectors
Nondurable tools	Factory clerical workers, timekeepers, etc.
Lubricants	Helpers and laborers
Unabsorbed freight and cartage	Storekeepers and assistants
	Chauffeurs and drivers
	Overtime payments of bonuses
	Elevator operators
	Idle time
	Athletics
	Sickness pay

OTHER INDIRECT COSTS

Maintenance	*Fixed Charges*
Building maintenance	Depreciation
Machinery and tool maintenance	Taxes
Furniture and fixture maintenance	Insurance
Transportation system maintenance	Shop vacations
Patterns	Group insurance
Auto and delivery equipment maintenance	Taking inventory
	Pensions
	Rentals

Power, Heat, and Light	*Special Service Department Costs*
Operating employees	Purchasing department
Operating supplies	Receiving department
Maintenance of equipment	Storeskeeping department
Fixed charges	Cost accounting department
	Medical department
	Cafeteria department
	Police and protection

Sundry Overhead Costs

Royalties	Interest on investment (when used)
Apportioned administrative expenses	Defective material losses
Special taxes, such as payroll, processing, and even income taxes	Spoiled goods
	Direct material inventory losses

Manufacturing overhead costs have also been classified as *fixed, variable, semivariable,* and *semifixed.* Total fixed manufacturing costs remain more or less constant in amount, regardless of the volume of production. Total variable costs fluctuate with, and in the same manner as, the volume of production, whereas semivariable costs fluctuate with the volume of production but not in the same manner—rather, by periodic steps. *The per unit cost of fixed overhead decreases in a given period as the number of units produced increases.* Few indirect costs are exactly fixed or 100 percent variable. Many of them are somewhere in between.

The following indirect costs may generally be classified as below:

Fixed Costs	*Variable Costs*
Rent	Compensation insurance
Taxes	Heat, light, and power
Fire insurance	Supplies
Depreciation	Repairs
Superintendence	Spoilage
	Freight-in
Semivariable Costs	Taxes on payroll
Inspection	
Indirect labor	*Semifixed Costs*
Factory clerical help	Rent
Supervision	Taxes
	Insurance

While this grouping of manufacturing overhead costs is important in order to obtain the maximum amount of managerial control, emphasis has been centered on the variable overhead costs as being the most satisfactory for control. However, it should not be overlooked that fixed overhead costs might also be controlled when grouped as follows:[1]

(1) *Capacity costs* such as depreciation, taxes, leasehold expenses. These could be controlled by the sale of some plants or equipment.
(2) *Organizational costs* relate primarily to key management personnel salaries such as secretaries, telephone operators, who may be dismissed in a studied reorganization.
(3) *Policy costs* which are based upon changes in long-term projected economic conditions. Research and development costs, engineering costs, etc. might be revised if economic conditions change.

These fixed costs must be given careful managerial attention in preparing a flexible budget.

---

[1] N.A.A. *Accounting Practice Report No. 10.*

CALCULATING THE PREDETERMINED MANUFACTURING OVERHEAD RATE

To calculate a predetermined overhead rate, the accountant must first of all determine whether there should be a single rate covering all the departments of a factory or whether there should be separate rates for each department. In a small plant with only a few departments similar in organization, all departments using either machine or hand labor exclusively and each product moving through all departments, a single rate might be practical. However, if some departments use machine work and others handwork and if all the products do not go through all the departments, then in the interest of more accurate costs it is advisable to have a predetermined overhead rate for each productive department in the factory. The procedure followed when manufacturing overhead is applied on a departmental basis is similar to that when but a single rate is used for the entire factory.

When the detailed budget of indirect factory costs is prepared for the coming year, this estimate assumes that there must also be an estimate of the *volume of production.* This volume may be expressed in terms of (1) units produced, (2) direct labor hours, (3) direct labor costs, (4) machine-hours, or (5) material costs.

If only a single product is being manufactured, it is possible to use the *units-produced* method. If a number of different products are manufactured, however, this method becomes impractical and some common base must be used to measure the volume of production such as labor hours, labor costs, or machine-hours.

Dividing the volume of production into the budgeted or estimated manufacturing overhead will produce the *predetermined overhead rate, expressed either as dollars* per unit, per direct labor hour, or per machine-hour, or as a *percent* of the direct labor costs or material costs.

Although the method may seem simple, the effectiveness of the cost system depends upon the reliability of *two estimates* — the indirect costs and the volume of production — both of which may be grossly miscalculated. As a result of long years of experience and through the use of carefully prepared budgets of sales and indirect costs, cost accountants have been able to calculate predetermined overhead rates with a surprising degree of accuracy.

NORMAL OPERATING CONDITIONS AND THE MANUFACTURING OVERHEAD RATES

When the manufacturer estimates his volume of production, he must do so in terms of *normal operating conditions,* since these affect the method of calculating a predetermined rate for manufacturing overhead. Accountants, engineers, and top management are not always in agreement as to the exact meaning of this term.

There are three concepts of normal operating conditions: (1) *total or ideal plant capacity*, (2) *practical plant capacity,* and (3) *expected actual volume.* When all is said and done, management must decide how it will measure the efficiency of its production.

Some accountants feel that in calculating the predetermined overhead rate the estimated volume of production should be the *maximum* or *total plant capacity.* In other words, if the plant has a full operating capacity at maximum efficiency (no idle time or machine breakdown) of 10,000 units even though business and factory conditions indicate that only 6,000 units will be produced, the former figure should be used in computing the predetermined factory overhead rate. It is obvious that the use of the 10,000 figure will result in applied manufacturing overhead very much less than the actual overhead, but these accountants maintain that the *underapplied* manufacturing overhead is due to *idle plant capacity* and is a proper charge to the Profit and Loss account. They consider it a management loss or expense chargeable either to the *sales* department because of its inability to sell the maximum amount of goods which would have kept the plant busy at capacity or to the *production* department for having too great an investment in plant and equipment or for not properly supervising the workmen or equipment to prevent machine breakdown and idle time. This basis is usually a *long-term* — five- or ten-year — measure of efficiency.

Other accountants maintain that few plants operate continuously at the maximum plant capacity. Therefore, they compute the predetermined overhead rates on the basis of *practical plant capacity.* This volume is based on the production estimated when the employees work on a regular shift, the usual number of hours per week, with due allowance for human inability to achieve maximum, 60-minutes-per-hour production, for machine breakdown, idle time, and other delays and interruptions which prevent maximum production. Some accountants estimate this volume at about 80 percent of the ideal or maximum volume. This procedure is also a long-term measure of efficiency.

A more reasonable interpretation of *normal operating conditions,* the one used in computing the predetermined rates in this text, assumes production at the *expected actual volume* for a period of a year or less. This volume may be based upon past performance, adjusted to the present business and economic outlook. The sales budget is usually the determining factor. This method results in an accurate measurement of managerial efficiency over a short period of time.

Top management must decide what basis should be used in measuring the effectiveness of production. So long as top management realizes that there are several bases on which to compute the predetermined overhead rate and then uses this information in analyzing the results as indicated by the over- or underapplied overhead, an intelligent interpretation of managerial efficiency will be possible.

For example:

1. If the estimate of maximum plant capacity for the next five years is 200,000 hours, 240,000 hours, 300,000 hours, 320,000 hours, and 400,000 hours, then the *ideal normal* plant capacity will average 292,-000 hours. Over the period of the next five years, management must strive to equal this figure during the first two years and should attempt to exceed it during the last three years. The production results will be interpreted in the light of the five-year period.

2. If the plant has 100 machines and there is a 15 percent allowance for delays, machine breakdowns, etc., the *practical plant capacity* would be computed as follows:

	Hours
100 machines × 40 hours per week × 50 weeks per year	200,000
Less: 15% for idle machines, etc.	30,000
Practical Plant Capacity for Computing the Predetermined Overhead Rate	170,000

This practical plant capacity is based on the *ability to produce,* not necessarily the ability to sell.

3. If it is assumed that the sales prospects indicate that during the coming year 5,000 units will be sold, that no attempt will be made to build up the finished goods inventory, and that 30 machine-hours will be required to produce each unit, the estimated capacity based upon *expected actual volume* (which in turn is based upon *estimated sales*) is 150,000 machine-hours.

In a year in which there is low production, the use of expected actual capacity will result in a high rate which is meaningless from the standpoint of measuring production efficiency and misleading in helping to set sales prices. When production is low, a higher rate would give the impression that a higher selling price is necessary; this would cause production to drop even lower. The effect of the capacity level on the manufacturing overhead rates may be illustrated as follows:

	Ideal	*Practical*	*Expected Actual*
Operating capacity	100%	85%	70%
Direct labor hours	1,000	850	700
Budgeted manufacturing overhead costs:			
Fixed	$2,000	$2,000	$2,000
Variable	2,000	1,700	1,400
Total	$4,000	$3,700	$3,400
Predetermined overhead rate	$4.00	$4.35	$4.85

CHARACTERISTICS OF A GOOD BASE FOR COMPUTING PREDETERMINED OVERHEAD RATES

The characteristics of a good base on which to compute the predetermined overhead rates are:

1. It should be computed easily.
2. It should be inexpensive to use in applying it to the cost of production.
3. It should have some relation to the time factor involved in many indirect costs (*period costs*).
4. It should be computed on a departmental basis, if possible, so that the causes of variations may be localized.
5. It should be reasonably accurate, that is, representative of the estimated overhead costs applicable to each unit.

In a survey conducted by the National Association of Accountants in one important industrial area, it was discovered that the methods of applying manufacturing overhead most commonly used were: *percentage of direct labor costs,* 41 percent of the firms surveyed; *per direct labor hour,* 11 percent; *per machine-hour,* 4 percent; *per unit rate,* 9 percent; and all other methods, 35 percent.

BASES FOR APPLICATION OF MANUFACTURING OVERHEAD TO PRODUCTION

Allocation of manufacturing overhead with reasonable accuracy over production for a month or a year is one of the major problems confronting a cost accountant and involves much study of cost data.

In ascertaining such a rate, manufacturing overhead is estimated for a given period and divided by the estimated base. In the following illustrations, a single-unit factory is assumed, undivided into production centers or departments. The methods used for a single-department factory, however, are also applicable to the individual departments or the operating units of production centers of a factory.

The bases used in determining the manufacturing overhead rate applicable to the cost of manufacturing are:

1. Unit.
2. Material costs.
3. Labor costs.
4. Prime costs.
5. Labor hours.
6. Machine-hours.
7. Machine-hours plus a supplementary rate.
8. Moving average.

Since production conditions and management control in business firms vary, each of the foregoing methods of applying manufacturing overhead will find application in some instances. To illustrate how each of these rates is computed, the following facts are assumed:

The *budgeted manufacturing overhead* for the
   year is:
    Fixed...$ 96,000
    Variable.. 360,000 $456,000
The estimated *number of units* to be produced in
   this period... 120,000 units
The estimated *direct material costs* are.............. $240,000
The estimated *direct labor costs* are................. $360,000
The estimated *prime cost* is........................... $600,000
The estimated *direct labor hours* are .... 180,000 man-hours
The estimated *machine-hours* are .... 84,000 machine-hours

The computation of the manufacturing overhead rates on the various bases is illustrated with only a blanket figure rather than a separate one for fixed and for variable manufacturing overhead.

UNIT BASIS

One of the simplest methods of distributing manufacturing overhead is on the per unit basis. The unit might be a pound, a foot, a machine, a hundred pieces, or, under the Bedaux incentive pay system, a "B." The formula for the determination of the rate is:

$$\frac{\text{Estimated manufacturing overhead}}{\text{Estimated number of units}} = \text{Overhead rate per unit (R).}$$

Using the figures given above, the unit burden rate is:

$$R = \frac{\$456,000}{120,000 \text{ units}} = \$3.80 \text{ per unit.}$$

The unit method of applying overhead is used most satisfactorily in small manufacturing concerns having relatively simple manufacturing processes or in large concerns manufacturing few articles in large quantities.

In foundry cost accounting, some firms use a predetermined rate based on the units of production (pounds of castings). Where a variety of castings are produced, the various products are grouped into classes, depending upon the size, and a predetermined rate per pound of casting is computed for each class.

MATERIAL COST BASIS

Some concerns find that a percentage of the cost of material used in production is a satisfactory method of determining the amount to add to the cost of direct materials and direct labor in computing the cost of manufacturing. The formula for determining the rate is:

$$R = \frac{\text{Estimated manufacturing overhead, \$456,000}}{\text{Estimated cost of material to be used, \$240,000}} = 190\% \text{ of material cost.}$$

This method is found in concerns *using materials of approximately the same value in each article being manufactured and also in concerns where the amount of material used per hour is uniform in value,* as in a firm whose output is controlled by automatic machines.

This method has limitations, however. First, since most of the factory overhead, such as superintendence, heat, light, power, insurance, rent, taxes, depreciation, and indirect labor, is consumed on a *time basis,* the value of the materials used must bear some direct relation to the amount of time used in manufacturing. This relationship is possible where the output is controlled by machines and where the cost of materials involved is more or less the same for each unit produced.

To illustrate the inaccuracies which may occur in the use of the material cost method when the cost of the materials consumed per hour or per day is not approximately the same, consider the jewelry manufacturer who uses, in the manufacture of rings of similar design, silver costing $1.80 per ounce, gold at $35 per ounce, and platinum at $65 an ounce. Rings to be manufactured from these three metals will require approximately the same amount of time and the same quantity of metal. Labor costs should be the same for each ring, since the designs are similar. If manufacturing overhead were charged to production on the basis of time, the applied overhead *should be essentially the same for each ring.* But the absence of any relationship between the time consumed in making the ring and the cost of materials used is shown by the following figures:

	Silver	Gold	Platinum
100 rings, materials	$90	$300	$520
100 rings, labor	25	30	30
100 rings, overhead (10% of material costs)	9	30	52
	$124	$360	$602

Although the amount of time used on each of these jobs was approximately the same and therefore the amount of the indirect overhead consumed on a time basis should also be the same, the resulting overhead applied on a materials cost basis varies widely.

From a theoretical viewpoint this method of computing the manufacturing overhead applicable to a given job is quite incorrect, but firms using this method argue that since the cost of the articles varies, the selling prices will vary accordingly and on the higher priced articles the amount of profit should be greater. Therefore, the amount of overhead to be borne by these higher priced articles should be greater. This is a practical answer, but it is not correct from any accounting viewpoint.

LABOR COST BASIS

The labor cost basis follows closely the materials cost method. Concerns having the same hourly pay rate for all direct laborers can best use this method. The formula is:

$$R = \frac{\text{Estimated manufacturing overhead, \$456,000}}{\text{Estimated labor costs, \$360,000}} = 126\tfrac{2}{3}\% \text{ of labor costs.}$$

The weakness of this method is apparent. If one skilled worker is paid $2.20 per hour and another worker who is more skilled but not necessarily performing the same kind of work is paid $3.30 per hour, the amount of overhead charged for the second worker per hour would be $1\frac{1}{2}$ times as much as the first. Yet when both have worked one hour they have used about the same amount of manufacturing overhead on a time basis. Simplicity of operation seems to be the main argument for such a method, and it finds very wide application. Since most workers in the same department will probably receive the same rate of pay, this method will be most practical when a separate rate is calculated for each department.

PRIME COST BASIS

The prime cost method is rather arbitrary and has the same weaknesses as the materials and the labor cost methods. Theoretically, it could be used where the increased cost of direct materials is offset by a proportionate decrease in the direct labor cost per article due to a proportionate decrease in the amount of time used by such workers. Such conditions, however, do not exist in business. The most that can be said for such a method is that it is simple and arbitrary — not sound.

The formula used in determining the rate is:

$$R = \frac{\text{Estimated manufacturing overhead, \$456,000}}{\text{Estimated prime cost of production, \$600,000}} = 76\% \text{ of prime cost.}$$

LABOR HOUR BASIS

To overcome the theoretical objections of the first three methods, some firms have resorted to the use of labor hours as a base for ascertaining the overhead rate. The labor hour method considers the time factor in applying overhead but involves additional clerical expense in computing the labor hours used on each job. It is sometimes known as the *man-hour* rate and can be effectively used where the work is of a manual and skilled nature, such as carpentering, painting, grinding, riveting, drilling, polishing, and assembling.

The formula used in determining the rate is:

$$R = \frac{\text{Estimated manufacturing overhead, \$456,000}}{\text{Estimated number of man-hours, 180,000}} = \$2.53\tfrac{1}{3} \text{ per man-hour.}$$

MACHINE-HOUR BASIS

The machine-hour basis is similar to the labor hour method and is used where the work is performed primarily on machines. In many concerns a large proportion of the manufacturing overhead is made up of depreciation on machines, power, and repairs to machines; overhead can therefore be charged more accurately to production on a machine-hour basis. The method does require additional clerical expense in computing the machine-hours on each job.

The formula used in computing the rate is:

$$R = \frac{\text{Estimated manufacturing overhead, \$456,000}}{\text{Estimated machine-hours, 84,000}} = \$5.42\tfrac{6}{7} \text{ per machine-hour.}$$

As in the case of the labor-cost-basis method, this machine-hour method can be used to advantage when a concern wishes to compute and apply manufacturing overhead to production on a departmental basis and where in some departments it might be desirable to use the percentage of labor cost method and in others the machine-hour method. It should be emphasized that both the labor hour and the machine-hour methods are desirable because they consider the time factor which influences the amounts of many overhead cost items.

MACHINE-HOUR PLUS A SUPPLEMENTARY RATE

The use of the machine-hour rate for applying manufacturing overhead is sometimes modified by a second, or "supplementary," rate. Under this method, there is a machine-hour rate for applying the overhead to production, and at the end of each month or year, the overapplied or underapplied manufacturing overhead is distributed by the use of a supplementary rate. This supplementary rate serves to correct the error in the predetermined rate; and when it has been used to take care of this adjustment, there no longer is any overapplied or underapplied overhead.

The objections to the use of this procedure are apparent. First, it is costly to readjust the job sheets for a given period, particularly when there are a great number of them. Second, the final costs on each job must be held up until the end of the month or the end of the year, when the adjustments by the supplementary rate are made. Finally, the particular value of this method is somewhat doubtful. If the overhead rates are carefully computed at the beginning of each period, the amount of the overapplied or underapplied manufacturing overhead should not be very large and this can be conveniently closed into the Cost of Goods Sold account.

There is a second interpretation of the *machine-hour rate plus a supplementary rate*. Where the factory has been departmentalized, it is possible to have a machine-hour rate for the various departments. In calculating this rate, only those indirect costs which originate in or are chargeable directly to the respective departments are used. In other words, the machine-hour rate is a direct departmental overhead rate. For all other manufacturing overhead, that is, general factory overhead, a second or supplementary rate can be used. This rate will be the same for the entire factory. Therefore, on each job sheet, in addition to the overhead applied on the basis of machine-hours, there will appear a second charge at the supplementary rate.

MOVING-AVERAGE METHOD

This method uses actual figures for the past 12 months in ascertaining overhead rates. No estimated or predetermined overhead figures are necessary. Actual manufacturing overhead for the past 12 months is totaled and averaged (by dividing by 12). The resulting average represents the amount of manufacturing overhead applicable to production for the following month. The overhead rate may be based upon the material cost, labor cost, labor hour, machine-hour, or production unit. However, this method has very little application in business today.

USING MORE THAN ONE MANUFACTURING OVERHEAD RATE IN COSTING PRODUCTION

In the interest of more accurate costing, some firms compute and use more than one manufacturing overhead rate in place of a single rate. This multirate procedure may involve several approaches:

1. *Departmental versus a single predetermined rate.* Instead of using a single plantwide rate, many firms analyze the manufacturing overhead costs by departments and then compute a separate rate for the work done in each department. These departmental rates usually apply only to the producing departments. The detailed procedure is discussed in more detail later in this chapter.

2. *Special rates for material handling costs.* In firms where materials are

used only in some of the departments, it is felt that the material handling costs—freight-in, storage, inventory recordings, delivery to factory costs, etc.—are really part of the costs of the materials used, and as such should be charged to the departments using the material on some predetermined rate basis such as a percent of the cost of materials used.

3. *General administrative expense costs* of a multiplant organization often requires the allocation of some of these costs to the various manufacturing plants. These must then be absorbed by the cost of manufacturing in these plants. This can best be done by a separate rate, unless the amount is included with the general factory overhead costs.

4. *Separate fixed and variable overhead cost rates.* In order to create the maximum control over the manufacturing costs, many firms analyze their overhead costs into the fixed and variable elements, using separate rates for each group.

INTERIM CHANGING OF GROSSLY INACCURATE OVERHEAD RATES

In some rare instances, manufacturing overhead rates computed at the beginning of an accounting period may be out of line with the actual operating conditions. This is usually due to some unforeseen contingencies arising during the accounting period. Management is faced with the question of what to do: should it continue to use the incorrect rate and report a large over- or underapplied overhead at the end of the period; should it go back over the cost reports completed and change the applied overhead to conform to the revised rate; or should a new rate be computed for the remainder of the accounting period using corrected figures? If there are not too many job orders or if this calculation error occurs early in the accounting period, the firm may use what is known as the *retroactive* method. Under this, a corrected rate is computed and used on the work completed so that it will be more comparable to normal production. If the rate originally computed was too high, a correction entry would be made, as follows:

```
Applied Manufacturing Overhead...............................................xxxxx
    Work-in-Process.................................................................         xxxxx
```

If the original rate is used for the production already completed and a new rate is computed for the remaining period, it is known as the *progressive method.* To illustrate this procedure, the following is given:

```
Budgeted manufacturing overhead, January 1 ...................................$60,000
Budgeted production for year, in terms of labor hours...................... 30,000 hrs.
Actual production during first three months.................................... 25,000 hrs.
Expected annual production for remainder of year........................... 60,000 hrs.
Additional overhead to be incurred because of increased volume
    of production ......................................................................... $8,000
```

On the basis of this data and using the *progressive* (*noncorrective*) method, the accounting entries would be:

March 31

Work-in-Process — Manufacturing Overhead 50,000
    Applied Manufacturing Overhead   50,000
    To record applied overhead on the basis of a predetermined rate
    of $2 (January 1) and 25,000 units.

The revised budgeted overhead for the remaining nine months would be $18,000 ($10,000 + $8,000), and budgeted production would be 60,000 direct labor hours. This results in a predetermined rate of 30 cents for the production during the next nine months. If a new rate is used for the remaining accounting period, then the original costing will be incorrect and the costing for the remaining period will also not be comparable. While this method may be more convenient, the cost accounting will have little managerial value as a measure of production efficiency. No correction entry is necessary when this method is used.

One well-known firm sets its manufacturing overhead rates at the beginning of the accounting period and does not change these no matter what happens. In instances where this results in a large over- or under-applied manufacturing overhead, criticism is placed with those responsible for budgeting the overhead costs and calculating the rates.

DEPARTMENTALIZATION OF THE MANUFACTURING OVERHEAD

Computing overhead rates on a departmental basis results in better cost control by localizing the variations from the budgeted and the actual costs. A *department or a production center* of a factory for cost accounting purposes has been defined as a group of machines or workers performing similar operations. For example, a group of employees working at benches assembling vacuum cleaners would be considered the *assembly department;* a group of men operating a large stamping machine would be considered the *stamping department;* and a group of employees painting the final product might be described as the *painting* or *finishing* department. Departments must be further classified as *producing* or *service* departments. A producing department is one in which the actual manufacturing operations are performed such as cutting, assembling, drilling, and painting. Service departments are those whose activities are necessary to facilitate the manufacturing operations, but in which no manufacturing work is actually performed, such as the materials handling department, the powerhouse activities, maintenance and repair of plant and equipment department, factory toolroom, factory hospital, and factory lunchroom. Since the service departments do not involve *directly* the manufacturing operations, it will be necessary to apply the overhead of the service departments on some rational basis. It may be done under three possible arrangements:

1. *Reciprocal basis* under which the service department expenses are distributed to the various other departments so that when it is completed, the entire manufacturing overhead costs are allocated to the *producing* departments.
2. *Direct basis* under which the manufacturing overhead costs are allocated only to the producing departments, with none to the service departments—thus making it unnecessary to redistribute the service department overhead costs to the producing departments.
3. *Nonreciprocal basis* under which there is an accumulation of the service departments overhead costs and under which a separate rate is computed for each service department as well as for each producing department.

However, although there are three basic methods for use in allocating the manufacturing overhead, the most practical method is the reciprocal method under which all the service department overhead costs are redistributed to the producing departments; and thus when completed, there are predetermined rates only for the producing departments.

PROCEDURE USED IN DEPARTMENTALIZING INDIRECT FACTORY COSTS

The procedure to be followed in departmentalizing manufacturing overhead may be outlined as follows:

A. SETTING DEPARTMENTAL RATES
1. Prepare a list of the estimated or budgeted overhead costs for the entire plant.
2. Decide what bases are to be used in allocating the various costs to the departments, service as well as production (such as floor space, production hours, etc.).
3. Prepare a factory survey (statistical summary) of these bases and use this information to distribute the budgeted overhead costs to the various departments.
4. Transfer the service department costs to the producing department so that all the budgeted costs will be assigned to producing departments only.
5. Estimate the number of labor hours, machine-hours, etc., to be used as the denominator in calculating departmental rates.
6. Compute the predetermined rates by dividing the estimated departmental overhead by the estimated base.

B. APPLYING OVERHEAD RATES
1. Apply the predetermined overhead rates to the finished jobs and the work-in-process on a departmental basis.
C. RECORDING ACTUAL OVERHEAD COSTS
1. Record overhead actually incurred in the Manufacturing Overhead Control account, posting details to the subsidiary ledger.
2. Prepare a work sheet analysis similar to the one used in distributing estimated costs by departments.
3. Calculate the over- or underapplied manufacturing overhead by department and dispose of this difference at the close of the fiscal year.

To amplify the procedures listed above, the following discussion should be carefully examined.

A–1 and A–2. Bases for Allocating and Prorating Manufacturing Overhead Departmentally. The first step in prorating the manufacturing overhead departmentally is the preparation of a list of the estimated or budgeted overhead costs for the entire plant, as shown in Illustration 10–1. After this has been done, the cost accountant is faced with the prob-

Illustration 10–1. Budgeted Overhead Costs and Bases for Allocation

Cost Item	Amount	Basis of Distribution to Departments
Indirect materials	$11,000	Estimated departmental use
Indirect labor	5,600	Estimated departmental use
Superintendence	5,000	Number of workers
Fire insurance on machinery	1,200	Value of equipment in department
Compensation insurance	1,600	Estimated department payroll
Light	800	Kilowatt-hours
Power	2,400	Horsepower-hours
Fuel	1,000	Heat Service Department in total
Repairs to machinery	4,000	To Maintenance Department in total
Depreciation of machinery	4,200	Value of equipment in each department
Rent	2,400	Square footage
Total Estimated Overhead Costs	$39,200	

lem of allocating these costs departmentally. Some of these overhead costs may be allocated *directly* to the various departments, both producing and service, since they may arise solely within the department affected or may be measured as a departmental direct charge. Others are plant-wide charges which must be *prorated* to the various departments on some equitable basis.

Those *indirect costs* which can be charged directly to the departments affected may be items such as indirect materials and indirect labor;

electricity where each department has a meter measuring arrangement; payroll taxes and compensation insurance costs based upon departmental payrolls; and depreciation charges based upon departmental equipment investment. The procedure of departmentalization of indirect costs directly to the departments affected is known as *allocation*.

Some indirect costs, however, do not lend themselves to accurate allocation. These must be prorated, and the results must be approximately correct. For example, in prorating the building maintenance costs, such as rent, taxes, insurance, and repairs, it is assumed that each location in the building is of equal value and that by using the square footage as a basis, a reasonable distribution of these costs to the various departments can be computed. There are many other charges which must be similarly treated.

Except for those indirect costs whose allocation is obtained by direct measurement, the basic procedure for allocating or prorating factory overhead requires the preparation of a *factory survey* which will give the information about the number of square feet, the number of employees, the investment, and other facts necessary for indirect cost distribution. Illustration 10–2 presents some suggested bases for overhead cost distribution.

A–3. Factory Survey for the Distribution of Indirect Costs to the Departments. After the bases for distribution have been agreed upon for a plant, a survey of the factory and adjoining facilities is made to ascertain how each of these bases affects each of the departments. The facts presented in the survey are first used in allocating the estimated indirect costs to the departments so that the predetermined departmental overhead rates may be computed. *The same survey is used as a basis for allocating or prorating the actual indirect costs to the departmental overhead accounts*, through a departmental analysis sheet or a work sheet.

This survey may be used year after year with slight adjustments for such items as investments, payroll, or electricity used. In using this survey it is necessary to estimate the total indirect manufacturing costs for a given period. A large number of these estimated costs, such as rent, insurance, superintendence, depreciation, etc., may be determined exactly.

A hypothetical factory situation is set up to illustrate the nature of a survey (see Illustration 10–3). There are four departments actually engaged in the manufacturing processes and three service departments: the maintenance and repair department, air-conditioning service, and heating service. It is assumed that the power is purchased rather than manufactured. The bases for prorating the estimated manufacturing overhead for the year are as given in Illustration 10–2.

The item of rent is used to illustrate how these estimated indirect costs are prorated to the departments in conjunction with a survey.

Illustration 10–2.   Bases of Departmentalization of Factory Overhead Costs

Basis of Distribution	Indirect Costs Distributed on this Basis
Square footage	Rent of factory Taxes on factory Depreciation of factory buildings Repairs to factory buildings Fire insurance on buildings Heat expense, where separately charged
Number of employees	Superintendence Factory lunchroom costs Factory hospital costs Cost accounting costs Toolroom costs
Pay of employees	Compensation insurance Payroll taxes
Rated capacity	Light (when not metered for each department)
Horsepower-hours	Power (when not metered for each department)
Investment in equipment	Fire insurance on machinery Depreciation on machinery Machinery repairs (if not charged directly) Personal property taxes
Direct departmental charges	Indirect labor Machinery repairs
Number of electric light bulbs	Light charges are distributed on this basis if all bulbs are of a uniform wattage

Illustration 10–3.   Factory Survey for Year 19—

Department	Basis					Invest-ment
	Square Feet	No. of Em-ployees	Total Pay to Employees	KW Hours	H.P. Hours	
Producing Department A	400	10	$12,000	800	3,200	$10,000
Producing Department B	500	10	10,000	800	800	5,000
Producing Department C	600	15	20,000	1,200		1,000
Producing Department D	800	20	30,000	2,000	1,600	7,500
Maintenance service	300	5	4,000	100	200	2,500
Air-conditioning service	200	3	2,000	50	100	1,000
Heating service	200	2	2,000	50	100	1,000
Total	3,000	65	$80,000	5,000	6,000	$28,000

Department A occupies 400 square feet out of a total of 3,000. This department, therefore, would be charged with 400/3,000 of $2,400, or $320; Department B, with an area of 500 square feet, would be charged with 500/3,000 of $2,400, or $400; etc.

A similar prorating method is used for each of the other indirect costs.

A–4. Transfer the Service Department Overhead Costs to the Producing Departments. Although a few firms use a separate predetermined rate for each of the service departments, this procedure is not practical because it becomes too complicated. Therefore, in most factories the budgeted manufacturing overhead costs for the service departments are prorated to the producing departments on the basis rendered to the respective departments. When the producing departments have been charged with all the prorated indirect costs as well as the *service* department's costs, a predetermined manufacturing overhead rate is calculated for each producing department, for use in determining the overhead charges to be entered on the job order cost sheets.

The apportionment of the service department overhead costs to the other departments may sometimes cause difficulty because some of the service departments may render service to other service departments. To avoid too many complications, the *sequence* in which the service department manufacturing overhead is to be distributed to the producing departments must be established. For example, the maintenance of equipment department serves not only the producing departments but also the other service departments; the air-conditioning and heating departments do likewise. A safe rule to follow in apportioning service department costs is to *first* close out the amount for that service department which affects the *greatest number of other service departments*. If such a distinction is not possible, as in the case above, close first the amount for the service department which involves *the largest amount of costs*. Once a service department overhead has been closed, no further items are distributed to it.

A list of estimated indirect costs shown in Illustration 10–1, together with the proration to the service and producing departments, is shown in the tabulation of Illustration 10–4. The proration is based upon the factory survey shown in Illustration 10–3.

In the table of distribution given in Illustration 10–4, the amount of maintenance department costs was distributed first because it involved the largest amount. The basis of distribution to the other departments was the *equipment investment* in each department. After the amount for the maintenance department costs was closed, the air-conditioning department costs were distributed. It should be noted that the amount distributed to the other departments included not only the original amount of $2,171.60 but the additional amount of $300 charged from the distribution of the maintenance department overhead. Air-conditioning costs were distributed to the other departments on the basis of *square*

Illustration 10–4. The Departmentalization of the Estimated Indirect Manufacturing Costs for the Year 19–

Cost Item	Service Departments			Producing Departments				Total
	Maintenance	Air Con.	Heating	A	B	C	D	
Indirect material	$1,000.00	$700.00	$300.00	$2,000.00	$1,200.00	$3,000.00	$2,800.00	$11,000.00
Indirect labor	1,200.00	800.00	1,100.00	700.00	800.00	1,000.00		5,600.00
Superintendence*	384.60	230.75	153.85	769.25	769.25	1,153.80	1,538.50	5,000.00
Fire insurance on machinery*	107.15	42.85	42.85	428.55	214.30	42.85	321.45	1,200.00
Compensation insurance	80.00	40.00	40.00	240.00	200.00	400.00	600.00	1,600.00
Light	16.00	8.00	8.00	128.00	128.00	192.00	320.00	800.00
Power	80.00	40.00	40.00	1,280.00	320.00		640.00	2,400.00
Fuel			1,000.00					1,000.00
Repairs to machinery	4,000.00							4,000.00
Depreciation of machinery	375.00	150.00	150.00	1,500.00	750.00	150.00	1,125.00	4,200.00
Rent	240.00	160.00	160.00	320.00	400.00	480.00	640.00	2,400.00
Total	$7,482.75	$2,171.60	$2,994.70					$39,200.00
Maintenance*		300.00	300.00	2,932.75	1,500.00	300.00	2,100.00	$7,482.75
Total		$2,471.60						
Air conditioning*			200.00	400.00	500.00	600.00	771.60	$2,471.60
Total			$3,494.70					
Heating*				665.00	835.00	1,000.00	994.70	$3,494.70
Total				$11,413.55	$7,616.55	$8,318.65	$11,851.25	$39,200.00
Basis of predetermining rate				11,500 direct labor hours	$30,464.00 direct labor costs	$41,598.00 direct labor costs*	47,400 machine-hours	
Predetermined departmental overhead rates				$1.00 per labor hour	25% of direct labor costs	20% of direct labor costs*	25¢ per machine-hour	

* Approximated calculations of the distributions.

footage. Although the usual basis for distributing air-conditioning and heat costs is the cubic footage, square footage is equally satisfactory if the ceilings are of a uniform height. Heating department costs were distributed to the producing departments, but the amount so distributed included the costs added from the maintenance and air-conditioning departments.

A–5 and A–6. Computing the Departmental Predetermined Overhead Rate. When the budgeted overhead costs have been properly allocated to the producing departments (including the distribution of the service departments' overhead costs), then a predetermined overhead rate must be computed for each producing department. To do this, management must decide what base is to be used in the various departments for this overhead application. It might be: *a percent of labor costs; a dollar and cents rate per direct labor hour; or a dollar and cents rate per machine-hour.* This then necessitates the *estimate* of the labor costs, the labor hours, or the machine-hours for the period covered by the budgeted overhead costs. In Illustration 10–5, the manufacturing overhead rates are computed

Illustration 10–5. Computation of Predetermined Overhead Rates

Department	Predetermined Overhead	Basis of Pre-determining Rate	Predetermined Overhead Rate on Departmental Basis*
Producing Department A	$11,413.55	11,500 direct labor hours	$1 per labor-hour*
Producing Department B	7,616.55	$30,464 direct labor costs	25% of direct labor costs*
Producing Department C	8,318.65	$41,598 direct labor costs	20% of direct labor costs
Producing Department D	11,851.25	47,400 machine-hours	25¢ per machine-hour

*Approximate calculation.

departmentally. In this illustration, it was estimated that in Department A there would be 11,500 direct labor hours; in Department B, $30,464 direct labor costs; in Department C, $41,598 direct labor costs; and in Department D, 47,400 machine-hours. Using this information together with the allocation of the budgeted overhead costs as shown in Illustration 10–4, it is possible to compute the departmental overhead rates as shown in Illustration 10–5 as follows:

Producing Department A...................$1 per man-hour
Producing Department B ....25% of direct labor costs
Producing Department C...................20% of direct labor costs
Producing Department D..................25¢ per machine-hour

B-1. Applying Manufacturing Overhead Costs Departmentally. When departmental overhead rates are used, the design of the job order sheets must be changed so that the overhead may be recorded in separate columns representing the different departments (Illustration 10-6). In this illustration, manufacturing overhead is applied departmentally:

1. Machine Department No. 1 on the basis of machine-hours.
2. Machine Department No. 2 on the basis of machine-hours.

Illustration 10-6. Cost of Production Report Showing Manufacturing Overhead and Labor Costs Departmentalized

PRODUCTION ORDER & JOB ORDER COST SHEET

FOR *Browning Mfg Co*   JOB NUMBER *10-142*

ADDRESS *Houston, Texas*   DATE *Oct 20, 19--*

DESCRIPTION *5 Special Machines*   CUSTOMER'S NUMBER *OM-7-487*

DATE COMPLETED *Nov. 11.19.*   SELLING PRICE *6500 00*   TOTAL COST *3,172 00*   UNIT COST *634 40*

DIRECT LABOR COSTS

DATE	MACH. DEPT. #1		MACH. DEPT. #2		ASSEMBLING		FINISHING	MATERIAL COSTS		
	Mach. Hrs.	Amount	Mach. Hrs.	Amount	Labor Hrs.	Amount	Amount	Date	Req. No.	Amount
Oct 28	30	90 00	10	33 00				Oct 20	651	160 00
Nov 4	25	80 00	10	33 00	32	100 00		30	658	200 00
Nov 11					60	200 00	600 00	Nov 7	690	400 00
Totals		170 00		66 00		300 00	600 00			760 00

APPLIED MANUFACTURING OVERHEAD COSTS

DATE	MACH. DEPT. #1			MACH. DEPT. #2			ASSEMBLING			FINISHING			SUMMARY	
	Hrs.	R.	Amt.	Hrs.	R.	Amount	Hrs.	R.	Amount	Cost	%	Amt.	Cost Element	Amount
Oct 28	30	2 00	60 00	10	1 80	18 00							MATERIAL	760 00
Nov 4	25	2 00	50 00	10	1 80	18 00	32	2 50	80 00				LABOR #1	170 00
Nov 11							60	2 50	150 00	600 00	150%	900 00	LABOR #2	66 00
													LABOR #3	300 00
													LABOR #4	600 00
													O.H. #1	110 00
													O.H. #2	36 00
													O.H. #3	230 00
													O.H. #4	900 00
Total			110 00			36 00			230 00			900 00	TOTAL COST	3172 00

3. Assembling department on the basis of labor hours.
4. Finishing department as a percent of labor costs.

Since in Machine Departments No. 1 and No. 2 it is necessary to record the machine-hours and in Assembling the labor hours, space must be provided for recording this data in the Payroll section of the job order cost sheet. Parallel columns are then provided for recording the manufacturing overhead.

Paralleling this procedure, applied manufacturing overhead accounts must be maintained for each producing department. The entry, made weekly or monthly, to record the applied manufacturing overhead would be:

Work-in-Process – Manufacturing Overhead 6,000		
Applied Manufacturing Overhead – Department No. 1		600
Applied Manufacturing Overhead – Department No. 2		100
Applied Manufacturing Overhead – Assembling......................		1,500
Applied Manufacturing Overhead – Finishing.........................		3,800
To record overhead applied to production.		

The above entry is a summary of the applied overhead costs recorded on the job order cost sheets for the period.

C-1, C-2, and C-3. Recording the Actual Manufacturing Overhead Costs. The procedures, problems, and methods of recording the actual overhead costs will be discussed in Chapter 11.

ANALYZING OVERHEAD COSTS INTO THEIR FIXED AND VARIABLE ELEMENTS

As previously indicated, *fixed overhead* costs do not fluctuate in response to fluctuations in volume. They may fluctuate from period to period. In fact, fixed overhead costs may exist when there is no production at all. *Variable* overhead costs fluctuate in the same direction and usually proportionately with the volume of production. *Semivariable* overhead costs while fluctuating in the same direction as volume, do so in less than the proportional changes in volume of production, and frequently in "steps" rather than in a continuous manner. It might be assumed that since a *basic* figure for semivariable overhead will exist with a minimum volume of production, this cost could be considered fixed.

On the theory that factory management and supervision has little or no control over the fixed or period overhead costs but has considerable control over the variable overhead costs, it becomes necessary to separate manufacturing overhead costs into their fixed and variable elements. This separation and the subsequent comparison of these costs from period to period, or from job to job, will provide a more reliable measurement of the managerial achievements in cost reduction through the variable overhead. By examining the fluctuation in costs and production of the semivariable overhead item of *inspection costs* – Illustration 10–7, showing figures arranged in order of the volume of production, not chronologically—it is possible to compute the increase in costs due to increase in volume of production—the *variable* element of the cost. To illustrate, the following data are used:

Month	Volume of Production (Units)	Inspection Costs
January	120,000	$ 8,000
February	120,000	8,000
March	145,000	9,500
April	142,000	9,300
May	150,000	9,800
June	130,000	8,300
July	135,000	8,750
August	157,000	10,392
September	155,000	10,200
October	100,000	7,000
November	140,000	9,200
December	140,000	9,200

The increase in the volume of production of 57,000 units over the base or minimum figure of the October production of 100,000 resulted in an increase in the inspection costs of $3,392, or the equivalent of 5.95 cents per unit ($3,392 ÷ 57,000 units). This 5.95 cents is assumed to be the *average* variable cost since it fluctuated with the volume of

Illustration 10–7. Analysis of the Inspection Costs for the Previous Year

Month	Volume of Production (Units)	Cost of Inspection	Increase in Volume of Production (Units)	Increase in Cost of Production Due to Inspection Costs
October	100,000	$ 7,000	...	...
January	120,000	8,000	20,000	$1,000
February	120,000	8,000	...	...
June	130,000	8,300	10,000	300
July	135,000	8,750	5,000	450
November	140,000	9,200	5,000	450
December	140,000	9,200	...	...
April	142,000	9,300	2,000	100
March	145,000	9,500	3,000	200
May	150,000	9,800	5,000	300
September	155,000	10,200	5,000	400
August	157,000	10,392	2,000	192
Total			57,000	$3,392

production. In prorating the inspection costs for each month between the fixed and variable amounts, the actual production is multiplied by this variable cost per unit and the balance is considered the *fixed* inspection cost. It should be noted that this is merely a mathematical procedure for dividing the costs into the controllable and noncontrollable factors. To illustrate this proration:

Production for October, 100,000 units, variable cost @5.95¢....................$5,950
Balance is fixed cost 1,050
Total Inspection Cost...$7,000

On the basis of these computations, it will be assumed that for each month the *fixed* portion of the inspection costs will be $1,050 and the balance variable. Following this procedure, it is possible to prepare a budget of the estimated manufacturing overhead costs, showing the fixed and variable parts of each item, and thereafter to compute a separate rate for the fixed and variable items, or a combined rate. Since management is interested in the *controllability* of the variable portion of the various manufacturing overhead costs, separation into two parts is desirable. The same procedure of separating the various manufacturing overhead costs into their fixed and variable portions, as was used above for inspection costs, has been used for the 16 items listed in Illustration 10–8.

In addition to the previous method of separating the semivariable and semifixed overhead into the fixed and variable portions (known as the

Illustration 10–8. Analysis of Manufacturing Overhead Estimated for Year Ending December 31, 19—

Overhead Cost Item	Fixed	Variable	Total
Indirect materials		$12,000	$ 12,000
Fuel...	$ 6,000	2,000	8,000
Superintendence..	12,000		12,000
Inspection..	12,600	2,500	15,100
Material handling	6,000	4,000	10,000
Indirect labor..		14,000	14,000
Payroll taxes	1,300	900	2,200
Maintenance of buildings	3,000		3,000
Repairs and maintenance of equipment		7,000	7,000
Telephone and telegraph....................................	500	2,500	3,000
Depreciation—machinery and equipment..............	10,000		10,000
Workmen's compensation insurance	200	800	1,000
Light...	500	3,500	4,000
Power		12,000	12,000
Rent...	10,800		10,800
Small tools		5,200	5,200
Total..	$62,900	$66,400	$129,300

high-low method), two other methods are used: (1) the scattergraph method and (2) the method of least squares.

The *scattergraph method* involves the plotting of the cost and volume data on a sheet of graph paper and fitting a line by sight to these data (see Illustration 10–9). The fixed element can be read from the graph at the point where the overhead cost line crosses the *Y*-axis.

Examining this graph, the following situations exist:

	Fixed Overhead	Variable	Total
January ...:.................................	$790	$7,200	$7,990
February	790	7,200	7,990
March.....................................	790	8,700	9,490

Illustration 10–9. Scattergraph of Fixed and Variable Overhead Costs (data in Illustration 10–7)

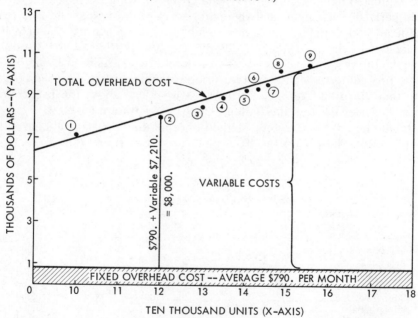

As is evident, these figures are approximate but would come out exactly were precise mathematical calculations involved. Here, the application and theory are important. Calculating the variable overhead cost on a unit basis results in a figure of approximately 6 cents per unit.[2]

The least squares method of separating overhead costs into their fixed

---

[2] 120,000 units × 0.06 = $7,200.

and variable elements is an application of statistics to accounting. This mathematical method eliminates the guesswork used in the scattergraph method, since it is unlikely that the 12 points in a scattergraph will result in a straight line. In this method, the line is determined by means of the statistical technique of least squares. The line represents a situation in which the sum of the squared deviations is a minimum. Two simultaneous linear equations are necessary to determine the fixed cost element and the variable cost per unit of activity. For any given month, the mathematical implication of these formulae is:

Fixed overhead cost + (Unit variable overhead allowance × Production)
= Total overhead.

The linear equations are:

(1) $$\Sigma XY = a\Sigma X + b\Sigma X^2$$
(2) $$\Sigma Y = na + b\Sigma X$$

in which

X = number of units of production.
Y = total overhead cost at a given level of production.
n = number of observations (months).
a = fixed cost amount.
b = variable cost per unit of production.

To illustrate this method of least squares, the data given for the scattergraph are used and will be tabulated in accordance with the formulae requirements (see Illustration 10–10).

Illustration 10–10

Month	X Units of Production (Thousands)	Y Inspection Costs	XY	X²
January	120	$ 8,000	$ 960,000	14,400
February	120	8,000	960,000	14,400
March	145	9,500	1,377,500	21,025
April	140	9,300	1,302,000	19,600
May	150	9,800	1,470,000	22,500
June	130	8,300	1,079,000	16,900
July	135	8,750	1,181,250	18,225
August	157	10,390	1,631,230	24,649
September	155	10,200	1,581,000	24,025
October	100	7,000	700,000	10,000
November	140	9,200	1,288,000	19,600
December	140	9,200	1,288,000	19,600
	1,632	$107,640	$14,817,980	224,924

Using this data in the formula, the equations would be:

(1)
$$\Sigma XY = a(\Sigma X) + b(\Sigma X^2)$$
$$\$14,817,980 = a(1,632) + b(224,924)$$

(2)
$$\Sigma Y = na + b(\Sigma X)$$
$$\$107,640 = 12a + 1,632b$$

Solving these two simultaneous equations, a will be the fixed inspection costs for the month, or $810,[3] and b will be the variable cost *per thousand units* of production, or $60.[3]

A shortcut procedure for the least squares method would be as shown in Illustration 10–11.

The variable rate *per thousand units* of production is as follows:

$$\frac{\$178,940}{2,972} = \$60.$$

The fixed element per month is computed as follows: Average total cost per month minus average total variable cost per month equals the total fixed cost per month.

$$\$8,970 - (\$60 \times 136) = \$810 \text{ approximate.}$$

Illustration 10–11

Month	(1) Difference from Average of Units of Production $1,632 \div 12 = 136$	(2) Column (1) Squared	(3) Difference from Average of Inspec- tion Costs $\$107,640 \div 12 =$ $\$8,970$	(4) Column 1 × Column 3
January	−16	256	$ −970	$ 15,520
February	−16	256	−970	15,520
March	+9	81	530	4,770
April	+4	16	330	1,320
May	+14	196	830	11,620
June	−6	36	−670	4,020
July	−1	1	−220	220
August	+21	441	1,420	29,820
September	+19	361	1,230	23,370
October	−36	1,296	−1,970	70,920
November	+4	16	230	920
December	+4	16	230	920
Total	0	2,972	0	$178,940

It should be noted that the high-low, statistical scattergraph and least squares methods of separating fixed and variable costs are all based on an analysis of past performance. From a control standpoint, this may

---

[3] Approximate figures.

perpetuate waste and inefficiency. We should encourage a fresh, engineering point of view which looks at what costs should be rather than what they were.

ABSORPTION COSTING VERSUS DIRECT COSTING

Under internal revenue rulings and the professional accounting societies, the cost of manufacturing must include both fixed and variable overhead costs in order to compute acceptable work-in-process and finished goods inventories and cost of sales. Having two rates, one fixed and one for the variable overhead costs, meets these requirements. This procedure of including the total manufacturing overhead costs as part of the manufacturing costs is known as absorption costing—that is, the total overhead costs are absorbed. For managerial control however, some firms in recent years have adopted in their cost reports what is known as direct or variable costing. Fixed overhead costs are not treated as part of the cost of production but are treated as operating expenses. The cost of goods manufactured and the work-in-process and finished goods inventories will then be composed of three variable costs: direct materials, direct labor, and variable overhead. Since the departmental foremen will be held responsible for the fluctuations in their costs over which they have some control, the cost reports will be more reliable as a measure of their work. Direct or variable costing will be discussed in greater detail in Chapter 20.

CONTROLLING COSTS THROUGH THE USE OF A FLEXIBLE MANUFACTURING OVERHEAD BUDGET

A budget is a plan of action. It is used to measure actual results. Material and labor costs are variable costs and therefore subject to control. Manufacturing overhead may be fixed with a limited amount of cost control or it may be flexible, in which case it is the area in which major cost control can be exercised. Therefore the manufacturing overhead budget is made up of two parts—the fixed and flexible costs. The fixed part is comparable to the static budget; the flexible part is the one which varies with production and is therefore subject to a certain amount of supervisory control.

Overhead rates are usually determined and used for a definite period of time—usually on an annual basis, subject to correction if they are extremely out of line with actual conditions.

By preparing and using a flexible manufacturing overhead budget as shown in Illustration 10–12, it is possible to compare the actual operating results with those that should have occurred because of fluctuating volume of production. From this comparison, it is possible to determine whether the variations in overhead costs are due to volume of production

Illustration 10–12

FLEXIBLE MANUFACTURING OVERHEAD COST BUDGET
FOR THE CUTTING DEPARTMENT*

For Year Ending December 31, 19—

Element of Overhead	Operating Capacity				
	40%	60%	80%	100%	110%
Variable overhead costs:					
Indirect materials........	$ 4,800	$ 7,200	$ 9,600	$ 12,000	$ 13,200
Fuel.....................	800†	1,000†	1,500†	2,000†	2,200†
Inspection...............	0	200†	300†	500†	600†
Materials handling.......	1,500†	2,600†	3,000†	4,000†	4,500†
Indirect labor...........	5,000	8,000	11,200	14,000	15,500
Payroll taxes...........	360†	540†	720†	900†	1,000†
Equipment repairs and maintenance..........	2,640	4,260	5,580	7,000	7,500
Telephone and telegraph	1,000†	1,500†	2,000†	2,500†	2,800†
Compensation insurance..	300†	500†	650†	800†	900†
Light...................	1,400†	2,100†	2,800†	3,500†	3,800†
Power...................	4,800	7,200	9,600	12,000	13,200
Small tools.............	2,000	3,000	4,000	5,200	5,800
Total Variable Costs	$ 24,600	$ 38,100	$ 50,950	$ 64,400	$ 71,000
Fixed overhead costs:					
Fuel.....................				$ 6,000‡	
Superintendence..........				12,000	
Inspection...............				8,000‡	
Materials handling.......				6,000‡	
Payroll taxes...........				1,300‡	
Building maintenance....				3,000	
Telephone and telegraph				500‡	
Depreciation—equipment				10,000	
Compensation insurance..				200‡	
Light...................				500‡	
Rent....................				10,800	
Total Fixed Overhead........	$ 58,300	$ 58,300	$ 58,300	$ 58,300	$ 58,300
Estimated direct labor costs.................	$140,000	$190,000	$250,000	$300,000	$340,000
Predetermined rate—variable	1.76%	2.00%	2.04%	2.15%	2.09%
Predetermined rate—fixed	4.16%	3.07%	2.33%	1.94%	1.71%

* Similar schedules must be prepared for each producing department.
† Variable portion of semivariable overhead costs.
‡ Fixed portion of semivariable overhead costs.

or to the cost of the overhead—thus serving as a tool of managerial control of costs.

In Illustration 10–12, if it is assumed that at the start of the accounting period the plant would be operating at 80 percent capacity during the coming year, then the predetermined rates for overhead would be 2.04 percent for the variable overhead and 2.33 percent of labor costs for the fixed overhead. These would be used during the coming year. Any over- or underapplied manufacturing overhead would then be reconciled to the overhead costs and the predetermined rates, to ascertain how much of the variation was due to costs and how much to the volume of production. The foremen would have some definite plan for measuring their operating efficiency.

QUESTIONS FOR REVIEW

1. Manufacturing overhead is a controllable cost which management must consider because it assumes a much larger part of the cost of manufacturing. Why is it increasing? How can management exert its controllable function? What must management do in order to control it?

2. Classification of manufacturing overhead costs is important. If an expense can be treated as manufacturing overhead, it may have to be capitalized in the form of work-in-process and finished goods inventory. If it is an expense and is treated as such, it may help to reduce the profit and the resulting income taxes. The following is a comprehensive list of possible expenses which may be treated accordingly: By using the letters OH, SE, AE, FE, indicate if these are to be treated as manufacturing overhead, selling expenses, administrative expenses, or financial expenses (other income).

Factory hospital expenses	Storeroom expenses
Heat, light, and power costs	Telephone
Machinery repairs	Building repairs
Rent of factory	Salesmen's salaries
Pension costs of factory workers	Bonus to factory workers
Apprentice learning costs	Unemployment insurance costs
Cost accounting department costs	Lunchroom expenses
Depreciation of office furniture	Watchmen's salaries
Factory supplies	Capital stock taxes
Garage expenses	Small tool expenses
Fire insurance	Purchasing department expenses
Advertising	Freight-in
Receiving department expenses	Stationery and printing
Foremen's salaries	Inventory shortage of raw materials
Bad debt expense	Sales tax
Sales discounts	Federal income taxes
Purchase discounts	Inspection costs
Office supplies	Royalties
Supervision costs	

Under what conditions would you recommend the treatment of an item as manufacturing overhead costs, instead of a deductible business expense if there is a choice?

3. In job order cost accounting, what is the relation of the following to the costing and accounting procedure: (a) job order cost sheet, Job. No. 145; (b) factory overhead control account; (c) work-in-process—factory overhead; and (d) applied manufacturing overhead.

4. Manufacturing overhead may be described under three titles. What are they? When are they used? For what purpose?

5. The Dije Manufacturing Company estimates its manufacturing overhead for the coming year at $200,000. It is estimated that 40,000 units will be produced at a material cost of $280,000. Production will require 50,000 direct labor hours at a wage cost of $200,000. The machines will operate at about 48,000 machine-hours. Compute the factory overhead rate to be used in costing the various jobs, using the following bases: (a) material costs, (b) direct labor hours, (c) direct labor costs, and (d) machine-hours.

6. Some firms use more than one manufacturing overhead rate in costing production. What are these different rates and why is it desirable to use them rather than merging them into a single rate?

7. Manufacturing overhead is usually a control account. How are the subsidiary records for this control maintained? How are the books of original entry affected by the controlling account arrangement?

8. The budgeted manufacturing overhead based upon 30,000 direct labor hours amounted to $90,000. The actual overhead totaled $96,000. Twenty-five thousand hours were used in production. Analyze the causes of the over- or underapplied manufacturing overhead.

9. Predetermined manufacturing overhead rates are based upon *normal operating conditions*. What is meant by this term? How does the interpretation of this term affect the managerial control of overhead costs?

10. The *moving-average* method of computing the manufacturing overhead rate has limited application. Under what conditions do you think it might be practical to use it?

PROBLEMS – GROUP A

Problem 10–1.   Purpose: *Comparative Study of Methods of Applying Manufacturing Overhead*

The Jiller Machine Company is making a study of the cost effects of using the various methods of applying manufacturing overhead to production.

The budgeted manufacturing overhead for the year ending June 30, 19 –, was $72,000. The budgeted production indicated that the direct material will cost $80,000; direct labor, $96,000; and that the manufacturing will require 48,000 direct labor hours, or 30,000 machine-hours.

There was no work-in-process at July 1, the beginning of the fiscal period. The actual cost and production figures for the month of July were as follows:

Job Order Number	Direct Material Costs	Direct Labor Costs	Direct Labor Hours	Machine-Hours	Job Completion
JL–101.........$ 800	$ 940	400	300	July 12
JL–103......... 1,000	1,400	600	460	July 18
JL–104......... 950	1,150	510	420	Incomplete
JL–106......... 960	1,000	495	430	Incomplete
JL–108......... 1,200	1,500	680	440	July 28

Required:

a) Calculate the predetermined manufacturing overhead rate based upon prime costs, direct labor costs, direct labor hours, and machine-hours.

b) Compute the comparative costs, in tabular form, of completing Jobs JL–101 and JL–108.

c) If the actual overhead for the month of July was $5,200, what is the amount of the over- or underapplied manufacturing overhead under each of the four methods?

d) Make journal entries for manufacturing costs for month using labor hours base.

Problem 10–2.   Purpose: *Combined Manufacturing Overhead and Payroll Problem Journal Entries; Overhead Calculated on the Labor Hours and Labor Costs Bases*

The Jackson Manufacturing Company does not use a factory journal in recording its cost accounting data. The firm uses a single rate for applying its manufacturing overhead to production.

The plant operates on a 40-hour week, with time-and-one-half pay for all hours over 40 in any one week. Overtime bonus is part of the manufacturing overhead cost.

The budgeted figures for the coming year are:

```
Budgeted manufacturing overhead..................$40,000
Budgeted direct labor costs........................... 16,000
Budgeted labor hours................................... 5,000 hours
```

An analysis of the payroll data and job time tickets for the week showed:

Employee	Hourly Pay	Job Number	Hours Worked						Federal Withholding Tax
			M	T	W	TH	F	S	
Allen........	$5.00	Supt.	8	8	8	8	8	6	$22.00
Butler.......	$3.00	501	6	8	5	6			$14.00
		502	2		2		6	4	
		N.W.			1	2	2		
Clark........	$2.80	501					8	4	$16.00
		502	8	8	8	6			
		N.W.				2			
Dawson....	$2.75	502					8		$18.00
		503	8	6	6	8	2		
		504		2	2				
Elfers	$3.00	503	8	4	4		4		$20.00
		504		4	2	4	2		
		505			2	4	2		
Frankel.....	$2.80	504	2	2	4	4	8		$18.00
		505	5	4	4	4			
		N.W.	1	2					
Grabel......	$3.00	504	3	4	5	6	1	4	$21.50
		505	4	4	6	2	6		
		N.W.	1				1		

Required:

a) Prepare the payroll for the week of March 10.

b) Make journal entries to summarize the payroll and distribute it to production (FICA tax rate is 5.2 percent). Prepare payroll recapitulation sheet.

c) Prepare a comparative table of direct labor costs and applied manufacturing overhead for each job if overhead is applied on direct labor hours and also on direct labor cost basis.

Problem 10–3. Purpose: *Computing Departmental Manufacturing Overhead Rates*

The Johnson Manufacturing Company departmentalizes its manufacturing overhead. In preparing its budgeted departmental overhead rates, it has prepared a survey of its plant facilities as follows:

Department	Area in Square Feet	Investment in Equipment	Estimated Materials to Be Used	Horse-power-Hours	Direct Labor Hours	Direct Labor Costs	No. of Employees
Department I 10,000		$40,000	$75,000	500	32,000	$80,000	16
Department II 12,000		30,000	15,000	300	12,000	30,000	6
Assembling 8,000		10,000	5,000	400	24,000	64,000	15
Finishing 4,000		20,000	5,000	600	22,000	50,000	13
Material 3,000		4,000					4
Handling..........							
Toolroom............ 2,000		16,000					2
Factory							6
Office.............. 1,000		2,000					

Material handling costs are prorated on the basis of the estimated cost of materials to be used; toolroom costs on the basis of the number of employees in the producing departments; and factory office costs equally to all the departments. The factory office costs are prorated first, the toolroom second, and the material handling third.

The budgeted manufacturing overhead costs for the period were:

Rent of factory........................	$14,400	Factory office salaries........	$12,000
Superintendent's salary	15,500	Factory office expenses......	2,410
Depreciation of equipment.........10% per year		Factory supplies:	
Machinery repairs....................	$2,440	Department I	600
Fire insurance on equipment......	1,220	Department II	800
Compensation insurance ($2.00		Assembling	300
per $100 of direct labor).........	$4,480	Finishing	700
Power..................................	5,400		
Fuel, light, and heat.................	6,000		

Indirect labor, overtime bonuses, and payroll taxes: Department I, $2,400; Department II, $3,600; assembling, $4,000; finishing, $1,200; material handling, $12,000; toolroom, $5,800.

Required:

a) Prepare a work sheet to departmentalize the manufacturing overhead to the producing and service departments.

b) Computation of predetermined overhead rates if overhead is applied on the labor hours basis in the assembling and finishing departments; and on the labor cost basis for Departments I and II.

Problem 10–4. Purpose: *CPA Problem Involving the Revision of Manufacturing Overhead Rates*

The Josceyn Manufacturing Company has decided to change its method of applied manufacturing overhead to its production, all of which is on a special job order basis.

The factory ledger trial balance for the six-month period ending June 30, 19 —, was as follows:

	Debits	Credits
Stores control	$ 86,000	
Work-in-process — materials	84,000	
Work-in-process — labor	82,000	
Work-in-process — manufacturing overhead	145,000	
Indirect labor	40,000	
Factory rent	12,000	
Insurance — machinery and equipment	4,000	
Compensation insurance	5,400	
Superintendence	15,000	
Factory clerical salaries	6,400	
Machinery repairs and maintenance	20,000	
Depreciation of machinery and equipment	57,900	
Fuel	3,600	
Electricity	4,200	
Manufacturing supplies used	3,800	
Payroll taxes	11,300	
Factory office supplies	1,200	
Miscellaneous factory expenses	1,500	
Applied manufacturing overhead		$206,000
General ledger control		377,300
	$583,300 =	$583,300

The manufacturing operations are carried on in three producing departments, A, B, and C, and two service departments, numbered I and II.

The allocation bases or amounts are as follows:

	Departments				
	A	B	C	I	II
Square footage of plant floor space ...	10,000	5,000	2,000	7,500	5,500
Number of employees	50	20	4	24	10
Number of labor hours	50,000	20,000	4,200	24,000	10,000
Number of machine-hours	32,000	10,000	600	6,000	0
Salaries and wages	$ 78,000	$ 28,000	$10,000	$ 38,000	$ 9,500
Cost of machinery and equipment	$600,000	$280,000	$20,000	$110,000	$12,000
Annual depreciation rates (percent)	12	10	12	10	20

In developing overhead rates, expenses not distributed according to the above table should be distributed as follows:

On the basis of floor space: factory rent, fuel, and one fourth of electricity.
On the basis of salaries: compensation insurance, superintendence, manufacturing supplies used, payroll taxes, factory office supplies, and miscellaneous factory expense.
On the basis of investment machinery: machinery insurance, machinery maintenance and repairs, and three fourths of electricity.

Factory clerical salaries and $5,000 of indirect labor are charged to Department II; the balance of indirect labor to Department I.

Overhead costs of Department I are to be distributed one tenth to Department II and the balance to all the other departments on the basis of machine-hours.

Expenses of Department II are to be distributed to Departments A, B, and C on the basis of labor hours.

The predetermined manufacturing overhead rates are to be based upon machine-hours for Departments A and B and for labor hours for Department C. For Job No. 717, the costs were:

> Materials $490
> Direct labor 500
> Machine-hours in Department A......... 60
> Machine-hours in Department B......... 15
> Labor hours, Department C.............. 25

Required:

a) Prepare a work sheet and determine appropriate manufacturing overhead rates on the basis of operating results for the six months ending June 30, 19—.

b) Compute the cost of Job No. 717, using the above calculated rates.

> (Adapted from AICPA Uniform Examination)

Problem 10–5.   Purpose: *Separating Manufacturing Overhead Costs into Their Fixed and Variable Elements*

The Judson Supply Company, in attempting to obtain more accurate costs, separates its various overhead costs which are of a semivariable nature into its fixed and variable components. By so doing it expects to obtain better managerial control over its departmental manufacturing overhead.

The following is a schedule of its inspection costs for the past year. On the basis of the analysis of these figures, it expects to determine how much of inspection costs may be considered fixed and how much variable.

Month	Direct Labor Hours	Inspection Costs
January...........................	1,800	$ 6,000
February........................	2,000	6,400
March.............................	3,200	8,400
April	4,000	10,000
May	2,800	7,800
June	4,800	12,000
July...............................	5,000	13,000
August............................	3,800	9,600
September......................	4,500	11,000
October	5,300	13,800
November......................	4,200	10,400
December	3,000	8,000
Totals...................	44,400	$116,400

Required:

Compute the fixed and variable overhead rates using—

a) The high-low method.
b) The shortcut least squares method.

PROBLEMS—GROUP B

Problem 10-6.   Purpose: *Various Methods of Applying Manufacturing Overhead to Production*

The Victory Manufacturing Company has been in business for two months. Its cost accounting system and procedure are still incomplete because it does not have enough accounting information nor cost accounting experience.

During the first two months of its existence, the accounting records showed the following:

Materials used	$12,500
Direct labor costs	27,000
Indirect materials used	2,000
Indirect labor including supervisory salaries	8,000
Labor fringe costs	1,500
Depreciation of plant	2,000
Depreciation of equipment	4,500
Taxes on plant	800
Plant insurance	1,300
Miscellaneous factory expenses	840
Power, heat, and light	1,260
Selling expenses	3,000
Administrative office costs	1,200
Advertising expenses	1,000
Miscellaneous general expenses	400

During this two-month period, four jobs were worked on, of which three were completed. The costs allocated to these jobs were as follows, with Job No. 704 still being in the process of completion:

Element of Cost	Job No. 701	Job No. 702	Job No. 703	Job No. 704
Materials cost	$2,200	$3,600	$4,000	$1,600
Direct labor costs	8,000	9,000	8,000	2,000
Direct labor hours	1,800 hrs.	2,000 hrs.	2,000 hrs.	200 hrs.
Machine-hours	500 hrs.	600 hrs.	700 hrs.	100 hrs.

The company has not set up or used a predetermined manufacturing overhead rate for charging production with the indirect manufacturing costs. However, it feels that now that the plant has been in operation for two months it might be desirable to set up and use a predetermined rate, assuming that operating conditions will continue or improve as indicated.

Required:

a)   Compute the cost of each job using as a basis for charging factory overhead, the following bases: (1) direct labor costs, (2) direct labor hours, and (3) machine-hours.

b)   Assuming that costs will continue in the same proportion as has been experienced in the first two months, which of the methods of applying manufacturing overhead would you recommend? Why?

Problem 10–7.   Purpose: *Accounting Cycle Journal Entries When the Actual Manufacturing Overhead Account Is Used for Both the Actual and Applied Manufacturing Overhead*

The trial balance of the Vortran Manufacturing Company as of January 1, 19—, is given below. This company operates its cost accounting system on a job order basis and applies manufacturing overhead on the basis of direct labor hours. The trial balance represents the accounts on the factory ledger, since its cost accounting records are segregated from the financial accounting.

VORTRAN MANUFACTURING COMPANY
Factory Trial Balance, January 1, 19—

Materials inventory.....................	$15,000	
Work-in-process inventory...........	22,000	
Finished goods inventory............	6,000	
General ledger control................		$43,000
Totals	$43,000	$43,000

Since this firm is using a separate factory journal, the following transactions for the month of January need recognition on the factory books. (No separate applied manufacturing overhead account is used):

1. Materials purchased on account, $14,000.
2. Factory supplies purchased on account, $6,000.
3. Materials requisitioned: $13,400, of which $1,400 was for indirect materials.
4. Payroll vouchered by the main office for the factory work was: Total: $21,000 on which the withholding income taxes were $4,800 and FICA taxes, $1,230. Of this amount, $15,400 was for direct labor.
5. Factory's share of payroll taxes, both FICA and unemployment and disability, totaled $2,640.
6. Other factory overhead costs vouchered and paid were for repairs, $100; rent, $420; power and light, $320.
7. Depreciation of machinery and equipment was $600.
8. Factory insurance that expired cost $80.
9. Factory overhead applied to production was 60% of direct labor costs.
10. Inventories at the end of the month were work-in-process, $10,640; finished goods, $5,400.
11. Sales on account totaled $84,500.

Required:

a) Factory journal entries for the foregoing transactions. The over- or under-applied manufacturing overhead is not closed out until the end of the fiscal accounting period.
b) Prepare T-ledger accounts for the Work-in-Process, Manufacturing Overhead, and Finished Goods.

Problem 10–8.   Purpose: *Departmental Overhead Rate Determination*

The Vallina Manufacturing Company is trying to compute a predetermined rate for its complicated manufacturing Department II. It is hoped to compute this rate on the basis of the machine-hours used in operating the plant in the previous year.

1. The machines occupy 30% of the factory space for Department II.
2. Cost of rent, insurance, and other equipment costs were $16,000 of which one eighth was allocated to Department II.
3. The foreman of Department II was paid $8,000.
4. Heating and lighting costs for Department II cost were $2,400.
5. Other departmental expenses which fluctuate with the production running hours amount to $5,400 for six machines.
6. The plant operates for 2,000 hours per year. During the year, each machine is required to be put down for repairs and oiling, etc., for 200 hours, thus providing for a productive time of operations of only 1,800 hours per machine.
7. The cost of each machine is (of which there are six) $15,000 with a scrap value after 10 years of service of $3,000. The estimated life of each machine is based upon 50,000 running hours.
8. Estimated repairs over the life of each machine is expected to be $600.
9. The power costs have been allocated at the rate of $0.25 per machine-hour.

Required:

On the basis of this information, you are asked to calculate the rate of manufacturing overhead for Department II on the basis of machine usage.

Problem 10–9.   Purpose: *Computation of Manufacturing Overhead Rates and Capacity Variations*

The fixed overhead of the Vorman Manufacturing Company is $60,000 based upon an expected operating capacity of 30,000 machine-hours. Variable overhead costs were $75,000. Normal capacity of the firm's plant is 40,000 machine-hours. Actual capacity used during the year, 36,000 hours. The actual overhead costs were fixed costs, $63,000; and variable costs, $93,600.

Required:

a) Computation of the predetermined manufacturing overhead rates on expected actual and on normal capacity.
b) Computation of budgeted and capacity variations for the expected actual and the normal capacity.

Problem 10–10.   Purpose: *Computation of Manufacturing Overhead Variations*

For the Volfram Manufacturing Company, the budgeted manufacturing overhead volumes and costs are: at a production budgeted at 4,000 hours, budgeted overhead is $9,600; at production budgeted at 6,000 hours, budgeted overhead is $11,600.

Actual production statistics are 5,500 hours and actual overhead costs, $12,200.

Required:

a) Variable overhead in the two different budgeted productions.
b) Budgeted fixed overhead.
c) Applied manufacturing overhead.
d) Over- or underapplied manufacturing overhead.
e) Capacity variation.
f) The cost or spending variation.

chapter 11

Accounting for the Actual Manufacturing Overhead Costs

ACCUMULATING ACTUAL MANUFACTURING OVERHEAD COSTS

In the previous chapter, discussion was centered upon estimating the manufacturing overhead costs on a departmental basis and applying them to production by means of a predetermined rate. Departmentalizing these indirect costs, as well as separating them into their fixed and variable amounts, results in better managerial control through more accurate costs on a job or production in a process type of manufacturing operations. Additional predetermined rates are sometimes used for materials handling charges and for central administration costs, thus providing even more accurate costs.

Predetermined overhead costs were considered first in the preceding chapter because they are used before the actual manufacturing overhead are or could be accumulated. The actual manufacturing overhead costs are accumulated during the fiscal period, and some are not recorded until the end of the fiscal period. In most instances, a *Manufacturing Overhead Control account* is used, supported by a subsidiary ledger of the individual overhead costs. How these costs are recorded in the various books of original entry will be discussed later in this chapter. A careful analysis of the various manufacturing overhead costs will indicate that these may be grouped under five headings: (1) indirect labor, (2) indirect materials, (3) valuation charges, (4) items for which cash must be expended, and (5) accruals and deferrals. Entries in journal form to illustrate the recording of these charges (these entries assume that no separate factory journal is used) are as follows:

Nature of Overhead Cost	Book in Which Recorded	Journal Entry to Record Overhead Cost Item		
1. Indirect labor	General journal	Manufacturing Overhead Control (Indirect Labor)...	200	
		Work-in-Process — Direct Labor	8,000	
		Payroll		8,200
2. Indirect materials	General journal	Manufacturing Overhead Control (Indirect Materials)	500	
		Work-in-Process — Materials	11,000	
		Stores		11,500
3. Depreciation or valuation charges	General journal	Manufacturing Overhead Control (Depreciation)	800	
		Allowance for Depreciation		800
4. Indirect costs involving payment of cash	Voucher register	Manufacturing Overhead Control (Power Costs)	900	
		Accounts Payable		900
5. Expiration of prepaid expense	General journal	Manufacturing Overhead Control (Insurance Costs)	520	
		Prepaid Insurance		520
6. Accrued charges	General journal	Manufacturing Overhead Control (Taxes)	560	
		Accrued Taxes Payable		560

RECORDING AND POSTING THE MANUFACTURING OVERHEAD COSTS

When a control account is used, postings must also be made to the subsidiary ledger for the detailed amounts. This will be accomplished by using special columns in the books of original entry and in exceptional cases by means of split postings. An analysis of the five types of manufacturing overhead cost entries just listed indicates that entries for these are made in the voucher register and in the general journal. Special columns for the manufacturing overhead are provided in each of these journals. This is illustrated in the paragraphs that follow.

VOUCHER REGISTER

A debit column is provided for the manufacturing overhead (see Illustration 11–1). The total of this column is posted to the Manufacturing Overhead Control account. The individual items are posted to the respec-

Illustration 11-1. Voucher Register Illustrating Entries Made for the Manufacturing Overhead Costs When No Factory Journal Is Used

Date	Explanation	Voucher No.	Paid Date	Paid Check No.	Accounts Payable, Cr.	Stores, Dr. Code	Stores, Dr. Amount	Payroll, Dr.	F.I.C.A. Taxes Payable, Cr.	Federal Withholding Taxes Payable, Cr.	State Withholding Taxes Payable, Cr.	Factory Overhead, Dr. Code	Factory Overhead, Dr. Amount	Selling Expense, Dr.	Administrative Expense, Dr.	Misc. Dr.	Misc. Cr.	L.F.	Explanation
Apr. 4	Aetna Realty Co,	100	4/4	210	800 00							903	800 00						
5		101																	
6		102																	
8	Morton Repairs Co.	103			260 00							906	260 00						
9		104																	
11		105																	
11		106																	
12	General Power Co.	107	4/15	270	480 00							907	480 00						
12		108																	
12		109																	
13		110																	
14		111																	
												√	4,840 00						
													(42)						

tive subsidiary ledger account. Since there are many different individual overhead costs, the nature of the expense is indicated by a code number. Assume that the code number of the Manufacturing Overhead Control account is 900 and the subsidiary ledger accounts are:

901   Indirect Materials
902   Indirect Labor
903   Rent of Factory
904   Depreciation of Equipment
905   Factory Insurance
906   Machine Repairs
907   Heat, Light, and Power

Examining the partial illustration of the voucher register, it will be noted that on April 4, the factory rent was paid. Entry is made in the Voucher Payable column, Cr., and a debit to the Manufacturing Overhead. Since the rent code number is 903, this is indicated in the proper column. This figure will be posted to the subsidiary ledger account for Factory Rent. Similarly entries are made for Machine Repairs, Code 906, and Heat, Light, and Power, Code 907. At the end of the month, the total in this column is posted to the Manufacturing Overhead Control account, thus agreeing with the total of the postings to the subsidiary ledger accounts.

FACTORY JOURNAL ENTRIES AND POSTINGS

In this illustration of the procedure, it is assumed that a separate factory journal is used. Entries are made in this journal for the manufacturing overhead costs, with a separate amount and code column for these charges to permit the dual postings (see Illustration 11–2). Sample entries are made for the indirect labor, indirect materials, depreciation transferred from the general office records, and the expired insurance also transferred from the general office.

The individual figures for indirect materials ($300), indirect labor ($800), depreciation ($480), and insurance ($160) are posted to the respective subsidiary ledger accounts; and the total of $4,600 is posted to the Manufacturing Overhead Control account.

POSTING TO THE SUBSIDIARY MANUFACTURING OVERHEAD ACCOUNTS

As has been indicated previously, the summary figures for the manufacturing overhead are maintained in the *Manufacturing Overhead Control account*. Since a subsidiary ledger is maintained, posting arrangements must be made for posting to these subsidiary ledger accounts.

*Illustration 11–2.   Factory Journal Illustrating Entries Made for the
Manufacturing Overhead Costs (Method 2)*

General Ledger, Dr.	Manufacturing Overhead Control, Dr.		Factory Ledger, Dr.	L.F.	Account and Explanation	L.F.	Factory Ledger, Cr.	General Ledger, Cr.
	Code	Amount						
			4,000 00		Jan. 6 Work-in-Process— Materials			
	901	300 00			Indirect Materials Stores Used during week.		4,300 00	
			5,000 00		6 Work-in-Process— Labor			
	902	800 00			Indirect Labor Payroll For week.		5,800 00	
	904	480 00			31 Depreciation General Ledger For period.	√		480 00
	905	160 00			31 Insurance—Factory General Ledger Expired for month.	√		160 00
10,000 00		4,600 00	30,000 00				38,000 00	6,600 00
(21)		(10)	(√)				(√)	(21)

The following arrangements indicate the various *methods* of postings
to the subsidiary ledger for manufacturing overhead:

1.   Entries in sufficient detail in the *general journal* and the *voucher
register* so that dual postings can be made — special columnar totals to
the Manufacturing Overhead Control account and the subsidiary ledger
postings by means of code numbers in the special columns. No factory
ledger is used.

2.   Prepare *factory journal or transfer vouchers* in sufficient detail so that the entries may be made therefrom on factory books and the subsidiary ledgers.

3.   Send the *original invoice* for the manufacturing overhead charge to the subsidiary ledger clerk so that he may make the entry therefrom. It would be better, however, to use the method of 2 whereby all charges to the subsidiary ledger are vouchered in a uniform manner.

4.   Place the subsidiary ledger charge on a punched card and have these accumulated from time to time for entry on the subsidiary ledgers. When either procedures 1 or 2 have been followed and completed, the Manufacturing Overhead Control account will show in total the details shown in the subsidiary ledger accounts. The columnar postings to the Manufacturing Overhead Control account will be as follows:

Manufacturing Overhead Control

Dec. 31	GJ.	4,500	Dec. 31	Applied manufacturing overhead	10,000
31	VR.	8,000			

Applied Manufacturing Overhead

Dec. 31	Closed to Manufacturing Overhead Control	10,000	Dec. 31	Applied to production	10,000

Departmentalization of the Actual Manufacturing Overhead.   It has been emphasized in the previous discussion that the predetermined rates for manufacturing overhead and the applied manufacturing overhead should, in the interest of more accurate costing and better managerial control of the manufacturing operations, be departmentalized. Therefore, for comparative purposes, the *actual* manufacturing overhead must also be recorded on a departmental basis. The most practical method of doing this is by means of the *work sheet method,* paralleling the procedure used in departmentalizing the estimated manufacturing overhead.

Under this method, a controlling account is set up for the total of the actual manufacturing overhead costs, with a subsidiary ledger for the individual expense accounts. At the end of the fiscal accounting period, a list of the individual manufacturing overhead accounts is entered on a work sheet on which there is a distribution column for each of the producing and service departments of the plant. *Using the same survey of plant facilities as was necessary in departmentalizing the estimated manufacturing overhead costs,* these overhead costs are then prorated or allocated to the various departments, the amounts being entered in the appropriate departmental columns.

Since the service departments do not involve any manufacturing operations, it is necessary to redistribute their overhead costs to the

Illustration 11-3

JOHANNSON MANUFACTURING COMPANY

WORK SHEET FOR THE PRORATION OF THE ACTUAL MANUFACTURING OVERHEAD COSTS
For the Year Ended December 31, 19—

Basis for Apportioning Various Overhead Costs		Total Amount	Cutting Dept.	Planing Dept.	Assembling Dept.	Finishing Dept.	Material Handling Dept.	Toolroom	Factory Office
No. of employees	Superintendent's salary	12,000.00	3,600.00	3,000.00	2,000.00	1,400.00	800.00	400.00	800.00
Area	Taxes on building	6,000.00	1,500.00	1,250.00	1,000.00	750.00	750.00	500.00	250.00
Investment	Depreciation of equipment	30,600.00	12,000.00	8,000.00	2,000.00	1,600.00	400.00	6,000.00	600.00
Area	Insurance of plant	600.00	150.00	125.00	100.00	75.00	75.00	50.00	25.00
Investment	Repairs to machinery	4,590.00	1,800.00	1,200.00	300.00	240.00	60.00	900.00	90.00
Area	Repairs to plant	400.00	100.00	83.33	66.67	50.00	50.00	33.33	16.67
Investment	Fire ins., machinery and equip.	612.00	240.00	160.00	40.00	32.00	8.00	120.00	12.00
Area	Depreciation of plant	5,000.00	1,250.00	1,041.67	833.33	625.00	625.00	416.67	208.33
Payroll	Compensation insurance	3,600.00	1,360.00	1,000.00	840.00	400.00			
Horsepower	Power costs	4,800.00	1,920.00	1,280.00	960.00	640.00			
Direct	Factory office salaries	10,500.00							10,500.00
Area	Fuel, heat, and light	2,400.00	600.00	500.00	400.00	300.00	300.00	200.00	100.00
Direct	Factory office expenses	2,000.00							2,000.00
Direct	Indirect materials used	2,000.00	500.00	300.00	600.00	600.00			
Direct	Indirect labor costs	23,800.00	1,800.00	2,000.00	2,400.00	2,800.00	10,000.00	4,800.00	
	Total	108,902.00	26,820.00	19,940.00	11,540.00	9,512.00	13,068.00	13,420.00	14,602.00
No. of employees	Factory office costs	14,602.00	4,693.50	3,911.25	2,607.50	1,825.25	1,043.00	521.50	14,602.00
							14,111.00		
Cost of materials used	Material handling costs	14,111.00	11,288.80	423.33	987.77	1,411.10	14,111.00		
								13,941.50	
No. of employees	Toolroom costs	13,941.50	5,018.94	4,182.45	2,788.30	1,951.81		13,941.50	
	Total	108,902.00	47,821.24	28,457.03	17,923.57	14,700.16			
	Applied manufacturing overhead	112,902.00	45,821.24	31,457.03	18,923.57	16,700.16			
	Over-( ) or underapplied mfg. overhead	(4,000.00)	2,000.00	(3,000.00)	(1,000.00)	(2,000.00)			

various departments to the extent to which these service departments render service to the other departments.

When this work sheet has been completed, *all* of the manufacturing overhead costs will have been allocated to the producing departments. In the following illustration, the total amount of the manufacturing overhead at the end of the accounting period was $108,902. The various overhead cost items are listed, and these have been allocated to the producing and service departments on the bases indicated in the plant survey. However, the amounts allocated to the *service departments* must then be redistributed to the other departments as shown, resulting in a *final* total, departmentally, of the actual manufacturing overhead as illustrated (see Illustration 11–3).

Cutting department	$ 47,821.24
Planing department	28,457.03
Assembling department	17,923.57
Finishing department	14,700.16
Total Actual Manufacturing Overhead	$108,902.00

When these actual departmental overhead cost figures are compared with the applied departmental manufacturing overhead costs, the over- or underapplied departmental manufacturing overhead is computed. This *applied* and the *over- or underapplied* departmentally may also be shown on this work sheet, as illustrated.

The journal entry to close the Manufacturing Overhead Control account into the various departmental manufacturing overhead accounts as shown on the work sheet would be:

Manufacturing Overhead — Cutting Department	47,821.24	
Manufacturing Overhead — Planing Department	28,457,03	
Manufacturing Overhead — Assembling	17,923.57	
Manufacturing Overhead — Finishing	14,700.16	
Manufacturing Overhead Control		108,902.00
To close the Manufacturing Overhead Control account per work sheet.		

To visualize the sequence of the entries made to record and departmentalize the *actual* manufacturing overhead, Illustration 11–4 is given. A study of this illustration reveals the following procedures:

1. Manufacturing overhead is recorded in a subsidiary ledger.
2. The Manufacturing Overhead Control account is a controlling account for the subsidiary ledger.
3. The Manufacturing Overhead Control account is closed into the departmental overhead accounts, both service and producing departments, by a journal entry. The figures used in this entry are obtained from a work sheet showing distribution of the actual manufacturing overhead.

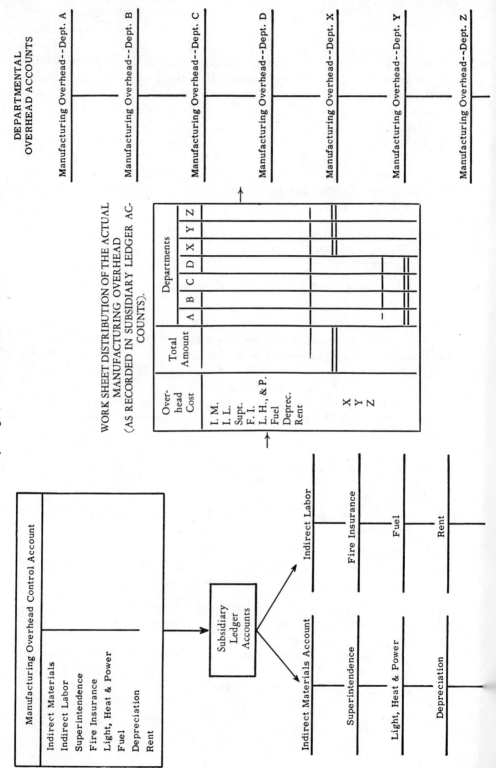

Illustration 11–4. Accounting Sequence of Manufacturing Overhead Accounts When the Manufacturing Overhead Control Account, Subsidiary Ledger, and Work Sheet Are Used

4. The service department overhead accounts are closed into the producing department overhead accounts by a journal entry.

A specific illustration of the journal entry made to close the controlling account into the departmental accounts is given below:

```
Manufacturing Overhead—Department A...............................7,000
Manufacturing Overhead—Department B...............................4,550
Manufacturing Overhead—Department C...............................6,400
Manufacturing Overhead—Department D ..............................8,000
Manufacturing Overhead—Department X...............................7,000
Manufacturing Overhead—Department Y...............................2,600
Manufacturing Overhead—Department Z...............................  880
    Manufacturing Overhead Control......................................        36,430
    To close Manufacturing Overhead Control account as per work
    sheet.
```

Following the procedure used with the estimated manufacturing overhead, the distributions to Departments X, Y, and Z Manufacturing Overhead accounts must be closed into the accounts of the producing departments, either singly or jointly. A summary of departmental distributions from work sheet is presented in Illustration 11–5 with the

Illustration 11–5. Showing the Method of Transferring the Service Department Overhead into the Producing Department Overhead

	Department							Total
	X	Y	Z	A	B	C	D	
Total.....................	$7,000.00	$2,600.00	$ 880.00	$ 7,000.00	$4,550.00	$6,400.00	$ 8,000.00	$36,430.00
Service Department X, overhead costs........		100.00	100.00	2,800.00	1,500.00	300.00	2,200.00	7,000.00
Total....................		$2,700.00						
Service Department Y, overhead costs........			200.00	450.00	600.00	650.00	800.00	$ 2,700.00
Total...................			$1,180.00					
Service Department Z, overhead costs........				280.00	340.00	390.00	170.00	$ 1,180.00
				$10,530.00	$6,990.00	$7,740.00	$11,170.00	$36,430.00

subsequent distribution of service department overhead so that the journal entries to close the service department overhead accounts may be understood more readily.

On the basis of this summary the individual entries necessary to close overhead accounts of Departments X, Y, and Z are:

(1)

Manufacturing Overhead – Department A	2,800	
Manufacturing Overhead – Department B	1,500	
Manufacturing Overhead – Department C	300	
Manufacturing Overhead – Department D	2,200	
Manufacturing Overhead – Department Y	100	
Manufacturing Overhead – Department Z	100	
Manufacturing Overhead – Department X		7,000

To close the overhead costs of Department X into the other departments.

(2)

Manufacturing Overhead – Department A	450	
Manufacturing Overhead – Department B	600	
Manufacturing Overhead – Department C	650	
Manufacturing Overhead – Department D	800	
Manufacturing Overhead – Department Z	200	
Manufacturing Overhead – Department Y		2,700

To close the overhead costs of Department Y into the other departments.

(3)

Manufacturing Overhead – Department A	280	
Manufacturing Overhead – Department B	340	
Manufacturing Overhead – Department C	390	
Manufacturing Overhead – Department D	170	
Manufacturing Overhead – Department Z		1,180

To close the overhead costs of Department Z into the producing departments.

However, since these data appear on the work sheet, the foregoing entries are usually combined into a *single entry*, that is, the three service department overhead accounts are closed simultaneously as follows:

Manufacturing Overhead – Department A	3,530	
Manufacturing Overhead – Department B	2,440	
Manufacturing Overhead – Department C	1,340	
Manufacturing Overhead – Department D	3,170	
Manufacturing Overhead – Department Y	100	
Manufacturing Overhead – Department Z	300	
Manufacturing Overhead – Department X		7,000
Manufacturing Overhead – Department Y		2,700
Manufacturing Overhead – Department Z		1,180

To close the service department overhead cost accounts into the producing departments.

In fact, some accountants avoid entirely the use of manufacturing overhead *accounts* for the service departments. The work sheet is completed showing the allocation of the actual manufacturing overhead to both producing and service departments, and then the redistribution of the service department overhead costs to the other departments. Then when the journal entry is made to close out the Manufacturing Overhead Control, the charges are made directly and only to the producing departments, viz:

Manufacturing Overhead—Department A 10,530
Manufacturing Overhead—Department B 6,990
Manufacturing Overhead—Department C 7,740
Manufacturing Overhead—Department D 11,170
    Manufacturing Overhead Control   36,430
    To close out the Manufacturing Overhead Control as per work
    sheet.

ALTERNATIVE METHOD OF TREATING SERVICE DEPARTMENT OVERHEAD COSTS

Sometimes some of the service department overhead is analyzed into its fixed and variable portions, such as heat, light, and power costs (powerhouse). The fixed portion is distributed to the other departments on the basis of area, number of lights, or horsepower. The variable portion is distributed to the other departments on the basis of services rendered or actual consumption. This method has certain advantages because of its greater accuracy, especially in those instances where the production and usage is not uniform throughout the plant. In some firms, some service department overhead costs are not redistributed to the other departments but instead a separate or supplementary rate is calculated for the service department involved. This rate is used as an additional overhead costing on the job sheets. Using this method will result in an over- or underapplied manufacturing overhead for the service department involved. This method has found limited application, since it is difficult to determine how much of the service department costs should be charged to a specific job without incurring a large amount of additional clerical work.

OVER- AND UNDERAPPLIED DEPARTMENTAL MANUFACTURING OVERHEAD

The departmental manufacturing overhead discussed thus far covers three phases of the subject: (1) *estimated manufacturing overhead*, from which the predetermined departmental rates are computed; (2) *applied manufacturing overhead*, which represents the departmental amounts charged to the work-in-process on the job order cost sheets by means of rate computed in (1); and (3) *actual departmental manufacturing overhead*, which is ascertained from the work sheet analysis. The difference between the actual manufacturing overhead and the applied manufacturing overhead accounts for each *producing* (and sometimes *service*) department represents the over- or underapplied manufacturing overhead.

The localization of errors in the estimate permits better managerial control of the overhead cost element. At the end of the accounting period, the applied departmental overhead accounts are closed into the actual departmental overhead accounts. Periodically a statement may be prepared, as shown in Illustration 11–6, showing the actual and the applied manufacturing overhead and the resulting variance for each producing department.

Illustration 11–6

MARTIN MANUFACTURING CO.
Summary of the Actual and Applied Manufacturing Overhead
January 1, 19— to December 31, 19—

Actual Manufacturing Overhead Charges					
	Dept. A	Dept. B	Dept. C	Dept. D	Total
Indirect material................	$ 1,989.00	$1,256.00	$2,800.00	$ 3,110.00	$ 9,155.00
Indirect labor..................	700.00	800.00	1,000.00	....	2,500.00
Superintendence................	769.25	769.25	1,153.80	1,538.50	4,230.80
Fire insurance..................	428.55	214.30	42.85	321.45	1,007.15
Compensation insurance..........	250.00	200.00	450.00	700.00	1,600.00
Light..........................	128.00	128.00	192.00	320.00	768.00
Power..........................	1,280.00	320.00	....	640.00	2,240.00
Depreciation on machinery.......	1,500.00	750.00	150.00	1,125.00	3,525.00
Rent...........................	320.00	400.00	480.00	640.00	1,840.00
Apportioned charges (service depts.)....................	3,050.00	2,800.00	1,000.00	3,865.00	10,715.00
Total actual overhead......	$10,414.80	$7,637.55	$7,268.65	$12,259.95	$37,580.95
Less:					
Applied mfg. overhead.........	10,366.08	7,740.15	7,378.85	12,331.60	37,816.68
Balance underapplied............	$ 48.72	....	....	....	....
Balance overapplied.............	....	$ 102.60	$ 110.20	$ 71.65	$ 235.73

The over- or underapplied manufacturing overhead on a departmental basis is disposed of in the same manner as previously discussed for indirect costs not departmentalized. In this illustration, to close out the variation to the Cost of Goods Sold account, the following entry is necessary:

Manufacturing Overhead – Department B.....................102.60
Manufacturing Overhead – Department C......................110.20
Manufacturing Overhead – Department D 71.65
    Manufacturing Overhead – Department A..............   48.72
    Cost of Goods Sold...   235.73
To close the balances in the departmental overhead
accounts into the Cost of Goods Sold account.

A similar procedure may be followed if it is desired at the end of the fiscal accounting period to prorate the over- or underapplied manufacturing overhead on a departmental basis to the Work-in-Process, Finished Goods, and Cost of Goods Sold accounts.

Closing out the over- or underapplied manufacturing overhead either into the Cost of Goods Sold account or prorating to the Work-in-Process, Finished Goods, and Cost of Sales accounts is usually not done until the end of the fiscal accounting period. This is true, since the over- or underapplied manufacturing overhead of one month may be offset by the reverse over- or underapplied manufacturing overhead of the following month. It is the over- or underapplied manufacturing overhead at the end of the fiscal accounting period that must be considered, not the monthly fluctuations, which may be only temporary.

ANALYZING THE OVER- AND UNDERAPPLIED MANUFACTURING OVERHEAD

Management wants to know why there was an over- or underapplied manufacturing overhead. This analysis becomes more effective if the overhead is first separated into its *fixed* and *variable* elements. In either instance, the causes for the over- or underapplied overhead may be traced to incorrect estimates of the *volume* of production expressed in terms of labor hours or labor costs, or incorrect estimates of the *cost* or spending for the overhead items, or a combination of both of these factors (see Illustration 11–7).

To illustrate this analysis, the following facts are assumed:

	Fixed Overhead	*Variable Overhead*
Estimated (budget) overhead	$24,000	$14,400
Budgeted plant capacity	24,000 labor hours	24,000 labor hours
Predetermined rate	$1	$0.60
Actual overhead	$25,440	$12,000
Actual labor hours (volume)	25,000 labor hours	25,000 labor hours
Applied overhead:		
25,000 hrs. × $1.00	$25,000	
25,000 hrs. × $0.60		15,000
Underapplied overhead (Dr.)	$440	
Overapplied overhead (Cr.)		$3,000

A more detailed analysis of these variations is given in Chapter 17 on standard cost accounting.

Illustration 11–7. Analysis of the Over- and Underapplied Manufacturing Overhead

VARIATIONS DUE TO COST FACTORS (SPENDING VARIATION)

	Fixed Overhead	Variable Overhead	Total
Budgeted overhead	$24,000	$14,400	
Actual overhead........................	25,440	12,000	
Difference due to costs:			
Favorable (Cr.)		$ 2,400 (Cr.)	
Unfavorable (Dr.)....................	$ 1,440 (Dr.)		$ 960 (Cr.)

VARIATIONS DUE TO VOLUME OF PRODUCTION

Budgeted labor hours	24,000 hrs.	24,000 hrs.	
Actual production hours	25,000	25,000	
Excess productions (favorable)	1,000 hrs.	1,000 hrs.	
Variation due to volume:			
1,000 hrs. × $1.00 (Cr.)............	$ 1,000 (Cr.)		
1,000 hrs. × $0.60 (Cr.)............		$ 600 (Cr.)	$1,600 (Cr.)
Net underapplied (unfavorable).....	$ 440 (Dr.)		
Net overapplied (favorable).........		$ 3,000 (Cr.)	$2,560 (Cr.)

SPECIAL MANUFACTURING OVERHEAD COST PROBLEMS

Special attention must be given to the allocation of some of the manufacturing overhead costs to the various departments. Among these are the following:

The fixed manufacturing overhead cost of *factory rent costs* is usually distributed departmentally on a square footage basis. When the building is owned, a charge equivalent to rent is sometimes built up out of the following: property taxes, insurance, depreciation, and maintenance and repair charges.

Light, heat, and power costs may be incurred by a direct charge from the utility company. In that event, the allocation is simple: *light* on the basis of kilowatt-hours and/or the number of bulbs in each department; *heat* on the basis of square or cubic feet in each department, or the number of radiators; *power* on the basis of the number of machines in each department, or the machine-hours of production, or the horsepower-hours used.

If, however, the firm has its own powerhouse, then more accurate cost accounting would divide the powerhouse house costs into its *fixed* elements (taxes, insurance, depreciation, and maintenance) and the *variable* costs (cost of actual power production) and prorate these to the various departments.

Taxes as manufacturing overhead creates no particular problem as far as taxes on plant and payroll taxes are concerned. But in recent years, a lively discussion has arisen as to the advisability of including state and federal income taxes in the cost of production. Some writers in the bulletins of the National Association of Accountants and in a study made by the National Industrial Conference Board have recommended the inclusion of these taxes in manufacturing costs. This recommendation has not as yet had very wide acceptance.

Indirect materials consist of materials not directly identifiable with the product — materials such as repair and replacement parts, packing materials, and cleaning and polishing supplies. Where large supplies of these materials are kept on hand, control through the use of inventory cards and requisition forms is desirable, the charges for indirect materials used being made direct to the departmental overhead accounts.

Tools and *tool expense* require special consideration. If a large quantity of tools is consumed in production, inventories may be taken monthly to determine the charge to manufacturing overhead. Some firms carry the tool inventory at a fixed basic figure, and all replacements of tools are treated as an overhead cost at the time of purchase.

Indirect labor is work which is not applied directly to the product and which cannot be charged to specific jobs or lots, such as work done by shop foremen, repairmen, sweepers, clerks, janitors, and timekeepers. Indirect labor may include labor costs for idle time due to lack of materials, nonfunctioning machinery, or any other cause which prevents men ordinarily engaged in direct labor from working on the product if such costs are not recorded in a separate Idle or Delay Time account.

In the case of *insurance,* a diversity of opinion exists as to whether or not the various insurance costs should be included in the computation of manufacturing costs. Some insurance costs, such as against forgery, holdup, and robbery, are treated as administrative expenses. These do not affect the factory operations directly. Insurance costs paid on automobiles may be variously treated. Insurance on trucks used for outgoing shipments is selling expense; insurance on trucks used to carry materials to the factory is factory overhead or part of the freight and cartage-in. If the trucks are used for both in and out shipments, it will become necessary to prorate on some equitable basis all the delivery expenses (including the insurance) between manufacturing overhead and selling expenses. Premiums for group life insurance and compensation insurance are treated as factory overhead costs if they are calculated on the wages paid employees in the factory, as selling expenses if on wages paid sales employees, and as administrative expenses if paid on wages of office force. The insurance costs applying to the factory payroll should be apportioned departmentally on the basis of departmental payrolls. The costs of fire and sprinkler insurance covering the factory equipment and materials used in manufacturing are treated as manufacturing overhead. If such insurance covers the finished stock, its cost is part of the selling expenses. The cost of fire insurance on the materials used in manufacturing is merged with the other storeroom costs and becomes part of the prorated charges of the service department. The cost of fire insurance and sprinkler leakage insurance on the buildings will be prorated over the departmental overhead accounts, usually on the basis of area occupied by each department. Some of these costs may be allocated to a sales department or an administrative department if such departments are located in the same building as the factory operations.

Conversion or *reconversion* costs raise a serious problem for many manufacturers. The cost of rearranging the plant and reinstalling machinery and lines of production may either be capitalized and written off over a long period of time or treated as a charge to be written off over the current year's production. The attitude of the Internal Revenue Service has not been definite in this matter. Until the time when a definite legal ruling is obtained, it would seem reasonable and conservative to write off the conversion or reconversion cost over the shortest possible period. It would therefore be an element of manufacturing cost and part of the manufacturing overhead for the current period. It would destroy the comparability of costs for that year with the subsequent years when no such charge will occur.

Normal *inventory shrinkages* in stores, resulting from evaporation, breakage, obsolescence, etc., are legitimate charges to production costs as manufacturing overhead. They are often discovered when inventory count is reconciled with perpetual inventory cards. Extraordinarily large losses, however, resulting from unforeseen, unusual circumstances would be charged to a special loss account with an appropriate title and then closed out to the Profit and Loss account. Raw materials market price changes call for no special consideration as price changes will be reflected in the costs of the *period of use* rather than the period of purchase.

The allocation of the indirect costs of a number of *special services* sometimes raises a problem. The costs of the *medical department,* the *cafeteria department* (loss due to costs being greater than income), *welfare department, general supervision, cost department, timekeeping and payroll, and the employment department* may well be distributed on the basis of either the number of employees or man-hours. *Purchasing department* costs and *storeroom* costs may well be allocated to the departments on the basis of tonnage or value of materials used in the various departments. Some accountants recommend the allocation on the basis of man-hours, but there seems little justification for this practice except perhaps its simplicity and the small amount involved. *General engineering costs,* unless identified with special jobs or currently manufactured products, may be capitalized and charged to some capital asset or deferred charge. *Building elevator* and *building operation costs* should be collected into one summary account and allocated on the basis of square footage. *Police, fire, and watchman service costs* should no doubt be prorated on the basis of the value of the property in each department—that is, investment. Interest on investment is discussed on pages 357–59.

DEPRECIATION AS MANUFACTURING OVERHEAD COST

Depreciation is not a method of evaluation of property but rather a method of allocating the cost of property to operating periods.

The Internal Revenue Code recognizes this allocation in the calculation of taxable income, and several methods of calculating the depreciation charge are permissible. The Internal Revenue Code of 1969 has focused attention on the so-called *accelerated* methods of depreciation with their income tax advantages to the manufacturer.

Formerly the *straight-line* method (cost less scrap value divided by the estimated life of the asset) was considered the most satisfactory method; now because of income tax and cash savings effected by the *sum-of-years' digits* and the *fixed-percentage-of-diminishing-value* methods, their use has increased. These two methods, forms of accelerated depreciation, permit a larger write-off in the earlier years of life of the asset than would be permissible under the straight-line method. Illustrations 11–8 and 11–9 present the comparative depreciation costs for the

Illustration 11–8

COMPARATIVE METHODS OF DEPRECIATION
As Authorized in Sec. 167 of Internal Revenue Code of 1969
(Illustrative Case. Item Cost of $100,000 with Ten-Year Estimated Useful Life. Salvage Not Considered.)

Ten-Year Life	Straight Line		Maximum Permissible Declining Balance*		Sum of the Digits		
	Annual Charge	Cumulative Allowance	Annual Charge	Cumulative Allowance	Sum Digits	Annual Charge	Cumulative Allowance
1.............	$10,000	$ 10,000	$20,000	$20,000	10	$18,182	$ 18,182
2.............	10,000	20,000	16,000	36,000	9	16,364	34,546
3.............	10,000	30,000	12,800	48,800	8	14,545	49,091
4.............	10,000	40,000	10,240	59,040	7	12,727	61,818
5.............	10,000	50,000	8,192	67,232	6	10,909	72,727
6.............	10,000	60,000	6,554	73,786	5	9,091	81,818
7.............	10,000	70,000	5,243	79,029	4	7,273	89,091
8.............	10,000	80,000	4,194	83,223	3	5,455	94,546
9.............	10,000	90,000	3,355	86,578	2	3,636	98,182
10.............	10,000	100,000	2,684	89,262	1	1,818	100,000
					55		

Prepared by American Appraisal Company

*Maximum rate cannot exceed twice the straight-line rate.

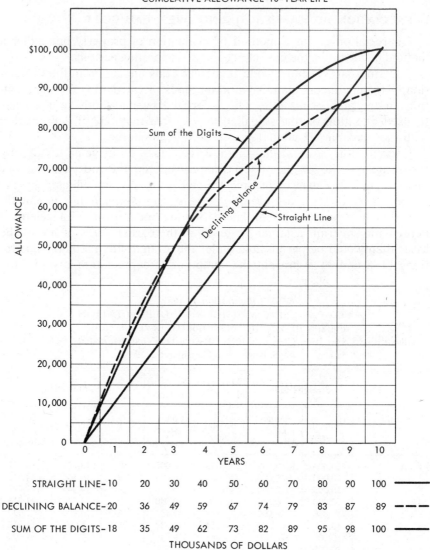

Illustration 11-9
COMPARATIVE METHODS OF DEPRECIATION
As Authorized in Sec. 167 of Internal Revenue Code of 1969
(Salvage Cost Not Considered. Item Cost, $100,000. Ten-Year Basis.)

CUMULATIVE ALLOWANCE-10-YEAR LIFE

	1	2	3	4	5	6	7	8	9	10	
STRAIGHT LINE-10		20	30	40	50	60	70	80	90	100	———
DECLINING BALANCE-20		36	49	59	67	74	79	83	87	89	- - - -
SUM OF THE DIGITS-18		35	49	62	73	82	89	95	98	100	———

THOUSANDS OF DOLLARS

Prepared by American Appraisal Company

three methods most frequently used under the new income tax regulations.

A change to one of the newer permissible methods will also raise some interesting and important questions: Do the higher depreciation charges in the earlier years, as part of manufacturing overhead, increase the cost of manufacturing to the extent that a selling price higher than that of competitors will become necessary? Are the current costs unduly burdened by the higher depreciation charges, and will some future periods benefit from the resulting lower manufacturing overhead charges?

Furthermore, the law permits the manufacturer using the declining-balance method to change to the straight-line method at any time, but this is not possible with the sum-of-years'-digits method. It becomes, therefore, a serious problem of management to select the method of depreciation which will most effectively reflect *comparable* costs, so that management may measure the effectiveness of production by plants, divisions, and products. These are some of the situations which may arise:

1. A product with a level sales trend will have few major capital requirements, whereas one with a rapid growth or with many style changes will have frequent major additions to capital requirements.
2. A narrow profit product produced on a highly mechanized line could well be changed into a losing product if a major addition in or replacement of equipment is to be made and a higher rate of depreciation used.
3. If replacements and additions occur at different times in various units of a company, then it will be a long time before all the fixed assets in all the plants of a company are on the same basis of depreciation.
4. Increased mechanization through greater application of automation in manufacturing will greatly increase the amount of depreciation application to cost of manufacturing, since a greater investment in machines and other equipment will be required. The importance of automation in planning for the future cannot be overemphasized.

ACCURACY OF DECLINING-BALANCE VERSUS STRAIGHT-LINE DEPRECIATION METHOD

It must be restated here that depreciation is not a method of evaluating property but rather a method of allocating the cost of property use to operating periods and finally to the product. The most logical and reasonable basis for allocating this cost would seem to be in relation to the net value of the service rendered in the various operating periods. *This assumption leads to the conclusion that depreciation should be on some declining-amount basis for several reasons:*

1. When property is purchased, it is with the expectation that the volume of production and the earnings for the reasonably immediate future will justify the purchase. It is not ordinarily expected that the property will be uniformly useful over its entire estimated life.
2. The physical efficiency of property ordinarily declines over its useful life, reducing gradually the quantity and/or the quality of its service. This may involve the loss of precision, more time out for repairs, and other factors. There are, however, some situations where this is not true. For example in the paper-making industry, the paper machines increase their efficiency for many years after their installation, producing more paper of a better quality.
3. There is the gradual encroachment of obsolescence, which reduces the value of even the same quantity and quality of service rendered in the successive periods.
4. Repairs and maintenance tend to increase each year and reduce the net value of the service rendered in successive periods.

Which declining-balance method should be used is still a difficult problem. In addition to the two methods — fixed-percentage-of-diminishing-value and sum-of-years'-digits method — there is the multiple-straight-line principle under which 150 percent of the straight-line method can be used during the first half of the useful life and only 50 percent of the straight-line rate for the last half; or 150 percent of straight-line during first third of useful life, 100 percent during second third, and 50 percent during the last third. The ultimate in the application of the multiple-straight-line method is a constantly declining rate with a uniform change each year — such as 145 percent of the straight-line rate or $14\frac{1}{2}$ percent the first year, 135 percent or $13\frac{1}{2}$ percent the second year, and 125 percent or $12\frac{1}{2}$ percent the third year, etc., until in the last year of a 10-year asset it would be $5\frac{1}{2}$ percent of the cost. The sum-of-years'-digits method is a very specific, inflexible application of this method.

In any given situation the method selected should be one which achieves best the following objectives: it should reflect best the periodic decline in the net value of the service rendered; it should produce the best cost figures for managerial purposes, including replacement policies; and, other things being equal, it should involve the least administrative and accounting costs. But the selection of a declining-amount method in a given situation and its application present extremely more difficult problems than those involved in the straight-line method.

A continuation of the straight-line method results in substantial errors in cost allocation greater than any that are likely to result from selection and application of any declining-amount method that seems reasonably appropriate to the given situation. For cost accounting to have any managerial significance, it is necessary to use the declining-amount method. But because of the conflict of tax accounting, straight-line book accounting, and more accurate cost accounting through a declining-amount method (other than fixed-percentage-of-diminishing-value or of sum-of-years'-digits method), most firms will probably continue to use the straight-line method for cost accounting.

GUIDELINE LIVES FOR DEPRECIATION

Not only is the selection of the method of depreciation important to the manufacturer but the determination of the *useful life* is also relevant.

In 1962, the Treasury Department issued Revenue Procedure 62–21 (later amended) which introduced the concept of *Guideline Life*. A taxpayer could adopt Guideline Lives for depreciating his assets without having to substantiate these lives as long as his replacement policy was consistent with the Guidelines. Generally, the useful lives in the 75 categories permitted under the Guidelines were liberal.

The fact that a Guideline Life has been adopted for tax purposes does not necessarily mean that the same useful life should be used in computing depreciation on the accounting records of the company. The useful life used by the company in its record-keeping should be that which clearly approaches reality, and guidelines are supposed to be realistic.

RECONCILING COST, BOOK, AND TAX ACCOUNTING DEPRECIATION METHODS

The retention of the straight-line depreciation for book accounting, with the adoption of a declining-amount method for income tax purposes, ordinarily demands the use of an account, *Deferred Income Taxes Payable*. In years when the depreciation deduction for tax purposes exceeds book depreciation, there should be added to this estimated liability an amount equal to this difference times the effective tax rate, with an offsetting charge to an expense account in lieu of taxes. In years when the book depreciation exceeds the depreciation deduction for tax purposes, there should be deducted from this estimate an amount equal to this difference times the effective tax rate, with an offsetting credit to an account which is contra to tax expense. This procedure is consistent with that recommended by the Committee on Accounting Procedure of the American Institute of Certified Public Accountants.

INTEREST ON INVESTMENT AS A COST ELEMENT

One of the controversial subjects in cost accounting is the treatment of *interest on investment*. Although some cost accountants are quite emphatic in stating that interest should or should not be included as an element in cost accounting, it must be pointed out here that interest on investment is one of those doubtful items which must be omitted from cost for some purposes and must be included in cost for other purposes. The items to be included in or excluded from cost depend entirely upon the purpose for which the cost figure is to be used. There is no such thing as *a* correct cost figure for *all* purposes.

Interest on investment as an element of cost refers to the amount to be included in the manufacturing overhead as a charge for the capital used in production. It assumes that if this capital had not been used in the business it would have been invested and would have earned a return called "interest on investment." The rate or amount of the return is an economic concept defined as the income derived from capital with a minimum of risk involved in the investment. This *economic* concept of interest, when applied to accounting, raises several difficulties.

The first difficulty lies in the definition of *investment*. Investment is not used with the same meaning by all concerns. For some, investment has been defined as the value of inventories plus the value of fixed assets less allowance for depreciation; for others, investment has been defined as the sum of all the assets except intangibles and investments in securities; for others it may be any variation of these values. A second difficulty is created by the question: *What rate of interest represents the economic concept of a return on investment with a minimum of risk?*

Many cost accountants have raised arguments favoring or opposing the inclusion of interest as an element of cost, assuming that a uniform procedure should be followed by all. This is not true. There are conditions under which interest on investment as an element of cost might be used; there are others in which it should not be used. Where interest on investment is to be included as part of the manufacturing overhead, it is probably better to treat costs as *statistical data*. The books will then not have to be adjusted when the cost statements are to be prepared in which interest on investment is not permitted to appear.

If costs are treated as statistical data and are not controlled by entries on the general accounting books, the interest item is recorded on the cost sheets as part of the manufacturing overhead, but no journal entries are made. If, however, the costs are controlled by the general accounting records, journal entries to record the interest on investment are:

(1)

Manufacturing Overhead Control (Interest Cost) xxxx
    Interest on Investment   xxxx
    To record the interest on investment charge as an element of cost.

(2)

Interest on Investment xxxx
    Retained Earnings   xxxx
    To record the amount of interest applicable to the cost of goods sold.

The effect of these two entries is to divide the usual net profit of a business into two parts: (1) interest on investment, which through the Manufacturing Overhead Control account increases the cost of goods manufactured and through the Retained Earnings account increases the net income; and (2) the *remaining* net income arising from the difference between the increased cost of goods manufactured and sold (increase due to the addition of interest on investment as an element of cost) and the selling price. If interest on investment were not used, the net income would equal the sum of the two parts thus mentioned.

Trade associations favor the inclusion of interest on investment because it provides a more uniform and accurate comparison of manufacturing efficiency of the various members. The interest charge acts as a measure of the effect of capital in large- and small-scale business operations.

In most accounting work there is no need for inclusion of interest on investment. The Internal Revenue Service does not permit the inclusion of interest on investment as an element of cost. For them the inclusion of interest on investment inflates costs, and because of the larger inventories, it understates the profits.

For managerial use, interest may or may not be included as an element of cost, but the treatment of interest must be consistent from year to year. If the firm owns and operates several plants with varying investments in plants and machinery, the inclusion of interest as an element of cost would allow a more reliable comparison of the relative efficiency of each than would its exclusion and a better comparison of the relative costs of manufacturing the different products. Very few concerns are organized in this manner. A survey of the members of the National Association of Accountants indicated that for this reason about four out of every five oppose the inclusion of interest on investment as a manufacturing cost.

DIAGRAMMATIC SUMMARY OF MANUFACTURING OVERHEAD ACCOUNTING

In order to visualize the complete sequence of the application of manufacturing overhead to production from the time the costs are incurred until they have been charged to a job order, Illustration 11–10 is presented on the following page.

A RECAPITULATION OF WHAT MANAGEMENT MUST DO RELATIVE TO MANUFACTURING OVERHEAD

From the discussion in this and the preceding chapter, it becomes apparent that management, through its cost accounting division, must make certain decisions relative to the calculation and application of

Illustration 11-10. Diagrammatic Summary of Manufacturing Overhead Accounting

Transaction	Forms Used	Book of Original Entry	Source of Entry	Journal Form of Entry	Cost Record or Summary Form Used	Entry on Cost Record or Summary Form
Recording indirect labor costs	Time tickets and recapitulation sheet	General journal	Recapitulation sheet	Dr. Mfg. Overhead Control (Indirect Labor) Cr. Payroll	Standing order sheet or subsidiary ledger	
Recording indirect materials used costs	Material requisitions	Requisition journal or general journal	Requisition journal or requisitions	Dr. Mfg. Overhead Control (Indirect Material Used) Cr. Stores	Standing order sheet or subsidiary ledger	
Incurring factory overhead through (1) Payment of cash	Voucher check	Voucher register	Invoice	Dr. Manufacturing Overhead Control (Heat, Light, and Power, Etc.) Cr. Accounts Payable / Dr. Accounts Payable Cr. Cash	Standing order sheet or subsidiary ledger	
(2) Decreasing prepaid charges		General journal	Memorandum	Dr. Manufacturing Overhead Control (Insurance, Etc.) Cr. Prepaid Expense	Standing order sheet or subsidiary ledger	
(3) Depreciation valuation charges		General journal	Memorandum	Dr. Manufacturing Overhead Control (Depreciation) Cr. Allowance for Depreciation	Standing order sheet or subsidiary ledger	
Distribution of manufacturing overhead to service and producing depts.	Summary of standing orders or work sheet analysis	General journal	Summary of standing orders or work sheet	Dr. Producing Dept. Overhead Accounts / Service Dept. Overhead Accounts Cr. Manufacturing Overhead Control		
Distribution of service dept. overhead	Summary of standing orders or work sheet analysis	General journal	Summary of standing orders or work sheet	Dr. Producing Dept. Overhead Accounts Cr. Service Dept. Overhead Accounts		
Manufacturing overhead applied to production	Summary of applied manufacturing overhead	General journal	Summary of applied manufacturing overhead	Dr. Work-in-Process—Mfg. Overhead Cr. Applied Mfg. Overhead—Producing Depts.	Job order sheet	Entry in the Applied Mfg. Overhead section of job order sheets

manufacturing overhead to production. Among these, but not necessarily in the order given, are the following:

1. Analysis of indirect costs into fixed (period) and variable, and the subsequent preparation of a flexible overhead budget.
2. Determination of whether the overhead costs are to be applied to the cost of production on an overall-plant, departmental, or work-center basis.
3. Determination of whether the costs of service departments are to be (*a*) collected by service departments or allocated directly to the producing departments or (*b*) distributed to production by means of a supplementary overhead rate.
4. The determination of the effect of calendar variations on the predetermined overhead rate.
5. Determination of the basis on which to apply overhead cost to production.
6. Determination of the accounting disposition of the over- or underapplied overhead costs whether on a factorywide or departmental basis.
7. Analysis of the causes of the manufacturing overhead variations into *cost* and *volume* factors.
8. Determination of method of correcting grossly inaccurate predetermined overhead rates.

MANAGERIAL CONTROL OF MANUFACTURING OVERHEAD COSTS

Compilation of manufacturing overhead data, with its many ramifications, is but one important phase of the work of the cost accountant. Another, and probably more important phase, is the prodding of management to use these data to create a more efficient plant.

Effective reports form the link between the factory and top management, and the preparation of many of these reports is often in the hands of the cost accountant. Among these reports, those on manufacturing overhead rank high as aids in possible effective control of some of the factory costs.

Effective manufacturing overhead reports must be in the hands of management promptly if the information is to be meaningful and usable. These reports must pinpoint to management the expected and actual costs with a study of possible reasons for differences. These differences between actual and applied overhead must be departmentalized wherever feasible to further localize performance.

Departmental foremen, too, are an important part of the management team in the collection of information in their respective departments. Two reports from the factory in Illustrations 11–11 and 11–12

Illustration 11–11. Controllable Overhead Report

CONTROLLABLE OVERHEAD REPORT 80% Operating Capacity Department No. 62—Drill Press			For Month Ending April 30, 19—		
F. A. Butler, Foreman			80% Capacity O.R.		
Expense	Actual This Month	Budget This Month	Difference for Month Between Actual and Budget	Actual Year to Date	Budget Year to Date
Power & Light	$ 50.00	$ 52.00	$ 2.00*		
Inspection	60.00	60.00	—		
Indirect Labor	245.00	250.00	5.00*		
Supplies	110.00	108.00	2.00†		
Repairs	65.00	60.00	5.00†		
Spoilage	40.00	47.00	7.00*		
Tool Expense	50.00	54.00	4.00*		
Total Variable	$ 620.00	$ 631.00	$11.00*		
Fixed Charges	870.00	870.00	—		
Total	$1,490.00	$1,501.00	$11.00*		
Direct Labor Hours	4,800	4,810	10*		

* Decrease.
† Increase.

emphasize the position of the factory foreman in managerial control. Foremen are also important in the later analysis and study of the cost data for their departments. Failure to reach expected goals must be sought in large measure at the operational level in the factory, in factors such as careless operation, inexperience, wasted time, idle men, idle machines, poor machines, poor lighting, poor tools, poor materials, spoilage and waste of materials, and even in poor supervision.

As manufacturing plants grow in size and the relationship of top management and factory personnel becomes more impersonal, these various reports, including those on manufacturing overhead, take on added significance in the line of communication between the factory and the executive offices.

Illustration 11-12. Idle Machine Report

| Ma-chine Num-ber | Stan-dard Hours | Actual Hours | | | Idle Hours | | | | | | | % of Stan-dard | Burden Rate for Idle Time | Cost of Idle Time | Remarks |
| | | Reg-ular | Over-time | Total | No Oper-ator | No Mate-rials | Re-pairs | Await-ing Set Up | Await-ing Tools | Await-ing Instruc-tions | Total | | | | |

IDLE MACHINE REPORT — For month ending July 31, 19—

DEPARTMENT #106   CUTTING — Foreman: A. B. Howard

Ma-chine Num-ber	Stan-dard Hours	Reg-ular	Over-time	Total	No Oper-ator	No Mate-rials	Re-pairs	Await-ing Set Up	Await-ing Tools	Await-ing Instruc-tions	Total	% of Stan-dard	Burden Rate for Idle Time	Cost of Idle Time	Remarks
C-108	160	160		160											O.K.
C-103	160	150		150	10						10	6.25	$3.10	$31.00	Material held up in drilling dep't.
C-104	160	160		160											
F-110	160	140		140				20			20	12.5	1.80	36.00	Improper Scheduling
F-111	130	160	15	175									1.80	27.00*	To make up loss of Mach. #110.
F-112	130	125		130					3	2	5	3.85	1.80	9.00	Job instructions not on hand.
Total	900	895	15	915	10			20	3	2	35	2.77		31.00	

*Credit for overtime.

QUESTIONS FOR REVIEW

1. What is the difference between the meaning of the terms *department* and *production center* when used in cost accounting? What is the nature of a service department?

2. Five steps are usually followed in departmentalization of the manufacturing overhead costs. What are these?

3. What is meant by a plant or factory survey for departmentalization of manufacturing overhead? What information is usually contained in such a survey? Who is responsible for its preparation?

4. What is meant by a departmental overhead cost sheet? How is it used? What is a more common procedure used in place of the departmental (standing order) cost sheets? Why?

5. Two methods can be used in allocating service department overhead costs to production. What are these? Which method is more preferable?

6. If none of the actual manufacturing overhead costs are allocated to service departments but all are charged only to producing departments, what effect will this have on the cost accounting data?

7. What procedure is followed in handling the over- or underapplied manufacturing overhead costs (*a*) at the end of the month and (*b*) at the end of the accounting period?

8. What is meant by a "supplementary rate" for prorating the overhead when it refers to (*a*) the service department overhead costs, and (*b*) when it refers to the over- or underapplied manufacturing overhead?

9. What method of computing factory depreciation of plant and equipment seems more desirable for cost accounting? Explain.

10. Over- or underapplied manufacturing overhead may be analyzed into two causes. What are these and how are they computed?

PROBLEMS—GROUP A

Problem 11-1.   Purpose: *Entries to Departmentalize the Manufacturing Overhead and Applied Manufacturing Overhead*

The Klamath Manufacturing Company's factory contains three producing and three service departments. The departmental overhead costs have been tabulated and distributed as follows:

Costs	Cutting	Assembling	Finishing	Storeroom	Maintenance	Toolroom
Indirect material................	$ 400	$ 500	$ 500	$ 200	$1,000	$ 100
Indirect labor..................	800	400	600	300	1,000	200
Taxes, plant	200	200	300	200	250	150
Insurance......................	100	200	200	250	250	150
Depreciation—plant.............	300	200	100	100	150	200
Depreciation—equipment.........	400	180	120	500	200	300
Heat and light.................	100	200	140	60	100	100
Power	250	150	200	–	100	–
Superintendence................	150	100	100	50	180	120
Plant repairs..................	50	40	30	60	120	–
Miscellaneous..................	150	130	110	80	150	80
Totals......................	$2,900	$2,300	$2,400	$1,800	$3,500	$1,400
Maintenance department.........	1,000	700	900	500		400
Toolroom.....................	750	550	350	150		$1,800
Storeroom....................	1,700	500	250	$2,450		
Totals......................	$6,350	$4,050	$3,900			
Applied overhead..............	6,000	4,000	4,150			
Difference...................	$ 350	$ 50	$ (250)			

Required:

a) Journal entry to close out the Manufacturing Overhead Control account.
b) Journal entry to distribute the service departments' overhead costs.
c) Journal entry to record the applied manufacturing overhead.
d) Journal entry to close out the over- or underapplied manufacturing overhead.

Problem 11-2.   Purpose: *Journal Entries to Apply Manufacturing Overhead and Correct Grossly Miscalculated Rates*

The Kwillard Manufacturing Company budgets its manufacturing overhead on an annual basis and calculates its predetermined rate in advance of its year's operation.

The budgeted statistics for the year ending December 31, 19—, were as follows:

Budgeted overhead.............................$150,000
Budgeted direct labor costs.................. 120,000
Budgeted overhead rate .... 125% of direct labor costs

Strikes hindered production in the first three months of the year. Labor costs for this period were only $10,000. A recalculation of the budgeted figures indicated that for the remaining nine months direct labor costs will be $70,000 and that the revised manufacturing overhead costs will be $120,000 for the entire year.

In view of the strike, the company felt that some corrective cost accounting action must be taken.

Required:

a)   Journalize the applied manufacturing overhead for the first three months.
b)   Journal entry to correct retroactively the applied manufacturing overhead.
c)   Compute the new manufacturing overhead rate, to be used for the manufacturing for the remaining nine months in the year if no retroactive entry is made.
d)   Comment on the advisability of using the retroactive rate versus a new rate for the remaining nine months.

Problem 11–3. Purpose: *Analysis of the Causes for Over- and Underapplied Manufacturing Overhead*

The management of the Kweenio Manufacturing company is anxious to determine the cause for the over- or underapplied manufacturing overhead for the year. An examination of the records indicated the following statistics:

1.   The actual manufacturing overhead for the year was $180,000.
2.   Actual machine-hours on which the overhead is applied to production was 52,000 hours.
3.   The budgeted manufacturing overhead was $200,000.
4.   The budgeted machine-hours were 50,000.

Required:

a)   Compute the amount of the over- or underapplied manufacturing overhead.
b)   Determine how much of this variation was due to the volume (capacity) of plant production. Indicate if it is favorable or unfavorable.
c)   Determine how much of this is due to cost (spending) and whether it is favorable or unfavorable.

Problem 11–4. Purpose: *Prorating Actual Service Department Costs to Producing Departments; Journal Entries*

The Kohanson Manufacturing Company, a manufacturer of parts for the automotive industry, has four manufacturing departments and three service departments, viz: machine department I, machine department II, assembling, finishing, maintenance, toolroom, and storeroom.

The departmental manufacturing overhead (standing order) sheets for the year ended December 31, 19—, have been completed and indicated the following:

Department	Departmental Overhead Costs	Applied Manu- facturing Overhead
Machine Department I $22,500		$20,000
Machine Department II 14 500		16,000
Finishing department......................... 9,800		12,800
Assembling department....................... 12,000		15,200
Maintenance 8,000		
Toolroom 6,000		
Storeroom 5,000		

The factory survey of the facilities which was used in prorating the factory overhead was as follows:

Department	Area in Square Feet	No. of Employees	Percentage
Machine Department I 5,000		30	35
Machine Department II 3,000		25	30
Finishing department........................2,000		10	15
Assembling department.....................1,000		4	20
Maintenance department 2,000		6	
Toolroom 1,200		4	
Storeroom 3,000		2	

The service departments' overhead costs are allocated to the other departments in the order given on the following bases:

1. Maintenance: square footage.
2. Toolroom: number of employees in the department excluding the storeroom.
3. Storeroom: percentage basis.

Required:

a) Prepare a summary of the work sheet showing the actual overhead for each department, the distribution of the service departments' costs to the other departments, the applied manufacturing overhead, and the amount of the over- or underapplied manufacturing overhead.
b) Prepare journal entries to close out the Manufacturing Overhead Control account, the allocation of the service departments' overhead, the applied manufacturing overhead, and the closing out of the over- or underapplied manufacturing overhead.

Problem 11–5. Purpose: *Journal Entries Affecting Departmentalization of Manufacturing Overhead and Its Application*

The Keenan Manufacturing Company's allocation of the manufacturing overhead for the year ending December 31, 19 —, was as follows:

Producing Departments	Service Departments
Machine Department I $15,000	Heat, light, and power.........$8,000
Assembling department......... 10,000	Factory maintenance 6,000
Finishing department............ 6,000	Toolroom......................... 5,000
	Storeroom........................ 4,000

The actual overhead for the service departments was distributed as follows:

Department	Dept. I	Assembling	Finish-ing	Store-room	Mainte-nance	Tool-room
Storeroom	$2,400	$1,600	$1,300			
Maintenance	2,100	1,900	1,500	$ 550	....	$ 800
Heat, light, and power	2,000	1,800	2,200	750	$850	400
Toolroom	2,500	2,200	1,500			
	$9,000	$7,500	$6,500	$1,300	$850	$1,200

Additional manufacturing overhead data for the year indicated the following:

Department	Budgeted Overhead	Budgeted Labor Hours	Applied Manufacturing Overhead on Labor Hours Basis
Machine department I	$28,500	19,000	14,000 hrs. at $1.50
Assembling	15,000	7,500	9,000 hrs. at $2.00
Finishing	12,500	12,500	11,500 hrs. at $1.00

Required:

a) Journal entries to close out the Manufacturing Overhead Control account.
b) Journal entries to record the Applied Manufacturing Overhead.
c) Journal entries to close out the Applied Manufacturing Overhead accounts and the over- and underapplied manufacturing overhead.
d) Complete the schedule indicating the amount of the over- or underapplied manufacturing overhead and the causes for the variation, and if it is a debit or credit item.

Department	Overapplied	Underapplied	Amount Due to Volume	Amount Due to Cost (Spending)
Department I				
Assembling				
Finishing department				
Totals				

PROBLEMS—GROUP B

Problem 11–6.   Purpose: *Computation of Manufacturing Overhead Rates; Analysis of Over- or Underapplied Overhead*

The Kallus Manufacturing Company applies manufacturing overhead on the basis of direct labor hours. The budgeted hours for the month of July are 10,000. Actual hours worked were 8,000.

The overhead cost data was as follows:

| Overhead Description | Budgeted Overhead Costs | | Actual Overhead Costs |
	Variable	Fixed	
Indirect labor	$1,200	$ 2,800	$ 3,200
Superintendence		3,000	3,000
Heat, light, and power	1,200	1,800	2,400
Indirect materials	1,000		1,200
Depreciation of equipment		2,200	2,200
Maintenance costs		500	700
Real estate taxes		400	400
Repairs	1,000	500	1,600
Insurance costs		800	1,000
Totals	$4,400	$12,000	$15,700

Required:

a) Compute the predetermined manufacturing overhead rates.
b) Compute the applied manufacturing overhead and make the journal entry to record this.
c) Compute the over- or underapplied manufacturing overhead costs.
d) Compute the causes and amounts of the variation in manufacturing overhead due to volume of production and due to cost factors.

Problem 11–7.   Purpose: *Journal Entries to Apply Manufacturing Overhead and to Correct Grossly Miscalculated Rates during the Year*

The Kramour Manufacturing Company budgets its manufacturing overhead costs on an annual basis since its operations involve the production of a single item.

The budgeted statistics for the year starting January 1, 19 –, were as follows:

```
Budgeted fixed manufacturing overhead.....................$100,000
Budgeted variable manufacturing overhead.................  60,000
Budgeted production is based upon direct labor
  costs of $250,000 spread uniformly
  throughout the year.
```

Strikes hindered production during the first three months of the year, and direct labor costs were only $12,500. A recalculation of the budget items indicated that for the remaining nine months, the direct labor costs will probably not exceed $125,000. A revision of some of the overhead costs indicated that adjustments and eliminations will change the budgeted statistics for the entire year as follows:

```
Budgeted fixed manufacturing overhead.................$80,000
Budgeted variable overhead...............................  25,000
```

In order to make the cost accounting for overhead more realistic, certain corrective action must be taken.

Required:

a) Journalize the applied manufacturing overhead for the first three months on the basis of the original budget.

b) Correct retroactively by entries the manufacturing overhead applied on the basis of revised budget figures.

c) Compute a new rate for the manufacturing overhead if no retroaction is taken for the first three months.

d) Comment on the two possible methods of applying manufacturing overhead on the basis of having reliable cost accounting figures.

Problem 11–8. Purpose: *Analysis of the Causes of the Over- or Underapplied Manufacturing Overhead*

The Kweenio Supply Company wishes to analyze the causes for the over- or underapplied manufacturing overhead at the end of its first year's operation, so that the same errors will not occur in the future.

The following information has been taken from the books of the firm for the past year:

1. Budgeted manufacturing overhead $180,000
2. Budgeted machine-hours on which the overhead
   is to be applied.. 45,000 hrs.
3. Actual manufacturing overhead costs were.........................$210,000
4. Actual machine-hours worked....................................... 50,000 hrs.

Required:

a) Compute the over- or underapplied manufacturing overhead for the year just ended.

b) Determine how much of this variation is due to the volume of production. Indicate if this is a favorable or unfavorable variation.

c) Determine how much of this variation is due to the cost factors. Indicate if this is favorable or unfavorable.

d) Managerially, indicate where the responsibility for these variations should be placed.

e) Indicate what procedure should be followed in the future to avoid any large variations.

Problem 11–9. Purpose: *Prorating the Actual Manufacturing Overhead on a Departmental Basis; Journal Entries*

At the end of the accounting period, the accounting records and the plant survey of the Kwollan Manufacturing Company presented the following information:

	Actual Overhead Allocated	Plant Survey Data		
		Square Feet	Number of Employees	Materials Used
Production departments:				
Cooking.............................$21,000		6,000	16	$20,000
Drying................................. 35,000		8,000	10	2,000
Mixing................................. 7,000		5,000	8	3,000
Packaging............................. 4,900		6,000	6	3,000
Service departments:				
Storeroom............................. 9,100		3,000	4	
Maintenance.......................... 8,400		2,000	5	
Factory office 4,500		1,000	3	
Totals.........................$89,900		31,000	52	$28,000

During the year, the applied manufacturing overhead was cooking department, $33,000; drying department, $40,000; mixing department, $10,000; and packing department, $6,500.

Paralleling the procedure followed in preparing the manufacturing overhead budget at the beginning of the year, the proration of the service departments followed this order and bases for allocation (to the nearest dollar):

1. The factory office costs are prorated to all the other departments equally.
2. Maintenance costs are prorated to the other departments on a square footage basis.
3. Storeroom costs are allocated on the basis of the cost of materials used.

Required:

a) Prepare a work sheet showing the distribution of the service departments' costs to the other departments.
b) Indicate the applied and the over- or underapplied overhead for the producing departments.
c) Prepare entries in journal form to close out the Manufacturing Overhead Control account; to close out the service departments' overhead costs and the applied manufacturing overhead; and to close out the over- or underapplied manufacturing overhead to the Cost of Sales account.

Problem 11–10. Purpose: *Departmental Analysis of the Over- or Underapplied Manufacturing Overhead*

The Kwenson Manufacturing Company has submitted the following manufacturing overhead data for the year ending June 30, 19—, and has asked you to analyze the causes of the over- or underapplied manufacturing overhead on a departmental basis.

	Department I	Department II	Finishing Department
Budgeted manufacturing overhead costs...	$30,000	$50,000	$ 75,000
Budgeted volume of production:			
Machine-hours...	12,000 hrs.	10,000 hrs.	
Labor costs...			112,500
Actual manufacturing overhead ...	$36,000	$42,000	60,000
Actual volume of production:			
Machine-hours...	13,000 hrs.	8,000 hrs.	
Labor costs...			108,000

Required:

a) Compute the over- or underapplied manufacturing overhead for each department.

b) Compute the amount of the variation due to volume of production indicating whether it is favorable or not.

c) Compute the amount of the variation due to cost factors, indicating if each of these is favorable or unfavorable.

chapter 12

Distribution Cost
Analyses and Control

INTRODUCTION

To complete the picture of cost determination, it is necessary to include a discussion of the costs of distributing the product manufactured, whether on a job or process basis. Cost determination extends beyond the manufacturing operations. It must include the sale and marketing of the products. This chapter relates to the discussion of the distribution cost analyses and compilation.

Distribution costs have been defined in two ways. The more common interpretation includes all costs incurred from the time the product is manufactured and placed in the stock room until it has been converted into cash. From this definition it is apparent that the term embraces not only what are commonly known as *selling expenses* but also the *administrative* and perhaps part of the *financial management expenses*. A second, more narrow definition sometimes used limits the term *distribution costs* to what is customarily called *selling and marketing expenses*. In the discussions and illustrations in this chapter, the broader connotation of distribution costs is used. These *distribution costs* might include:

1. *Packing and shipping expenses*—packing materials, packing labor, apportioned building expenses, delivery equipment expenses, and clerical expense.
2. *Selling expenses*—salesmen's salaries, salesmen's travel expenses, commissions, advertising, postage, collection expenses, apportioned charges, rent, taxes, insurance, depreciation, and office expense.
3. *Administrative and financial expenses*—applicable to the conversion of manufactured goods into cash.

Distribution costs may also be grouped into two major categories:

1. *Order-getting costs* which include all cost items involved in the functions of obtaining an order. Included in this category would be salesmen's costs, commissions, and advertising.
2. *Order-filling costs* include costs incurred in getting the goods to the customer and collecting the cash from the customer. Included in order-filling costs are the functions of packing and shipping, billing, and collection expense.

PURPOSES OF DISTRIBUTION COST ANALYSES

At the beginning, *curiosity* was the primary reason for pioneering in this area; but the recent, rapid strides made in marketing research coupled with the increasingly high costs of distribution have added new stimulus to the further study and application of distribution costs analyses as another valuable tool for management control. Furthermore, federal legislation in the matter of price fixing and marketing practices makes a knowledge of distribution costs a necessity. The Robinson-Patman Act, for example, administered by the Federal Trade Commission, is an act under which manufacturers may at any time be called upon to justify, on the basis of *cost,* quantity discounts or price concessions given to large quantity purchasers.

The development of accounting procedures for the costs of distribution has lagged somewhat compared to the progress made in industrial *production cost* accounting. One reason for this has been the difficulty in establishing uniform rules of accounting for the many possible variations of application. The cost of distributing a product, for example, will vary not only with the product distributed but also with the territory in which the sale is made, the type of customer, the method of sale, and the method of delivery. Recently, increased attention has been given to the area of distribution costs as these costs may make up a significant portion of total costs. In some industries, distribution costs are greater than production costs.

Analysis of distribution costs may lead to the implementation of responsibility accounting concepts. Cost data should be accumulated in accounts that are grouped by function so that the person in charge of the function knows his costs. For example, all costs of the billing function such as salaries, supplies, and postage should be determinable so that the manager of the billing department could be held accountable for his costs. The concepts of departmentalizing costs in the factory should be carried over to the distribution effort by functionalizing the costs under the order-getting and order-filling categories.

CLASSIFYING DISTRIBUTION COSTS

For the most effective managerial control, distribution costs must be classified as either *direct* or *indirect,* distinguishing between those which can be allocated directly to a product, a sale, a territory, or a method of distribution, and those which must be apportioned. There must be a further analysis of the distribution costs into those which are *fixed* and those which are *variable.* Some, such as salesmen's commissions, vary with the sales; others, such as rent of sales facilities, are fixed or period costs. As in the case of manufacturing overhead costs, distribution costs must be carefully analyzed and grouped, and become part of the computations of *marginal income, contribution margin,* and *break-even point.*

Effective distribution cost control also requires that periodically, actual expenses be compared with predetermined standards; hence, standards must be established. A flexible budget showing the fixed and variable distribution costs at various sales volumes permits ready comparison with actual to determine the causes of variations from the predetermined or standard distribution cost rates.

ACCUMULATING AND RECORDING DISTRIBUTION COSTS

The concept of distribution costs involves a threefold task which in its final analysis resolves itself into (1) *accumulating and recording the costs of distributing the product,* (2) *analyzing the costs of distribution on some acceptable basis,* and (3) *the control and interpretation of distribution costs through the use of predetermined standards and budgets.*

Distribution costs may be grouped under the following major functions and then further subdivided according to the salaries, supplies, rent, and other expenses within the group:

Order-getting costs:
1. Direct selling costs.
2. Advertising and sales promotion.

Order-filling costs:
1. Transportation and delivery.
2. Warehouse and storage expense.
3. Credit and collection expense.

Each of these five categories represents a control account with a subsidiary ledger for the detailed accounts. A section of such a Code of Accounts is shown in Illustration 12–1. This Code of Accounts is by no means complete; it is merely indicative of accounts found in the subsidiary ledger.

If no subsidiary ledgers are desired, it is possible to record the individual expenses of selling and distribution in their respective accounts and

Illustration 12-1

SUGGESTED CODE OF CHART OF ACCOUNTS OF THE DISTRIBUTION COSTS

Control Account		Subsidiary Ledger	
Acct. No.	Account	Acct. No.	Account
510	Direct Selling Expense Control		
		511	Salesmen's Salaries
		512	Salesmen's Commissions
		513	Salesmen's Bonuses
		514	Salesmen's Traveling Expenses
		515	Sales Office Expenses—Supplies
		516	Sales Office Salaries
		517	Sales Office Telephone
		518	Sales Office Rent
520	Advertising and Sales Promo- tion Control		
		521	Salaries
		522	Office Supplies
		523	Rent of Office
		524	Samples—Cost and Distribution
		525	Newspaper Advertising
		526	Magazine Advertising
		527	Direct Mail
		528	Billboard Advertising
530	Transportation Expense Control		
		531	Freight-Out
		532	Shipping Department Salaries
		533	Shipping Department Supplies
		534	Delivery Expense
		535	Depreciation Delivery Equipment
		536	Salaries of Drivers
		537	Freight-In on Returned Sales
540	Warehouse and Storage Expense Control		
		541	Supplies
		542	Salaries
		543	Rent or Taxes
		544	Repairs
		545	Depreciation of Buildings or Equipment
		546	Insurance
		547	Heat and Light
550	Credit and Collection Expense Control		
		551	Collection Department Salaries
		552	Collection Department Supplies
		553	Credit and Collection Rent
		554	Credit Services and Expense
		555	Legal Fees
		556	Heat and Light
		557	Losses from Bad and Doubtful Accounts
570	General Distribution Costs		
		571	Prorated Administrative Expenses

at the end of regular periods to close them out to summary accounts. The diagrammatic effect is somewhat like that shown in the illustration which follows:

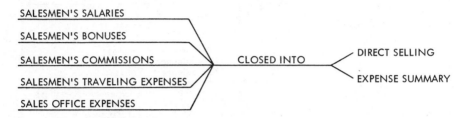

This procedure is similar to that used in summarizing the individual manufacturing overhead costs in a Manufacturing Overhead Control account.

ANALYZING THE COSTS OF DISTRIBUTION

The purpose of distribution cost analysis is to enable management to determine the answers to some or all of the following questions: "What *customers'* accounts are profitable?" "What *products* are most profitable to sell?" "In which *territories* are the most profitable sales made?" "What are the most profitable *methods* of distribution?" "What *salesmen* are making the most profitable sales?" These questions indicate to a certain degree the nature of the analyses which are required. Management must decide under which bases it desires to have distribution costs analyzed and whether such analysis is to be the result of a *statistical study carried on periodically* or whether the analysis is to be part of a *continuous, routine accounting function.* If it is to be a statistical study, then the accounting department will merely furnish the expense figures and the marketing or statistical sections will analyze these data and prepare reports for management. Our discussion will be based on the assumption that the distribution cost analysis is an integral part of the accounting system.

Distribution costs may be classified to expedite the following analyses:

1. The cost of distribution *of each product.*
2. The cost of distribution *within each territory.*
3. The cost of distribution for *classes of customers,* which may be further subdivided as follows:
    a) According to *size of sale.*
    b) According to *territorial classification* — urban or rural.
    c) According to *type of customer organization* — chain stores, mail-order houses, and independents.
    d) According to *type of store* — drugstore, department store, variety store, etc.

4. The cost of distribution for each *method of sale,* which may be subdivided into—
   a) Branch offices.
   b) Salesmen.
   c) Mail.
   d) Unsolicited,
   or as an alternative classification, as—
   a) Cash sales.
   b) Credit sales.
   c) Installment sales.

The *first two* of the foregoing types of analyses are most reasonably and accurately determined because the number of variables is smaller than when the customer factor is considered. The many individual differences in types of customers cause the greatest complication in distribution cost analysis; and that is why, so frequently, most concerns leave methods 3 and 4, above, to a method of statistical analysis of accounting data rather than to a method based on recorded continuous data, such as might be used for methods 1 and 2.

PRODUCT METHOD OF DISTRIBUTION COST ANALYSES

Distribution cost analyses on the basis of *products sold* may be advantageously used if the nature of the products, the selling effort, and the size of order are such as to prevent the use of a uniform basis, such as sales dollar volume, quantity of units, or weight. This method could be used by sellers of few products, each of which is produced and sold in large volume and each of which has different characteristics that prevent a uniform analysis of distribution costs. Companies selling many products might group products by *product line.* For example, a manufacturer of motor vehicles might classify his distribution costs by type of vehicle. A company that manufactures many products but has a distinctly seasonal demand for some products might well benefit from an analysis of costs *by product* to provide necessary data to determine whether or not the company should encourage off-season orders at reduced prices.

The "product" method of distribution cost analyses lends itself most readily to continuous accounting records and statements. The distribution costs can be recorded under (1) direct selling costs, (2) advertising and sales promotion, (3) transportation, (4) warehousing and storage, (5) credit and collection, (6) general administrative expenses, and (7) all other distribution costs. A subsidiary ledger may be provided for each expense group. Periodically—weekly, semimonthly, or monthly—the expenses can be allocated to each product by the use of product expense analysis sheets corresponding to the departmental expense analysis or standing order sheets used for manufacturing expenses.

The allocation of the various expenses requires further explanation. Expenses for allocation may be classified as: *direct,* chargeable directly to the product or territory; *semidirect,* such as advertising copy which may cover several products; and *indirect* expenses.

A suggested basis for the allocation of the various distribution costs is shown in Illustration 12–2.

The same basis of allocation can be used if it is desired to compile distribution costs *by territories;* here, the total sales in each territory rather than the sales of each product would be the basic factor. However,

Illustration 12–2

Expense or Cost Functionally Grouped	Basis of Allocation
Direct selling expenses:	
Salesmen's salaries........................	Sales value of product
Salesmen's commissions....................	Sales value of product
Salesmen's bonuses........................	Sales value of product
Sales or branch office expenses, including supplies, salaries, telephone, rent or building maintenance, entertainment......	Sales value of product
Advertising and sales promotion expense:	
Salaries and office expenses................	Sales value of products
Samples..................................	Specific cost of each product samples
General company advertising..............	Sales value of products
Direct product advertising, newspaper, magazine, and direct mail...............	Directly to product being advertised
Transportation expenses:	
Freight-out.............................	Apportioned on the basis of one of the following: (*a*) sales value of each product, (*b*) relative weight of product sales, or (*c*) size of product weighted by quantity sold
Shipping department salaries and supplies	
Delivery expenses.......:...............	
Warehouse and storage:	
Supplies and salaries....................	Number of units sold and shipped or on basis of relative size of product weighted by number handled
Depreciation...........................	
Insurance.............................	Average cost value of each product on hand
Credit and collection expenses:	
Salaries...............................	Sales value of each product sold
Supplies...............................	Sales value of each product sold
Rent..................................	Sales value of each product sold
Legal fees.............................	Number of accounts and products sold to each
Heat and light.........................	Sales value of each product sold
Loss on bad and doubtful accounts.........	Number of accounts and the value of products sold to each
Administrative expenses:	
Salaries and expenses of bookkeeping department..........	Either number of sales invoices or lines per invoice for each product
Other administrative expenses..............	Either on sales value of each product, or the number of orders received for each product

when it is desirable to analyze the costs of distribution by classes of customers or by method of sale, some modifications in procedure must be made for certain expenses.

To illustrate the method used to record as accounting data the distribution costs accumulated and analyzed on a product basis, the case of the Harvey Paint Manufacturing Company is used. This firm produces three main groups of products: (1) white lead and oils; (2) paints; and (3) enamels, lacquers, and varnishes. Although these are distributed to dealers and jobbers, that fact is not pertinent to our present problem. An analysis of the books and records for the past three months brings forth the following necessary information concerning business operations:

	White Lead and Oils	Paints	Enamels, Lacquers, Varnishes	Total
Sales for past three months	$150,000	$400,000	$250,000	$800,000
Number of orders received	1,500	3,800	2,200	7,500
Volume of sales in gallons	70,000	150,000	80,000	300,000
Specific product advertising	$ 10,000	$ 30,000	$ 20,000	$ 60,000

The distribution costs for the period were:

Code No.	Accounts		
510	Direct Selling Expense Control		$40,000
511	Salesmen's Salaries and Commissions	$32,000	
512	Sales Office Expenses	8,000	
	Total	$40,000	
520	Advertising and Sales Promotion Expense Control		68,200
521	Product Advertising	$60,000	
522	Company Advertising	3,200	
523	Samples (Paints, $3,000; Lacquers, $2,000)	5,000	
	Total	$68,200	
530	Transportation Expense Control		18,000
531	Freight-Out	$ 3,000	
532	Shipping Salaries and Supplies	9,000	
533	Delivery Expenses	6,000	
	Total	$18,000	
540	Warehousing and Storage Expense Control		6,600
541	Salaries and Supplies	$ 4,800	
542	Rent and Maintenance	1,800	
	Total	$ 6,600	
550	Credit and Collection Expense Control		4,200
551	Salaries and Supplies	$ 3,000	
552	Legal Fees	900	
553	Loss on Bad Debts	300	
	Total	$ 4,200	

Illustration 12–3. Control Accounts and Subsidiary Ledger Accounts for Distribution Costs

CONTROL ACCOUNTS

SUBSIDIARY LEDGER ACCOUNTS

510 DIRECT SELLING EXPENSE CONTROL
40,000.00

511 Salesmen's Salaries & Commissions
32,000.00

512 Sales Office Expenses
8,000.00

520 ADVERTISING AND SALES PROMO-TION EXPENSE CONTROL
68,200.00

521 Direct Product Advertising
White lead and oils 10,000.00
Paints 30,000.00
Lacquers 20,000.00

522 Company Advertising
3,200.00

523 Samples
Paints 3,000.00
Lacquers 2,000.00

530 TRANSPORTATION EXPENSE CONTROL
18,000.00

531 Freight-Out
3,000.00

532 Shipping Salaries & Supplies
9,000.00

533 Delivery Expense
6,000.00

540 WAREHOUSING AND STORAGE EXPENSE CONTROL
6,600.00

541 Salaries and Supplies
4,800.00

542 Rent and Maintenance
1,800.00

550 CREDIT AND COLLECTION EXPENSE CONTROL
4,200.00

551 Salaries and Supplies
3,000.00

552 Legal Fees
900.00

553 Loss on Bad Debts
300.00

570 ADMINISTRATIVE EXPENSE CONTROL
5,250.00

561 Supervision of Office Work
3,000.00

562 Bookkeeping and Clerical Expense
2,250.00

560	Administrative Expense Control		5,250
561	Supervision of Office Work	$ 3,000	
562	Bookkeeping and Clerical Work	2,250	
	Total	$ 5,250	

As is evident, this list of expenses is only partially complete and is used for illustrative purposes only. In a complete distribution cost accounting system, there would be six controlling accounts, with a subsidiary expense ledger for each group. However, the controlling accounts may be dispensed with if the individual expense accounts are not too numerous. In either case, it should be noted that this illustration is one of *historical costs,* not predetermined standard costs, which will be illustrated later in the chapter. Furthermore, no matter what method is used, it will be necessary to accumulate the distribution costs by products, and the simplest method is by use of *distribution cost product analysis sheets.* Continuing the illustration, the relationship of the control accounts and the subsidiary ledger are shown (see Illustration 12–3) and then the use of the standing order sheets (Illustration 12–4) and the product distribution cost analysis summary accounts (Illustration 12–5).

One of these standing order sheets is used each month, with sufficient columns for each group of products. It is also possible to prepare this

Illustration 12–4. Distribution Cost Analysis Sheet by Products

DISTRIBUTION COST ANALYSIS

For Month of March, 19—

Date	Code No.	White Lead and Oils	Paints	Enamels, Lacquers, and Varnishes	Total
		Amount	Amount	Amount	Total
3/31	511	$ 6,000.00	$16,000.00	$10,000.00	$ 32,000.00
	512	1,500.00	4,000.00	2,500.00	8,000.00
	521	10,000.00	30,000.00	20,000.00	60,000.00
	522	600.00	1,600.00	1,000.00	3,200.00
	523	.....	3,000.00	2,000.00	5,000.00
	531	562.50	1,500.00	937.50	3,000.00
	532	1,687.50	4,500.00	2,812.50	9,000.00
	533	1,125.00	3,000.00	1,875.00	6,000.00
	541	1,120.00	2,400.00	1,280.00	4,800.00
	542	420.00	900.00	480.00	1,800.00
	551	600.00	1,520.00	880.00	3,000.00
	552	181.00	454.00	265.00	900.00
	553	60.00	152.00	88.00	300.00
	561	600.00	1,520.00	880.00	3,000.00
	562	450.00	1,140.00	660.00	2,250.00
		$24,906.00	$71,686.00	$45,658.00	$142,250.00

Illustration 12–5

DISTRIBUTION COST ANALYSIS SHEETS

One for Each Product for Which Distribution Costs Are Being Analyzed

One of these may be used each month or quarter, or one with twelve columns can be used for an entire year. For basis of cost allocation see footnotes.

Standing Order Sheet No. 1
PRODUCT: White Lead and Oils

Date	Code No.	Amount
3/31	511	$ 6,000.00[1]
	512	1,500.00[1]
	521	10,000.00[2]
	522	600.00[1]
	531	562.50[1]
	532	1,687.50[1]
	533	1,125.00[1]
	541	1,120.00[3]
	542	420.00[3]
	551	600.00[4]
	552	181.00[4]
	553	60.00[4]
	561	600.00[4]
	562	450.00[4]
	Total	$24,906.00

Standing Order Sheet No. 2
PRODUCT: Paints

Date	Code No.	Amount
3/31	511	$16,000.00[1]
	512	4,000.00[1]
	521	30,000.00[2]
	522	1,600.00[1]
	523	3,000.00[2]
	531	1,500.00[1]
	532	4,500.00[1]
	533	3,000.00[1]
	541	2,400.00[3]
	542	900.00[3]
	551	1,520.00[4]
	552	454.00[4]
	553	152.00[4]
	561	1,520.00[4]
	562	1,140.00[4]
	Total	$71,686.00

Standing Order Sheet No. 3
PRODUCT: Enamels, Lacquers, and Varnishes

Date	Code No.	Amount
3/31	511	$10,000.00[1]
	512	2,500.00[1]
	521	20,000.00[2]
	522	1,000.00[1]
	523	2,000.00[2]
	531	937.50[1]
	532	2,812.50[1]
	533	1,875.00[1]
	541	1,280.00[3]
	542	480.00[3]
	551	880.00[4]
	552	265.00[4]
	553	88.00[4]
	561	880.00[4]
	562	660.00[4]
	Total	$45,658.00

[1] On basis of sales value. [2] Direct product charges. [3] On basis of physical volume. [4] Number of sales orders.

Distribution Costs—White Lead and Oils
March 31 24,906.00

Distribution Costs—Paints
March 31 71,686.00

Distribution Costs—Enamels, Lacquers, Varnishes
March 31 45,658.00

sheet so that there would be one for each group of products, with columns for each month, so that the sheet could be used for a three-month, six-month, or one-year period.

The journal entry made from the summary of the standing order sheets, based on distribution costs analyzed and recorded by products, would be:

```
Distribution Costs—White Lead and Oils ................................24,906
Distribution Costs—Paints ....................................................71,686
Distribution Costs—Enamels, Lacquers, and Varnishes ..............45,658
    Direct Selling Expense Control.........................................          40,000
    Advertising and Sales Promotion Expense Control...............          68,200
    Transportation Expense Control........................................          18,000
    Warehousing and Storage Expense Control .........................           6,600
    Credit and Collection Expense Control ..............................           4,200
    Administrative Expense Control........................................           5,250
To close out the distribution expense control accounts to the
product analysis summary accounts.
```

The same effect is realized without the use of the control accounts by crediting the expense accounts and charging the product summary distribution expense accounts. When this point has been reached in recording distribution costs on a historical cost plan, the distribution cost product summary accounts are closed out to the Profit and Loss account, to wit:

```
Profit and Loss Account .....................................................142,250
    Distribution Costs—White Lead and Oils........................          24,906
    Distribution Costs—Paints ............................................          71,686
    Distribution Costs—Enamels, Lacquers and Varnishes........          45,658
To close out the distribution cost summary accounts.
```

ANALYSIS OF DISTRIBUTION COSTS BY TERRITORIES

The territorial analysis of distribution costs should be made as this may be desirable to control the costs of definite territorial areas. Naturally, when distribution costs are analyzed by territories, sales and costs of sales would follow the same pattern. The plan of this type of distribution costing and analysis is the same as that for product analysis. Frequently, within a given territory, the method of distribution of the products includes sales from warehouses, sales from branch offices, and sales made directly to customers. When these variations are not the same for each territory, the analysis can become complex. Computers may be of help here by providing the necessary data. The analysis of territorial distribution assumes a more or less uniform procedure in each territory. The final summary of distribution costs will show: Distribution Costs, Territory I; Distribution Costs, Territory II; and Distribution Costs, Territory III.

In allocating certain expenses to the respective territories, the following should be taken into consideration:

Expense	*Method of Allocation*
Salesmen's salaries and expenses.........	Time spent in each territory
Billing and office expenses.................	Number of billing items or direct charge
Advertising....................................	Territory covered by media
Transportation	Either direct, or on the basis of mileage
Credit and collection........................	Number of accounts in each territory or number of sales

OTHER METHODS OF DISTRIBUTION COST ANALYSIS

Distribution cost analysis may be continued under the headings of *classes of customers* and *methods of sales*. As a general rule they are not recorded on the books as functional or dynamic costs. They represent studies made by the marketing department to aid management.

Distribution costs collected by *classes of customers* might be analyzed and interpreted in one of five ways:

1. The distribution costs might be analyzed or allocated to the sales according to the *size of the sale* made. Sales might be grouped: $1 to $50, $51 to $100, $101 to $200, and over $200. Such an analysis would be fundamentally useful to manufacturers who sell to both large-volume and small-volume customers and who wish to give inducements to the large buyers.
2. The distribution costs might be analyzed or allocated to the sales on the basis of the *territorial* distribution of the customers. Customers might be grouped as rural and urban, by states, or by cities. This method of collecting distribution costs would be useful in justifying different selling prices in the various territories.
3. The distribution costs might be analyzed or allocated to the sales on the basis of the *size of the community* in which sold. This method is similar to the territorial.
4. The distribution costs might be analyzed or allocated to sales on the basis of type of *customer organization.* Customers might be grouped as *chain stores, mail-order houses,* and *independents.*
5. The distribution costs are sometimes analyzed or allocated to sales on the basis of the *type of customers,* such as drugstores, department stores, grocery stores, etc.

In each of the foregoing methods, distribution cost analysis can become complex. Here again, the computer should be of help.

If the distribution costs are to be determined on the basis of customers, it is necessary to apportion or allocate the various expenses on the basis of the amount of service which each customer or class of customer receives. This type of cost analysis is important to large distributors who wish to have data to justify special price concessions or discounts to certain customers. Illustration 12–6 shows a summary of the costs of

Illustration 12–6

THE CHAPELA COMPANY
COST TO HANDLE SALES OF VARIOUS SIZES
Expressed as a Percentage of Sales Prices

	Sales under $200	Sales between $201 and $500	Sales between $501 and $5,000	Total
Number of sales.......	400	150	50	600
Percent of total	66⅔	25	8⅓	100
Sales volume $45,150		$61,580	$157,270	$264,000
Percent of total 17.10		23.33	59.57	100
Cost to handle ....$ 2,265		$ 1,875	$ 2,160	$ 6,300
Cost to handle as percent of sales 5.02		3.04	1.37	2.39

handling accounts of varying sizes in terms of percentage of sales. It is comparatively easy to determine the number of sales in the various price classifications and the total sales for each group. The cost of handling the sales in each group must be determined by charging against each its share of the 15 previously listed marketing expenses. Expenses such as advertising may be charged directly; several of the others must be allocated. Often, detailed studies must be made to determine an equitable basis of allocation. To determine the portion of sales office expense applicable to each group it is necessary to make a detailed study of the cost of taking an order, entering an order, billing and accounting for the sale, etc. Similarly, the cost of general company advertising must be apportioned on some fair basis. The total of the distribution expenses for each group of sales is known as the total *cost to handle*. This figure is also shown as a percentage of sales.

A simpler method of computing the costs of handling the sales to certain customers may be used. Instead of apportioning the expenses according to the size of the sale, the average cost of handling all the sales, expressed as a percentage of the total sales, is determined. The final result tells the manufacturer approximately what percentage to add to the selling price to cover distribution costs. However, this amount is not accurate; it does not cost as much to sell a large quantity of goods to a single buyer as it does to distribute the same quantity to 50 different customers. Furthermore, greater sales effort may be required to sell certain commodities. The result obtained by using total expenses and total sales is an average cost and, like all averages, may be misleading.

These average costs, obtained by dividing each expense by the total sales, are shown in Illustration 12–7.

Illustration 12–7

THE CHAPELA COMPANY
Cost of Distribution as a Percentage of Sales

	Percent of Sales
Advertising	2.12
Salesmen's salaries	5.48
Salesmen's traveling expenses	2.41
Sales office expenses	3.79
Shipping and transportation	1.61
Warehousing	0.80
Credit and collection expense	0.40
Allowance for bad debts	0.60
General administrative expenses apportioned	4.85
Total Cost of Distribution Expressed as Percentage of Sales	22.06

A few organizations analyze their marketing costs on the basis of the *methods of distribution,* which might be either:

1. Costs of direct selling by company representatives:
   a) To wholesalers.
   b) To large retailers.
2. Costs of unsolicited or mail orders.

Sometimes the methods of distribution are based on the *credit terms* of the sales. Distribution expenses are then allocated to sales by:

1. Cash sales.
2. Credit sales.
3. Installment sales.

No matter what the basis is for allocating marketing and distribution costs, the total costs are usually expressed as a percentage of the net sales; and when so expressed, distribution cost analysis becomes useful to management in fixing selling prices, in attempting to eliminate unprofitable practices, and in determining the size of quantity or cash discounts. Total costs may also be reduced to a cost per unit of product or per sales order.

To illustrate distribution costs on the basis of *methods of distribution,* an analysis could be made of the sales of a large wholesaler. The types of sales made by a wholesale dealer in hardware might be (1) retail—cash and carry; (2) country sales—truck delivery; (3) country sales—freight delivery; and (4) mail-order sales—shipped by freight. In order to analyze cost of marketing in this manner, it is necessary to ascertain the amount of the sales in each class.

It is also necessary to compute the amount of the distribution costs applicable to each kind of sales. This procedure requires a statistical analysis similar to that made in the other methods of allocating distribution costs. Illustration 12–8 shows, in condensed form, the method of presenting this information. In analyzing the data in this illustration, the following meaningful conclusions are drawn:

Illustration 12–8. Statement of Distribution Costs and Profits

	Retail Cash Sales	Country Sales, Truck Delivery	Country Sales, Freight Delivery	Mail-Order Sales	Total
THE CHAPELA COMPANY STATEMENT OF DISTRIBUTION COSTS AND RATIOS For the Month of August, 19—					
Sales volume................	$40,000	$60,000	$30,000	$70,000	$200,000
Percent of total sales........	20%	30%	15%	35%	100%
Distribution costs...........	$12,000	$ 7,200	$ 2,100	$ 3,500	$ 24,800
Percent of total distribution costs....................	48.39%	29.03%	8.47%	14.11%	100%
Distribution costs expressed as percent of sales..........	30%	12%	7%	5%	12.4%
Net income................	$ 3,600	$ 7,200	$ 3,000	$ 9,100	$ 22,900
Percent of total net profit	15.7%	31.4%	13.1%	39.8%	100%

1. Retail sales are responsible for 48.25 percent of the distribution costs, yet furnish only 15.7 percent of the profit.
2. Retail sales furnish 20 percent of total sales, but only 15.7 percent of the net income.
3. Country sales—truck delivery are above average in profitability. They consume 29.03 percent of the distribution costs and still produce 31.4 percent of the net income.
4. Country sales—freight delivery consume 8.62 percent of the distribution costs and produce 13.1 percent of the net income.
5. Mail-order sales required 14.1 percent of the distribution costs but supplied 39.8 percent of the income.

DISTRIBUTION COSTS AND THE DIRECT OR VARIABLE COSTING CONCEPT

Companies using direct costing procedure have stated that the usefulness of a *decision-making* cost report is greatly enhanced by separating those period costs which are specifically traceable to a product from those

Illustration 12–9. Product Line Income Statement

Product Line Income Statement

	Total		No. 1		No. 2		No. 3	
	Amount	Pct.	Amount	Pct.	Amount	Pct.	Amount	Pct.
Net sales	$600,000.00	100.0	$300,000.00	100.0	$200,000.00	100.0	$100,000.00	100.0
Direct costs								
Manufacturing								
Direct materials	$150,000.00	25.0	$ 75,000.00	25.0	$ 55,000.00	27.5	$ 20,000.00	20.0
Direct labor	90,000.00	15.0	30,000.00	10.0	30,000.00	15.0	30,000.00	30.0
Direct overhead	60,000.00	10.0	30,000.00	10.0	20,000.00	10.0	10,000.00	10.0
Selling								
Freight-out	12,000.00	2.0	9,000.00	3.0	3,000.00	1.5	----	---
Salesmen's commisions . . .	24,000.00	4.0	12,000.00	4.0	8,000.00	4.0	4,000.00	4.0
Total direct costs	$336,000.00	56.0	$156,000.00	52.0	$116,000.00	58.0	$ 64,000.00	64.0
Marginal income	$264,000.00	44.0	$144,000.00	48.0	$ 84,000.00	42.0	$ 36,000.00	36.0
Period costs specific to product lines								
Depreciation	$ 40,000.00		$ 20,000.00		$ 10,000.00		$ 10,000.00	
Property taxes and insurance . . .	20,000.00		10,000.00		2,000.00		8,000.00	
Advertising	24,000.00		20,000.00		---		4,000.00	
Total	$ 84,000.00		$ 50,000.00		$ 12,000.00		$ 22,000.00	
Margin after specific period costs	$180,000.00	30.0	$ 94,000.00	31.3	$ 72,000.00	36.0	$ 14,000.00	14.0
Allocated general period costs								
Manufacturing	$ 40,000.00		$ 20,000.00		$ 13,320.00		$ 6,680.00	
Selling	30,000.00		15,000.00		10,000.00		5,000.00	
Administrative	30,000.00		15,000.00		10,000.00		5,000.00	
Research and development . . .	20,000.00		10,000.00		6,666.00		3,334.00	
Total	$120,000.00		$ 60,000.00		$ 39,986.00		$ 20,014.00	
Income (loss) before taxes . . .	$ 60,000.00	10.0	$ 34,000.00	11.3	$ 32,014.00	16.0	($ 6,014.00)	(6.0)

Product Lines

SOURCE: Adapted from *N.A.A. Research Report 37, Current Application of Direct Costing.*

which are shared in common with other products. See Illustration 12–9.

Reference to the statement will illustrate an important point. The period costs have been divided among those that are *specific to product lines* and those that are *allocated general period costs*. Although the allocation of general period (or fixed) costs is necessary in order to achieve a "full-cost" concept, the results of allocation may be misleading. For example, see the results of Product Line No. 3 in Illustration 12–9. This product line shows a loss of $6,014 which could lead to a conclusion by management that Product Line No. 3 is unprofitable and should be dropped. Further analysis, however, is necessary.

An examination of the sales and cost structure of Product Line No. 3 shows that the amount left to contribute to period costs is $36,000. Even after the fixed costs applicable to Product Line No. 3 are deducted, there is still $14,000 left to cover the general fixed costs. If Product Line No. 3 is discontinued, the $14,000 would disappear and the loss would be increased to $20,014 as the general period costs would go on.

The validity of allocating the general fixed expenses is thus subject to question. Of course, eventually, *all* fixed costs must be covered by the company, but for managerial usefulness in the short run, it might be desirable *not* to allocate common costs that will continue even if a product or product line is discontinued.

THE USE OF STANDARDS AND BUDGETS

Historical analysis is not sufficient for effective managerial control. As in industrial accounting, management must know what the distribution costs *should have been,* as well as *what they are.* The utilization of budgets and predetermined standard costs are as necessary for effective distribution cost control as for manufacturing cost control. If distribution costs are to be prorated and determined on the basis of *products* or on the basis of *territory,* the predetermined distribution cost rate can be based on the estimated sales value by products or by territories. Standards must be set for each function of order getting and order filling.

Standard costs make use of a single predetermined rate for each group of distribution costs, and later the individual expenses are analyzed on a statistical report. For example, an estimate of the various expenses by Products A, B, and C for a certain manufacturer resulted in the calculation of the predetermined distribution cost rates, expressed as a percentage of sales as shown in Illustration 12–10.

Although these predetermined rates for selling and distribution expenses might be used in a manner similar to the predetermined rates for manufacturing overhead—that is, make entries and have accounts for both the actual expenses and the applied expenses—this is not always done. In many cases, the various selling and distribution expenses by

Illustration 12–10

PREDETERMINED RATES FOR APPLYING SELLING AND DISTRIBUTION EXPENSES TO THE COST OF GOODS SOLD

(percentage based upon cost of sales)

Expense	Product A	Product B	Product C
Direct selling expenses	4.61%	4.20%	4.15%
Advertising and sales promotion	3.41	3.14	3.60
Transportation	2.72	2.70	2.60
Warehousing and storage	.90	.90	.90
Credit and collection	2.75	2.15	2.20
General administrative expenses	8.71	8.51	7.05
Totals	23.10%	21.60%	20.50%

groups are analyzed *statistically* and compared regularly in the same manner as any other budgeted figures. The statistical analysis is usually made by the marketing analysis division in cooperation with the accounting department. For example, it is assumed that the distribution expenses are to be grouped under the following headings:

Order-getting costs:
1. Direct selling expenses.
2. Advertising and sales promotion.

Order-filling costs:
1. Transportation.
2. Warehousing and storage.
3. Credit and collection.
4. General administrative expenses.
5. Miscellaneous distribution expenses.

A statistical analysis can be made monthly showing the distribution of these actual expenses to the various products, territories, etc. In the illustrations which follow, these analyses are by *products.* On the basis of the sales made during the month and the predetermined rates previously calculated, the over- or underapplied expenses are computed. The preceding illustrations show:

1. The schedule of the direct selling expenses by products (Illustration 12–11).
2. The schedule of the advertising and sales promotion expenses by products (Illustration 12–12).
3. A recapitulation sheet showing the actual and the applied expenses by the seven groups for each of the three products sold (Illustration 12–13).

Illustration 12–11. Schedule of Actual and Applied Direct Selling Expense

THE CHAPELA COMPANY

SCHEDULE OF ACTUAL AND APPLIED

DIRECT SELLING EXPENSES

For Month of August, 19—

Expense	Product A	Product B	Product C	Total
Salesmen's Salaries	$ 600.00	$ 800.00	$1,000.00	$ 2,400.00
Salesmen's Commissions	800.00	1,200.00	1,800.00	3,800.00
Salesmen's Bonus			250.00	250.00
Salesmen's Traveling Expense	120.00	160.00	170.00	450.00
Sales Office Supplies	50.00	55.00	60.00	165.00
Sales Office Salaries	200.00	210.00	220.00	630.00
Sales Office Telephone	45.00	48.00	52.00	145.00
Sales Office Rent	60.00	60.00	60.00	180.00
Direct Selling Expense Total	$1,875.00	$2,533.00	$3,612.00	$8,020.00
Applied Direct Selling Expense	1,720.00	2,400.00	3,800.00	7,920.00
Underapplied Direct Selling Expense	$ 155.00	$ 133.00	$ 188.00*	$ 100.00

* Overapplied.

Illustration 12–12. Schedule of Actual and Applied Advertising and Sales Promotion Expense

THE CHAPELA COMPANY

SCHEDULE OF ACTUAL AND APPLIED

ADVERTISING AND SALES PROMOTION EXPENSES

For Month of August, 19—

Expense	Product A	Product B	Product C	Total
Salaries	$ 150.00	$ 160.00	$ 170.00	$ 480.00
Office Supplies	100.00	90.00	200.00	390.00
Rent of Office	60.00	60.00	60.00	180.00
Samples	400.00	375.00	600.00	1,375.00
Newspaper Advertising	4,000.00			4,000.00
Magazine Advertising			700.00	700.00
Direct Mail Advertising		300.00		300.00
Billboard Advertising	100.00	100.00	100.00	300.00
Advertising and Sales Promotion Expense Total	$4,810.00	$1,085.00	$1,830.00	$7,725.00
Applied Advertising and Sales Promotion Expense	4,600.00	1,000.00	1,600.00	7,200.00
Underapplied Advertising and Sales Promotion Expense	$ 210.00	$ 85.00	$ 230.00	$ 525.00

Illustration 12–13. Summary of Distribution Costs

THE CHAPELA COMPANY

SUMMARY OF DISTRIBUTION COSTS—CLASSIFIED BY PRODUCTS

For the Month of August, 19—

Expense	PRODUCT A Actual	Applied	Under-Applied	PRODUCT B Actual	Applied	Under-Applied	PRODUCT C Actual	Applied	Under-Applied	TOTAL FOR ALL PRODUCTS Actual	Applied	Under-Applied
Direct selling expense..	$ 1,875.00	$ 1,720.00	$155.00	$2,533.00	$2,400.00	$133.00	$ 3,612.00	$ 3,800.00	$188.00*	$ 8,020.00	$ 7,920.00	$100.00
Advertising and sales promotion.	4,810.00	4,600.00	210.00	1,085.00	1,000.00	85.00	1,830.00	1,600.00	230.00	7,725.00	7,200.00	525.00
Transportation.	3,760.00	3,500.00	260.00	870.00	950.00	80.00*	1,560.00	1,710.00	150.00*	6,190.00	6,160.00	30.00
Warehouse and storage.	186.00	200.00	14.00*	245.00	200.00	45.00	353.00	300.00	53.00	784.00	700.00	84.00
Credit and collection...	433.00	400.00	33.00	544.00	600.00	56.00*	610.00	580.00	30.00	1,587.00	1,580.00	7.00
General administrative expenses....	1,189.00	1,180.00	9.00	1,540.00	1,500.00	40.00	1,845.00	1,880.00	35.00*	4,574.00	4,560.00	14.00
Miscellaneous distribution costs........	843.00	900.00	57.00*	1,034.00	1,000.00	34.00	1,160.00	1,030.00	130.00	3,037.00	2,930.00	107.00
Total Cost of Distribution......	$13,096.00	$12,500.00	$596.00	$7,851.00	$7,650.00	$201.00	$10,970.00	$10,900.00	$ 70.00	$31,917.00	$31,050.00	$867.00

* Overapplied expense.

ANALYSIS OF OVER- OR UNDERAPPLIED DISTRIBUTION COSTS

The over- or underapplied expense is analyzed further in a manner similar to what was done in the case of factory overhead. If the standard costs for the distribution effort were established with the use of flexible budgets, the *controllable* or *spending* variations and the *volume* variation are isolated. An illustration will help bear this out. Illustration 12–13 showed $1,875 as actual direct selling expense for Product A.

Suppose that the monthly flexible budget appeared as given in Illustration 12–14.

Illustration 12–14

THE CHAPELA COMPANY
FLEXIBLE BUDGET

DIRECT SELLING EXPENSE — PRODUCT A

Level of sales	$18,000	$20,000	$22,000
Expense:			
Salesmen's salaries	$ 450	$ 450	$ 450
Salesmen's commissions	720	800	880
Salesmen's traveling expenses	90	110	140
Sales office supplies	40	50	70
Sales office salaries	150	150	150
Sales office telephone	38	40	54
Sales office rent	60	60	60
Total Expense	$ 1,548	$ 1,660	$ 1,804
Standard rate per $100 sales	$8.60	$8.30	$8.20

If the planning budget for the month of August anticipates $18,000 in sales of Product A, the rate of $8.60 becomes *the* standard distribution cost rate for the period. As a result, when actual sales of Product A registered $20,000 for the month of August, $1,720 was applied for direct selling expense ($8.60 per $100 sales × $20,000 sales).

A comparison of the $1,720 applied with the actual of $1,875 shows $155 as underapplied. If the analysis is carried a step further as in Illustration 12–15, comparisons are made between what the *budget should have been* at the $20,000 sales level with the actual expense. In addition, the budget and applied are compared.

The difference between the adjusted or allowable budget and the amount applied is the *volume* variance. In the illustration, the favorable volume variance of $60 resulted from the fact that more units of Product A were sold than had been planned. The planning budget called for $18,000 of sales with a resulting $8.60 rate. If the level of sales had been estimated correctly at $20,000, the standard cost rate would have been $8.30. The $0.30 difference in rate multiplied by the $2,000 increase in sales accounts for the $60 volume variance.

The difference between the adjusted budget and the actual expense

Illustration 12–15

THE CHAPELA COMPANY
VARIANCE REPORT — MONTH OF AUGUST, 19—

DIRECT SELLING EXPENSE — PRODUCT A

Expense	Budget Adjusted to $20,000 Sales	Applied	Actual	Net Variance	Volume Variance	Controllable Variance
Salesmen's salaries	$ 450		$ 600			$150
Salesmen's commissions	800		800			0
Salesmen's traveling expenses	110		120			10
Sales office supplies	50		50			0
Sales office salaries	150		200			50
Sales office telephone	40		45			5
Sales office rent	60		60			0
	$1,660	$1,720	$1,875	$155 unfavorable	$60 favorable	$215 unfavorable

denotes the *controllable* or *spending* variance. This variance has important control implications since it is the resultant of a comparison between what was spent and what should have been spent. In the Chapela Company illustration, $1,875 was incurred as expense compared to the $1,660 allowable when the budget is adjusted to the actual sales level of $20,000. The result of the comparison is a $215 unfavorable controllable variance. Further analysis discloses excesses were incurred as follows:

Salesmen's salaries	$150
Salesmen's traveling expenses	10
Sales office salaries	50
Sales office telephone	5
	$215

Investigation should then be undertaken to determine *why* the variances arose with the result that steps may be taken to see that they are eliminated or reduced in the future.

DISTRIBUTION COSTS AND THE ROBINSON-PATMAN ACT

The general purposes of the Robinson-Patman Act are: (1) to prohibit discrimination in price or in terms of sale between competitive purchasers of commodities of like grade and quality, (2) to prohibit the payment of brokerage or commissions under dummy brokerage firms, (3) to suppress pseudo-advertising allowances, and (4) to provide a presumptive measure of damages in certain cases.

Price discrimination in price or in terms of sale between purchasers of commodities of like grade and quality implies that a businessman must first *classify his products or commodities* into groups. Identical products with different brand labels may frequently be considered as different products because of the imputed value interpreted as a return on an investment in the brand name. Price discrimination further implies competition between purchasers within a given area or market. Therefore, the manufacturer must define his competitive markets. A manufacturer who sells women's handbags to retailers in Syracuse and in New York City would not have to consider these cities as being in the same market area. The sales prices to retailers in New York City need not be identical to prices to retailers in Syracuse.

Within a given area or market, in handling the same product, there can be no price discrimination. (*Differentials* are permitted, but not *discrimination*.) Variations in price are allowed for variances arising in the cost of manufacturing different quantities, the cost of sale, or cost of delivering certain quantities. A large cheese manufacturer had the following price differentials, based upon varying distribution costs in selling quantities of five-pound boxes of cheese for a single delivery.

1 to 30 lbs....................	list price
30 to 150 lbs....................	1¢ off list
150 to 750 lbs....................	2¢ off list
Over 750 lbs....................	2½¢ off list

The Robinson-Patman Act does not define the meaning of *cost*. The businessman presumably does not have specific costs for each article or quantity produced; for the most part, his costs are average costs. In one case the Federal Trade Commission held that the Goodyear Rubber Company had to average its overhead items, such as credit department expenses and general company advertising, over the entire production whether or not it related to the Goodyear–Sears, Roebuck & Company business. The foregoing case implies that in compliance with the act, costs of manufacturing and distribution must be analyzed on a *product* and on an *area* or *market* basis.

Advertising allowances, either in the form of services or facilities furnished to the buyer by the seller or in payment for such services when undertaken by the buyer, except when made to all buyers on *proportionately equal terms,* are prohibited under this act.

But the meaning of *proportionately equal terms* is debatable and has not yet been finally settled by the courts. It might mean:

1. The manufacturer will pay 50 percent or any other percentage of the advertising cost to any customer who advertises his product—if he does the same for everyone else.

2. The manufacturer might pay the advertising allowance in proportion to the value of the sales of the products.
3. The manufacturer may agree to pay a definite amount based upon the circulation of the advertising media used, the area and location of window displays, or the number of people passing the windows each day.

Whatever the final interpretation, the accountant for distribution costs must now find some way of controlling and accounting for a previously unchecked advertising expense.

Quantity discounts are allowed to mass buyers, but the same discounts must be given to all customers buying the same quantity. This law permits *differentials* but not *discrimination*. For example, if a firm sold the same product to Customer A on orders each for 10 carload lots and to Customer B on a standing order of one carload each month and to 10 other customers each on a single order for one carload, it should not be difficult to justify quantity discounts on the basis of cost of distribution.

In the Federal Trade Commission case against Bird & Sons and Montgomery Ward & Company for violation of the Robinson-Patman Act, the manufacturer (Bird & Sons) was able to submit comparative selling costs on mail-order sales of $65,000 and direct-to-retailer sales of $68,000, as shown in Illustration 12–16. The differential that could have been allowed to mail-order sales was a discount of 28.07 percent (36.81 percent minus 8.74 percent).

Illustration 12–16

	Mail Order		Retailer	
	Dollars	Percent of Sales	Dollars	Percent of Sales
Advertising	$ 443.41	0.68	$ 2,769.20	4.02
Warehousing	229.98	0.35	10,311.35	14.96
Freight	3,111.61	4.75	7,036.88	10.21
Administration	1,934.76	2.96	5,247.97	7.62
	$5,719.76	8.74	$25,365.40	36.81

The classification of these expenses should be noted. Higher warehousing costs were due to the discontinuance by Bird & Sons of direct-to-retailer sales, and hence the existence of unusual expenses in adjusting warehousing contracts. The use of a special trade name on the Montgomery Ward product reduced considerably the amount of specific product or general company advertising allocable to the mail-order sales. The difference in freight costs was due to quantity shipments by cheaper water routes. Administration costs of the accounting and credit departments were determined on a per invoice basis.

Where only a few buyers are able to purchase certain large quantities that are available to them but not to others and such practice tends to give the preferred buyer a monopolistic advantage, the Federal Trade Commission is permitted to fix the quantity limits of the purchases.

Exceptions under the act are permitted in the case of perishable products, obsolete or seasonable goods, distress sales in good faith, or goods sold under court order.

The burden of proof under this act is on the seller; and at the initiation of a case by a competitor or customer who alleges injury through unfair competition, the seller may be required to present publicly before the Federal Trade Commission his cost figures for production and distribution. As has been indicated throughout this chapter, the cost of selling goods in varying quantities must be regularly and carefully accounted for and verified.

QUESTIONS FOR REVIEW

1. Distribution costs may be defined in two ways. Indicate the basic differences in these two definitions. Which seems to be most satisfactory from a managerial control viewpoint?

2. Distribution costs for managerial control purposes are usually divided into six groups. What are these?

3. A company has three major groups of products each supervised by an assistant sales manager. How would you allocate the following distribution costs to the products?

   a) Advertising on a national scale.
   b) Salesmen's commissions.
   c) Salesmen's salaries.
   d) Warehouse expenses.
   e) Sales manager's salary.
   f) Sales office expenses.
   g) Credit and collection costs.
   h) Delivery costs where the firm hires trucks by the month.

4. Some firms use a predetermined rate for distribution costs. How are these used?

5. What are the main provisions of the Robinson-Patman Act? Why was this law enacted?

6. The Lucky Motor Company conducts regular visitors' tours throughout its plant for the advertising value it may provide. How should such an expense item be prorated when distribution costs are allocated on (a) a product basis, and (b) on a territorial basis?

7. Should the distribution costs be allocated on the books of the firms or treated on a statistical basis? Why?

8. In the future, distribution cost analyses will become increasingly important to business managements? Why?

9. Distribution costs may be analyzed on three different bases? For most businesses, which seems to be the more desirable? Why?

10. The Latell Manufacturing Company manufactures four groups of products which are distributed on a national basis. A sales group is assigned to six exclusive territories to contact regular customers and to attempt to secure new orders. Advertising is centralized and on a national basis. The central administrative office maintains customers' records and is responsible for all collections and billings. Warehouses are located in California, Illinois, and New York. Outline a possible method of determining the distribution costs and allocating them to the four groups of products.

PROBLEMS – GROUP A

Problem 12–1.   Purpose: *Distribution Cost Analysis on Basis of Sales Prices*

The Lennox Manufacturing Company feels that it should analyze its distribution costs to ascertain changes in methods and sales emphasis. This firm produces three main products: refrigerators, air conditioners, and gas ranges.

For the past year, the distribution costs incurred were as follows:

Distribution Cost	Amount	Basis for Allocation
Salesmen's salaries	$ 60,000	Direct charge
Salesmen's commissions	36,000	Amount of sales
Sales office expenses	12,800	Number of orders
Advertising and sales promotion:		
Product	130,000	Direct charge
General	30,000	Amount of sales
Packing and shipping	15,000	Size of product
Transportation and delivery costs	24,000	Size of product
Warehouse and storage	6,000	Size of product
Credit and collection costs	8,000	Number of orders

An analysis of the accounting and clerical records produced the following statistics:

	Refrigerators	Air Conditioners	Ranges
Number of salesmen, all paid same salary	4	5	1
Number of orders	700	800	100
Percentage of direct product advertising budget	40%	45%	15%
Space in cubic feet per $100 of sales value	30 cu. ft.	10 cu. ft.	15 cu. ft.
Sales value	$210,000	$96,000	$114,000
Average price per order	$300	$120	$240

Required:

a) Prepare a schedule showing in detail the cost of distributing each product per $100 of sales.

b) Compute the average cost of distributing the per $100 of sales; and the percentage of distribution costs of sales.

c) What conclusions or recommendations do you make relative to distribution costs in this instance?

Problem 12–2.   Purpose: *Distribution Cost Analysis on a Territorial and Sales Basis*

The Larkin Manufacturing Company manufactures infra-red electric ranges for home and industrial use. The average sales value per order is:

Apartment size	$ 500
Home size	400
Industrial or commercial	2,000

The following statement of operations for the year ended December 31, 19—, is given to you for your distribution cost analysis:

LARKIN MANUFACTURING COMPANY
STATEMENT OF INCOME
For Year Ended, December 31, 19—

Sales		$1,060,000
Cost of Sales		630,000
Gross Profit		$ 430,000
Distribution Costs:		
Salesman's Salaries	$ 90,000	
Salesmen's Commissions	53,000	
Advertising	120,000	
Warehouse and Storage	8,368	
Transportation and Delivery	25,704	
Credit and Collection	7,740	
Packing and Shipping	12,852	
Sales Office Expenses	5,700	323,364
Net Selling Profit		$ 106,636
General and Administrative Expenses		12,000
Net Income for the Year		$ 94,636

There are 15 salesmen working for the company, and they cover the entire eastern part of the United States which is divided into three districts: New England and New York, Pennsylvania, and Virginia.

Five salesmen are allotted to each district, each being paid the same basic salary plus 5 percent commission on all sales.

The analysis of sales and cost of sales for the year was as follows:

District	Apartment Cost of Sales	Sales	Home Cost of Sales	Sales	Industrial Cost of Sales	Sales
New England......	$ 90,000	$155,000	$130,000	$190,000	$130,000	$260,000
Pennsylvania.......	55,000	85,000	55,000	80,000	60,000	110,000
Virginia.............	35,000	50,000	35,000	50,000	40,000	80,000
	$180,000	$290,000	$220,000	$320,000	$230,000	$450,000

An analysis of the direct product advertising for the year showed:

	Apartment	Home	Industrial
New England district:			
Newspaper advertising........................	$ 3,500	$ 6,000	–
Magazine advertising..........................	4,000	5,000	$14,000
Pennsylvania district:			
Newspaper advertising......................	3,500	8,000	4,000
Magazine advertising..........................	3,000	4,000	10,000
Virginia district:			
Newspaper advertising......................	3,000	6,000	6,000
Magazine advertising..........................	3,800	8,200	6,000
Direct mail advertising......................	4,200	2,800	–
Totals....................................	$25,000	$40,000	$40,000

Transportation and shipping expenses cannot be analyzed. However, a sample investigation indicates that apartment ranges would take up 10 cubic feet; home ranges, 15 cubic feet; and industrial, 35 cubic feet of space per $100 of sales value; and that the weight of each product was in the same proportion as the size or amount of space occupied.

Required:

Prepare an analysis of the distribution costs on the basis of territory and sales values.

Problem 12–3. Purpose: *Analysis of Distribution Costs by Products and by Order-Size Classes*

The Loran Manufacturing Company is anxious to make a study of the income by products and by order-size classes.

In apportioning distribution costs by *products,* sales commissions were at the rate of 5 percent; sales salaries by sales times number of customers; credit management expenses and bookkeeping and billing on the basis of volume of sales; packaging and shipping and warehousing on the basis of weight times the number of units. All other distribution costs were not allocated. Advertising was $40,000 for each product.

In allocating distribution costs by *order-size classes,* the bases for apportionment were:

1. Sales salaries – by sales times the number of customers in the class.
2. Sales traveling expenses ⎫
   Sales office expenses   ⎬ Number of customers in each class.
   Credit management   ⎭
3. Sales commissions on basis of 5 percent of sales.
4. Packing and shipping ⎫ Number of orders weighted in ratio of
   Warehousing   ⎬ 1, 4, 8, and 10.
5. Bookkeeping and billing – number of orders.
6. Advertising and general administrative expenses – not allocated.

Three products are sold: *Product Alpha,* weighing one pound each, of which 100,000 were sold at a cost of sales of $250,000; *Product Gamma,* weighing five pounds each, of which 80,000 were sold at a cost of sales of $400,000; and *Product Omega,* of which 200,000 were sold weighing three pounds each at a cost of sales of $220,000.

The distribution costs for the year were:

Salesmen's salaries	$ 33,000
Salesmen's commissions	82,500
Salesmen's traveling expenses	24,750
Sales office expenses	82,500
Credit and collections	14,850
Packing and shipping	33,000
Warehousing	22,000
Advertising	120,000
Bookkeeping and billing	49,500
General selling and administrative expenses	100,000
Total	$562,100

An analysis of the sales activity revealed the following:

Order-Size Class	No. of Customers	No. of Orders	Total Sales	Product Sales		
				Alpha	Gamma	Omega
Under $50	1,000	7,000	$ 110,000	$ 42,000	$ 45,000	$ 23,000
$50–$200	400	4,000	330,000	115,000	130,000	85,000
$200–$400	200	2,000	660,000	230,000	260,000	170,000
Over $400	50	1,000	550,000	190,000	210,000	150,000
	1,650	14,000	$1,650,000	$577,000	$645,000	$428,000
Number of customers	1,650			550	600	500
Number of orders		14,000		5,000	5,500	3,500

Required:

a) An income statement by products, with the proration of the selling and administrative expenses by products. Where not allocated, apportion expense equally.

b) An income statement by order-size classes with the proration of distribution and administration costs. Indicate the net income percent of sales in each of the above statements.

c) What managerial implications are indicated in two statements prepared above?

PROBLEMS—GROUP B

Problem 12–4.   Purpose: *Distribution Cost Analysis on Basis of Sales Prices*

The Lucerne Refrigerator Company wishes to analyze the distribution costs of its refrigerators sold under the trade name of *Frost Free*. Three sizes are produced for three different market areas: home (12 cubic feet), apartment (8 cubic feet), and industrial (24 cubic feet).

The distribution costs for the past year were:

Distribution Cost	*Amount*	*Basis for Apportionment*
Salesmen's salaries..	$ 60,000	Direct charge
Salesmen's commission and bonuses..............	36,000	Amount of sales
Sales office expenses....................................	12,800	Number of orders
Advertising and sales promotion:		
Direct product.......................................	97,500	Direct charge
General...	30,000	Amount of sales
Packing and shipping....................................	15,000	Size of product
Transportation and delivery..........................	24,000	Size of product
Warehouse and storage.................................	12,000	Size of product
Credit and collection....................................	8,000	Number of orders
Total...	$295,300	

Statistics taken from the records of the company relating to sales of the three sizes were:

	Total	*Apartment Size*	*Home Size*	*Industrial Size*
No. of salesmen, all paid same salary...................	12	3	8	1
No. of orders...........................	1,600	350	1,200	50
Percentage of direct advertising budget..................	100%	20%	55%	25%
Space in cubic feet per $100 of sales value................	60 cu. ft.	10 cu. ft.	15 cu. ft.	35 cu. ft.
Sales values...........................	$600,000	$210,000	$300,000	$90,000
Average sales price per order.......................	$ 600	$ 250	$ 1,800	

Required:

a) A schedule showing in detail the cost of distributing each product, per $100 of sales.

b) Compute the percent of sales of distributing each product.

c) Comment on managerial reaction to this analysis.

Problem 12–5.   Purpose: *Distribution Cost Analysis by Products, Districts, Jobbers, and Dealers*

The Landersone-Phillips Corporation manufactures hand drills, light electric drills, and heavy-duty electric drills which are sold by its own sales force to customers in various lines of business.

Sales are departmentalized on a territorial basis into two areas: eastern and western territories.

The firm's net income from operations, after a charge of $6,000 for general administrative expenses for the last fiscal period, was only about $1\frac{1}{2}\%$ on net sales, and a negligible amount on the return of capital. The firm obtains a fairly large volume of business as compared with the rest of the industry, and maintains a one-price policy, pricing all goods at a uniform markup of 25% on factory cost.

The firm pays its salesmen as a travel expense allowance, a flat rate of 7 cents per mile for the use of their own automobiles. In the eastern territory salesmen reported 58,000 miles; and in the western territory, 70,000 miles, during this past year; and the salesmen were paid accordingly.

The following schedules and accounting data were prepared for the year just ended by the treasurer's office staff:

SCHEDULE OF DISTRIBUTION COSTS

Packing and shipping expenses	$ 8,600
Warehouse operations	8,100
Cartage to railroads	6,720
Credit investigations	1,980
Bookkeeping and billing	2,600
Advertising	32,440
Traveling expense reimbursement	8,960
Salesmen's commissions	38,800
Total	$108,200

	Hand Drills	Light Electrics	Heavy-Duty Drills
Cost to make	$2.00	$16.00	$48.00
Shipping weight—each	2 lbs.	16 lbs.	40 lbs.
Unit packing and shipping cost	$0.05	$ 0.20	$ 0.90
Salesmen's commission rates	6%	5%	10%
Warehouse space used	270,000 Cu. ft.	450,000 Cu. ft.	180,000 Cu. ft.

DISTRIBUTION STATISTICS—SALES AND ADVERTISING
BY TERRITORIES

	Eastern Territory	Western Territory
Unit sales:		
Hand drills	55,000	17,000
Light electrics	6,000	10,000
Heavy duty...	1,200	800
Orders from new customers:		
Hand drills	200	300
Light electrics	100	400
Heavy duty...	700	100
Total New Customers Orders	1,000	800
Repeat orders:		
Hand drills	4,300	500
Light electrics	900	1,600
Heavy duty...	800	100
Total Repeat Orders..	6,000	2,200
Total New and Repeat Orders	7,000	3,000
Advertising expenditures:		
Featuring hand drills only..	$ 6,000	$ 3,000
Featuring light electrics only..	4,000	5,000
Featuring heavy duty only	3,000	4,000
Total Direct Product Advertising	$13,000	$12,000
General "firm name" advertising $7,440		
Total Advertising Costs $32,440		

Required:

a) A columnar comparative statement showing the sales revenue, gross profit margins, and detailed distribution cost allocations for each product in each territory. (Indicate the bases used in allocating the various distribution costs — do not distribute the general administrative expenses.)

b) What in your opinion are the important facts brought out by your statements? Interpret your analysis by summarizing and explaining the effects of such factors as you think management might consider significant.

Problem 12–6. Purpose: *Analysis of Distribution Costs*

The Lawson Meat-Packing Company finds that its distribution costs — selling, administrative, and general expenses — constitute 65% of the cost of doing business and feels that a study of these costs is necessary.

An analysis made to determine the basic causes of the cost variations in selling, administrative, and general expense items discloses that each expense item varies according to one of these three bases: (1) number of orders, (2) number of items per order, and (3) weight of orders expressed in hundredweight (cwt.).

The analysis of each class of distribution expenses discloses that these expenses are attributable to each of these three factors as follows:

Distribution Cost Control	Totals	Expenses Based on		
		No. of Orders	No. of Items	No. of Cwt.
Selling expense control............................	$4,076.00	$2,464.00	$1,262.00	$ 350.00
Packing and delivery...............................	1,050.00	200.00	300.00	550.00
Administrative and general expense control.................................	2,151.20	1,200.00	580.00	371.20
Total Distribution Costs.................	$7,277.20	$3,864.00	$2,142.00	$1,271.20

The following represents the data by order size:

Order Size	No. of Orders	Total No. of Items	Total Cwt.
Under 50 pounds	3,000	4,000	800
50–199 pounds	2,800	8,400	2,600
200–499 pounds	600	2,250	1,880
500–999 pounds	400	2,400	2,800
1,000 pounds and over................................	100	800	1,000
All Orders	6,900	17,850	9,080

Required:

a) Prepare a statement showing the allocation of the total distribution costs per hundredweight (cwt.) of meat products for each class of order (expressed in pounds per order). Carry unit costs to hundredths of a cent.

b) How does the solution to this problem apply to the Robinson Patman Act.

(Adapted from AICPA Uniform Examination)

chapter 13

Electronic Data Processing for Cost Determination and Control

INTRODUCTION

Electronic data processing is becoming increasingly important in modern business as the means of preparing information for use by management because of the promptness in accumulating the information and reporting it for managerial decisions. Computers and related data processing equipment can record and store vast quantities of business operating data, retrieve the accumulated data almost instantly upon demand, and transmit the data speedily over both short and long distances. Already numerous applications can be found in which electronic data processing via the computer is being used in such financial accounting work as preparing business records, payrolls, and financial statements. Because of the importance of accumulating and controlling costs to improve the profit and competitive picture of a business firm, the prompt and complete use of cost data by management becomes a *must* today.

As is customary with modern inventions, the original product is large and complicated. Later it is simplified and applied to more situations. So it has been with the computers. To date most computers used in business have been relatively large machines, too costly for the average business. Necessity to create a wider use of the service rendered by these machines has resulted first in business sharing the use of larger machines; and second in the development of special purpose minicomputers. This is part of the evolutionary process. The purpose of this chapter is to describe in a generalized manner the adaptation of the computer to the cost determination and control business process. It is merely introductory; the future holds many more possibilities, but the computer is to be recognized as an important phase of cost determination and control. In this chapter, our specific purposes are (1) to present the fundamentals of computer operations; and (2) to discuss the current and the probable uses of the computer in future cost determination and managerial control through costs.

NATURE OF COMPUTERS IN DATA PROCESSING

Computers are part of the system of automatic compilation and reporting of business information for managerial control. Business information thus compiled has been classified as (1) *financial information,* (2) *personnel information,* and (3) *logistics information.* Financial information relates to sales, payrolls, operating expenses, and other data used in the preparation of the financial statements of operations; personnel information refers to the records about the personnel employed in an organization. The logistics information with which cost accounting is primarily concerned relates to the procurement, production, and distribution of physical goods within an organization. It includes information about the manufacturing operations such as inventory control, production planning and operating controls, scheduling of production, and transportation. All three systems use recurring documentary data, internal and historical, and sometimes projected budgetary information. The financial and logistics systems report the information in monetary terms.

The need of the computer in data processing is emphasized by the high speed with which large amounts of repetitive data and information required in cost accounting control are processed with a reasonable accuracy for prompt managerial interpretation and action.

The logistics system is a well-planned program made up of many subsystems. It includes information relating to the procurement of materials and the labor force, raw materials inventory control, production scheduling and control, and finished goods inventory control. These are both quantitative, operational, and financial data. Additional financial information can be compiled relating to the comparisons of actual with predetermined costs and actual with budgeted data.[1]

FUNDAMENTALS OF THE COMPUTER DATA PROCESSING SYSTEMS

The Computer System. There are two basic types of electronic data processing computers—*digital* and *analog.* The digital computer is used with mathematical data such as inventory control, payrolls, and other accounting data; whereas the analog deals with the continuous quantities

---

[1] For more detailed description, see John Dearden and F. Warren McFarlan, *Management Information Systems,* Homewood, Ill.: Richard D. Irwin, Inc., 1966, pp. 7–11.

such as power control in a public utility, machine operation controls in a factory, and pressure and measurement controls in storage and transmission industries. Since the information of these two types of computers must be used together in some management decisions, it is possible to turn one kind of information to the other computer by means of analog to digital or digital to analog transducers. In this chapter, our interest is in the use of a digital computer for cost and production control.

The digital computer system as used in this chapter may be outlined as follows:

1. A *control unit*—a centralized electronic unit which directs, co-ordinates, and summarizes the operations.
2. An *input unit* which provides the data to be processed as well as the operating instructions for processing or transferring the data.
3. An *internal storage* or *memory unit* which stores data for current or subsequent processing.
4. An *arithmetical unit* which performs the required mathematical calculations of the data processing.
5. An *output unit* which issues the results of the data processing either in temporary or permanent form (magnetic tape or printed).

These five functional units require auxiliary equipment to support or facilitate the operations. This auxiliary equipment is known as *hardware* and includes card punch devices, special typewriters, magnetic tapes and disks, optical character readers, and data communication or transmission equipment.

In addition, to make this system operational, there is what is known as *software,* which consists of the instructions for operating the computer automatically and for the accounting data to be used with the instructions. These input instructions are known as *programs.* There are *application* programs and subprograms relating to the determination of costs, payrolls, or inventories; and *supervisory* programs for directing and coordinating the various units of the computer. The *application* programs are usually written by a specially trained programmer in the employ of the firm using the computer. He must be familiar with the particular computer language to be used. The *supervisory directing* and *coordinating programs* which involve a completely planned system for computer action are usually prepared by the computer manufacturer. Illustration 13–1 presents diagrammatically the arrangement and interrelation of the computer units.

The following is a brief description of the functional units of the computer system:

The *control unit* coordinates the programmed instructions and the input data of the source data and directs it through the various units of the computer until the appropriate reports or material stored for future use are issued as output.

Illustration 13–1. *The Electronic Computer Data Processing System*

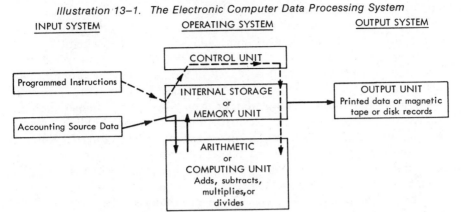

INPUT SYSTEM   OPERATING SYSTEM   OUTPUT SYSTEM

Programmed instructions enter storage unit under direction of control unit, transferred to control unit, "decoded," and give instructions to control unit to direct the other units in processing the accounting data in producing the output.

Accounting source data by direction of the control unit, entered in the memory unit, transferred to arithmetic unit if computations are necessary, and ultimately sent to the output unit. The control unit may require a number of sequential back and forward movements through the various units.

Input to the computer is of two types: (*a*) the programmed instructions, and (*b*) the accounting or source data. Some of the source data may have to be stored in the memory unit for future use, or they may be transferred to the arithmetic unit for computation work and then temporarily stored in the memory unit. There are many different procedures that may be programmed into the system, depending upon the firm's requirements. Also, there may be several "in-and-out" operations between the memory and arithmetical units before the information is in output status. Programmed instructions for the input are usually in magnetic tape on which the instructions are recorded as magnetic impulses. The source data may be entered into the computer system in various forms and procedures. The following are some of the methods of entering the source data into the computer: (*a*) *via punched cards* — timecards, requisitions, manufacturing overhead costs, sales invoices which may first be recorded on punched cards and then converted to magnetic tape or read directly into the computer; (*b*) *via special typewriter* recordings on tapes; (*c*) by *optical scanning* or reading of printed or written information or magnetic ink recordings. Whatever method of recording the source data, it must finally be in compatible form for machine operation. Thus far, the procedure has involved the instructions to the control unit and the input of the operating data.

The storage or memory unit is an intermediary, operating, and facilitating unit. It will store information which may be required currently or later in the computer operations. There are two kinds of storage — internal and external. In this paragraph, the discussion relates to internal storage. The input must be stored in the computer for its operations. Programmed instructions are fed into the machine and stored so that when the input is placed in the computer, it can be properly directed, controlled, and operated on. When the input is placed in the machine, the program will direct its operation—it may be held up temporarily in some unit until some other operation is completed, or it may be directed immediately to some other unit such as the arithmetical unit. It is the "holding" operation in the computer cycle that is known as temporary or internal storage.

When a particular computer cycle is completed, it may be necessary to remove from the computer certain data for use in some future operation. In such cases, the data thus removed will be recorded via the output unit on magnetic tapes or disks. These externally stored tapes or disks will be used for the input operation at some future date.

The *arithmetic unit* is made up of a series of electronic calculators which accepts the input data and follows the programmed instructions to produce the mathematical calculations and/or accumulations either for further storage or for the output data.

The *output unit* produces the reports that are the result of the computer operations used. This output may be in the form of printed reports; or the data, if it is to be used in future computer operations, may be stored in the form of magnetic tapes or disks. For example, in payroll accounting, the computer may print out the weekly payroll sheet showing the gross earnings and deductions for each employee, and it may also print out the payroll checks with the corresponding information. However, since the individual's earnings must be accumulated from week to week so that at the end of the year the W-2 income tax forms can be prepared, it is necessary each week to update on a master tape the previous cumulated earnings plus the current week's earnings. This magnetic updated tape is a form of external storage. In the next payroll period it becomes part of the input data.

Programmed Instructions.   As indicated previously, input to the computer is of two types: (*a*) source data, and (*b*) programmed instructions. Programmed instructions often require a long period of planning and development by experts familiar with charting procedures and the computer language. There are a number of computer languages in use today: COBOL (Common Business Oriented Language) used for accounting and business transactions; and FORTRAN used primarily for scientific and mathematical work, although it may be used with business transactions. The use of these two languages has been developed in an attempt to make the computer work of machines of the different manufacturers more compatible. It will also simplify the preparation of programs and thereby reduce the cost of this most important phase of computer operations. Because of the skill required in programming, many computer equipment manufacturers will prepare a suitable program for a specialized installation if the firm does not have its own programmers. Since some manufacturers have made a number of installations for payroll accounting, sales accounting, and inventory control, they have developed a file of programs which can be adapted to the requirements of the prospective user. However, where a special system installation is required, a lengthy period of study and experimentation may be necessary before a workable program can be developed. For example, in the installation of a computerized system for stock brokerage firms, the program and its operating system were developed, installed, and used parallel with the traditional manual system for a period of a year to be sure that the computer system would function as planned. At the end of the year, a comparison was made of the operating results of both systems to be sure that the computerized system was satisfactory before abandoning the manual system. Once this program has been perfected, it could be used with modification by a large number of other stock brokerage firms.

Source Data. The source data for cost and production control are the time clock cards, requisitions, and sales invoices. To be usable by the computer, they must be in compatible form—recorded in code as electrical impulses on such media as punched cards, magnetic tapes, or perforated paper tapes. Punched card preparation requires a keypunch machine to perforate a specially designed card with the required accounting information. The location of the perforations on the card indicate the numerical or alphabetical information as shown in Illustration 13–2a.

Illustration 13–2a. Punched Card

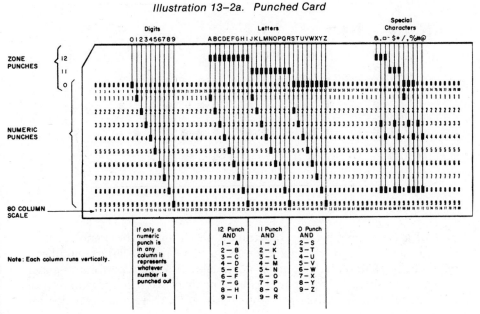

Courtesy: Honeywell Inc.

Sometimes the source data is recorded on *punched or perforated paper tapes* prepared simultaneously with the source document by a perforating mechanism on a typewriter, bookkeeping machine, adding machine, or cash register. These perforated tapes can then be converted to a magnetic tape for use in the computer. These perforated tapes are also known as common language tapes to indicate the code used. The width of the tape indicates the number of "channels" used. Illustration 13–2*b* shows

Illustration 13–2b

	A	B	C	D	E	F	G	H	I	J	K	L	M	N	O	P	Q	R	S
Figures				3				8							9	0	1	4	
Letters	A	B	C	D	E	F	G	H	I	J	K	L	M	N	O	P	Q	R	S
	1	1		1	1	1			1	1							1		1
	2		2				2		2	2	2	2				2	2	2	
CODE	·	·	·	·	·	·	·	·	·	·	·	·	·	·	·	·	·	·	·
CHART			3		3		3	3					3	3		3			3
		4	4	4		4	4			4	4		4	4	4		4	4	
		5					5	5				5	5		5	5			

Code as applied to tape

part of a five-channel tape; Illustration 13–3 shows the complete five-channel and an eight-channel code as used to record letters, numbers, and special characters. The main advantage of using a perforated paper tape is that since it is prepared simultaneously with the preparation of the original source document (requisitions, etc.), there is less chance for error, it saves clerical cost and time, and the use of the perforated paper tape permits transmission via Teletype or telephone lines to a central administrative office for use with the computer.

Computer Machine Language.   For the computer to be able to use the input it receives (programmed instructions or source data), it must be captured as electronic impulses or recorded and stored as magnetic spots. The electronic computers are based almost universally on the *binary system* of counting because of its simplicity. Under this system all letters and digits can be expressed as zero (0) or one (1), similar to the on-and-off electric switch. On a punched card or paper tape, a one (1) is expressed as a perforation and a zero (0) as a blank space. On a magnetic tape, a magnetic spot becomes a (1) and a blank space a zero (0). The columnar location of these ones and zeros translates the codes into meaningful program instructions or source data.

Illustration 13–4 details briefly this binary code. It should be noted that four binary digits are required for each decimal digit and six for each letter of the alphabet. This binary system has been expanded and modified to meet the increased speed and capacity of modern computer operations; but basically, the binary system here illustrated indicates the principles on which all such codes are developed and used.

One foot of magnetic tape can contain 2,400 characters; one reel of 2,400 feet will contain 5,760,000 characters; and at the speed of many computers, 15,000 characters can be written or read into the machine in one second.

Various Input and Output Devices Used in the Computer System.   There are a number of different procedures that can be used in preparing input data for the computer and for reporting the output. Among these are:

1. *Magnetic tape typewriters* used to record data on magnetic tapes for speedier entry into the computer. These are called typewriter-to-magnetic tape data recorders.
2. *Converters* used to convert punched cards to tape, tape to punched cards, tape to tape.
3. *Perforated tape preparation devices.* Tape punching typewriters, bookkeeping machines, adding machines, and cash registers may have attachments which will simultaneously prepare a perforated tape when the source documents are prepared or source data is recorded in manual records. These can also be used in the preparation of punched cards.
4. *Senders and receivers* using telephone, telegraph, microwave, and radio circuits to transmit data to a central operating computer.
5. *Visual display units* or terminals used to get information into and out of the computer, e.g., airline reservation system.
6. *Typewriters* to enter data in magnetic disks.

7. *Optical mark readers* used in entering sales, cash receipts, and utility meter reports into the computer.
8. *Optical scanners or readers* to record information directly from printed forms into the computer.
9. *Printout devices* to record in printed form the information that might otherwise be shown on the visual display units.

From this partial listing, it becomes evident that while the basic operations of the computer are as outlined earlier in the chapter, the use of the above hardware may vary the procedure to meet the needs of the particular firm. For this reason, the most effective installation of a costly computer system should make use of a feasibility study by experienced consultants, and perhaps require the leasing of the equipment on a trial basis before an actual purchase is made.

Illustration 13-3. Five-Channel and Eight-Channel Codes Used in Perforated Paper Tape Preparation

5-CHANNEL TAPE CODE

LETTERS POSITION	5 CHANNEL TAPE CODES						FIGS. POSITION	
							4 BANK KEYBOARD	3 BANK KEYBOARD
	1	2	.	3	4	5		
A	1	2	.				-	-
B	1		.		4	5	$	$
C		2	.	3	4		N.P. CODE	N.P. CODE
D	1		.		4		TAB.	TAB.
E	1		.				3	3
F	1		.	3	4		'	'
G		2	.		4	5	&	&
H			.	3		5		(
I		2	.	3			8	8
J		2	.		4		ERROR	ERROR
K		2	.	3	4		P.R. CODE	P.R. CODE
L		2	.			5		)
M			.	3	4	5	.	.
N			.	3	4		'	'
O			.		4	5	9	9
P		2	.	3		5	0	0
Q	1	2	.	3		5	1	1
R		2	.		4		4	4
S	1		.	3			/	/
T			.			5	5	5
U	1	2	.	3			7	7
V		2	.	3	4	5	PUNCH OFF	PUNCH OFF
W	1	2	.			5	2	2
X	1		.	3	4	5		PUNCH ON 2
Y	1		.	3		5	6	6
Z	1		.			5		PUNCH ON 1
CARR. RET.			.		4		CARR. RET.	CARR. RET.
SPACE			.	3			SPACE	SPACE
———	1	2	.	3	4	5	LTRS. SHIFT	LTRS. SHIFT
FIGS. SHIFT	1	2	.		4	5		
PUNCH ON 2—L.F.		2	.				PUNCH ON 1	LINE FEED
STOP CODE			.				STOP CODE	STOP CODE

Courtesy: Singer Co., Friden Division

Illustration 13–3 (continued)

8-CHANNEL TAPE CODE

TAPE TO CARD PUNCH	8 CHANNEL TAPE CODES									FLEXOWRITER AUTOMATIC WRITING MACHINE
	EL	X	O	CH	8	•	4	2	1	
0 (ZERO)			O			•				0 (ZERO)
1						•			1	1
2						•		2		2
3				CH		•		2	1	3
4						•	4			4
5				CH		•	4		1	5
6				CH		•	4	2		6
7						•	4	2	1	7
8					8	•				8
9				CH	8	•			1	9
A		X	O			•			1	A
B		X	O			•		2		B
C		X	O	CH		•		2	1	C
D		X	O			•	4			D
E		X	O	CH		•	4		1	E
F		X	O	CH		•	4	2		F
G		X	O			•	4	2	1	G
H		X	O		8	•				H
I		X	O	CH	8	•			1	I
J		X		CH		•			1	J
K		X		CH		•		2		K
L		X				•		2	1	L
M		X		CH		•	4			M
N		X				•	4		1	N
O		X				•	4	2		O
P		X		CH		•	4	2	1	P
Q		X		CH		•				Q
R		X			8	•			1	R
S			O	CH	8	•		2		S
T			O			•		2	1	T
U			O	CH		•	4			U
V			O			•	4		1	V
W			O			•	4	2		W
X			O	CH		•	4	2	1	X
Y			O	CH	8	•				Y
Z			O		8	•			1	Z
SPACE				CH		•				SPACE
–		X				•				–
/			O	CH		•			1	/
#					8	•		2	1	STOP
$		X		CH	8	•		2	1	$
,			O	CH	8	•		2	1	,
.		X	O		8	•		2	1	.
@				CH	8	•	4			NP CODE
%			O		8	•	4			PRINT-PESTR
*		X			8	•	4			PUNCH 1 ON
		X	O		8	•	4			UPPER CASE
&		X	O	CH		•				&
SKIP			O	CH	8	•	4	2		TAB
END CARD 1					8	•	4	2		
END CARD 2			O		8	•	4	2	1	PUNCH OFF
COR. TAB		X		CH	8	•	4	2	1	
ERROR		X			8	•	4	2	1	ERROR
PI 1				CH	8	•		2		PI 1(2, 8, SP)
PI 2					8	•		2		PI 2(2, 8, –1)
PI 3			O		8	•		2		PI 3 (2, 8, 01)
PI 4			O	CH	8	•	4		1	PI 4(5, 2)
PI 5		X	O		8	•	4		1	PI 5 (N, Z)
PI 6		X		CH	8	•	4		1	PI 6 (9, N)
PI 7					8	•	4		1	PI 7 (1, 4, B)
SP–1		X	O	CH	8	•		2		LOWER CASE
SP–2		X	O		8	•	4	2		PUNCH 2 ON
CR		X		CH	8	•	4	2		SPECIAL CODE
TAPE FEED		X	O	CH	8	•	4	2	1	TAPE FEED
END LINE						•				CAR NET

Courtesy: Singer Co., Friden Division

Illustration 13–4. Binary Code

Decimal Digit or Letter or Character	Electrical Binary Notation	
0	0000	
1	0001	
2	0010	(each movement to the left doubles the preceding digit as in geometric progression)
3	0011	(one plus two)
4	0100	(double of two)
5	0101	(four plus one)
6	0110	(four plus two)
7	0111	(four plus two plus one)
8	1000	(double of four)
9	1001	(eight plus one)
A (first letter in alphabet)	01 0001	
B (second letter)	01 0010	
C (third letter) etc.	01 0011	
$	11 1011	
%	11 1100	

Two illustrations, 13–5 and 13–6, visualize the computer system: Illustration 13–5 indicates the functional system; and Illustration 13–6 presents a system where most of the source data is first entered on punched cards.

The Feasibility Study for the Installation of a Computer System. The purposes of computerized data processing for production control and manufacturing cost accumulation are (*a*) a reduction in the administrative cost of data compilation, (*b*) provision for better and more complete managerial information promptly, and (*c*) the use of this information in the reduction of manufacturing costs, more efficient production, and increased profits.

Because of these exciting advantages, many firms may make the mistake of installing an expensive computer system which just does not function as it was hoped and thus achieve the above results. Therefore the answer to the question of "Is the installation of a computer system for production control and cost determination a necessary managerial decision?" is best determined by the so-called *feasibility study or report.* It answers the question: Should the firm install a computer system for a particular purpose? Ultimately the answer will be YES; but presently, it may be NO.

The firm may already have a computerized accounting system for such financial accounting as payrolls, sales, and inventory control. Should it be extended to cover production control and cost determination? If so, what will it cost? Is it worth it? The answers to these questions can best be given by a preliminary *feasibility study and report.*

Illustration 13–5. *Diagram Indicating the Work Performed in Each Section of Electronic Data Processing*

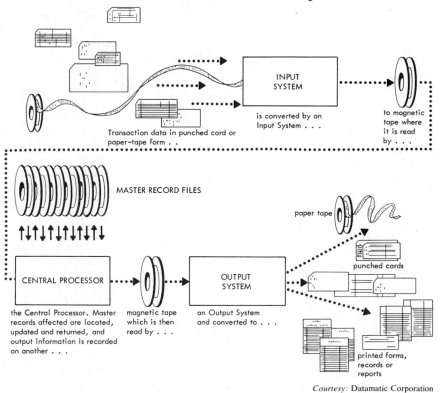

Courtesy: Datamatic Corporation

This study may supplement one previously made for the installation of financial accounting for sales, payrolls, and inventory control.

While a feasibility study can be completed by the controller and his staff, it is often less biased and prejudicial if completed by outside experts and computer consultants.

Such a study would cover the following information:

1. What is to be automated?
2. What equipment will be necessary?
3. Comparative costs of leasing and purchase of necessary equipment. This data should be obtained from not more than two or three manufacturers.
4. What software (programs, employee training, etc.) will be provided by the manufacturer?
5. Personnel problems that will arise. A determination of which new employees must be hired; which present employees can be retrained for computer work; which transferred to other work or released.

Illustration 13–6

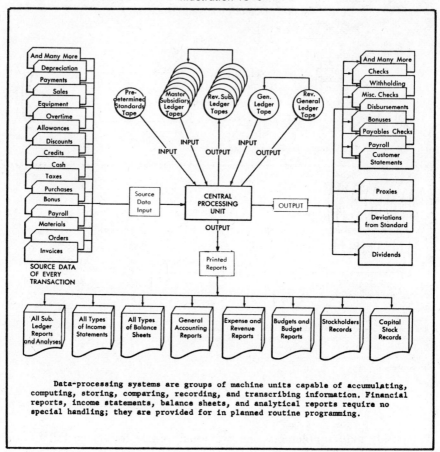

6. Determination of what operating management will be responsible for the performance of the computer system; reporting what is being accomplished; and the percent of time that the equipment will actually be used.

With such a study, management is in a better position to decide if a computer for cost control is necessary.

COMPUTER APPLICATIONS OF PRODUCTION AND COST CONTROL

The variety of complete and at times partial computerized production and cost control varies with the size of the organization, the number of manufacturing departments, and the nature of the products being manufactured. Therefore in this chapter it is possible merely to present what some firms are doing in this area of managerial and accounting control. It should be remembered that cost determination and control is inseparable from production control, so that an effective computer system must be related to both. Each computerized system has to be practically tailor-made with certain standardized procedures for material, labor, and manufacturing overhead cost determination, with adaptation to the budgetary and standard cost system.

With the increased concentration on minicomputers (those selling for less than $50,000), the future will no doubt result in the creation and use of separate computer systems for the production and cost control with the summary or final administrative reports tied in with the central unit, if and when this is necessary. It is primarily a question of how important is production and cost control for the successful operation of a business and how much can be spent for this control. Presently the arguments favoring the use of computers for this business function are (1) the vast amount and variety of information that management can obtain from its use; (2) the promptness with which this information is made available; and (3) the low cost of its availability compared with the benefits to be derived. No attempt is made in this chapter to describe what a sound feasibility study should reveal, nor the type or model of equipment to be selected, nor whether the equipment should be leased or purchased. It is related to the application of routine financial and accounting control of material costs, factory labor costs, factory overhead application, and the budgetary and standard cost comparisons.

The following computerized applications of production and cost control are given:

1. A computerized cost accumulation installation.
2. Production control integrated with cost control via EDP.
3. Electronic data processing inventory control in a manufacturing company:
   a) *Application 1* — computerized inventory control for multiplant.
   b) *Application 2* — computerized inventory control.
4. Computerized labor cost analysis.
5. Illustration of use of computer in labor cost analysis.
6. Computerized maintenance work authorization and control.
7. Computerized distribution costs.

A Computerized Cost Accumulation Installation.[2]   This is a large industrial corporation which has many governmental contracts and accumulates its cost data with the use of a computer. Planning for production control requires the production of a number of parts. This requires the

---

[2] For more detailed description of this installation see Michael R. Tyran, "Computerized Cost Accumulation," *Management Accounting,* June 1970, pp. 27–33.

placement of purchase orders, labor cost distribution, factory payrolls, manufacturing overhead costs, and cost ledgers. Plans and budgets are prepared initially. The operating data must be summarized for management to measure the operating results against the plans and budgets to permit necessary corrective action.

The use of the computer by this firm for cost determination and control resulted in —

1. Establishment of a comprehensive cost data bank after mechanizing most of its record-keeping.
2. Proper cost classification into those which are direct, and the indirect which must be apportioned.
3. Supervision and control of cost input data and inventory control.
4. Constant studies for possible need for changing the recording and reporting procedures.
5. Provision for prompt operating reports of costs in summary and in detail, as well as performance reports.

This firm uses four inventory classifications for storage and reporting in the record files. This grouping simplifies the inventory control function. In the work-in-process account, there are 21 levels of data segregation to permit more detailed and accurate production control, since this work-in-process is constantly being updated for retrieval, reporting, and adjusting needs.

Production Control Integrated with Cost Control via EDP. An electronic data processing system for *production control* makes use of a comprehensive program that integrates all production activities — both planned and operational. *Cost accounting control* is the evaluating medium of production control. Its purpose is to report what jobs are being worked on, what jobs have been completed, what jobs are behind schedule, and what jobs are meeting the schedule. To produce a computerized system to meet the particular needs of a firm will require a great deal of time and expense. Most of the systems thus developed in the past and tested on the factory floor have been unsuccessful because they have been too difficult to use, too expensive to operate, and too delicate for the factory environment.

Studying some of the specialized, computer-controlled (called numerically control) machines built for modern industry by such firms as the Cincinnati Tool Company, one realizes that modern manufacturing operations can be put under a controlled system: controlling manufacturing or production operations by machines and by departments; controlling the movement and transfer of the work-in-process; and controlling the quality of the work as it moves through the manufacturing cycle. Through computerized tapes, this system controls and monitors the jobs and the machines. Computerized tapes control the operations and output of the various machines such as the drill presses and milling and grinding machines, and they keep track of the millions of component parts.

This production control system cannot be tacked on to the existing inventory, billing, and payroll computer system but must be integrated as a completely new system from the ground up. It will be comprised of a number of production control features, the results of whose operations will show up in the cost accounting data. These will include the following planned programs:

1. *Engineering data control* for maintaining standard bills of materials and standard routing of the work.
2. *Inventory planning* for controlling the inventory levels of raw materials, component parts, and subassemblies.
3. *Operations scheduling* of the sequence in which the jobs are to be run in each machine center, including the purchases from outside vendors.
4. *Shop floor control* to provide information for management as to how the manufacturing operations are functioning.

To illustrate this briefly, one firm manufactures 80 different machine models with 150 different combinations. Three assembly lines are used to provide parts from which these machines are produced. These lines are used in conjunction with the sales forecasts and customers' orders to establish the parts and subassembly requirements on a *weekly* basis. More than 15,000 inventory items—raw materials, parts, and subassemblies—are included in the requirements planning. This planning cycle is on a yearly basis which is updated or adjusted as orders come in. *Scheduling* is then programmed on a five-day week throughout the year with adjustments for exceptions due to the unique conditions which may arise. Each week previous order data and substituted new information are entered into the capacity planning program to measure and forecast the manpower and machine requirements to meet customer shipments requirements. All this production data and operating data must be integrated with the cost accounting reports.

It may be generalized that in the future as the need for this computerized production control increases and as the manufacturers of computers will have accumulated a large amount of experience and a number of successful instruction programs, methods will be developed to reduce the cost of the computerization, simplify the computer operations, and become readily adaptable to the many prospective users of computers. In production planning, properly established and controlled production orders can be effectively supervised in the manufacturing cycle. Deviations from scheduled work are immediately reported for corrective action. Engineering changes or cutbacks in sales requiring revised production schedules will be *immediately* available, so that production orders may be split, material reserved may be released, and open jobs may be re-scheduled. Job delinquency reports may be issued to establish managerial control and responsibility. Material requisitions can be properly sched-uled to expedite the manufacturing operations. Labor efficiency reports can be produced, examined, and acted upon. Continuous comparisons can be made of the budgeted and actual operating results. It is the con-stant updating of this information and the speed with which it can be retrieved from the files connected with the computer that makes the com-puter such a necessary tool of successful modern production manage-ment. It should be added, however, that the use of the fourth-generation minicomputer for cost determination in this production control system will produce more precise and timely control information than ever be-fore at a minimum of cost, since the minicomputers will localize and specialize the production and cost control data processing.

Electronic Data Processing Inventory Control in a Manufacturing Com-pany. More than 30% of the working capital of most industrial concerns is tied up in the inventory investment. Yet in many concerns inventory control is one of the most neglected managerial controlled activities. Few firms feel that their inventory control programs represent a satis-factory answer to the inventory problems.

The choice of a specific inventory control system will depend upon the size and the diversity of the inventory, the volume of activity, the geo-graphic dispersion of the manufacturing operations, and the need for in-ventory information. Manufacturers of electronic data processing equip-ment have a number of standard programs that can be adapted with considerable effort to the particular needs of a business. The inventory control system will provide management with figures of the factory usage of the various materials and parts, will forecast the inventory require-ments, and will compute the most economic purchase (EOQ) order quan-tity. Management must compare the cost of having a certain inventory on hand versus the lost sale costs of not having it; the dollar costs of order-ing the material, as well as the investment costs of maintaining a given stock level. By computerizing the inventory control, management is able to continuously and quickly determine "how much to order" and "when to order" each of the thousand inventory items needed.

In addition, the master file of the inventory (on magnetic tapes, disks, or drums) continuously records the receipts and issues of all material and maintains for managerial control four balances for each item:

1. Quantity or balance on hand for immediate use.
2. Quantity on order.
3. Quantity reserved for scheduled use.
4. Quantity or balance available to be reserved.

The programs for inventory management may be further developed to indicate when special management action is needed: *stock out* when reserved stock becomes due to be issued and there is insufficient material; and *potential shortages* whereby two weeks prior to reservation issue date, the inventory record is examined to determine if enough material has been received and made available for production. The quantity short is indicated by a "potential shortage" message. The program provides a *rescheduling* of factory production whereby the supply of material is compared with the demand in time sequence. If there is enough material on order to meet the required demands but delivery is not scheduled soon enough, there may be need for rescheduling the production. This again requires management action. Special inventory problems can be aided by *simulation*. Simulation is a managerial method whereby under different situations the possible variables are programmed and answers or solutions arrived at either by observation, interpretation, or mathematical calculation. This simulation process can with the use of computer render its results in a matter of seconds based upon historical data and can indicate inventory forecasting accuracy, inventory turnover, average inventory investment, and such other information as management may require.

Application 1—Computerized Inventory Control for Multiplant.[3] In this firm of machine equipment manufacturing on a multiplant basis, the units costs of many purchased parts were higher for one plant than for another. Investigation showed it was due to decrease in the average purchase order size. A computerized program was developed to calculate EQP (economic order to be placed) for each of the parts and to project the average inventory balance based upon the EQP calculations. Comparisons were made of the price differential of different quantity purchases and the inventory carrying costs (obsolescence, taxes, insurance, storage, and interest) to ascertain the savings if any in using EQP data. These comparisons were made periodically to be sure that they were up to date.

Application 2—Computerized Inventory Control. This firm has more than 800,000 items of printers' types. Because of the large number of items, the hierarchy inventory (subclassifications) control was necessary; and this was especially efficient when set up on a computer. A computerized master product file was set up for the plant's hot metal matrices which are used in casting type for the printing industry. The major classifications of the inventory file shows the sales statistics by font and character, character activity, and reorder point. The major classifications for a brass matrix is the family with a hierarchy of subfamilies. It shows the group fonts, subdivided into (*a*) *character* such as italics, bold, etc.; and (*b*) *sizes* such as the point sizes. The installation of this system required the elimination of a large number of inactive or obsolete matrices. As a result, the inventory was reduced to 2,000 fonts containing a sum of at least 100,000 characters.

[3] See Jack Rinehard, "EQP Calculations," *Management Accounting,* September 1970, pp. 18–20.

Computerized Labor Cost Analysis. Labor costs like material costs are essentially variable costs, and as such they are controllable. The high-speed operations and storage facilities of the electronic computer can be used to store and accumulate vast amounts of important labor cost information and make it available almost instantly. For many concerns, either through the use of their own computers, or a service bureau, or leased time, the preparation of the many financial accounting records and reports for payroll accounting is quite a common practice today. It is permissible for firms which have appropriate computerized records and a large enough volume of operations to send to the Internal Revenue Service magnetic tapes prepared by the computer reporting the gross pay, withholding income taxes, social security deductions in place of the

Illustration 13–7. IBM Punched Cards for Use as Basis of Labor Cost Input

Individual Job Card

Continuous Job Card

usual typewritten reports. Obviously, this eliminates a large amount of clerical and paper work which would be necessary to issue the manually prepared reports, at the same time enabling the IRS to process the data immediately by using their compatible computers.

As a by-product of this financial accounting for labor, the computer can be used in the preparation of a series of management reports for controlling the production costs of labor. Programs must be written to direct the compilation of the data for these reports. The input source data for these reports are the job, group, or departmental timecards (Illustration 13–7).

The punched card is a most satisfactory labor cost record because of the speed with which it may be sorted and the convenience in converting

Illustration 13–7 (continued)

Group or Gang Job Card

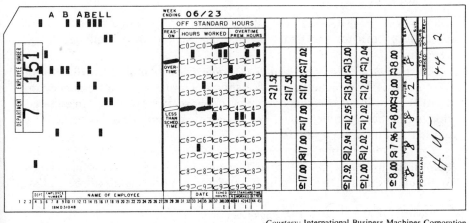

Daily Job Timecard

Courtesy: International Business Machines Corporation

its data to magnetic tape. With modern transmission equipment, these cards can be prepared and controlled in a centralized computer department as follows:

Each employee in a plant will have a laminated prepunched identification card for use in transmitting the necessary personnel information to the computer department. When production orders are sent to the initial manufacturing department, prepunched job order cards are also attached. In the factory, input and automatic transmission stations are located, connected with the computer department. At the start of each job, the employee selects the most conveniently located station, inserts the prepunched job card and the worker's identification punched card. This information is automatically transmitted for recording to the computer. The information may be fed directly into the computer or used to prepare punched cards for subsequent use with the computer.

The information thus transmitted will include the job number or departmental identification, employee identification number, time starting on the job, and rate of pay. At the completion of the job, the same information will be transmitted for the final manufacturing operation, plus the quantity of units completed, spoiled and rejected.

These data are available daily for immediate and cumulative processing. Supplementary data may indicate the predetermined production standard and costs for comparison with the actual results reported.

From these data, when processed by programmed instruction tapes, management can obtain reports in addition to the comparisons of actual with standard labor costs such as:

1.   What are the average hourly wages by occupation or departments?
2.   What is the daily, weekly, or monthly idle time cost?
3.   What are the average incentive or overtime earnings?
4.   A comparison of the indirect labor costs with the budgeted amounts.
5.   The labor turnover, the absentee rate, and other personnel control information.

Illustration 13–8 shows diagrammatically the computerized payroll procedure both for the financial records and for the job allocation and reporting.

Illustration of Use of Computer in Labor Cost Analysis.[4] In Illustration 13–9, two IBM punched cards are shown. Card A is for attendance, and Card B is for job order cost accounting. These cards are used in conjunction with the Calculagraph Time Recording-Computing Recorder discussed and illustrated in Chapter 9.

Card A (attendance) is prepunched by employee, and any hours other than standard must be authorized in one of the lower left-hand boxes. Without overtime, the keypunch operator simply makes three (or six

---

[4] Courtesy of J. A. Neal, Calculagraph Company.

Illustration 13–8. Computerized Payroll and Job Cost Accounting

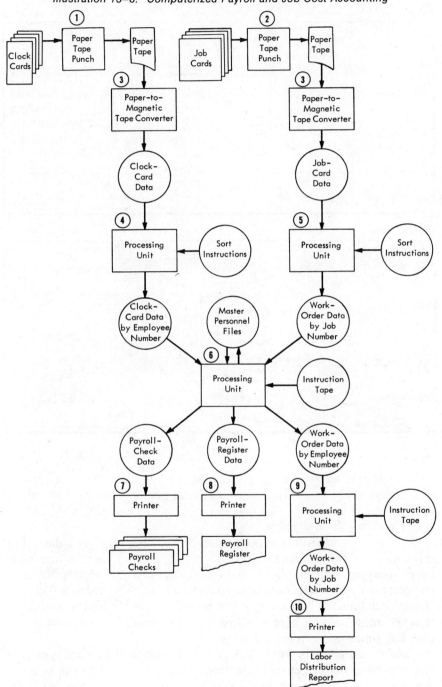

Courtesy: Haskins & Sells, *Data Processing by Electronics*, p. 61.

Illustration 13–9. IBM Cards Used in Computer System for Job Costing

CARD A

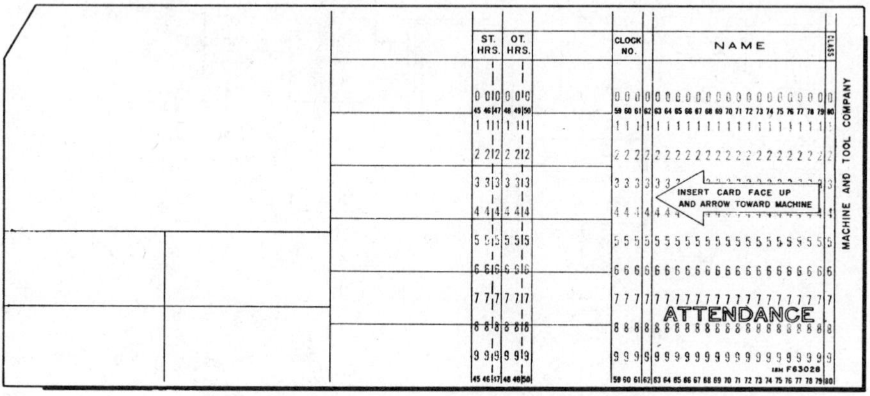

CARD B

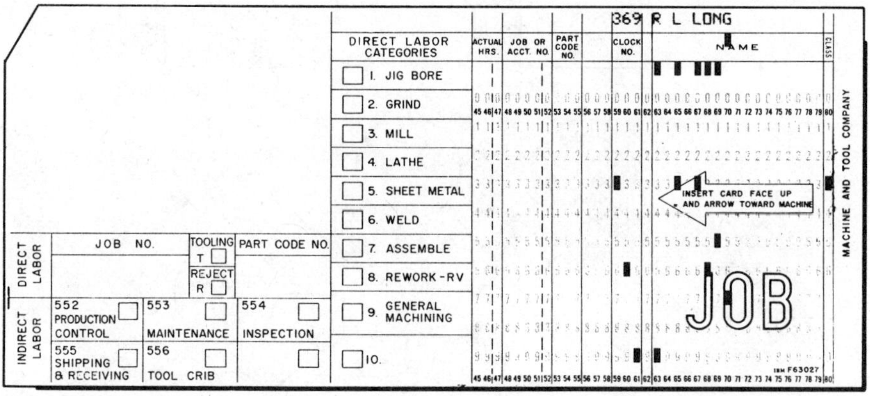

with overtime) keystrokes into the card. This is done daily and results in a steady daily work load and no critical peaks when payroll writing time arrives. In addition, this makes it possible to balance, *daily,* payroll hours against job cost hours.

To prepare a payroll for 100 people, this system requires a daily time investment of approximately 10 to 15 minutes. (This figure is arrived at by multiplying 100 employees by 3 keystrokes, which equals 300 keystrokes per day.) A reasonable keypunch operator's speed is 6,000 keystrokes per hour. (Thus $300/6,000 \times 60$ minutes $= 5$ minutes. However, to make allowance for card handling time, overtime, keypunching errors, etc., this time has been tripled.)

Card B, the labor or job ticket, is also prepunched by employee. The nine most popular direct labor operations are preprinted on the ticket so that the employee simply ticks off the proper category. No. 10 is for operations not included in the preprinting. This card can also serve for indirect labor when the employee is working on indirect labor. The labor cards, both direct and indirect, are returned to the data processing department daily where the information is keypunched. Keypunching involves only 14 (14) keystrokes per labor ticket. A comparison listing of job hours against the attendance hours (Card A) is made. The comparison ensures that one balances against the other. This listing is returned to the production management department before noon each day, and any corrections are made by them (such as cards without numbers, or operation numbers, etc.). Data processing is made aware of the corrections which are then entered. The responsibility for correct input lies with the production personnel rather than with data processing. This keeps the errors to a minimum because if the foreman realizes that he is going to be required to make the correction even if it's the next day, he makes sure that the information is correct the first time. This auditing procedure is done by the foreman throughout the workday. Every so often he checks the completed jobs of his employees. He is assisted in this by two separate time-card racks in the time recording center. One rack is designated for the job tickets that are currently being worked on, and the other contains the employee's attendance card and all completed job tickets.

By making the foreman responsible for correct job information on the labor ticket, clean input to both the cost and payroll system is ensured, and the foreman must examine each work ticket since he must initial it. This makes him aware of the department output and "instant production control."

Once this procedure has been completed, the computer system takes over to produce the results and reports.

Computerized Maintenance Work Authorization and Control.[5] A large industrial concern computerized the maintenance work authorization and control of its own equipment and that serviced for its customers. The following program related to its own equipment. To forecast and control the maintenance departments costs, records were set up for (*a*) preventive maintenance, (*b*) lubrication schedules, (*c*) stores inventory of spare parts, (*d*) inspection schedules, and (*e*) spare parts requirements.

This was accomplished by having a work order system set up on a priority basis. Estimating cost procedures, work schedules with provision for time recording of actual costs, and a comparative report of actual versus estimated costs were used in controlling maintenance costs.

A historical cost record is used for each type of equipment. As a result the firm is able to note excessive maintenance costs of the various types or pieces of equipment; and based upon the management reports, the need for redesign or replacement of equipment.

---

[5] See "Babcock & Wilcox Co. Staff," *Management Accounting,* May 1970, pp. 19–22.

All of this information was maintained through use of electronic data processing to reduce the maintenance costs and improve the quality of its equipment.

Computerized Distribution Costs. In the financial accounting for sales using a computer, the preliminary input of source data will often be on punched cards. These can be so designed and supplemented by other distribution-cost punched cards, so that it will be possible to maintain a continuous record of distribution costs by products, territories, salesmen, and/or size of product (see Chapter 12), and to compare these data with the budgeted figures. The master magnetic tape file can contain the yearly budgeted figures by product lines or by territories. A second master file can accumulate the actual distribution costs on the same basis as the budgeted figures. Monthly and cumulative figure comparisons can be made and printed out in report form for control purposes. Because of the high speed of processing by the computer in which carefully planned programs have been inserted, this information becomes readily available for managerial action. It is in reality a prompt and detailed statistical analysis and comparison of accounting and budgeted data for distribution sales.

QUESTIONS FOR REVIEW

1. What is the nature of the common language tape?
2. What are the five units that comprise the electronic data processing system?
3. What advantages are there in using electronic data processing in cost determination?
4. The binary code is used in electronic data processing. What is the significance of the word *binary?* What is a *bit?* How many are used to make or record a *digit?* A *letter?*
5. What are the various methods used for transferring data into the computer?
6. What is meant by the term "memory" in the computer system? How is it used?
7. What are the various memory or storage media used with the computer?
8. In electronic data processing systems for accounting control, at least two sets of tapes are used. What are these, and what is the purpose of each?
9. In many large business firms, management control is today aided by the use of electronic computers. Indicate how the computer can be useful in cost determination.

PROBLEMS

Problem 13–1.   Purpose: *Computerizing the Payroll Accounting for a Small Industrial Firm*

The ABC Manufacturing Company has 200 factory workers. It manufactures a number of small electrical tools. It is increasing its factory production at the rate of 25 employees a year, with a maximum capacity number in its present plant of 300.

This firm is planning to use a Computer Service Bureau for its payroll and its labor cost work.

Required:

a) How should the payroll data be submitted to the service bureau?

b) How should the labor costs be prepared for the service bureau?

c) What are the advantages and disadvantages in using a service bureau?

Problem 13–2.   Purpose: *Preliminary Study for Installing a Computer System for Payroll, Inventory Control, and Sales*

The Mooranco Steel Company is considering the installation of an electronic data processing system to account for and control payroll, inventory, and sales. The company asks you to indicate the best procedure to follow in making a selection of a system to meet its requirements.

Required:

How do you think the firm should proceed before installing such a system?

part II

PLANNING AND CONTROL OF COSTS

Part I of this text was devoted to a discussion of the cost determination for both job order and process or departmental cost systems. This discussion was expanded to cover not only the procedures and practices of these two systems but also the cost determination problems arising in the areas of material costs, labor costs, manufacturing overhead costs, and distribution costs.

This second section is devoted to the procedures and practices used in planning efficient manufacturing operations and controlling costs to provide better managerial supervision and analyses. For these purposes, discussion centers on the use of budgetary procedures in controlling costs, estimated cost procedures, standard cost practices, direct or variable cost procedures, and installing a cost accounting system with provision for managerial reports for control.

chapter 14

Managerial Cost Control through Budgetary Procedures

NATURE OF BUDGETARY PROCEDURES IN A MANUFACTURING BUSINESS

In modern business, management must always look to and plan for the future. Historical past performance is helpful in planning for the future — it provides the factual basis which must be considered with the probable future business and operating conditions. This projected planning through numerical and financial statements is known as budgeting. A budget is a carefully prepared estimate of future business operations used for managerial decisions to maintain or improve a firm's profit results. Since cost determination is an important factor in profit realization, planning for reliable future cost determination is a prerequisite for successful business management. Since budgeting is forecasting in the uncertain future business area, it involves some risk. The more factual, historical data available in making the forecasts, the less chance for serious errors.

Planning for future business operations may be in terms of *operational* or *period planning,* and/or in terms of *project planning.* Planning for the material and direct labor requirements for the coming year would constitute operational planning — that is, requirements for the estimated production for this period. Planning for the construction of a new plant or modernizing an older plant would be considered as project planning budgeting. The more nearly the actual business operations conform to the budgeted figures, the more successful business management is rated. The budget is an action guide for management which measures or finalizes the accountability of management's performance. Ideally, a budget for a business firm should be all-inclusive and encompass revenue, costs, expenses, and funds flow.

Budgets are designed to assist management in the planning, coordination, and control of the various business functions of sales, production, and administration. Since conditions in businesses vary, the budgets prepared will also vary. The basic principles, however, will be the same for any size business and for almost any type of industry.

Operating budgets are classified under two categories: (1) *static* or *fixed,* and (2) *variable* or *flexible.* The fixed budget is based upon a single (estimated as probable) volume of business activity, while the flexible budget is based on a *series* of possible volumes, all considered within the range of probability. The fixed budget, therefore, will be prepared from a relatively constant set of figures, using figures for the sales and expenses for a single definite estimated volume. Of course, these figures will be presented in great detail for each period (usually a month) so that maximum managerial control may be exerted by making comparisons with the actual operating figures.

The *flexible* or *sliding scale* budgets are a series of comparable budgets prepared for a *series* of volumes, one of which is the standard volume and represents the 100 percent figure. Budget figures will then be prepared for 90 percent volume of sales or production and for the 80 percent, 70 percent, as well as 110 percent and 120 percent. Thus a flexible budget can readily be used for making comparisons with the actual operating conditions without preparing a completely new budget. Whether a budget is static or flexible, it is always desirable to have all manufacturing overhead costs and selling and administrative expenses grouped into fixed, variable, and semivariable classifications, so that when making comparisons of the budgeted with the actual figures, management can evaluate to what extent the variations in costs or income were controllable.

ADVANTAGES IN USING BUDGETS

The use of budgets by the business firm may be advantageous for the following reasons:

1. The preparation of budgets forces management personnel to engage in *planning;* management must become forward-looking. In addition, the objectives of the firm have to be defined and stated in financial terms.

2. The use of budgets lends itself to *coordinating* the activities of the various segments of the business. For example, the use of budgets may have the effect of coordinating distribution effort with the sales effort as well as with the production effort.

3. The implementation of budgets may provide an instrument for *control.* Deviations from a prescribed course of action may be determined, and management may take steps to eliminate the causes for the deviations.

4.   The techniques used in budgeting force management to examine carefully the uses of labor and capital with the result that a more efficient use of resources may result.

5.   The use of budgets results in a management team that is *"cost conscious"* before funds are committed. The emphasis in budgeting is not in cost reduction per se but rather in the maximization of long-run profit. Additional costs will be incurred if these costs can be expected to produce additional profits.

6.   The use of budgets provides the machinery to aid in choosing among *alternative courses of action*. Better decisions may be reached when such problems as make or buy, lease or build, etc., are being considered.

LIMITATIONS OF BUDGETS

The limitations of the use of budgets must be understood if the advantages of budgets discussed in the preceding paragraphs are to be achieved.

First and foremost, one must remember that at best a budget is a sophisticated estimate; no one knows what will happen in the future. That does not mean budgets are useless; on the contrary, they can be very useful if one doesn't lose sight of the fact that they are estimates.

Second, the budgetary system should not be a device that would take the place of management. A budget cannot be a substitute for management but should be used by management.

Third, the benefits to be derived from the use of budgets will only be as good as the effort expended to establish the budget. Even though a budget is an estimate, there are various degrees of reliability of the estimation.

Fourth, a budgetary system will provide desired results only if the system is reviewed continuously and amended as needs and activities change. An antiquated system provides little benefit.

THE BUDGET PERIOD

The *budget period* is an important factor in developing a complete budgetary plan. For the most effective results, all three of the following time plans should be used:

1.   A *long-range* planning period covering several years. Such a program would affect company expansion policy regarding new products and the matter of investing in new plant and equipment.

2.   Overall planning for the *fiscal accounting period*. Usually this covers a period of one year and refers to the master budget, since it sets

forth the operating plans and profit objective for the next fiscal period. This budget phase includes all areas of the business and coordinates the sales, production, distribution, and finance functions.

3. A *month-to-month basis budget* gives the detail, by months, of the overall planning budget for the fiscal accounting period. This plan will be the most effective in controlling costs, sales, and expenses because of the shortness of the period. The month-to-month budget is used as a major guide to action by the businessman.

Most budgets are prepared on both long-term and short-term bases. A total budget for the year gives a complete picture of estimated conditions; and a short-period budget is prepared in greater detail to cover the requirements of the immediate period. Some companies engage in continuous budgeting. For example, each month a budget is prepared for the same month of the following year. Thus, at any one time, the company has an operating budget for a full year. Obviously, the businessman that has this is at a considerable advantage; the plan for an entire year is always there.

REQUIREMENTS OF A SUCCESSFUL BUDGET PROGRAM

For a budget program to achieve the desired results, the firm's responsibility organization must be carefully planned. Each person in a supervisory capacity from the foreman to the president must have his duties defined. The firm's organization chart serves as the center of focus for a well-defined organization. The chart should be accompanied by a manual of job classifications.

The budgets that are prepared must be realistically attainable. A budget that is not realistic affects employee morale and disrupts the efforts toward coordination. Budgets have to be implemented by *people*. Therefore, budgets will produce desired results only when people are motivated properly; realistically attainable budgets help.

The chief executive of the firm must give his complete support to the budget program if it is to achieve success. The need for using budgetary control must originate with top management.

ORGANIZATION FOR BUDGETARY CONTROL

Generally, the direction and execution of the budget is delegated to a budget committee which reports directly to top management. The actual preparation of the budget, however, should be started as far down the line as possible. One member of the budget committee is the *budget director* who is in charge of preparing a budget manual of instruction and the accumulation of the budgeted and actual figures and reports. Customarily, other members of the budget committee are the functional department heads and include the sales manager, the production manager, the treasurer, and the controller. The controller or an assistant is frequently appointed to serve as the budget director. The duties of the budget committee under the leadership of the director would include:

1. Receiving from the various executives, department heads, and supervisors, estimates for the long- and short-term periods, and where necessary to supply the previously used figures to these employees;
2. Assembling this budget data in accordance with a previously organized master plan;
3. Evaluating and revising, where necessary, the data thus collected before preparing the final budget; and
4. Issuing periodically—daily, weekly, monthly, quarterly—reports showing the comparisons of the actual with the budgeted figures.

A MANUFACTURER'S COMPLETE BUDGET PLAN

A complete budgetary control system in a manufacturing concern should cover the following types of budgets, each of which can be broken down into smaller units:

I. Selling function: sales or income budget.
II. Production function:
   a) Cost of production budget:
     1. Materials budget.
     2. Labor budget.
     3. Manufacturing overhead cost budgets.
   b) Inventory budget.
   c) Purchases budget.
III. Operating expense functions:
   a) Distribution cost budget.
   b) General and administrative expense budget.
   c) Financial expense budget.
IV. Financial budgets:
   a) Cash receipts budget.
   b) Cash expenditures budget.
V. Capital expenditures budget:
   a) Plant and equipment proposals.
   b) Other proposals.

A complete budgetary system is shown diagrammatically in Illustration 14–1.

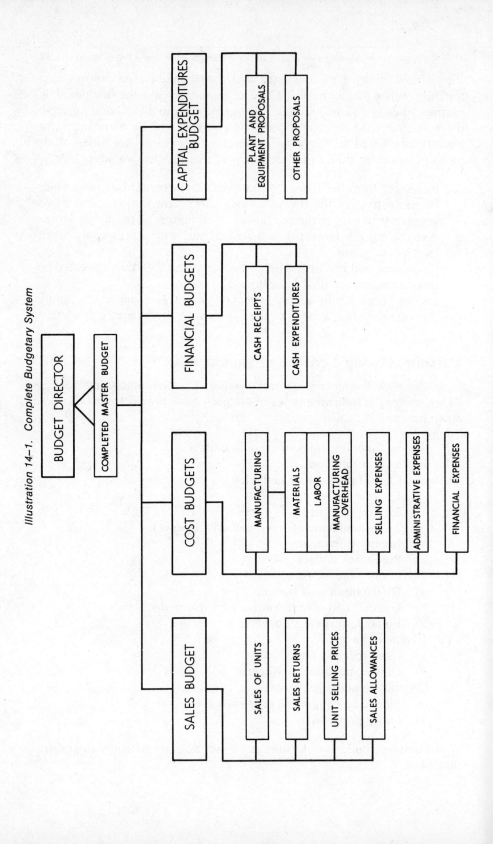

Illustration 14–1. Complete Budgetary System

THE SALES BUDGET

The most important budget upon which all others are contingent is the *sales budget* – the forecast of goods to be sold. Four classes of information are usually considered in preparing the sales estimates:

1. Quantity and value of past sales, usually by products and territories.
2. General business and market conditions.
3. Conditions within the particular industry.
4. Plans and policies of the company.

The detailed method used in preparing sales budgets varies with each individual company. For example, one very successful machine manufacturer has been able to forecast in August, and based almost entirely upon the orders received in August, the probable sales for the following February. In February the actual orders received are used to predict sales for the next August. Some companies have the sales personnel submit budgets of expected sales in each of their territories. The success of this forecast over a period of years has been surprising.

Ideally, a firm should combine all three techniques. Sales personnel who are in contact with the customers should aid in the preparation of sales budgets. Top management, although not as close to the customers as the salespeople, might have a better overall view of the market and competition and would be in a position to evaluate the sales picture. Economic indicators must also be examined and considered in the formation of the sales budget.

A variation of the traditional budget procedure was described for the sales as used by a large industrial firm. This firm makes three plans in budgeting sales: (1) anticipated sales, (2) if sales run ahead of plans, and (3) if sales should fall below projections. This multiple budget system forces the executives to keep two of their most important functions in mind: (1) how to handle unanticipated increase in demand, and (2) how to handle a decline.[1]

THE PRODUCTION BUDGET

Supplementing the sales budget, and subsidiary to it, is the *production budget*. When it is estimated how many units of each product will probably be sold, provision must be made for their production. This involves budgeting the figures for the manufacturing department. The completed budget of this department is known as the *production budget*. Studying the actual and the budgeted production figures is one of the most important tasks of managerial control because by analyzing the unfavorable variations and their causes it should be possible to correct inefficient pro-

[1] E. M. de Windt, *Forbes Magazine*, July 1, 1970.

duction costs and even reduce costs. The production budget starts with a weekly or monthly estimate of the number of units to be produced, as indicated by the sales budget and by the most efficient number of units that can be produced at one time. This could be followed by a *standard cost sheet* for each product, although a production budget may be used in an organization that does not employ a standard cost system. On this would be shown the estimated amount of material, labor, and manufacturing overhead for each product. Considering the predetermined costs for each product and the quantity of each product to be produced, it is possible to prepare budgets showing the materials requirements, the labor budgets, and the manufacturing overhead budgets for the entire plant and by departments.

Although the foregoing are listed as separate budgets, they are all closely interrelated. From the sales budget and the inventories of finished goods, it is possible to determine the quantity of each product that must be produced. When the number of units to be produced has been established, the materials, labor, and overhead costs can be determined. Purchases budgets may also be prepared. In certain instances, it will be necessary to study and prepare a plant and equipment budget showing to what extent the plant will or will not be used on the basis of budgeted production figures. Upon the completion of the sales and the production budgets, that portion of an estimated income statement which will indicate the estimated gross profit on sales may be prepared.

To illustrate how the sales budget may be converted into a production budget, Illustration 14-2 gives the estimated plant load in direct labor hours—a production budget for the year. This budget must take into consideration (1) the quantity in finished goods inventory, (2) the quantity on order and in process, and (3) the quantity to be manufactured in each of the next four quarters of the fiscal year. These production statistics can then be converted into labor hours per week, material requirements, and the flexible manufacturing overhead cost budget.

Flexible Budgeting. A basic consideration in the preparation of a budget is the expected level of operations. In the case of a manufacturing situation, production might be the major consideration whereas the level of sales might be the major consideration in budgeting distribution costs.

The level of operations would not be a serious problem in the budgeting process if one of the following two conditions were present:

1. The level of operations was always the same; no fluctuations in production or sales occurred, or
2. All costs and expenses behaved in the same manner.

Obviously, these conditions do not exist in the majority of companies. Not only does the level of operations vary from one year to the next but variations within the year may also occur. To complicate matters, not all

Illustration 14–2

COMPUTATION OF ESTIMATED DIRECT LABOR HOUR PLANT LOAD FOR YEAR 19—
BASED ON SALES FORECAST AND INVENTORY ANALYSIS
(Prepared in November for Next Year)

	On Order and in Process at Time Budget Is Prepared	To Be Manufactured in 19— (Budgeted)		
		First Quarter	Second Quarter	Last Half of Year
Total amount to be produced per inventory analysis as at November, 19—..................	$750,000.00	$400,000.00	$370,000.00	$700,000.00
Less: Work-in-process inventory, November, 19—..............	400,000.00	....	....	....
Balance to be manufactured.......	$350,000.00	$400,000.00	$370,000.00	$700,000.00
Total estimated direct labor hours required.....................	76,000	91,000	84,500	169,000
Direct labor hours required per week.......................	9,500 (8 weeks)	7,000 (13 weeks)	6,500 (13 weeks)	6,500 (26 weeks)
Plant capacity in direct labor hours per week, November, 19—: First shift................. Second shift...............	8,200 1,300	8,200 1,300	8,200 1,300	8,200 1,300
Total capacity............	9,500	9,500	9,500	9,500
Percent of plant capacity to produce budgeted sales: Two-shift basis.............. One-shift basis..............	100% 116%	73.7% 85.4%	68.4% 79%	68.4% 79%

costs behave in the same manner. Generally, an assumption is made that direct material and direct labor costs are *variable,* i.e., these costs vary in direct proportion with production.

Although the *total* costs of direct material and direct labor are considered variable, the *unit* costs would be constant or fixed especially if proper controls for the quality of materials purchased have been used and if, as is so frequently the case, the volume of work per hour is controlled by the speed of the machines. However, with the long list of items making up the *manufacturing overhead* or *indirect manufacturing costs,* the cost per unit may or may not vary as the volume for a given period changes, i.e., not all these costs behave in the same manner. It is with these manufacturing overhead costs that management is primarily concerned. Management has, therefore, grouped these manufacturing overhead items into *fixed* and *variable* and then attempted to indicate their effect on the budget at different operating volumes. For example, if a firm rents its buildings, then the rental cost will be fixed regardless of the volume of production. At all capacities of production, the budget will show the same figure. The same would probably be true if the firm owned the buildings and included the charge for real estate taxes in place of the rental cost. However, as the volume of production increases, the *per unit cost* for rent or taxes will decrease, and vice versa.

There are, however, many manufacturing overhead costs which will fluctuate as the volume of production increases or decreases. The rate or degree of variability is not the same for each of these. Some, variable costs, will fluctuate consistently and at the same rate as production increases or decreases; others, semivariable, will fluctuate intermittently or only when the change has reached a certain volume. Most of the costs which are characterized as having variability are of the semivariable nature.

To avoid the problem, many firms prepare annually a *flexible budget* which is nothing more than a series of alternative budgets prepared at various operating (volume) capacities such as 60, 80, 100, and 120 percent of capacity. A brief illustration of a flexible budget for factory overhead costs follows:

	Capacity Used		
	Theoretical	Practical	Normal
Percentage of productive capacity	100%	80%	60%
Capacity expressed in terms of direct labor hours	1,500 hrs.	1,200 hrs.	900 hrs.
Budgeted overhead costs:			
Fixed costs...	$3,000	$3,000	$3,000
Variable costs	3,000	2,400	1,800
Total	$6,000	$5,400	$4,800
Budgeted manufacturing overhead rate based on direct labor hours	$4.00	$4.50	$5.33

SEPARATING COSTS INTO FIXED AND VARIABLE[2]

A flexible budget presents the estimated indirect costs, both manufacturing, selling, and administrative, at varying levels of production. For those costs which are fixed, management can only plan to increase the

------

[2] See Chapter 10 for a discussion of the methods of separating semivariable overhead costs into their fixed and variable elements.

volume of production so that the *per unit* overhead cost will be reduced. But there are a number of costs which are semivariable in nature—that is, they contain some element of both fixed and variable costs. For example, even with a minimum of production, some *inspection* costs must be incurred. As production increases, it may become necessary to increase this cost, but not immediately, nor consistently, with the increase in the volume. *However, the relation of the increase in inspection costs to the increase in the volume of production must be established by management so that the variable part of the cost may be identified and separated from the basic or fixed amount.* In Chapter 10 relating to applied manufacturing overhead, several methods (high-low, scattergraph, or method of least squares) of separating the semivariable overhead costs into their fixed and variable elements were given and illustrated. In substance, these methods indicated that *the increase in any indirect manufacturing overhead cost divided by the corresponding increase in the volume of production would produce the average variable UNIT cost increase.*

MANAGERIAL SIGNIFICANCE OF SEPARATING THE SEMIVARIABLE OVERHEAD COSTS INTO ITS TWO COMPONENTS

Some, but not necessarily all, of the variable elements of manufacturing overhead, selling, and administrative expenses may be controllable—that is, subject to reduction. To properly evaluate managerial effectiveness in cost reduction, it is first necessary to separate the *semivariable* overhead costs into that which is relatively fixed and beyond the control of the *supervisory* staff and that which is variable and may be subject to reduction.

Therefore, in most effective cost accounting systems some form of budgetary procedure must be used in which projected costs and realized costs will be compared. Since in many concerns production fluctuates from month to month or from season to season, a *flexible budget* not only for the manufacturing overhead but also for selling and administrative expenses is desirable. This will permit better managerial control through comparisons of the budgeted and actual costs and expenses at various volumes of production and sales.

The principles of flexible manufacturing overhead budgets are continued in the use of *standard or predetermined costs.* As will be discussed in the following chapters, standard costs are detailed figures of what the material, labor, and manufacturing overhead costs should be under normal operating conditions. This *estimated cost* presumes forecasting or budgeting material and labor costs in addition to manufacturing overhead. For a proper *control of costs*, there should be standard costs—*estimated costs under normal operating conditions*—which can be compared with the *actual costs* in order to control manufacturing operations.

The same principles apply to a study of the *distribution* and *administration cost analyses*. It is, therefore, fundamental that the reader understand the need for a budgetary system and the method of preparing and using it as a management tool in reducing the cost of production and distribution in order to increase income.

The specific relationships of the budget department and the cost accounting department may therefore be listed as follows:

1. The establishment of *predetermined manufacturing overhead cost rates*.
2. The preparation and use of *standard costs* (predetermined costs) for materials, labor, and also manufacturing overhead.
3. The preparation and control of predetermined distribution and administration costs.
4. The preparation of reports showing the comparison of budgeted cost figures with actual costs.
5. The use of forecasting charts—the break-even graph—showing the point at which a certain sales volume and its profit will break even with the expenses and costs.

ADVANTAGES OF FLEXIBLE BUDGETS

A company president once remarked, "I don't understand flexible budgets; it seems to me that a budget is fixed and that for any one given time period there can be but one budget." If what the president says is true, what, if any, are the advantages of using flexible budgets?

Three main advantages may be attributed to the use of flexible budgets. The first has to do with the budgetary process. The use of flexible budgets simplifies the task of preparing a budget for a particular period. For example, Department A has established a monthly flexible overhead budget in the amount of $10,000 in fixed costs plus 50 cents per machine-hour of variable costs. If the budget estimate is that 50,000 machine-hours will be the level of operations for a particular period, the preparation of the overhead budget is a mechanical operation. The budgeted amount for overhead for Department A for the time period would total $35,000.

Second, the use of flexible budgets may result in the preparation of more accurate budgets. Flexible budgeting techniques require that consideration be given to the volume factor in budget preparation. The basic idea underlying flexibility is that budgets are established for various levels of activity. Since all costs do not behave in the same manner as some costs rise faster than others when production increases, a budget giving consideration to the volume factor is bound to be more accurate than one where volume is not considered.

Third, the use of flexible budgeting techniques results in a more meaningful comparison between actual and budgeted data as *comparable* data are compared. An illustration will aid in pointing out the advantage.

A monthly overhead budget of 50 cents per machine-hour plus $10,-000 for fixed costs had been established. Fifty thousand machine-hours had been budgeted for a particular period resulting in a dollar budget of $35,000 (50¢ × 50,000 + $10,000). The actual costs incurred by the department amounted to $33,000. An immediate reaction would be that efficient procedures resulted in a cost saving of $2,000. If flexible budgeting techniques had not been utilized, the analysis would have ended at this point.

To continue the illustration, suppose that 42,500 were the actual number of machine-hours worked in the department. A budget adjusted to the actual number of hours worked showed that 42,500 × 50¢ + $10,000 or $31,250 was the amount allowable. A comparison of the $33,000 costs incurred with the $31,250 allowable shows that $1,750 more was incurred than should have been. Thus, flexible budgeting techniques provide the machinery to achieve better control over overhead costs.

CONTROL THROUGH THE USE OF FLEXIBLE BUDGETS

By the preparation of reports showing the actual versus the budgeted standard cost figures and analyzing these as to volume and price causes, it is possible to make available a management control that will help reduce losses and permit the business operations to be conducted more efficiently. The preparation of periodic (monthly) comparisons of the budgeted (standard) total and unit costs with the actual total and unit costs is desirable. These comparison reports must follow the same plan as the original budget preparation. Therefore, the comparisons in this instance, adequately supported by detailed schedules analyzing each important fact, will cover the following:

1. Budget report of sales.
2. Budget report of cost of production, supported by:
   a) Budget report of material costs.
   b) Budget report of labor costs.
   c) Budget report of manufacturing overhead costs.
3. Budget reports of the operating expenses:
   a) Distribution costs, supported by:
       (1) Selling expense reports.
       (2) Administrative expense reports.
       (3) Financial expense reports.

Two illustrations are given—a budget report of monthly sales (Illustration 14–3) and a budget report of the cost of production (Illustration 14–4).

Illustration 14–3
BUDGET REPORT OF MONTHLY SALES

Territory   1   Month of   March   Operating Rate   60%

Product	Quantities		Values		Increase or Decrease*	Remarks
	Budget	Actual	Budget	Actual		
A	1,000	1,100	$16,500	$18,150	$1,650	Increased quantity
B	800	800	16,500	18,000	1,500	Increased price
C	800	700	7,000	5,250	1,750*	Smaller quantity at lower price
Total.....	2,600	2,600	$40,000	$41,400	$1,400	

THE CASH BUDGET

An important aspect of the budgetary procedure is the preparation of the cash budget—a schedule of the expected cash receipts and how the cash will be expended. Properly prepared, it will indicate shortages and excesses for proper managerial action. Generally, cash budgets should be prepared a year in advance, subdivided into monthly figures. Monthly comparisons with the actual cash receipts and expenditures will permit prompt corrective action.

One procedure in preparing a cash budget is to estimate directly each expected source and amount of cash for the given time period and the expected disbursements. To illustrate, a cash budget for the month of June is to be prepared. The only source of cash is from accounts receivable, since all sales are on account. Ninety-eight percent of the accounts are collected in the following manner (2% are considered uncollectible):

20% in month of sale
50% in month following sale
20% in second month following sale
10% in third month following sale

Budgeted sales for June.................$1,000,000
Actual sales:
    March.....................................   900,000
    April...................................... 1,200,000
    May....................................... 1,300,000

Accounts payable are paid in the month following their incurrence since purchase discounts are not available in this industry.

May purchases..............................$400,000
June purchases.............................. 700,000

Illustration 14–4

BUDGET REPORT OF THE COST OF PRODUCTION

Cost Element	Product A			Product B			Product C		
	Budget	Actual	Increase Decrease*	Budget	Actual	Increase Decrease*	Budget	Actual	Increase Decrease*
Material—Cutting Department	$ 3,600.00	$ 4,000.00	$ 400.00	$ 3,000.00	$ 2,900.00	$100.00*	$ 900.00	$ 675.00	$ 225.00*
Material—Finishing Department	240.00	260.00	20.00	600.00	610.00	10.00	300.00	200.00	100.00*
Labor—Cutting Department	2,400.00	2,600.00	200.00	2,000.00	2,000.00	....	1,600.00	1,280.00	320.00*
Labor—Stamping Department	1,200.00	1,300.00	100.00	1,000.00	1,200.00	200.00	400.00	320.00	80.00*
Labor—Finishing Department	2,160.00	2,340.00	180.00	1,800.00	1,700.00	100.00*	800.00	640.00	160.00*
Manufacturing Overhead—Cutting Department	692.64	975.00	282.36	577.20	577.20	....	461.76	460.00	1.76*
Manufacturing Overhead—Stamping Department	432.00	468.00	36.00	360.00	432.00	72.00	144.00	115.20	28.80*
Manufacturing Overhead—Finishing Department	756.00	819.00	63.00	630.00	567.00	63.00*	280.00	224.00	56.00*
Total Costs	$11,480.64	$12,762.00	$1,281.36	$9,967.20	$9,986.20	$ 19.00	$4,885.76	$3,914.20	$971.56*
Number of Units	1,200	1,300	100	1,000	1,000	0	1,000	800	200*

Wages and salaries expense of $600,000 includes $40,000 accrued at the end of June to be paid in July. Wages of $30,000 were accrued at the end of May and were paid in June.

Other cash payments to be made in June:

Semiannual interest payment...............$60,000
Dividends....................................... 80,000
Tax payment, covers 6 months............ 70,000

The cash budget for the month is given in Illustration 14–5.

Illustration 14–5

ABC MANUFACTURERS

CASH BUDGET

For Month of June, 19—

Estimated cash balance, June 1		$ 360,000
Estimated cash receipts:		
From June sales, 20% × (98% of $1,000,000)	$196,000	
From May sales, 50% × (98% of $1,300,000)	637,000	
From April sales, 20% × (98% of $1,200,000)	235,200	
From March sales, 10% × (98% of $900,000)	88,200	
Total cash receipts		1,156,400
Cash available		$1,516,400
Estimated cash payments:		
On accounts payable		$ 400,000
Wages and salaries:		
Expense	$600,000	
To be paid in July	40,000	
	$560,000	
May expense, paid in June	30,000	590,000
Interest		60,000
Dividends		80,000
Taxes		70,000
Total estimated cash payments		$1,200,000
Cash Balance, June 30		$ 316,400

Another method of cash budgeting, the adjusted net income method, begins with the budgeted net income figure and adjusts this figure to reflect cash transactions. It is a method similar to the one used to prepare a statement of sources and applications of funds. Costs and expenses such as depreciation and amortization which do not require cash outlays are added back to the projected net income. Cash outlays that are not reflected in the income statement are subtracted. Examples would be cash dividends or sums to be spent on the purchase of equipment. Expected excesses of collections over sales are added. Any excess of accounts receivable over sales is subtracted. Any decrease in payables is also subtracted. The resultant figure is the expected increase or decrease in cash.

THE CAPITAL EXPENDITURE BUDGET

Project or *capital expenditure budgeting* is an important area of long-term managerial planning, particularly in the manufacturing business. In many instances, it is an area where action may be taken or postponed without seriously affecting current operating results. On the other hand, capital expenditures may require long-term planning which makes it more difficult to forecast with any degree of accuracy.

Illustrations of the types of capital expenditure projects are:

1. Replacement of obsolete or worn-out facilities.
2. Expansion of facilities.
3. Expansion of products, services, and sales territories.
4. Improvements in products and processes.

In some instances, management may not have a choice of whether or not to make the capital expenditure, such as in the case of replacement of worn-out steam boiler. In other cases, it may be necessary to make a decision of whether or not to purchase new, more efficient machines to replace some old but still operating machines. In this discussion, applications are to be made to those situations where the management has a choice of whether or not to make the capital expenditure. Management will usually invest in a given project if there is a likelihood that an acceptable return on the investment will be realized. This return on the investment may be in the form of a cost saving resulting from replacing an old machine with a newer more efficient model, or in purchasing equipment with which to manufacture a new product. Such decisions indicate what is termed as the *operating advantage*. Estimates of the operating advantage and investment evaluations are based on the funds that must be expended NOW with the expectation that some profit advantage will be derived in the FUTURE. Therefore management must analyze the relative importance of each of these factors before making a capital expenditure decision. The methods of capital budgeting analysis frequently used are: (1) the *payback* method of analysis, or (2) the *simple rate of return* analysis, or (3) the *time adjusted rate of return* analysis.

Although capital expenditure proposals in a modern company originate at all levels of administration, final evaluation of the proposals is made by the staff of the chief financial executive. Once management selects the desired proposals, these are then incorporated into the master budget of the company. Post-completion audits should be conducted to learn whether or not the project actually developed in the manner that was forecast; that is, the operating advantage that was expected.

PAYBACK EVALUATION

The *payback* method measures the length of time necessary to recoup the investment. It is primarily a method used to measure the return *of* the investment. An illustration will be of help. Management of the ABC Plating Company has the opportunity to purchase a new machine for $19,000 plus $1,000 of installation, etc., costs. A cost study has shown that the operating advantage is expected to amount to $2,000 per year over the life of the new machine. The new machine's estimated life is 10 years, and the combined federal and state tax rate is 50 percent.

The payback period is computed as follows:

$$\frac{\text{Net investment}}{\text{Operating advantage} + \text{Depreciation} - \text{Income tax}} = \text{Payback period.}$$

$$\frac{\$20,000}{\$2,000 + \$2,000 - \$1,000} = 6.67 \text{ years.}$$

Note that depreciation is added back to the operating advantage. This is necessary because this method measures the full amount that flows into the business, i.e., the cash flow. Each year $3,000 of new cash is generated; and at that rate, 6.67 years are necessary to recoup the $20,000 new investment. The fact that the depreciation and the savings each amount to $2,000 is coincidental but a possibility as shown here.

Most businessmen have at some time relied on the payback method as it discloses how fast one will get his money back and thus has some use in evaluating risk, especially if it is possible that the new machine may become obsolete before the end of the 10 years estimated as the useful life. Payback computations also are of help in determining the liquidity of the company as the new cash generated is determinable. However, the method does not show how much will be earned; profitability is not shown.

SIMPLE RATE OF RETURN EVALUATION

The simple or accounting rate of return method measures the profitability of the investment proposal; the return *on* the investment is computed. The calculation is made as follows:

$$\frac{\text{Operating advantage (after tax)}}{\text{New initial investment}} = \text{Rate of return on investment.}$$

If the same data are used as in the preceding illustration, the simple rate of return is:

$$\frac{\$1,000}{\$20,000} = 5 \text{ percent.}$$

Of the $3,000 of new cash generated each year, $1,000 is profit and $2,000 is the return *of* the investment, i.e., depreciation. Since $2,000 of the investment is recouped each year via depreciation, the *average* investment is $10,000. Some analysts thus use the average investment rather than the initial investment:

$$\frac{\$1,000}{\$10,000} = 10 \text{ percent.}$$

Not only does a difficulty arise in determining whether to use initial investment or average investment but the simple rate of return treats each year's savings the same as any other year's savings. Also, a comparison is made between savings to be received in the future with an investment to be made now; the two are not comparable. The time adjusted rate of return method solves the problems created by the simple rate of return method.

TIME ADJUSTED RATE OF RETURN METHOD

The time adjusted rate of return method brings in the time element, and the investment is evaluated on a comparable basis with the stream of future payments. A dollar to be received sometime in the future is worth less than $1 today. For example, if one wants $1 a year from now and the going rate of interest is 4 percent (compounded annually), the present value table on page 455 shows that $0.962 invested now will yield $1 a year from now. That $1 is worth only $0.962 today. Similarly, if an investor wants $1 per year for 10 years and the going rate of interest is 4 percent, the investor would need $8.111 now as per the table on page 454. Note the difference between the two tables. The one on page 455 measures the present value of $1, and the one on page 454 measures the present value of $1 *per year* for N years, i.e., a flow.

The table on page 454 is useful in determining the time adjusted rate of return. The stream of future payments must be discounted to present value and compared to the investment. Using the data from the illustration, the net investment was $20,000 with an operating advantage of $2,000 less taxes of $1,000. Depreciation was $2,000. The $20,000 of investment is compared with the stream of $3,000 which is the saving plus depreciation minus taxes. If $20,000 is expected to yield $3,000 per year for 10 years, $20,000/$3,000 or $6.667 of investment is needed to produce $1 per year for 10 years. (The tables are in the form of $1.) If $6.667 is the present value of the future stream of $1 payments to be received in each of the next 10 years, what is the rate of return? The table on page 454 shows the following under 10 years in searching for 6.667:

$$8\% = 6.710$$
$$10\% = 6.145$$

Present Value of $1 Received Annually for N Years

Years (N)	1%	2%	4%	6%	8%	10%	12%	14%	15%	16%	18%	20%	22%	24%	25%	26%	28%	30%	35%	40%	45%	50%
1	0.990	0.980	0.962	0.943	0.926	0.909	0.893	0.877	0.870	0.862	0.847	0.833	0.820	0.806	0.800	0.794	0.781	0.769	0.741	0.714	0.690	0.667
2	1.970	1.942	1.886	1.833	1.783	1.736	1.690	1.647	1.626	1.605	1.566	1.528	1.492	1.457	1.440	1.424	1.392	1.361	1.289	1.224	1.165	1.111
3	2.941	2.884	2.775	2.673	2.577	2.487	2.402	2.322	2.283	2.246	2.174	2.106	2.042	1.981	1.952	1.923	1.868	1.816	1.696	1.589	1.493	1.407
4	3.902	3.808	3.630	3.465	3.312	3.170	3.037	2.914	2.855	2.798	2.690	2.589	2.494	2.404	2.362	2.320	2.241	2.166	1.997	1.849	1.720	1.605
5	4.853	4.713	4.452	4.212	3.993	3.791	3.605	3.433	3.352	3.274	3.127	2.991	2.864	2.745	2.689	2.635	2.532	2.436	2.220	2.035	1.876	1.737
6	5.795	5.601	5.242	4.917	4.623	4.355	4.111	3.889	3.784	3.685	3.498	3.326	3.167	3.020	2.951	2.885	2.759	2.643	2.385	2.168	1.983	1.824
7	6.728	6.472	6.002	5.582	5.206	4.868	4.564	4.288	4.160	4.039	3.812	3.605	3.416	3.242	3.161	3.083	2.937	2.802	2.508	2.263	2.057	1.883
8	7.652	7.325	6.733	6.210	5.747	5.335	4.968	4.639	4.487	4.344	4.078	3.837	3.619	3.421	3.329	3.241	3.076	2.925	2.598	2.331	2.108	1.922
9	8.566	8.162	7.435	6.802	6.247	5.759	5.328	4.946	4.772	4.607	4.303	4.031	3.786	3.566	3.463	3.366	3.184	3.019	2.665	2.379	2.144	1.948
10	9.471	8.983	8.111	7.360	6.710	6.145	5.650	5.216	5.019	4.833	4.494	4.192	3.923	3.682	3.571	3.465	3.269	3.092	2.715	2.414	2.168	1.965
11	10.368	9.787	8.760	7.887	7.139	6.495	5.937	5.453	5.234	5.029	4.656	4.327	4.035	3.776	3.656	3.544	3.335	3.147	2.752	2.438	2.185	1.977
12	11.255	10.575	9.385	8.384	7.536	6.814	6.194	5.660	5.421	5.197	4.793	4.439	4.127	3.851	3.725	3.606	3.387	3.190	2.779	2.456	2.196	1.985
13	12.134	11.343	9.986	8.853	7.904	7.103	6.424	5.842	5.583	5.342	4.910	4.533	4.203	3.912	3.780	3.656	3.427	3.223	2.799	2.468	2.204	1.990
14	13.004	12.106	10.563	9.295	8.244	7.367	6.628	6.002	5.724	5.468	5.008	4.611	4.265	3.962	3.824	3.695	3.459	3.249	2.814	2.477	2.210	1.993
15	13.865	12.849	11.118	9.712	8.559	7.606	6.811	6.142	5.847	5.575	5.092	4.675	4.315	4.001	3.859	3.726	3.483	3.268	2.825	2.484	2.214	1.995
16	14.718	13.578	11.652	10.106	8.851	7.824	6.974	6.265	5.954	5.669	5.162	4.730	4.357	4.033	3.887	3.751	3.503	3.283	2.834	2.489	2.216	1.997
17	15.562	14.292	12.166	10.477	9.122	8.022	7.120	6.373	6.047	5.749	5.222	4.775	4.391	4.059	3.910	3.771	3.518	3.295	2.840	2.492	2.218	1.998
18	16.398	14.992	12.659	10.828	9.372	8.201	7.250	6.467	6.128	5.818	5.273	4.812	4.419	4.080	3.928	3.786	3.529	3.304	2.844	2.494	2.219	1.999
19	17.226	15.678	13.134	11.158	9.604	8.365	7.366	6.550	6.198	5.877	5.316	4.844	4.442	4.097	3.942	3.799	3.539	3.311	2.848	2.496	2.220	1.999
20	18.046	16.351	13.590	11.470	9.818	8.514	7.469	6.623	6.259	5.929	5.353	4.870	4.460	4.110	3.954	3.808	3.546	3.316	2.850	2.497	2.221	1.999
21	18.857	17.011	14.029	11.764	10.017	8.649	7.562	6.687	6.312	5.973	5.384	4.891	4.476	4.121	3.963	3.816	3.551	3.320	2.852	2.498	2.221	2.000
22	19.660	17.658	14.451	12.042	10.201	8.772	7.645	6.743	6.359	6.011	5.410	4.909	4.488	4.130	3.970	3.822	3.556	3.323	2.853	2.498	2.222	2.000
23	20.456	18.292	14.857	12.303	10.371	8.883	7.718	6.792	6.399	6.044	5.432	4.925	4.499	4.137	3.976	3.827	3.559	3.325	2.854	2.499	2.222	2.000
24	21.243	18.914	15.247	12.550	10.529	8.985	7.784	6.835	6.434	6.073	5.451	4.937	4.507	4.143	3.981	3.831	3.562	3.327	2.855	2.499	2.222	2.000
25	22.023	19.523	15.622	12.783	10.675	9.077	7.843	6.873	6.464	6.097	5.467	4.948	4.514	4.147	3.985	3.834	3.564	3.329	2.856	2.499	2.222	2.000
26	22.795	20.121	15.983	13.003	10.810	9.161	7.896	6.906	6.491	6.118	5.480	4.956	4.520	4.151	3.988	3.837	3.566	3.330	2.856	2.500	2.222	2.000
27	23.560	20.707	16.330	13.211	10.935	9.237	7.943	6.935	6.514	6.136	5.492	4.964	4.524	4.154	3.990	3.839	3.567	3.331	2.856	2.500	2.222	2.000
28	24.316	21.281	16.663	13.406	11.051	9.307	7.984	6.961	6.534	6.152	5.502	4.970	4.528	4.157	3.992	3.840	3.568	3.331	2.857	2.500	2.222	2.000
29	25.066	21.844	16.984	13.591	11.158	9.370	8.022	6.983	6.551	6.166	5.510	4.975	4.531	4.159	3.994	3.841	3.569	3.332	2.857	2.500	2.222	2.000
30	25.808	22.396	17.292	13.765	11.258	9.427	8.055	7.003	6.566	6.177	5.517	4.979	4.534	4.160	3.995	3.842	3.569	3.332	2.857	2.500	2.222	2.000
40	32.835	27.355	19.793	15.046	11.925	9.779	8.244	7.105	6.642	6.234	5.548	4.997	4.544	4.166	3.999	3.846	3.571	3.333	2.857	2.500	2.222	2.000
50	39.196	31.424	21.482	15.762	12.234	9.915	8.304	7.133	6.661	6.246	5.554	4.999	4.545	4.167	4.000	3.846	3.571	3.333	2.857	2.500	2.222	2.000

Present Value of $1

Years Hence	1%	2%	4%	6%	8%	10%	12%	14%	15%	16%	18%	20%	22%	24%	25%	26%	28%	30%	35%	40%	45%	50%
1	0.990	0.980	0.962	0.943	0.926	0.909	0.893	0.877	0.870	0.862	0.847	0.833	0.820	0.806	0.800	0.794	0.781	0.769	0.741	0.714	0.690	0.667
2	0.980	0.961	0.925	0.890	0.857	0.826	0.797	0.769	0.756	0.743	0.718	0.694	0.672	0.650	0.640	0.630	0.610	0.592	0.549	0.510	0.476	0.444
3	0.971	0.942	0.889	0.840	0.794	0.751	0.712	0.675	0.658	0.641	0.609	0.579	0.551	0.524	0.512	0.500	0.477	0.455	0.406	0.364	0.328	0.296
4	0.961	0.924	0.855	0.792	0.735	0.683	0.636	0.592	0.572	0.552	0.516	0.482	0.451	0.423	0.410	0.397	0.373	0.350	0.301	0.260	0.226	0.198
5	0.951	0.906	0.822	0.747	0.681	0.621	0.567	0.519	0.497	0.476	0.437	0.402	0.370	0.341	0.328	0.315	0.291	0.269	0.223	0.186	0.156	0.132
6	0.942	0.888	0.790	0.705	0.630	0.564	0.507	0.456	0.432	0.410	0.370	0.335	0.303	0.275	0.262	0.250	0.227	0.207	0.165	0.133	0.108	0.088
7	0.933	0.871	0.760	0.665	0.583	0.513	0.452	0.400	0.376	0.354	0.314	0.279	0.249	0.222	0.210	0.198	0.178	0.159	0.122	0.095	0.074	0.059
8	0.923	0.853	0.731	0.627	0.540	0.467	0.404	0.351	0.327	0.305	0.266	0.233	0.204	0.179	0.168	0.157	0.139	0.123	0.091	0.068	0.051	0.039
9	0.914	0.837	0.703	0.592	0.500	0.424	0.361	0.308	0.284	0.263	0.225	0.194	0.167	0.144	0.134	0.125	0.108	0.094	0.067	0.048	0.035	0.026
10	0.905	0.820	0.676	0.558	0.463	0.386	0.322	0.270	0.247	0.227	0.191	0.162	0.137	0.116	0.107	0.099	0.085	0.073	0.050	0.035	0.024	0.017
11	0.896	0.804	0.650	0.527	0.429	0.350	0.287	0.237	0.215	0.195	0.162	0.135	0.112	0.094	0.086	0.079	0.066	0.056	0.037	0.025	0.017	0.012
12	0.887	0.788	0.625	0.497	0.397	0.319	0.257	0.208	0.187	0.168	0.137	0.112	0.092	0.076	0.069	0.062	0.052	0.043	0.027	0.018	0.012	0.008
13	0.879	0.773	0.601	0.469	0.368	0.290	0.229	0.182	0.163	0.145	0.116	0.093	0.075	0.061	0.055	0.050	0.040	0.033	0.020	0.013	0.008	0.005
14	0.870	0.758	0.577	0.442	0.340	0.263	0.205	0.160	0.141	0.125	0.099	0.078	0.062	0.049	0.044	0.039	0.032	0.025	0.015	0.009	0.006	0.003
15	0.861	0.743	0.555	0.417	0.315	0.239	0.183	0.140	0.123	0.108	0.084	0.065	0.051	0.040	0.035	0.031	0.025	0.020	0.011	0.006	0.004	0.002
16	0.853	0.728	0.534	0.394	0.292	0.218	0.163	0.123	0.107	0.093	0.071	0.054	0.042	0.032	0.028	0.025	0.019	0.015	0.008	0.005	0.003	0.002
17	0.844	0.714	0.513	0.371	0.270	0.198	0.146	0.108	0.093	0.080	0.060	0.045	0.034	0.025	0.023	0.020	0.015	0.012	0.006	0.003	0.002	0.001
18	0.836	0.700	0.494	0.350	0.250	0.180	0.130	0.095	0.081	0.069	0.051	0.038	0.028	0.021	0.018	0.016	0.012	0.009	0.005	0.002	0.001	0.00
19	0.828	0.686	0.475	0.331	0.232	0.164	0.116	0.083	0.070	0.060	0.043	0.031	0.023	0.017	0.014	0.012	0.009	0.007	0.003	0.002	0.001	
20	0.820	0.673	0.456	0.312	0.215	0.149	0.104	0.073	0.061	0.051	0.037	0.026	0.019	0.014	0.012	0.010	0.007	0.005	0.002	0.001	0.001	
21	0.811	0.660	0.439	0.294	0.199	0.135	0.093	0.064	0.053	0.044	0.031	0.022	0.015	0.011	0.009	0.008	0.006	0.004	0.002	0.001		
22	0.803	0.647	0.422	0.278	0.184	0.123	0.083	0.056	0.046	0.038	0.026	0.018	0.013	0.009	0.007	0.006	0.004	0.003	0.001	0.001		
23	0.795	0.634	0.406	0.262	0.170	0.112	0.074	0.049	0.040	0.033	0.022	0.015	0.010	0.007	0.006	0.005	0.003	0.002	0.001			
24	0.788	0.622	0.390	0.247	0.158	0.102	0.066	0.043	0.035	0.028	0.019	0.013	0.008	0.006	0.005	0.004	0.003	0.002	0.001			
25	0.780	0.610	0.375	0.233	0.146	0.092	0.059	0.038	0.030	0.024	0.016	0.010	0.007	0.005	0.004	0.003	0.002	0.001	0.001			
26	0.772	0.598	0.361	0.220	0.135	0.084	0.053	0.033	0.026	0.021	0.014	0.009	0.006	0.004	0.003	0.002	0.002	0.001				
27	0.764	0.586	0.347	0.207	0.125	0.076	0.047	0.029	0.023	0.018	0.011	0.007	0.005	0.003	0.002	0.002	0.001	0.001				
28	0.757	0.574	0.333	0.196	0.116	0.069	0.042	0.026	0.020	0.016	0.010	0.006	0.004	0.002	0.002	0.002	0.001	0.001				
29	0.749	0.563	0.321	0.185	0.107	0.063	0.037	0.022	0.017	0.014	0.008	0.005	0.003	0.002	0.002	0.001	0.001					
30	0.742	0.552	0.308	0.174	0.099	0.057	0.033	0.020	0.015	0.012	0.007	0.004	0.003	0.002	0.001	0.001	0.001					
40	0.672	0.453	0.208	0.097	0.046	0.022	0.011	0.005	0.004	0.003	0.001	0.001										
50	0.608	0.372	0.141	0.054	0.021	0.009	0.003	0.001	0.001	0.001												

Interpolating yields the following results:

$$\frac{0.043}{0.565}(2\%) = 0.0152 + 8\%, \text{ or } 8.015\%.$$

The 8 percent return is what the investor expects to receive on his investment when the element of time is considered. The time adjusted rate of return incorporates both the return *of* the investment and the return *on* the investment. The use of this method has resulted in the various investment proposals being placed on comparable bases. Today, many companies use the time adjusted rate of return method in evaluating investment opportunities.

APPLICATIONS OF CAPITAL EXPENDITURE ANALYSIS

The type of analysis presented earlier pertaining to the purchase of a new machine may be used to evaluate other types of proposals; any type of investment opportunity may be evaluated. For example, the analysis may be of help in a situation where the replacement of facilities is being contemplated. An illustration will be of help.

Assume a situation where operating expenses before depreciation are expected to amount to $2,900 per year if manufacturing is continued with the present machine. For an investment of $6,000 in a new machine lasting 10 years, the operating expenses before depreciation can be cut to $1,500. The dismantling cost of the old would about equal any revenue realized from its sale. The income tax rate is 50 percent.

Should the company buy the new one or keep the old? Computation of the payback and time adjusted rate of return would show:

	Annual Cost of New	Annual Cost of Old
Operating expenses	$1,500	$2,900
Depreciation	600	0
	$2,100	$2,900

Saving, $800 (before tax)
Tax, $400
Net saving, $400

$$\text{Payback} = \frac{\$6,000}{\$600 + \$400} = 6 \text{ years.}$$

The time adjusted rate of return method shows that for the $6,000 investment, $1,000 is returned each year, or $1 for each $6 of investment. The table on page 454 discloses a rate of return of approximately 11%.

Note that in the above computation, depreciation on the old machine was ignored. The decision whether or not to replace the machine should be based on *future* costs and not on past costs. The cost of the old machine is a *sunk cost,* and whether the amount is written off over one day, one year, or several years is not relevant for the decision of whether or not to buy the new one. What is relevant is any future cost. If the old machine had a resale value, that amount would be depreciated over its remaining life. The reason is that if the company kept the old machine, it gave up the opportunity to receive the proceeds from its sale.

RESEARCH AND DEVELOPMENT COST BUDGETS

In many modern growth industries, progress is measured by the results of continuous research and development work to improve the products currently being produced or to create new products. Many firms capitalize these expenditures. Management in collaboration with the research director will regularly budget the amount to be spent on this work which is usually classified as basic research, development research, or applied research, and allocated to cost reduction, improved products, or new products.

As in the case of capital budgeting, research and development budgeting is somewhat flexible, since in many instances both activities and expenditures can be postponed if the financial conditions, high interest rates, and economic business conditions warrant retrenching.

THE OPERATING BUDGET ILLUSTRATED

To help the understanding of the complete budget plan, an illustration is used to show the interrelation of the various budgets thus prepared.

The Jordan Manufacturing Company produces three products, A, B, and C, similar in size and weight. These products are sold to dealers. Six salesmen operate in territory 1 and four salesmen in territory 2, under the direction of the sales manager, who supervises the sales function from the home office. Some sales are also made direct from the warehouse, adjacent to the home office.

The sales budget in summary form is presented in Illustration 14–6.

Illustration 14–6
SALES INCOME BUDGET
For Year Ended December 31, 19—

Territory	Net Sales	Product A	Product B	Product C
1	$300,000	$150,000	$100,000	$ 50,000
2	400,000	120,000	200,000	80,000
Warehouse	100,000	60,000	30,000	10,000
Total	$800,000	$330,000	$330,000	$140,000

This budget was prepared from a compilation of the monthly sales estimates, supported by detailed estimates of the *quantities* to be sold.

From the sales figure of $800,000 the budget director is able to compute the desired net income in order to place a limit on the total amount of costs and expenses. If it is assumed that the net income on these sales should be $56,000, or 7 percent, then the balance of $744,000 represents the limit on cost of production plus operating expenses.

The cost of production budget corresponding to the above sales would appear in summary form as shown in Illustration 14–7.

Illustration 14–7

ESTIMATED COST OF PRODUCTION

For Year Ended December 31, 19–

Cost Element	Total	Product A	Product B	Product C
Materials..	$194,000	$ 80,000	$ 90,000	$24,000
Labor	296,000	120,000	120,000	56,000
Manufacturing overhead......................	74,000	30,000	30,000	14,000
Total	$564,000	$230,000	$240,000	$94,000

Illustration 14–8

ANALYSIS OF ESTIMATED UNIT PRODUCTION COSTS BY DEPARTMENTS

For the Year 19—

	Total	Cutting Department	Stamping Department	Finishing Department
Product A:				
Material......................	$3.20	$3.00	....	$0.20
Labor.......................	4.80	2.00	$1.00	1.80
Manufacturing Overhead.......	1.20	0.50	0.25	0.45
Total....................	$9.20	$5.50	$1.25	$2.45
Product B:				
Material......................	$3.60	$3.00	....	$0.60
Labor.......................	4.80	2.00	$1.00	1.80
Manufacturing Overhead.......	1.20	0.50	0.25	0.45
Total....................	$9.60	$5.50	$1.25	$2.85
Product C:				
Material......................	$1.20	$0.90	....	$0.30
Labor.......................	2.80	1.60	$0.40	0.80
Manufacturing Overhead.......	0.70	0.40	0.10	0.20
Total....................	$4.70	$2.90	$0.50	$1.30

However, this is merely a condensed summary of the detailed reports, which would include: (1) a schedule of estimated production costs by elements per unit in each *department,* i.e., the material and labor and overhead costs; and (2) a detailed manufacturing overhead budget, broken down into variable, fixed, and semivariable overhead costs. These two important schedules are shown in Illustrations 14–8 and 14–9.

The analysis of estimated unit costs (see Illustration 14–8), coupled with the number of units to be produced, as indicated by estimated sales, should give the total estimated cost of production for the year, reanalyzed by months.

A *manufacturing overhead cost budget* may be used so that effective budgetary control is realized. As indicated in the first half of this text, it is practically necessary for a manufacturer to estimate his manufacturing overhead costs and his production for the year in order to calculate a predetermined rate for applying manufacturing overhead to production

Illustration 14–9
BUDGET ESTIMATE OF MANUFACTURING OVERHEAD COSTS
For the Year Ended December 31, 19—

	Total	Producing Departments			Service Departments	
		Cutting	Stamping	Finishing	X	Y
Variable Overhead Costs:						
Indirect Materials	$ 2,000.00	$ 300.00	$ 200.00	$ 1,000.00	$ 350.00	$ 150.00
Indirect Labor	10,000.00	1,000.00	500.00	1,000.00	3,750.00	3,750.00
Fuel	2,500.00	500.00	400.00	300.00	650.00	650.00
Light and Power	3,000.00	1,300.00	900.00	200.00	300.00	300.00
Compensation Insurance	7,000.00	3,000.00	1,500.00	1,000.00	750.00	750.00
Telephone and Telegraph	500.00	100.00	....	....	200.00	200.00
Fixed and Semivariable:						
Rent of Factory	5,000.00	1,400.00	900.00	900.00	900.00	900.00
Fire Insurance	4,000.00	1,000.00	800.00	900.00	600.00	700.00
Superintendence	20,000.00	7,000.00	2,000.00	7,000.00	2,000.00	2,000.00
Depreciation	10,000.00	3,500.00	1,000.00	2,300.00	1,500.00	1,700.00
General Administrative Expenses	5,000.00	1,100.00	800.00	700.00	1,400.00	1,000.00
Amortization of Patents	5,000.00	3,000.00	....	2,000.00	....	....
Total						
	$74,000.00				$12,400.00	$12,100.00
Apportioned Charges, Department X	$12,400.00	5,000.00	3,000.00	4,400.00		
Apportioned Charges, Department Y	12,100.00	4,800.00	2,500.00	4,800.00		
	$74,000.00	$33,000.00	$14,500.00	$26,500.00		

costs. *This implies a budgetary process.* By use of special forms, the actual and budgeted figures should be compared frequently and cumulatively to note variations and the reasons therefor. Similar procedures can be followed for selling and administrative expenses or for distribution costs. To make the illustration complete, both the manufacturing overhead and the selling and administrative expense budgets are shown; see Illustrations 14–9 and 14–10. To be most effective, these budgets must first be prepared on a *monthly basis by departments.*

Illustration 14–10
BUDGET ESTIMATES OF SELLING AND ADMINISTRATIVE EXPENSES
For the Year Ended December 31, 19 –

	Total	Selling Expenses	Administrative Expenses
Variable Expenses:			
Traveling expenses.............................	$ 5,000	$ 4,000	$ 1,000
Office expenses.................................	14,000	6,000	8,000
Warehouse expenses...........................	16,000	16,000	....
Delivery costs...................................	15,000	15,000	....
Postage...	4,000	2,250	1,750
Telephone and telegraph......................	8,000	5,000	3,000
Office supplies..................................	3,000	750	2,250
Miscellaneous....................................	2,000	1,000	1,000
Total Variable Expenses	$ 67,000	$ 50,000	$17,000
Fixed and Semivariable:			
Salaries..	$ 60,000	$ 30,000	$30,000
Rent...	25,000	15,000	10,000
Administration...................................	10,000	4,000	6,000
Insurance...	8,000	6,000	2,000
Depreciation.....................................	10,000	7,500	2,500
Total Fixed Expenses....................	$113,000	$ 62,500	$50,500
Total Expenses......................................	$180,000	$112,500	$67,500

Once the budget has been completed to this point, it is possible to project the income statement for the period and break it down into monthly statements for comparisons with the actual operating results. When the budget is prepared, only the first columns can be completed. As the actual figures are received, they may be inserted and the variations computed and analyzed. Illustration 14–11 shows how the budgeted and actual figures of the income statement may be compared and analyzed.

The analysis of the departmental manufacturing overhead requires a study of the variations, in addition to facts indicated in the Remarks column. Manufacturing overhead variations are caused, in part, by *inefficiency* of production; that is, more hours may have been required to complete a job than were provided for. In addition, there may be further variations because the overhead incurred might cost more than was anticipated and is known as a *budget overhead variation*. If the plant as a unit operates at a greater capacity than was anticipated in the production budget, there will be a favorable variation because of greater plant activity. This is known as a *capacity variation*. The sum of the budget variation and the capacity variation, whether positive or negative, will equal the over- or underapplied manufacturing overhead for the period.

Illustration 14—11
ESTIMATED INCOME STATEMENT
For the Year Ended December 31, 19—

	Budget		Actual		Difference†		Remarks
	Amount	%	Amount	%	Amount	%	
Net Sales............	$800,000.00	100.0	$900,000.00	100.0	$100,000.00	12.5	
Cost of Sales........	560,000.00*	70.0	650,000.00	72.2	90,000.00	16.0	
Gross Profit on Sales..	$240,000.00	30.0	$250,000.00	27.8	$ 10,000.00	4.16	
Selling Expenses......	$112,500.00	14.06	$135,000.00	15.0	$ 22,500.00	20.0	
Administrative Expenses..........	67,500.00	8.44	63,000.00	7.0	4,500.00†	6.6†	
Total Expenses.......	$180,000.00	22.50	$198,000.00	22.0	$ 18,000.00	10.0	
Operating Income....	$ 60,000.00	7.5	$ 52,000.00	5.8	$ 8,000.00†	13.3†	
Financial Expenses...	4,000.00	.5	4,500.00	.5	500.00	12.5	
Estimated Net Income (7% of Sales)......	$ 56,000.00	7.0	$ 47,500.00	5.27	$ 8,500.00†	15.1†	

* Inventory of Finished Goods, $4,000.
† Indicates decrease.

Controlling overhead costs by such an analysis is a fundamental purpose of a budget. It enables management to understand why there are variations and then to act in correcting unfavorable procedures. Illustrations 14–12 and 14–13 are examples of reports pointing out variations. In the chapter on standard costs, methods of how to compute them will be illustrated and methods showing how to place responsibility for their existence so that corrective action may be taken will be discussed.

Illustration 14-12

BUDGETARY REPORT ON MANUFACTURING OVERHEAD COSTS

For Month Ending March 31, 19—

Department: Cutting

Foreman: Allen K. Marmon

Costs	Budget This Month	Actual This Month	Variation This Month	Budget Year to Date	Actual Year to Date	Variation Year to Date	Remarks
Variable Overhead Costs:							
Indirect Materials	$ 25.00	$ 30.00	+$ 5.00	$ 75.00	$ 90.00	+$ 15.00	Weather conditions
Indirect Labor	83.33	83.33	....	250.00	240.00	– 10.00	
Fuel	46.67	50.00	+ 3.33	140.00	160.00	+ 20.00	Special orders
Light and Power	108.33	120.00	+ 11.67	325.00	450.00	+ 125.00	Higher wages
Compensation Insurance	250.00	270.00	+ 20.00	750.00	800.00	+ 50.00	
Telephone and Telegraph	8.33	7.00	– 1.33	25.00	20.00	– 5.00	
Fixed and Semivariable:							
Rent of Factory	116.67	116.67	....	350.00	350.00	....	
Fire Insurance	83.33	83.33	....	250.00	250.00	....	
Superintendence	583.33	583.33	....	1,750.00	1,750.00	....	
Depreciation	291.60	291.60	....	875.00	875.00	....	
General Administration	91.67	85.00	– 6.67	275.00	210.00	– 65.00	Salary cuts
Amortization—Patents	250.00	250.00	....	750.00	750.00	....	
Apportioned Charges, Department X	416.67	380.00	– 36.67	1,250.00	1,300.00	+ 50.00	See schedule
Apportioned Charges, Department Y	400.00	450.00	+ 50.00	1,200.00	1,220.00	+ 20.00	See schedule
Total	$2,754.93	$2,800.26	+$45.33	$8,265.00	$8,465.00	+$200.00	

Illustration 14–13

BUDGETARY REPORT ON PRODUCTION COSTS
BY PRODUCTS AND BY ELEMENTS OF COSTS*
For Month Ending March 31, 19—

Cost Elements	Budget for Month	Actual Cost for Month	Variation	Remarks
Material Cost:				
Product A..........	$ 6,666.67	$ 7,000.00	+$ 333.33	
Product B..........	7,500.00	7,600.00	+ 100.00	
Product C..........	2,000.00	2,000.00	....	
Labor Cost:				
Product A..........	10,000.00	11,000.00	+ 1,000.00	
Product B..........	10,000.00	12,000.00	+ 2,000.00	Strike
Product C..........	4,666.67	5,000.00	+ 333.33	
Manufacturing Over-head Cost:				
Product A..........	2,500.00	2,750.00	+ 250.00	
Product B..........	2,500.00	3,000.00	+ 500.00	
Product C..........	1,166.66	1,250.00	+ 83.34	
Total..........	$47,000.00	$51,600.00	+$4,600.00	

*These may be further analyzed by departments. The extent to which analyses and comparisons will be made will depend upon the size of the organization and the amount the company is willing to spend for budgetary control.

To illustrate the flexible budgets, sets of facts paralleling those given for the static budget are used but changed where necessary. Reduced to a monthly basis, the flexible sales budget for the Jordan Manufacturing Company would appear as shown in Illustration 14–14.

Illustration 14–14

MONTHLY FLEXIBLE SALES BUDGET*
FOR THE JORDAN MANUFACTURING COMPANY
For Year 19 —
(Approximate Figures)

Product	Operating Capacity					
	40%	60%	80%	100%†	120%	140%
Product A........	$ 11,000.00	$ 16,500.00	$ 22,000.00	$ 27,500.00	$ 33,000.00	$ 38,500.00
Product B........	11,000.00	16,500.00	22,000.00	27,500.00	33,000.00	38,500.00
Product C........	4,666.67	7,000.00	9,333.33	11,666.67	14,000.00	16,333.33
Monthly Total ..	$ 26,666.67	$ 40,000.00	$ 53,333.33	$ 66,666.67	$ 80,000.00	$ 93,333.33
Annual Total* ..	$320,000.00	$480,000.00	$640,000.00	$800,000.00	$960,000.00	$1,120,000.00

*These figures arrived at by considering the budget of standard quantities for each month and the standard selling prices (standard price × standard quantities = foregoing figures).

†Compare this annual figure with the static budget figure given on page 461. The 100 percent operating capacity figure is the same as the static budget figure.

The flexible cost of production budgets involve a great amount of detailed budgeting. A standard direct material cost budget is prepared. The material cost per unit will usually be the same no matter what the operating capacity. The same is true of the per unit direct labor costs. These figures will be comparable to those appearing on the standard cost sheets for the various products. The per unit manufacturing overhead, particularly the fixed and semivariable overhead costs, will tend to be affected by different operating capacities. Therefore, for the computation of unit manufacturing overhead costs, the flexible or sliding budget is of paramount importance. To illustrate the standard material and labor budgets, are taken from the table on page 458, Illustration 14–15 and 14–16 are presented. Illustration 14–17 presents the flexible manufacturing overhead budget.

It should be pointed out that the flexible overhead budget found in Illustration 14–17 is but one way of showing a flexible budget. Illustra-

Illustration 14–15
STANDARD DIRECT MATERIAL COST BUDGET
For Year Ending December 31, 19 –

Standard Quantity	Description of Material	Standard Price	Department in Which Used	Product A	Product B	Product C
3	Sheet Steel	$1.00	Cutting	$3.00	$3.00	....
1	Sheet Steel	0.90	Cutting	....	....	$0.90
12	Rivets	0.10	Finishing	0.10	0.10	0.10
4 oz	Enamel	0.10	Finishing	0.10	0.10	....
1 set	Fittings	0.40	Finishing	....	0.40	....
8 oz	Wax	0.20	Finishing	....	....	0.20
Standard Unit Cost..	....	....	....	$3.20	$3.60	$1.20

Illustration 14–16
STANDARD DIRECT LABOR COST BUDGET
For Year Ending December 31, 19—

Standard Quantity	Description of Labor Operation	Standard Rate	Department in Which Used	Product A	Product B	Product C
4 hours............	Cutting Machine	$2.50	Cutting	$ 5.00	$ 5.00	....
4 hours............	Cutting Machine	2.40	Cutting	....	....	$ 9.60
2 hours............	Stamping Machine	2.50	Stamping	2.50	2.50	....
1 hour.............	Stamping Machine	2.40	Stamping	....	....	2.40
4 hours............	Finishing Work	2.45	Finishing	4.90	4.90	....
2 hours............	Finishing Work	2.40	Finishing	....	....	4.80
Standard Unit Labor Cost.......	....	....	....	$12.40	$12.40	$16.80

tion 14–17 presents the elements of overhead at certain selected levels of operating capacity, i.e., at 40, 60, 80, 100, 120, and 140 percent of capacity. Another way of stating the flexible budget is in fixed and variable components. Each cost is analyzed and its fixed and variable components isolated. For example, fuel expense in the assembly department may be $350 at the 5,000 direct labor hour level and $440 at the

Illustration 14–17

FLEXIBLE MONTHLY MANUFACTURING OVERHEAD COST BUDGET
FOR CUTTING DEPARTMENT*
For Year Ending December 31, 19—

Element of Overhead	Operating Capacity					
	40%	60%	80%	100% (Std)	120%	140%
Variable Overhead Costs:						
Indirect Materials.....	$ 100.00	$ 150.00	$ 200.00	$ 250.00	$ 300.00	$ 350.00
Indirect Labor........	333.30	518.00	666.70	833.30	1,036.00	1,166.70
Fuel.................	....	....	....	466.70	....	....
Light and Power.......	450.00	600.00	860.00	1,083.30	1,180.00	1,500.00
Compensation Insurance	1,000.00	1,400.00	1,900.00	2,500.00	3,000.00	3,200.00
Telegraph and Telephone.............	30.00	49.00	70.00	83.30	96.70	112.00
Apportioned Overhead Costs:						
Department X.......	4,100.00	4,100.00	4,166.70	4,166.70	4,166.70	4,220.00
Department Y.......	3,900.00	3,900.00	4,000.00	4,000.00	4,000.00	4,100.00
Variable Overhead Total.	$ 9,913.30	$10,717.00	$ 11,863.40	$ 13,383.30	$ 13,779.40	$ 14,648.70
Fixed and Semivariable:						
Rent of Factory........	$ 1,166.70	$ 1,166.70	$ 1,166.70	$ 1,166.70	$ 1,166.70	$ 1,166.70
Fire Insurance.........	833.30	833.30	833.30	833.30	900.00	900.00
Superintendence.......	583.33	583.33	583.33	583.33	583.33	583.33
Depreciation of Equipment..............	2,916.70	2,916.70	2,916.70	2,916.70	3,000.00	3,000.00
Administrative Expenses.............	850.00	850.00	916.70	916.70	916.70	1,000.00
Amortization of Patents	250.00	250.00	250.00	250.00	250.00	250.00
Semivariable and Fixed Overhead Total.......	$ 6,600.03	$ 6,600.03	$ 6,666.73	$ 6,666.73	$ 6,816.73	$ 6,900.03
Estimated Direct Labor Costs................	$50,000.00	$60,000.00	$110,000.00	$120,000.00	$140,000.00	$150,000.00
Standard Rate—Variable Overhead............	19.83%	17.86%	10.78%	11.15%	9.84%	9.76%
Standard Rate—Semivariable and Fixed Overhead............	13.20%	11.00%	6.06%	5.55%	4.87%	4.6%

*Similar schedules must be prepared for each producing department.

8,000 direct labor hour level. Analysis of the cost by the use of the high-low point method of separating fixed and variable components discloses variable costs of $0.30 per direct labor hour and fixed costs of $200. Budgeting for fuel cost is then possible for any level between 5,000 and 8,000 direct labor hours. Illustration 14–18 presents a flexible budget for a department where each of the costs has been analyzed in a manner similar to fuel cost:

Illustration 14–18
FLEXIBLE MONTHLY MANUFACTURING
OVERHEAD COST BUDGET FOR
ASSEMBLY DEPARTMENT
For Year Ending December 31, 19—

	Variable per Labor Hour	Fixed
Indirect material	$0.50	
Indirect labor	1.50	$4,000
Fuel....................................	0.30	200
Light and power......................	0.20	300
Rent		800
Fire insurance		600
Depreciation		700
Other expenses.......................	0.10	600
	$2.60	$7,200

Illustration 14–19
STANDARD COST OF PRODUCTION BUDGET
Reduced to Unit Cost Basis

Month: March, 19—   Operating Capacity: 60%

Cost Element and Department	Product A	Product B	Product C
Material—Cutting Department....................	$ 3.00	$ 3.00	$ 0.90
Material—Finishing Department...................	0.20	0.60	0.30
Labor—Cutting Department.....................	5.00	5.00	9.60
Labor—Stamping Department....................	2.50	2.50	2.40
Labor—Finishing Department...................	4.90	4.90	4.80
Manufacturing Overhead—Cutting Department (28.86% × $5.00 or $9.60)....................	1.44	1.44	2.77
Manufacturing Overhead—Stamping Department (36% × $2.50 or $2.40)....................	0.90	0.90	0.86
Manufacturing Overhead—Finishing Department (35% × $4.90 or $4.80).....................	1.72	1.72	1.68
Total Standard Unit Costs......................	$19.66	$20.06	$23.31
Standard Quantity of Production.................	100	150	200

The flexible budget thus becomes $7,200 plus $2.60 per labor hour.

Once these standards and budgets have been prepared by determining the anticipated operating capacity for any month at the beginning of the month, it is possible to prepare a standard cost of production budget. To illustrate, assume that the firm will operate at 60 percent capacity during March. Compiling figures at the 60 percent capacity rate, the standard cost of production per unit for this month should be as shown in Illustration 14–19.

The combined cost of production report comparing budgeted with actual figures will probably be quite voluminous. It therefore becomes necessary to subdivide it into separate sections for materials, labor, and manufacturing overhead, and subsequently to consolidate these into a single summary report. These variations, it should be noted, are the same as those that will be presented in the discussion under standard costs, and therefore they can be recorded on the books as operating data. The consolidated report for the end of any month would appear as shown in Illustrations 14–3 and 14–4 on pages 448 and 449.

QUESTIONS FOR REVIEW

1. Is the concept of the budget compatible with the principle of *management by exception?* Explain.

2. What kinds of variances from the budget are determinable? Whom would you hold responsible for these variances?

3. What are the limitations of budgets? Why do you think the advantages outweigh the disadvantages?

4. Distinguish between *theoretical capacity, normal capacity,* and *practical capacity.* How do these terms affect the preparation of budgets?

5. When is a capital budget necessary in business? Describe each of the following methods and the advantages of each, if any, of using the following methods of determining the desirability of capital expenditures:
    a) The payback method.
    b) The simple rate of return.
    c) The time adjusted rate of return.

6. Distinguish between the two methods of cash budgeting. Which do you prefer? Why?

7. A good manufacturing budget separates the semivariable and semifixed overhead into their fixed and variable elements. What methods are used to accomplish this separation? What assumptions are made when you separate the overhead costs into their fixed and variable amounts?

8. How often should the actual and budgeted figures be compared? Explain.

9. How can a capital budget be used as a cost control device? What alternative does a firm have to capital budgeting?

10. Why is a flexible budget more desirable than a fixed budget for most manufacturing concerns?

PROBLEMS—GROUP A

Problem 14–1.   Purpose: *Analysis of Budgeted and Actual Costs*

The Martin Manufacturing Company presented the following budgeted and actual figures of the operating results for the three months ending March 31, 19—:

> *Budgeted data:*
> Sales, 420,000 units at $6 each.
> Budgeted production:
> 400,000 units for which the following costs were budgeted:
> 200,000 pounds of material at a cost of 35 cents.
> 300,000 direct labor hours at $2.50 per hour.
> $100,000 fixed manufacturing overhead.
> $50,000 variable manufacturing overhead.
> *Actual operating results:*
> Sales, 400,000 units at a cost of $6.10 each.
> Production costs:
> 420,000 units, using the following costs:
> 220,000 pounds of material at a cost of 32 cents.
> 290,000 direct labor hours at $2.60 per hour.
> $185,000 total of manufacturing overhead.

Required:

a)   Prepare an income statement and a schedule indicating the variations between the budgeted and actual figures.

b)   What managerial action, if any, do you think should be taken as a result of this comparison?

Problem 14–2.   Purpose: *Comparative Statements of Budgeted and Actual Operating Results; Variation Analyses*

The Moriches Manufacturing Company manufactures a single product known as *Morfax*. The budgeted costs for producing one unit of *Morfax* are as follows:

Material costs:		
10 pounds of *Orion* at $2.00	$20.00	
8 gallons of *Querian* at $3.00	24.00	$ 44.00
Labor costs:		
Department 1: 10 hours at $3.00	$30.00	
Department 2: 12 hours at $2.50	30.00	60.00
Manufacturing overhead:		
Department 1: fixed, 10 hours at $1.00	$10.00	
Department 1: variable, 10 hours at $1.20	12.00	
Department 2: fixed, 12 hours at $1.00	12.00	
Department 2: variable, 12 hours at $1.20	14.40	48.40
Total Cost to Make, Budgeted at		$152.40

The budgeted production for the quarter was 12,000 units.
Actual production was 10,000 units.
There were no work-in-process or finished goods inventories at the beginning of this period.

The budgeted and actual operating results were:

	Budgeted	Actual
Materials:		
Orion, purchased 130,000 pounds $260,000		$273,000
Querian, purchased 100,000 gallons 300,000		280,000
Materials used:		
Orion...		98,000 lbs.
Querian...		88,000 gals.
Direct labor costs:		
Department 1, 100,000 hours at $3.05		$305,000
Department 2, 124,000 hours at $2.80		347,200
Manufacturing Overhead Incurred Totaled		515,200

Required:

a) Prepare a statement of the cost of goods manufactured as budgeted and at actual.
b) Prepare a statement of the variations from the budgeted figures.
c) Indicate what action if any management should take as a result of the statement of variations.

Problem 14–3.   Purpose: *Budget Preparation*

The Marshall Manufacturing Company makes two products, X and Y. X sells for $12 per unit, and Y for $25 per unit. Production of one unit of X requires two units of Material A and one unit of Material B. Production of one unit of Y requires two units of Material B and three units of Material C.

Inventories on March 1 were as follows:

	Units
Product X	20,000
Product Y	20,000
Material A...................	25,000
Material B...................	22,000
Material C...................	20,000

Budgeted sales for the month of March were:

	Units
Product X 100,000
Product Y 50,000

Budgeted inventory, March 31:

	Units
Product X	10,000
Product Y	5,000
Material A...................	18,000
Material B...................	10,000
Material C...................	15,000

The purchasing department has budgeted the cost of materials for March at the following prices:

	Per Unit
Material A	$1.20
Material B	1.80
Material C	2.40

Budgeted direct labor costs are:

	Per Unit
For making Product X	$3.00
For making Product Y	3.50

Manufacturing overhead is estimated at 100 percent of direct labor costs. Selling and administrative expenses are budgeted at 20 percent of the sales.

Required:

a) Compute the quantity of material that will have to be purchased if the future prices will probably not increase and the final inventory on hand should be as budgeted.

b) Compute the budgeted cost of goods manufactured and sold for the month of March.

c) Prepare a proforma income statement of the budgeted figures for the month of March.

d) What is your managerial reaction to this budget?

Problem 14–4. Purpose: *Budgeting Capital Expenditures*

The Norma Manufacturing Company has in its plant two boring machines which have a combined book value (original cost less accumulated depreciation to date) of $11,000. The sound value is $8,500; and the remaining useful life, five years. At the present time the machines could probably be sold for a total of $1,000, but scrap value five years from now would be negligible. Each of these machines requires one operator, who is paid $3 per hour, 40 hours per week, 50 weeks per year, and can produce 60 units per hour (i.e., 2 × 60 = 120 units of production per hour for both machines). This firm is considering the purchase of a new type of boring machine to replace the two presently in use. This machine would cost $50,000 and have an estimated useful life of 10 years, with almost no residual value at the end of the 10 years. The "practical" capacity of this machine is three times as great as each of the present boring machines, i.e., 180 units would require but one operator who would be paid $4 per hour.

The production forecast for the next 10 years indicates that 252,000 work units will be required each year.

Required:

Assuming an income tax rate of 50 percent, show by various computations whether or not this firm should make this capital investment. (This firm would need to continue depreciation for unrecovered cost of old machines.)

Problem 14–5.   Purpose: *Cash Budgeting (CPA Problem)*

The Naramore Corporation ends its fiscal year on December 31. You have been requested early in January, 1973, to assist in making a cash budget or forecast. The following information is available from the company's records and interviews:

1. Management feels that the sales pattern for 1972 is a reasonable basis for budgeting the sales for 1973. Sales for 1972 were as follows:

January ....$	360,000
February	420,000
March	600,000
April.......................	540,000
May........................	480,000
June........................	400,000
July	350,000
August	550,000
September..................	500,000
October....................	400,000
November..................	600,000
December..................	800,000
Total...............$	6,000,000

2. The accounts receivable, December 31, 1972, totaled $380,000. Sales collections are generally made as follows:

During month of sale............................	60%
In first subsequent month......................	30
In second subsequent month..................	9
Uncollectible	1

3. Cost of goods purchased averages 60 percent of the selling price. The cost of the inventory on hand December 31, 1972, is $840,000, of which $30,000 is obsolete. Arrangements have been made to sell the obsolete inventory in January at half its normal selling price on a c.o.d. basis.

    The company wishes to maintain the inventory as of the first of each month at a level of three months' sales as determined by the sales forecast for the next three months. All purchases are paid for on the 10th of the following month. Accounts payable December 31, 1972, were $370,000.

4. Recurring fixed expenses amount to $120,000 *per month,* of which $20,000 is for depreciation. For accounting purposes the company apportions the recurring fixed expenses to the various months in the same proportion as the month's estimated sales bears to the total estimated annual sales. Variable expenses amount to 10 percent of the sales. Payment for expenses are made as follows:

	During Month Incurred	*Following Month*
Fixed expenses........................55 percent		45 percent
Variable expenses....................70		30

5. Annual property taxes amount to $50,000 and are paid in two equal installments on December 31 and March 31. These taxes are in addition to the expenses in item 4.
6. It is anticipated that a cash dividend of $20,000 will be paid on the 15th day of the third month in each quarter.
7. In addition to the expenses indicated in 4 above, unusual advertising expenses will require cash payments in February of $10,000 and in March of $15,000.
8. Equipment replacements are made at the rate of $3,000 per month. The equipment has an average estimated life of six years.
9. The company's income tax for 1972 is $230,000. Balance due on 1972 tax must be paid by March 15, 1973. The estimated income tax payments made by the firm for 1972 were $210,000. For 1973, the estimated income tax will total $220,000. Required quarterly payments for 1973 are computed as follows: total estimated tax liability for 1973 less special temporary exemption of $4,400 [$220,000 − (80 percent of $5,500)] ÷ 4. Such quarterly corporate estimated tax payments are due for a calendar year corporation on the 15th day of the third month of each calendar quarter, except that the first quarter estimated tax payment is due on April 15th. The Naramore Corporation elected to make such deposit of payment on March 15, before the due date, as allowed by law.
10. At December 31, 1972, the company had a bank loan with an unpaid balance of $280,000. The loan requires a principal payment of $20,000 on the last day of each month, plus interest at ½ percent per month on the unpaid balance at the first of the month. The entire balance is due March 31, 1973.
11. The cash balance December 31, 1972, is $100,000.

Required:

Prepare a cash forecast statement by months for the first three months of 1973 for the Naramore Corporation. All computations and supporting schedules should be presented in good form. The statement should show the amount of cash on hand (or deficiency of cash) at the end of each month.

(Adapted from AICPA Uniform Examination)

PROBLEMS—GROUP B

Problem 14–6.   Purpose: *Comparative Statements of the Budgeted and Actual Data for a Manufacturing Concern*

The budgeted and actual operating data for the Norbert Manufacturing Company for the year ending December 31, 19—, were as follows:

	Budgeted	Actual
Sales.................................	32,000 units @ $120	36,000 units @ $130
Purchases:		
Material X.......................	64,000 lbs. @ $3.30	50,000 lbs. @ $3.50
Material Y	40,000 lbs. @ $6.00	50,000 lbs. @ $5.80
Used in production:		
Material X.......................	72,000 lbs.	75,000 lbs.
Material Y	48,000 lbs.	54,000 lbs.
Labor costs.........................$256,000		$306,000
Manufacturing overhead........$172,000		$200,000
Production.......................... 25,000 units		30,000 units
Selling expenses...................$224,000		$259,200
Administrative expenses........$160,000		$198,000
Interest on bank loans...........$ 16,000		$ 14,800
Inventories, January 1, 19—:		
Material X.......................		40,000 lbs. @ $3.30
Material Y		30,000 lbs. @ $6.00
Work-in-process...............		0
Finished goods		15,000 units at $40

Required:

On the basis of this information, you are asked to —

a) Prepare a schedule of budgeted and actual inventories, December 31, on the Fifo basis.

b) Prepare a comparative income statement at budgeted and actual on a *per unit* basis.

c) Prepare a comparative income statement at budgeted and actual on a *total sales* basis.

(Adapted from AICPA Uniform Examination)

Problem 14–7. Purpose: *Cost Analysis in Capital Budgeting Decision Making*

The Northeastern Computer Service Company renders a computer service to its various clients. Because of the rapid growth of its service income, it feels that it must obtain an additional computer on January 1, 1973. The feasibility study of the best method of obtaining this equipment provided the following information:

1. The purchase price of the new computer is $230,000. Maintenance, property taxes, and insurance will be $20,000 per year. If the computer is rented instead of purchased, the annual rent will be $85,000 plus 5 percent of annual billings. The rental price includes maintenance.
2. Due to technical improvements and newer models, the company feels that it will be necessary to replace this computer, if purchased, at the end of three years with a larger, more advanced model. It is felt that in 1976, the resale value of this computer will be $110,000. Meanwhile, the computer will be depreciated on a straight-line basis both for financial reporting and income tax purposes. The income tax rate is assumed to be 50 percent.

3. In addition to the expenses mentioned above, the following income and operating expenses will be incurred during the three years:

	1973	1974	1975
Start-up expenses ....$	10,000	0	0
Operating expenses.........................	80,000	$ 80,000	$ 80,000
Estimated income – billings..............	220,000	260,000	260,000

4. If the computer is purchased, the firm expects to pay cash for it. If the computer is rented, it is expected that the firm can invest the cost of $230,000 at a 15 percent rate of return.

5. If the computer is purchased, the amount of the investment recovered during each of the three years can be reinvested immediately at a 15 percent rate of return. Each year's recovery of investment in the computer will have been reinvested for an average of six months by the end of the year.

6. The present value of $1 due at a constant rate during each year and discounted at 15 percent is:

Year	Present Value
0–1....................	$0.93
1–2....................	0.80
2–3....................	0.69

The present value of $1 due at the end of the year and discounted at 15% is:

End of Year	Present Value
1	$0.87
2	0.76
3	0.66

Required:

a) Prepare a schedule comparing the estimated annual income from the new computer under the purchase plan versus the rental plan. The comparison should include a provision for the opportunity cost of the average investment in the computer during each year.

b) Prepare a schedule showing the annual cash flows under the purchase plan and also under the rental plan.

c) Prepare a schedule comparing the net present values of the cash flows under the purchase plan and also the rental plan.

d) Comment on the results obtained in (a) and (c). How should the computer be financed? Why?

(Adapted from AICPA Uniform Examination)

Problem 14–8.   Purpose: *Budgetary Procedure for a Manufacturing Concern*

The Neumann Electrical Company manufactures a single product. The following information relates to the operations for the three months ending June 30,

19—. All inventories are costed on the Fifo basis. There was no work-in-process inventory, April 1, 19—.

The budget for the firm was based upon the following costs for each unit of manufacture:

Material costs:
  10 pounds of *Queron* at $2.00....................$20.00
  8 gallons of *Syphot* at $2.60..................... 20.80 $ 40.80
Direct labor:
  Department 1: 8 hours at $3.00..................$24.00
  Department 2: 6 hours at $3.50.................. 21.00   45.00
Manufacturing overhead:
  14 hours at $2.50....................................   35.00
       Total $120.80

	Budget	Actual
Materials:		
Queron:		
Inventory, April 1, 19— $24,000		$24,000
Price per pound............................ $2.00		$2.00
Inventory, June 30, 19— $21,000		$27,000
Price of current purchases............... $2.10		$2.25
Syphot:		
Inventory, April 1, 19— $13,000		$13,000
Price per gallon............................. $2.60		$2.60
Inventory, June 30, 19— $19,200		$25,000
Price of current purchases............... $2.40		$2.50
Production Statistics:		
Finished units, April 1, 19—	2,000 units	2,000 units
Sold	15,000	18,000
Inventory, June 30, 19—	1,000	3,000

Supplemental Information:

1. The actual material used was 10% more than budgeted.
2. Direct labor costs were:
     Department 1, 159,600 hours at $3.00.
     Department 2, 102,600 hours at $3.40.
3. Actual manufacturing overhead costs were $419,520.

Required:

Prepare a comparative statement of the cost of sales at actual and at budget.

Problem 14–9. Purpose: *Separation of the Semivariable Overhead Costs into Their Fixed and Variable Elements*

The following data represents the volume of production and the cost of the semivariable overhead of the Newhouse Manufacturing Company:

Month	Volume of Production	Overhead Costs
January 20,000		$28,500
February 17,200		26,550
March.........................18,200		26,400
April..........................15,000		30,000
May............................14,200		21,600
June...........................12,000		21,000
July 12,600		21,700
August 12,800		21,600
September 13,600		22,100
October......................16,000		23,600
November 19,200		28,000
December...................20,700		29,300

Required:

From the above data you are asked to compute the fixed and variable amounts using the following methods:

a) The average of the three highest and the three lowest volumes as the basic fixed figure.

b) The high-low method of determining the fixed and variable costs for each month.

c) In addition to the above requirements, prepare a budget of fixed and variable for the coming year based upon:

	Estimated Volume
January 18,000	
February 22,000	
March 30,000	

Problem 14–10.   Purpose: *Analysis of Manufacturing Overhead Variation Causes*

The Nurgent Company is engaged in the production of heavy equipment. The firm has applied manufacturing overhead to its product on the basis of an average rate of 115% of direct labor costs. This rate at the time it was established was based on the following information as to its expected operations:

Direct labor hours		150,000 hrs.
Direct labor costs..		$450,000
Average labor costs per hour..........................		$3.00
Fixed overhead...	$ 90,000	
Variable overhead	427,500	$517,500

On December 31, 19 —, the end of the accounting period, the records disclosed the following information:

Direct labor hours		140,000 hrs.
Direct labor costs		$392,000
Average labor cost per hour		$2.80
Fixed overhead	$100,000	
Variable overhead	392,200	
Total Actual Overhead Costs		$492,200
Applied manufacturing overhead		450,800
Underapplied manufacturing overhead		41,400

The management is concerned with the fact that it failed to absorb overhead to the extent of $41,400.

Required:

a) Prepare an explanation of why the $41,400 underapplied manufacturing overhead existed. You are to compute and show the effect of the direct labor rates and the direct labor hours on the absorption of both the fixed and the variable overhead. (Computations should be correct to the nearest dollar.)

b) Criticize the current system being used to absorb the overhead.

(Adapted from AICPA Uniform Examination)

chapter **15**

Managerial Control
through Estimated
Cost Accounting

NATURE OF COST ESTIMATES

Some firms have simplified their cost work and records through the use of an *estimated cost system.* It is a form of *predetermined costs* used by firms who must calculate their costs in estimated form in advance of the actual manufacture of the goods or the completion of a special construction contract for the purpose of subsequent comparison with actual costs. The estimated cost figures actually appear in the Work-in-Process, Finished Goods, and Cost of Goods Sold accounts, though they must later be adjusted to the actual cost figures. Manufacturers of clothing, shoes, and furniture, among others, may use estimated costs. Contractors engaged in construction and engineering work also use a modified form of estimated costs.

Cost estimates are sometimes known as *formula costs,* especially in firms engaged in the manufacture of chemicals, patent medicines, or candy.

Cost estimates are also known as *predetermined costs,* since the cost of each element of cost — materials, labor, and manufacturing overhead — is estimated and computed before the manufacturing operations are started. Such an interpretation has led many cost accountants to believe that estimated costs are merely a type of standard costs. However, the difference between standard and estimated costs will be indicated later in the chapter.

There are two basic reasons for having estimated costs:

1. The nature of the manufacturing and selling operations requires the determination of selling prices sometime in advance of the actual

manufacturing. Orders for men's suits and for shoes, for example, are taken months in advance of actual production and shipment. To fix the selling prices, estimates of cost must be prepared.

2. The use of an estimated cost accounting system reduces the expense of the clerical work of cost keeping because most requisitions and job time tickets are eliminated. It is true that the cost figures obtained under an estimated cost system are not so accurate nor so reliable as those obtained under the historical job order cost method. Estimated costs represent a practical method adapted to peculiar business conditions, i.e., advance sale of goods not yet manufactured.

The disadvantage of a slight inaccuracy in costs may be greatly outweighed by the advantage of a much smaller clerical expense in cost keeping.

MANAGERIAL IMPLICATIONS OF ESTIMATED COSTS

Two managerial aspects of estimated costs should be discussed before proceeding with the accounting treatment of estimated costs. These are (1) budgetary aspects of estimated costs, including PERT; and (2) engineering aspects of estimated costs.

Cost estimating especially in the large manufacturing plants must be performed by carefully trained personnel. They must be familiar with the product engineering and design, manufacturing operations, and possess a knowledge of methods of cost allocations especially of the *fixed and variable* manufacturing overhead. Cost estimating is a form of forecasting under certain given conditions, and as such is closely akin to budgeting. Cost estimating procedures require a comparison of the estimates with the actual costs and a study of the differences. In this respect, it parallels budgeting when budgeted figures are compared with the actual figures. In recent years, a newer production and cost accounting procedure known as PERT (program evaluation and review technique) for planning, scheduling, and controlling complex manufacturing or construction projects has been developed. This also is an important phase of estimating costs and is closely related to budgeting.

The factors involved in cost estimates emphasize the engineering background that an estimator should possess. For example, for reliable estimates to be developed, he should have complete drawings and specifications of the product to be manufactured, the approximate volume of production, and a budget of the material, labor, and overhead costs. These must be supplemented by a knowledge of the manufacturing operations. Use will be made of previous estimates and previous actual cost records. When these characteristics have been accepted, a definite organization for estimating should be set up. Usually a centralized department organized under the supervision of the general manager has proven most effective.

DETERMINATION OF COST ESTIMATES

Cost estimates are usually broken down into estimates of the elements of cost, viz: materials, labor, fixed charges, and apportioned charges. These estimates may be secured from records of past experience, from computations, from mathematical or chemical formulas, or simply from approximations. They must be computed for each different product. If there are many different products, the use of an estimating cost procedure becomes as expensive as a more complete system, with results that may be less accurate.

Estimates are prepared at the beginning of the manufacturing season; at the beginning of a fiscal period; or in the case of construction work, such as shipbuilding and tunnels, bridge, or building construction, when the contract is accepted.

The most common method of preparing estimates is by the *elements of cost*, viz:

ESTIMATED COST PER UNIT OF
MANUFACTURING
MEN'S FINE SUITS—STYLE J-47

Materials	$13.25
Supplies (linings, buttons, etc.)	3.75
Labor	10.00
Factory overhead (50% of labor cost)	5.00
Total	$32.00

Whether or not this detail is necessary will depend upon the method or possibility of verifying *actual* figures with the *estimates*. In the case above, it is presumed that verification by the elements of cost will be possible and desirable.

Sometimes verification of actual with estimated costs will be on the basis of *elements of cost* figured departmentally and sometimes by *total costs*.

The figures given above are again presented to illustrate the estimates based upon the elements of costs, but this time they are analyzed on a departmental basis:

ESTIMATED COST PER UNIT OF MANUFACTURING
MEN'S FINE SUITS—STYLE J-47

	Cutting Department	Tailoring Department	Total
Materials used	$13.25	—	$13.25
Supplies (linings, buttons, etc.)	—	$ 3.75	3.75
Labor	3.00	7.00	10.00
Factory overhead (50% of labor)	1.50	3.50	5.00
Total	$17.75	$14.25	$32.00

Illustration 15—1

DETROIT MACOID CORPORATION
COST ESTIMATE SHEET FOR PLASTICS

Acme Motor Car Co.

Address: Detroit   Date: April 30,

Name of Part: Knob   Part No. S-4930

Description	Quan-tity	Unit Cost	Total Cost	Cost per C Pcs.
Material Cost				
Material Delivered	79.00	70	55.30	
Credits: Sprue 15.5%	12.25	45	5.51	
Scrap 0.3%	0.25	45	0.11	
Burn 11.4%	9.00	0	0	
Total Credits	21.5	26	5.62	
Net Material Cost	57.5	.864	49.68	.998
Production				
Gross 100.0%	5,006			
Scrap 0.5%	27			
Burn %	0			
Total Scrap 0.5%	27			
Net Prod. Pieces 99.5%	4,979			

Description	Hours	Rate	Total Cost	Cost Per C Pcs.
Labor and Burden Cost				
Molding Labor	17	4.00	68.00	1.366
Finishing Labor			70.00	1.406
Finishing Burdens 75%			52.50	1.054
Total Operating Cost			190.50	3.826
Summary:				

Statistics:		Total Cost	Cost Per C Pcs.
	Material Cost	49.68	0.998
Number in Mold 2	Operation Cost	190.50	3.826
Mach. Prod. per Hr. 290	Cost of Inserts	10.01	0.20
Wgt. of 1 Piece 5 Grams			
Wgt. of C Pieces 500 Grams	Total Cost Without Molds	250.19	5.025
Material No. AW1702 M.S.	Sales & Adm. @ 30%	72.05	1.447
Estimator	Mold Cost @ 10,000 Pcs.		5.000
Est. Mold Cost $500.00	Mold Cost @ 50,000 Pcs.		1.000
	Mold Cost @ 100,000 Pcs.		0.500

Prices Quoted	Cost	Profit	Price	Total Cost @ 10,000 Pcs.			11.472
Without Dies	$ 6.472	0.647	7.12	Total Cost @ 50,000 Pcs.			7.472
With Dies @ 10 M.	11.472	1.294	12.766	Total Cost @ 100,000 Pcs.			6.972
With Dies @ 50 M.	7.472	0.970	8.442	Remarks: Prices and costs are	in	ter	ms o f C pie ces
With Dies @ 100 M.	6.972	0.647	7.619				

*Taken, with permission, from Robert W. Peden. "Cost Accounting in the Plastic Molding Industry." *N.A.(C.)A. Bulletin.* Vol. 20, No. 9.

If the verification of estimates is by total costs, the figure $32 is used without reference to the figures for material cost, labor cost, or overhead cost. Emphasis should again be laid on the fact that the nature of the estimates is governed by the method to be used in verifying actual costs with the estimates.

Many concerns have specially prepared forms on which the estimated figures are inserted. These forms are adapted to the products and processes of the particular business and thus simplify the estimating work. These estimated cost sheets may be used for computing the selling prices or for the purpose of recording the costs on an estimated basis. However, it is possible to have an estimated cost sheet and still use job order costs or process costs as a matter of record.

Illustration 15–1 shows a sample of an estimated cost sheet used in a plastics concern and is given as an illustration because of its completeness.

RESPONSIBILITY FOR SETTING ESTIMATED COSTS

Setting estimated costs is primarily an engineering job, supplemented by aid from the purchasing, budget, and accounting departments. Product design or improvements will be made by the engineering department aided by the sales or marketing divisions. Effective production procedures and flow of work will be estimated or established by the engineers and the factory supervisory force. Occasionally test runs may be used in the factory in which a large volume of production is anticipated. Through these test runs, the speed of production and the estimated labor costs can be established; and if necessary revisions in the flow of work through the factory can be made. Time and motion studies may be necessary also to determine estimated labor costs. By means of sales and production budgets and manufacturing overhead budgets, careful estimates can be made of the per unit overhead costs. These budgets require the cooperation of the engineering, factory supervisory, and the accounting and budget personnel. How expensive this procedure for setting the standards is will be determined by the scope of the manufacturing operations, the volume and variety of products, and thoroughness with which it is done. This cost of determining estimates must be weighed against the savings resulting from the use of an estimated cost accounting system as compared with a traditional, integrated cost accounting system.

LEARNING OR IMPROVEMENT CURVE IN COST ESTIMATING

With the event of automating machinery and the progressive assembly line, *direct labor costs* tend to decrease as the employees become more experienced. In a competitive price situation, the manufacturer must be able to estimate this change in direct labor costs. Several studies have been made of the influence of *learning with practice* on direct labor costs. In the large-scale manufacturing of television sets, it was found that —

a) The larger the group size, that is, the length of the assembly line, the more complex the learning curve, since the line cannot progress faster than the slowest worker.

b) The more complex the operations, the longer it takes to improve the volume of production.

c) The extent of change in work procedures or flow of work from previous operations will influence the relearning.

d) Wage incentives influence the speed in which to achieve maximum production.

e) Supervisory pressure and union restrictions affect the speed of the learning process and the improved production.

f) Labor turnover rate and level of operators' skill influence the learning curve. If there is a constant labor turnover, the slowdown of the newer, inexperienced workers affects the volume of production.

In an estimating cost system, the work measurement engineers set the standard production at 100 percent efficiency as the ultimate objective of the production line, as well as the initial production of the inexperienced workers. As the employees become more experienced in their tasks, the ultimate objective may be approached. However, this is restricted if there is a large labor turnover resulting in a constant retraining of new employees.

Studies seem to indicate that as the employee on an assembly line or at a production area becomes more experienced, the time required for a task may be reduced 15 percent to 40 percent with the most common reduction about 20 percent. The learning curve is based on the principle that as the cumulative quantities double, the average time per unit should decrease 20 percent as illustrated:

| | | Time in Minutes | | |
Production in Units	Cumulative Production	Cumulative	Percent Improvement of Previous Production	Time per Unit (Minutes)
10	10	600	0	60
20	30	1,440	80*	48
40	70	2,688	80	38.4
80	150	4,608	80	30.72
160	310	7,619	80	24.58
320	630	12,512	80	19.86

*Twenty percent improvement in production time.

The graph in Illustration 15–2 shows the effect of these changes in production and time.

It should be noted that the relationship between the assembly labor hours and the machine-hours generally determines the percentage decline in unit costs—the higher the ratio of assembly labor to total cost, the greater the decline in unit costs.

The learning curves are used as the basis for setting prices in such large-scale industries as the automobile, television industries, and in

Illustration 15–2.   Learning Curve Showing 20% Time Reduction

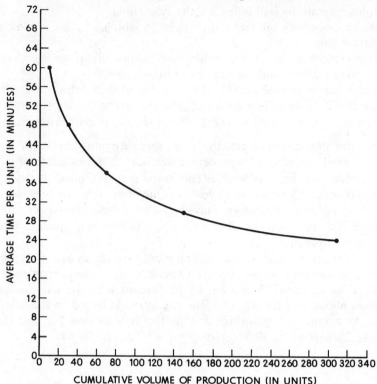

CUMULATIVE VOLUME OF PRODUCTION (IN UNITS)

subcontracting at fair prices in the aerospace industries. It also is an important consideration in budgeting labor costs for the factory.

ACCOUNTING PROCEDURES FOR ESTIMATED COSTS

The estimated cost procedures discussed here are those which are used as the basis of the journal entries with a minimum of clerical expense. They may be summarized briefly as—

1. Charge the *work-in-process* for the *actual* costs of materials, labor, and manufacturing overhead incurred.
2. Charge the *finished goods* and cost of *sales accounts* for the *estimated* cost of the goods completed or sold, crediting either the *work-in-process* or *finished goods* accounts accordingly.
3. Take a physical inventory of the work-in-process at *estimated costs.* Find the difference between this figure and the amounts in the work-in-process accounts and transfer the differences to the *Adjustment account.* (These differences represent the errors due to incorrect estimates.)

4. Prorate the amount of the adjustments to the work-in-process, finished goods, and cost of goods sold, usually on the basis of units.

Applying these four rules of procedure to the specific elements of costs, the following discussion is given:

1. Materials Accounting. Purchases of materials are recorded in the voucher register by debiting the Stores account and crediting Accounts Payable. Where practical, a perpetual or book inventory of stores should be maintained. When the foregoing debit to Stores is posted at the end of the fiscal period—whether it be a month, six months, or a year—the Stores account will contain on the debit side the *inventory of materials at the beginning of the period and the purchases for the period.*

Thereafter, materials will be issued to the factory upon properly authorized requisitions specifying the quantities only, not the prices. These requisitions are not recorded unless a perpetual inventory is kept. At the end of a month, six months, or a yearly period, a physical inventory is taken of the direct materials on hand. The difference between the inventory of materials at the beginning of the period plus the purchases during the period and the inventory of the materials at the end of the period represents the cost of the materials used. This figure is used for the following entry:

```
Work-in-Process—Materials.....................................................xxxx
    Stores...............................................................                 xxxx
```

The value stated in this entry is presumed to be *actual cost of the materials used.*

2. Labor Accounting. The *actual cost* of the factory labor, both direct and indirect, is transferred to the Work-in-Process—Labor account at the end of the fiscal accounting period.

3. Manufacturing Overhead Cost Accounting. This follows the same procedure as that for the labor accounting, namely, the transfer of the *actual overhead costs* to the work-in-process account at the end of the period.

4. Finished Goods Accounting. This is recorded at the end of the fiscal period by debiting the Finished Goods account and crediting the work-in-process accounts for the *estimated cost* of the goods completed, viz:

```
Finished Goods.........................................................................xxxx
    Work-in-Process—Materials...............................................     xxxx
    Work-in-Process—Labor ....................................................     xxxx
    Work-in-Process—Manufacturing Overhead...........................     xxxx
```

When this entry is posted, the Finished Goods account will represent the *estimated cost value* of the finished work but the work-in-process accounts will have debit figures on an *actual* cost basis and credit figures on an *estimated* cost basis.

5. *Cost of Sales Accounting.* Since the Finished Goods account has debit figures at the estimated costs, the transfers to the Cost of Sales account must of necessity be at the estimated costs, the entry being:

```
Cost of Sales (estimated cost)...................................................xxxx
        Finished Goods (estimated cost) .........................................     xxxx
```

At this stage of the accounting work, the estimated and actual costs of the accounting entries would be as follows:

Work-in-Process

Materials used *at actual*	xxxx	Finished goods *at estimated*	xxxx
Payroll costs *at actual*	xxxx		
Overhead costs *at actual*	xxxx		

Finished Goods

From work-in-process *at estimated*	xxxx	Cost of sales *at estimated*	xxxx

Cost of Sales

From finished goods *at estimated*	xxxx

Since the Work-in-Process account is the only account of the three above in which the debit (at actual) and the credit (at estimated costs) are not on the same cost basis, some adjustment of this conflict is necessary so that the Work-in-Process account will be on a comparable basis with the Finished Goods and Cost of Sales accounts in which both the debit and credit are at estimated costs.

6. *Determining the Variation from Estimates.* To adjust the conflict of bases indicated in the work-in-process accounts, a physical inventory is taken of the work-in-process priced at the *estimated cost value* for the *proportion of work done*. This physical inventory uses the *equivalent production* method described in chapters on process costs. For example, if the estimated cost of manufacturing a suit of clothes is:

```
            Materials and supplies..............................$17
            Labor.................................................... 10
            Factory overhead (50% of labor).................  5
                                                              $32
```

and the physical inventory of work-in-process showed 200 suits on which all the necessary material but only one fourth of the labor and overhead had been added, then the value of the inventory at estimated costs for the proportion of work done is calculated thus:

200 suits at $17 (material)...$3,400
200 suits at $\frac{1}{4}$ of $10 (labor).. 500
200 suits at $\frac{1}{4}$ of $5 (for overhead)..   250
    Inventory of Work-in-Process for Proportion of Work Done............$4,150

The difference between this physical inventory of work-in-process priced at *estimated costs* and the inventory of work-in-process as recorded in the work-in-process accounts represents the *variation due to incorrect estimate*. This error may be adjusted in several ways:

a) The error may be spread over the *cost* of the effective production for the period, i.e., over the work-in-process, finished goods, and cost of sales priced at *estimated cost value*. This method has the effect of correcting the estimates and adjusting the inventories which will appear on the balance sheet and are used in determining the cost of goods sold on the income statement. When this adjustment has been made, the work-in-process inventory, the finished goods inventory, and the cost of sales will then be stated at the amounts that would have been secured if the original estimates had been correct and therefore had coincided with the actual costs.

b) The error may be spread over the cost of the work-in-process, finished goods, and cost of goods sold on the basis of the *number* of completed units or equivalent units. This method has the same effect as the first, but the error is corrected on the basis of *quantities* rather than *costs*.

To summarize the accounting procedure of an estimated cost system: (1) charge the Work-in-Process account with the *actual* cost of materials, labor, and overhead used in production; (2) charge the Finished Goods account, crediting the Work-in-Process account, for the *estimated* cost of work completed; (3) take a physical inventory of work-in-process at *estimated cost;* and (4) find the difference between the book and physical inventory of work-in-process and prorate the error over work-in-process, finished goods, and cost of goods sold on the basis of estimated cost or on the basis of equivalent production quantity of each.

ILLUSTRATIONS OF ESTIMATED COST ACCOUNTING

Since the accounting for estimated costs revolves around the method of handling the work-in-process, illustrations of estimated cost procedures must be classified on the basis of the work-in-process accounts. Accounting procedures have therefore been classified according to the following work-in-process conditions: (1) the use of a single Work-in-Process account; (2) the use of a Work-in-Process account for each element of cost —material, labor, and manufacturing overhead; (3) the use of a single

Work-in-Process account for each producing department; and (4) the use of a Work-in-Process account for each element of cost in each producing department.

To a certain extent, these methods overlap. Furthermore, the accounting work is considerably simplified if at the end of the cost accounting period no unfinished work remains in process; under such conditions, the variations from estimates can be closed out to the finished goods inventory and the cost of goods sold on the basis of the number of units manufactured and sold during the period if a single product is being manufactured. Illustrations of the accounting procedure will be given for (2) since that overlaps and practically includes (1), and for (4) which overlaps and includes (3).

THE USE OF A WORK-IN-PROCESS ACCOUNT FOR EACH ELEMENT OF COST

The estimated cost sheet for producing article B is:

ESTIMATED COSTS – ARTICLE B

Materials and supplies	$ 4
Labor	5
Manufacturing overhead	3
Total Estimated Cost	$12

From the books and records the following information was secured:

Inventory of materials and supplies, September 1	$ 1,200
Purchases of materials and supplies during September	15,800
A physical inventory of materials and supplies on September 30	600
Sales for the month	60,000
Payroll for month	16,310
Manufacturing overhead, including indirect labor	11,900

The production records for the month of September showed that 4,000 units were started into production. Of these, 3,000 were completed and 1,000 were still in process. But of the unfinished work, all the required material had been applied but only one half of the required labor and overhead. Of the units completed, 2,500 were sold at $24 each.

Entries in journal form to record the transactions for the month and the ledger accounts prepared therefrom would be as follows:

(1)

Materials and Supplies	15,800	
Accounts Payable		15,800
To record purchases for the month.		

(2)

Work-in-Process—Materials 16,400
    Materials and Supplies...   16,400
To record the actual cost of materials and supplies used. Computed as follows: inventory at beginning plus purchases, minus inventory at end, or $1,200 + $15,800 − $600 = $16,400.

(3)

Work-in-Process—Labor...16,310
    Payroll...   16,310
To close out the payroll into the work-in-process.

(4)

Work-in-Process—Manufacturing Overhead 11,900
    Manufacturing Overhead..   11,900
To close out the manufacturing overhead to the work-in-process.

(5)

Finished Goods..36,000
    Work-in-Process—Materials   12,000
    Work-in-Process—Payroll   15,000
    Work-in-Process—Manufacturing Overhead   9,000
To record the value of the finished goods computed on the basis of estimated costs, 3,000 units at a total cost of $12 each.

(6)

Cost of Sales 30,000
    Finished Goods...   30,000
Twenty-five hundred units sold at an estimated cost of $12 each, or a total value of $30,000.

(7)

Accounts Receivable...60,000
    Sales   60,000
Twenty-five hundred units sold at a selling price of $24 each, or $60,000.

It is now necessary to adjust the Work-in-Process, Finished Goods, and Cost of Goods Sold accounts for any variations between actual costs and estimated costs. Before doing so, it is advisable to post the foregoing transactions to determine the status of each of the ledger accounts. To the ledger accounts on the following pages there have been posted not only the foregoing transactions but also certain adjusting entries not yet discussed. By ignoring these adjustment entries for the moment, it is possible for the student to determine the status of each ledger account at this point in the procedure.

Materials and Supplies

Sept.	1	Inventory	1,200	Sept. 30	Used (2)	16,400
	30	Purchases (1)	15,800	30	Balance	600
			17,000			17,000
Sept.	30	Inventory	600			

Accounts Payable

| | | | Sept. 30 | Purchases (1) | 15,800 |
| | | | 30 | Payroll direct labor | 16,310 |

Work-in-Process — Materials

Sept. 30	Materials (2)	16,400	Sept. 30	Finished goods (5)	12,000
30	Adjust (9a)	100	30	Adjust (8a)	400
			30	Balance	4,100
		16,500			16,500
Sept. 30	Inventory	4,100			

Work-in-Process — Labor

Sept. 30	Payroll direct labor (3)	16,310	Sept. 30	Finished goods (5)	15,000
30	Adjust (8b)	1,190	30	Adjust (9b)	170
			30	Balance	2,330
		17,500			17,500
Sept. 30	Inventory	2,330			

Payroll

| Sept. 30 | Accounts payable | 16,310 | Sept. 30 | To close (3) | 16,310 |

Work-in-Process — Manufacturing Overhead

Sept. 30	Applied (4)	11,900	Sept. 30	Finished goods (5)	9,000
30	Adjust (9c)	200	30	Adjust (8c)	1,400
			30	Balance	1,700
		12,100			12,100
Sept. 30	Inventory	1,700			

Finished Goods

Sept. 30	Completed (5)	36,000	Sept. 30	Sold (6)	30,000
30	Adjust (9a)	50	30	Adjust (9b)	170
30	Adjust (9c)	200	30	Balance	6,080
		36,250			36,250
Sept. 30	Inventory	6,080			

Cost of Sales

Sept. 30	Finished goods (6)	30,000	Sept. 30	Adjust (9b)	850
30	Adjust (9a)	250			
30	Adjust (9c)	1,000			

Accounts Receivable

Sept. 30 Sales (7)	60,000	

Sales

	Sept. 30 Accounts receivable	60,000

The *book* inventory of work-in-process as of September 30 (before adjustment for errors in estimates) and the physical inventory priced at estimated cost are presented in Illustration 15–3.

Illustration 15–3

	Present Book Inventory as Shown in the Accounts	Computed Inventory on Estimated Cost Basis	Variation
Work-in-process — materials.................................$4,400		—	—
Work-in-process — materials (1,000 equivalent production at $4 each unit)	—	$4,000	$ 400*
Work-in-process — labor.......................................	1,310	—	—
Work-in-process — labor (1,000 units ¹/₂ completed at $5)	—	2,500	1,190†
Work-in-process — manufacturing overhead	2,900	—	—
Work-in-process — manufacturing overhead (1,000 units ¹/₂ completed at $3)	—	1,500	1,400*

*Indicates estimated costs too low.
†Indicates estimated costs too high.

In order to adjust the balances in the work-in-process accounts to an estimated cost basis, the variations shown above are transferred to an Adjustment account. The necessary entries are:

(8a)

Adjustment	400	
Work-in-Process — Materials...		400

(8b)

Work-in-Process — Labor...1,190		
Adjustment		1,190

(8c)

Adjustment 1,400		
Work-in-Process — Manufacturing Overhead		1,400

To adjust the work-in-process accounts to the estimated cost figures. Separate entries were made for each, since each figure will have to be prorated separately later.

When these entries have been posted, the work-in-process accounts will be costed on the same basis as the Finished Goods and the Cost of

Sales accounts — *the estimated cost basis.* Therefore, the adjustment amounts must be prorated over all of these accounts in order to bring them to the amounts that would be there if the estimated costs had been absolutely correct. Entries are made for each adjustment separately. Proration may be on the basis of equivalent units or cost values; in this case, the results on either basis are the same. The entries are:

(9a)

Work-in-Process — Materials	100	
Finished Goods	50	
Cost of Sales	250	
Adjustment		400

To prorate the material cost variation arising from estimates that were too low. The ratio used was work-in-process, 1,000; finished goods, 500; cost of sales, 2,500; these figures represent the number of units or equivalent production for the material cost.

(9b)

Adjustment	1,190	
Work-in-Process — Labor		170
Finished Goods		170
Cost of Sales		850

To prorate the labor cost variation arising from estimates which were too high. The ratio used was work-in-process, 500 (1,000 × $\frac{1}{2}$ complete); finished goods, 500; and cost of sales, 2,500; these figures represent the number of units or the equivalent production for the labor cost.

(9c)

Work-in-Process — Manufacturing Overhead	200	
Finished Goods	200	
Cost of Sales	1,000	
Adjustment		1,400

To prorate the manufacturing overhead cost variation arising from estimates which were too low. The ratio used was the same as that for labor.

The Adjustment account is not always used; instead, the net amount taken from or added to the work-in-process accounts is prorated directly to the Finished Goods and Cost of Sales accounts, for example:

Finished Goods (+$50 − $170 + $200)	80	
Cost of Sales (+$250 − $850 + $1,000)	400	
Work-in-Process — Labor	1,020	
Work-in-Process — Materials		300
Work-in-Process — Manufacturing Overhead		1,200

To prorate the adjustment amounts to the Finished Goods and Cost of Sales accounts directly from the work-in-process accounts.

The financial statements prepared for managerial use when estimated costs are used enables management to evaluate the results of their estimates. The statements sent to the stockholders or used for financial purposes show only the actual costs, that is, the costs after adjustment. The managerial statements prepared when estimated costs are used are shown in Illustrations 15–4 and 15–5; these are based on the amounts in the foregoing entries.

Illustration 15–4. One Form of Cost of Goods Manufactured Statement When Estimated Costs Are Used

Schedule B-1

ALTON MANUFACTURING COMPANY

SCHEDULE OF COST OF GOODS MANUFACTURED

For Month of September, 19—

Material Cost, at Estimate			$16,000.00
Labor Cost, at Estimate			17,500.00
Manufacturing Overhead Cost, at Estimate			10,500.00
Total Estimated Cost			$44,000.00
Adjustments:			
Material Cost, at Actual	$16,400.00		
Material Cost, at Estimate	16,000.00		
Underestimate		$ 400.00	
Manufacturing Overhead, at Actual	$11,900.00		
Manufacturing Overhead, at Estimate	10,500.00		
Underestimate		1,400.00	
Total Underestimate		$1,800.00	
Labor, at Actual	$16,310.00		
Labor, at Estimate	17,500.00		
Total Overestimate		1,190.00	
Net Underestimate			610.00
Actual Manufacturing Cost Put into Production			$44,610.00
Less: Inventory, Work-in-Process:			
Material Cost, at Estimate	$ 4,000.00		
Labor Cost, at Estimate	2,500.00		
Manufacturing Overhead, at Estimate	1,500.00		
Total at Estimate	$ 8,000.00		
Add: Adjustment for Underestimate:			
Material	$100.00		
Labor	170.00*		
Manufacturing Overhead	200.00	130.00	
Adjusted Work-in-Process Inventory			8,130.00
Actual Cost of Goods Manufactured to Exhibit B, Income Statement			$36,480.00

* Overestimated figures.

Illustration 15–5.   A Second Form of Cost of Goods Manufactured Statement When Estimated Costs Are Used

Schedule B-1

ALTON MANUFACTURING COMPANY

SCHEDULE OF COST OF GOODS MANUFACTURED
For Month of September, 19—

	Estimated Cost	Adjustment Cost	Actual Cost
Material Costs.........................	$16,000.00	$ 400.00	$16,400.00
Labor Costs............................	17,500.00	1,190.00*	16,310.00
Manufacturing Overhead Costs............	10,500.00	1,400.00	11,900.00
Total..............................	$44,000.00	$ 610.00	
Total Actual Manufacturing Cost.......................................			$44,610.00
Less: Inventory of Work-in-Process:			
Material Costs.........................	$ 4,000.00	$ 100.00	
Labor Costs...........................	2,500.00	170.00*	
Manufacturing Overhead Costs..........	1,500.00	200.00	
Total..............................	$ 8,000.00	$ 130.00	8,130.00
Actual Cost of Goods Manufactured......................................			$36,480.00

* Overestimated figures.

Exhibit B

ALTON MANUFACTURING COMPANY

INCOME STATEMENT
For Month of September, 19—

Sales..			$60,000.00
Cost of Sales:			
Cost of Goods Manufactured per Schedule B-1................		$36,480.00	
Less: Inventory of Finished Goods:			
At estimate...............................		$6,000.00	
Add: Adjustments:			
Material...........................$ 50.00			
Labor............................. 170.00*			
Manufacturing Overhead............. 200.00			
Net Underestimate..................———	80.00		
		6,080.00	
Cost of Sales, at actual (adjusted)......................................			30,400.00
Gross Profit on Sales...			$29,600.00†

* Overestimate.
† From this figure must be subtracted the selling and administrative expenses.

ESTIMATED COSTS WHERE THE WORK-IN-PROCESS IS KEPT BY ELEMENTS OF COSTS AND BY DEPARTMENTS

A more complicated cost accounting situation arises where the manufacturing operations go through several departments and where the work-in-process accounts are maintained by elements of cost for each department. To illustrate the procedure, the following information, entries, and ledger accounts are used.

The estimated cost card for manufacturing a certain article is represented in Illustration 15–6.

Illustration 15–6

	Dept. A	Dept. B	Total by Elements
Estimated Cost Card No. 8 Product X-Y Style: Large		Date of Estimate 9/1/—	
Materials and Supplies:			
5 yds. of material @ $0.60	$ 3.00		
Supplies	0.60		$ 3.60
Labor:			
2 hours @ $1.50	3.00		
1½ hours @ $1.20	1.80		
3 hours @ $1.60		$4.80	9.60
Manufacturing Overhead:			
3½ hours @ $0.80	2.80		
50% of $4.80		2.40	5.20
Total Estimated Cost	$11.20	$7.20	$18.40

From the books of record the following data have been ascertained:

Inventory of materials and supplies at beginning of month	$ 1,300
Purchases of materials and supplies during month	13,260
Materials and supplies on hand at the end of the month (determined by physical inventory)	2,500
Sales for the month	50,000

Departmental Charges for the Month	Dept. A	Dept. B	Total
Direct labor payroll*	$13,300	$13,500	$26,800
Indirect labor payroll*	210	230	440
Fixed charges	4,026	3,000	7,026
Apportioned manufacturing overhead costs	4,820	3,200	8,020

*In this illustration, factory payroll is separated into direct and indirect labor, the latter being part of overhead.

Illustration 15–7 shows the production record for the month.

Illustration 15–7

	Dept. A	Dept. B	Total
Number of units in process at the beginning of the month — all materials and supplies have been issued against them, but labor and overhead averaged 60 percent completion...	100	200	
Number of units completed during month including those in process at the beginning.....................................	3,000	3,100	
Units in process at the end of month on which all the material had been issued, but labor and overhead averaged 40 percent completion...	200	100	
Number of units sold			2,500

SOLUTION

The value of the initial inventory of the work-in-process is analyzed and computed as shown in Illustration 15–8.

Illustration 15–8

	Dept. A	Dept. B Transfer Account	Dept. B
Materials and supplies:			
100 units at $3.60..	$360		
200 units at $3.60 (Department A costs)..................		$ 720	
Labor:			
100 units × 60 percent × $4.80..........................	288		
200 units × 100 percent × $4.80 (Department A costs)...		960	
200 units × 60 percent × $4.80..............................			$576
Factory overhead:			
100 units × 60 percent × $2.80..............................	168		
200 units × 100 percent × $2.80 (Department A costs)...		560	
200 units × 60 percent × $2.40..............................			288
Total Initial Work-in-Process Inventories..............	$816	$2,240	$864

The journal entries necessary to record some of the transactions for the month to illustrate the procedures of estimated cost are:

(1)

Purchases — Materials and Supplies..	13,260	
Accounts Payable..		13,260
To record the purchases of materials and supplies for the month.		

(2)

Work-in-Process—Materials, Department A.............................12,060
   Materials and Supplies...   12,060
To record the actual cost of the materials and supplies used,
computed as follows: inventory at beginning plus purchases,
minus inventory at end, or $1,300 + $13,260 − $2,500 = $12,060.

(3)

Work-in-Process—Labor, Department A 13,300
Work-in-Process—Manufacturing Overhead, Department A.........   210
   Payroll Accrued   13,510
To record actual amounts expended for payroll in Department A,
for both direct and indirect labor.

(4)

Work-in-Process—Manufacturing Overhead, Department A......... 8,846
   Manufacturing Overhead...   8,846
To record the actual fixed and apportioned manufacturing over-
head incurred during the month.

(5)

Work-in-Process—Transfer, Department B[1] 33,600
   Work-in-Process—Materials, Department A........................   10,800
   Work-in-Process—Labor, Department A   14,400
   Work-in-Process—Manufacturing Overhead, Department A...   8,400
By the use of the Work-in-Process—Transfer account, to record
the cost of the goods transferred to Department B, computed
on the basis of 3,000 units which were transferred to Department
B from Department A:
   Materials............................3,000 @ $3.60 = $10,800
   Labor ....3,000 @ 4.80 = 14,400
   Manufacturing overhead.........3,000 @ 2.80 =   8,400

(6)

Work-in-Process—Labor, Department B...................................13,500
Work-in-Process—Manufacturing Overhead, Department B.........   230
   Payroll Accrued   13,730
To record actual amounts expended for payroll during month in
Department B, both direct and indirect labor.

(7)

Work-in-Process—Manufacturing Overhead, Department B......... 6,200
   Manufacturing Overhead...   6,200
To record the actual fixed and apportioned manufacturing over-
head incurred during the month in Department B.

(8)

Finished Goods...57,040
   Work-in-Process—Transfer, Department B   34,720
   Work-in-Process—Labor, Department B............................   14,880
   Work-in-Process—Manufacturing Overhead, Department B...   7,440
To record the value of the finished goods transferred from
Department B. 3,100 units at a cost as follows: Department A at
$11.20; labor, Department B, $4.80; and manufacturing over-
head, Department B, $2.40.

---

[1] When a *Work-in-Process—Transfer account* is used, this account is considered as
the Finished Goods account when related to the work done in Department A and as the
Work-in-Process—Materials account when related to the work done in Department B.

(9)

Costs of Sales 46,000
    Finished Goods   46,000
    To record the sale of 2,500 units at an estimated cost of $18.40
each, or total, $46,000.

(10)

Accounts Receivable 50,000
    Sales   50,000
    To record the selling price of the goods sold during the month.

The final inventory of work-in-process in analyzed form, priced at *estimated cost* per unit, is calculated as shown in Illustration 15–9.

Illustration 15–9

	Dept. A	*Dept. B Transfer Account*	Dept. B
Materials and supplies:			
200 units at $3.60	$ 720		
100 units at $3.60 (Dept. A cost)		$ 360	
Labor:			
200 units 40% × $3.00	240		
200 units 40% × $1.80	144		
100 units 100% × $3.00 (Dept. A cost)		300	
100 units 100% × $1.80 (Dept. A cost)		180	
100 units × 40% × $4.80			$192
Factory overhead:			
200 units × 40% × $2.80	224		
100 units 100% × $2.80 (Dept. A cost)		280	
100 units × 40% × $2.40			96
Total Closing Work-in-Process Inventories, at Estimated Cost	$1,328	$1,120	$288

*This Transfer account is similar in theory to the Finished Goods account of Department A. Adjustments must first be made for Department A before considering adjustments for Department B accounts.

In order to ascertain the variation between the work-in-process inventory accounts at estimated cost, as shown above, and the *book* inventory of the work-in-process accounts, it is necessary to reconstruct the accounts from the entries made during and at the end of the period:

Work-in-Process — Materials, Department A

Inventory at beginning	360	(5)	10,800
(2)	12,060	Balance	1,620
	12,420		12,420
Balance before adjustment	1,620		

Work-in-Process — Labor, Department A

Inventory at beginning	288	(5)	14,400
(3)	13,300		
Balance	812		
	14,400		14,400
		Balance before adjustment	812

Work-in-Process — Manufacturing Overhead, Department A

Inventory at beginning	168	(5)	8,400
(3)	210	Balance	824
(4)	8,846		
	9,224		9,224
Balance before adjustment	824		

Work-in-Process — Transfer, Department B

Inventory at the beginning	2,240	(8)	34,720
(5)	33,600	Balance	1,120
	35,840		35,840
Balance before adjustment	1,120		

Work-in-Process — Labor, Department B

Inventory at beginning	576	(8)	14,880
(6)	13,500		
Balance	804		
	14,880		14,880
		Balance before adjustment	804

Work-in-Process — Manufacturing Overhead, Department B

Inventory at beginning	288	(8)	7,440
(6)	230		
(7)	6,200		
Balance	722		
	7,440		7,440
		Balance before adjustment	722

Finished Goods

(8)	57,040	(9)	46,000

Cost of Sales

(9)	46,000		

Illustration 15–10

Account	Book Inventory Taken from the Accounts	Computed Inventory on Estimated Cost Basis per Schedule, p. 498	Variation
Work-in-Process—Materials, Department A	$1,620	$ 720	$ 900†
Work-in-Process—Labor, Department A	812 Cr.	384	1,196‡
Work-in-Process—Manufacturing Overhead, Department A	824	224	600†
Work-in-Process—Transfer, Department B	1,120	1,120	0*
Work-in-Process—Labor, Department B	804 Cr.	192	996‡
Work-in-Process—Manufacturing Overhead, Department B	722 Cr.	96	818‡

* Before adjustment for Department A variations.
† Indicates estimates too low.
‡ Indicates estimates too high.

A comparative summary of the book inventory of the work-in-process taken from the foregoing accounts and the work-in-process computed on the basis of *estimated costs* (see schedule, page 498) presents the figures shown in Illustration 15–10, but attention is directed to the fact that the Work-in-Process—Transfer, Department B, account shows no variation and will not until adjustments have been made in Department A.

As previously stated, the variations from estimates may be closed out by apportioning the amounts to the Work-in-Process, Finished Goods, and Cost of Sales accounts or by transferring the entire amount to the Cost of Sales account. The former seems more desirable for estimated costs; the latter more practical for standard costs. The use of an Adjustment or Estimated Cost Variation account simplifies the accounting work. The entry to transfer the variations to the Adjustment account is:

(11)

Work-in-Process—Labor, Department A	1,196	
Work-in-Process—Labor, Department B	996	
Work-in-Process—Manufacturing Overhead, Department B	818	
Work-in-Process—Materials, Department A		900
Work-in-Process—Manufacturing Overhead, Department A		600
Adjustment		1,510

To transfer the estimated cost variations to the Adjustment account, thus leaving the balances in all work-in-process accounts at estimated cost.

Although the Adjustment account may be closed by apportioning the amount to the Work-in-Process, Finished Goods, and Cost of Sales accounts on the basis of the equivalent number of units produced in each, it is usually easier, where the accounting for estimated costs is quite involved, as in this instance, to make the corrections of the estimated costs on the basis of the estimated cost values in each account.

In order to do this, the amount of each variation must be apportioned between the Work-in-Process accounts, the Finished Goods account, and the Cost of Goods Sold account. The simplest way to do this is to set up a detailed tabulation showing the estimated cost figures in each account, and then to compute the proration. In this tabulation, for example, the variation in the Work-in-Process — Materials, Department A, is $900 (see Illustration 15–11). The balances at estimated material cost in the respective accounts are:

Work-in-Process — Materials, Department A (see p. 498)..........................$ 720
Work-in-Process — Transfer, Department B (see p. 498)   360
Finished Goods, 600 units at $3.60 (see estimated cost sheet, p. 495)   2,160
Cost of Goods Sold, 2,500 units at $3.60 (see cost sheet, p. 495)   9,000
    Total Basis of Proration for Material Cost Variation.....................$12,240

The same procedure is followed for labor costs in Department A, labor costs in Department B, manufacturing overhead in Department A, and manufacturing overhead in Department B. Illustration 15–12 (p. 503) shows the estimated cost figures now in the accounts, the amount of the adjustments, and the verification.

Below is the summary adjustment entry which should be made to close out the variations of the estimated costs from the actual costs (in other words, to adjust the estimated figures to the actual):

Work-in-Process — Materials, Department A..........................   52.94
Work-in-Process — Manufacturing Overhead, Department A.....   14.63
Work-in-Process — Transfer, Department B..........................   8.29
Adjustment...1,510.06
    Work-in-Process — Labor, Department A 29.18
    Work-in-Process — Labor, Department B.......................   12.69
    Work-in-Process — Manufacturing Overhead,
        Department B...   10.42
    Finished Goods..   296.81
    Cost of Sales 1,236.82

When this entry is posted, the inventory accounts will all have been adjusted to correct the error caused by inaccurate estimates. The same procedure will be followed at the close of each succeeding accounting period. However, the Transfer account may cause some difficulty if after adjustment for this period the estimated costs for the next period are revised. In that event the adjustment must be made on the basis of the revised estimates and the actual costs as adjusted for the previous period.

Illustration 15–11

TABULATION SHOWING THE ESTIMATED COST FIGURES IN THE VARIOUS ACCOUNTS, THE AMOUNT OF THE ADJUSTMENTS AND THE ADJUSTED TOTAL (ACTUAL) FOR EACH ACCOUNT

	MATERIAL PUT INTO PROCESS IN DEPARTMENT A			LABOR COSTS IN DEPARTMENT A			LABOR COSTS IN DEPARTMENT B			MANUFACTURING OVERHEAD, DEPARTMENT A			MANUFACTURING OVERHEAD, DEPARTMENT B		
	Balance at Estimated	Adjustment*	Adjusted to Actual	Balance at Estimated	Adjustment	Adjusted to Actual	Balance at Estimated	Adjustment	Adjusted to Actual	Balance at Estimated	Adjustment	Adjusted to Actual	Balance at Estimated	Adjustment	Adjusted to Actual
Department A	$ 720.00	$ 52.94	$ 772.94	$ 384.00	$ 29.18*	$ 354.82				$ 224.00	$ 14.63	$ 238.63			
Department B—Transfer	360.00	26.47	386.47	480.00	36.47*	443.53				280.00	18.29	298.29			
Department B							$ 192.00	$ 12.69*	$ 179.31				$ 96.00	$ 10.42*	$ 85.58
Finished Goods:															
600 @ $3.60															
600 @ 4.80															
600 @ 4.80	2,160.00	158.83	2,318.83	2,880.00	218.79*	2,661.21	2,880.00	190.30*	2,689.70	1,680.00	109.76	1,789.76	1,440.00	156.31*	1,283.69
600 @ 2.80															
600 @ 2.40															
Cost of Goods Sold:															
2,500 @ $3.60															
2,500 @ 4.80															
2,500 @ 4.80	9,000.00	661.77	9,661.77	12,000.00	911.64*	11,088.36	12,000.00	792.96*	11,207.04	7,000.00	457.31	7,457.31	6,000.00	651.30*	5,348.70
2,500 @ 2.80															
2,500 @ 2.40															
TOTAL	$12,240.00	$900.01	$13,140.01	$15,744.00	$1,196.08*	$14,547.92	$15,072.00	$995.95*	$14,076.05	$9,184.00	$599.99	$9,783.99	$7,536.00	$818.03*	$6,717.97

* Credit.

COMPUTATIONS

$$\frac{\$ 900.00}{12,240.00} = .07353$$

$720.00 X .07353 = $ 52.94
360.00 X .07353 = 26.47
2,160.00 X .07353 = 158.83
9,000.00 X .07353 = 661.77
$900.01

$$\frac{\$ 1,196.00}{15,744.00} = .07597$$

$ 384.00 X .07597 = $ 29.18
480.00 X .07597 = 36.47
2,880.00 X .07597 = 218.79
12,000.00 X .07597 = 911.64
$1,196.08

$$\frac{\$ 996.00}{15,072.00} = .06608$$

$ 192.00 X .06608 = $ 12.69
2,880.00 X .06608 = 190.30
12,000.00 X .06608 = 792.96
$995.95

$$\frac{\$ 600.00}{9,184.00} = .06533$$

$ 224.00 X .06533 = $ 14.63
280.00 X .06533 = 18.29
1,680.00 X .06533 = 109.76
7,000.00 X .06533 = 457.31
$599.99

$$\frac{\$ 818.00}{7,536.00} = .10855$$

$ 96.00 X .10855 = $ 10.42
1,440.00 X .10855 = 156.31
6,000.00 X .10855 = 651.30
$818.03

Illustration 15–12

TABLE SHOWING THE SUMMARY OF ADJUSTMENTS OF ESTIMATED COSTS TO ACTUAL

(Prepared from Tabulation on Page 502)

Account	Amount of Adjustment	Work-in-Process Accounts						Finished Goods	Cost of Goods Sold
		Materials, Dept A	Labor, Dept. A	Overhead, Dept. A	Transfer Account, Dept. B	Labor, Dept. B	Overhead, Dept. B		
Materials Used in Department A..	$ 900.01 Dr.	$52.94			$26.47			$158.83	$ 661.77
Labor Used in Department A......	1,196.08 Cr.		$29.18*		36.47*			218.79*	911.64*
Manufacturing Overhead, Department A..	599.99 Dr.			$14.63	18.29			109.76	457.31
Labor Used in Department B......	995.95 Cr.					$12.69*		190.30*	792.96*
Manufacturing Overhead, Department B..	818.03 Cr.						$10.42*	156.31*	651.30*
	$1,510.06 Cr.	$52.94	$29.18*	$14.63	$ 8.29	$12.69*	$10.42*	$296.81*	$1,236.82*

* Credit.

ESTIMATED COSTS WHEN TWO OR MORE PRODUCTS ARE MANUFACTURED

When two or more products are manufactured at the same time, a similar procedure as discussed above is followed. A separate work-in-process account for each product is necessary however.

Since the total cost of the materials used is determined by computation, i.e., inventory at beginning plus purchases minus inventory at the end, some method must be used whereby the material costs are allocated to the several work-in-process accounts. If the same quantity of each product is produced, a ratio of the estimated material cost of each may be used. For example:

Estimated Costs	Product A	Product B
Material	$ 7	$ 3
Labor	6	5
Overhead	4	4
	$17	$12

Materials used for the period cost $8,500. The *same number of units* of Product A and Product B were started into process. Material costs are charged to the Work-in-Process—Product A and Product B accounts on a 70 percent and 30 percent basis, i.e., on the basis of unit cost of material for each. If the volume started into process for each product is not the same, the estimated value of the material to be used in each product must be weighted by the quantity started into process and be used in calculating the percentages for apportioning the actual material costs for a given period.

A similar procedure is followed in apportioning the actual labor and manufacturing overhead costs to Work-in-Process—Product A and Product B accounts. *Physical* inventories of the Work-in-Process—Product A and Product B, taken at estimated costs and compared with the book inventories, indicate the amount of the material, labor, and overhead adjustment. The adjustment is made to the Work-in-Process and Finished Goods accounts in the manner previously discussed for each product on the basis of the percentages previously used. For example, the materials adjustment for the work-in-process is $1,200. Of this amount, 70% is applicable to Product A and 30% to Product B.

This procedure becomes quite complicated, especially when many different products are produced at the same time. A more complete historical or standard cost system would not be much more expensive to operate than such a complicated estimated cost system, and the results would certainly be more satisfactory.

If a number of similar products of varying *sizes* or *styles* are manufactured, apportioning the amount of the adjustments to the various styles or sizes is impractical. The adjustments are then made through the accounts representing the work-in-process, finished goods, and cost of sales for the *total* production of a given period.

PERT-TIME AND PERT-COST AS A PHASE OF ESTIMATING COSTS

PERT began as a technique to help solve the problems of developing the Polaris Missile by setting out in logical fashion the sequence and time of the steps necessary for the completion of the project. PERT is a recent tool of management associated with cost control. PERT, defined as Program Evaluation and Review Technique, is a development of the governmental agencies for cost control of defense purchases and contracts. In 1961 PERT was used for only 19 percent of private commercial work. By 1963, PERT users showed over 50 percent in private commercial work; and in a study of 44 companies, it was found that time savings for more than 75 percent of the firms ranged from 10 percent to more than 31 percent. PERT has been used in designing, developing, and using new machines; streamlining paper-work systems; and scheduling commercial aircraft transport production.

PERT must be separated into its two elements—PERT-Time and PERT-Cost. PERT may also be described as a phase of systems management aiming at greater efficiency through lower costs. It is therefore an important element of cost accounting especially in the area of estimated costs and budgeting.

PERT-Time is the basic analysis by management of the problem of producing a maximum volume with a minimum delay of time. PERT-Time is based on the principle that there may be a number of operations which can be completed simultaneously rather than sequentially, thus reducing the time of the finished product manufacture when the simultaneous operations are merged. The planning of the sequence and merging of the various operations is known as the Critical Path Method (CPM). The integration of the sequence and merging is shown in the PERT-Network.

Two illustrations of the use of PERT-Time and PERT-Costs and the cost reduction implications are given:

1. In the area of prefabricated, factory-produced private home dwellings or even plant construction, it is possible in the former case to construct simultaneously in different sections of the plant, a complete kitchen, several complete bathrooms, and the other individual rooms and truck these to the building sites, where they can be assembled into a completed home in the matter of a few days. This procedure has

eliminated more than 40% of the time required for on-site sequential construction.

2. In the more modern shipbuilding concerns, procedure has resulted in reducing the time required for construction as well as the costs. A number of separate parts of the ship under construction are built simultaneously in the shipyards and then welded together into the completed vessel.

PERT-TIME OPERATIONS

The culmination of PERT-Time is a diagram known as the network, which represents the beginning and ending of activities representing a finished product or finished project. The activities represent the various tasks to complete the job and are timed. The sequence and flow of these tasks follows the critical path outlined by management and engineering. The network is a well-thought-out plan upon which is superimposed the activities time and the flow of work. The most satisfactory achievement indicates the maximum time required to complete the job along the critical path.

The network (see Illustration 15–13) pictures all the activities which

Illustration 15–13.   Critical Path Network—The Plan

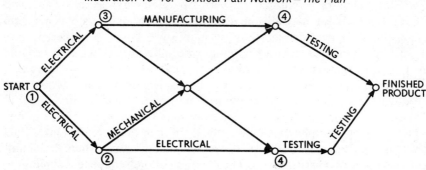

must be performed before the final product is completed. It also pictures the times required for each so that the date of completion can be set. Thus a budget is projected and the probable costs are estimated. PERT-Cost is part of this budget program, but it is based upon activity time, not on the fiscal accounting period. Emphasis is placed on the projected work packages, not the annual budget. It is predicated on *activity time*—the time to complete a project or some phase of the project. This network diagram is the cornerstone of PERT-Time. It is a logical plan incorporating the events and activities. In this illustration, the work packages might be:

1. Electrical work.
2. Mechanical work.
3. Assembling (manufacturing).
4. Testing.

The costs can be estimated once the network has been established. These costs can be estimated in various ways: (1) a single expected actual cost estimate; (2) a triple cost estimate as the *best estimate,* the *most likely estimate,* and the most *pessimistic* costs; or (3) the *optimum* time for completing the project with the resulting effect on costs.

The Critical Path Network indicates the plan or flow of work of operations, indicating those that can be completed simultaneously. A second network should be prepared indicating the time requirements for each activity and the optimum time for completing the project. (See Illustration 15–14.)

Illustration 15–14. The Network—Time Estimate

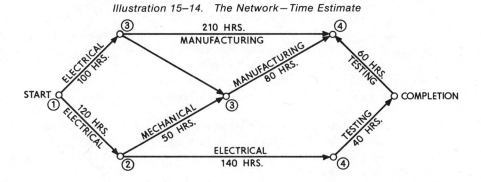

Two of the electrical activities can be completed simultaneously, thus saving 100 hours. Some of the mechanical, manufacturing, assembling, and electrical work can be completed simultaneously, as can some of the testing. The maximum time should be electrical, 120 hours; manufacturing, 210 hours; testing, 60 hours—total 390 hours when allowance is made for simultaneous manufacturing activities.

Once this time estimate has been computed, it is possible to prepare a manufacturing schedule indicating the operations, the time when the various activities are to be started and completed, and the date of completion. All of these seem to be estimated costs and budgeted operations.

PERT-COSTS

As may have been noted, PERT-Cost is the managerial tool which must be coordinated with PERT-Time in estimating costs in project planning and control. PERT-Cost results not only in financial reporting both on the cost accounting and individual manager's level but it is basic in decision making in the planning and managerial control phases of the project. Some of the problems of PERT-Cost which have not yet been resolved are:

1. A lack of sophisticated analysis of costs for decision making in many firms.
2. Lack of historical cost data for many of the projects involved in the network because the products have not been manufactured previously.
3. Since PERT-Time often overlaps the fiscal accounting period, there may be a conflict in reconciling PERT-Costs with those of the fiscal accounting period.

QUESTIONS FOR REVIEW

1. How and when are cost estimates determined?
2. Outline the accounting procedure to be followed when an estimated cost system is used. What effect would the lack of a work-in-process inventory at the end of the period have on this procedure?
3. How is the procedure outlined in 2 changed when —
   a) Two products are manufactured simultaneously in a single operating department, and
   b) When a single product is produced in two successive departments.
4. The *Work-in-Process—Materials* account is charged with the actual cost of materials used. How does a firm ascertain this figure? Does it include factory supplies and indirect materials?
5. What procedure is followed when no Adjustment account is used? How can the figures be computed for the entry when no Adjustment account is used?
6. Why does the estimated cost system seem impractical for a firm making a large number of different products?
7. What is the nature of PERT-Time and PERT-Cost procedures? What are the advantages of these two procedures?
8. What is the nature of the Critical Path Network? In what way do PERT-Time, PERT-Cost, and CPN relate to estimated costs?
9. The Oliver Manufacturing Company estimates its cost of manufacturing its single product at $4. The actual costs of operating for the year were materials and supplies used, $3,000; direct labor, $5,000; and manufacturing overhead, $4,600. Twenty-five hundred units were completed; 2,200 were sold, and 500 were in process, 60 percent complete as to materials, labor, and manufacturing overhead. What is the variation from the estimated cost for this period? (Use one work-in-process account.)
10. Are material requisitions necessary when an estimated cost system is used? Explain. How will the cost of materials used in an estimated cost system be determined when there is no perpetual book inventory?

PROBLEMS—GROUP A

Problem 15–1.   Purpose: *Estimated Cost Procedures, Single Product, One Department*

The Orienta Manufacturing Company uses an estimated cost system. Costs are estimated for the single product every three months, making corrections for any necessary changes. Quarterly summary entries are made with the variations transferred to an adjustment account, prorated to the production for the month, so that costs will be at actual.

The estimated unit costs for the first quarter, ending March 31, 19—, were:

Materials	$400	
Labor costs	250	
Manufacturing overhead	50	$700

Operating costs for this quarter were:

Materials inventory, January 1, 19—	$ 25,000
Materials inventory, March 31, 19—	30,000
Materials purchased, 1/1/— to 3/31/—	114,440
Factory payroll	68,250
Manufacturing overhead costs	8,400

Production statistics showed:

	Units
Started into production	240
Completed	180
In process, March 31, 19— (80% complete as to materials, 50% complete as to labor and overhead)	60
Sold	150

Required:

a) Journal entries to record the manufacturing operations for the first three months, using three work-in-process accounts and an Adjustment account.

b) Prepare a cost of goods manufactured and sold statement.

c) Calculate a revised estimated cost statement per unit for the second quarter based upon the actual costs for the first quarter.

Problem 15–2.   Purpose: *Estimated Cost Accounting for Two Products Manufactured in a One-Department Plant; Journal Entries; Revised Estimated Unit Costs*

The Othican Corporation manufactures two products simultaneously in its one-department factory and uses an estimated cost accounting system.

The estimated costs per unit for the coming year are:

	Product Orax	Product Opan
Material costs	$ 6	$10
Labor costs	5	12
Manufacturing overhead	4	8
Total	$15	$30

Production statistics (in units) for the year were:

	Orax	Opan
Started into production	10,000	8,000
Completed	7,000	7,000
In process, 80% material, 50% labor and overhead	3,000	
In process, 100% material, 60% labor and overhead		1,000
Units sold	6,000 @ $45.00	5,000 @ $55.00

Production costs included the following:

Purchases during year	$310,000
Inventory at end of year	105,400
Factory payroll	160,440
Manufacturing overhead costs	85,320

Required:

a) Journal entries by products to cover the production cycle for the year including the proration of the adjustment account amounts, using three work-in-process accounts for each product.

b) A combined statement of the cost of sales and gross income for the year (by products and in total).

c) Estimated unit costs for each product for the next year based upon corrected figures for this year.

Problem 15–3. Purpose: *Estimated Cost Accounting Problem Involving One Product, but Two Consecutive Manufacturing Departments; Journal Entries*

The Outhroud Manufacturing Company uses an estimated cost accounting system in the manufacture of its single product which goes through two manufacturing departments. Costs are kept separate by departments by elements of cost. The estimated costs per unit of manufacturing for the coming year are:

	Department A	Department B	Total
Material costs	$ 50	—	$ 50
Labor costs	30	$40	70
Manufacturing overhead	20	10	30
Totals	$100	$50	$150

The volume of production (in units) for the year were:

	Department A	Department B
Started into production	2,000	
Completed and transferred	1,600	1,200
In process:		
100% material, 50% labor and overhead	400	
40% labor and overhead		?
Sold		1,000

The manufacturing costs for the year were:

Materials used in Department A $120,000
Labor costs, Department A........................ 45,000
Labor costs, Department B........................ 50,320
Overhead costs, Department A................. 30,600
Overhead costs, Department B................. 16,320

Required:

a) Prepare entries in journal form to record the information given, using departmental work-in-process accounts by elements of cost.
b) Entries to close out the adjustment accounts.
c) Detailed statement of the revised estimated costs to be used for the next year if these estimates are to be based upon the adjustments made this year.

Problem 15–4. Purpose: *Estimated Cost Statements and Analysis*

The Orthington Manufacturing Company is engaged in the production of piece goods and has no cost system. Its sales were made on the basis of estimated costs, adding 15 percent to estimated direct cost to cover overhead, then adding to the total so estimated a profit equal to 12 percent of the selling price.

At the end of the year 19 —, the trial balance was as follows:

Buildings...$	276,000	
Machinery...	310,000	
Spools and other similar items	33,000	
Accounts receivable.....................................	110,000	
Accounts payable..		$ 27,000
Allowances for depreciation to January 1, 19—:		
Buildings..		36,000
Machinery...		71,000
Sales		2,013,000
Inventory—January 1, 19—	157,000	
Purchases—raw material...............................	1,200,000	
Labor—direct	480,000	
Labor—foremen, etc.	213,000	
Office payroll...	76,000	
Factory overhead	280,000	
Office and administration expenses..................	113,000	
Capital stock		1,000,000
Cash in bank	18,000	
Retained earnings—January 1, 19—		119,000
	$3,266,000	$3,266,000

An estimated cost, which may be taken as representative of all the estimated costs, was as follows:

Cost per yard:
Raw material...$0.89
Weaving—piecework.. 0.38
Winding, warping, etc. 0.03
Foremen and supervision 0.10
                                                                            $1.40
Factory and office overhead—15% of $1.40.................. 0.21
                                                                            $1.61
Profit—12% of $1.83 .... 0.22
    Selling Price per Yard.......................................$1.83

Inventories were principally of raw material, and for the present purpose may be considered as consisting entirely of raw material at cost. The inventory at December 31, 19—, was valued at $376,000.

The annual rate of depreciation on buildings was 2 percent, and on machinery, $7\frac{1}{2}$ percent; spools, etc., were not depreciated; replacements were charged to operations (factory overhead).

Before the books were closed, it was realized that a heavy loss had been sustained. Suggestions were made—a defalcation, material stolen, etc.

What was the amount of the loss and to what do you ascribe it? Indicate briefly what is needed to prevent a repetition of such conditions.

(Adapted from AICPA Uniform Examination)

Problem 15–5.   Purpose: *Estimated Cost Accounting Procedures When Three Products Are Being Manufactured Simultaneously; Journal Entries and T-Ledger Accounts*

The Orapeous Products Company manufactures three different products simultaneously. The factory is not departmentalized, so costs are computed on an estimated basis as though the plant were a single operating unit.

For the coming year, the estimated costs for each of these products are as follows:

Element of Cost	Product X	Product Y	Product Z
Material costs	$ 60	$ 80	$ 70
Labor costs	40	50	60
Manufacturing overhead costs	20	30	30
Totals	$120	$160	$160

For each product, three work-in-process accounts are maintained—one for each element of cost (total nine accounts).

Inventories at the beginning of the year were:

Stores...$15,000
Finished goods, adjusted for the actual
    cost of the preceding period:
    Product X—20 units at $100
    Product Y—10 units at   180
    Product Z—15 units at   160

During the year the production statistics were as follows:

	Product X	Product Y	Product Z
Started into production	200 units	150 units	300 units
Completed	180 units	130 units	260 units
In process, end of year	20 units	20 units	40 units
Stage of completion:			
Materials	100%	80%	100%
Labor and overhead	50%	50%	25%
Sales on a Fifo basis	150 units	125 units	250 units
	@ $280	@ $300	@ $300

```
Materials purchased...................................$65,000
Labor costs............................................. 36,960
Manufacturing overhead costs...................... 14,490
Materials inventory at end of year................. 12,980
```

All costs for materials, labor, and overhead are to be prorated to the various products on the basis of the weighted average of the equivalent production and the estimated costs.

Required:

a) Journal entries to record the cost of production and to close out the adjustment accounts.

b) T-ledger accounts for the manufacturing operations.

c) Corrected estimated costs for the next period based upon the corrected estimated costs for this period.

PROBLEMS—GROUP B

Problem 15–6. Purpose: *Estimated Cost Procedures for a Single Product*

The Outlook Manufacturing Company operates a machine shop and manufactures a single product. Simple cost control is developed by using estimated cost accounting procedures. This product sells at a unit price of $640.

The current estimated costs are:

```
50 pounds of raw material at $2.00.......................     $100
100 hours of direct labor at $2.50..........................      250
100 hours of applied manufacturing overhead:
    Fixed ........................................................$60
    Variable.......................................................  80      140
        Total .....................................................            $490
```

Raw material inventory at the beginning of the period was 1,000 pounds at $2. Work-in-process inventory at the beginning of the period represented 40 units:

```
Materials in process..............................$4,000
Labor in process ................................. 3,000
Manufacturing overhead ......................... 1,480
        Total........................................$8,480
```

During the current period, 150 additional units were put into production; 160 units were completed and the balance was in process, 50% complete as to materials, 40% completed as to labor and manufacturing overhead.

Materials purchased were:

```
3,500 pounds at $2.20
4,000 pounds at $2.40
6,000 pounds at $2.80
```

Materials issued on Fifo basis and used in production were 8,400 pounds. Direct labor costs were 18,200 hours at a total cost of $36,400.

Actual manufacturing overhead costs incurred:

$$
\begin{array}{lrl}
\text{Fixed} & \$16,000 & \\
\text{Variable} & \underline{4,000} & \$20,000
\end{array}
$$

Of the units completed, 130 were sold.

Required:

a) Prepare journal entries and ledger accounts to record the above information and to close out the adjustment account.
b) Compute the estimated costs per unit for the next period if the current actual costs become the estimated costs for the next period.

Problem 15–7. Purpose: *Estimated Cost Procedures for a Two-Department Manufacturing Plant*

The Orinoco Manufacturing Company is engaged in manufacturing a single product in two successive departments. The estimated costs of each of these are:

	Department I	Department II
Material costs	$12	0
Labor costs	6	$10
Manufacturing overhead costs	2	4
Totals	$20	$14

During the current manufacturing period, the following represent the production (in units):

	Department I	Department II
Started into production	3,800	
Completed and transferred to Department II	3,000	
In process in Department I, 60% complete as to materials and 50% completed as to labor and overhead	800	
In process in Department II, 50% complete as to labor and manufacturing overhead		200
Completed in Department II		2,800
Units sold		2,500
Selling price per unit, $80.		

The actual operating costs for this period were:

	Department I	Department II
Material costs	$48,720	0
Labor costs	17,000	$36,250
Manufacturing overhead costs	6,800	17,400

Required:

a) Journal entries to record the above information.

b) Journal entries to close out the adjustment accounts.

c) Revised estimates for the next period based upon the actual costs for this period.

Problem 15–8.   Purpose: *C.P.A. Problem Involving Statements of Estimated Costs for a Process Industry*

From the following information concerning the Oldton Company, prepare a statement showing the estimated cost of producing 13,500 tons of X product for the purposes of bidding on a government contract.

The Oldton Company manufactures X, a main product, and *Yappo*, a by-product. Product X is produced and sold by the ton (2,000 pounds). The raw materials used in production consists of three ingredients: H, I, and J. They are contained in both the finished product and in the finished by-product in proportion and at estimated cost per ton set forth as follows:

H, 40% at $8 per ton;	I, 36% at $5 per ton;	J, 24% at $7 per ton.

The contract for 13,500 tons of Product X represents 60 percent of the budgeted 1972 production of X by the Oldton Company.

The main Product X is manufactured through four operating departments, viz:

Department I. Materials H and I are put into production at the beginning of operations. Completed work is transferred to Department II.

Department II. Material H suffers a 5 percent loss in weight due to evaporation at the end of the processing in this department, and 10 percent of the remaining work-in-process is sold as waste at a nominal amount of $6 per ton. Completed work is transferred to Department III.

Department III. Material J is mixed with the material received from Department II at the beginning of operations in this department. Material J looses 4 percent of its original weight due to evaporation at the end of operations in Department III.

Department IV. In this final department, the material is separated into the main Product X and the By-product *Yappo* in the proportion of 80 percent and 20 percent, respectively; and such products are placed in salable form.

Estimated direct labor costs per ton on a departmental basis and the manufacturing overhead costs at normal capacity (i.e., 75 percent of total plant capacity of 25,000 tons annually of X) are as follows:

Department	Direct Labor per Ton	Variable Overhead	Fixed Overhead
I.........................$5.00		$ 60,000	$30,000
II......................... 2.50		62,000	18,000
III 3.00		50,000	20,000
IV....................... 4.00		40,000	16,000
Total		$212,000	$84,000

At normal capacity level, general manufacturing overhead costs applicable to the factory as a whole amount to $60,000, of which 40 percent is fixed. It is expected that the units called for by the government contract, coupled with the company's curtailed production during 1972, will reach 90 percent of total plant capacity measured in finished units of Product X.

By-product *Yappo* is expected to sell for an estimated $20 per ton before deductions for handling, selling, and administrative expenses of $2.50 per ton. (Carry all computations correct to two decimal places.)

(Adapted from AICPA Uniform Examination)

Problem 15–9.   Purpose: *CPA Problem Using Estimated Cost Procedures*

On the basis of the following data, prepare a statement of factory accounts showing costs, variances, and inventory balances.

The Oroten Manufacturing Company has a contract to manufacture 10,000 units of its product *Copon,* a regular-line product, for a lump-sum price. This price was determined on the basis of estimates of manufacturing cost, selling, administrative, and general expenses and provision for net profit.

Management desires to check manufacturing cost estimates against corresponding actual costs through the factory accounting records and decides to make use of procedures followed under estimated cost systems in which estimated and actual costs are reflected in opposition in cost accounts and variations are developed thereby. These comparisons are to be made monthly so that differences between estimated and actual costs can be detected and controlled currently.

Product *Copon* has been manufactured by two major processes developed in the fabricating and finishing departments. Estimated costs per unit of product for each of these departments follow:

PRODUCT COPON
ESTIMATED COST PER UNIT

	Fabricating Department			Finishing Department		
	Quantity or Time	Estimated Value	Total	Quantity or Time	Estimated Value	Total
Direct materials....................3 units		$1.20	$3.60	....	....	....
Direct labor........................2 hours		0.90	1.80	1.5 hours	$1.00	$1.50
Manufacturing overhead ....2 hours		0.60	1.20	1.5 hours	0.50	0.75
Total			$6.60			$2.25

Product and cost data for operations during the first month under the contract are as follows:

	Fabricating Department	Finishing Department
Beginning inventory:		
Quantity..	200 units	80 units
Average state of completion	35%	55%
Costs:		
Direct materials.........................$720		
Transfer materials from fabricating department		$528
Direct labor............................. 126		66
Manufacturing overhead.............. 84	$ 930	33 $ 627
Materials purchased and issued	9,100	
Direct labor incurred........................	3,810	3,860
Manufacturing overhead incurred	3,180	2,105
Ending inventory:		
Quantity.....................................	300 units	240 units
Average state of completion	60%	70%

Note. The amounts in the above tabulation are at actual cost, with the exception of the beginning inventories which are stated at estimated cost.

During the month, 2,000 units were completed of which 1,800 were shipped to the purchaser under contract. Goods are assumed to be produced and sold on a first-in, first-out basis.

(Adapted from AICPA Uniform Examination)

Problem 15–10.   Purpose: *CPA Problem Involving Journal Entries Ledger Accounts and Adjustments for Estimated Costs*

The Olcrest Manufacturing Company estimates its cost for a unit of its product *Dabon* to consist of the following:

> Material—5 pounds at $1.22 per pound
> Labor—7 hours at $1.30 per hour

Overhead is applied on a direct labor cost basis and need not be considered in this problem.

The company takes the raw materials purchased into inventory of raw materials at $1.22 per pound, recording any difference between that price and actual purchase cost in a Price Variation—Materials account. The actual raw material used is issued to production at $1.22 per pound. The material cost and the actual direct labor cost for the month are recorded in separate work-in-process accounts. Finished Goods Inventory is debited, and these process accounts are credited with the estimated cost of completed units. At the end of the month the Finished Goods account and the work-in-process accounts are adjusted to actual cost by spreading the differences between actual costs and estimated costs over the accounts in proportion to the amounts of estimated costs applicable to each of the accounts. Material price variation is spread over inventory of raw materials, work-in-process, and finished goods in the same manner as other variations, but the amount applicable to inventory of raw materials is left in the variation account.

Account balances after adjustment for March 31, but before adjustment to actual costs for April 30, were as follows:

Account	Debit Balances 3/31/— after Adjustment	Debit Balances 4/30/— before Adjustment
Inventory of Raw Materials	$10,485.90	$10,673.78
Price Variation—Materials	723.55	973.28
Work-in-Process—Materials	770.80	1,091.90
Work-in-Process—Labor	731.15	758.94

The 3/31/— balance of Work-in-Process—Materials includes $49.78 of price variation. Status of the work-in-process was as follows:

	March 31, 19—		April 30, 19—	
	Units	Percent Completed	Units	Percent Completed
Materials	60	50	50	30
Materials	80	90	100	75
Labor	60	25	50	10
Labor	80	80	100	60

During the month of April, 19—, 510 units of product *Dabon* were completed and transferred to Finished Goods.

You are to set up skeleton ledger accounts for all of the accounts affected by these transactions and prepare and post the adjustment necessary for the company at the end of April, 19—.

(Adapted from AICPA Uniform Examination)

chapter 16

Standard Cost Accounting — Materials and Labor

THE NATURE OF STANDARD COSTS

When costs are defined on a time basis, cost determination and managerial control may be described under two headings:

1. *Historical costs* which are computed upon the completion of the manufacturing operations. Costs thus determined are used in evaluating past performance and as the basis for future planning. Historical costs are retrospective, and whatever errors or inefficiencies are reported will become known some time after their occurrence — oftentimes too late to be of much managerial control help. This unfavorable aspect of historical costs has encouraged the development of a more satisfactory managerial cost determination approach, namely, *predetermined costs.*

2. *Predetermined costs* are computed before the actual production. These may be estimated costs or standard costs. The former has already been discussed. In this and the following chapters, standard costs will be discussed as a form of predetermined costs. Predetermined standard costs have such universal acceptance today that any firm that does not use some form of them seems outmoded, because when standard costs are used management will know before production starts, "What the costs should be"; and soon after the completion of the job, management will know "What the costs actually were," "What was the difference between the predetermined and actual costs," and "WHY there was a difference." Historical costs do not supply answers to these managerial control questions, so corrective action cannot be taken in time to benefit the firm. Standard costs may be job order costs or process costs. The term "standard" merely refers to the predetermined nature of the costs.

Standard costs are a supplementary part of the manufacturing concern's budget. Their predetermined nature has resulted in some accountants calling them budgeted costs. While the budget is usually a plant-wide compilation of figures, the standard costs are related to materials, labor, and manufacturing overhead data, on a departmental basis, for more localized control and action. Variations from standard costs permit more immediate corrective action than the more inclusive firm's budget variations.

Standard costs, when most effectively used, are scientifically predeterminations of the direct material; the direct labor, variable manufacturing overhead, and fixed overhead costs that should be incurred in completing a certain job or certain manufacturing process operations. Standard costs are made up of two factors: a *predetermined quantity* of materials or number of labor hours or machine-hours; and a *predetermined cost* for each of these elements. Variations of actual costs from standard costs will therefore be due either to the *quantitative* or *cost* factors or a combination of them.

ADVANTAGES OF STANDARD COST SYSTEMS

There are several reasons for using standard costs. The first of these has already been mentioned, namely, the effective analysis of cost data. Through the use of standards, it can be determined why costs are not what they should have been because the standard serves as a measuring device focusing attention on cost variations. Suppose an accountant reports that 10 model X machines shipped to the Granite Motor Company cost $250 each. The executive does not know whether this total cost or the individual costs for material, labor, and overhead represent efficient or inefficient operation. If, on the other hand, this executive has a detailed report of material, labor, and overhead costs which indicates that the standard cost should have been $240 per machine, then he knows that the producing department is not so efficient as was expected. He may then proceed to uncover the causes for this difference. Thus, the moving, changing nature of cost figures is brought clearly into view and the fluctuations of cost can be more easily controlled.

A second reason for using standard costs is that the use of standards reduces bookkeeping costs which have for years been important factors restricting the use of cost accounting by businessmen. A complete standard cost system is usually accompanied by standardization of production operations in that a standard production order calling for a standard quantity of product is prepared in advance of actual production. All production orders for a given product involve identical components so that material requisitions, labor time tickets, cost sheets, and operating instructions can be prepared on standard forms. Whenever an order is placed in the factory to manufacture a certain product, a standard cost sheet already complete with the standard amounts for materials, labor, and overhead is processed. The requisitions are sent to the storeroom for the standard amount of materials, and the job time tickets for the standard labor charges are forwarded to the factory. The historical costing procedure is reversed, since it will not be necessary to sort and tabulate the

Illustration 16–1

Excess Labor Cost Report				
Clock Number & Name	Excess minutes	Excess cost	Total	Explanation
Total Cost—Failure to Make Standard				
Departmental Lost Time				
701—Waiting for setup or adjustment				
702—Machine breakdown				
703—Waiting for material				
704—Waiting for order or assignment				
705—Reworking				
706—Nonstandard operation				
707—Nonstandard material				
708—Salvage nonstandard material				
710—Other				
Total Departmental Lost Time				
Unaccounted for Time				
Cost of Overtime Premium				
Total Excess Labor Cost for the Day				

SOURCE: *N.A.A. Accounting Practice Report No. 9, Reports Which Managements Find Most Useful.*

Illustration 16–2

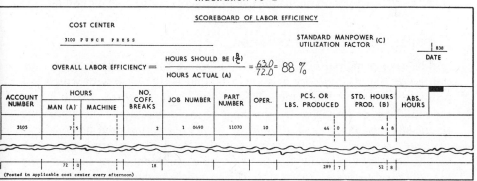

| SCOREBOARD OF LABOR EFFICIENCY | | | | | | | | | | |

COST CENTER

3100 PUNCH PRESS

STANDARD MANPOWER UTILIZATION FACTOR (C)   .838   DATE

$$\text{OVERALL LABOR EFFICIENCY} = \frac{\text{HOURS SHOULD BE } (\frac{B}{C})}{\text{HOURS ACTUAL (A)}} = \frac{63.0}{72.0} = 88\%$$

ACCOUNT NUMBER	HOURS		NO. COFF. BREAKS	JOB NUMBER	PART NUMBER	OPER.	PCS. OR LBS. PRODUCED	STD. HOURS PROD. (B)	ABS. HOURS	
	MAN (A)	MACHINE								
3105	7	5		2	1 0490	11070	10	44	0	4	8
	72	0		18				289	7	52	8

(Posted in applicable cost center every afternoon)

Daily departmental report detailed by operation is tied in to budgeted hours which have been related to budgeted labor dollars. The efficiency ratio of 88% at the top is the result of dividing actual hours (72) into the quotient of standard hours produced (528) divided by a "manpower utilization factor" for the particular cost center (.838). The factor reflects the relationship of budgeted direct hours to budgeted total hours. Review of operation detail shown may disclose the cause of the "score" or outcome.

SOURCE: *N.A.A. Accounting Practice Report No. 9, Reports Which Managements Find Most Useful.*

many material requisitions and job time tickets because the *standard* amounts are already recorded on the summary cost sheets. When an order is completed, credit slips are issued for unused materials or unused labor time tickets. Should additional material or labor be required, a special colored requisition or job time ticket is prepared. This means that when an order is completed, entries on the standard job sheets are necessary only for the amount of material or labor *above* or *below* standard; this notation takes but a few moments after the last manufacturing operation. Both job sheet and manufacturing operation are completed almost simultaneously.

Other important advantages may be claimed for standard cost systems. Because of the emphasis on cost variations, the entire organization is made cost-conscious; foremen and workmen can readily see the importance of efficient operations, and costs can be reduced by concerted effort. The use of standard costs places emphasis upon budgetary control because of the close relationship between budgets and standards. The use of standard costs and the attempt to apply them to factory operations necessitates close cooperation between the engineering and costing departments in developing and improving the standardization of product design, quality, and methods of manufacture. These advantages inherent in standard cost systems represent but one type of benefit being derived from the general standardization movement throughout industry.

Presented in Illustration 16–1 is a daily excess labor cost report used by one company to ascertain the reasons for labor inefficiency and to emphasize to accountable management their responsibility to "realign manpower or adjust production schedules to produce the best efficiency possible." This report is distributed to foremen within four hours after the current shift starts and covers operations of the preceding day. Illustration 16–2 shows and explains the use of a "scoreboard" of labor efficiency.

DIFFERENT TYPES OF STANDARDS

The two principal considerations affecting the classification of standards are: (1) *attainability* of standard—that is, the ease with which it is possible to achieve the standards set—and (2) the *frequency* with which the standards are revised. On the basis of these two factors, it is possible to classify standards as *ideal, normal, expected actual,* and *basic.*

Ideal Standards. These represent the level of performance which would be achieved under the best possible combination of factors—the most favorable prices for materials and labor, highest output with best equipment and layout, and maximum efficiency in the utilization of the manufacturing resources—in other words, maximum output at minimum cost. Such standards are engineering standards in the strictest sense. Once set, they are rarely changed unless radical changes are made in the product or the manufacturing processes.

Normal Standards. Costs predicated upon normal operating conditions for a company *over the period of a complete business cycle* are called *normal standards.* While these are more likely to be attainable, they are difficult to compute because of the probable errors in predicting the extent and duration of cyclical effects. They are also troublesome in that cyclical economic effects may cause *large variation from standard* at certain periods in the cycle. Many of these variations are, for the most part, beyond the control of the individual firm and are, therefore, of little significance in controlling cost variations. Normal standards are based upon an attainable goal and serve to isolate the effects of the business cycle on costs.

Current or Expected Actual Standards. These standards are based on *current business conditions* and represent the achievement level at which management aims for the ensuing accounting period. The standards that are set are attainable. Any deviation from this standard represents inefficiency in the manufacturing operations, unless due to uncontrollable factors. If the factors are not controllable, it must be assumed that the standards are not correct and must be revised accordingly. These current standards represent a *short-run* point of view and are prepared with the understanding that they will be revised when necessary. These current standards are easily understood and have proved most useful in managerial control.

Basic or "Bogey" Standards. These represent a special class of standards of a statistical nature, prepared for some base year, and used in much the same way as the statistician uses commodity price indices. These standards merely serve as a yardstick with which to compare actual performance and are not revised unless the products or the manufacturing operations or processes are changed.

To illustrate this method, the year 1960 is assumed to be the basis for comparison and calculation. The raw material used by this firm is copper sheeting, the price of which during most of that year was 68 cents a pound. This figure is then used to represent the 100 percent figure. In the year 1970, the average price of copper is $1.02 a pound. The *basic standards* for the copper material to be used must first be adjusted by 150 percent before a comparison with the actual costs can be made. Similarly, standard labor costs and manufacturing overhead charges must first be adjusted for their relationship to the basic standard before making comparisons with the actual costs. The main advantage of the basic standard is that it minimizes the number of revisions which would be required because of changes in cost of materials or labor. When *expected actual standards* are used, revisions must be made whenever conditions or costs change. When *basic standards are used,* no change is required other than a computation of the cost relationships between the basic period and the current period. This computation is used in adjusting the standard costs before making comparisons with the actual costs. In view of the statistical nature of the basic or "bogey" standards, they are not recorded in the regular accounting records but they may be recorded in memoranda columns to facilitate the computation of the percentage relationships between standard and actual. The use of basic standards is usually confined to the study of cost variations by statistical rather than accounting methods. Basic standards are less commonly used than *expected actual* or *current standards*.

Comparative Illustration of Ideal, Normal, and Current Standards. In the illustration that follows, an assumption is made that under ideal conditions the maximum operating capacity will permit a larger volume of purchases, resulting in a price reduction of 10 percent under the regular price. Labor costs per unit will not change with increased volume of production, but idle time costs are eliminated from the manufacturing overhead charges. On the basis of these assumptions, the comparative standard costs might be as follows:

PRODUCT: *Steel Cabinets—Per Unit Standard Cost*

Type of Standard	Material Cost	Labor Cost	Overhead Cost	Total Cost
Ideal standard	$18.00	$10.00	$7.00	$35.00
Normal standard	19.00	11.60	8.50	39.10
Current standard	20.00	12.20	9.20	41.40

In selecting the type of standards to be used, management must consider these two basic questions:

1. Which type of standard will be most effective for control purposes?
2. Should the standard cost accounting information be incorporated into the records or treated as statistical data?

While all of the methods have found some application in industry, the method most widely used by firms having a complete standard cost accounting system is that of *expected actual standard or current costs*.

RESPONSIBILITY FOR SETTING STANDARDS

For standard costs to be used successfully, definite authority and responsibility must be placed with some person or group of persons. To be effective, the authority so assigned must be at least commensurate to the level of authority delegated to those who are responsible for variations from standards. This is frequently accomplished by means of a *standards committee* or the organization of a *standards division*. The *product engineering department* must be represented on the *standards committee* or *division,* since this department designs the product and determines what materials to use. The *purchasing department* must be represented in this group, since the purchasing agent must be able to indicate the standard cost of the materials to be used during the period. The production management people who are responsible for the routing and scheduling of the manufacturing operations must be represented in the setting of standards. The personnel manager must be represented since he is responsible (adhering to union contracts) for the labor rates. The cost accounting personnel are interested in the work of this committee because they must tie all the standard cost figures together. Because so many different persons and departments are interested in setting standards, there must be one person who coordinates, summarizes, and interprets the results of standard cost accounting. He is usually the *controller.* He is responsible for the preparation of the statement of variations, and he is responsible for suggestions regarding revision of the standards.

METHODS OF DETERMINING STANDARDS

The success of a standard cost system depends upon the reliability and accuracy of the physical standards as well as the standard costs. But the problem of determining what an item should cost is not easily solved. In many cases, averages of past experience taken from costs of previous periods are used as standards. Unfortunately, relying exclusively upon past experience may have the effect of perpetuating inefficiencies. What has happened in the past should not be indicative of what should have happened in the past. It is better to take the "grass-roots" approach where standards will be set on the basis of each aspect of the production process. The process of determining standards is one of the more important aspects of standard cost accounting as the benefits to be derived will vary in direct proportion with the care with which standards have been established.

Standards are usually computed for use over a 12-month period. Some firms use the same standards year after year until some drastic change in the price or nature of the product occurs. Some of the more progressive firms are constantly reviewing their standards and standard costs and view this function as a continuing process.

PARTIAL USE OF STANDARDS

Many accountants believe that standard costs, if used, must be adapted to the complete manufacturing cycle. Although desirable, this is not necessary. In one concern it was extremely difficult to allocate the labor in the cutting and shearing department to the various jobs. The amount of work in handling the job time tickets was so great that this department always held up the cost work of all the other departments. And, what was more important, the volume was so great as to cause all kinds of inaccuracies in the labor cost allocations. It was suggested that in this department standards for labor costs be set up and each job charged with the standard cost of work done. At the end of each month the difference between the standard charges and the actual labor costs was the variation from standard. This amount was then prorated to all the jobs worked on during the month on the basis of the value of materials used on the jobs. By this partial use of standards it was possible to reduce by more than 80 percent the volume of clerical work connected with labor costs and still have reasonably accurate and acceptable costs.

Similarly, in some instances, the partial use of standards can be applied to materials. Some accountants study the variations of only the most important materials used in the manufacturing operations. In other instances, a firm may desire to study the labor cost variations only in some of the departments. The partial use of standards will help reduce the volume of cost accounting work and at the same time permit a study of cost variations of the most important components of the costs of manufacturing.

Standards for materials are more tangible and may be easier to establish than the so-called "operating" standards of labor and manufacturing overhead. Methods of determining the various standards will be discussed separately under the headings of the respective elements of cost.

DIRECT MATERIAL QUANTITY STANDARDS

In setting standards for the direct material costs of manufacturing a certain product, two factors must be considered:

1.   The *quantity* of material to be used.
2.   The *price* or *cost* of this material.

It is comparatively simple to ascertain the *quantity of material* to be used in a given unit of manufacture. These standards may be established from records of past experience, from test runs, from mathematical or scientific computations, or through the use of standard bills of material. Current material quantity requirements and their costs are subject to constant examination and revision if necessary — both as to the *kind* of material and the *quantity*. An important factor that must be considered in some industries in setting material quantity standards is the standard allowance for waste, shrinkage, and scrap. This spoilage and shrinkage allowance is more important in firms using a raw material which must pass through one or more converting stages than when a firm is merely using a number of purchased parts in assembling a finished product.

In determining *material quantity standards,* past records may be analyzed and an average quantity of materials used may be selected as the standard. The average may be computed in several ways: (1) using an *average* of all similar jobs for a given period such as a month or three months, or (2) using an *average* of the best and poorest performance in the period preceding the setting of the standards, or (3) using the *best* previous performance with reference to material used quantities.

If the product to be manufactured is new, or if the past records are not considered a reliable basis on which to predicate future costs, quantity standards may be set by the engineering department after due consideration has been given to the most economical size, shape, and quality of the article and the results to be expected from the use of various kinds and grades of materials. These standards may be established by either of two methods: *test runs* or *mathematical and technological analysis.* Where the test-run method is used, a quantity of material or units are put into process and the results carefully noted and studied. Results obtained in this manner are usually somewhat artificial because workmen tend to focus undue attention upon the test lots and use greater than ordinary care in using materials. These factors result in better performance on tests than can be expected in actual future operations. With union supervision of test runs, the reverse may also be true.

In some cases the processing is of such nature as to make possible fairly exact predictions of material consumption. Chemical processes are of this kind. One concern engaged in chromium plating metal containers placed a measured quantity of chromium salts in an electrolytic solution and then found out how many containers could be plated with this quantity of the chemical. This number could be checked scientifically by measuring the thickness and area of the plating; quantitative chemistry would indicate the theoretically perfect result. Such computations are often used to check standards set by other methods.

In some industries the materials issued from the stock room for the various manufacturing operations are fairly well standardized. This is particularly true in firms assembling a finished product, such as a television set, a sewing machine, a typewriter, or some such product. In some departments it is possible to use a single requisition for all the necessary material. It can be adapted to many concerns which use a variety of raw materials for manufacturing operations, such as foundries and plastic manufacturers. Such a form adapted to standard cost accounting procedures is known as the *standard bill of materials.* On it are listed the *standard quantities* and detail of all materials that should be used in various departments on various jobs or in various processes. Most good standard cost accounting systems will sooner or later attempt to use a standard bill of materials to save time in issuing materials to the factory, to reduce the clerical work in handling but a single requisition form, and to have better *quantity control* over materials used. There are no special forms for these standard bills of materials because each firm prepares a form adapted to its business. It is simply a composite requisition standardized in the same way that the production is standardized. The standard bill of materials may be on a deck of punched cards or on magnetic tape. The form of the document does not alter its purpose. For foundries, bakeries, and similar types of manufcturing, there are *standard mixture sheets* which indicate the quantity of each kind of material necessary to make the various products. These formula sheets are similar to standard bills of materials.

MATERIAL COST STANDARDS

Setting *material cost* standards involves quite a different problem. The type of material cost standards to be used is determined by the type of standard costs to be used. Three types of standards for material prices or costs are in use:

1. *Current or expected price standards* are the most desirable and effective. When these are used, the purchasing department must determine in advance either by long-term commitments or forecasting what the expected actual costs are to be during the ensuing accounting period. The accuracy of these price standards is a measure of the efficiency of the purchasing department. One well-known manufacturer sets these standards in November of each year for the following year. The price standards are not changed, once they are set, until the following year when they may again be revised. The purchasing department is held accountable for any variations.

2. *Normal price standards* are more in the line of statistical or average price standards for materials. Usually these are not recorded on the books because the prices cover a period of years, allowing for seasonal variations and long-term trends. Under such conditions inventories of materials, work-in-process, and finished goods must be based upon the actual, not standard, costs for materials.

3. *Fixed price standards* are usually part of a system which uses basic or bogey standards. Once the prices have been set for materials, these are used as the standards as long as that product is being manufactured. Here again, inventories of materials, work-in-process, and finished goods must be based upon the actual cost, not the standard cost, of the material, since the variations are not indicative of current practices but of a trend over a relatively long period of time.

When *current or expected price standards* are in use, standard costs for materials may be set by the purchasing or stores department as follows:

1. Through prices agreed upon in *long-term purchase* contracts, usually sufficient to take care of the manufacturing requirements for three to six months in the future.
2. Through the use of a *statistical forecasting* group either within or without the business organization. This group will attempt to forecast probable prices during the coming period.
3. Through the computation of the *weighted average* of purchase prices on the most recent purchase orders, or
4. Through the use of the *median price* paid on recent orders.
5. Through the use of *arbitrary estimates* based upon knowledge and experience in this type of business.

It should not be overlooked in setting these price standards that the best standards should take into consideration the price advantages to be obtained by determining the most economical quantity to buy, the best methods of delivery and storage at the lowest cost, and the credit terms which will result in cost or price savings.

ILLUSTRATIONS OF MATERIAL COST STANDARDS

To illustrate more specifically the nature of material cost standards, the standard material costs for two manufacturers are shown, namely, (1) a candy manufacturer, operating on a formula cost basis, producing 100 pounds of any one type of candy on each job (Illustration 16–3); and (2) a clothing manufacturer, producing a standard quantity of one dozen articles of each style (Illustration 16–4). On both of these illustrations, both the *standard quantities* and the *standard costs* of the materials to be used are shown. These two illustrations represent the *Material sections* of the standard cost sheets.

Illustration 16–3. Standard Material Costs for Candy Manufacturer

STANDARD COST SHEET PRODUCT: *Coconut BonBons, Formula 42*			
	Quantity	Price	Total
Materials:			
Corn Syrup..............................	50 lbs.	$0.13	$ 6.50
Sugar......................................	30	0.08	2.40
Chocolate.................................	10	0.30	3.00
Coconut...................................	20	0.60	12.00
Flavoring and Coloring....................	1	1.00	1.00
Total Material..........................	111 lbs.	$2.11	$24.90
Percentage of Waste, 10%..............	11	0.38	......
Total Material.........................	100 lbs.	$2.49	$24.90

Illustration 16–4. Standard Material Costs for Clothing Manufacturer

STANDARD COST RECORD					
Product: Hunting Coat *Manufacturing Unit:* 1 Dozen				*Date* 3/4/— *Size Scale:* 37–49	
Direct Materials:				Standard Cost per Dozen	
Code	Description	Width	Quantity	Price	Extension
23	*Body Materials* 11 oz. Army Duck............	40 in.	40 yds.	$0.65	$26.00
	Total.......................				$26.00
610 420	*Trim* Thread..................... Size Tickets................. 36/E Br. Buttons............	*Unit* M G	 12 108	 $0.80 0.60	$ 0.93 0.01 0.45
	Total..................... Total Materials..............				$ 4.00 $30.00

DIRECT MATERIAL COST VARIATIONS

Differences between the *standard cost* of material as shown on the standard cost sheets for the various products being manufactured and the *actual cost* of materials used are known as *variations* or *variances*. The two basic types of such variations may be described as follows:

1. *Material cost or material price variations* which result from paying more or less for the materials purchased than was anticipated when the standard cost sheets were prepared. The causes of these variations or differences include:
   a) Unfavorable or favorable purchasing contracts and terms.
   b) Unforeseen changes in market prices.
   c) Higher or lower delivery costs than were expected.
   d) Miscalculation of amount of purchase discounts expected.
   e) Proper or improper timing of purchases.
2. *Material quantity or material usage variations* which result from using more or less material on the various jobs or in the various operations than was estimated on the standard cost sheets. These variations may be attributable to—
   a) Using a different grade or a substitute material.
   b) Better control or lack of control of waste or spoilage.

c) Efficient or inefficient plant operations which result from supervision of type of tools used and the workers' capabilities.

d) Variations in the yield of materials used.

Material cost variations may be computed and recorded either (1) at the *time of the purchase* of the materials, or (2) at the *time that the material is used.* In the first procedure, the Stores account is kept on the books at the *standard price* of the materials. The *total cost or price variation* is recorded on the books *before* the materials are used. Unless there is an adjustment at the end of the accounting period for that portion of the material price variation related to the unused portion of the materials purchased, there may be a distortion in the cost of the final stores inventory. This distortion may be eliminated by recording the material price variation only at the time when the material is used. This method meets with the approval of the income tax authorities who are interested in the more accurate costing of inventories. However, recording the price variation only at the time of the usage of the material involves additional expense. Even more important an item to consider is the control feature. Isolating the material price variance at the time of purchase highlights the variance early. Management becomes aware of the differences between actual and standard costs.

ILLUSTRATION OF MATERIAL COST VARIATIONS

To compute the material cost variations, four items of information are necessary:

1. The *standard quantity* of material required to produce a given unit or number of units. This will appear on the standard cost sheet.
2. The *standard cost* of the material required in production. This also appears on the standard cost sheet.
3. The *actual quantity* of material used as shown by the requisitions.
4. The *actual cost* of the materials used as shown on the accounting records or purchase invoices.

To illustrate the computation of the material cost variations, the following facts are assumed:

> To manufacture 100 units of Product X on one job, 200 pounds of Material A are required, as shown on the standard cost sheet, at a standard cost of $2 per pound. During the month, 10 jobs were completed. The *actual* material used, as shown by the requisitions, was 2,250 pounds. Latest invoices indicated that this material cost $2.10 per pound.

The procedure followed in computing the material variations is as follows:

Quantity or usage variation:
Actual quantity of material used.. 2,250 lbs.
Standard quantity of material used (10 jobs × 200 pounds) 2,000

Excess quantity of material used, resulting in an unfavorable
    quantity variation... 250 lbs.
250 pounds × $2 (standard cost of material)................................$ 500

Material cost or price variation:
Actual cost of materials used (actual quantity × actual price)
    2,250 pounds × $2.10...$4,725
Standard cost of materials used (actual quantity × standard price)
    2,250 pounds × $2... 4,500

Difference represents material price variation, which is unfavorable ...$ 225

Proof or total material cost variation:
Actual costs: 2,250 pounds × $2.10...$4,725
Standard costs: 2,000 pounds × $2 4,000

    Total material variation..$ 725

Material quantity or usage variation...$ 500
Material price variation... 225

    Total Variations (All Unfavorable) ....$ 725

Sometimes a further refinement is made. The material cost or price variation is made up of two components: (1) the price change due to the standard quantity used; and (2) the price change due to the additional quantity used.

To illustrate, the total material price variation of $225 resulted from a price rise of 10 cents per pound times the 2,250 pounds used. Of the 2,250 pounds used, 2,000 pounds represented the standard quantity. If there had been no quantity variation, the price variation of the materials used would have been 2,000 pounds times 10 cents, or $200. Since 250 additional pounds were used, 250 times 10 cents or $25 of the price variation was due to the increased quantity used. This is often referred to as the *price-quantity* variation.

Although the *price-quantity* variation is of interest to management and should be computed, it is rarely stated separately in a standard cost accounting system. The remainder of the discussion in the text will assume that the *price-quantity* variation is incorporated in the *price* variation.

MATERIAL MIX AND YIELD VARIANCES

In some continuous process manufacturing operations, the material quantity variations have required a more detailed analysis for better managerial control. In some industries such as textiles, foundries, rubber manufacturing, and chemical industries which use predetermined formulas for mixing certain materials, the resulting output results in variations. These variations are of two kinds and closely related: a *mix* variation, and a *yield* variation. A favorable mix variation may have an effect on the yield and cause a yield variation. In the manufacture of castings, a certain mixture will yield a certain volume of finished castings. In the manufacture of sugar, canning fruits, and vegetables, the yields may vary with the mixtures or with the grading of the output. A change in the mixture may also have an effect on the cost of direct labor used. In certain specialized industries, a study of the mix and yield variations is an important phase of production and cost control.

To illustrate these mix and yield variations, a hypothetical illustration is used:

To produce 2,000 pounds of a finished product, the following raw materials quantities and prices at standard are:

Material A................................	1,500 pounds at $0.30......................	$450.00
Material B	500 pounds at 0.20......................	100.00
Material C	400 pounds at 0.425	170.00
Total Cost of Materials Used		$720.00
Cost per pound ($720 ÷ 2,400 pounds)...		$0.30
Cost per pound of finished product ($720 ÷ 2,000 pounds)		0.36

Actual quantities of raw materials used at standard prices:

Material A	8,000 pounds at $0.30........................	$2,400
Material B..............................	2,400 pounds at 0.20........................	480
Material C..............................	2,800 pounds at 0.425......................	1,190
Total............................	13,200 pounds	$4,070

To compute the *yield* variation, it will be noted that for the quantity of material used, the output was less than the formula called for and hence the variation is unfavorable, for example,

Actual quantity at standard material costs:	
13,200 pounds at $0.30..	$3,960*
Actual output at standard material costs:	
10,000 pounds at $0.36...	3,600
Material Yield Variation (Unfavorable, Debit)............................	$ 360

*According to the formula, the use of 13,200 pounds of materials should have produced 11,000 pounds of finished production:

(13,200 × 2,000/2,400, or 11,000.   11,000 − 10,000 × $0.36 = $360.)

To compute the *mix* variation, it must be realized that the quantities of the various raw materials used did not conform to the formula, and therefore the variations are due to the change in the mixture, for example,

Actual quantities used at standard prices (see
  above 13,200 pounds) $4,070
Actual quantities at standard material costs:
  13,200 at $0.30 3,960
      Mix Variation (Unfavorable, Debit)..$ 110

NATURE OF LABOR STANDARDS

As in the case of direct materials, labor standards are established for both *cost* and *quantity* (efficiency). These may be computed in the same manner used for direct materials. For standard cost purposes, *direct labor* is treated separately from *indirect labor,* which is included in the manufacturing overhead cost. Conditions under which labor standards must be set vary from firm to firm. Each company requires a detailed study of the payroll procedures, payroll rates, and the labor supervision conditions under which the standards are to be used. The same basic approach should be taken for labor as was taken for materials.

This discussion is primarily concerned with the basic principles and practices which are used in setting labor standards.

LABOR EFFICIENCY STANDARDS

The determination of how much time workers should use in performing the various manufacturing operations represents one of the most important phases of managerial control. Therefore, the *labor efficiency or quantity or time standards* are an important phase of any standard cost accounting system. Through the careful preparation of time standards, management is able to *measure and control the productivity* of labor, a significant cost element. Great care must be exercised in setting these standards so that their comparison with the actual results will be realistic and meaningful.

Preceding the determination of direct labor time standards must come the standardization of *conditions of work,* in addition to the standardization of the *products* and the *quantity to be manufactured* on each manufacturing order. Specific prerequisites to effective labor time standards include:

1. Efficient plant layout with modern equipment to provide maximum production at minimum cost.
2. Development of a planning, routing, scheduling, and dispatching staff to provide a smooth flow of production without undue delay and confusion.

3. Provision for the careful purchase of materials to flow into production at the proper time, when workmen and machines are available.
4. Standardization of labor operations and methods, with adequate instructions to and training of workers so that the manufacturing will be performed under the best possible conditions.

Labor *time* or *quantity* or *efficiency standards* may be developed by:

1. Averaging past performance records as shown on the cost sheets for the preceding periods. Care must be exercised so that no existing inefficiencies are perpetuated.
2. Making experimental test runs of the manufacturing operations under expected normal conditions.
3. Making time and motion studies of the various labor operations under expected actual conditions. As a result of these the engineering department prepares routing sheets indicating the standard amount of time to be used for each labor operation.
4. Making a reasonable estimate based upon experience and knowledge of the manufacturing operations and the product.

To illustrate the forms used in setting these labor time standards, a *route sheet* (Illustration 16–5), a *time-study observation sheet* (Illustration 16–6), and the Labor Cost section of the standard cost sheet (Illustration 16–7) are shown.

Illustration 16–5. Simple Route Sheet

ROUTE SHEET				
Part Name: _Motor Shaft_			Part No.: _1255_	
Material: _SAE 2315_				
Approve: _J. B. Corkin_			Date: _2/12/_	
No.	Operation Description	Hours per C	Pieces per Hr.	Tools Needed
5	Pick up piece and place in jig	0.47	213	Jig #1255
10	Drill ¼″ hole	0.95	105	H.S. Drill ¼″
15	Remove piece from jig	0.20	500	
20	Blow out chips	0.19	526	
	Total base time	1.81	55	
	Allowance for personal and unavoidable delay	0.36		
	Total standard	2.17	46	

Illustration 16–6. Time-Study Observation Sheet

STUDY NO. 275 — OPERATION Drill 1/4" holes — PART NAME Motor Shaft — PART NO. 1255

TIME STUDY OBSERVATION SHEET — SHEET 1 OF 1 SHEET

NO.	ELEMENTS DESCRIPTION	1 T	1 R	2 T	2 R	3 T	3 R	4 T	4 R	5 T	5 R	6 T	6 R	7 T	7 R	8 T	8 R	9 T	9 R	10 T	10 R
1	Pick up piece and place in jig	19	19	16	216	19	398	18	681	20	765	19	847	19	1027	20	1108	21	1293	19	1477
2	Tighten Set Screw	(23)	42	20	236	20	418	20	701	19	84	19	66	18	46	20	28	19	1312	19	96
3	Advance drill to Work	8	50	9	245	10	28	9	10	10	94	9	75	10	56	10	38	9	21	9	1505
4	Drill 1/4" hole	94	144	89	334	90	518	92	802	90	884	89	964	88	1144	90	1228	92	1413	90	95
5	Raise drill from hole	(11)	155	5	339	6	24	5	07	5	89	6	70	5	49	5	33	5	18	5	1600
6	Loosen Set Screw	9	164	10	349	9	33	9	16	10	99	9	79	9	58	8	41	9	27	9	09
7	Remove piece	14	178	11	360	12	45	10	26	11	810	10	89	11	69	11	52	12	39	10	19
8	Blow out chips	22	200	19	379	18	63	19	45	18	28	19	1008	19	88	20	72	19	58	19	38

FOREIGN ELEMENTS

I	T	R	DESCRIPTION
A			
B			
C			
D			
E			
F			
G			
H			
I			
J			
K			
L			
M			
N			

ELEMENT NUMBER →	1	2	3	4	5	6	7	8
TOTAL "T"	190	174	93	904	47	91	112	192
No. OBS	10	9	10	10	9	10	10	10
AVER. "T"	19	19	9	90	5	9	11	19
MIN. "T"	16	18	8	88	5	8	10	18
MAX. "T"	21	20	10	94	6	10	14	22
RATING								
LEVELING FACTOR	0	0	0	0	0	0	0	0
SELECTED TIME	19	19	9	90	5	9	11	19
% ALLOWANCE								
NORMAL TIME								

	SKILL			EFFORT	
	SUPER	+15		KILLING	+15
	EXCELL.	+10		EXCELL.	+10
	GOOD	+6		GOOD	+6
✓	AVERAGE	0	✓	AVERAGE	0
	FAIR	−7		FAIR	−7
	POOR	−15		POOR	−15

	CONDITIONS			CONSISTENCY	
	EXCELL.	+6		EXCELL.	+4
	GOOD	+4		GOOD	+2
✓	AVERAGE	0	✓	AVERAGE	0
	FAIR	−4		FAIR	−2
	POOR	−7		POOR	−4

COMB. RATING FOR STUDY	SKILL	EFFORT	COND.	CONS'CY.

STUDY STARTED	STUDY FINISHED	OVERALL TIME

Illustration 16–7. *Part of Standard Cost Sheet, Showing Labor
Costs for Manufacturing of Motor Shaft**

STANDARD FACTORY COST PER 100				
Part Name: *Motor Shaft*			Part No.: *1255*	
LABOR COSTS				
Operation Number	Operation Description	Standard Hours	Rate	Standard Labor Cost
1	*Place in jig*	*0.56*	*$1.50*	*$0.84*
2	*Drill ¼" hole*	*1.14*	*1.50*	*1.71*
3	*Remove from jig*	*0.24*	*1.50*	*0.36*
4	*Blow out chips*	*0.23*	*1.50*	*0.345*
	Total labor cost	*2.17*	*1.50*	*$3.255*

*Prepared from routing sheet and time-study observation sheet.

LABOR COST OR RATE STANDARDS

Standard cost *rates* for direct labor may be determined on the basis of—

1. Union contracts.
2. Past experience data. The average, weighted average, or median labor cost for the preceding period might be used as standard.
3. Computations involving *normal operating conditions.*
4. Arbitrary or estimated rates. The person setting the standard costs uses his experience or judgment.

The type of wage system in use also influences the standard cost *rates.* The basic types are (1) day or hourly wage systems, (2) straight piece rates, and (3) multiple piece rates or bonus systems.

Daily or Hourly Wage Systems. When daily or hourly wage systems are used, the standard costs may be affected by the union contracts. Frequently this simplifies matters, especially if it is a long-term contract, because there will be little variation in the rate during this period. On the other hand, the volume of production of hourly wage employees may be controlled by the speed of the automatic machines in use. Changing the rate of speed of the machine will affect the standard labor cost per unit of production.

Straight Piece Rates. These result in the payment of a flat amount per unit of production. Subject to correction for the effect of the minimum wage and hour regulations applicable to these employees, when straight piece rates are used the direct labor cost of manufacturing a unit or number of units is fixed and will not be subject to any variation. Theoretically it is ideal for standard costs, but from a practical viewpoint, this type of wage payment is frequently opposed by labor unions.

Multiple Piece Rates or Bonus Systems. These usually involve several wage rates depending upon the volume of the worker's production. Among such plans are the Halsey, Gantt, Bedaux, and the "differential" piece-rate systems. When this type of wage system is in use, the cost accountant must ascertain from management answers to questions such as:

Is the premium or bonus to be considered as part of the direct labor cost?

Will the standard used in computing the bonuses be the same as the standard used on the cost sheets? If not, what differences or adjustments must be considered?

In studying material standards, it was pointed out that variations were of two kinds: those involving the *quantity* of materials used, and those involving the *price* or *cost* of the materials used. Similarly, in studying labor standards, two types of variation must be considered: those involving the *quantity* of labor to be used in producing a certain quantity, thus indicating the *efficiency of labor;* and those involving the *cost* of the labor to be used, thus indicating the *labor cost variation.*

The *labor efficiency variation* is computed as follows:

Difference between the *standard* hours and the *actual* hours multiplied by the standard labor rate. If the standard hours are more than the actual hours, the variation is considered favorable; if less, it is unfavorable.

The *labor cost or rate variation* is computed in one of two ways:

1. The difference between the *standard wage rate* and the *actual wage rate* multiplied by the number of direct labor hours used in production.
2. The difference between the *actual costs of direct labor incurred* and the product of the *actual number of direct labor hours* and the *standard labor cost rate.*

ILLUSTRATION OF THE COMPUTATION OF LABOR VARIATIONS

As in the case of material variations, four types of information are required to compute labor variations. These are obtained from the standard cost sheets, job time tickets, and payroll records. The data required are:

1. The *standard time or hours* allowed for each operation.
2. The *standard labor cost rate* per hour or per piece.

3. The *actual time or hours* spent in the manufacturing operations.
4. The *actual labor costs* paid for the work.

Continuing the illustration used in computing the material cost variations, the following operating and standard cost data are used:

> On the standard cost sheet for manufacturing 100 units of Product X on a single job, 35 hours of direct labor at a standard cost of $2.40 per hour are required. During the month 10 jobs were completed, on which 360 direct labor hours were used at an average cost of $2.25 per hour.

To compute the two labor cost variations, namely, *efficiency,* based upon the time used, and the *cost or rate variation,* based upon the rate of pay used, the procedure would be:

Standard number of hours (10 jobs × 35 hours) ....350 hrs.
Actual number of hours 360
Excess hours (time or inefficiency variation)...................... 10 hrs. (unfavorable)
10 hours × standard rate of $2.40 shows that the *time or in-*
    efficiency variation cost..$ 24 (unfavorable)
Actual cost of labor, 360 hours × $2.25............................$810
Standard cost of labor, 360 hours × $2.40......................... 864
Savings or favorable cost variation is 15¢ per hour (or 360
    hours × 15¢)...$ 54 (favorable)
        Net Favorable Labor *Cost* Variation ($54 − $24) ......$ 30

Proof or total labor cost variation:
    Standard cost to complete 10 jobs (35 hours × 10 jobs ×
      $2.40)...$840
    Actual cost to complete 10 jobs (360 hours × $2.25) 810
    Net Labor Cost Variation ....$ 30

A *cost-efficiency* variation for labor may be computed in a manner similar to the *price-quantity* variation for materials.

To illustrate, the $54 savings indicated by the cost variation was due to a 15 cents an hour savings over the 360 actual hours used. Had there been no difference between the actual and standard hours worked, the savings would have been 15 cents times 350 hours, or $52.50. The additional 10 hours times the 15 cents or $1.50 was due to the additional hours worked times the savings. Had there not been a 15 cents an hour saving, the additional hours used would have cost $1.50 more.

As in the case of the *price-quantity* variation for materials, the *cost-efficiency* variation for labor is important to management and should be computed. The variation, however, is rarely stated separately in the accounts. The remainder of the discussion in the text will assume that the *cost-efficiency* variation is incorporated in the *cost* variation.

ILLUSTRATION OF STANDARD COSTS AND VARIATIONS

To illustrate the general nature of standard costs as they affect direct material and direct labor, a hypothetical situation is presented so that variations from standard can be computed and so that it is possible to discuss how responsibility for these variations might be placed within a manufacturing organization.

In the first illustration, the standard and actual costs are shown in comparative form (Illustration 16–8), so that in a second illustration (Illustration 16–9) the quantity and cost (price) variations might be indicated. Since the manufacturing overhead is applied on the basis of direct labor hours, any variation due to labor inefficiency will be reflected in a single variation figure for overhead. A more detailed analysis of manufacturing overhead variations will be discussed in the following chapter.

Illustration 16–8

COMPARATIVE COST RECORD July 26, 19—		Article: _A_ Standard Quantity: _100_		
Cost Components	Standard Cost	Actual Cost	Variation	
Materials:				
50 lbs. @ $0.32....................	$ 16.00			
52 lbs. @ $0.30....................		$ 15.60	$ 0.40*	
Labor:				
Operation No. 1:				
18 hrs. @ $2.50....................	45.00			
16 hrs. @ $2.45....................		39.20	5.80*	
Operation No. 2:				
20 hrs. @ $2.40....................	48.00			
24 hrs. @ $2.42....................		58.08	10.08†	
Operation No. 3:				
10 hrs. @ $2.60....................	26.00			
15 hrs. @ $2.55....................		38.25	12.25†	
Manufacturing overhead:				
48 hrs. @ $0.70....................	33.60			
55 hrs. @ $0.70....................		38.50	4.90†	
Total..............................	$168.60	$189.63	$21.03†	

*Under standard.   † Over standard.

An examination of the comparative cost statement indicates that the variations are due either to *price* (*cost*) or *quantity* (*efficiency*) factors. Some variations are due to the fact that the actual costs were higher than the standard, in which case they are *unfavorable;* or less than standard, in which case they are *favorable.*

A detailed statement of the variations is shown in Illustration 16–9.

Illustration 16–9
SUMMARY OF VARIANCES
Article A
(per 100 units)
July 26, 19—

Variance Factor	Amount of Variations			
			Net Variation	
	* Variance over Standard	† Variance under Standard	* Over Standard	† Under Standard
Materials:				
Quantity: 2 lbs. more @ 32¢	$ 0.64			
Price: 2¢ per lb. less for 52 lbs		$1.04		
Net Variation				$0.40
Labor:				
Efficiency (quantity):‡ 2 hrs. less @ $2.50		$5.00		
Cost: 5¢ less for 16 hrs		0.80		
Net Variation				5.80
Efficiency (quantity):‡ 4 hrs. more @ $2.40	$ 9.60			
Cost: 2¢ more for 24 hrs	0.48			
Net Variation			$10.08	
Efficiency (quantity):‡ 5 hrs. more @ $2.60	$13.00			
Cost: 5¢ less for 15 hrs		$0.75		
Net Variation			12.25	
Manufacturing Overhead:				
Efficiency (quantity):‡ 7 hrs. more @ 70¢			4.90	
			$27.23	$6.20
Final Net Variation ($27.23 − $6.20)			$21.03	

* Unfavorable variations if the standards are properly set.
† Favorable variations if standards are properly set.
‡ Labor quantity variation is usually known as labor efficiency variation.

Placing Managerial Responsibility for Variations.   One purpose of standard costs is to permit a comparison of the actual costs with those predetermined so that managerial or supervisory personnel may be held accountable for unfavorable results and credit may be given for favorable performance. Just how this responsibility might be placed will be explained in the following paragraphs. It must always be remembered, however, that the standards may have been incorrectly or improperly computed.

Material.   Responsibility for material cost variations lies in either the *purchasing department* or the *manufacturing department*. The purchasing department may have experimented by buying a different grade or kind of material at a lower price, and because of this it was necessary to use more material. But, nevertheless, even though more material was used, the saving in price might be greater than the cost of the additional quantity.

However, it is also possible that the purchasing department was able to purchase the standard grade of material at less than standard prices, although through waste or spoilage in the manufacturing department the effect of the savings was somewhat nullified, since more than the standard quantity was used in production.

Labor.   Responsibility for labor cost variations belongs to either the *personnel department* or the *manufacturing department.*

The fact that fewer hours were used in manufacturing may be attributable to more careful supervision, better machine arrangement, or to the fact that the personnel department selected more efficient workmen and is perhaps paying a higher wage to some of them.

The increased cost of labor may be due to labor market conditions or to a sudden increase in production volume, necessitating higher wages or the employment of poorly trained workers. Improper supervision or machine setup might also cause labor cost variations by requiring the use of more than the standard number of hours. An inferior grade of material might have required more labor for proper processing. The exact reasons can usually be found with a little careful investigation. In many large concerns there will be no cost variation for labor due to wage rates since they have long-time contracts with labor unions fixing the hourly rates of pay for a definite period of production. In other firms the union contracts fix the labor piece rates, and this also eliminates the labor cost variation. The variations will be due primarily to inefficiency resulting from poor supervision, poor tools, or poor materials.

Manufacturing Overhead.   Since manufacturing overhead costs in this illustration are computed on the basis of labor hours, the amount of manufacturing overhead charged to the order is affected directly by the number of direct labor hours. Therefore, the overhead variation shown for the order is only a quantity variation. The price variation of manufacturing overhead does not appear on specific orders but is part of the over- or underapplied manufacturing overhead at the end of the period, which must be separately analyzed.

Again it must be emphasized that this illustration was used to bring out the nature of variations and does not clearly indicate the clerical routine of standard cost accounting.

STATISTICS AND VARIANCE ANALYSIS

In order to effectively study variances from standard costs, it is necessary for a company to accumulate experience. The cost accountant must have accumulated variances for extended periods of time or from a large number of jobs. Only after some experience has been obtained can the standards and standard costs become defensible and the variances meaningful as quite often the cost accountant will find that a particular standard cost is not realistic and therefore needs adjustment.

Statistical methods may be used by the cost accountant in the area of variance analysis. A problem that comes up again and again in industry is that of determining which variances should be investigated by management. Earlier discussions have shown that even though scientifically determined, a standard is an average and that in any one period, actual performance may vary from the average. Since the standard represents an average, it might be said that variations that occur within the *range* of where the standard was set need not be investigated. For example, if stamping 300 units per hour is standard and the normal range goes from 290 to 310, then only variances above 310 and below 290 need to be investigated, i.e., only those above or below the limits as shown in Illustration 16–10.

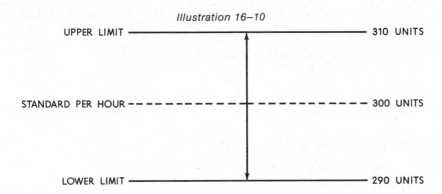

Illustration 16–10

UPPER LIMIT ———————————————————— 310 UNITS

STANDARD PER HOUR — — — — — — — — — — — — — — — — — 300 UNITS

LOWER LIMIT ———————————————————— 290 UNITS

QUESTIONS FOR REVIEW

1. "Standard costs are widely used because they serve as an effective tool for managerial control." Explain briefly.

2. Are standard costs equally applicable to job order costs as to process costs? Explain. Since the printing business is usually on a job order basis, how do you set standards for printing jobs?

3. The material costs variation may be recorded at the time of purchase or at the time of usage. Explain the procedures involved in each case. Which is desirable? Why?

4. Since the Internal Revenue Service does not approve of the materials inventory at standard cost, explain how this objection may be overcome in standard cost procedures.

5. Management is undecided whether to record its standard costs as statistical data or as operating data. What are the arguments for and against each method?

6. What objections are there to the use of the ideal and normal standards in place of expected actual standards? Why are the two former in use?

7. What two types of labor cost variations are used? Which is the more important managerially? Why?

8. How are standards for materials and labor set? For how long a period should they be set? How often revised?

9. In the manufacture of fireproof doors, two pieces of steel measuring 84 inches × 42 inches and having a standard cost of $3.50 each are used. During the month of March, 1,000 doors were completed for which 2,200 pieces of steel costing $8,240 were used. What was the material cost variation and the material quantity variation?

10. The Standard Supply Company produces a single article which goes through two operating departments. The standard cost card for this article indicated the following labor costs:

Department A: Standard time 2.2 hours at a standard rate of $3.60 per hour
Department B: Standard time 1.6 hours at a standard rate of $4.00 per hour

During the month of June, 1,000 units were produced. The actual labor costs in the two departments were:

Department A: 2,000 hours at a cost of $7,600
Department B: 1,500 hours at a cost of   5,700

What was the labor cost and the labor efficiency variation?
What journal entry would be made to close out the Payroll account?

PROBLEMS—GROUP A

Problem 16–1. Purpose: *Material and Labor Cost Variances*

The Plymouth Corporation manufactures a product which is nationally advertised as *Brechtol.* It is manufactured in standard bundles of 1,000 units. A standard cost accounting system is used.

The following data were obtained from the accounting and manufacturing departments for a recent operating period:

1. Standard cost per bundle of 1,000 units:

Direct materials, 80 pounds at $0.50.............................$	40
Direct labor, 40 hours at $3.00......................................	120
Manufacturing overhead, 40 hours at $2.00......................	80
Total Standard Cost..$	240

2. Operating budget:

240 bundles

Direct materials, 19,200 pounds at $0.50.........................$	9,600
Direct labor, 9,600 hours at $3.00.................................	28,800
Manufacturing overhead, 9,600 hours at $2.00	19,200
Total Budgeted Manufacturing Costs ....$	57,600

3. Actual operating results:

> 220 bundles produced
> Direct materials used, 18,500 pounds at $0.48..................$ 8,880
> Direct labor, 8,420 hours at $3.25................................ 27,365
> Manufacturing overhead 19,000
>   Total Manufacturing Cost $55,245

Required:

a) Prepare a statement showing the variances for material and labor costs.
b) Indicate the persons who might be held responsible for these variations.

Problem 16–2. Purpose: *Preparation of Comparative Standard Cost Sheets for Ideal, Normal, and Expected Actual Standards*

The Pitchburg Manufacturing Company is interested in making a comparison of its standard costs under *ideal, normal,* and *expected actual* conditions. This firm manufactures a single product in lots of 1,000. In manufacturing each unit, the standard material and labor costs are:

> Material X...................20 pounds per unit
> Material Y...................30 pounds per unit
> Labor costs:
>   Department 1: 2 hours at $2.80 per unit
>   Department 2: 3 hours at $2.50 per unit
>   Department 3: 5 hours per unit at $3.00

The flexible manufacturing overhead budget was as follows, based upon a maximum production of 52,000 units at 100 percent capacity:

Plant operating						
capacity	100%	90%	80%	70%	60%	50%
Direct labor hours	520,000	468,000	416,000	364,000	355,200	319,000
Budgeted manufacturing						
overhead..................	$780,000	$753,800	$749,000	$728,000	$710,400	$559,000

The plant is presently operating at 60 percent of capacity, and it is expected that this rate will continue during the present year.

Materials are contracted for on a three-month basis but are delivered monthly as needed. Special prices and discounts are offered for purchases in larger quantities, as indicated in the following schedules:

MATERIAL X		MATERIAL Y	
Quantity Contracted for:	Price per Lb.	Quantity Contracted for:	Price per Lb.
Less than 150,000 lbs............$1.20		Less than 200,000 lbs...........$2.00	
150,000–200,000 lbs.............. 1.00		200,000–300,000 lbs. ....Discounts of 20% and 20%	
200,000–1,000,000 lbs. 0.75		300,000–1,200,000 lbs.........Discounts of 20% and 30%	
Over 1,000,000 lbs................ 0.60		Over 1,200,000 lbs. ....$0.90 per lb.	

Required:

Prepare a standard cost sheet for 1,000 units with parallel vertical columns so that comparative costs may be shown under each of the following conditions:

a)   *Ideal* standards at 100 percent operating capacity.
b)   *Normal* standards at 80 percent operating capacity.
c)   *Expected actual* standards.
d)   Which do you consider the most practical method?

Problem 16–3.   Purpose: *Preparation of Standard Cost Sheet; Variance Analysis*

The Peeman Laboratories, Inc., has just produced a new product known as FY–100, a rejuvenation cream liquid. Cost and production studies indicate the following:

This product is to be sold in an 8-ounce bottle at a suggested retail price of $3. Costs and production studies were as follows:

CONTAINER COST

Item	Description	Cost	Comments
2147......8 oz. bottles		$6.00 per gross	Waste and breakage allowance, 2%
315......Labels		$3.30 per M	Waste and spoilage allowance, 3%

Product will be reshipped in bottles, cased.

RAW MATERIALS

Item No.	Description	Cost	Quantity Used per 125-Gallon Batch*
4200 ....Special compound 3X		$42 per 100 lbs.	70.0 lbs.
2136 ....Alcohol and glycerine		$40 per 100 lbs.	80.0 lbs.
3136B ....Perfume oil (secret formula)			4.0 lbs.

* A gallon contains 128 oz.

Standard costs of a 90-pound batch of perfume oil are as follows:

Ingredients...$2,200.00
Direct labor, 4.4 hours at $3 ....   13.20
Manufacturing overhead — $8 per batch plus $2 per
standard labor hour

Allowance for lost materials:
Overfilling, waste, and breakage, allow 4 percent of standard material cost.
Direct labor per gross:
Compounding ....0.12 hours at $2.00
Filling and packing ....1.00 hour at $1.80
Manufacturing overhead:
Compounding ....$2.60 per standard labor hour
Filling and packing .... 1.30 per standard labor hour
plus $0.80 per gross

Required:

a) You are asked to prepare a standard cost sheet for one gross of bottles, arranging the data under the five subheadings listed. Calculations to nearest cent per gross.

b) The company expected to produce 1,000 gross of FY–100 in its first week of production but actually produced only 800 gross. Its direct labor cost of filling and packing was $1,000.40 based upon 820 hours. Prepare an analysis of labor cost variance from standard showing the causes of the variances.

(Adapted from AICPA Uniform Examination)

Problem 16–4. Purpose: *Computation of Variances*

The Pioneer Manufacturing Company produces a chemical detergent in standard batches of 100 units, and in its cost work it uses a standard cost accounting system. The standard cost for a batch of 100 units is as follows:

Materials, 40 pounds at $0.35 per pound	$ 14
Direct labor, 20 hours at $3	60
Manufacturing overhead 20 hours at $2.50	50
Total	$124

Production for the month of September amounted to 220 batches. The relative cost data were as follows:

Budgeted standard output per month	24,000 units
Materials used	9,000 lbs.
Cost of materials used	$ 4,050
Direct labor costs, 4,200 hours	14,700
Overhead costs, actual	10,752
Budgeted overhead per month	$12,000

Management feels that the actual costs per batch varied somewhat from the standard costs calculated at the beginning of the year.

Required:

a) Prepare a statement which will contain a detailed explanation of the variations of the actual costs from the standard costs.

b) Indicate the causes for these variations.

(Adapted from AICPA Uniform Examination)

Problem 16–5. Purpose: *Computation of Material Variances of Price, Mix, and Yield*

The Puritex Chemical Company manufactures a special automotive oil additive which it produces in monthly runs of 10,000 quarts. In the manufacture of this product, production fluctuates because the mix and yield do not always come out to the specified standard figures because of the chemical reactions.

During the month of June, six runs were put through the plant, each expected to produce 2,000 quarts, because the firm had planned to build up an inventory of 2,000 quarts.

The standard product mix for making 2,000 quarts is:

Material A: 1,000 quarts at $1.00 per quart
Material B: 800 quarts at 0.80 per quart
Material C: 750 quarts at 0.40 per quart

June's production of 12,000 quarts were as follows:

Material A: 6,250 quarts at actual cost of $1.10 per quart
Material B: 4,850 quarts at actual cost of 0.84 per quart
Material C: 4,680 quarts at actual cost of 0.35 per quart

Required:

Prepare a schedule showing the variations due to costs and yield for the production runs during June.

PROBLEMS — GROUP B

Problem 16–6. Purpose: *Determining Actual Costs from Standard Cost Records for Material and for Labor Costs*

The Portian Manufacturing Company which started operations in January, 1972, for the manufacture of a specially designed multiplex electronic switching device uses a standard cost accounting system in which all inventories are maintained at standard cost.

However, for financial accounting, the financial statements are prepared at the actual costs. This means that at the end of the fiscal accounting period the cost accounting records must be adjusted to actual costs for the financial statements, but these adjustments are not recorded on the books, only on work sheets.

The inventory accounts at standard cost showed the following balances and entries on December 31, 1972:

Materials		**Materials Price Variance**	
15,000		25,000	

Work-in-Process — Materials		**Materials Usage Variance**	
60,000		25,000	

Work-in-Process — Labor		**Labor Cost Variance**	
40,000		15,000	

Labor Efficiency Variance		**Cost of Sales**	
5,000		Material costs	
		420,000	
		Labor costs 250,000	

Finished Goods	
Labor costs 20,000	
Material costs 30,000	

Required:

a) Compute the actual cost of materials in the cost of goods manufactured.
b) Compute the actual cost of labor in the cost of goods manufactured.
c) Compute the actual cost of the materials portion in the inventories December 31, 1972.
d) Compute the actual cost of the labor portion in the inventories December 31, 1972.

Problem 16–7.   Purpose: *Determination of Variances from Standard, and the Managerial Responsibility Therefor*

The Proudfoot Manufacturing Company submits the following data relative to the completion of Job PR–717. This firm uses a standard cost system, and the standard quantity of production each such job is 200 items.

STANDARD COST SHEET		
JOB PR–717		QUANTITY: 200
		Total Standard Cost
MATERIAL COSTS	Material X, 160 pounds at $4.40	$ 704
	Material Y, 100 pounds at 3.00	300
	Material Z, 50 pounds at 1.60	80
	Total Material Cost...............	$1,084
LABOR COSTS	Department I, 100 hours at $2.50....	$ 250
	Department II, 120 hours at 2.00....	240
	Department III, 60 hours at 3.00....	180
	Total Labor Costs.................	$ 670
MANUFACTURING OVERHEAD	280 hours at $3.50....	$ 980
TOTAL STANDARD COST FOR 200 UNITS......................................		$2,734

The following data represents the quantity and costs applicable to the completion of 10 of these jobs of 200 units each:

Material	Quantity Purchased	Purchase Price	Quantity Used on These 10 Jobs of 200 Units
X...............	800 lbs.	$4.30	800 lbs.
X...............1,200 lbs.		4.60	1,000 lbs.
Y...............1,400 lbs.		3.30	950 lbs.
Z...............	800 lbs.	1.80	550 lbs.

The labor costs incurred for the completion of these 10 jobs were:

Department	Hours	Hourly Pay Rate
I............................800		$2.60
I............................350		2.30
II............................800		2.00
III............................500		3.10
III............................130		3.00

Required:

a) A statement showing comparatively the standard cost, the actual costs, and the variations listed separately for quantity (efficiency) and cost (price), and whether favorable or unfavorable.

b) A supplemental statement showing the possible causes and the managerial responsibility for each variation.

Problem 16–8.   Purpose: *Computation of Actual Costs When Standard Cost Data Is Given; a CPA Problem Adaptation*

The Praderite Corporation was established in 1972. This firm manufactures a single product which passes through several departments. This firm uses a standard cost system. The company's inventories at standard cost are as follows:

	December 31, 1972
Raw material................................	0
Work-in-process:	
Material..................................	$ 75,000
Labor......................................	7,500
Overhead.................................	15,000
Total.....................................	$ 97,500
Finished goods:	
Material..................................	$ 60,000
Labor......................................	20,000
Overhead.................................	40,000
Total.....................................	$120,000
Total Inventories..................	$217,500

The company's preliminary income statement for the year ended December 31, 1972, prior to any year-end inventory adjustments, follows:

Sales	$900,000
Cost of goods sold:	
Standard cost of goods sold:	
Material...	$300,000
Labor	100,000
Overhead	200,000
Total	$600,000

Variances:

Material	$ 25,400	
Labor	25,500	
Overabsorbed overhead	(16,500)	
Total	$ 34,400	634,400
Gross profit		$265,600

Selling expenses:

Salaries	$ 28,000	
Commissions	72,000	
Shipping expense	18,000	
Other	7,000	
Total	$125,000	
General and administrative expenses	50,000	175,000
Profit from operations		$ 90,600

Other income:

Purchases discount	$ 8,000	
Scrap sales	9,000	17,000
Net Income before Taxes		$107,600

All purchase discounts were earned on the purchase of raw materials. The company has included a scrap allowance in the cost standards; the scrap sold cannot be traced to any particular operation or department.

Required:

a) Prepare a schedule computing the actual cost of goods manufactured. The schedule should provide for a separation of costs into material, labor, and overhead costs.

b) Prepare a schedule comparing the computation of ending inventories at standard cost and at actual cost. The schedule should provide for a separation of costs into material, labor, and overhead costs.

(Adapted from AICPA Uniform Examination)

Problem 16–9.   Purpose: *Preparation of Standard Cost Sheets Revisions*

The Panwall Supply Company uses a standard cost system. It produces five basic products, each in lots of 200. The standards have been set after careful studies and tests, supplemented by past experience of manufacturing these unique products. The standard cost sheets are changed only when conditions warrant it. Sometimes these same standards have been in use for a long period of time. On other occasions when business is rather erratic, changes have had to be made.

The standard cost sheets have extra columns for the insertion of four possible revisions of the standards either in part or in total.

The standard cost sheet for the manufacture of Article B, in lots of 200, prepared January 1, was as follows:

Element of Cost and Description	Standard Cost Extensions			
	Jan. 1, 19—	Aug. 1, 19—	Oct. 31, 19—	Jan. 1, 19—
Material Costs:				
180 Lbs. Material X @ $2.00...	$ 360.00			
100 Lbs. Material Y @ 2.50...	250.00			
90 Lbs. Material Z @ 1.50...	135.00			
Total Material Costs.............	$ 745.00			
Labor Costs:				
30 Hrs. in Department I @ $2.00	$ 60.00			
70 Hrs. in Department II @ 2.10	147.00			
50 Hrs. in Department III @ 1.80	90.00			
Total Labor Costs................	$ 297.00			
Manufacturing Overhead Costs:				
150 Hrs. @ $2.00	$ 300.00			
Total Standard Cost per 200 ...	$1,342.00			
Standard Cost per Unit.........	$ 6.71			

On August 1, the price of Material X was increased to $2.40 and Material Y was decreased to $2.08. A substitute material, Material O, was used in place of Material Z. One hundred pounds were required at a cost of $1.10.

In October, due to a strike, labor costs in Department I were increased to $2.10 per hour and in Department III to $2 per hour. In Department II, they remained the same.

In January of following year, it was decided to install a new machine in Department II, which would require only 20 hours of labor at a cost of $2.50 per hour.

Required:

You are asked to show the cost sheet as revised on August 1, October 31, and on January of the following year.

Problem 16–10. Purpose: *Preparation of Comparative Standard Cost Sheets for Ideal, Normal, and Expected Actual Conditions*

The Pristone Manufacturing Company manufactures a single product in lots of 1,000. The maximum capacity of the plant is 36,000 units per year. At the present time, the plant is operating at 70 percent capacity, and it is expected that this will be the rate for the coming year.

To manufacture this product, two raw materials are used—Lartex and Reezon. In the manufacture of each unit, 15 pounds of Lartex and 20 pounds of Reezon are used. Materials are contracted for on a three-month basis but are delivered monthly, as needed. Special prices and discounts are offered for purchases in large quantities, as indicated by the following schedule:

Quantity Contracted For	Lartex	Reezon
Less than 100,000 pounds......	$1.00 per lb.	
100,000 to 130,000 pounds.....	0.75 per lb.	
Over 130,000 pounds	0.60 per lb.	
Less than 100,000 pounds......		$1.50 per lb.
100,000 to 150,000 pounds.....		Discounts of 20% and 10%
Over 150,000 pounds		$0.90 per lb.

The per unit standard labor cost is as follows:

Department I ....2 hours at $1.50 per hour
Department II..1 hour at $2.00 per hour
Department III ....3 hours at $1.60 per hour

The manufacturing overhead cost budget for the year called for the following items on a flexible basis. These costs are applied to the standard cost sheet on the basis of labor hours, a single rate being used for the entire factory.

ESTIMATED MANUFACTURING OVERHEAD COSTS AT VARIOUS OPERATING CAPACITIES

Direct Labor Hours....	108,000	129,600	151,200	172,800	194,400	216,000
Percentage of Capacity	50	60	70	80	90	100
Factory Supervision....	$ 5,000.00	$ 5,000.00	$ 5,000.00	$ 6,000.00	$ 6,000.00	$ 8,000.00
Indirect Labor........	14,000.00	15,000.00	15,000.00	16,000.00	18,000.00	18,000.00
Indirect Materials.....	2,000.00	4,000.00	4,500.00	5,000.00	5,800.00	6,000.00
Repairs..............	1,000.00	1,000.00	1,000.00	1,500.00	1,500.00	1,500.00
Insurance, Fire........	500.00	500.00	500.00	500.00	500.00	500.00
Insurance, Compensa-tion................	300.00	400.00	500.00	600.00	700.00	800.00
Depreciation..........	1,500.00	1,500.00	1,500.00	1,500.00	1,500.00	1,500.00
Heat, Light, and Power	400.00	450.00	500.00	550.00	600.00	650.00
Taxes................	150.00	150.00	150.00	150.00	150.00	150.00
Total............	$24,850.00	$28,000.00	$28,650.00	$31,800.00	$34,750.00	$37,100.00

Required:
From this information prepare in comparative form the standard cost sheets under each of the following conditions (computations to nearest fourth decimal):
a) *Ideal* standards, 100 percent operating capacity.
b) *Normal* standards, 80 percent operating capacity.
c) *Expected actual* standards are to be used.

chapter 17

Standard Cost Accounting — Manufacturing Overhead

NATURE OF MANUFACTURING OVERHEAD IN STANDARD COSTS

Manufacturing overhead cost standards are much more complex than those of direct material and direct labor. The standard cost of materials and the standard cost of labor for each article produced are much more definite in that these costs do not vary greatly with changes in the capacity of the plant, nor with the volume of production. In fact, direct material and direct labor costs are generally assumed to be variable costs. Manufacturing overhead costs, however, while applied to specific jobs or departments, and as such are standard costs for the article produced, are nevertheless also affected by certain *plant* factors rather than *job* factors. The *total plant volume* of production must be a consideration in computing overhead standards. Manufacturing overhead costs include many definite items, but all of these do not follow the same pattern. Some are closely related to the manufacturing operations. Power, indirect materials, supplies, and compensation insurance vary in the same manner as the volume of production, i.e., the *variable overhead* costs. Other manufacturing overhead costs have no direct relation to the volume of the manufacturing operations but are incurred for the *period* whether there is a large or small volume of production. These are classified as *fixed* charges and relate specifically to the overall plant rather than to specific jobs. *Period costs* or *fixed costs* include such items as rent, taxes on building, fire insurance of building, and the superintendent's salary. Between these two groups of overhead costs are a number of indirect costs which are neither definitely fixed nor completely variable, but the amounts incurred will increase less than in proportion to volume increases, or at irregular intervals as the volume of production increases. This group includes such items as indirect labor and inspection costs. This complexity in the makeup of the total manufacturing overhead must be taken into consideration when setting standard costs.

THE PREDETERMINED NATURE OF OVERHEAD COSTS

Long before many firms used standard costs for materials and labor, they were using a predetermined rate for manufacturing overhead. This form of standard was the forerunner of a broader application of standards to materials and labor. The analysis of the over- and underapplied overhead into detailed factors is one of the managerial advantages of a more complete system of standard costs.

The predetermined manufacturing overhead rate is primarily related either to the overall plant or to the various departments within the plant rather than to specific jobs. It is only after the plant or departmental rate has been first determined that it is possible to compute an applied cost for overhead for a specific product. In other words, setting a predetermined overhead rate which subsequently becomes the basis for the standard overhead cost for each product involves certain plant factors. These factors are the *budgeted capacity* or production expressed in terms of direct labor hours or machine-hours or some other base and the overall standard *indirect costs* of operating the plant at this budgeted capacity or volume of production.

The *budgeted capacity* used in setting overhead standard costs for managerial control involves agreement on what is to be considered *normal output* for setting standards, and then developing a *flexible budget* to show the effect on costs for fixed, variable, and semivariable items at varying operating capacities. In other words, setting standard overhead costs requires the determination of (1) *standard capacity* and (2) *standard overhead costs* for this capacity.

STANDARD OR PREDETERMINED OVERHEAD RATES

Predetermined overhead rates, previously discussed in Chapter 10, related to historical costs, but the concept of predetermining overhead costs started the development of standard costs for managerial control. There is an increasing tendency to use *separate* predetermined overhead rates for fixed overhead and for variable overhead. The purpose of this breakdown is to permit a more effective analysis and control of variations by function.

To compute a standard or predetermined overhead rate, the formula used is:

$$\frac{\text{Budgeted manufacturing overhead}^1}{\text{Budgeted production}} = \text{Predetermined rate.}$$

The budgeted production in a plant may be measured in various ways. For some firms in which there are a few uniform products, this production may be expressed in terms of *units*. Where there are many different products requiring different amounts of material and productive time, production may be expressed in terms of *hours*, either *direct labor* or *machine*. Sometimes, either due to the uniformity of the wage payment per hour or the difficulty in computing the labor or machine-hours, the production may be measured in terms of *direct labor wage payments* or *labor costs*.

Predetermined *standard* overhead rates may be set in various ways depending on the circumstances in a given company as one company-wide rate may not be enough. If operations are carried on in various departments, a predetermined rate for each department is necessary. Production may be expressed in labor hours in some departments and in machine-hours in others. In some companies, the departmental rates are further divided between fixed and variable.

In addition to these, if a firm has a large number of factories scattered throughout the country, all or part of the general administrative overhead from the central main office may be allocated to each plant as an element of manufacturing overhead costs. This may also require a separate predetermined overhead rate.

CONTROLLING STANDARD OVERHEAD COSTS

Because *comparison* is a necessary element of control, a standard cost system is a good control technique. Because certain costs tend to vary with changes of activity while others ordinarily do not, *volume* is an important consideration in attempting to control manufacturing overhead costs.

To determine proper standards for the comparison of predetermined estimated costs with actual costs at various volume levels, manufacturing overhead must be accumulated in such fashion that the relationship of cost to volume of activity may be readily ascertained. Therefore, in addition to classification by *department* or function or cost center, costs must be further classified as to *behavior*. *Cost behavior* is determined through the process of distinguishing between *fixed* and *variable* costs. Understanding *cost behavior* is an important phase of managerial control.

Manufacturing overhead costs, grouped first by department and then

---

[1] The budgeted manufacturing overhead is calculated upon the *normal operating capacity*, whether this is at theoretical, average, or expected actual capacity.

by behavior, fixed or variable, are further reduced to a predetermined or standard basis for each unit of production — either units of product, per labor hour, per machine-hour, or per labor cost dollar. Since the *per unit* fixed overhead cost will increase as the volume of production decreases, and vice versa, adequate control of the overhead costs can best be established by using a *flexible* or *sliding* budget instead of one based on an arbitrarily selected "normal" volume.

The development and application of *flexible budgets* (discussed in Chapter 14) facilitates more effective cost control and improved management planning by:

1. Recognizing the elements of cost behavior at varying levels of production, thus providing the total estimated overhead costs at each output level so that throughout a given period, proper standard overhead rates which will most nearly represent the anticipated volume of production can be used, and
2. Providing data for management's extension of *cost behavior relationships* to the overall planning of the company.

Timely analysis and interpretation of the *effect of volume on costs* have done much in aiding progressive management to institute better techniques of cost control to maintain and improve profits.

Illustration 17–1 shows the flexible budget for overhead costs for Machine Department No. 1. It is assumed that these figures represent hypothetically a period of one year. In studying this illustration it should be noted:

1. A standard rate should be used for an entire year. The flexible budget is used for comparative purposes if the volume of production or the cost of the overhead items do not equal those used in computing the standard overhead rate.

2. The various manufacturing overhead costs are grouped functionally. Within each group there may be fixed or variable costs. This grouping aids in managerial control of the costs.

3. The effect of the volume of production on these various overhead cost items and groups is shown for plant operating capacities of 50, 60, 70, 80, 90, and 100 percent.

4. Total overhead costs are shown for each operating capacity so that a predetermined standard overhead cost rate may be computed for each.

5. The various predetermined overhead cost rates determined for the different operating capacities, based upon direct labor hours (approximate computations), are:

At   50% capacity, $1,937 ÷ 4,000 hours = $0.48 per direct labor hour

Illustration 17–1

MANUFACTURING OVERHEAD COSTS
AT VARIOUS OPERATING CAPACITIES

Machine Dept. No. 1
E. J. Fuller, Foreman

Direct Labor Hours		4,000	4,800	5,600	6,400	7,200	8,000
Per Cent of Capacity........		50	60	70	80	90	100
Code No.	Overhead Cost Items						
	Supervision and Clerical Expense:						
01	Foreman.................	$ 360.00	$ 360.00	$ 360.00	$ 400.00	$ 500.00	$ 500.00
02	Inspectors...............	....	....	....	....	....	....
03	Clerical.................	196.00	196.00	196.00	196.00	220.00	220.00
	Total Supervision and Clerical Expense......	$ 556.00	$ 556.00	$ 556.00	$ 596.00	$ 720.00	$ 720.00
	Indirect Labor:						
10	Oilers, Sweepers, and Cleaners...............	$ 140.00	$ 148.00	$ 156.00	$ 164.00	$ 172.00	$ 180.00
11	Internal Transportation...	28.00	28.00	28.00	36.00	36.00	36.00
12	Idle or Lost Time.........	....	....	....	....	....	....
13	Other Indirect Labor......	240.00	264.00	288.00	312.00	336.00	360.00
	Total Indirect Labor....	$ 408.00	$ 440.00	$ 472.00	$ 512.00	$ 544.00	$ 576.00
	Operating Supplies:						
20	Fuel....................	....	....	....	....	....	....
21	Nails, Rods, and Wire....	....	....	....	....	....	....
22	Grinding and Polishing Wheels...............	$ 116.00	$ 120.00	$ 124.00	$ 128.00	$ 132.00	$ 136.00
23	Paints, Lubricants, and Waste.................	120.00	120.00	124.00	128.00	128.00	132.00
24	Stationery and Office Supplies..............	14.00	14.00	14.00	18.00	18.00	18.00
25	Miscellaneous Supplies	20.00	20.00	20.00	20.00	24.00	24.00
	Total Operating Supplies.............	$ 270.00	$ 274.00	$ 282.00	$ 294.00	$ 302.00	$ 310.00
	Maintenance and Repairs:						
40	Machinery...............	$ 120.00	$ 144.00	$ 168.00	$ 192.00	$ 216.00	$ 240.00
41	Motors.................	24.00	28.00	32.00	36.00	40.00	44.00
42	Tools...................	360.00	432.00	504.00	568.00	648.00	720.00
43	Miscellaneous Equipment..	16.00	16.00	16.00	16.00	16.00	18.00
	Total Maintenance and Repairs.............	$ 520.00	$ 620.00	$ 720.00	$ 812.00	$ 920.00	$1,022.00
	Miscellaneous:						
50	Machinery Setup.........	$ 11.00	$ 14.00	$ 18.00	$ 20.00	$ 23.00	30.00
51	Telephone..............	5.00	5.00	5.00	5.00	5.00	5.00
52	Inventory Adjustment.....	....	....	....	....	....	....
53	Employee Welfare........	8.00	8.00	12.00	12.00	12.00	12.00
54	Liability Insurance.......	20.00	24.00	28.00	32.00	36.00	40.00
59	Miscellaneous Expense....	16.00	16.00	16.00	16.00	20.00	20.00
	Total Miscellaneous....	$ 60.00	$ 67.00	$ 79.00	$ 85.00	$ 96.00	$ 107.00
	General Charges:						
70	Depreciation.............	$ 100.00	$ 100.00	$ 100.00	$ 100.00	$ 100.00	$ 100.00
71	Insurance................	9.00	9.00	9.00	9.00	9.00	9.00
72	Taxes...................	14.00	14.00	14.00	14.00	14.00	14.00
	Total General Charges......	$ 123.00	$ 123.00	$ 123.00	$ 123.00	$ 123.00	$ 123.00
	Total All Overhead Costs	$1,937.00	$2,080.00	$2,232.00	$2,422.00	$2,705.00	$2,858.00

At 60% capacity, $2,080 ÷ 4,800 hours = $0.43 per direct labor hour
At 70% capacity, $2,232 ÷ 5,600 hours = $0.40 per direct labor hour
At 80% capacity, $2,422 ÷ 6,400 hours = $0.38 per direct labor hour
At 90% capacity, $2,705 ÷ 7,200 hours = $0.37 per direct labor hour
At 100% capacity, $2,858 ÷ 8,000 hours = $0.36 per direct labor hour

As a general rule, the rates should be lower at each successive level of increased volume, since the fixed costs are allocated over more units.

6.   Some of these budgeted overhead costs are fixed, such as telephone, depreciation, insurance, and taxes. Others are variable, but even part of the variable is fixed—that is, would be incurred if there were no production at all. Among such we have the wages of oilers, sweepers, cleaners, and supervisors. Analyzing a few of the fixed or semivariable overhead items into their fixed and variable elements, the following table might be prepared for the *90% capacity rate:*

	Fixed Portion	Variable Portion
Supervision and clerical expense	$556	$164
Internal transportation	28	8
Employee welfare	8	4
Miscellaneous expense	16	4

To be most effective, the changes in the fixed and semivariable overhead costs must be studied to determine whether or not they are controllable items.

7.   This illustration indicates the overhead costs for Department No. 1. Although it is possible to prepare such a budget on a plantwide basis, for most effective managerial control it is desirable to compute predetermined overhead cost rates and variations for each group of costs on a *departmental* basis.

8.   Although in this illustration a single composite rate for the department is computed for the total of the fixed, variable, and semivariable overhead costs, many firms prefer a more detailed control by establishing separate rates for the fixed, variable, or semivariable overhead items, or by having separate rates for each group within the department, such as supervision, indirect labor, operating supplies, maintenance and repairs, general charges, and miscellaneous. This procedure is much more costly than having a single departmental rate, and therefore can be justified only if the managerial control and economies effected through the use of many rates results in higher profits.

VARIATIONS IN OVERHEAD COSTS

Variations from standard costs for manufacturing overhead fall into two general classifications:

1. Those that have to do with the *level of operations.*
2. Those that have to do with the *level of performance.*

The variations from standard costs may be computed by using the three-variance or the two-variance method. The method that is chosen will depend on the data available and the information desired. The three-variance method is based upon a budget for *actual* hours while the two-variance method is based upon a budget for *standard* hours for the production attained. Both methods will be illustrated in the following paragraphs.

MANUFACTURING OVERHEAD VARIATIONS WITH A FLEXIBLE BUDGET

Manufacturing overhead variations become *more meaningful* as control devices when flexible budgeting techniques are used. The budget may be adjusted to the level of operations that existed during the period. A three-variance system and a two-variance system may be utilized. Both will be illustrated.

The three-variation system utilizing a *flexible budget* is similar to the three-variation system where a fixed budget is being used. The difference is that the budget is adjusted for the *actual hours* worked. The variations computed under this method are:

1. *Budget* or *spending* variation.
2. *Capacity* or *plant volume* variation.
3. *Efficiency* variation.

In lieu of the three-variation system, a two-variation system may be utilized. Under this system, the following two variations are isolated:

1. *Plant Volume Variation.* This variation is the difference between what was applied to production and the budget adjusted to *standard production.*
2. *Controllable or Spending Variation.* This variation is the difference between actual manufacturing overhead and the budget adjusted to the *standard production.* This is an important variation for control purposes as the difference between what costs were and what costs should have been is highlighted.

Illustrations of both the three- and two-variation methods follow using the same basic data:

The following cost data affecting the manufacturing overhead costs are obtained from the records of the Efandee Manufacturing Company for the period under study. This firm expects to operate at 100 percent capacity and is using a flexible budget, separating the overhead costs into the fixed and variable.

Budgeted manufacturing overhead costs for the period at the 100 percent capacity were:

Fixed $150,000		
Variable.. 100,000	$250,000	

Budgeted volume of production at 100 percent capacity, in terms of direct labor hours...125,000 hrs.

Standard overhead rate for period:
$0.80 variable cost rate
$\underline{1.20}$ fixed cost rate $2.00 per hr.

Standard direct labor hours for production for period ....126,000 hrs.
Actual hours worked on production for period...................................126,710 hrs.
Actual manufacturing overhead costs for period:

Fixed $150,000		
Variable.. 103,200	$253,200	

THREE VARIATIONS—FLEXIBLE BUDGET

The budget or spending variation is determined as follows:

Actual manufacturing overhead................	$253,200	
Budget adjusted to *actual* hours:		
Variable costs (126,710 × $0.80)...........$101,368		
Fixed costs..................................... 150,000	251,368	
Budget or Spending Variation	$ 1,832	unfavorable

The $1,832 is the difference between actual factory overhead costs and budgeted costs. Note that the budget has been *adjusted* to the actual hours worked.

The *capacity* or *volume* variation is computed in the following manner:

Budget at actual hours $251,368	
Actual hours at standard rate (126,710 × $2) 253,420	
Capacity or Volume Variation........................$ 2,052	favorable

The capacity or volume variation has the same meaning as in the case of the static budget except that the budgeted figure has been adjusted for actual hours worked. The plant worked 1,710 hours above the budgeted volume that was used in setting the standard rate. The plant worked 126,710 hours instead of the 125,000 hours that was used in setting the budget. The difference of 1,710 hours multiplied by a rate of $1.20 which is the fixed expense rate equals $2,052, the amount of the capacity variance.

The *efficiency* variation is determined in the following manner:

Actual hours at standard rate $253,420
Standard hours at standard rate (applied to work-in-
  process) (126,000 × $2)..................................... 252,000
      Efficiency Variation................................$ 1,420 unfavorable

The efficiency variation indicates that 710 hours in excess of standard was necessary to complete the production.

Summary of the three variations:

Budget variation..$1,832 unfavorable
Capacity variation .... 2,052 favorable
Efficiency variation .... 1,420 unfavorable
      Net Variation ....$1,200 unfavorable

TWO VARIATIONS – FLEXIBLE BUDGET

The *controllable* or *spending* variation is computed as follows:

Actual manufacturing overhead................ $253,200
Budget adjusted to the *standard* hours:
  Variable costs (126,000 × $0.80)...........$100,800
  Fixed costs..................................... 150,000   250,800
      Controllable or Spending Variation... $ 2,400 unfavorable

The $2,400 is the difference between actual cost and what was allowed for the budget based on standard production. It represents the difference between what was incurred and what should have been incurred for the production that was made. This is the variation that can be used to measure operating management especially if the controllable variation is further analyzed into price and volume variations. The $2,400 may be due to changes in volume and changes in cost of overhead items.

The *volume* variation is computed as follows:

Budget adjusted to standard hours...........................$250,800
Standard hours × standard rate (applied to work-in-
  process: 126,000 × $2)..................................... 252,000
      Volume Variation.......................................$ 1,200 favorable

The $1,200 arose because the company operated at more than 100% of capacity. In fact, the volume variance under the two-variation method arises because of the behavior of fixed costs. The standard rate of $2 per hour included $1.20 of fixed costs and $0.80 of variable costs. The $1.20 rate was established at a level of 125,000 hours. Since the company worked 126,000 standard hours, 1,000 hours more × $1.20 was applied than had been budgeted resulting in the favorable volume variation of $1,200.

The two variations are summarized:

Controllable variation..$2,400 unfavorable
Volume variation.. 1,200 favorable
Net Variation (Underapplied)...........................$1,200 unfavorable

The two-variation system has been becoming more popular since it is the one that the businessman can understand; variations are isolated for changes in performance and for changes in volume. Until a company adopts flexible budgeting techniques, however, it is precluded from using the two-variation method. Furthermore, the two-variance method results in tighter control because it measures performance against a budget for completed production and not just for putting in time.

ILLUSTRATION OF DEPARTMENTAL OVERHEAD VARIATIONS

Having observed the general methods and principles of computing manufacturing overhead variations on a plantwide basis, it is desirable to show this on a departmental basis. The departmental unit is considered best for effective managerial control. In the following illustration the data shown for the flexible budget for *Machine Department No. 1* are used in computing the two manufacturing overhead variations:

1. Manufacturing overhead budget for Department 1 for the period at the expected operating capacity of 100 percent, or 10,000 direct labor hours:

	Fixed Amount	Variable Amount*	Total
Supervision...	$ 556	$150	$ 706
Indirect labor	408	200	608
Operating supplies..............................	270	50	320
Maintenance and repairs.....................	520	300	820
Miscellaneous costs...........................	60	50	110
Depreciation	100	–	100
Insurance..	9	–	9
Taxes..	14	–	14
Total..	$1,937	$750	$2,687

* Variation due to increased volume over 50 percent capacity.

2. Budgeted hours for Machine Department 1 for month, 10,000 hours.

3. Standard predetermined overhead rate for department for month at operating capacity of 100 percent:

> Fixed overhead costs: $1,937 ÷ 10,000 hours = $0.1937
> Variable overhead costs: $ 750 ÷ 10,000 hours = 0.0750
> Total Departmental Overhead Rate, per Labor Hour...$0.2687

4. Actual hours worked during month in Department 1, 9,200 hours.
5. Standard hours called for by the *actual production* in Department 1 during the month, 9,000 hours.
6. Budgetary report showing actual and budgeted overhead costs for the month for Department 1:

Dept. *Machine Department No. 1 (E. J. Fuller, Foreman)*			Planning Budgeted Hours *10,000*
			Actual Hours *9,200*
For Month of ____ *June* ____ 19—			Standard Hours *9,000*

Overhead Cost Items	Adjusted Budget (9,000 Hours)	Actual	Controllable Variation
Supervision.............................	$ 691.00	$ 730.00	+$39.00
Indirect labor.........................	588.00	680.00	+$92.00
Operating supplies....................	315.00	290.00	−$25.00
Maintenance and supplies..............	790.00	850.00	+60.00
Miscellaneous factory expense...........	105.00	90.00	−15.00
Depreciation..........................	100.00	100.00	0
Insurance.............................	9.00	9.00	0
Taxes.................................	14.00	14.00	0
Total............................	$2,612.00	$2,763.00	+$151.00
Applied to production for month (9,000 hours × $0.2687)....................		2,418.30	
Underapplied.........................		$ 344.70	

The two manufacturing overhead cost variations computed on a departmental basis from these data are:

> *Controllable variation:*
> Actual manufacturing overhead $2,763.00
> Budget adjusted to 9,000 hours ($750 × 90% + $1,937)... 2,612.00
>   Unfavorable ....$ 151.00
>
> *Volume variation:*
> Budget adjusted to 9,000 hours..............................$2,612.00
> Applied: standard hours × standard rate (9,000 hours × $0.2687)... 2,418.30
>   Unfavorable ....$ 193.70

Summary:

Controllable variation—unfavorable	$ 151.00
Volume variation—unfavorable	193.70
Net Variation (Underapplied)	$ 344.70

The determination of the variances on a departmental basis is a common procedure in practice as better managerial control is achieved than if the variances had been determined for the company as a whole. The departmentalization of the variances permits the pinpointing of responsibility for the variances. For example, in the above illustration, E. J. Fuller, foreman, should be asked why the indirect labor expense was $92 more than anticipated, etc.

MANUFACTURING OVERHEAD VARIATIONS WITH A FIXED OR STATIC BUDGET

If a company uses a fixed or static budget for overhead instead of a flexible budget, the *three-variation system* is the only one that may be used. These three variations are:

1. *Budget or Spending Variations.* These are overhead *cost* variations and are due primarily to the fact that the overhead costs were higher or lower than the estimate as shown in the budget. They indicate that the various items of overhead for the plant cost more or less than anticipated. The causes may be due to change in volume of production or to improperly estimating the cost of the various items which make up the overhead. It is computed by taking the difference between the *estimated* or *budgeted* overhead costs and the *actual* overhead costs.

2. *Capacity or Volume Variations.* These represent *volume* variations for the plant as a unit. Volume may be measured in terms of units produced, direct labor hours, machine-hours, or some other base. This variation arises because the estimated volume of production in the plant as a unit differs from the actual. For example, if the estimated volume of production for a given period was 100,000 direct labor hours on the basis of the standards set for the various products and the firm worked 106,000 hours, then the firm worked 6,000 hours more than the anticipated capacity. Ordinarily this would be a favorable condition, unless this increase in capacity was due to the inefficiency of the workers on the jobs. In other words, increased capacity to be considered favorable must result in increased production; otherwise it merely offsets the inefficiency due to excess labor hours. This variation is computed by multiplying the excess hours (6,000) by the predetermined standard rate for overhead.

3. *Efficiency Variations.* These variations arise because more or less time or effort was expended on the production than should have been expended.

The sum of these three manufacturing overhead variations is equal to the over- or underapplied manufacturing overhead. Hence, these variations represent an analysis of over- or underapplied manufacturing overhead into variations due to changes in costs and variations due to changes in the volume of production.

An illustration that will aid in the computation of the variations follows:

The following cost data affecting the manufacturing overhead costs are obtained from the records of the Milden Manufacturing Company. This firm uses a fixed budget.

Budgeted manufacturing overhead costs for the period.........$250,000
Budgeted volume of production .... 125,000 hrs.
Standard overhead rate (based upon the budget)................ $2 per hr.
Standard direct labor hours for production......................... 126,000 hrs.
Actual hours worked on production................................. 126,710 hrs.
Actual manufacturing overhead costs for period $253,200

The *budget* or *spending* variation is determined as follows:

Actual manufacturing overhead $253,200
Budgeted manufacturing overhead..................... 250,000
    Budget or Spending Variation.................$ 3,200 unfavorable

The $3,200 is the difference between what was budgeted and what was incurred. Since actual costs were greater than anticipated costs, the variation is considered unfavorable.

A weakness in the usefulness of this budget variation is that no recognition is given to changes in production volume. The budget was 125,000 hours, and the actual hours worked were 126,710. The use of flexible budgeting techniques will help solve the problem as a budget adjusted for actual production will be prepared. This is illustrated in the next section.

The *capacity* or *volume* variation is determined as follows:

Budgeted manufacturing overhead $250,000
Actual hours at standard rate (126,710 × $2)................. 253,420
    Capacity or Volume Variation ....$ 3,420 favorable

The $3,420 indicates that more hours were worked than had been anticipated and that the $250,000 had been allocated over too few hours. The standard rate of $2 had been determined by dividing $250,000 by 125,000. The $250,000 should have been divided by the 126,710. The $3,420 is considered favorable as more work had been done in the plant than had been planned.

The *efficiency* variation is determined as follows:

Actual hours at standard rate (126,710 × $2)..................$253,420
Standard hours at standard rate (this is the amount
applied to work-in-process under a standard cost
system) (126,000 × $2)... 252,000
      Efficiency Variation ....$ 1,420 unfavorable

The $1,420 indicates that more hours were used to complete the units than the standard called for. Seven hundred and ten more hours were used than should have been used; the efficiency variation in this illustration was unfavorable. It measures the production efficiency of the work done.

The three variations are summarized as follows:

       Budget variation ....$3,200 unfavorable
       Capacity variation... 3,420 favorable
       Efficiency variation....................................... 1,420 unfavorable
          Net Variation (Underapplied)..................$1,200 unfavorable

The net variance of $1,200 may also be computed by subtracting the amount applied to production ($252,000) from the actual ($253,200). Since $1,200 less was applied to production than should have been, the amount is underapplied. The causes of the underapplied are explained by the three variations.

ILLUSTRATIONS OF STANDARD COST SHEETS

Illustration 1.   In the manufacture of ice cream, candy, cereals, and similar process cost products, it is possible to have *test runs* to determine the standard costs of definite quantities, lots, or batches, and to determine the *allowable or standard* amount of waste or spoilage. The products indicated are representative of *continuous process* or of operation costs, as contrasted with job order or job lot costs. Once the standards of such a test run have been set up, it will not be necessary to change the standards unless wide variations result in the manufacturing operations, at which time new standards and new test runs will be necessary. This type of standard cost sheet (see Illustration 17–2) is characteristic of the ease and simplicity of setting continuous process standards.

Illustration 2.   This represents the standard cost sheet of a company which manufactures a variety of trousers, coats, and vests used in hunting or as work clothes. The products manufactured by this firm are divided equally between those for stock and those made to the order of the customer. The company uses a job-lot plan of manufacturing be-

Illustration 17–2

			February 14, 19—

STANDARD COST SHEET
(HARD CANDIES AND BULK PACKAGES)
PRODUCT: *Coconut Bonbons, Formula 42*

	Quantity	Price	Amount
Material:			
Corn Syrup..	50 lbs.	$0.13	$ 6.50
Sugar...	30	0.08	2.40
Chocolate...	10	0.30	3.00
Fruits and Nuts....................................	20	0.60	12.00
Flavoring and Coloring..............................	1	1.00	1.00
Total Material..................................	111 lbs.		$24.90
Percentage of Waste, 10%.........................	11		.....
Total Material.................................	100 lbs.	$0.249	$24.90

	Labor		Manufacturing Overhead	
	Hours @	Amount	Rate	Amount
Labor and Manufacturing Overhead:				
Heating and Boiling..................		$18.00	50%	$ 9.00
Whipping and Mixing................		3.00		1.50
Coating...........................		1.50		0.75
Mix Coating.......................		2.10		1.05
Hand Dipping......................		15.40		7.70
Hand Packing......................		.....		.....
Machine Dipping...................		.....		.....
Machine Packing...................		.....		.....
Subtotal.......................		$40.00		$20.00
Percentage of Waste...............		.....		.....
Cartoning........................		2.00		1.00
Total Labor and Manufacturing Overhead.....................		$42.00		$21.00
Boxes and Labels......................		$ 3.00		$.....
Cases and Cartons.....................		1.10		.....
Material as Above.....................		24.90		.....
Total Material Cost...............		$29.00		$.....
Total Factory Cost...............		$92.00		$.....
Commercial Expense...................		30.00		.....
Interest and Discounts.................		.....		.....
Total Cost per Pound..............		$ 1.22		$.....
Total Cost per Unit...............		$ 1.22		$.....
Selling Price.....................		2.00		.....
Profit.........................		$ 0.78		$.....

*Adapted with permission from C. W. Bennett and W. P. Fiske, "Cost Accounting for Hattie Hicks Sweets Co.," *N.A.A. Bulletin.*

cause of the constantly changing design of a diversified line of more than 200 to 250 separate items. The standard cost sheet shown in Illustration 17–3 is used to record the cost of producing *one dozen* garments and is a rather simple form of standard cost sheet.

Illustration 3. In some firms, a large number of small parts must first be manufactured before the main product can be assembled. In the production of sewing machines, vacuum cleaners, pianos, washing machines, and various motors, a separate standard cost sheet must be used for each part manufactured, and finally an assembly standard cost sheet for the final product. The cost control of the individual parts manufactured is often more important than the cost control of the final assembly because the latter may not offer much variation from the standard. This is emphasized even more when one considers the manufacturing process of a piano, which requires more than *four hundred* different parts, and for each part there is a standard cost sheet for control of production costs.

Illustration 17–3.   Standard Cost Record*

STANDARD COST RECORD											
DESCRIPTION					DATE		CUSTOMER		STYLE NO.		
Hunting Coat—1 dozen					SIZE SCALE *37–49*		SIMILAR TO		CODE NO.		
DIRECT MATERIALS					STANDARD COST PER DOZEN		ESTIMATED		ESTIMATED		
CODE	DESCRIPTION	WIDTH	QUANTITY	PRICE	EXTENSION		PRICE	EXTENSION	PRICE	EXTENSION	
	BODY MATERIALS			$	$		$	$	$	$	
23	*11 oz. Army Duck*	*40"*	*40*	.65	26.00						
	TOTAL				26.00						
	TRIM	UNIT									
	Thread				.93						
610	*Size Ticket*	*m*	*12*	.80	.01						
420	*36/E Br Buttons*	*g*	*108*	.60	.45						
	TOTAL				4.00						
	TOTAL MATERIALS				30 00						
	TRANSPORTATION IN				%		%		%		
LABOR AND EXPENSE		COST CENTER	RATE	SAH	EXTENSION		SAH	EXTENSION	SAH	EXTENSION	
CUTTING		51	2.00	$1.00	$ 2.00		$	$	$	$	
SEWING		51	1.50	12.00	18 00						
INSPECTION		51	1.50	.50	.75						
TOTAL LABOR AND EXPENSE					20.75						
STANDARD MANUFACTURING COST					50.75						
ADMINISTRATION SELLING—CHAIN—JOBBER—RETAIL											
PROFIT AND LOSS					9.00						
TOTAL STANDARD COST					59.75						
COMMISSION %											
DISCOUNT %											
MARK-UP %					5.30						
STANDARD SELLING PRICE					65.05						

* With permission, from *N.A.A. Bulletin.*

The illustration of the standard cost sheet for this type of procedure is based upon the manufacture of 100 motor shafts. (See Illustration 17–4.) The material costs used in this work can be ascertained fairly easily, either by measurement, test runs, or past experience. The computation of the standard costs for labor is not so simple. Management must first standardize the *flow of work* in the factory to create the most efficient work. This is done by preparing a *job routing sheet.* Industrial

Illustration 17–4. Standard Cost Sheet Prepared from Routing Sheet and Time-Study Observation Sheet

STANDARD FACTORY COST PER 100				
Part Name: *Motor Shaft*				Part No.: *1255*
LABOR COSTS				
Operation Number	Operation Description	Standard Hours	Rate	Standard Labor Cost
1	Place in jig	0.56	$1.50	$ 0.84
2	Drill ¼" hole	1.14	1.50	1.71
3	Remove from jig	0.24	1.50	0.36
4	Blow out chips	0.23	1.50	0.345
	Total labor cost	2.17	$1.50	$ 3.255
MATERIAL COSTS				
Entry Point	Description	Gross Quantity	Standard Price	Standard Cost
Oper. 1	SAE 2313	250#	$0.10	$25.00
	Total material cost			$25.00
STANDARD COST SUMMARY				
		8/1/—		
Material		$25.00		
Labor		3.255		
Mfg. overhead 160% D.L.		5.208		
Total		$33.463		

engineers and the production manager usually are responsible for this phase of the work. Once the job routing sheets have been completed, it becomes necessary to set *job time or operation standards*. This is done most effectively by having time and motion studies made of each operation.

FACTORS INTERFERING WITH THE SUCCESSFUL USE OF STANDARDS

Some of the factors which tend to interfere in the successful use of standards as reported in the *N.A.A. Research Series No. 12* ("Standards to Aid Control of Manufacturing Costs") are:

1.   *Lack of interest or understanding of the usefulness of standard costs by management.* Some companies have well-developed standard cost plans for product costing but make little use of the standard costs for managerial control purposes. One glaring and almost unbelievable example is that of an important valve manufacturing concern that had been collecting labor cost variations by departments for several years and yet did not know what to do with them. When a discussion of these variations with the foreman in the department in which they occurred was suggested, the cost accountant could not believe that he had overlooked such obvious procedure for managerial control.

2.   Some standards are out of date or unreliable and are therefore not taken seriously.

3.   Some standards are designed to give product, rather than operation, costs. This prevents management from making effective use of the standards, since it is difficult to determine the source of the variances. And when these sources are eventually discovered, so much time has elapsed since they occurred that the managerial effectiveness of control is lost.

4.   Reports are not prepared in terms which management understands. Using technical accounting terminology will not help executives having a production background.

5.   Changing conditions make it necessary to revise standards more often. Many firms do not do this.

QUESTIONS FOR REVIEW

1.   Why might the manufacturing overhead costs be the logical area in which a firm might begin working toward a standard cost system if one had never been used before?

2.   In what way are the variances relating to manufacturing overhead costs basically different from those isolated for labor and material costs?

3. Distinguish between the two- and three-variance system when referring to manufacturing overhead. Why is the two-variance system not practical when a fixed overhead budget is used?

4. The cost department's figures allowed 1,200 hours for the completion of Job JN–42. The overhead for this firm is applied on the basis of direct labor hours. Budgeted overhead for the period is $60,000 based upon 80,000 budgeted hours. Of the total of $60,000 for overhead, $40,000 is considered variable overhead costs. When the job was completed, the report showed 1,500 hours worked. Actual overhead charged to the job, $1,250. What were manufacturing overhead variations applicable to Job JN–42 when the three-variance method is used and when the two-variance method is used?

5. A firm is undecided what method to follow in setting up a predetermined overhead rate for its standard cost system. The following have been suggested: (a) budgeted sales volume for the year, (b) 85 percent of maximum plant capacity production, (c) maximum plant capacity with allowance for normal repairs and maintenance which would be operative if the plant were not in operation, or (d) some other basis. Which method would you recommend, and why?

6. At 100 percent operation, a firm's overhead is $400,000 based upon 10,-000 units. The flexible budget indicated the following changes in the overhead at different operating capacities:

> 80 percent capacity.................$360,000
> 60 percent capacity.............,....... 325,000
> 50 percent capacity................. 310,000

What are the dollar amounts of controllable and volume variances if the firm produced 6,000 units (60 percent capacity) and the actual overhead incurred was $348,000?

7. "The determination of the manufacturing, labor, and material variances on a departmental basis results in better managerial control than when these variations are determined for the company as a whole." Explain why this is so.

8. From the following information, determine the fixed and variable components of the indirect labor costs:

Month	Direct Labor Hours	Indirect Labor Costs
January	500	$360
March	800	480
June........................1,000		600

9. How does the calculation of a mix variation differ from that of a quantity variation?

10. In some process industries, the cost standard is often based upon an assumed yield. What is the basis for managerial control in using this figure? How may this yield variance be expressed in formula form?

PROBLEMS—GROUP A

Problem 17–1. Purpose: *Statement of Variation Analysis When Flexible Budget Is Used*

The Queensboro Manufacturing Company uses a standard cost system in its single-product manufacturing operations.

The standard cost sheet for this period was as follows:

Direct materials....................50 lbs. at $3.00.................$150		
Direct labor..........................10 hrs. at 3.50................. 35		
Fixed overhead ....10 hrs. at 1.00................. 10		
Variable overhead.................10 hrs. at 0.30................. 3		
Total...$198		

The monthly factory overhead flexible budget used by this firm was as follows:

	Operating Capacity			
	60%	*80%*	*100%*	*120%*
Direct labor hours.........................	30,000	40,000	50,000	60,000
Fixed overhead.............................	$50,000	$50,000	$50,000	$50,000
Variable overhead	9,000	12,000	15,000	18,000
Total Factory Overhead.........	$59,000	$62,000	$65,000	$68,000

Operating data for the month of April:

1. Work-in-process inventory, April 1, 100 units, all material, 50% labor.
2. Work-in-process inventory, April 30, 100 units, all materials, 50% labor.
3. Planned production, 5,000 units.
4. Started into production, 4,500 units.
5. Materials put into production, 235,000 pounds of material at an average cost of $2.90.
6. Direct labor, 46,400 hours at an average labor cost of $3.40 per hour.
7. Actual factory overhead, $67,320.

Required:

a) A variance analysis for materials costs.
b) A variance analysis for labor costs.
c) A variation analysis for manufacturing overhead (three-variation method).

Problem 17–2. Purpose: *Statement of Variations with Three Variations for Manufacturing Overhead*

Each plant of the Quario Manufacturing Company specializes and produces a single product. The standard cost records are maintained in one central location for better managerial control. From the following information prepare a statement of variations from standard costs for each plant. Seven variations should be used: materials price and quantity; labor cost and efficiency; and manufacturing overhead efficiency, budget, and capacity.

Budget production data for each plant were as follows:

Plant No.	Units	Labor Hours	Manufacturing Overhead Based upon Labor Hours
101.................10,000	60,000	$45,000
501.................12,000	60,000	30,000
751.................50,000	50,000	75,000

The standard costs for the accounting period were:

	Plant No. 101	Plant No. 501	Plant No. 751
Cost of materials all used ....$ 38,700	$ 33,600	$ 90,000
Quantity of material used by job at standard cost...... 37,200	35,400	88,000
Cost of labor...................... 189,000	139,200	104,000

The actual operating costs for the accounting period were:

Units produced................... 12,000	9,600	50,000
Material costs all used $36,900	$30,000	$96,000
Labor costs per hour........... $2.50	$2.80	$2.20
Labor hours...................... 70,000 hrs.	49,000 hrs.	52,000 hrs.
Manufacturing overhead.......$48,000	$31,250	$72,000

Required:

Statement of variations using the seven variations indicated above.

Problem 17–3.   Purpose: *Revision of Standard Cost Sheets*

The standard cost sheet for Product *Acme* of the Quincy Manufacturing Company indicated the following costs:

Element of Cost	Prime Costs	Applied Manufacturing Overhead (40 percent)	Total
Material A.......................................$12.00		
Material B 6.00		
Material C....................................... 4.00		
Direct labor, cutting department.......... 10.00	$4.00	
Direct labor, shaping department......... 6.00	2.40	
Direct labor, assembling.................... 3.00	1.20	
Direct labor, boxing department 2.00	0.80	
	$43.00	$8.40	$51.40

The budget called for the manufacture of 12,000 units of Product *Acme* at a cost of $616,800.

The following variance accounts relating to Product *Acme* appear on the books for the period:

	Debit	Credit
Material price variances, Material A		$26,500
Material usage variances...		4,500
Labor cost variances:		
10% wage increase in direct workers..................................	$10,000	
Labor productivity variation—strike loss..............................	21,000	
Manufacturing overhead, fixed, strike loss.............................	8,000	
Manufacturing overhead, variable, due to elimination		
of certain variable costs		10,000
Totals..	$39,000	$41,000

The inventories at the end of the period were as follows:

200 units of Material A at $12...	$ 2,400
300 units of Material B at $6..	1,800
100 units of Material C at $4..	400
200 units of Product *Acme*, cut, at $36..	7,200
300 units of Product *Acme*, shaped, at $44.40	13,320
150 units of Product *Acme*, assembled, at $48.60	7,290
100 units of Product *Acme*, finished and boxed, at $51.40	5,140

Required:

a) A schedule of revised standard cost which will clearly indicate the cumulative standard for each successive operation.

b) A schedule applying the revised standard to the ending inventories.

(Adapted from AICPA Uniform Examination)

Problem 17–4. Purpose: *Computation of Manufacturing Overhead Variances*

The Quinlain Furniture Company uses a standard cost accounting system for its manufacturing operations. The standard cost of its dining room set of furniture is as follows:

Lumber materials, 500 feet at $150 per 1,000 feet.......................................	$ 75
Direct labor, 20 hours at $4 per hour..	80
Manufacturing overhead:	
Fixed, 30% of direct labor..	24
Variable, 60% direct labor..	48
Total Cost per Set of Furniture..	$227

The flexible manufacturing overhead budget indicated the following:

Direct Labor Hours	Budgeted Overhead
25,000	$86,400
24,000	81,600
22,000	76,800
20,000 (100%, normal capacity)	72,000
18,000	67,200

The actual costs for the month of June for one set of dining room furniture were:

Lumber and materials (550 feet at $120 per M) ....$ 66.00
Direct labor 21¼ hours at $4.16.. 88.40
Manufacturing overhead ($84,480 ÷ 1,200 units)................. 70.40
     Total Actual Unit Cost per Set $224.80

Required:

a) Prepare a schedule analyzing material, labor, and manufacturing overhead variations using a three-variation system for the manufacturing overhead supported by journal entries.
b) Recompute the manufacturing overhead variations using a two-variance system.
c) Interpret managerially the standard cost variations.

Problem 17–5. Purpose: *Preparation of Journal Entries from Incomplete Data*

The QMC Manufacturers, Inc., produces a single product that has the following standard costs:

Material (5 pieces)...................$ 5.50
Labor (1 hour)....................... 3.50
Overhead (1 hour)................. 3.00
                  $12.00

The units put into production were 100,000: 80,000 were completed and transferred to finished goods; 20,000 were complete as to materials but 25 percent complete as to labor and overhead.

The following variances were isolated during the period:

Labor rate variation ....$16,000 (cr.)
Labor efficiency variation... 8,000 (dr.)
Manufacturing overhead volume variation......................... 4,000 (dr.)
Manufacturing overhead budget variation.......................... 12,500 (dr.)
Manufacturing overhead efficiency variation .... 6,000 (dr.)
Material cost variation (520,000 pieces bought)................. 5,200 (dr.)
Material quantity variation .... 6,000 (cr.)

Required:

Prepare journal entries that were made to record the above variations.

PROBLEMS–GROUP B

Problem 17–6. Purpose: *Analysis of Manufacturing Overhead Variances Using Two- and Three-Variance Methods*

The Quonset Manufacturing Company manufactures a single product for each of which the standard are 30 direct labor hours. During the year 20,000 units were manufactured, for which 580,000 direct labor hours were required. The actual manufacturing overhead costs, $510,000.

The budgeted manufacturing overhead hours and costs at 90 percent and 100 percent capacity were as follows:

	90% Capacity	100% Capacity
Budgeted hours	630,000 hrs.	700,000 hrs.
Budgeted overhead costs	$504,000	$525,000

Required:

a) An analysis of the manufacturing overhead by the two-variance method.
b) An analysis of the manufacturing overhead by the three-variance method.

Problem 17–7. Purpose: *Computation of Standard Cost Variations for Materials, Labor, and Manufacturing Overhead*

The Quintescence Manufacturing Company manufactures a single product and uses a standard cost accounting system. The budget for the year calls for the production of 75,000 units, for which 150,000 labor hours are budgeted.

The standard cost for this product has been set as follows:

Materials, 10 pounds at $0.40 per pound		$ 4
Direct labor, 2 hours at $3		6
Manufacturing overhead, 2 hours at $2		4
		$14

The budgeted manufacturing overhead rate is based upon the following:

Fixed overhead	$165,000
Variable overhead	135,000
Total	$300,000
Predetermined rate on the basis of 150,000 hours	$2.00

Production for the month of April called for the production of 22,000 units and 44,000 direct labor hours. The manufacturing overhead budget for this production was as follows:

Fixed overhead, $\frac{1}{12}$ of $165,000	$13,750
Variable overhead	39,600
Total	$53,350

During April, 42,800 hours of direct labor were used and the production was as follows:

	Units
In process, complete as to materials, and one-half complete as to labor and overhead	400
Started into production	20,700
Total	21,100

Accounted for as follows:

	Units
Completed in April	20,600
In process, complete as to materials and 80% complete as to labor and overhead	500
Total Accounted For	21,100

Costs incurred during April: Materials used, 210,000 pounds which cost $75,600.

Labor costs, 42,800 hours	$117,600
Manufacturing overhead	55,000

Required:

a) Calculate the material price and the material quantity variations.

b) Calculate the labor cost and the labor efficiency variations.

c) Determine the manufacturing overhead variations—

    (*A*) Assuming a flexible budget on the three-variance method and the two-variance method.

    (*B*) Assuming a fixed or static budget.

Problem 17–8.   Purpose: *Computation of Variations from Standard Costs for Material, Labor, and Manufacturing Overhead*

The Quaker Manufacturing Company uses a standard cost accounting system in the production of one of its products. The standard cost sheet for this product indicated the following:

Material X, 5 pounds at $2	$10
Material Y, 3 pounds at $3	9
Direct labor, 3 hours at $3	9
Manufacturing overhead 3 hours at $4	12
Total	$40

The costs for Material X were:

Inventory at beginning, 2,000 units at $2.10
Purchases, 30,000 units at $2.40
Material X used, 9,500 units

The costs for Material Y were:

Inventory at beginning, 1,000 units at $2.90
Purchases, 12,000 units at $3.30
Material Y used, 5,200 units

The production statistics were:

Work-in-process inventory at beginning (all material and
    40 percent labor and overhead)................................... 500 units
Cost of this work-in-process inventory was.....................$13,700
Started into production.. 1,800 units
Work-in-process at end of period (all material,
    ⅔ labor and overhead).. 300 units
Completed production.. 2,000 units

Actual direct labor costs for 6,300 hours were $18,270.
Actual manufacturing overhead costs were $20,000.

Required:

a) Compute the material cost and quantity variations.
b) Compute the labor cost and efficiency variations.
c) Compute the manufacturing overhead efficiency variation.

Problem 17–9. Purpose: *Computation and Analysis of Standard Cost Variations;*
CPA Problem

The Queensland Manufacturing Company uses a standard cost system in
accounting for the cost of one of its products.

The budget calls for a monthly production of 100 units per day for 22 days
each month. Standard unit cost for labor is 16 hours at $3 per hour.

Standard overhead costs are based on the following:

Fixed overhead per month...$ 58,080
Variable overhead per month 79,200
    Total Budgeted Overhead..$137,280

Budgeted direct labor costs..$105,600
Budgeted overhead rate based on labor costs........................ 130%
Standard overhead cost per unit $62.40

During the month of September the plant operated only for 20 days. For the
2,080 units produced the costs were:

Direct labor, 32,860 hours at $3.04 ....$99,894.40
Fixed overhead 58,600.00
Variable overhead 78,130.00

Required:

a) Compute the labor cost variations for September.
b) Compute the manufacturing overhead cost variations.
c) Analyze the variations from identifiable causes for –
    (1) Direct labor.
    (2) Fixed and variable overhead.

(Adapted from AICPA Uniform Examination)

Problem 17–10.   Purpose: *Computation of Price, Mix, and Yield Variations*

The Quaranty Manufacturing Company manufactures a special lubricant additive used in the automotive industry. Each month this firm has to supply its customers with 7,500 gallons of this product. It requires a week to complete each run of this product, and during the month four manufacturing cycles are completed involving 1,875 gallons.

The standard product mix for making 1,875 gallons of this product are:

Material A:	1,000 gallons at $1.00
Material B:	600 gallons at 0.80
Material C:	400 gallons at 1.80

During the month of March, 7,500 gallons were produced using the following materials:

Material A:	5,200 gallons at $1.20
Material B:	3,000 gallons at 0.82
Material C:	1,900 gallons at 1.20

Required:

a) Compute the material price variation.
b) Compute the mix variation.
c) Compute the yield variation.

chapter 18

Accounting Procedures
for Standard Costs

INTRODUCTION

In the great majority of companies using standard costs, it will be found that the standard costs are integrated into the regular accounting records. Exceptions are occasionally encountered where standards are used only as an analytical measuring device to provide statistical data without incorporating the standard costs in any way in the books of account.

There are three possibilities of recording standard costs:

1. Standard costs may be recorded as *statistical* data without appearing in the books of account at all.
2. Standard costs may be recorded as *operating* data with the work-in-process accounts at standard—both debits and credits. This is the most common method and the one discussed in this chapter.
3. Standard costs may be recorded as *memoranda* data—the work-in-process accounts will show both the standard and actual costs, but the standard costs are merely memoranda figures.

RECORDING THE STANDARD COSTS AS STATISTICAL DATA

When standard costs are treated as statistical data, the actual costs are recorded in the same manner as was discussed in the sections on job order and continuous process costs. The standard costs are developed as statistical data for comparison with the actual costs thus computed. The comparisons and analyses would be similar to those discussed in the previous chapter with reference to the statement of variations.

RECORDING THE STANDARD COSTS AS OPERATING DATA

This method of recording standard costs is usually restricted to those firms whose standards are *expected actual*. This is true because the budget and standard cost variations can be related more closely and because it focuses attention on the *controllable* cost variations.

Two procedures may be followed in recording standard costs as operating data, viz:

Procedure 1. Two separate variations are recorded for materials — one for the *price* or *cost variation,* recorded at the time materials are purchased, and one for *quantity variation* recorded when the materials are used.

An ideal time to isolate the material price variation is at the time of purchase if maximum control is desired. Considerable time may elapse before materials that have been purchased are used, and if the price variation is not isolated until the materials are used, it may be too late to correct any undesirable situation.

Two variances are recorded for labor — one for *cost* variations and one for *efficiency* or *quantity.*

Three separate variations may be recorded for manufacturing overhead: one for *manufacturing overhead — efficiency variation,* computed and recorded at the time jobs are completed; the *budget* or *cost* variation; and the *volume* or *capacity* variation. Both the budget and volume variations are computed at the end of the accounting period. If the two-variation method is used, the *volume* variation is recorded at the end of the accounting period. The *controllable* variation may be computed whenever a job is finished, or periodically in the case of a process type of operation.

Procedure 2. One combined *price and quantity* variation is recorded for the materials when the materials are used. When materials are purchased, they are recorded at *actual* cost. However, when materials are used, the difference between the actual and standard cost of materials used is recorded as the variation. It represents a combined price and quantity variation.

A similar combined variation account for *labor cost* and *labor efficiency* may be set up for labor, but it is permissible to have a single variation for materials and two variations for labor.

Under this method, as well as under the first method described, the same three variations are recorded for manufacturing overhead — *efficiency, capacity,* and *budget.*

Combining the cost and quantity variations for materials and/or the cost and efficiency variations for labor is not so effective for managerial cost control as when separate variations are recorded. Therefore, Procedure 1 should be used whenever possible. If the cost or price variation is not computed at the time purchases are recorded, it is still possible to compute a *price* variation when the materials are used. This is done simply by comparing the actual with the standard price for the materials. Subtracting this price variation figure from the total material cost variation will indicate the variation arising from the material usage.

Procedure 1 is illustrated on the following pages.

A recent study of 62 companies by N.A.A. shows the following number using material price standards under various conditions:

	Number of Companies
Materials costed at standard price at receipt	36
Materials costed at standard price at issue	12
Materials costed at standard price on completion of manufacturing process	3
	51

The frequency at which material price variations are reported often indicates the importance placed on this type of variance for managerial control. Most companies prepare material price variation reports monthly, as indicated by the following survey of 62 companies by the N.A.A. showing the frequency of *material price* variation reports:

	Number of Companies
Quarterly	3
Monthly	43
Weekly	2
Irregularly	2
Not showing price variations	12
	62

The survey of 62 firms by the N.A.A. indicated that *labor variances* were reported as follows:

	Number of Companies
Reporting variances monthly	25
Reporting variances weekly	21
Reporting variances daily	7
Not reporting regularly	9
	62

RECORDING MATERIAL PRICE VARIATIONS AT TIME OF PURCHASE

When this method is used, the *Stores* account is maintained at standard cost. The Work-in-Process—Materials account is also maintained at standard cost. The procedure is summarized as follows:

1.   When materials are purchased, the Stores account is debited at the *standard cost* of the materials and the difference between the standard and actual cost is debited or credited to a *Material Price Variation account*.

2.   When materials are used, the *standard quantity* at the *standard price* is charged to the Work-in-Process — Materials account and the difference between the *standard quantity* and the *actual quantity used* at standard cost is debited or credited to the *Material Quantity Variation account*.

To illustrate these two material variations, the following data are assumed and must be recorded:

Standard cost price of material budgeted by the purchasing
    department and recorded on cost card, per unit............ $ 3
Purchases for the month:
    3,000 units at $3.15...   9,450
    2,000 units at $3.225   6,450
Requisitions:
    3,000 units at $3.15...$9,450
    1,200 units at $3.225 3,870   13,320
Standard number of units allowed for the job orders put into
    production ....   4,000 units

Material price variations recorded at time of purchase are computed as follows:

Purchases:
    3,000 units at $3.15...$9,450
    2,000 units at $3.225... 6,450
Total cost at actual $15,900
Purchases at standard cost:
    5,000 units at $3...   15,000
        Unfavorable Purchase Price Variation................... $ 900 (debit)

Material quantity variation shows that 4,200 units were used when the standard quantity called for on the job sheets was 4,000, making an unfavorable quantity variation of 200 units at the standard price of $3 each, or $600.

Entries in journal form to record this information would be as follows:

Stores..15,000
Material Price Variation   900
    Accounts Payable...   15,900
    To record purchase of 3,000 units at $3.15 and 2,000 units at
    $3.225.

The entry made to summarize the issuance of materials to the factory would be as follows:

Work-in-Process—Materials 12,000
Material Quantity Variation... 600
    Stores.. 12,600
    To record the requisitions for the month.

The Work-in-Process account is kept at the standard cost—that is, the *standard quantity* of material at the *standard price*.

RECORDING LABOR VARIATIONS

The variations for labor costs are similar in nature to those just recorded for materials and involve both *cost* and *efficiency* (quantity or number of labor hours).

To obtain the *labor cost variation*, the difference is computed as follows:

Actual quantity of labor (hours worked) × Standard labor rate per hour.
Actual quantity of labor (hours worked) × Actual labor rate or cost.

This difference will be recorded in the *Labor Cost Variation account*. If the actual labor cost *rate* is higher than the standard set, it is unfavorable and is recorded as a debit. If the actual is less, then it is favorable and is recorded as a credit in the variation account.

The Work-in-Process account is maintained at the standard cost—that is, the standard hours for labor × the standard labor rate. To obtain the *labor efficiency variation*, the difference is computed as follows:

Actual quantity of labor (hours worked) × Standard labor rate per hour.
Standard quantity of labor (hours allowed) × Standard labor rate per hour.

If the actual *hours* used are greater than the standard hours allowed, then the variation is *unfavorable* and is recorded as a debit. If the actual hours used are less, then the variation is *favorable* and is recorded as a credit.

To illustrate the computation and recording of these two labor variations, the following data are assumed:

Actual hours worked..................4,250 hrs.
Actual payroll costs $8,925
Actual rate per hour...................$2.10
Standard hours allowed...............4,000 hrs.
Standard rate per hour................$2.25

The labor cost or rate variation computed on the basis of the foregoing data and instructions is as follows:

4,250 actual hours × $2.25 (standard labor rate) $9,562.50
4,250 actual hours × $2.10 (actual labor rate).............................. 8,925.00
    Favorable Cost (Rate) Variation for Labor ....$ 637.50 (cr.)

The labor efficiency or quantity variation is computed as follows:

```
4,250 actual hours × standard rate of $2.25................................$9,562.50
4,000 standard hours × standard rate of $2.25.............................  9,000.00
        Unfavorable Labor Efficiency (Quantity) Variation..............$   562.50 (dr.)
```

When the FICA tax rate is assumed to be 5.2 percent, the entries in journal form to record these two labor variations would be as follows:

```
Payroll.............................................................8,925.00
    FICA Taxes Payable ..............................                464.10
    Withholding Taxes Payable .......................                981.75
    Accounts Payable.................................              7,479.15
    To record actual payroll costs in voucher register.

Work-in-Process—Labor...............................9,000.00
Labor Efficiency Variation .............................. 562.50
    Labor Cost Variation ..............................               637.50
    Payroll...........................................             8,925.00
    To distribute the payroll and to record labor variations.
```

It is also possible but not always *practical* to record the *labor cost variation* directly in the payroll book or voucher register, in which case the two variations will appear in separate records, viz:

```
Payroll (actual hours × standard rate)..................9,562.50
    FICA Taxes Payable ..............................                464.10
    Withholding Taxes Payable .......................                981.75
    Labor Cost Variation ............................                637.50
    Payroll Accrued .................................              7,479.15
    To record payroll in payroll book at standard.

Payroll Accrued .....................................7,479.15
    Accounts Payable.................................              7,479.15
    To record the preparation of the voucher for payroll.

Work-in-Process—Labor...............................9,000.00
Labor Efficiency Variation .............................. 562.50
    Payroll...........................................             9,562.50
    To record labor efficiency variation when distributing
    the payroll charges.
```

RECORDING MANUFACTURING OVERHEAD COST VARIATIONS

Under the three-variation system, the manufacturing overhead cost variations fall into two separate groups: those determined *when the job is completed,* and those determined at the *end of the accounting period.* The former relate to the *job;* the latter to the *plant.* The job variation is called *manufacturing overhead—efficiency variation;* the plant variations are known as *manufacturing overhead—budget variation* if they are cost variations and *manufacturing overhead—capacity variation* if they are volume variations.

To illustrate the manufacturing overhead variations, the following data will be used:

Normal capacity, budgeted hours ....15,000 hrs.
Budgeted manufacturing overhead at this capacity:
    Fixed costs $15,000
    Variable costs.. 15,000
                                   $30,000

Standard overhead rate per labor hour $2.00
Standard hours for actual production for period...............................11,600 hrs.
Actual hours used for actual production ....14,000 hrs.
Actual manufacturing overhead costs incurred..................................$32,500

To compute and record the *three manufacturing overhead variations* from these data, the following procedure is used:

1. *Manufacturing overhead — efficiency variation* (difference between standard hours and actual hours × predetermined or standard rate):

Actual hours × standard rate (14,000 × $2)....................................$28,000
Standard hours × standard rate (11,600 × $2)................................ 23,200
    Manufacturing Overhead Efficiency Variation, Unfavorable
      (2,400 hours × $2) ....$ 4,800 (dr.)

Entries in journal form to record this variation:

Manufacturing Overhead Control 32,500
    Sundry Credits...   32,500
    To record actual manufacturing overhead incurred.

Work-in-Process — Manufacturing Overhead 23,200
Manufacturing Overhead — Efficiency Variation......................... 4,800
    Applied Manufacturing Overhead......................................   28,000
    To record applied manufacturing overhead and the
    efficiency variation.

2. *Manufacturing overhead — budget variation* (difference between the budgeted and actual manufacturing overhead costs):

Actual manufacturing overhead costs $32,500
Budgeted manufacturing overhead costs....................................... 30,000
    Budget or Cost Variation, Unfavorable..............................$ 2,500 (dr.)

3. *Manufacturing overhead — capacity variation* (difference between budgeted hours and actual hours times the predetermined rate):

Budgeted hours, 15,000 × $2.00 ....$30,000
Actual hours, 14,000 × predetermined rate $2 28,000
    Capacity Variation, Unfavorable (1,000 Hours × $2)..............$ 2,000 (dr.)

Summary of variations equaling over- or underapplied overhead:

Budget variation	$2,500	unfavorable
Capacity variation	2,000	unfavorable
Efficiency variation	4,800	unfavorable
Net variation (underapplied)	$9,300	unfavorable

The journal entry to record the budget and capacity variations is:

Applied Manufacturing Overhead	28,000	
Manufacturing Overhead – Budget Variation	2,500	
Manufacturing Overhead – Capacity Variation	2,000	
Manufacturing Overhead Control		32,500

To close out applied and actual overhead accounts and to record the budget and capacity variations.

If the two-variance system is used, the budget is adjusted to the *standard hours* of production. A *volume* variance and a *controllable* or *spending* variance are computed. To compute and record the two manufacturing overhead variations from these data, the following procedure is used:

1. Manufacturing overhead – controllable variation:

Actual manufacturing overhead costs		$32,500	
Budget adjusted to standard hours:			
Variable costs, 11,600 hours × $1	$11,600		
Fixed costs	15,000	26,600	
Controllable variation (spending or cost)		$ 5,900	unfavorable

2. Manufacturing overhead – volume variation:

Adjusted budget	$26,600	
Applied (standard @ standard) 11,600 hours × $2	23,200	
Volume variation	$ 3,400	unfavorable

Entries to record the data are:

Manufacturing Overhead Control	32,500	
Sundry Credits		32,500

Work-in-Process – Manufacturing Overhead	23,200	
Controllable Variation (spending or cost)	5,900	
Volume Variation	3,400	
Manufacturing Overhead Control		32,500

ILLUSTRATION OF ENTRIES FOR STANDARD COSTS

To present a comprehensive illustration of standard cost accounting, the following data are assumed:

1. Balances, June 1, 19—, were:

	Standard Cost
Materials	$2,800
Work-in-process—materials	1,500
Work-in-process—direct labor	1,000
Work-in-process—overhead	1,000
Finished goods	1,500

2. Purchases for the month were:

	Actual Cost	Standard Cost
Purchase order No. 869 (900 units)	$ 750	$ 720
Purchase order No. 870 (5,000 units)	3,700	4,000

3. Materials issued to production department, at standard cost:

Standard quantity (4,000 units)	$3,200
Additional materials (100 units)	80

4. Materials returned to stores, 30 units at standard cost, $24.
5. Direct labor time tickets:

Standard for orders actually put into production	9,600 hrs.
Excess time	30
Total	9,630 hrs.

6. Actual wages for direct labor (standard wage rate, $1.90 per hour):

3,420 hours at $1.92	$ 6,566.40
5,860 hours at $1.88	11,016.80
350 hours at $1.80	630.00
9,630 hours	$18,213.20

7. Manufacturing overhead (a fixed budget is used):

Total of manufacturing overhead budget	$12,250
Budgeted direct labor hours	9,800
Standard rate per direct labor hour	

$$\frac{\$12,250}{9,800} = \$1.25$$

7a. Actual manufacturing overhead, $12.670.
8. Cost of goods completed during the month at standard cost:

Material costs	$ 4,000
Direct labor costs	19,000
Manufacturing overhead costs	12,500
	$35,500

9.   Cost of sales at standard cost amounted to $30,000.

The entries for these data would appear, in journal form, as follows:

(1)

Stores..	720.00	
Material Price Variation	30.00	
Accounts Payable...		750.00
To record invoice on purchase order No. 869.		

(2)

Stores..	4,000.00	
Material Price Variation		300.00
Accounts Payable...		3,700.00
To record invoice on purchase order No. 870.		

(3)

Work-in-Process — Materials...	3,200.00	
Material Quantity Variation	80.00	
Stores..		3,280.00
To record materials issued during the month.		

(4)

Stores..	24.00	
Material Quantity Variation		24.00
To record materials returned to stores.		

(5a)

Payroll	21,013.20	
Withholding Taxes Payable.....................................		2,311.45
FICA Taxes Payable (5.2%)		1,092.69
Accounts Payable..		17,609.06
To record wages earned.		

(5b)

Direct Labor	18,213.20	
Indirect Labor	2,800.00	
Payroll		21,013.20
To record and analyze factory payroll.		

(5c)

Accounts Payable...	17,609.06	
Cash		17,609.06

(5d)

Work-in-Process — Direct Labor.....................................	18,240.00	
Direct Labor Efficiency Variation	57.00	
Direct Labor Cost Variation		83.80
Direct Labor		18,213.20
To close out Direct Labor account.		

(6)

Work-in-Process — Manufacturing Overhead......................	12,000.00	
Manufacturing Overhead — Efficiency Variation	37.50	
Manufacturing Overhead Applied.............................		12,037.50
To record manufacturing overhead applied to production and efficiency variation for the month.		

(7)

Manufacturing Overhead Summary	12,670.00	
Taxes		900.00
Supplies		680.00
Repairs		820.00
Depreciation of Machinery and Building		3,400.00
Indirect Labor		2,800.00
Power		3,700.00
Superintendence		300.00
Miscellaneous Manufacturing Overhead		70.00

To close manufacturing overhead accounts.

(7a)

Manufacturing Overhead Applied	12,037.50	
Manufacturing Overhead—Capacity Variation	212.50	
Manufacturing Overhead—Budget Variation	420.00	
Manufacturing Overhead Summary		12,670.00

To close the Manufacturing Overhead and the Manufacturing Overhead Applied accounts and record idle capacity and budget excess variations.

The idle capacity variation is 170 hours (9,800 − 9,630) at $1.25 per hour; the budget excess variation is the difference between actual and budgeted manufacturing overhead costs ($12,670 − $12,250).

(8)

Finished Goods	35,500.00	
Work-in-Process—Materials		4,000.00
Work-in-Process—Labor		19,000.00
Work-in-Process—Manufacturing Overhead		12,500.00

To record the cost of goods completed at standard cost.

(9)

Cost of Sales	30,000.00	
Finished Goods		30,000.00

To record the cost of goods sold at standard cost.

When these entries have been posted, the general ledger accounts will appear as follows:

Stores

June	1	Inventory	S*	2,800.00	June 30		S	3,280.00
	30	Purchases	S	720.00				
	30	Purchases	S	4,000.00				
	30	Return to stores	S	24.00				

*S indicates at *standard* cost; A indicates at *actual* cost.

Material Price Variation

June 30		S	30.00	June 30		S	300.00

Accounts Payable

June 30		A	17,609.06	June 30	A	750.00
				30		3,700.00
				30		17,609.06

Work-in-Process — Materials

June 1	Inventory	S	1,500.00	June 30	S	4,000.00
30		S	3,200.00			

Material Quantity Variation

June 30	(Act. Qty. — Std. Qty.)	S	80.00	June 30	S	24.00

Direct Labor

June 30	A	18,213.20	June 30	A	18,213.20

Direct Labor Cost Variation

		June 30	83.80

Payroll

June 30		A	21,013.20	June 30	A	21,013.20

Work-in-Process — Labor

June 1	Inventory	S	1,000.00	June 30	S	19,000.00
30		S	18,240.00			

Direct Labor Efficiency Variation

June 30	57.00	

Manufacturing Overhead Summary

June 30		A	12,670.00	June 30	A	12,670.00

Work-in-Process — Manufacturing Overhead

June 1	Inventory	S	1,000.00	June 30	S	12,500.00
30		S	12,000.00			

Manufacturing Overhead—Efficiency Variation

June 30	37.50		

Manufacturing Overhead Applied

June 30	12,037.50	June 30	S	12,037.50

Manufacturing Overhead—Capacity Variation

June 30	212.50		

Manufacturing Overhead—Budget Variation

June 30	420.00		

Finished Goods

June 1	S	1,500.00	June 30	S	30,000.00
30	S	35,500.00			

Cost of Sales

June 30	S	30,000.00	

On the books of this firm there are now seven variation accounts, with debit balances of $783 and credit balances of $353.80. These balances serve to point out what costs in total were different from the expected standard cost, and they may be summarized as follows:

Material costs were less than expected by...$270.00
Labor costs were less than expected by.. 83.80
    Total Variations under Standard..$353.80

The quantity of materials used was greater than expected by ....$ 56.00
The quantity of labor required was greater than was expected by.............. 57.00
Because of the inefficiency of labor, and the use of more than the standard
    hours, manufacturing overhead costs were excessively used by 37.50
Facilities, measured by 170 hours, were not utilized, and this wasted capacity
    cost in manufacturing overhead... 212.50
The cost of the manufacturing overhead exceeded the budget by 420.00
    Total Variations Over Standard $783.00

If a *flexible budget* had been used for manufacturing overhead and two variances isolated, the following would have been changed in the preceding illustration (all data and entries not shown below remain the same):

7. Manufacturing overhead (a flexible budget is used).

> Variable overhead is $0.60 per direct labor hour.
> Fixed overhead is $6,370
> 9,800 direct labor hours are budgeted at $0.60 + $6,370 = $12,250
> The standard rate per direct labor hour is:

$$\frac{\$12,250}{9,800} = \$1.25.$$

The following entries are made in lieu of those made in the preceding illustration:

(6)

Work-in-Process — Manufacturing Overhead	12,000.00	
Manufacturing Overhead Applied		12,000.00
To record overhead applied to production.		

(7a)

Manufacturing Overhead Applied	12,000.00	
Manufacturing Overhead — Controllable Variance	540.00	
Manufacturing Overhead — Volume Variance	130.00	
Manufacturing Overhead Summary		12,670.00
To close the Manufacturing Overhead and Manufacturing Overhead Applied accounts and to record the controllable and volume variations.		

The total number of variations appearing on the books would be six since the controllable and volume variances were determined in lieu of the capacity, efficiency, and budget variances.

THE DISPOSITION OF VARIATION ACCOUNTS

The disposition of variation account balances is an area in which accountants are not entirely in agreement. There seem to be two general points of view.

One group of accountants maintains that standard cost is not the *actual* cost and that, therefore, the variation should be prorated over the cost of sales, finished goods inventory, and work-in-process inventories. For example, if the labor variance amounted to $600 for the 6,000 equivalent units that were put into production, 1,000 were still not finished, 2,000 were finished and on hand, and 3,000 were sold, $100 of the variance should be added to work-in-process, $200 to finished goods, and $300 to cost of goods sold.

This prorating process, if accurately computed, would result in a sufficient amount being added or subtracted from the various inventory accounts and Cost of Sales account to bring these figures to an approximation of *actual* cost. This procedure has the advantage of meeting the requirements of federal income tax regulations.

The other group of cost accountants takes the position that if standards are carefully determined and revised when necessary, the variation accounts will reflect losses and gains due to efficiency factors; such losses and gains are not normal items in manufacturing cost. Therefore, variation accounts should be closed to the Cost of Sales or the Revenue and Expense account and shown on the statements accordingly. Inventories valued at standard cost are, to this group of accountants, properly valued, since efficiency and inefficiency are not values to be recorded on balance sheets in inventories but are income-determining factors.

From a theoretical point of view, at least, there is much to be said for the second method. Income tax regulations need not determine the general accounting methods, and suitable adjustments can serve effectively to meet the legal stipulations. The argument for prorating variations over the inventories and Cost of Sales accounts is theoretically wrong, for there is a distinction between *cost* and *loss,* however difficult it may be to make such a distinction in practice. If standards are carefully established and their adequacy is maintained by making revisions where uncontrollable factors upset the initial estimates, *and* if management *uses* the variation data as a basis for improvement of methods, the variation balances should be small indeed. The question of the disposition of variation account balances may thus resolve itself into another and more significant one: "How well-planned and administered is this particular business?"

In the case of the extended illustration found on pages 591–93, the entry to close the variation accounts into the Cost of Sales or Profit and Loss account would be:

```
Cost of Sales (Revenue and Expense) .....................................429.20
Material Price Variation ....................................................270.00
Direct Labor Cost Variation................................................ 83.80
      Material Quantity Variation.............................................      56.00
      Labor Efficiency Variation ..............................................      57.00
      Manufacturing Overhead – Efficiency Variation...................      37.50
      Manufacturing Overhead – Budget Variation ......................     420.00
      Manufacturing Overhead – Capacity Variation.....................     212.50
   To close variation accounts into the Cost of Sales account.
```

Shown on the income statement, these variations tell management in a broad way why the cost of sales was not the standard cost of $30,000, and in so doing call attention to the need for improved methods and procedures to eliminate inefficiencies.

OPERATING STATEMENTS UNDER STANDARD COST ACCOUNTING

Examples of statements of cost to manufacture prepared from a standard cost system are shown in Illustration 18–1 or as arranged in Illustration 18–2.

Illustration 18-1
POWERS MANUFACTURING COMPANY
COST OF GOODS MANUFACTURED
For the Year, 19—

Standard cost:		
Materials used		$ 7,500
Direct labor..		15,000
Variable manufacturing overhead		3,000
Fixed manufacturing overhead..		2,000
Cost of production at standard..		$27,500
Deduct:		
Increase in work-in-process inventory at standard..................		7,200
Cost of goods finished at standard.....................................		$20,300
Deduct: Variations under standard costs:*		
Labor quantity variation $2,000		
Material price variation 3,400		
Idle capacity variation... 2,600		8,000
Total..		$12,300
Add: Variations over standard costs:		
Labor cost variation...$1,750		
Material quantity variation... 2,300		
Manufacturing overhead—efficiency variation......................... 2,650		
Manufacturing overhead—budget excess variation.................. 1,400		8,100
Total Cost of Goods Manufactured		$20,400

* Variations may also be added or subtracted from cost of goods sold.

Illustration 18-2
POWER MANUFACTURING COMPANY
COST OF GOODS MANUFACTURED
For the Year, 19—

	Standard Cost	Variation from Standard	Actual Cost
Costs of production:			
Materials used ....$ 7,500			
Material quantity variation		+$2,300	
Material price variation		− 3,400	$ 6,400
Labor costs	15,000		
Labor cost variation....................................		+ 1,750	
Labor efficiency variation...........................		− 2,000	14,750
Manufacturing overhead	5,000		
Manufacturing overhead—efficiency variation		+ 2,650	
Manufacturing overhead—budget excess variation		+ 1,400	
Manufacturing overhead—capacity variation...		− 2,600	6,450
Total...$27,500		+$ 100	$27,600
Less: Increase in work-in-process inventory, at standard..	7,200		7,200
Cost of Goods Manufactured $20,300		+$ 100	$20,400

For many companies, interim as well as annual income statements are prepared. The question of what to do with the variations from standard on these statements must receive attention, even though the procedures used by the various firms are not uniform. One suggested procedure relating to the interim — monthly or quarterly — statements would be:

1. Those variations which are an indication of managerial or supervisory inefficiency should be charged to the cost of goods sold for the period. These are losses and should be charged in the period when realized. These include labor efficiency, manufacturing overhead budget, and manufacturing overhead efficiency variations. Material price variation might better be prorated over the inventories of work-in-process, finished goods, and stores.
2. When the variations are favorable (credit balances), they should first be used to offset the negative or debit variations. Any unused balance should be used to reduce the inventory balances in some pro rata manner.
3. To meet the requirements of the Internal Revenue Service, material price variations should be prorated over the work-in-process, finished goods, and cost of sales in proportion to the amount of purchased materials used for each during the current period.

At the end of the fiscal period, all variations should be closed into the cost of goods sold, except that proportion of the material cost variation which relates to the unused inventory of purchases for the period.

However, it should be remembered that since uniformity is not practiced by managements, decisions on how to treat the variations in the interim as well as fiscal statements should give consideration to the following: (1) nature of variation, (2) amount involved, (3) regularity of occurrence in the manufacturing cycle, (4) cause of variation, (5) effect of method used on the income statement and balance sheet, (6) reasonableness of such treatment — what does management want to indicate to its employees?

QUESTIONS FOR REVIEW

1. Management is undecided whether to record its standard costs as statistical data or as operating data. How would you suggest the firm record its standard costs? Why?
2. Manufacturing overhead variations fall into two major groups — job variations and plant or period variations. Explain the difference.
3. "We cannot use standard costs in our firm because we are afraid that the standard costs would complicate our accounting work." Explain.
4. What is meant by "partial use of standards"? Why do some firms use this procedure?

5. When firms price materials at standard cost at time of purchase and the inventory is therefore maintained at standard cost, how do they reconcile their statements to meet the requirements of the Internal Revenue Service?

6. What arguments favor the disposition of all variation accounts by closing them into the Cost of Sales account? What effect does the closing out of the variation accounts have on the inventory values? Explain.

7. Part of the standard cost sheet for the Laurel Manufacturing Company's single product shows:

Overhead, 10 labor hours at $3..................$30

The flexible budget for October shows:

Labor Hours	Overhead Budget
20,000	$ 80,000
30,000	100,000
40,000	120,000
50,000	140,000

During the month of October, 3,500 units of its product were manufactured. Thirty-eight thousand labor hours were used, and the actual overhead for the month was $122,000.

Compute the overhead variances for October using the two-variance system.

8. Using the data in 7, compute the overhead variances using the three-variance system.

9. What arguments favor prorating the standard cost variations over the Work-in-Process, Finished Goods, and Cost of Sales? When this method is used, how does the Work-in-Process account differ from that used when there are estimated costs?

10. Material cost and labor cost variations are not too important for many concerns using standard costs. Explain why this might be so.

PROBLEMS—GROUP A

Problem 18–1. Purpose: *Income Statements for Firm Using Standard Costs; T-Ledger Accounts*

The Ramasees Manufacturing Company uses a standard cost accounting system in its manufacturing operations, in which it produces a single product in lots of 100 each. During the next six months, it is expected that 72 lots (7,200 units) will be produced. The standard cost sheet for each lot of 100 units is as follows:

200 pounds of material at $5	$1,000
80 hours direct labor at $3	240
80 hours manufacturing overhead at $1.50	120
Total	$1,360
Standard selling and administrative expenses—25% of cost of sales	340
Total Cost to Make and Sell	$1,700

The following transactions occurred during the six months ending June 30, 19—:

1.
Purchases of Materials	Payroll Costs
4,000 pounds at $5.00	2,000 hours at $3.00
5,200 pounds at 4.60	3,000 hours at 3.25
6,000 pounds at 5.25	1,000 hours at 3.40
3,000 pounds at 5.40	

2. Actual manufacturing overhead incurred, $9,840.
3. Actual materials used, 13,830 pounds.
4. Seventy jobs were started and completed during this period. There were no work-in-process inventories.
5. Selling and administrative expenses totaled $22,500.
6. Sales were 66 lots at $3,000 each lot.

Required:

a) T-ledger accounts to record the foregoing information.
b) Statement of the *cost of goods manufactured and sold* indicating the amount of seven variations, all chargeable to the Cost of Sales. The material price variation is charged to production on the basis of the actual usage, on an average cost (not Fifo) basis.
c) Condensed income statement indicating the selling and administrative expense variation.
d) Comment on the standard costs used in this problem.

Problem 18–2. Purpose: *Journal Entries for the Cost Accounting Cycle When Standard Costs Are Used*

The Roman Electrical Manufacturing Company produces a single product for which the standard costs are:

Materials, 5 pounds at 62¢	$ 3.10
Labor, 2 hours at $3.50	7.00
Manufacturing overhead, 4 machine-hours at 50¢	2.00
Standard Cost per Unit	$12.10

Normal capacity of plant is 40,000 machine-hours (10,000 units).
Budgeted production for the period is 10,000 units.

Production Data:

Put into production	9,800 units
Completed	9,300 units
Work-in-process—80% complete as to material and 60% complete as to labor and overhead	500 units
Actual machine-hours incurred	39,500 hrs.

Operating Transactions:

1. Purchased 52,000 pounds of material at 64 cents.
2. Materials used in production, 48,400 pounds.
3. Payroll for the period (direct labor): 19,800 hours at $3.40.
4. Manufacturing overhead costs for the period totaled $21,760.

5. Manufacturing overhead was applied to production.
6. Sales were 9,000 units at $25 each.
7. Selling and administrative expenses totaled, $18,000.

Required:

a) Journal entries to record the above transactions using three variance accounts for the manufacturing overhead and prorate the material cost variation in accordance with the amount used. Close the variation accounts into the Cost of Sales.
b) Prepare income statement.

Problem 18–3. Purpose: *Journal Entries for Standard Costs from Ledger Accounts*

The Roliver Supply Company manufactures a single product with the following standard costs:

Materials, 10 gallons	$ 8.00
Labor, 2 hours	7.50
Manufacturing overhead, 2 hours	5.50
Total	$21.00

During the month of March, 100,000 units were started: 80,000 were completed and transferred to the finished goods storeroom; 20,000 were in process at the end of the period, with 90% of the material and 50% of the labor and overhead.

During the period, 1,200,000 gallons of materials were purchased.

The ledger contained the following balances in the variance accounts:

Material Price Variance	Material Quantity Variance	Labor Cost Variance
8,000	10,000	2,300

Labor Efficiency Variance	Manufacturing Overhead — Budget Variance	Manufacturing Overhead — Capacity Variance
14,000	9,800	36,600

Manufacturing Overhead — Efficiency Variance
10,267

Required:

Prepare journal entries which covered the transactions which resulted in the above variations in the standard cost accounting cycle.

Problem 18–4. Purpose: *Journal Entries Covering the Cost Accounting Cycle at Standard Costs*

The RacCall Manufacturing Company operates an integrated standard cost accounting system. The differences between the actual and the standard costs are recorded in *variation accounts,* namely, Material Cost Variation, Material Quantity Variation, Labor Cost Variation, and Labor Efficiency Variation, and three variance accounts for the manufacturing overhead costs.

Material price variations are recorded at the time of purchase but are charged to production on the basis of amount of material used, thus conforming to the Internal Revenue Service rulings.

The firm is budgeting its production for the next year as follows: 60 jobs of 100 units per job, *per month.* On this basis, the standard cost figures presented by the engineering and standards department are as follows:

Materials, 300 pounds at $1.50 per pound..............................$450
Labor, 80 hours at $2.50.. 200
Manufacturing overhead, 80 hours at $1.80 per hour................. 144
Total Standard Cost per 100 units $794

Budgeted fixed overhead is $5,000.
During the period, direct materials purchased were as follows:

8,000 pounds at $1.50 per pound
8,400 pounds at 1.60 per pound
9,000 pounds at 1.00 per pound

The manufacturing operations indicated the following:

Direct labor costs:
2,100 hours at $2.60
1,000 hours at 2.80
900 hours at 2.50
800 hours at 2.40
Actual manufacturing overhead, $10,000
Materials requisitioned, 17,300 pounds

Sixty-two jobs were completed during the period. There was no work-in-process at the beginning or end of the month.

Sales for the period totaled 6,000 units at $24 each.

Selling expenses were $16,000; administrative expenses, $12,000.

Required:

a) Journal entries to record the above information for the month, showing all variations, closed out to the Cost of Sales account.

b) Criticize the standard cost of this firm.

Problem 18–5. Purpose: *Journal Entries for Manufacturing Overhead Variations*

The following are two independent situations for recording the manufacturing overhead variations on the two- and three-variation bases.

Situation 1: From the following data, prepare journal entries for the manufacturing overhead variations, using the two-variance and then the three-variance methods:

Standard hours for the actual production ....20,000 hrs.
Budgeted direct labor hours ....24,000 hrs.
Actual direct labor hours..............................22,500 hrs.
Budgeted overhead costs, at normal capacity:
  Fixed..$ 9,600
  Variable... 18,000
Actual overhead costs:
  Fixed..$ 9,500
  Variable... 16,000

Situation 2: From the following data, you are asked to prepare journal entries to record the two- and three-manufacturing overhead variations:

The Rates Manufacturing Company manufactures a single product. Part of the standard cost is based upon the following:

Direct labor, 1 hour at $3.60 per hour..............$3.60
Factory overhead:
  Fixed, 1 hour at $0.40 per hour.................... 0.40
  Variable, 1 hour at $0.60 per hour................ 0.60

During the month of April, 10,000 units were completed. On April 30, 500 units were in process, 80 percent complete as to materials and 60 percent complete as to labor and overhead. Normal budgeted operations called for 12,000 units per month.

Actual labor hours for the month of April were 10,650 hours, and the payroll costs, $36,210.

Actual manufacturing overhead for the month was $12,500.

PROBLEMS—GROUP B

Problem 18–6. Purpose: *Standard Costs for Process Type of Business. Journal Entries; Proration of Material Cost Variation*

The Resources Manufacturing Company produces a single product in two successive departmental operations. This firm uses a standard cost accounting system. However, to meet the IRS requirements, material price variations are charged to the cost of sales on the basis *of the amount of materials used during the period.*

The standard costs in lots of 200 each for the ensuing accounting period are as follows:

Cost Element	Department I	Department II
Materials costs.................	80 lbs. Mat. A at $0.90 = $ 72	60 gals. of Mat. Z at $1.20 = $ 72
Labor costs	50 hrs. at $3 = 150	40 hrs. at $3.25 = 130
Manufacturing overhead.....	50 hrs. at $1 = 50	40 hrs. at $1.25 = 50
Total Standard Costs	$272	$252

Transactions during the accounting period ending July 31 were:

1. Material purchases:

2,000 lbs. of Material A at $1.00	1,000 gals. of Material Z at $1.10
3,000 lbs. of Material A at 0.95	2,000 gals. of Material Z at 1.20
5,000 lbs. of Material A at 0.82	3,000 gals. of Material Z at 1.40

2. Labor and manufacturing overhead costs, departmentally are:

	Department I	Department II
Labor costs incurred..........	4,000 hrs. at $2.80	2,500 hrs. at $3.40
Manufacturing overhead:		
Budgeted	$4,500	$3,750
Actual.........................	4,200	4,250

3. Production statistics:

Started in Department I, 80 jobs (200 units each).
Transferred to Department II, 65 jobs.
In process in Department I, 15 jobs on which 80 percent of the material and 60 percent of the labor had been applied.
Materials used: 6,400 lbs. of A; 3,300 gals. of Z.
Added materials in Department II do not increase the volume of units.
Completed and transferred to finished stock room in Department II, 45 jobs.
The 20 jobs still in process are 60 percent complete as to materials and 50 percent complete as to labor and overhead.

4. Of the jobs completed (45 jobs at 200 units each), 8,000 units were sold at an average price of $9 each.

Required:

a) Journal entries to record the transactions, using seven variations (three for manufacturing overhead).
b) T-ledger accounts to record the work-in-process, finished goods, cost of sales, and the variation accounts.
c) Statement of cost of goods sold at actual with the proration of the material price variation on basis of usage.

Problem 18–7.   Purpose: *Journal Entries Covering Manufacturing Cost Accounting Cycle; Three Variances for Manufacturing Overhead*

The Reston Manufacturing Company uses a standard cost accounting system in the production of its specialized *Transometer,* in lots of 100 units each.

The standards set for the production of one job of 100 units for the coming accounting period are:

Materials, 300 pounds at $2.60..............................$	780
Labor costs, 80 hours at $3.00	240
Manufacturing overhead, 80 hours at $2..................	160
Total..$1,180	

Seven variance accounts are used in recording the accounting and operating data. Material cost variations at the time of purchase are charged to production through the Cost of Sales account at the end of the accounting period.

The budget for the accounting period under examination calls for the production of 90 jobs of 100 units each. Eighty jobs were started and completed during the period. There was no work-in-process at either the beginning or the end of the accounting period. Seven thousand *Transometers* were sold during this period at a unit price of $25 each.

Other transactions affecting the cost accounting were:

1. Materials purchased were:

> 4,000 pounds at $2.70   3,000 pounds at $2.80
> 10,000 pounds at $2.30   6,000 pounds at $2.40
> 5,000 pounds at $2.50

(Summarize these purchases in a single entry.)
2. Materials used were 26,250 pounds.
3. Payroll costs were:

> 2,000 hours at $3.20
> 3,000 hours at 3.40
> 1,600 hours at 3.10

4. Actual manufacturing overhead costs incurred totaled $13,800.
5. Selling expenses totaled $3,000; and administrative office costs were $2,800.

Required:

a) Journal entries to record the above transactions.
b) A statement of the cost of goods sold adjusted to actual, and a condensed statement of income.

Problem 18–8. Purpose: *Journal Entries for a Standard Cost Accounting Cycle Using Two-Variation Method for Manufacturing Overhead*

The Rubrya Chemical Company uses a standard cost accounting system in its continuous process manufacturing of a fresh water detergent known as *Antipolut*.

The standard costs for producing a barrel of 50 pounds of this product are as follows:

20 pounds of Material Alpha at $1.50 ....$30.00		
8 gallons of Material Zeta at $1.25.................. 10.00	$40.00	
8 hours of direct labor at $3..........................	24.00	
8 hours of manufacturing overhead:		
Fixed overhead at $0.60 .... $4.80		
Variable overhead at $0.40.......................... 3.20	8.00	
Total Standard Cost of One Barrel		
(50 lbs.)	$72.00	

Normal operating capacity of the plant is 16,000 hours with a manufacturing overhead budget of $16,000.

Transactions for the month were as follows:

Materials purchased:
  Material Alpha, 40,000 pounds at $1.60
  Material Zeta, 18,000 gallons at $1.20
Materials used:
  Material Alpha, 38,600 pounds
  Material Zeta, 15,000 gallons
Labor costs:
  15,200 hours at an average cost of $2.85 per hour.
Factory overhead incurred:

Fixed	$ 4,800
Variable	10,000

Volume of production:

Units completed	1,500
Units in process, 80 percent complete as to materials, and 60 percent complete as to labor and overhead	500
Units sold at $150 each	1,200

Required:

a) Journal entries to record the above information, using the two-variance system for the manufacturing overhead and closing all variances into the Cost of Sales account.

b) Compute the manufacturing overhead variances using the three-variance system.

Problem 18–9.   Purpose: *CPA Problem Requiring T-Ledger Accounts and Statement of Standard Cost Work-in-Process Inventories*

The Rirkon Company began operations on January 1, 19—. It manufactures a single product. The company installed a standard cost system but plans to adjust inventories to actual costs for financial statement purposes at the end of the year.

Under this system, the stores inventory is maintained at actual costs. Work-in-Process—Materials is charged for materials used at the standard prices. Material variance accounts are used for the difference.

One half of the material for each unit is put into production at the start of manufacturing operations, and the balance when the processing is about one-third completed.

Standard costs are computed on the basis of 256,000 direct labor hours with a production of 1,600 units. The standard cost sheet is as follows:

Materials, 100 pounds at $2.00	$200
Direct labor, 160 hours at $1.25	200
Manufacturing overhead based on direct labor hours, 160 hours at $0.25	40
Total Standard Cost per Unit	$440

A summary of the transactions for the year ended December 31 shows the following:

Materials purchased, 180,000 pounds at $2.20	$396,000.00
Direct labor, 247,925 hours at $1.30	322,302.50
Manufacturing overhead	49,585.00
Materials issued to production	177,600 lbs.

Production statistics:

Units complete...	1,500
Units one-half complete..	150
Units one-fourth complete..	30

Required:

a) Using *only* the following accounts, record the above transactions indicating for each entry the nature of the item recorded: Stores, Direct Labor, Manufacturing Overhead, Work-in-Process, Finished Goods, Material Price Variation, Material Quantity Variation, Labor Rate Variance, Labor Hours – Efficiency Variance, Manufacturing Overhead – Efficiency Variance, Manufacturing Overhead – Capacity Variance, Manufacturing Overhead – Budget Variance.

b) Using the proper accounts listed above, make the entries necessary to adjust the finished goods to actual costs for material. Give identifiable supporting computations showing clearly the method of arriving at each adjustment. (Do not adjust for labor or manufacturing overhead.)

c) Prepare a statement showing details of the material cost included in work-in-process inventory adjusted to actual cost.

(Adapted from AICPA Uniform Examination)

Problem 18–10.   Purpose: *Journal Entries for Standard Cost System Statements*

The Rolsin Company manufactures a confidential military product which it identifies as Product M. Three successive, continuous operations namely, M–10, M–11, and M–12, are made in which the manufacturing of each unit is developed as shown by the following tabulation of percentages of cost to manufacture. The company does not record the actual labor charges applicable to each operation.

PERCENTAGES OF COST OF MANUFACTURE
OF UNIT M

Operation	Material	Labor	Manufacturing Overhead
M–10.........................	20	20	40
M–11.........................	–	35	40
M–12.........................	80	45	20
Totals	100	100	100

The Rolsin Company operates a cost accounting system based on the standard costs which are incorporated into the manufacturing cost accounts. The difference between standard costs and actual costs are reflected in appropriate variance accounts, namely, material price, material usage, direct labor rate, direct labor time, and overall manufacturing overhead. The material price variance is assumed to be realized at the time of purchase, irrespective of time of usage.

The standard manufacturing costs used for unit M (based on a planned monthly production ranging between 8,000 and 12,000 units M) are as follows:

	Per Unit M	
	Quantity or Hours	*Amount*
Material:		
Item M–a (issued in operation M–10)	1	$0.50
Item M–b (issued in operation M–12)	1	2.00
Direct labor (total for all operations at uniform rate of $5 per hour)	¼ hr.	1.25
Overhead (applicable to operations as a whole):		
Variable expenses		0.60
Fixed expenses		0.90
		$5.25

The inventories applicable to unit M as at December 31, 19—, stated in accordance with the foregoing schedule of standard costs, are as follows:

> Material: item M–a—100 units; item M–b—100 units.
> Work-in-process: 50 units complete through operation M–10.
> Finished goods: none.

Transactions during January, 19—, are submitted as follows:

The voucher register reflects applicable transactions incurred and paid as follows:

	Amount
Material purchases:	
Item M–a—12,000 units at $0.45 per unit	$ 5,400
Item M–b—12,000 units at $2.10 per unit	25,200
Payroll for all operations:	
Direct labor—3,100 hours at $1.2625 per ¼ hour	15,655
Indirect labor	1,500
Manufacturing overhead, other than indirect labor	15,000
Selling, administrative, and general expenses	25,000

Other facts are:

During January, 19—, 11,000 units M were transferred to the finished goods warehouse and 10,500 units were sold at $9 per unit M.

As at January 31, 19—, 100 units of work-in-process are complete through operation M–11.

Stores requisitions indicate issuances of material items M–a and M–b in the quantities required for the production carried through the respective operations. A supplementary stores requisition, however, indicates that item M–a actually used was 2% in excess of standard quantity required.

(Adapted from AICPA Uniform Examination)

Required:

a) Journal entries for the month to record the manufacturing and operating data.

b) An income statement showing the appropriate cost variances for the month of January.

chapter 19

The Installation of the Cost Accounting System and Managerial Reports

ADMINISTRATIVE AND MANAGERIAL DIRECTION IN THE INSTALLATION OF A SYSTEM

The cost accounting system may be installed by the firm's public accounting firm, or by a firm of management engineers, or by the chief cost accountant under the direction of the controller. Regardless of who has the responsibility for installing the system, it is necessary first of all to obtain the approval and direction of top management of the objectives to be achieved through the cost accounting system.

This direction and control from top management should include the following:

1. What products are or will be produced?
2. The estimated profitability of these products.
3. The relative product mix of the production and sales.
4. The type of costing to be used—historical or predetermined standard; job order or departmental process.
5. The approximate cost of operating the system.
6. The reports to be issued and the use to be made of these reports—responsibility accounting and control.
7. The acceptable accounting procedures to be used in such matters as—
   a) Inventory control and pricing methods.
   b) Depreciation methods of plant and equipment.

Having obtained appropriate direction from top management, the second step requires the survey of the plant and manufacturing procedures.

PRELIMINARY SURVEYS TO BE COMPLETED

Surveys must be made at the outset of what is being done and what should be done in the matter of planning, operating, and accounting. These surveys are guides for planning the cost accounting system. It has already been determined what type of system will be installed— job order, process, historical, or standard.

In planning a new or revising the current cost accounting system, the *first* survey will involve:

a) A study of the plant layout and the flow of work.
b) Preparation of flow charts of the operations in each department, and should cover—
    (1) Receipt, movement, and transfer of production;
    (2) The working personnel involved;
    (3) The forms used or suggested to be used;
    (4) Controlling the operations.
c) Survey of the production and service departments in the matter of floor area, equipment investment, number of employees, equipment horsepower ratings.

A *second* survey should develop a chart of accounts for the general and subsidiary ledgers. These accounts must be properly coded and would cover the—

a) General ledger chart and code.
b) Factory ledger and code.
c) Subsidiary ledger accounts for the factory overhead on a cost center basis.

A *third* survey will cover the compilation of the present or contemplated forms to be used in completing the cost accounting cycle. This survey may have to include the mechanical devices such as punched card or electronic computers which are to be used with the forms.

A *fourth* survey will indicate the present and proposed personnel required for the general and factory accounting work with a clear definition or description of the duties and routines to be followed.

On the basis of these preliminary surveys, the firm is now ready to proceed with the installation of the cost accounting system.

DESIGNING THE COST ACCOUNTING SYSTEM

The preliminary work has resulted in the determination of the kind of cost accounting system that will be used—job order or departmental (process); historical or predetermined. Modern cost accounting thinking seems to favor the use of a predetermined standard cost accounting system as the most effective for managerial control. On this latter acceptance, it now becomes necessary to agree on how the standards are to be determined. What type of standards will be used—past experience, test runs, or scientifically set standards? If the latter, then the firm must organize a standards department. Will it be a full-time or part-time organization, and who will be on it? The larger the firm, the greater the need for a separate group of industrial engineers, properly directed by a senior official of the firm, to operate this department. A flexible budget should be set up for the manufacturing overhead costs at different operating levels. This flexible budget could very well be reviewed monthly or quarterly in order to have the most responsible costs and control.

With these preliminary matters settled, the design of the cost system will proceed with the planning of the paper work to be instituted.

First on this will be the design of the job order cost sheet or the cost of production report. These will be necessary to summarize the job or periodic costs. The design will be influenced by the nature of the manufacturing operations and departmentalization of the labor and overhead costs.

Second will be the design of the forms to be used for the materials acquisitions and usage, with due consideration of the internal control. Where possible, preprinted standard bills of materials should be used for controlling the materials used. Inventory records should be maintained for all important materials. Mechanical methods for computing, recording, and summarizing these forms should be carefully studied, especially if punched-card accounting equipment is available.

Third, the forms for compiling labor costs by jobs or by departments should be planned and simplified. Using a Calculagraph to expedite payroll cost computations for the job order system, as well as telephone or telegraph or teletypewriter methods of transferring labor costs to a central department, should be considered.

Fourth, manufacturing overhead forms should be designed and routines planned for their use. These would include:

a) Survey of plant facilities by departments or work centers as a basis for allocating the overhead costs.
b) Separating the overhead into its fixed and variable items both for the budgeted as well as the actual costs should be developed if such managerial control is desirable.
c) Flexible budgeting procedures should be outlined—both the preparation as well as the use and revision.
d) Determining the bases to be used in applying the manufacturing over-

head to production or to departments. Questions of whether to use more than one rate for each department, whether to use a separate rate for materials handling, and whether to use a rate for central administration must all be considered when planning the forms and procedures to be instituted for this phase of costing.

SPECIAL MANAGERIAL DECISIONS BEFORE INSTALLING THE COST SYSTEM

Is it planned to have the cost accounting integrated with the regular financial accounting records or merely treated as a statistical compilation? If only partial cost accounting is to be used—that is costing and control only of the major products or the activities of the most important departments, then it will not be possible to integrate the cost accounting records with the financial records. And this means that some of the internal control of accounting which results from an integrated accounting system will be lost.

Pricing the materials used will have an effect on the unit costs of production. Should Fifo, Lifo, average, or standard costs be used in such pricing? From the management viewpoint, which represents the more accurate costing method? This also will revert back to the first point mentioned—namely, integration of the cost accounting with the regular accounting records—because the income tax effects of the various inventory pricing methods must also be considered.

In a few concerns at present, management must also decide whether in the matter of accountability, it feels that *direct costing* should be used. If so, because of the Internal Revenue Service's disallowance of inventories on the direct costing basis, the cost systems must be maintained independently of the financial accounting records.

UPDATING THE COST ACCOUNTING SYSTEM[1]

With the constant and rapid changes in communication in modern business and the use of electronic data processing equipment to aid in this communication, attention must be given to the question of when, how, and why the cost accounting system should be constantly updated in order to make it most effective in managerial control and accountability at the lowest operating costs.

There is always an opportunity for improving the managerial control of the operations of a modern business concern. Cost control is one of the basic areas for improving the profit-making opportunities. The informa-

---

[1] Adapted with permission from an article by R. W. Holmes, *Management Accounting*, February 1970.

tion system of a business today provides the control and accountability measure for managerial success. Therefore the cost accounting system requires constant attention for measuring its effectiveness and for improving manufacturing efficiency. The *first* consideration in updating the cost accounting system is a study of the organization chart with suitable job descriptions. This will fix responsibility and avoid overlapping responsibilities. The *second* consideration requires the setting of objectives or goals for the company — both short term and long term. The use of budgets with computerized analyses will create measures of responsibility performance. These goals will also focus attention on the problems that may arise and their solution to provide measurable results. These analyses must be specific, factual, and extend beyond the mere comparisons of the cost and budgeted data. Furthermore, these analyses require the compilation of costs, not at the actual end of production but at the points where these costs are incurred. This means analyses of the variations from material and labor cost standards on the basis of operations, departments, employees, or products. Flexible budgets should be used to measure volume fluctuations. Costs of spoiled and effective work should be measured and analyzed. As is evident, these suggestions imply the necessity of fixing cost responsibility so that performance can not only be measured but identified. A flexible but detailed chart of accounts to localize each element of cost with daily or weekly reports of the variations of the most volatile elements of the budgeted versus the actual cost of labor and variable overhead is necessary.

Since the operation of a cost accounting system is usually an expensive administrative and clerical procedure, the system should also be reviewed continually to improve its information control without increasing its operating costs. This can be achieved in many cases by using the computer system which the firm already operates. By creating sophisticated programs with cost data already available, management information and control can be established by determining the finished goods turnover; the stores inventory versus requirements; quality control measurements; labor efficiency, labor turnover, and labor absenteeism; product line profit contribution; product servicing costs; and alternative managerial decisions affecting special price concessions, elimination of product lines, and decisions of whether to make or buy.

MANAGEMENT REPORTS

Along with the variety of managerial decisions which will require special studies such as break-even point, variable product mix of sales, to buy or to manufacture, and to modernize the equipment or to use present equipment, management must be supplied a series of periodic reports which will measure the supervisory and employee accountability.

These reports should be planned when the accounting system is first installed; should be checked upon when later used to determine their usefulness; and should be revised or eliminated if necessary.

The basic reports to be considered relate to the elements of materials, payroll, manufacturing overhead, and overall profitability of the manufacturing operations.

For *material cost control,* the following reports might be considered as useful when installing a cost accounting system:

1. *Material cost variations from the standards set up.* This report should indicate the material price and the material quantity variations, and the causes therefore. Whether this report should be prepared monthly, quarterly, or at less frequent intervals will be determined by the nature of the manufacturing operations and the customary fluctuations in the kind of materials used.
2. *Spoiled materials reports* may be necessary where spoilage affects the output and sales of the firm. This spoilage report may be part of the previous report on material variations from standard.

The use of these two types of reports is one form of managerial measurement of the accountability of the supervisory personnel in the various departments.

For *payroll cost control* the following might be considered:

1. *Efficiency* reports by workers or departments—a measurement of the variations of the actual payroll costs from the standard costs.
2. *Idle time reports* or machine *setup cost reports* may be necessary if not already a part of the efficiency report in 1.
3. Ratio of indirect labor to total labor costs or the ratio of the payroll costs to total cost of production may also be an important index of operating efficiency.

However, it must be remembered both in the case of material cost accounting and payroll cost accounting, reports and analyses should only be made in those instances where the material costs or the labor costs are an important phase dollarwise of the total cost of production, and if the material or labor costs are subject to fluctuation without justification. In the matter of increased automation, reports on labor costs or efficiency become unnecessary or meaningless.

Manufacturing overhead cost reports should be concerned with the analysis into the fixed and variable items, since the latter are controllable. It should further be concerned with arranging these overhead costs on a departmental basis. After meeting these two prerequisites, the cost accountant can determine what reports should be prepared. Presumably the control center is the department, and therefore the reports should be prepared departmentally. If the material and labor reports are

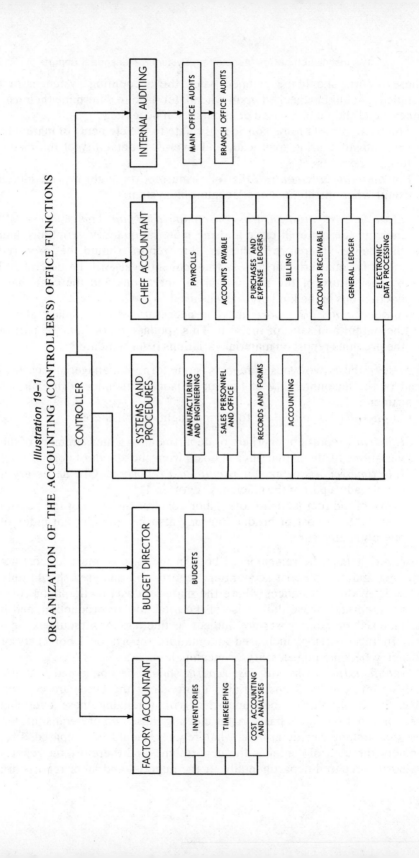

Illustration 19-1

ORGANIZATION OF THE ACCOUNTING (CONTROLLER'S) OFFICE FUNCTIONS

Illustration 19-1 (continued)

ORGANIZATION OF THE FACTORY COST ACCOUNTING STAFF

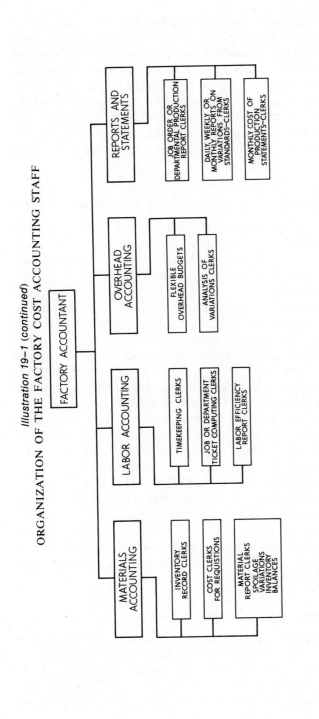

prepared monthly or quarterly, then the manufacturing overhead reports must follow a similar time pattern. The reports for manufacturing overhead will show the actual and applied for each department and the amount of the difference. Departmentally, the causes of the over- or underapplied manufacturing overhead should be ascertained. They may be due to faulty cost estimates or improper estimate of the volume of production. Furthermore, the variation of the applied overhead from the standard job or departmental overhead (efficiency variation) must also be shown. These reports measure the effectiveness of the production supervisory staff.

ORGANIZATION CHART OF COST ACCOUNTING FUNCTION

Having planned the accounting records for the cost system, it is well also to plan the personnel and functional organization of the various segments of this system — materials control, payroll costs, overhead costs, statements, reports, standards, and budgets. Both the divisions and the staff should be diagrammed.

First of these charts would be the place of the cost accounting department within the framework of the accounting (controller's) department. This might be as shown in Illustration 19–1.

Although surveys have indicated that the number of clerks engaged in the compilation of the costs of production as compared with the number of factory employees decreased as the size of the company increased, it is still desirable to have some criterion by which to gauge the maximum size of the clerical force required in cost accounting. Automation in the plant and automation in compiling cost accounting data no doubt seriously alter these figures. The following is given as a guide subject to adjustment for automation or special factors.

In smaller companies employing up to 600 factory workers, one cost clerk for each 80 employees was the average, whereas in larger firms the average was one cost clerk for each 150 employees. When this ratio is reconciled with the ratio of the total cost of operating the cost accounting function in business (approximately one fourth of 1 percent of sales), management should have a definite idea of the maximum cost of operating the cost accounting department.

EVALUATING THE COST ACCOUNTING SYSTEM

Either before or after the cost accounting system has been installed, management will probably want to evaluate the job. Before doing so, it might be necessary to outline the personnel, forms, and routines to be used in completing the work and the cost of its operation. This will answer the first question: "How much does it cost to operate the system?" Some years ago a study was made of the cost of all accounting work related to the sales income of the firms. It was found that the cost of operating an accounting system was 0.82 percent of the sales—less than 1 percent of sales. In this same study, the cost of operating a cost accounting system was 0.27 percent of sales, a little more than one quarter of 1 percent of sales. Times and conditions have changed, but these percentages are an average of 11 types of manufacturing firms covering 59 plants having sales of $346 million. This cost ratio might be suggestive of how to evaluate a cost accounting system.

A second method of evaluating a cost accounting system is "Does it work?" This means does it produce usable cost accounting information in time for proper managerial action. Does it indicate not only what the costs are but what they should be and the causes for the differences? Finally, the valuation must answer the question: "Does it pinpoint responsibility?" Has or will it permit cost reduction through increased efficiency?

And as part of this evaluation is the question: "Are the cost reports such that they will be used by top management to direct supervisory management to do a better job?"

IMPORTANCE OF MANAGERIAL REPORTS

As a company grows and expands its activities, proper reports must be made available to all levels of management. The reports must be accurate, useful, and timely as many a decision regarding the firm's future will be made based on the reports. The report is generally the only means of communicating financial information within the business firm.

In a dynamic economy containing a large number of industries, no one system of reports will be applicable to every business. Much ingenuity, research, planning, and judgment must be exercised in developing an integrated report system which will be of greatest benefit to an individual company. Obviously, the selection of proper reports is a continuing task so that obsolete reports will be dropped.

If the report system is to be effective, a clear understanding of the definite lines of authority and responsibility is a prerequisite to determining the specific reports required in a company. Illustration 19–2 presents in condensed form an administrative organization chart indicating the lines of authority followed by one corporation.

In addition to understanding the functional and supervisory organization, the *duties* of the executives must be clearly set forth so that proper reports may be given to the right people. Illustration 19–3 describes some of the typical duties of various executives in a manufacturing company.

Illustration 19–2. *Administrative Organization Chart of a Manufacturing Company (with Detail of Controller's and Production Departments)*

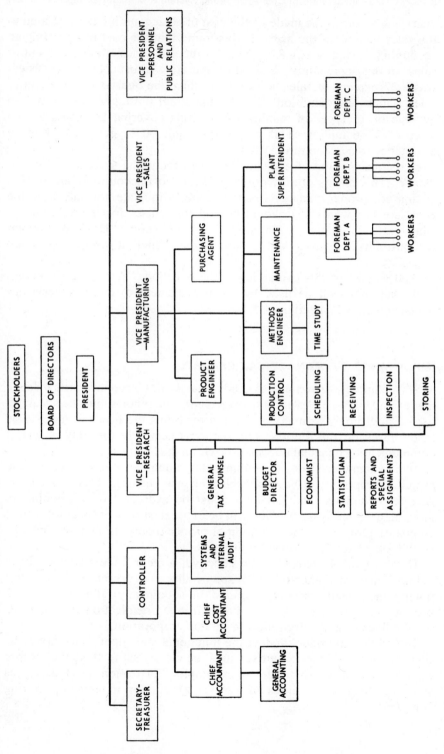

Illustration 19-3

Executive	Typical Duties
President, vice president, treasurer, and corporate secretary	General administrative and supervisory, by establishing policy and providing means of checking on adherence to these policies.
Controller	Organization of detailed and summary accounting procedure, supervisor of semisenior executives, such as chief accountant and cost accountant.
Budget director	Preparation and control of budget.
Chief engineer	Engineering and technical supervisor.
Production manager	Organization and coordination of those activities relating to planning and scheduling, purchasing, factory personnel, and inspection.
Sales manager	Organization and supervision of sales force.
Chief accountant	Under the controller; responsible for general accounting work.
Cost accountant	Responsible to controller for cost data to be used in preparing some of the reports; assist controller in installing cost system.
Purchasing agent	Under supervision of manufacturing vice president; responsible for receipt and storage of materials.
Factory superintendent	Responsible to manufacturing vice president for the use of materials, men, and factory facilities in efficient production of the finished products.
Foremen	Line deputies assisting the superintendent in creating efficient production.

This chapter considers primarily those reports which deal with cost and efficiency that serve as the basis for better cost control. Chapter 20 deals with the direct costing method of facilitating cost control and planning. Chapter 21 examines analytical and graphic methods of portraying the probable effect on profits of future policies of manufacturing and distribution which management has under consideration. Chapter 22 deals with specific managerial problems which require cost data for solution and discusses the manner in which the cost accountant selects the type of cost data appropriate to the solution of a specific problem.

OBJECTIVES OF REPORTS

A primary objective of a report is to communicate desired information to management. The various reports summarize, in understandable and usable form, essential facts of the functional areas of production and distribution, as found in the details of cost accounting systems, so that management may:

1. Study the trend of operating costs of material, labor, and overhead costs.
2. Measure the effectiveness of the various manufacturing and distribution functions.
3. Measure the efficiency of supervisory personnel held accountable for control of specific costs.
4. Plan future production and distribution policies for the entire firm.
5. Make specific price, production, financial, and labor policy decisions based on adequate cost information appropriate to the particular problem.

A basic objective of reports is the CONTROL of operations. For example, management is put into a position where manufacturing operations may be controlled when actual cost figures are compared with predetermined costs and the variances explained.

Cost accounting should furnish the necessary details of production and efficiency through the medium of reports. The number of these reports and their arrangement and content vary with the individual concern.

If the system of cost and efficiency reports is adequate, management should be able to answer questions such as:

Are the variations in material costs due to changes in the quantity used or to a change in the price of the material?

Are variations in labor costs due to a change in the number of workers, rate of wages, or efficiency?

Are increases in factory expenses due to idle time, waste, inaccurate budget estimates, or poor supervision?

Where does spoilage occur and why?

What department has inefficient workers and why?

Reports should be prepared for the three levels of management: the *proximate*—the foremen; the *intermediate*—the plant superintendent; and the *remote*—the president and board of directors. A different type of information may be required for each level. The closer the recipient is to the activity, the greater the amount of detail that must be provided. The top level of management should receive information that has been greatly condensed and summarized.

SCOPE OF REPORTS

Although there are many kinds of reports that are supplied to management, this discussion will concern itself with a coordinated system of cost reports whose basic purpose is to provide data necessary for control. A coordinated system of accounting reports to management provides historical data indicating the results of *past operations,* measures the degree of management control of *current operations,* and anticipates the estimated results of *future operations.* Reports are an aid to management, never a substitute for it. The accountant must not only determine and interpret significant information accurately but he must also translate the information in the best possible manner for users. Specialists in the fields of engineering, production, and sales do not usually have an extensive background in accounting principles and procedures. The unimportant should be deleted, repetitive data should be consolidated, and appropriate comments should be included emphasizing the significance of the report figures.

The effective report serves an *immediate purpose* and is a composite of many ingredients, including visual attractiveness; language that is simple, clear, and "to the point"; and a format that is neither overdetailed nor too brief. Reports should be comparative in form whenever possible, and adequate data should be presented in support of suggestions as to possible courses of action. Developments in the area of electronic computers and integrated data processing provide countless techniques that tend to improve and simplify the job of reporting financial data to management, but the lack of a carefully conceived plan of presentation may create considerable confusion which results in costly inefficiency.

As mentioned earlier, cost accounting reports and statements must be prepared for and distributed to three different levels of management. Each type of management — the *general executives,* the *departmental executives,* and the *foremen* — comes within a special sphere of influence; and the reports sent to a man should deal with matters falling within his sphere, thus providing him an effective tool for facilitating his particular management tasks. Primarily, the foreman is interested in the performance of his workers; the department head desires knowledge of the progress of a section; and the general executive requires information concerning all departments. The scope of a report, therefore, is determined by its expected use.

Cost accounting reports may be classified as *financial* or *efficiency.* Financial reports include cost statements of material, labor, and expenses; summary costs of production; and budgeted statements. Efficiency reports include those relating to idle machines, machine repairs, spoiled goods, employee productivity, plant productivity, or consumable tool expense.

Cost reports may be further classified as to *frequency* — i.e., daily, weekly, monthly, semiannual, or annual. The greater the degree of control required, the shorter the period of time covered in the report.

A list of the reports intended to provide adequate data for effective control customarily includes:

1. *For top management (board of directors and corporate officers):*
   a) Comparative monthly, quarterly, and annual income statements.
   b) Master budget covering the entire company.
   c) Summaries of as many of the more detailed cost and efficiency reports listed below as may be desirable or necessary in a particular company.
2. *For senior department executives (controller, production manager, sales manager, etc.):*
   a) Comparative income statements.
   b) Master budget and detailed departmental budgets.
   c) Weekly, monthly, and cumulative comparisons of budgeted and actual figures by department.
   d) Weekly and/or monthly reports on purchases, inventories, labor costs, idleness, repairs, spoilage, expenses, and production.
   e) Sales — actual versus budgeted.
3. *For semisenior departmental executives (including the factory superintendent, chief accountant, purchasing agent, etc., who are the liaison or connecting links between the senior executives, on the one hand, and the foremen or department managers, on the other):*
   a) Material reports showing receipts, issuances, and balances on hand.
   b) Material reports showing budgeted and actual figures.
   c) Labor reports showing budgeted and actual figures.
   d) Indirect labor costs, both budgeted and actual.
   e) Indirect material and small tool expenses on a budgeted and actual basis.
   f) Budgeted and actual figures of controllable expenses.
   g) Spoilage reports.
   h) Idle labor and idle machine reports.
   i) Reports on variation from standard costs of materials, labor, and overhead.
   j) Machine repair cost reports.
4. *For foremen:*
   a) Comparisons of budgeted with actual costs of their section(s).
   b) Various efficiency reports, limited in scope.
   c) Summaries of other controllable conditions within their departments or within related or comparative departments.

Many of the cost and operating reports are prepared through the cooperation of the semisenior executives and the cost accountant. The chief accountant will participate in preparing the financial and cost statements; the purchasing agent in preparing material reports and budgets; and the factory superintendent in preparing efficiency reports on labor, machines, and expenses.

Whether or not a report will be used in a given company is determined by the degree of control desired and whether its use justifies the expense of preparation.

TYPES OF REPORTS

A report may include *financial statements* as for example an interim income statement. Illustration 19–4 presents a comparative income statement.

A report often used is the *product activity* report, an example of

Illustration 19–4

COMPARATIVE STATEMENT OF INCOME FOR MONTH ENDED MARCH 31, 19— (Thousands of Dollars and Pounds)						
	Current Period			Year to Date		
	Budget	Actual	% of Budget	Budget	Actual	% of Budget
Net sales—pounds: Product A.....	100	110	110%	400	300	75%
Product B.....	150	150	100	300	350	117
Total..............................	250	260	104%	700	650	93%
Net sales: Product A.................	$200	$220	110%	$ 800	$600	75%
Product B.................	150	150	100	300	350	117
Total..............................	$350	$370	106%	$1,100	$950	86%
Less: Variable cost of sales.........	$190	$200	105%	$470	$450	96%
Freight on sales..................	10	20	200	30	30	100
Total variable cost.............	$200	$220	110%	$ 500	$480	96%
Contribution margin: Product A...	$ 90	$ 90	100%	$ 360	$160	44%
Product B...	60	60	100	240	310	129
Contribution margin—total..........	$150	$150	100%	$ 600	$470	78%
Less: Fixed costs:						
Plant operations.....................	$ 10	$ 10	100%	$ 30	$ 30	100%
Corporate management............	30	30	100	30	30	100
Research.............................	10	20	200	90	100	111
Selling.................................	10	10	100	30	40	133
Administration......................	10	10	100	30	30	100
Depreciation........................	30	30	100	90	90	100
Total fixed costs................	$100	$110	110%	$ 300	$320	107%
Income before Taxes	$ 50	$ 40	80%	$ 300	$150	50%

Illustration 19-5

Analysis of Orders Received and Shipments

	Week Includes 8/7-8/13						Cumulative to Date			
	Unfilled Orders Beginning of Week	Weekly Orders Received	Weekly Capacity	Per Cent Activity	Weekly Shipments	Unfilled Orders End of Week	Unfilled Orders Beginning of Year	Cum. Orders Received	Cum. Shipments	Unfilled Orders End of Week
A Division										
X Product	4,000	2,000	2,500	80	1,800	4,200	4,500	59,700	60,000	4,200
Y Product	3,000	1,000	1,000	100	950	3,050	3,200	29,850	30,000	3,050
Z Product	2,000	500	750	67	600	1,900	2,500	14,400	15,000	1,900
Total A Division	9,000	3,500	4,250	82	3,350	9,150	10,200	103,950	105,000	9,150
E Division										
X Product	2,000	500	550	91	500	2,000	2,400	24,600	25,000	2,000
Y Product	3,000	1,000	1,200	83	800	3,200	3,600	29,600	30,000	3,200
Total E Division	5,000	1,500	1,750	86	1,300	5,200	6,000	54,200	55,000	5,200
Grand Total	28,000	11,000	12,500	88	9,750	29,250	33,400	316,850	321,000	29,250
Wkly. Avg. (32 Wks. This Yr.)		9,901			10,031			9,901	10,031	
Wkly. Avg. (32 Wks. Last Yr.)		9,500			9,800			9,500	9,800	

SOURCE: Adapted from N.A.A. Accounting Practice Report No. 9, Reports Which Managements Find Most Useful.

which is shown in Illustration 19–5. Related to the product activity report is the group of reports disclosing *labor efficiency*. The labor efficiency report needs to be more detailed for the foreman than for the factory manager. Illustrations 19–6 and 19–7 are labor efficiency reports; Illustration 19–6 is for the factory manager while Illustration 19–7 is for the foreman.

Illustration 19–6

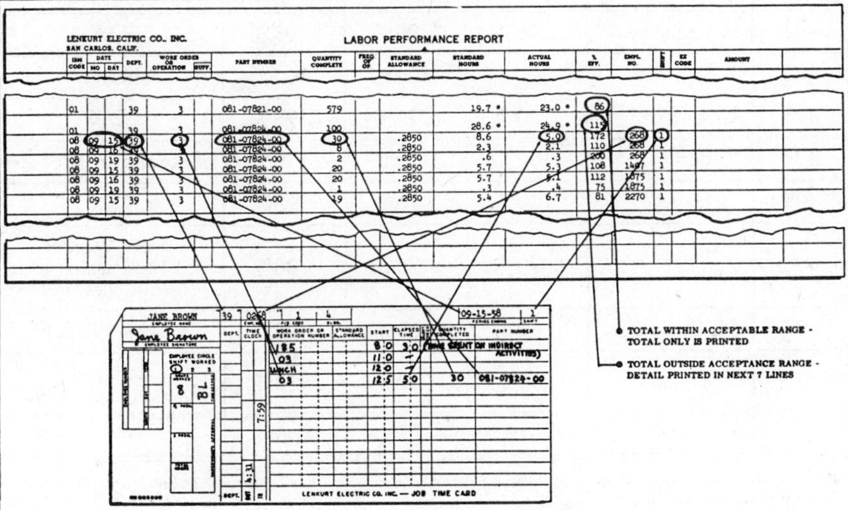

A Labor Performance Report (distributed weekly to factory managers and foremen) involving the use of a computer programmed to print out operations detail for a part when it shows efficiency outside of ranges established individually for each part by the department foremen.

SOURCE: *N.A.A. Accounting Practice Report No. 9, Reports Which Managements Find Most Useful.*

Analyses of manufacturing overhead represent another category which may be used. Illustration 19–8 is an example of the type of report that might be prepared in this category.

Quite often, selected items need to be reported to a particular level of management. Obviously, the items to be included will vary among the companies. Illustrations 19–9, 19–10, and 19–11 are examples of this type of report. Cost and usefulness are the only limits as to the type of information that could be reported under this category.

IMPORTANCE OF GRAPHIC PRESENTATION

Graphic illustrations should possibly supplement the reports of cost data. The graphic illustrations are not a substitute for the report but a

Illustration 19–7

DEPARTMENTAL EFFICIENCY REPORT

Department No. 78   Week Ending April 12, 19—

Ford A. Waters, Foreman

No.	Name	This Week	Last Week	Previous Month	Remarks
401	J. Columbus	96%	98%	95%	O.K.
402	R. Donlon	99%	100%	100%	O.K.
403	C. Cohen	90%	92%	95%	O.K.
404	R. Burton	100%	100%	102%	Exceptional Worker
405	F. George	100%	96%	98%	O.K.
406	A. Flint	70%	76%	80%	New Worker Not Familiar with Machine
407	M. Barb	80%	85%	90%	Machine Repairs
408	S. Chensi	80%	82%	80%	Delayed Waiting For Work
	Average	89.3%	91%	92.5%	

90% to 100% operating efficiency considered good. Above or below this figure some comment should be made by foreman in "remarks" column.

simple, more emphatic and perhaps more easily understood presentation, and hence, more usable. For this reason, perhaps, graphs and charts arouse the interest of executives.

Graphic presentation is most effective in showing comparisons, whether they are historical, current, or prognostic. The pictorial display of graphic presentation appeals to the different types of minds among the various grades of employees, from the unskilled factory worker to the trained corporate executive.

TYPES OF GRAPHIC PRESENTATION

Many different types of graphic presentation exist, but not all are suitable for industrial use. The following will be described and illustrated in this section: bar graphs, curve charts, strata charts, semilogarithmic charts, area or volume charts, and special graphs.

Bar graphs (see Illustrations 19–12 and 19–13) use *horizontal* columns to present values, the length of the bar indicating the value. Bars arranged *vertically* are known as *column* graphs. If these bar graphs present but

Illustration 19-8

DEPARTMENTAL COST STATEMENT

Unit of measure: Machine hours

Actual: 1,118
Normal: 980
% of normal: 114.1

Dept.: 942
Period: 3-19XX

EXPENSE	NORMAL STANDARD	PERCENTAGE		REVISED STANDARD	ACTUAL EXPENSE	VARIANCE—GAIN OR (LOSS)			
		Variability	Revision			Controllable	Volume		Controllable Year to Date
							Per Cent of Normal Standard	Amount	
.01 Direct labor—applied	$3,575	100	114.1	$4,079	$4,296	($217)			($605)
.02 Direct labor—unapplied	160	100	114.4	183	150	33			(4)
.03 Indirect labor	1,642	60	108.5	1,782	1,805	(23)	5.6	$ 92	(97)
.04 Supervision and clerical	735	20	102.9	756	740	16	11.3	83	90
Total wages and salaries	$6,112			$6,800	$6,991	($191)		$175	($616)
.11 Belting	133	90	112.8	150	158	(8)	1.4	2	(28)
.12 Machine parts	445	90	112.8	502	453	49	1.4	5	(10)
.13 Chemicals	496	90	112.7	559	516	43	1.4	7	159
.14 Miscellaneous supplies	164	75	110.4	181	205	(24)	3.5	6	(5)
.21 Maintenance department charges	265	70	109.8	291	405	(114)	4.2	11	33
.22 Power and light	470	60	108.5	510	530	(20)	5.6	26	19
.31 Spoiled work	530	100	114.1	605	502	103			196
Total direct costs	$8,615			$9,598	$9,760	($162)		$232	($252)
.61 Fixed charges	646				646				
Total expense	$9,261				$10,406				

PROOF

Variance above:
Volume.......... 232
Controllable.... (162)

Total...... 70

Direct expense absorbed:
8,615 × 114.1% = 9,830
Actual direct expense. 9,760

70

Source: David R. Anderson and Leo A. Schmidt, *Practical Controllership* (Homewood, Ill.: Richard D. Irwin, Inc.).

Illustration 19-9

MONTHLY REPORT TO TOP MANAGEMENT

INCOME STATEMENT

For the Two Months Ended February 28, 19—

(In Thousands of Dollars)

	This Month		This Year to Date		Last Year
	Actual	Budget	Actual	Budget	Actual
Net trade sales:					
Dollars.....................	$100	$120	$180	$250	$170
Number of cases..............	50	60	90	125	85
Cost of trade sales:					
Standard cost..................	$ 60	$ 70	$110	$150	$100
Manufacturing variances........	5	...	7	...	6
Purchase price variances........	2	...	3	...	2
Other costs....................	3	4	6	8	7
Research costs.................	2	2	4	4	5
Engineering...................	2	4	4	8	5
Total cost of trade sales.......	$ 74	$ 80	$134	$170	$125
Gross profit on trade sales........	$ 26	$ 40	$ 46	$ 80	$ 45
Operating expenses:					
Selling......................	$ 5	$ 8	$ 10	$ 16	$ 10
Advertising—budget basis......	2	2	4	4	5
Stock and shipping.............	2	3	4	6	4
Transportation................	2	2	4	4	4
Administrative.................	3	3	6	6	6
Corporate and legal...........	1	2	1	4	1
Total operating expenses....	$ 15	$ 20	$ 29	$ 40	$ 30
Operating profit..................	$ 11	$ 20	$ 17	$ 40	$ 15
Other income....................	2	3	4	6	2
Other expenses..................	1	1	2	2	1
Income before taxes.............	$ 12	$ 22	$ 19	$ 44	$ 16
Tax provision...................	4	5	5	10	8
Net Income.....................	$ 8	$ 17	$ 14	$ 34	$ 8
Percentages to trade sales:					
Gross profit....................	26%	33%	26%	32%	26%
Operating expenses.............	15	17	16	16	18
Income before taxes...........	12	18	11	18	9

SUMMARY OF FINANCIAL CONDITION

As at February 28, 19—

	This Month	Last Month	Beginning of This Year
Cash....................................	$60	$50	$65
% of total current liabilities..............	30%	27%	25%
Due from customers.......................	$80	$80	$70
Number of days sales....................	20	20	18
Current ratio...........................	2½:1	2½:1	2:1

Illustration 19–10

```
                        STATISTICAL DATA
                   As at February 28, 19—

                                        This      Last    February,
                                        Month     Month   Last Year
NUMBER OF EMPLOYEES:
   Salaried:
      New York
      Chicago
      Dallas

   Salaried Employees with Base Salary
      of $9,000 a Year or More

   Employed at Straight Time Hourly Wage Rates:
      New York
      Chicago
      Dallas

NUMBER OF CASES SHIPPED (000's omitted):
   New York
   Chicago
   Dallas
      Total

UNSHIPPED ORDERS AT SALES VALUE   (000's omitted):
   New York
   Chicago
   Dallas
      Total

BACK ORDERS AT SALES VALUE (000's omitted):
   New York
   Chicago
   Dallas
      Total

PRICES PAID FOR PRINCIPAL COMMODITIES:
   Cotton, strict middling    lb.
   Crude Rubber               lb.
   Talc                       lb.
```

SOURCE: Adapted from *N.A.A. Bulletin*, Volume 36, No. 4.

a single fact, they are known as *simple* bar charts; if several facts are presented in each bar, by means of coloring or crosshatching, the graph is known as a *composite* bar graph. If two or more bars are used for a single accounting period, the chart is known as a *grouped* bar graph. Bar graphs are most useful in presenting simple facts but are not so satisfactory as other graphic forms in presenting comparative data. Bar graphs have been used in cost accounting to:

a) Show the elements of cost for a unit or a period.
b) Show inventory figures for each kind of material, that is, the amount on hand and the amount used during a month.
c) Show the relationship between the sales price and the cost of sales for a unit or a given period.

Illustration 19–11

Comparison of Significant Figures					
DIRECT LABOR PERFORMANCE	BASE PERIOD	JANUARY	FEBRUARY		DECEMBER
Machining Division	00%	00%	00%		00%
Welding Division	00%	00%	00%		00%
Total Manufacturing Department	00%	00%	00%		00%
RATIO OF INDIRECT TO DIRECT LABOR HOURS					
Machining Division	00%	00%	00%		00%
Welding Division	00%	00%	00%		00%
Total	00%	00%	00%		00%
VOLUME (in 000's)					
Actual Direct Labor Hours	000	000	000		000
Standard Direct Labor Hours	000	000	00		000
Total Standard Dollars of:					
Prime Products Produced	0000	0000	0000		0000
Transfers to Other Plants	000	000	000		000
DEPARTMENT CONTROLLABLE COST/STD. DIR. LABOR HR.					
Accounting	$ .00	$ .00	$ .00		$ .00
Manufacturing	0.00	0.00	0.00		0.00
Total	$ 0.00	$ 0.00	$ 0.00		$ 0.00
OTHER COST INDEXES					
Spoilage Due to Defective Labor (in 000's)	$ .00	$ .00	$ .00		$ .00
Per Std. Direct Labor Hour	.00	.00	.00		.00
Purchases of Materials & Supplies	0,000	0,000	0,000		0,000
Material Variance (in 000's)	---	$ 000	$ 000		$ 000
Material Variance Percent	---	0.0%	0.0%		00.0%
EMPLOYMENT AND HOURS					
Hires	00	0	0		000
Separations	00	000	00		00
Employment By Department					
Accounting	000	000	000		000
Manufacturing	0000	0000	0000		0000
Total	0000	0000	0000		0000
Actual Hours Worked (in 000's)					
Hourly Roll—Direct	000	000	000		000
Hourly Roll—Indirect All Departments	000	000	000		000
Hourly Roll—Total	000	000	000		000
Weekly Roll	00	00	00		00
Total Hourly and Weekly Rolls	000	000	000		000
Overtime Hours Worked (in 000's)					
Hourly Roll	0.0	0.0	0.0		0.0
Weekly Roll	0.0	.0	.0		.0
Total	00.0	0.0	0.0		0.0
INVENTORIES AT STANDARD COST (in 000's)					
Production Stores	$ 0,000	$ 0,000	$ 0,000		$ 0,000
Indirect Inventories and Supplies	000	000	000		000
Prime Product Inventories	0,000	0,000	0,000		0,000
Total	$ 0,000	$00,000	$00,000		$00,000

SOURCE: *N.A.A. Accounting Practice Report No. 9, Reports Which Managements Find Most Useful.*

Illustrations 19–12 and 19–13 show but two of the many applications of the bar graph. Illustration 19–12 reflects the total costs for a given period, and Illustration 19–13 shows the comparative costs by products. These graphs may be prepared on the basis of either unit costs or total costs.

Curve graphs are used to present data in a continuous line, joining the various points on cross-section paper. These points usually indicate the time factor of a series of comparative data and, in this particular instance, cost data. If but one curve appears on the chart, the chart is

Illustration 19–12. Simple and Composite Bar Graphs Showing the Amount of the Various Elements of Cost at a Given Date*

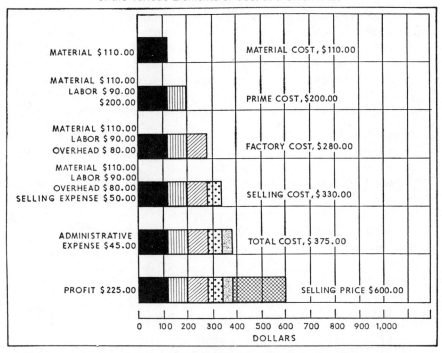

* SOURCE OF DATA: A manufacturing, income, and profit and loss statement at a given date.

Illustration 19–13. Simple Bar Graphs Showing Cost Elements on a Percentage Basis*

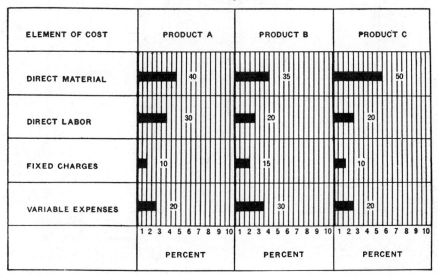

* SOURCE OF DATA: Detailed comparative statement on percentage basis of unit of total costs for each product.

known as a *single curve chart;* if two or more appear on the same chart, it is a *multiple curve chart* (see Illustration 19–14). By cumulating the data before preparing the curve graph, a *cumulative* curve chart can be prepared (see Illustration 19–15). Curve graphs are by far the most widely used in submitting business statistics and are most useful in showing comparative data, at the same time indicating historical data and long-time trends. Almost every type of cost data can be plotted in this form. The time interval may consist of weeks, months, or years.

Some purposes for which this type of display may be used include:

1. Plotting the high and low cost of direct labor per unit of manufacture.
2. Plotting the actual and budgeted manufacturing expenses for each department and for the factory as a whole on a monthly basis.
3. Showing the trend of the cost of manufacture for various articles.
4. Showing the relationship between the sales and the cost of sales of individual articles on a monthly or yearly basis.
5. Showing relationship between total sales and total cost of sales on a monthly or yearly basis.

Illustration 19–14.   Curve Graph Showing the Monthly Comparison of the Actual versus Budgeted Manufacturing Expenses*

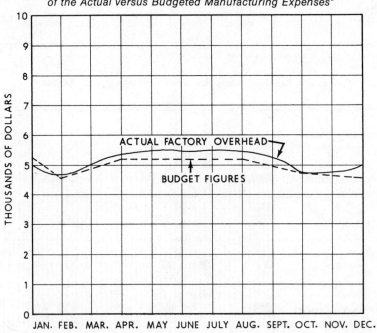

*This chart may also be prepared by plotting the percentages of variation. In that case the center horizontal line would be 0%, and the plus variations above the line and minus below the line.

Source: Monthly statements showing the relationship of budgeted versus actual manufacturing expenses.

*Illustration 19–15.   Curve Graph Showing the Relationship
between the Budgeted Manufacturing Expenses
on an Accumulated Basis*

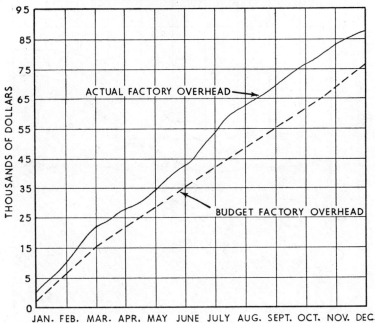

* SOURCE: The cumulative figures in the monthly statement of actual versus budgeted manufacturing expenses.

6. Showing on a monthly basis the inventory of direct materials, finished
    goods, and work-in-process.

Strata graphs are combinations of curve and area charts, the area
being variously colored or shaded to show the component parts. They
are most useful in showing comparisons over a long period of time, since
the shading or coloring is more effective than the use of simple cumulative
line curves. In cost accounting they are most practical in showing the
component parts of certain figures over a relatively long period of time,
such as the elements of cost of the cost of goods manufactured for each
month of the year or an analysis of the various items on the monthly balance sheets. Illustration 19–16 is an example of this type of graph.

The *semilogarithmic curve* chart is sometimes called a *ratio graph*. It
is most useful when rates of change, rather than absolute changes, are
desired or when the data of two or more related graphs, the quantitative
units of which are different, are to be shown. For example, the amount of
manufacturing expense incurred and the number of units manufactured
during a given month have a direct relationship, but one item is expressed

Illustration 19–16.   Strata Chart Showing the Elements of Cost
over a Period of Years*

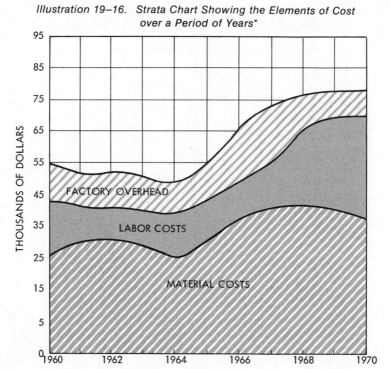

*SOURCE: Annual cost of manufacturing statements.

in dollars and the other in units. The logarithmic graph shows not the direct effect of the absolute figures but the ratio relationship of these figures.

The semilogarithmic curve chart is useful in presenting graphically the comparative relationship of all cost accounting data which involve a time or trend period, whether or not the data are expressed in terms of the same unit.

It must be kept in mind that the horizontal lines are drawn on a percentage scale. The distance from 5 to 10 represents a 100% increase over 5; the distance from 10 to 20, or 20 to 40, also represents a 100% increase and therefore must be equal to the distance from 5 to 10.

The scale figures on such a graph may represent 1,000,000 to 100,000,-000 bushels or $1 to $100 and, when plotted, actually indicate the percentage relationship of the figures in a given series.

Illustration 19–17 shows the semilogarithmic curve chart. The figures are cumulative.

Area or volume charts present data on a two-dimensional scale. Because of the illusory optical effects created, most of these displays have been discarded in the presentation of business and accounting data. A circle could be used to show the amount of each element of cost—the

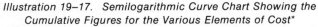

Illustration 19–17. Semilogarithmic Curve Chart Showing the Cumulative Figures for the Various Elements of Cost*

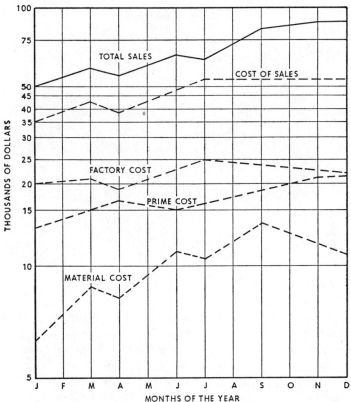

*Each line is related to the one immediately above and to the total sales. For example, in April, although the price of materials used dropped, as did the sales and cost of sales, the prime cost increased because of higher labor costs. The decrease in factory expenses more than offset the increase in labor.

entire circle representing the selling price and the various segments, proportionately divided, showing the material cost, labor cost, factory expense, administrative expense, selling expense, and profit. Similarly, trees, people, cars, and other characters have been used to portray quantities or values.

The circle or pie chart shows the analysis of a manufacturer's monthly cost of sales. See Illustration 19–18.

AUTOMATION AND MANAGEMENT REPORTS

Two unfortunate obstacles that formerly caused much concern in connection with report preparation have been greatly minimized by office automation. The *high cost of preparation* and the *undesirable time lag*

Illustration 19–18. *Area or Volume Chart Showing the*
*Analysis of the Cost of Sales**

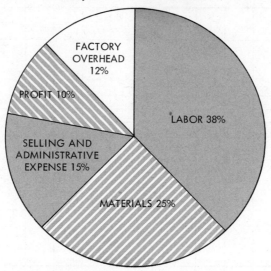

* Also called "circle or pie chart."

between the completion of the operation and the reporting thereof to personnel affected can now be overcome in a number of companies.

As indicated in Chapter 13, many industrial concerns have installed automatic data processing equipment to handle the normal accounting routine procedures, and this equipment is also available to produce cost control reports for management at little or no added expense. Even more important is the fact that these reports are now made available for distribution within a matter of *hours,* rather than the days or weeks previously required.

See Chapter 13, Illustrations 13–8 and 13–9, for a diagrammatical presentation of computerized report preparation and control.

In an adequate integrated data processing system, available instant reference to accounting data required for proper control permits the automatic presentation of data in the form of unit, product, department, individual plant, and/or companywide operating results and, if desired, in comparative form. Inventory control of stores and finished products are available immediately. No substantial delay is necessary in receiving from or distributing to distantly located plants any required information.

Reports that were formerly considered too expensive to prepare, reports that lost their effectiveness because they arrived too late to permit corrective action, and reporting problems created by the distance factor of multiplant locations might soon be considerations of the past.

Automatic data processing can permit the expeditious preparation and distribution of timely, comparative reports at a minimum of additional expense.

REPORT REVIEW

Periodically, accounting reports should be reviewed to determine their continued usefulness. The number of reports issued has a habit of increasing, and diligence must be exercised to see that only useful reports are prepared; a useful report two years ago may not be necessary today.

Those receiving reports should be asked whether or not they are still considered necessary, and if the answer is in the affirmative, to suggest how the form(s) might be revised to provide greater benefit. The controller's department frequently initiates accounting report changes, but to assure the effectiveness of any reporting program it is of utmost importance that both accounting and nonaccounting managerial personnel participate actively in proposed revisions.

AN INCOME AND COST CONTROL REPORT PROGRAM

A large textile manufacturing concern has developed a program of control through a series of 11 income and cost reports under the direction of the controller. These reports are properly calendarized and scheduled, and the executives who are to receive and study these file them in an executive's handbook for constant reference.

This report program included the following:

1. Monthly operating statement, supported by—
   a) Sales analysis both in dollars and in percents.
   b) Sales returns and allowances.
   c) Gross profit analysis by types of outlet and by products.
   d) Selling expenses analysis, budgeted and actual.
2. Manufacturing operating reports
   a) Material price variations.
   b) Material usage variations.
   c) Analysis of cost variations by cost centers, both service and productive.
   d) Budget comparison of yarn preparation cost center.
   e) Spoiled or damaged finished products.
   f) Idle machine report.

These reports are illustrated in Appendix A. They are distributed to the following executives:

1   and 1(*a*) to the vice president in charge of sales.

1   (*b*) to the vice president in charge of mill operations, who writes a letter of comment and sends a copy to the mill foreman.

1   (*c*) to the vice president in charge of sales and vice president in charge of manufacturing.

1   (*d*) to the vice president in charge of sales and to the branch managers.

2   (*a*) to the mill vice president and the purchasing agent.

2   (*b*) to the vice president in charge of mill operations, to the superintendent of the weaving room, and to the department supervisors handling the material.

2   (*c*) to the vice president of the mill operations and to the supervisors of the various production and service centers.

2   (*d*) to the vice president of the mill operations and to the foreman of the particular center (yarn preparation).

2   (*e*) to the vice president in charge of mill operations and the foremen of the finishing and weaving departments.

QUESTIONS FOR REVIEW

1. The installation of a cost accounting system seems academic since most manufacturing concerns have such a system. Why then should a chapter be devoted to such a topic?

2. The discussion of the installation of a cost accounting system should be used to evaluate a system presently used. Explain its significance.

3. What decisions should management make before installing a cost accounting system?

4. Managerial reports are a basic consideration when installing a cost accounting system. How does this affect the installation procedure?

5. What is the place of the organization charts in the systems installation procedure? The cost accounting report schedule?

6. How would you attempt to evaluate the effectiveness and usefulness of a cost accounting system?

7. The revision of the cost accounting system is frequently a sensitive yet often a necessary managerial procedure. Explain why it is necessary and how you might be able to handle this managerial problem effectively.

8. Cost reports, and in fact all accounting reports, are a means of managerial control. Explain what this means. What are the problems in the use of managerial reports?

9. Cost reports may be classified as *financial* and *efficiency*. Distinguish between these two. Which do you consider more important from a cost control viewpoint?

10. "Automatic data processing has resulted in the expeditious preparation and distribution of time, and comparative reports at a minimum of additional operating expense." Explain your reaction to this statement if you were

executive vice president of a manufacturing company whose sales totaled $5,000,000 per year with a net income of $450,000 per year.

PROBLEMS—GROUP A

Problem 19–1.   Purpose: *Revision of the Payroll Cost Accounting Procedure*

The So-Called Manufacturing Company is interested in revising some of its cost accounting procedures. It seems that in its job order cost accounting work, the phase that involves the greatest amount of clerical cost is related to the payroll and labor costs for the various jobs. This firm has a large number of jobs (300 a month) going through the firm each month. There are five operating departments, but the jobs are varied and rarely are affected by the labor costs in more than three departments in the completion of the job. The average cost of each job completed is approximately $600, thus making the cost volume $180,000 a month.

In the past, labor costs have been accumulated on the handwritten job time tickets. In some departments these are individual job tickets; in others they are on the daily job time basis. The number of these tickets, the cost of compiling them to obtain the labor costs, and the delay in obtaining the final results have discouraged management in this procedure.

There are approximately 3,600 job time tickets a month (300 jobs × 3 departments × 4 employees). You are asked to revise the labor job cost accounting procedure in order to (a) reduce the clerical labor cost, and (b) expedite the cost accounting results and reports.

What possible procedures would you suggest to improve this system of labor cost accounting? Indicate the alternatives and the recommended system.

Problem 19–2.   Purpose: *Revision of Material Used and Inventory Control System of Cost Accounting*

The Sequoia Company manufactures a product in which one half of the materials used in production are raw materials and the other half consist of parts to be assembled. In the past, whenever a job is started, and there are 200 a month, involving 10 different finished products, material requisitions are prepared in the planning, routing, and engineering department for each individual job. For most of these jobs, the basic raw material is the same but the quantity differs. The assembled parts may have as many as 150 different combinations—color, size, and extra equipment.

The present system is cumbersome. There are too many individual requisitions. It is hoped to be able to standardize the material issuance procedures to simplify the procedure and to reduce the clerical and accounting costs involved.

The firm has been considering the use of punched card accounting procedure or an electronic data processing procedure to handle this situation, or just a continuance of the manual preparation procedure.

Required:

A report indicating the possible alternative procedures which might be used in handling this cost accounting problem, assuming that the parts used involve approximately 160 different parts or combinations.

Problem 19–3.   Purpose: *Preparation of Statements for Management*

The Sine Gravel Company mines and processes rock and gravel. It started in business on January 1, 1972, when it purchased the assets of another company. You have examined its financial statements at December 31, 1972, and have been requested to assist in planning and projecting operations for 1973. The company also wants to know the maximum amount by which notes payable to officers can be reduced at December 31, 1973.

The adjusted trial balance follows:

THE SINE GRAVEL COMPANY

ADJUSTED TRIAL BALANCE

December 31, 1972

Cash	$ 17,000	
Accounts receivable	24,000	
Mining properties	60,000	
Accumulated depletion		$ 3,000
Equipment	150,000	
Accumulated depreciation		10,000
Organization expense	5,000	
Accumulated amortization		1,000
Accounts payable		12,000
Federal income taxes payable		22,000
Notes payable to officers		40,000
Capital stock		100,000
Premium on capital stock		34,000
Sales		300,000
Production costs (including depreciation and depletion)	184,000	
Administrative expense (including amortization and interest)	60,000	
Provision for federal income taxes	22,000	
	$522,000	$522,000

You are able to develop the following information:

1. The total yards of material sold is expected to increase 10 percent in 1973, and the average sales price per cubic yard will be increased from $1.50 to $1.60.
2. The estimated recoverable reserves of rock and gravel were 4,000,000 cubic yards when the properties were purchased.
3. Production costs include direct labor of $110,000, of which $10,000 was attributed to inefficiencies in the early stages of operation. The union contract calls for 5 percent increases in hourly rates effective January 1, 1973. Production costs, other than depreciation, depletion, and direct labor, will increase 4 percent in 1973.
4. Administrative expense, other than amortization and interest, will increase $8,000 in 1973.
5. The company has contracted for additional movable equipment costing $60,000 to be in production on July 1, 1973. This equipment will result in a direct labor hour savings of 8 percent as compared with the last half of

1972. The new equipment will have a life of 20 years. All depreciation is computed on the straight-line method. The old equipment will continue in use.

6. The new equipment will be financed by a 20 percent down payment and a 6 percent three-year chattel mortgage. Interest and principal payments are due semiannually on June 30 and December 31, beginning December 31, 1973. The notes payable to officers are demand notes dated January 1, 1972, on which 6 percent interest is provided for and was paid on December 31, 1972.

7. Accounts receivable will increase in proportion to sales. No bad debts are anticipated. Accounts payable will remain substantially the same.

8. Percentage depletion allowable on rock and gravel is to be computed at 5 percent of gross income and is limited to 50 percent of net income before depletion.

9. It is customary in the rock and gravel business not to place any value on stockpiles of processed material which are awaiting sale.

10. Assume an income tax rate of 50 percent.

11. The company has decided to maintain a minimum cash balance of $20,000.

12. The client understands that the ethical considerations involved in preparing the following statements will be taken care of by your letter accompanying the statements. (Do not prepare the letter.)

Required:

a) Prepare a statement showing the net income projection for 1973.

b) Prepare a statement which will show cash flow projection for 1973 and will indicate the amount that notes payable to officers can be reduced at December 31, 1973.

Note: Round all amounts to the nearest $100. If the amount to be rounded is exactly $50, round to the next highest $100.

(Adapted from AICPA Uniform Examination)

PROBLEMS—GROUP B

Problem 19–4.   Purpose: *Projected Operations Report for Management*

The Suller Company, Inc., is engaged in manufacturing and wholesaling two principal products. As their accountant, you have been asked to advise management on sales policy for the coming year.

Two different plans are being considered by management, either of which, they believe, will (1) increase the volume of sales, (2) reduce the ratio of selling expense to sales, and (3) decrease unit production costs. These proposals are as follows:

Plan 1—Premium Stamp Books:

It is proposed that each package of Product A will contain eight premium stamps and each package of Product B will contain four premium stamps. Premium stamp books will be distributed to consumers, and when a book is filled with stamps (100 stamps) it will be redeemed by the award of a cash prize in an amount indicated under an unbroken seal attached to the book at the time of distribution. Every 10,000 books distributed will provide for prizes in accordance with the following schedule:

Number of Books	Prize for Each	Total Prizes
1	$150.00	$ 150
5	50.00	250
14	20.00	280
50	10.00	500
160	5.00	800
1,020	1.00	1,020
8,750	0.40	3,500
10,000		$6,500

This schedule is fixed and not subject to alteration or modification. The cost of this plan will be as follows:

Books, including distribution cost.................$ 15 per 1,000 books
Stamps...$ 1 per 1,000 stamps
Prizes...$650 per 1,000 books

The premium stamp book plan will take the place of all previous advertising, and previously established selling prices will be maintained.

Plan 2 — Reduced Selling Prices:
It is proposed that the selling price of Product A will be reduced by $8\frac{1}{3}$ percent and of Product B by 5 percent and to increase the advertising expenditures over those of the prior year. This plan is an alternative to Plan 1, and only one will be adopted.

Management has provided you with the following information as to the previous year's operations and as to anticipated changes:

Prior Year's Operations	Product A	Product B
Quantity sold ....200,000 units		600,000 units
Production cost per unit........................ $0.40		$0.30
Selling price per unit 0.60		0.40

Selling expenses were 18 percent of sales, of which one third was for advertising.

Administrative expenses were 5 percent of sales.

	Product A	Product B
Expected changes:		
Increase in unit sales volume:		
Plan 1	50%	50%
Plan 2	40%	25%
Decrease in unit production cost:		
Plan 1	5%	10%
Plan 2	$7\frac{1}{2}\%$	$6\frac{2}{3}\%$

	Product A	*Product B*
Advertising:		
Plan 1	None	None
Plan 2	8% of sales	7% of sales
Other selling expenses:		
Plan 1	15% of sales	12% of sales
Plan 2	12% of sales	12% of sales
Premium book expenses:		
Plan 1	As indicated	
Plan 2	None	None
Administrative expenses:		
Plan 1	4% of sales	4% of sales
Plan 2	Same dollar amount as prior year	

Required:

Prepare a report for submission to management comparing operations of the previous year with those under both proposed plans.

(Adapted from AICPA Uniform Examination)

Problem 19–5.   Purpose: *Reports to Management: Pricing*

Shulton Electronics Corporation's sole activity in 1972 was a federal government fixed-price incentive contract awarded in January, 1972. The corporation's prior government contracts were cost-plus-fixed-fee or firm fixed-price contracts which were completed by December, 1971.

Provisions of the fixed-price incentive contract include the following:

1. Shulton is to construct eight identical digital computers, deliveries to be made between July, 1972, and June, 1973.
2. The total contract target price is $780,000, which includes a target cost of $700,000. The total adjusted price cannot exceed a ceiling of $810,000.
3. The incentive clause states:
    The total adjusted price (final contract price) shall be established by adding to the total adjusted cost (final negotiated cost) an allowance for profit determined as follows:

When the total adjusted cost is:	*The allowance for profit is:*
Equal to the total target cost	Total target profit.
Greater than the total target cost	Total target profit less 20% of the amount by which the total adjusted cost exceeds the total target cost.
Less than the total target cost	Total target profit plus 20% of the amount by which the total adjusted cost is less than the total target cost.

The following information is available at December 31, 1972:

1. Costs accumulated on the contract:

Direct materials	$170,000
Direct labor	192,000
Overhead	240,000
Total	$602,000

2. The estimated costs to complete the contract:

Direct materials	$ 30,000
Direct labor	48,000
Overhead	60,000
Total	$138,000

3. Past experience indicates that 1 percent of the gross amount of accumulated overhead charges will be disallowed by government auditors as contract costs. No provision has been made for this disallowance.
4. In addition to the estimated 1 percent disallowance in (3), the following 1972 costs will probably be disallowed:
    a) Depreciation on excess equipment, $1,000. The equipment was sold in January, 1973.
    b) Special nonrecurring recruiting costs, $4,000.
5. The corporation failed to take cash discounts totaling $2,000 in 1972. Lost discounts are credited to costs when found by government auditors. The corporation treats cash discounts, when taken, as a reduction of costs.
6. All costs that will probably be disallowed have been treated consistently as period costs by the corporation. Estimated allowable costs have been consistently allocated equally to identical units being manufactured under a contract.
7. Five computers were delivered in 1972 and billed at the target price. Progress payments of $75,000 were received for each computer delivered.

Required:
a) Prepare a schedule computing the estimated total adjusted price (estimated final contract price) for the fixed-price incentive contract.
b) Prepare a schedule computing the work-in-process inventory at estimated cost at December 31, 1972.
c) Assume that the estimated total adjusted price determined in (a) was $800,000. Prepare a schedule computing the estimated total amount receivable from the federal government at December 31, 1972, for the computers that were delivered.

(Adapted from AICPA Uniform Examination)

Problem 19–6.   Purpose: *Report on Cost Accounting Problems of a System Installation*

In the course of a Systems Installation assignment, the most serious problem has related to the manufacturing overhead. This phase of the system assignment has been given to you for solution.

A careful investigation indicates the following facts:

1. The company manufactures a line of bric-a-brac such as bookends, ornamental lamps, etc. The material costs vary from 15 to 60 percent of the total factory cost depending upon the kind of material, metal, or fabric used in its manufacture.

2. The business is subject to wide cyclical fluctuations due to the depression or prosperity of the area. Sales fluctuate accordingly.
3. About 60 percent of the manufacturing is normally done in the first quarter of the year.
4. For the whole plant wage rates fluctuate from $2 to $4 an hour. However, within each of the eight departments, the spread between the high and low wage rates is less than 5 percent.
5. All production goes through the eight departments but not in the same proportion of work.
6. Within the individual manufacturing departments, factory overhead ranges from 30 to 80 percent of the conversion cost.

Required:

On the basis of the foregoing information and such as may have to be assumed, you are asked to solve the manufacturing overhead systems problem for this assignment by indicating the following with supporting reasons for your recommendations:

a) Should the firm use a manufacturing overhead rate at all?
b) Should the predetermined or actual overhead rate be used if a rate is to be used?
c) Should overhead rate be based upon direct labor hours, direct labor costs, or prime costs, or on some other basis?

Problem 19–7.   Purpose: *Systems Installation Problem Involving Inventory Control*

In the process of installing a cost accounting system for the Slavinisk Manufacturing Company, the problem of the inventory control system has been assigned to you for your research, solution, and recommendation. The firm feels that in the past too much capital has been tied up in its inventory investment. They wish to have a more reliable determination of "how much" and "when" to order the various requirements for its manufacturing operations.

1. The most important, costwise, of the components purchased for use in the manufacturing operations is a *Migrafon,* which is sold in gross lots (144 units) at a price of $820 less a trade discount of $320.
2. The firm purchases 5,200 *Migrafons* during the production year which involves 260 working days. An additional allowance for breakage is necessary so that the purchases are usually increased to allow for this by increasing the purchases to 5,460 *Migrafons.* The firm uses about 20 *Migrafons* a day; the usage varies between 12 and 28 per day.
3. Normal delivery time to receive an order is 20 days from the date a purchase order is initiated. A rush order by airfreight costs an extra $144 a gross. Regular freight costs $30 per gross.
4. Clerical and receiving costs have been computed as follows: placing an order, $25; and receiving an order, $50.
5. Space storage costs are $24 per year per gross stored.
6. Insurance and taxes are approximately 12 percent of the net delivered cost of average inventory, and this firm expects a return of at least 10 percent on its average investment.

Required:

a) Prepare a schedule computing the total annual cost of *Migrafons* based on uniform order lot sizes of one, two, three, four, five, and six gross purchases.
b) Indicate the economic order quantity (EOQ).
c) Prepare a schedule computing the minimum stock reorder point for *Migrafons*.

chapter 20

Managerial Control through Direct or Variable Costing

NATURE OF DIRECT OR VARIABLE COSTING

Direct or variable costing is a method of costing which assumes that for proper managerial control, only those costs which vary directly with the volume of production should be considered. Translated, this means that to material and labor costs, both of which are variable, only the variable manufacturing overhead costs should be added to obtain the true or variable cost of goods manufactured, since only these three variable elements relate to the product; the fixed manufacturing overhead relates to the plant and equipment. Such items as depreciation, insurance, rent, and property taxes are *period and plant,* not product, costs. This evolutionary concept of managerial control of production has been gaining the logical interpretation of business executives in recent years, especially since it was first established by one of the largest industrial chemical manufacturing concerns. They feel it is a more accurate measurement for controllable operating conditions and for fixing credit and responsibility for the departmental and divisional supervisors.

In matching cost and revenue to determine periodic income, conventional cost systems distinguish between manufacturing and nonmanufacturing costs. These systems, commonly referred to as "absorption costing," because the product "absorbs" manufacturing overhead costs, use predetermined overhead rates which apply both fixed and variable costs to production without recognition of the amount of the fixed application or the amount of the variable application.

In contrast, "direct costing" systems, in matching cost and revenue to determine periodic income, recognize the distinction between direct (variable) and period (fixed) costs. It is this distinction between direct and period costs that is the basis of the direct costing concept. "Direct costs" (or "variable costs") tend to vary directly with the volume of production; "period costs" are incurred to keep facilities ready for manufacturing and marketing.

Period costs include not only costs customarily associated with plant and equipment but also research costs, some advertising costs, and costs required to maintain a basic organization. They are the costs—both manufacturing and nonmanufacturing—that must generally be incurred once facilities are being operated whether these facilities are functioning at 60 percent or 90 percent of capacity. Because they represent the fixed costs *of the period in which they are incurred,* period costs are charged against income of the period. *Direct costs* include the *additional* costs required only if specific products are manufactured and sold.

Under direct costing, fixed costs are distinguished from variable costs not only in the budget statements but also in the ledger accounts. Costs of direct materials and direct labor are handled in exactly the same manner under both absorption costing and direct costing. It is the manufacturing overhead that is treated differently.

Management of companies successfully employing direct costing techniques are able to offer several reasons for their use of this method. A company that pioneered the cause of direct costing and developed one of the first effective systems over 30 years ago did so in response to objections from its president that the income statements continued to show profits even though sales had declined considerably—a result he could not comprehend.

Even in companies having limited experience with direct costing, it is felt that management decisions have been expedited and improved since the accounting department has been able to supply timely information regarding the relationship of cost, volume, sales prices, and profit. If management is to benefit from the data furnished by cost accounting analyses, the information not only must be as complete and as nearly accurate as possible but also it must be prompt and presented in such a fashion that members of the management team who have not been schooled in the basic fundamentals of accounting can readily interpret the significance of the operating results. The major benefit, proponents of direct costing contend, is the prompt availability of cost data in an uncomplicated, usable form suitable for sound profit planning.

Direct costing procedures permit the presentation of data that is useful to various levels of management in current cost control; in the establishment of sound pricing policy if the market conditions for the firm's products are such as to give the company some degree of control over price; and in guiding management in the making of specific decisions relating to materials, labor, equipment, and financial policy. This is particularly true where *physical* production and sales volume do not coincide.

MATCHING OF COSTS AND REVENUES

A basic goal of accounting is to bring about a proper matching of income and expense in order to arrive at a clear determination of net income. The process of matching cost and revenue under direct costing may be outlined as:

```
Revenue from products sold this period ................................................... xxxx
Less: Variable costs of manufacturing and selling these products ................. xxxx
Marginal income or contribution margin ................................................. xxxx
Less: Fixed costs ............................................................................... xxxx
Net Income ...................................................................................... xxxx
```

Careful analysis of the above-described "matching process" reveals this fact: Within any volume range in which period costs are constant (i.e., *not* variable), marginal income per unit also tends to remain constant; and, therefore, if the marginal income rate is determined, it is possible to forecast with a reasonable degree of accuracy the increase in net income which will result from any specified increase in volume. This is accomplished by multiplying the estimated volume increase by the applicable rate of marginal income.

The marginal income ratio may also be used in determining other significant answers such as the volume of sales necessary to "break even," the volume of sales required to yield a desired rate of return on investment, or a product selling price to yield a desired rate of return.

"Marginal income" is sometimes called "contribution margin" on the theory that this figure represents the *contribution* provided by the "revenue from products sold this period" to meet the "period costs" of providing manufacturing and marketing capacity.

Direct costing may be used to provide information to management on the profitability of products. A direct costing income statement may be prepared analyzing operations by product or product line. Illustration 20–1 is an example of a direct costing income statement by products.

The statement points out the profitability of each of the products in dollar and percentage terms. Arbitrary decisions having to do with the allocation of fixed costs are eliminated, and only the variable costs are assigned to the products. The statement highlights the *contribution margin* of each of the products. In Illustration 20–1, if excess capacity exists and if the demand is present, the company might do well to push Product B, as $0.60 from each sales dollar contributes toward fixed costs and

Illustration 20–1
XYZ COMPANY
INCOME STATEMENT – DIRECT COSTING
For Month of August 19 –

	Total	Product		
		A	B	C
Sales..	$1,000,000	$500,000	$300,000	$200,000
Variable Cost of Sales	$ 600,000	$400,000	$100,000	$100,000
Variable Selling and Administrative.....	100,000	50,000	20,000	30,000
Contribution Margin	$ 300,000	$ 50,000	$180,000	$ 70,000
		10%	60%	35%
Period Costs:				
Manufacturing	$ 100,000			
Selling and Administrative	50,000			
Net Income....................................	$ 150,000			

profit. The illustration also points out that *all* of the products are profitable as they contribute to fixed costs and profit.

The same type of analysis as was done by product may be done by sales territory, plants, distribution areas, etc. Direct costing procedures permit the determination of the most profitable territory, plant, etc.

It is not only helpful to have *actual* cost and income information presented with variable costs treated separately from fixed costs, it is also helpful in portraying probable *future* cost and income. The direct costing approach is helpful in deriving and presenting future cost information which management can use in the following ways:

1. In considering the costs of changing production requirements and alternative production methods.
2. In grasping the probable effect on production and distribution costs of the anticipated changes in prices and wage rates.
3. In understanding the effect by product lines and for the total firm of changes in the volume and composition of demand.
4. In formulating marketing plans related to:
   a) Price setting on individual products and the revision of the firm's total pricing structure.
   b) The discontinuance of unprofitable items or the addition of new ones.
   c) The selection of improved methods of promotion and distribution.

Some cost accountants and businessmen contend that direct costing has its limitations and doesn't provide all the answers or necessarily the best answer in certain business situations or problems. For instance, improper management action might be taken when sales substantially exceed current production and inventories are being reduced. Under such conditions direct costing profits will be substantially higher than under conventional absorption cost accounting. During the early stages of a business reaction when sales lag behind production, the direct profit will be minimized or the direct loss aggravated. This may unduly impress management as to the severity of the reaction and cause them to take actions which may mean missing profit opportunities in the near future or which may have the effect of depressing the market even more.

In some situations the full cost of a product or a more complete cost of a function must be determined to provide management with proper information. In working out pricing policy, management in certain instances needs variable cost and marginal income information and at other times needs full cost information. How these costs are used depends upon the operating conditions of individual firms and the management need for information involved. Using variable costs alone would be improper when additional volume or new projects are being considered which may require the use of existing equipment during overtime or extra shift periods or the expansion of facilities. For long-run pricing policy, management should endeavor to set prices which will recover full cost and provide a profit on those products which constitute the bulk of the firm's volume. In certain special contract situations management will want to determine either full cost or full cost less certain commercial promotional expenses.

Sometimes questions are raised as to the future usefulness of direct costing with increased automation and the spread of guaranteed annual wage contracts. With such changes the portion of costs which are fixed to the firm will increase and those that are variable will decrease. An increased dollar portion of the overhead costs related to plant and equipment will tend to be fixed and more of the labor costs will tend to be fixed. Such a shift in the cost characteristics of the firm will obviously reduce the scope of usefulness of direct costing for current cost control since fewer costs will be controllable at the plant operating level. However, since more dollars of investment in machinery and plant will be at stake and the firm will have less flexibility in incurring direct labor cost, it will become more imperative that management understand the impact of fixed costs and make plans for the most effective utilization of the available high-speed machinery and the available labor force. This will mean that management will have to deliberate more carefully over the expansion of productive facilities and labor force. It will require more adequate information as to the size and stability of additional demand for its various products over an extended future period and as to the expected cost of securing that demand and producing to meet it.

COMPARISON OF DIRECT AND ABSORPTION COSTING METHODS WHEN STANDARD COSTS ARE USED

So that a proper comparison can be made between direct costing and absorption costing procedures when standard costs are used, Illustration 20–2 is provided, based on the following standard cost data for the months of May and June:

STANDARD COST

	Per Unit
Direct materials	$1.00
Direct labor	1.50
Variable manufacturing overhead	0.50
Total direct (or variable) manufacturing costs	$3.00
Variable selling expenses (salesmen's commissions)	0.25
Fixed overhead costs (period costs)	0.90
Standard volume of production for year	1,200,000 units
Fixed overhead costs for year	$1,080,000
Fixed overhead costs per unit	$0.90
Sales price per unit	$6.25

PRODUCTION STATISTICS

	May	June
Units sold	80,000	120,000
Units produced	120,000	84,000
Fixed overhead assigned each month	$ 90,000	$ 90,000
Fixed overhead applied to production	108,000	75,600
Overapplied (volume variance)	18,000	–
Underapplied (volume variance)	–	14,400
Fixed selling expenses	25,000	25,000
Fixed administrative expenses	20,000	20,000
Fixed research and development expenses	4,000	4,000

In studying Illustration 20–2, observe these important points:

1. Under direct costing, the ending inventory is costed at a smaller figure because only variable costs are charged to the product.
2. Net income in May under direct costing is $36,000 lower than under absorption costing because none of the fixed (period) costs have been included in the ending inventory.
3. Under the direct costing concept, cost of sales (direct costs) and marginal income vary directly with sales volume if fixed and variable costs are stable. Hence, an increase in sales volume (without a change in sales price) will result in a corresponding increase in profits. In the illustration, sales increased 50 percent in June. Note that total direct costs (cost of sales) were $260,000 in May and $390,000 in June—an increase of 50 percent. Note further that marginal income was

Illustration 20–2

COMPARISON OF DIRECT AND ABSORPTION COSTING METHODS WHEN STANDARD COSTS ARE USED

INCOME STATEMENT FOR THE MONTHS OF MAY AND JUNE
(Direct Costing Method)

	May	June
Sales: 80,000 Units @ $6.25........	$500,000.00	
120,000 Units @ 6.25........		$750,000.00
Direct Costs:		
Manufacturing:		
Inventory at Beginning of Month	0	$120,000.00
Direct Materials	$120,000.00	84,000.00
Direct Labor	180,000.00	126,000.00
Variable Overhead	60,000.00	42,000.00
Total	$360,000.00	$372,000.00
Less: Inventory, 40,000 Units @ $3.00	120,000.00	
Inventory, 4,000 Units @ $3.00		12,000.00
	$240,000.00	$360,000.00
Selling:		
Salesmen's Commissions	20,000.00	30,000.00
Total Variable Costs	260,000.00	390,000.00
Contribution Margin	$240,000.00	$360,000.00
Period Costs:		
Fixed Manufacturing Overhead	$ 90,000.00	$ 90,000.00
Fixed Selling Expenses	25,000.00	25,000.00
Fixed Administrative Expenses	20,000.00	20,000.00
Research and Development Expenses	4,000.00	4,000.00
Total Period Costs	139,000.00	139,000.00
Net Income	$101,000.00	$221,000.00

INCOME STATEMENT FOR THE MONTHS OF MAY AND JUNE
(Absorption Costing Method)

	May	June
Sales: 80,000 Units @ $6.25........	$500,000.00	
120,000 Units @ 6.25........		$750,000.00
Cost of Sales:		
Inventory at Beginning of Month	0	$156,000.00
Direct Materials	$120,000.00	84,000.00
Direct Labor	180,000.00	126,000.00
Direct Manufacturing Overhead	60,000.00	42,000.00
Applied Fixed Overhead	108,000.00	75,600.00
Total	$468,000.00	$483,600.00
Less: Inventory, 40,000 Units	156,000.00	
Inventory, 4,000 Units		15,600.00
Cost of Sales at Normal	$312,000.00	$468,000.00
Less: Overapplied Fixed Overhead	18,000.00	
Add: Underapplied Fixed Overhead		14,400.00
Cost of Sales at Actual Costs	294,000.00	482,400.00
Gross Profit on Sales	$206,000.00	$267,600.00
Operating Expenses:		
Salesmen's Commissions	$ 20,000.00	$ 30,000.00
Other Selling Expenses	25,000.00	25,000.00
Administrative Expenses	20,000.00	20,000.00
Research and Development Expenses	4,000.00	4,000.00
Total	69,000.00	79,000.00
Net Income	$137,000.00	$188,600.00

	May	June
Sales in relation to normal of 100,000 units	80%	120%
Production in relation to normal of 100,000 units	120%	84%

$240,000 in May and $360,000 in June—an increase of 50 percent.
4. Under absorption costing, even though sales increased 50 percent in June, gross profit on sales increased only 30 percent (approximately) —leading to the criticism of absorption costing that this result appears most unrealistic and confuses management in its attempt to understand and use accounting statement data. Profits are not created by production alone; it is only when the production has been converted into sales income that a realistic picture is presented.
5. In abbreviated form, an alternative form of income statement setup under direct costing would be:

	May
Net sales	$500,000
Less: Variable manufacturing cost of sales	240,000
Manufacturing margin	$260,000
Less: Variable selling expenses	20,000
Marginal Income (or Merchandising Margin)	$240,000

SEPARATION OF VARIABLE AND FIXED COSTS

Direct costing procedures were developed to provide better cost control for the guidance of enlightened industrial management through a more reliable system of assigning and fixing responsibility for controllable costs, pricing, planning, and related decisions.

The primary difference in the accounting techniques of direct costing, as distinguished from other costing methods, is that direct (variable) costs must be separated from the period (fixed) costs. Therefore, successful application of direct costing is dependent upon an adequate knowledge of *cost behavior* so that *cost responsibility* may be properly assigned.

Four typical patterns of cost behavior are found. These are: fixed, semifixed, semivariable, and variable. It is a common contention that any cost may be separated as direct or period (variable or fixed), depending upon the department involved and the purpose for which such cost was incurred.[1] However, it can be a task far from simple to distinguish between every variable and fixed cost, and occasionally certain parts of the separation process will be decided on the basis of practicability or expediency rather than on the basis of strict adherence to an established accounting principle. Whatever the decision may be, it should be adhered to consistently. The fixing of accounting policies is necessary in order that the net income be determined on a basis that is consistent from period to period, thereby making comparisons between periods truly valid. Of course, this does not mean that a change is precluded if conditions warrant or justify a change.

---

[1] See Chapters 10 and 14 for segregating fixed and variable costs.

Sound departmentalization is a prerequisite for the control of costs because it permits the separation of direct and period costs so that supervisory effort may be properly directed and rated. Proper departmentalization facilitates the achievement of the objectives of cost accounting in the following ways:

1. By following more closely the specific functional productive and service efforts of the firm, more reasonable and accurate bases for tracing and assigning costs to functions become evident and can be used.
2. By obtaining more accurate costing of each function or operation, more accurate assignment of costs to any product or products passing through each function can be achieved.
3. Cost control is aided by localizing the cost performance of the various individuals who are responsible for initiating actions for spending the firm's money through their functions. The performance of each function tends to be free from influence by the performance of other functions so that responsibility can be pinned down.
4. The breaking down of the effort to the level of just one particular type of activity means that costs will tend to fluctuate if they are affected by changes in volume of productive effort in some discernible relationship to this one activity variable. This permits more valid study of cost behavior which will aid cost control and various types of planning.
5. With the productive effort subdivided into a number of operational steps, there will be smaller in-process inventories at any stage of production, and their degree of completion can be more accurately evaluated. This leads to more accurate and easier costing of inventories which gives better support for statement figures.

ACCOUNTING PROCEDURES WHEN DIRECT COSTING IS USED

Because they are entirely variable (varying with volume of production), direct materials and direct labor costs are handled in exactly the same manner under direct costing as under absorption costing. The segregation between period (or fixed) and direct (or variable) costs, however, necessitates a change in overhead accounting technique.

Conventional cost systems separate manufacturing and nonmanufacturing costs but do not distinguish between fixed and variable, and a predetermined overhead rate is used to charge *both* fixed and variable costs to production. Under direct costing, fixed overhead costs and expenses are charged directly against income when incurred; and, therefore, separate accounts must be maintained to account for variable overhead.

When direct costing is to be incorporated in the accounting records, the following control accounts, supported by adequate subsidiary records, may be used:

Account	*Income Statement Presentation*
Variable Manufacturing Overhead Costs Control	Part of cost of manufacturing.
Variable Selling Overhead Control	Combine with other variable costs to arrive at marginal income (*or*, deduct from manufacturing margin to arrive at marginal income).
Variable Administrative Overhead Control	
Fixed Manufacturing Overhead Costs Control	
Fixed Selling Overhead Control	Combine and deduct from marginal income to arrive at net income.
Fixed Administrative Overhead Control	

In the above account titles, the term "direct" might well be substituted for "variable" and "period" used instead of "fixed." Each of the above accounts functions as follows:

Actual costs incurred (supporting detail accumulated on subsidiary cost analysis records)	Closed to Revenue and Expense account (Profit and Loss account)

If standard costs are used, variable overhead is accounted for by using:

Variable Manufacturing Overhead Control		Applied Variable Manufacturing Overhead	
Actual costs incurred	Close against Applied Variable Manufacturing Overhead and record variance, if any	Close against Variable Manufacturing Overhead Control, recording variance, if any	Predetermined manufacturing overhead rate × production (debit: Work-in-Process)

The variance(s) between the control, representing actual expenditures, and the applied, representing standard, must be further analyzed as to cause. The variance adjustment is periodically charged to Cost of Sales, as in other costing methods, but because under direct costing fixed expenses are considered a cost of the accounting period rather than a cost of the manufactured product, over- or underapplied manufacturing overhead is normally minimized.

For each production department a monthly manufacturing variance statement may be prepared showing for each class of cost the actual costs incurred and the variance from standard. In addition, for each nonproduction department, a statement may be prepared comparing actual expenses with budgeted expenses. In one company, it is a monthly requirement that foremen and plant managers explain the manufacturing variances, that sales managers attempt to account for volume variances, and that staff department heads analyze their budget variances.

Illustration 20–3, presented in *N.A.A. Research Report 37* described earlier, indicates how an operating statement may be prepared showing an analysis of period expenses by functional responsibilities.

If a company wishes to report operating results in published statements and tax returns on an absorption costing basis, conforming to generally accepted accounting principles, direct costing statements may be converted to more conventional accounting results by charging part of the period, or fixed, manufacturing overhead costs to the work-in-process and finished goods inventories. The principles involved are demonstrated in Illustration 20–4.

Illustration 20–3

Operating Statement Showing Period Expenses
by Functional Responsibilities

Details	Actual	Budget	Variance Favorable or (Unfavorable)	Responsibility of Name	Title
Sales	$3,100,000.00	$3,400,000.00			
Cost of sales (at standard)	1,922,000.00	2,040,000.00			
MARGINAL INCOME (at std.)	$1,178,000.00	$1,360,000.00	($ 182,000.00)	J. Smith	V.P. of Sales
Variations from standard:					
On purchasing materials	5,000.00	--------	5,000.00	T. Brown	V.P. of Pur.
On processing materials	(28,950.00)	--------	(28,950.00)	W. Lowe	V.P. of Mfg.
MARGINAL INCOME (Actual)	$1,154,050.00	$1,360,000.00	($ 205,950.00)		
Period expenses:					
Manufacturing	$ 185,400.00	$ 182,000.00	($ 3,400.00)	W. Lowe	V.P. of Mfg.
Personnel	125,400.00	124,500.00	(900.00)	C. Downs	V.P. of Per.
Accounting	89,100.00	84,000.00	(5,100.00)	B. Brown	Controller
Marketing	90,175.00	82,000.00	(8,175.00)	J. Smith	Mgr. of Mkt.
Purchasing	67,800.00	62,900.00	(4,900.00)	T. Brown	V.P. of Pur.
Plant engineering . . .	38,225.00	40,500.00	2,275.00	R. Roy	Dir. of Eng.
Legal	43,290.00	38,750.00	(4,540.00)	A. Wiley	Secretary
Treasury	35,410.00	37,200.00	1,790.00	W. Cash	Treasurer
Public relations	25,200.00	26,800.00	1,600.00	D. Cole	Dir. of P.R.
Research and development	21,850.00	18,300.00	(3,550.00)	A. Mack	V.P. of Res.
Total period costs .	$ 721,850.00	$ 696,950.00	($ 24,900.00)		
PROFIT BEFORE TAXES . .	$ 432,200.00	$ 663,050.00	($ 230,850.00)		

Illustration 20-4

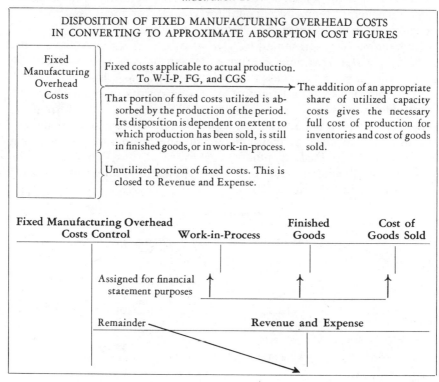

EFFECT OF DIFFERENT COSTING METHODS ON NET INCOME

The difference between the amount of net income of any accounting period computed by absorption costing and the net income under direct costing will be equal to the change in the amount of period costs deferred in inventory under the different methods. Both methods, of course, will result in identical amounts of *total* net income over a complete cycle of inventory buildup and liquidation.

If *inventory* of manufactured goods:

1. DOES NOT FLUCTUATE from period to period,
   net income under "absorption costing" is identical to net income under "direct costing."
2. DOES FLUCTUATE from period to period,
   net income will differ somewhat under the two methods because the absorption costing theory requires that part of the period costs be

deferred in inventory, whereas direct costing defers no period costs, therefore:

a) When inventory is *increased,*
    net income will be higher under absorption costing because inventory includes a portion of the period costs, while under direct costing all period costs are charged against current revenues.

b) When inventory is *decreased,*
    net income will be lower under absorption costing because the period costs previously included in inventory are now being charged against current revenues, whereas under direct costing only *current* period costs are being charged against current revenues.

A reconciliation of net income determined under direct costing procedures with net income under conventional absorption costing is demonstrated in Illustration 20–5 using the following basic standard cost data:

Normal capacity ....100,000 units	Selling price per unit...............$10.00
Production this period.... 90,000 units	
Sales this period .... 95,000 units	
Standard variable costs per unit:	Fixed costs for period:
Material and labor.................$4.00	Production* $200,000.00
Factory overhead.................. 1.00	Selling........................ 75,000.00
Selling expense..................... 0.50	Administration 50,000.00
	Others 25,000.00
Operating variances:	* Equal to $2 per unit if spread over normal
Representing excessive incur-	capacity of 100,000 units.
rence of variable costs $4,500.00	

In comparing absorption and direct costing, one factor of absorption costing should not be overlooked. In absorption costing income is influenced not only by the sales revenue but also by production for the period. Income can be influenced under absorption costing by an inventory buildup even if such inventory buildup is not justified or warranted by business conditions. By building up the finished goods and work-in-process inventories, it is possible to defer large amounts of the fixed overhead to a subsequent period, and thus manipulate the income for the current period. However, this would be the exception rather than the usual practice, since it would be assumed that top management would not sanction such a procedure.

Illustration 20–5

INCOME STATEMENT–ABSORPTION COSTING

Net sales...		$950,000
Less: Standard cost of sales (95,000 × $7)......................		665,000
Standard gross profit		$285,000
Less: Variances:		
Operating variances...	$ 4,500	
Volume variances (10,000 × $2)...............................	20,000	
Total variances..		24,500
Gross profit		$260,500
Less: Selling expenses ($47,500 + $75,000)......................	$122,500	
Administrative expenses	50,000	
Other expenses..	25,000	
Total expenses		197,500
Net Income		$ 63,000

INCOME STATEMENT–DIRECT COSTING

Net sales..		$950,000
Less: Standard variable cost of sales (95,000 × $5)............		475,000
Manufacturing margin..		$475,000
Less: Variable selling expenses (95,000 × $0.50)...............		47,500
Distribution margin		$427,500
Less: Operating variances		4,500
Contribution margin		$423,000
Less: Fixed costs:		
Production...	$200,000	
Selling expenses	75,000	
Administrative expenses	50,000	
Other expenses...	25,000	
Total fixed costs..		350,000
Net Income		$ 73,000

Reconciliation of Direct Costing Income to Absorption Costing Income

Direct costing net income..$73,000
Less: Reduction of fixed costs in inventory*.................................... 10,000
Absorption Costing Net Income...$63,000

* More units were sold than produced. This caused a 5,000-unit reduction in inventory. Each of these units sold resulted in a charge to standard cost of sales this period of $2 per unit, fixed production cost, which was carried forward from last period in the absorption cost method.

GENERAL ACCEPTANCE OF DIRECT COSTING

The National Association of Accountants in 1961 published *Research Report No. 37* entitled: *Current Application of Direct Costing* in which is summarized the experience of 50 companies that participated in the study by contributing information about their applications of direct costing. These companies indicated that their experience with direct costing has been quite favorable.

Critics of direct costing charge that oversimplification of operating results to aid management in making decisions is illogical because we are dealing with relationships that, of necessity, are complicated. Others argue that the problem of distinguishing between direct and period costs can become very involved and that it is not necessary to include direct costing procedures in the accounting records to obtain data. With flexible budgets and standards incorporated into an absorption cost system, the same basic information is available that a direct costing system provides.

The American Accounting Association in releases of its Committee on Accounting Concepts and Standards holds that: ". . . the cost of a manufactured product is the sum of the acquisition costs reasonably traceable to that product and should include both direct and indirect factors. The omission of any element of manufacturing cost is not acceptable." Because direct costing requires the omission of all fixed manufacturing costs from inventory, it is not considered an "acceptable" concept.

Neither the American Institute of Certified Public Accountants nor the Internal Revenue Service has recognized direct costing as *generally acceptable* for inventory valuation. While not specifically mentioning direct costing, the use of the term "indirectly incurred" would seem to include items of period cost which must be utilized in order to obtain production.

The Internal Revenue Service in its regulations defines inventory cost to include (a) raw materials and supplies entering into or consumed in connection with the product, (b) expenditures for direct labor, and (c) indirect expenses incident to and necessary for the production of the particular item. Here again, the inclusion of "indirect expenses necessary for production" would seem to include many items of capacity or period cost which are excluded from inventory in the direct costing method. Court decisions have not provided a definite answer as to the acceptability of direct costing for tax purposes because the decisions have been based on issues other than direct costing. For example, in Geometric Stamping Company (26 TC 301), the Commissioner of Internal Revenue did not contest the propriety of the direct costing method used by the taxpayer, and the court specifically excluded the question of acceptability of direct costing in its decision. In Frank G. Wikstrom & Sons, Inc. (20 TC 45), the court upheld the Commissioner's objection to the taxpayer including in inventory only direct labor and material applicable to specific jobs and deducting all other expenses from income in the year incurred. In Montreal Mining Company (2 TC 688), exclusion of certain overhead expense from inventory was advocated by the Commissioner and upheld by the court. It would appear that if it is to the government's advantage to disallow the use of direct costing as applied by the taxpayer that the Commissioner might well challenge the acceptability of the method.

The fact that statements prepared under the concept of direct costing may not be acceptable by the Internal Revenue Service or for published reports by some public accountants does not mean that these statements are not useful. A company may prepare *both* direct costing and absorption costing income statements. Each has its use.

If direct costing is used for purposes beyond statistical purposes in evaluating managerial effectiveness, management may be faced with certain evaluations of the work-in-process and finished goods inventories. If these inventories are recorded on the books as being composed of direct material, direct labor, and variable overhead, then these results may arise:

1. In computing the working capital ratio for credit purposes, the use of direct costing for work-in-process and finished goods inventories at the end of the period will produce a more unfavorable ratio than under absorption costing.
2. In the event of a fire or casualty loss affecting these inventories, claim settlements based upon the work-in-process and finished goods inventories will be unfavorable and understated.
3. The book value of the capital stock will be understated.
4. In some industries which have a proportionately large investment in plant and automatic machinery per employee, the omission of fixed costs affecting plant and machinery, such as depreciation and property insurance from the work-in-process and finished goods inventories, may produce a distorted picture of the income.

It becomes evident that unless self-balancing factors are present such as uniform sales and production and inventories from period to period, the use of direct costing in recording the work-in-process and finished goods inventory results in a distorted operating picture. However, for managerial control and supervisory evaluation, the use of direct costing has reasonable and acceptable recognition.

CONCLUSIONS

In our present complex economic system which is constantly undergoing changes in markets, materials, labor requirements, and methods of production and distribution, it is important that management be supplied with information that will be a guide in carrying out their cost control and planning responsibilities. Flexible budgets, standards, and direct costing can be used as separate or complementary devices in the attainment of these objectives. Most cost systems, either through the use of flexible budgets or flexible budgets and standards, can provide information for cost control and planning purposes. The chief advantage of the direct costing method seems to lie in the fact that presentations to management for internal use can be more readily prepared and are more readily understood and used by management in taking action or in making plans.

Current control of costs requires that costs within functional areas of responsibility be identified as to their fixed and variable characteristics in the short run. This separation is a prerequisite and is reflected in all direct costing statements prepared for management. This identification of costs aids the individual immediately responsible for controlling those costs to detect excesses and take corrective action. It also aids higher level supervisory personnel in evaluating the performance of men responsible to them. The impact of fixed costs in specific functions and in the firm as a whole is conveyed to management in a more forcible manner. Through successive reports management gradually achieves a better understanding of the effect of certain functional fixed costs and the firm's combined fixed costs upon the income result. This leads to management proposals to achieve better utilization of existing facilities and personnel.

The direct costing method strives to compile both manufacturing and nonmanufacturing costs in such a way as to determine the variable costs of each product or product line and the fixed costs by cost center, division, or the entire plant, whichever classifications are appropriate to the particular industrial situation. This provides the basis for furnishing management with timely information as to each product's contribution to combined marginal profit, that is, dollar sales of product less its variable costs.

QUESTIONS FOR REVIEW

1. The IRS does not approve of direct costs (direct materials, direct labor, and variable manufacturing overhead) as the basis of cost of sales. Why is this so?

2. What effect does the use of direct costing have on the income tax for a corporation? Explain in detail by using an illustration.

3. A firm has been reporting its income tax to the federal government on the basis of the direct material and direct labor costs constituting the cost of sales and treating all of its other indirect manufacturing costs as operating expenses. This has been approved in a few instances. Explain why.

4. Indicate how each of the following conditions would affect the amount of net profit under the conventional absorption costing and the direct (variable) costing:

   a) Sales and production are in balance at standard volume.
   b) Sales exceed production.
   c) Production exceeds sales.   (AICPA Uniform Examination)

5. What is meant by "period costs"? How does this affect unit costs in manufacturing? What is its significance in direct costing?

6. It has been stated that "there is no volume variance when direct costing is used in connection with a standard cost accounting system." Explain your agreement or disagreement with this statement.

7. "Cost responsibility may be properly assigned when direct costing versus absorption costing is used." Explain this statement as to its accuracy.

8. "Under absorption costing, profits are tied in with the production; whereas under direct costing, profits are related to sales." Which is more important from a managerial viewpoint?

9. "Direct costing is not important when a firm makes a single product. Managerial control is better exercised in a multiproduct firm when a firm produces a variety of different products." Explain.

10. Why have accountants been reluctant to accept direct costing as a "generally accepted" procedure when valuing inventories for certified statements?

PROBLEMS – GROUP A

Problem 20–1.   Purpose: *Preparation of Direct Costing and Absorption Costing Statements*

The Warren Manufacturing Company is making a comparison of its present traditional absorption costing cost accounting practices with the use of direct costing methods.

An examination of its accounting records produced the following information:

Maximum capacity of the plants	400,000 units
Normal capacity used as budgeted	360,000 units
Manufacturing overhead, fixed	$1,152,000
Selling and administrative expenses, fixed	467,500
Sales price per unit of product	100
Variable manufacturing cost per unit	40
Variable selling expenses per unit	10

For the year 1973, the following represent the accounting and budgeted data:

Budgeted production	360,000 units
Actual production	300,000 units
Sales	280,000 units
Inventory, January 1, 1973	10,000 units
Unfavorable variance from standard variable manufacturing cost	$50,000

Required:

On the basis of this information, you are asked to prepare income statements for 1973, using the following procedures:

a) Absorption costing.
b) Direct costing.
c) Which method would you prefer? Why?

Problem 20–2.   Purpose: *Preparation of Direct Costing Income Statement*

The Woodstock Manufacturing Company prepares its managerial control statements of cost on a direct costing basis. This firm closes its books on June 30 of each year.

On the ledger as of June 30, 19—, the following account balances appeared:

Material Quantity Variance...$	1,800 (dr.)
Material Price Variance...	2,000 (dr.)
Labor Cost Variance	2,200 (dr.)
Labor Efficiency Variance	2,800 (cr.)
Manufacturing Overhead Variance	2,000 (dr.)
Materials Purchased	75,000
Selling Expenses – Variable..	20,000
Selling Expenses – Fixed	28,000
Direct Labor Costs..	65,000
General Administrative Expenses – Variable............................	19,500
General Administrative Expenses – Fixed................................	21,000
Manufacturing Overhead Costs – Variable	30,000
Sales..	460,000
Fixed Manufacturing Overhead	75,000
Inventories:	
July 1, 19— (*beginning*):	
Materials	8,000
Labor..	10,000
Variable manufacturing overhead	12,000
June 30, 19— (*final*):	
Materials	9,000
Labor..	4,800
Manufacturing overhead (variable)	6,000

Required:

a) On the basis of this information, you are asked to prepare an income statement for the year using the direct costing accounting system.

b) What if any use might be made of the statement prepared in (a)?

Problem 20–3. Purpose: *Comparative Statements of Income under Direct Costing and Absorption Costing Procedures*

The Wilbur Manufacturing Company wishes to make a comparative study of the profit and loss for the past three years when absorption and direct costing procedures are used.

The quantitative production and sales figures for the three years were as follows:

Production and Sales Figures	First Year	Second Year	Third Year
Units in the opening inventory.........	0	0	8,000
Units produced during the period 30,000		40,000	42,000
Units sold during the period 30,000		32,000	45,000
Units on hand at end of period.........	0	8,000	5,000

The operating costs incurred during this three-year period were as follows:

Description	First Year	Second Year	Third Year
Actual material costs ....$	59,000	$ 83,000	$ 92,000
Actual direct labor costs	90,000	123,000	144,000
Actual direct labor hours.................	60,000 hrs.	84,000 hrs.	106,000 hrs.
Variable overhead costs ....$	30,000	$ 42,000	$ 60,000
Fixed overhead costs......................	40,000	40,000	40,000
Variable selling and administrative costs.......................................	120,000	128,000	180,000
Fixed selling and administrative costs..	20,000	20,000	20,000

The selling price per unit was $30.

Required:

a) Prepare comparative income statements using Fifo method of inventory issuance for each of these three years, first on the absorption costing basis, and then on the direct (variable) costing basis. Indicate percent of profit on sales for each year under each method.

b) Analyze the difference in income under the two methods.

Problem 20–4. Purpose: *Comparative Income Statements Using Absorption and Direct (Variable) Costing with Standard Costs*

The Wascott Manufacturing Company uses a standard cost accounting system. It is anxious to make a comparison of its income statements when direct costing procedures are used and when traditional absorption costing procedures are used.

The standard cost sheet for the single article produced by this firm was as follows:

Material costs $2.25
Direct labor costs 3.75
Variable manufacturing overhead............................... 2.60
Variable selling and administrative expenses.................. 1.05
Variable Cost to Make and Sell....................................$9.65

Production statistics:

Budgeted capacity of plant... 200,000 units
Actual production.. 185,000 units
Units sold during period at $25 each .... 170,000 units

Cost statistics:

Budgeted fixed manufacturing overhead $130,000
Fixed manufacturing overhead incurred...................................... 130,000
Fixed selling costs... 120,000
Fixed administrative expenses 88,000
Standard cost variations other than volume variations:	
Over standard... 12,000
Under standard.. 8,000

Required:

a) Prepare an income statement on the absorption costing basis.

b) Prepare an income statement on the direct or variable costing basis.

Problem 20–5. Purpose: *Comparative Statements Using Both Absorption and Direct (Variable) Costing Procedures*

The Warrentown Manufacturing Company has prepared the following budget on a quarterly basis for the year:

THREE-MONTH BUDGET USED ON AN ANNUAL BASIS

		Total Cost	Per Unit
Budgeted sales for three-month period, 40,000 units		$60,000	$1.50
Cost of sales:			
Direct material	$10,000		$0.25
Direct labor	12,000		0.30
Variable overhead	8,000		0.20
Fixed overhead applied	6,000		0.15
Total		36,000	$0.90
Gross profit		$24,000	$0.60
Fixed selling and administrative costs	$10,000		$0.25
Variable selling and administrative costs	4,000		0.10
		14,000	0.35
Net Income		$10,000	$0.25

The production and sales for the year in units were as follows:

	First Quarter Units	Second Quarter Units	Third Quarter Units	Fourth Quarter Units	Total for Year (Units)
Opening inventory	0	0	8,000	6,000	0
Production	40,000	40,000	28,000	30,000	138,000
Sales	40,000	32,000	30,000	32,000	134,000
Closing inventory	0	8,000	6,000	4,000	4,000

The following is the income statement under absorption costing for the first two quarters of the year:

	First Quarter	Second Quarter	Third Quarter	Fourth Quarter	Total for Year
Sales..	$60,000	$48,000			
Cost of Sales:					
Initial Inventory	0	0			
Material Costs..	$10,000	$10,000			
Labor Costs..	12,000	12,000			
Variable Manufacturing Overhead	8,000	8,000			
Fixed Overhead Applied	6,000	6,000			
Total...	$36,000	$36,000			
Less: Closing Inventory	0	7,200			
Cost of Sales (Normal)	$36,000	$28,800			
Under or (Over) Applied Fixed Overhead..........	0	0			
Cost of Sales, Actual...................................	$36,000	$28,800			
GROSS PROFIT ON SALES	$24,000	$19,200			
Fixed Selling and Administrative Costs...	$10,000	$10,000			
Variable Selling and Administrative Costs..........	4,000	3,200			
Total Selling and Administrative Costs	$14,000	$13,200			
Net Income, Absorption Costing.....................	$10,000	$ 6,000			

Required:

From the information given:

a) Complete the income statement using *absorption costing* for the periods and in total.

b) Prepare an income statement for the four quarters using the direct costing techniques.

PROBLEMS–GROUP B

Problem 20–6. Purpose: *CPA Problem on Effect of Direct Costing on Financial Statements and Audit Certificates*

You have a client engaged in a manufacturing business with relatively heavy fixed costs and large inventories of finished goods. These inventories constitute a very material item on the balance sheet. The company has a departmental cost accounting system that assigns all manufacturing costs to the products each period.

The controller of the company has informed you that the management is giving serious consideration to the adoption of direct costing as an integrated method of accounting for plant operations and inventory valuation. The management wishes to have your opinion of the effect, if any, that such a change would have on:

a) The year-end financial position.
b) The net income for the period.
c) The audit certificate used with the year-end statements.

State your reply to the request and the reasons for your conclusions.

(AICPA Uniform Examination)

Problem 20–7. Purpose: *Comparison of Inventory and Unit Costs; Direct and Absorption Costing*

The following costs and expenses were incurred by the Wenting Manufacturing Company during July, the first month of the new model year. No inventory was on hand at the beginning of the year.

	Fixed Costs	Variable Costs
Production, 105,000 units		
Materials...		$420,000
Direct labor...		315,000
Manufacturing overhead costs.................$210,000		129,150
Selling expenses	14,000	25,000
Administrative expenses	28,000	12,500
Units sold, 75,000 at a unit price of $24		

Required:

a) Compute the final inventory under direct costing.
b) Compute the final inventory under absorption costing.
c) Compute the net income under the two costing methods.
d) Explain the reason for the difference in the net income in (c).

Problem 20–8. Purpose: *Comparative Income Statements under Three Costing Methods*

The Warburton Manufacturing Company produces a single product which sells for $18 per unit. For the month of July, the cost and operating data are as follows:

Budgeted and standard costs:

Production scheduled.......................................	120,000 units
Standard direct material costs	$180,000
Standard direct labor costs	120,000
Standard variable overhead costs........................	240,000
Fixed manufacturing overhead...........................	180,000
Variable selling and administrative costs	60,000
Fixed selling and administrative costs..................	30,000

Actual cost data:

Units produced...	108,000 units
Material costs	$167,400
Direct labor costs	108,000
Variable manufacturing overhead costs...............	200,000
Fixed manufacturing overhead costs	188,000
Variable selling and administrative costs..............	54,000
Fixed selling and administrative costs.................	35,000
Units sold..	100,000 units @ $14 each

All variances are added to or subtracted from the Cost of Sales account.

a) Income statement on the historical cost basis.
b) Income statement using absorption standard costs.
c) Income statement using direct standard costs.

Problem 20–9. Purpose: *Comparative Study of Absorption and Direct Costing Procedures*

The Winthrop Manufacturing Company wishes to make a comparative study of the effect of direct costing versus absorption costing on its net income. The following data is submitted to you for the four quarters of the past year:

QUARTERLY BUDGET

	Total Cost	Per Unit
Sales, 36,000 Units	$54,000	$1.50
Cost of Sales:		
Direct Materials..................................$ 9,000		$0.25
Direct Labor..................................... 10,800		0.30
Variable Overhead 7,200		0.20
Fixed Overhead................................. 5,400		0.15
Total...	32,400	$0.90
Gross Profit...	$21,600	$0.60
Selling and Administrative Costs, Fixed.................	12,600	0.35
Net Income	$ 9,000	$0.25

NUMBER OF UNITS PRODUCED AND SOLD DURING YEAR

	First Quarter (Units)	Second Quarter (Units)	Third Quarter (Units)	Fourth Quarter (Units)	Total Units for Year
Opening Inventory	0	0	8,000	6,000	0
Production	36,000	40,000	28,000	30,000	134,000
Sales..............................	36,000	32,000	30,000	36,000	134,000
Closing Inventory.............	0	8,000	6,000	0	0

INCOME STATEMENT FOR THE YEAR ENDED DECEMBER 31, 19—
(Absorption Cost Accounting with Predetermined Fixed Overhead Rates)

	First Quarter	Second Quarter	Third Quarter	Fourth Quarter	Total for Year
Sales..	$54,000	$48,000			
Cost of Sales:					
Opening Inventory......................	0	0			
Material Costs............................	$ 9,000	$10,000			
Labor Costs...............................	10,800	12,000			
Variable Overhead Costs	7,200	8,000			
Applied Fixed Overhead..............	5,400	6,000			
Total	$32,400	$36,000			
Less: Closing Inventory...............	0	7,200			
Cost of Sales *at Normal*	$32,400	$28,800			
Under or (Over) Applied Fixed					
Overhead	0	(600)			
Cost of Sales Adjusted to Actual					
Costs.....................................	$32,400	$28,200			
Gross Profit.................................	$21,600	$19,800			
Fixed Selling and Administrative					
Expenses..............................	12,600	12,600			
Net Income	$ 9,000	$ 7,200			

Required:

a) Complete the income statements on a quarterly basis for the year, using the absorption costing.

b) Prepare an income statement showing the same information using direct costing techniques.

part III

PROFIT PLANNING BY MAKING SPECIAL COST ANALYSES

Part I covered 13 chapters related to cost determination for the two basic systems—job order and continuous process or departmental. In Part II, the subject of planning and control of these costs was presented. This involved the subjects of budgeting, predetermining costs, installing a cost accounting system, and using administrative reports, and direct costing procedures for fixing managerial accountability. Both of these sections have been developed from the accountant's or controller's viewpoint— that is, an explanation of how it is or should be done. In this Part III, the study of costs is further extended to indicate to management how cost data as compiled above may be used in making managerial decisions. This also is from the accountant's viewpoint—that is, how costs can be used, as contrasted with the managerial viewpoint in which management tells the cost accountant what it wants to know and asks him how this information may be obtained. This section contains the following three major topics:

Profit Planning through Break-Even and Cost-Volume-Profit Analyses
Cost Analyses for Special Purposes
Nonmanufacturing Cost Applications and Analyses

chapter 21

Profit Planning through Break-Even and Cost-Volume-Profit Analyses

BREAK-EVEN CHARTS AND PROFIT PLANNING

The success of a business is generally attributable in great measure to the ability of its management personnel to cope with probable conditions of the future. Short-range as well as long-term plans must be made *today* for the business operations of *tomorrow,* and this is accomplished by sound management evaluation of not only the potentials of tomorrow but also its pitfalls.

The success of a business is most frequently measured in terms of *profit.* Profit is dependent on three basic factors — the selling price of the product, the costs of manufacturing and distributing the product, and the volume of sales. No one profit factor is independent of the others because cost determines the selling price to arrive at a desired rate of profit; the selling price affects the volume of sales; the volume of sales directly influences the volume of production; and the volume of production influences the cost. This relationship of COST-VOLUME-PROFIT, frequently abbreviated to C-V-P, means that accounting must play a vital role in the planning function because management must have adequate data to properly appraise the probable effects of tomorrow's profit opportunities.

The direct costing procedures, as discussed in Chapter 20, are most conducive to the simplification of C-V-P analysis. A popular starting point in C-V-P analysis which has been used for many years is the *break-even chart*. Its practical applications have gone beyond just the determination of the break-even point — the volume level at which the income from sales is just sufficient to cover all costs.

Cost-volume-profit analyses are helpful to management in appraising the effect of changes in selling prices, fixed costs, and variable costs upon the earnings. (See Illustration 21–1.) The break-even chart constitutes a useful starting point for these analyses. The determination of a firm's break-even point supported by related volume, selling price, and cost analyses is an important aid in anticipating and meeting current problems. It involves techniques of assembling, coordinating, and inter-

Illustration 21–1

PROFIT STRUCTURE CHART
(SHOWING MAJOR SEGMENTS OF COSTS)

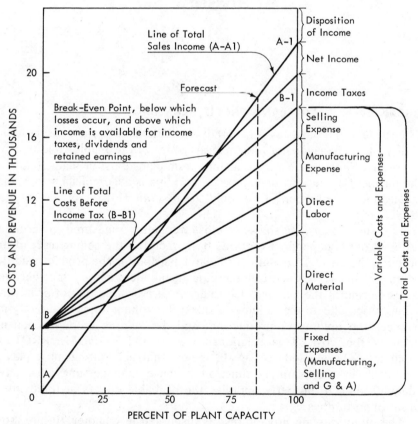

SOURCE: J. D. Wilson, Controller of Tidewater Oil Company. *Practical Applications of Cost-Volume Profit Analysis, N.A.A. Bulletin.*

preting quantitative production and distribution data to assist management in arriving at informed decisions. It is frequently the responsibility of the top financial executive to derive and summarize such data.

In any study looking toward the determination of the break-even point and other cost and profit facts or probabilities, the starting point is the estimation of costs at various levels of output. Thus, in order to tackle any phase of profit planning, it is necessary to provide for separation between fixed and variable costs through all of the firm's functions. If flexible budget information is derived periodically and a standard cost or direct costing system is used, such separation has been the basis of these devices; therefore, they serve as a most satisfactory point of departure in developing the current cost information necessary for profit planning. While the controller coordinates and assembles cost and market data, in a large firm the measurement and prediction of probable prices and sales volumes for the firm's products is the primary responsibility of a marketing research department, the sales manager, staff economists, or some combination of these.

Costs, volume, profit, and the break-even point may be expressed graphically and mathematically. Either of these devices may be helpful in communicating the underlying data to management and in explaining the probable effects of alternative proposals. By presenting this information in chart or graphic form, its effectiveness is increased since management is more readily able to grasp the significance of the related quantitative data.

To illustrate a simple break-even chart, it is assumed that management is budgeting its sales and production costs for the year on an estimated sales volume of 100,000 units of one product. With the related budgetary and unit information as it is given in Illustration 21–2, the

Illustration 21–2

ANY MANUFACTURING COMPANY
BUDGETED INCOME STATEMENT
For Year Ended December 31, 19—

Sales (100,000 at $20)			$2,000,000
Costs:	*Fixed*	*Variable*	
Direct Material...	0	$ 450,000	
Direct Labor..	0	750,000	
Manufacturing Overhead..............................	$100,000	160,000	
Administrative Expenses..............................	28,000	73,200	
Selling Expenses...	108,000	90,000	
Total...	$236,000	$1,523,200	1,759,200
Budgeted Net Income...................................			$ 240,800

(Capacity production, 140,000 units)

break-even point and income at various volume levels are presented.

This information is shown graphically in the charts given in Illustrations 21–3 and 21–4. In these charts, the following procedures are used:

1. The *vertical* scale is expressed in dollars and indicates the fixed and variable costs and revenue.

2. The *horizontal* scale is used to indicate the volume and may be expressed in terms of dollar volume, volume in units, percentages of capacity, direct labor hours, or some other suitable index of volume.

3. On these two charts, three lines are drawn—one for the *fixed costs,* one for the *variable* costs, and one for the *sales income,* showing these elements for the different volumes. The sequence of these items on the chart may vary. On the *first* chart, the base area is representative of fixed costs and indicated by drawing a line parallel to the base scale, since *fixed* costs are the same regardless of the *volume.* The *cumulative*

Illustration 21–3

BREAK-EVEN CHART WITH SALES VOLUME AS BASE

(Fixed Costs Plotted on Base or Horizontal Line)

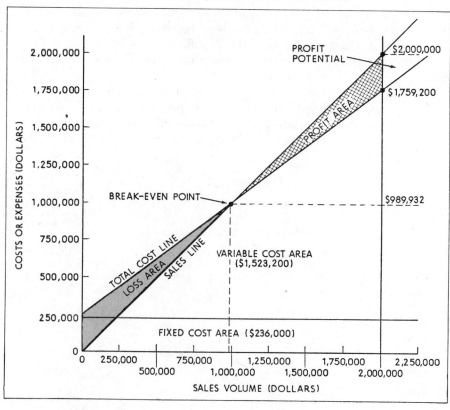

Illustration 21–4

BREAK-EVEN CHART WITH SALES VOLUME AS BASE

(Variable Costs Plotted on Base or Horizontal Line)

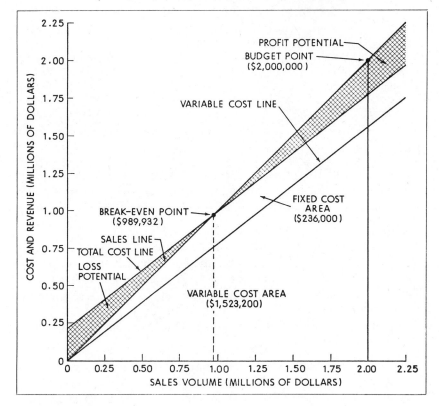

effect of adding the *variable* costs to the fixed cost area is now drawn. Finally the *sales income* line must be drawn from the point where there are no sales (zero intersection of horizontal and vertical scales) to the point where there are $2,000,000 in sales. Where the *total cost* (cumulative effect of the fixed and variable costs) and the *sales income* lines intersect, that is the *break-even point* (the volume of sales at which there is neither a profit nor a loss).

On the second chart, the *variable costs* are *first* plotted on the base or horizontal line and then the *fixed costs* are recorded. Since the fixed costs are the same for all volumes of production, this line will be parallel to the variable cost line and will represent the *cumulative total of variable plus fixed costs*.

In studying and analyzing the statements and charts, it should be noted that it is necessary to have costs and expenses grouped into *fixed and variable.* If an expense is semivariable, it is separated into its fixed and variable components as previously indicated in this text.

To illustrate the computation of the break-even point on the basis of sales volume, the statement previously used is presented in condensed form, viz:

Sales income (100,000 at $20)	$2,000,000	100.00%
Variable costs total	1,523,200	76.16
Contribution margin	$ 476,800	23.84%
Fixed costs	236,000	11.80
Net Income	$ 240,800	12.04%

Interpreting this information, it is observed that:

1. Out of every $100 of sales, $76.16 is required for variable expenses or costs. If there is no production, these costs will not be incurred.
2. Out of every $100 of sales, $23.84 is left to meet the fixed expenses or costs.

Therefore, to compute the dollar volume of sales necessary to meet the fixed charges, that is, just break even, the fixed charges of $236,000 must be divided by the 23.84 percent, viz: $236,000/0.2384 = $989,932.

This amount, $989,932, represents the amount of sales under the budgeted operating conditions which will result in just breaking even. Any amount of sales above this should produce a profit. However, these conclusions assume that:

1. Any changes in *sales volume* will not affect the price per unit.
2. That *fixed costs* will be the same in total for all volumes.
3. That *variable costs* will all vary in direct proportion to sales volume.

It is possible to construct the break-even chart with the sales line curved to indicate that the price per unit is not necessarily constant at different volume levels. It is also possible to reflect any changes in the fixed cost behavior over the wide range of volume between shutdown and 100% of capacity operations by showing appropriate step-up changes in the diagram. Changes in variable cost behavior can be shown by altering the slope of the variable cost line at different volume levels.

If more than one product is included in the sales analysis, then management is faced with the problem of *sales mix,* that is, the volume of each product to be included in the sales total. This problem can be solved satisfactorily by preparing several analyses and charts, assuming different sales mixes for each, thus indicating to management the effect on the break-even point and on net income of promoting or failing to promote the more profitable lines. Management usually needs more than one analysis because there are numerous possible combinations of sales volume and sales mix; different degrees of variability of costs as the sales volume and mix changes; and different fixed costs for alternative plans. Break-even analyses and charts must be kept current and not attempt to reflect probable operating circumstances over a period longer than a year because not only the mixture of variable cost and income elements may change but also fixed costs gradually shift over extended periods of time.

A *static* break-even analysis, or one such as in the foregoing illustration that simplifies the actual production and distribution circumstances, has limitations for profit planning which many firms have not always recognized. These limitations arise from four different causes:

1. Inaccuracies in estimating cost behavior for certain costs in certain functions of the firm.
2. Oversimplification of the revenue probabilities as to volume and market price of each product in a multiproduct firm.
3. Dynamic forces outside the firm in the market for materials, supplies, and labor and in productive technology which may cause unanticipated shifts in prices, rates, and productive conditions.
4. The impossibility of anticipating certain specific production and distribution problems which will confront management as the period ahead unfolds and to which management will have to adapt its forecast policy.

Awareness of these causes of limitations in usefulness can lead to improved and extended analysis which may sharpen the interpretation and application of the resulting projections. It must be kept in mind that any single break-even analysis or cost-volume-profit study will only show profit expectations under a single set of assumed conditions—external market conditions and internal management planning.

Various claims have been made concerning the managerial usefulness of break-even analysis. These claims include not only profit planning but also cost control both in the short and long run and assistance in the development of pricing policy. For these purposes, as well as for profit planning, the existence of the foregoing limitations must be taken into account.

Illustration 21–5 sets forth a simple device for within-the-month reference to probable results, a *profit determination chart*.

DERIVING DATA TO ASSIST MANAGEMENT IN PROFIT PLANNING

In order to plan effectively, the management of a firm must have some approximate profit goal or goals in mind. Is it striving for a certain rate of return on the investment in the total firm? Is it striving for certain rates of return on investment for each product division? Is it striving to get above-average profits in the coming period when volume is expected

Illustration 21–5

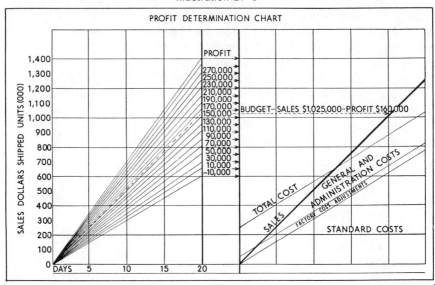

PROFIT DETERMINATION CHART

The righthand half constitutes a break-even chart and identifies budgeted volume and profits. A battery of alternative sales volume lines are plotted on the lefthand half in such a manner that the profit results for the month, implied by volume achieved to any date in the month, can be read from the chart. . .where volume and cost ratios remain relatively constant, some form of this chart can be an indication of performance before the formal reports are prepared.

SOURCE: *N.A.A. Accounting Practice Report No. 9, Reports Which Managements Find Most Useful.*

to be relatively high? The particular profit goals should be set by those top executives who are responsible for the financial management of the firm.

Management must have some ideas as to various ways to achieve the particular profit goal or goals set for the firm. Some responsible planning group, consisting of executives or representatives from each major function, must be established. Proposals from all functional sources — sales, product design and engineering, production departments, purchasing, etc. — must be considered. These proposals must be discussed by the planning group and those that seem feasible recommended for further study and development. *At this point the top financial executive has the responsibility of taking those proposals recommended for study and showing the probable effects on costs and/or income of each proposal.*

The group participation necessary to develop figures for the various proposals enlists the cooperation of at least the head of each staff and operating function involved. Much the same procedure is followed as that described previously for the development of figures for a flexible budget. If up-to-date flexible budget data are already available, many of the cost figures related to proposals can be derived directly. However, for profit planning it may be necessary to derive additional figures because some of the proposals being considered involve different assumptions as to price, labor rates, manufacturing method, etc., than those upon which the flexible budget figures are based. Through regular budgeting procedures and these special studies for profit-planning purposes, the responsibilities and problems of each function in the business become more familiar to each participant. This usually leads to the type of working relationship that will permit more thorough and more nearly accurate analyses in terms of the effect of a particular proposal upon a specific function.

A more detailed explanation of the typical procedures used in developing the probable revenue and cost effects of proposed changes is given in the following paragraphs.

DETERMINING ATTAINABLE VOLUME AND PRICE ALTERNATIVES

The first step in the development of cost-volume-profit studies and break-even analyses is the determination of the probable *volume levels* at which the firm would operate if certain recommended marketing plans were adopted. The level finally selected as the overall volume goal for the firm, or the levels selected for each individual product line, will be influenced by the general economic condition of the nation and by the characteristics of the particular business and the industry of which it is a member. For example, a business producing necessity items would expect more gradual and less drastic change in its volume than a business producing luxury items. Other basic considerations in deriving and evaluating the validity of volume figures are the degree of market maturity that has been reached for each line of product and the firm's competitive position as compared to the other firms in the industry. With respect to market maturity, it must be determined which of the following stages applies to each line of product to be offered for sale in the coming year:

1. *Low volume:* Customer acceptance of the firm's particular design and quality of product, or for this type of product throughout the industry, is not yet certain.
2. *Expanding volume:* Customer acceptance of the product has been achieved, and each firm in the industry producing the product is striving to service that portion of the future potential market which seems to be consistent with sound expansion plans for production and distribution facilities.
3. *Rather stable volume:* The bulk of the customers in the potential market have made their first purchase of the product, and the total demand is now made up partly of new customers and partly of those acquiring replacement units of the product.

4. *Declining volume:* Few new customers in the market, some replacement customers, with suitable substitutes making inroads on volume.

In order to formulate a production volume and price policy, it is also necessary to consider the type of competition that will be encountered by the firm. Three general types of relative competitive position are customarily found. They are:

1. The firm is but one of many suppliers producing for a broad market where the actions of any one of the firms does not have much impact on the total market.
2. The firm is one of several large competitors each having a substantial share of the market, but it is not controlling or leading the market.
3. The firm is in a dominating position in the market where it can at least maintain its large share of the total volume and even set prices for the industry.

Even though a firm understands these basic conditioning circumstances affecting the volume of product it may sell, the task of forecasting product-volume levels for a multiproduct firm is far from simple. In a dynamic and competitive economy, the problem of determining total volume is complicated further by these factors: (1) a live firm is periodically making changes in the quality and design of existing products and the degree of acceptance of these changes varies; (2) any newly developed products are in the trial stage where demand is uncertain; and (3) in order to achieve maximum utilization (least waste) of basic materials, it is constantly seeking to expand the use of existing by-products or to develop marketable by-products. Despite these difficulties *some forecasting must be done;* otherwise, the firm will drift aimlessly without a goal.

In companies not having market research specialists, the president, sales manager, and controller ordinarily are those most frequently called upon to estimate the probable volume levels for each product and in total. In larger organizations the volume levels to be projected are developed by market research specialists and are subsequently reviewed, perhaps modified, and approved by executive management.

The planning group may adopt a final sales budget or may request information on the relative costs and relative profitability of several different volume levels and product mixes. At this point other departments in the organization and the controller begin active work to determine how they would meet the forecasts and what costs would probably be incurred in so doing. First, the production departments should compute the production and time demands on each operation in order to determine the adequacy of present facilities and needs, if any, for new equipment or plant. For the sales department, it may mean more advertising, sales promotion, increased sales personnel and facilities, and expanded territories to increase or maintain sales levels. For research and engineering, it may mean greater activity on development and improvement of new products and helping manufacturing departments improve methods to increase production, reduce down time, and reduce repairs. If new products are involved, the production engineering and purchasing departments will have to work cooperatively in preparing estimates of new material and equipment needs, their availability and cost.

DETERMINING THE COSTS OF MEETING SELECTED VOLUME ALTERNATIVES

The costs of meeting a particular volume level will depend upon and vary with (1) the product mix; (2) the proposed promotional and distribution plans for securing the volume of each type of product; (3) the way in which manufacturing capacity will be used; (4) the effect of concurrent plans to improve efficiency of men and machines; and (5) the effect of the changing prices of various types of material, of changing rates of various classifications of labor, and of changing costs for replacement, maintenance, and repair of machines. The probable effect of such contemplated or expected changes must be estimated for each type of fixed, semifixed, semivariable, and variable cost in each producing and distribution function of the firm.

In obtaining information on cost behavior which will serve as a point of departure for projecting costs for the coming period, a variety of methods are used. These range from the simplest interpretations of past operating results to intensive cost accounting and engineering studies similar to the methods already discussed which are used in developing each element of cost in establishing flexible budgets.

The most simple, but least exact, approach is to analyze a series of operating statements for that span of recent years which will be useful in projecting coming year experience. Each selected year's sales and corresponding costs are plotted against the sales volume. This provides points on a scatter chart to which straight lines are fitted. The result is two lines representing the basic historical relationship between sales and costs and the resultant profits in relation to volume levels experienced by the company in the past. Refer to Chapter 14 on budgetary control for a detailed illustration of the scatter graph. In order to refine such studies, the effects of price level changes must be removed by appropriate index number techniques to achieve even a fair degree of accuracy. Unfortunately, except for some small single-product concerns, price change is only one of the possible distortions present in this type of analysis. For most concerns changes in plant size and production methods are almost certain to have taken place over the period of years studied. These different conditions of production cannot appropriately be intermingled in an historical analysis without careful adjustment if the objective is to arrive at the volume-cost relationship which exists now and will probably be effective in the year ahead. In spite of these difficulties, this approach has some usefulness where changes in various productive and distributive efforts have not been substantial and when only approximate results are desired.

If the management of the firm needs more nearly accurate information but has not yet adopted the practice of preparing periodic flexible budgets, then it must engage in more detailed analysis of the type which is preliminary to the establishment of a flexible budget. While this procedure has been discussed previously, a brief review of the steps involved will be helpful. A typical starting point is the historical analysis of monthly data over the past year or so when the operating conditions of particular functions have been substantially the same. A study of each specific type of cost is made department by department (or cost center by cost center) in order to determine the existing cost behavior pattern (cost to output relationship) for that type of cost in relation to the activity measure of that department. From this a scatter chart is prepared for each cost element. A linear relationship between the measure of output (activity measure) and the cost element is derived by visual inspection of the pattern or by statistical techniques. With the pattern of each cost in each factory function identified, there has been established a satisfactory point of departure for projecting each element of future cost of production.

Selling and administrative expenses and other nonfactory expenses can likewise be related to levels of product or service activity or sales in order to get an approximate pattern of their change with different levels of volume.

The two foregoing approaches are widely used, but in those situations where up-to-date cost standards and flexible budget data are available, the task of determining costs for different volume alternatives can be done more quickly and accurately. Some of the cost elements may be derived directly from the standards or flexible budget, or these may be readily modified to take into account any changes which are expected to be effective in the period ahead.

Once the detailed quantitative data are derived, they may be used in various combinations to present to management cost-volume-profit and break-even analyses. Before management decides upon a profit plan for the coming year, it will want to know the probable profit results of the several alternatives under consideration. For example, it may want a comparison of these two alternatives:

1.   The maintenance of present volume and product mix in the coming

year with the effect of various price and wage rate changes on cost elements.

2. The increase of volume to certain forecast volumes for each product line. In addition to taking into account the effect of various price and wage rate changes, this analysis should reflect: (*a*) the effect on income of any selling price or policy changes, (*b*) the effect on costs of the changes in nature and extent of promotional effort and other additional distribution services planned to attain the forecast volume, and (*c*) the effect on costs of production of the change in operating level.

These alternatives are suggestive of just two possible sets of conditions for which management would like to see the effects on cost, volume, and profit carefully analyzed and summarized. Illustrative data and charts for various combinations of changes in selling price, volume, fixed costs, and variable costs are presented later in this chapter.

When certain proposals have been adopted and constitute the profit plan for the coming year, the standards and budgets vital to their development can be used as *control* devices to guide and coordinate management action and to measure performance as the operations of the year take place. Previous chapters on budgetary control and the use of standards have described in detail how this might be accomplished. Carefully prepared cost-volume-profit analyses thus become an indispensable management tool for *profit planning* and *control*.

THE USE OF COST-VOLUME-PROFIT ANALYSES BY MANAGEMENT

Cost-volume-profit relationships are influenced by five factors or a combination of them. These are the result of changes in (1) *selling prices,* (2) *volume of sales,* (3) *product mix of the sales,* (4) *variable costs per unit,* and (5) *total fixed costs.* The preliminary marketing and cost analysis work provides management personnel with an improved understanding of each of these factors. Different combinations of these factors will be involved in each alternative proposal for profit improvement being considered by management. To permit effective profit planning, management must foresee the part that each of these factors plays, or will play, in changing the net income, the break-even point, and the return on investment for the firm. Carefully developed budgetary figures for income and costs and the graphic portrayal of these in break-even charts are the most effective means of providing the necessary information to management. This enables management to anticipate the effects of proposed actions and of changes in market conditions. The responsible group of executives are then in a position to select those proposals which will contribute most to the profit pattern in the year ahead. This is profit planning.

Before proceeding to the detailed study of the various cost-volume-profit relationships, two terms frequently used in this connection must be examined. These are *marginal income* or the *contribution margin* and *margin of safety (M/S) ratio*.

The *contribution margin* or *marginal income* is the difference between the *sales income* and the total of *variable costs and expenses*. A statement showing separately the marginal income is today an important management tool used in studying the effect of *changes* in volume (income) of sales. The ratio of the marginal income to sales is known as the *marginal income ratio* or *profit-volume ratio*.

Margin of safety ratio is computed by dividing the difference between the *total sales income* and the *break-even sales point* by the *total sales*. It merely indicates what portion of the sales are available to create profits for the firm.

To illustrate these two definitions more specifically, the following data are used:

Sales (10,000 units × $125)	$1,250,000	100%
Variable costs and expenses	800,000	64
Marginal income or contribution margin	$ 450,000	36%
Fixed costs and expenses	400,000	32
Net Income	$ 50,000	4%

The *marginal income* is $450,000. The *marginal income ratio* (marginal income to sales) is $450,000/$1,250,000, or 36 percent.

The *margin of safety ratio* is total sales income − break-even sales ÷ total sales income, or more specifically, $1,250,000.00 − $1,111,111.11 ÷ $1,250,000.00. This results in a margin of safety ratio of 11.1 percent, which is rather low. (Break-even sales are computed by dividing 36 percent into $400,000.)

BREAK-EVEN ANALYSES FOR CHANGING CONDITIONS

Break-even analysis as previously illustrated represented certain static conditions. It is possible to superimpose on such charts the effect on the break-even point of certain changing conditions which may be expected in the future such as:

1. Increase in variable costs.
2. Decline in sales.

In order to compare the existing situation with a future situation in which there will be increases in variable costs, the first step is the cost analysis necessary to derive the new variable cost figures. Then, the existing income and costs and the projected income and costs can be presented on a break-even chart or charts. It is probably easier for management to see the effect of the change in variable costs if both situations are presented on one chart, as in Illustration 21–6.

To illustrate such a comparative break-even chart when there is a *10%* increase in variable costs due to such items as materials, labor, etc., but no change in selling price of product, the following data are assumed:

Sales $2,500,000
Fixed costs 800,000
Variable costs before increase.................................. 1,600,000
Variable costs after increase................................... 1,760,000

Break-even point before increase:
  Variable costs of $1,600,000 equals 64% of sales.
  Profit margin is 36%. B.E. point is $800,000 ÷ 36%, or $2,222,222.22.

Break-even point after increase:
  Variable costs of $1,760,000 equals 70.4% of sales.
  Profit margin is 29.6%. B.E. point is $800,000 ÷ 29.6%, or $2,702,702.70.

This is presented graphically in Illustration 21–6. A similar procedure

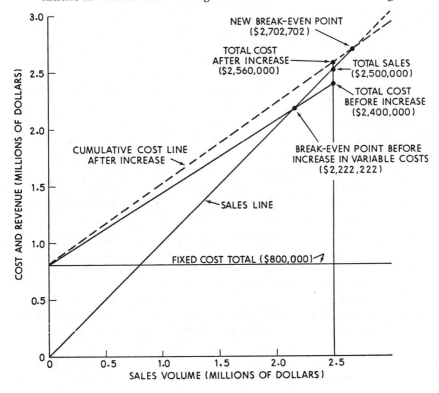

Illustration 21–6
BREAK-EVEN CHART FOR CHANGING CONDITIONS
Increase in Variable Costs—Selling Price and Fixed Costs Do Not Change

may be followed in presenting the data when a decline in sales is anticipated or a change is expected in any of the other factors affecting cost,
volume, and profit.

COST-VOLUME-PROFIT ANALYSIS FOR PLANT EXPANSION

If a plant is operating at full capacity and management is confronted
with the problem of meeting a substantial increase in demand for the
product, a choice must be made between overtime, extra shift operation,
and plant expansion. This may involve the entire plant or only those departments in which production bottlenecks are serious.

Overtime and extra shift operation will result in better utilization of
existing plant and equipment facilities and some reduction in fixed overhead costs per unit of production. Offsetting this saving there will be
certain increases in labor costs on overtime and extra shift operation.
Because of time and a half and shift differential premiums on wages, the
out-of-pocket unit costs for direct labor will be higher. This effect is
far-reaching and includes the indirect labor involved in the job or process
being operated and the various types of service and maintenance labor
supporting the operation, to the extent that overtime or extra shift work
is required in these areas. In addition, certain factors tending to lower
efficiency may be involved, such as worker fatigue on overtime work or
the lower productive skill of the employees added for extra shifts. If
all of the departmental equipment is not operated and less than a full
staff of direct labor is used, such additional time operation may involve
disproportionate supervision, materials handling, timekeeping, and other
types of indirect labor costs both within and without the departments
operating additional time. The advisability of using these methods of
producing additional volume will depend on the relationship of the reduction in fixed cost per unit to the extra cost per unit incurred for certain labor and service costs.

Plant expansion is an alternative means of obtaining the increased
volume to meet a demand which is taxing plant facilities. It involves
long-term investments in additions to building and equipment and additional periodic outlays for maintenance, taxes, and insurance that are
of a fixed nature. It will be considered by management if the outlook is
for rising demand over an extended future period with little possibility
of severe demand cutbacks to below the present level. Only with sustained utilization of the additional facilities will it be possible to maintain or improve production efficiency and to match or reduce production
cost per unit.

To illustrate the effect of plant expansion, the following data are used:

1. Present plant facilities (assumed to be 100 percent capacity) result in —

        Sales...$2,500,000
        Fixed costs   400,000
        Variable costs................................ 1,600,000

2. Proposed increase of plant facilities will increase production 25 percent and fixed charges by $150,000.

Using this information it is possible to compute the break-even points before and after expansion and then plot them in the graph.

At 100% plant capacity:
  Variable costs are $1,600,000, or 64% of sales.
  Profit margin is 36%.
  Break-even sales point is $400,000 ÷ 36%, or $1,111,111.11.
  When present plant facilities are increased 25%:
  It is assumed that variable costs will remain at same ratio to sales, namely, 64%.
  Profit margin is still 36%.
  Break-even sales point is $550,000 ÷ 36%, or $1,527,777.77.

On the respective graphs (Illustration 21–7) it is possible to compute, by measuring the vertical distance between the total cost line and the sales line in the profit area, the sales volume that will produce a certain desired profit.

In developing this graph, the same procedure was followed as in the previous illustrations, with the fixed costs forming the base to which the variable costs are added to obtain the line showing the total costs. The dotted line represents the break-even data for the increase in plant and equipment. To determine at what point the new plant capacity will create the same amount of profit as is presently being produced, the sales line and the total cost lines for the proposed 125 percent plant facility operations must be extended until the vertical distance between them on the graph equals $500,000. This point will be approximately at 114 percent.

In the illustration presented, it was assumed that the variable costs would continue at the same rate of variability as in the original plant and that the rate of gross profit and sales mix would also continue uniformly as before. This may not be so. The added plant facilities might permit increased labor efficiency so that the variable cost per unit would change for the added production. Other modifications might also result from the added facilities. However, this should not change the importance of the break-even analysis to management. It merely means additional cost analysis and the preparation of two separate, almost independent, charts on the same sheet of graph paper, or separately, taking into account the changed conditions at the two different operating levels.

Illustration 21–7

BREAK-EVEN CHART WHEN PLANT FACILITIES ARE INCREASED

(Fixed Charges Are Increased; Other Costs and Income Do Not Change)

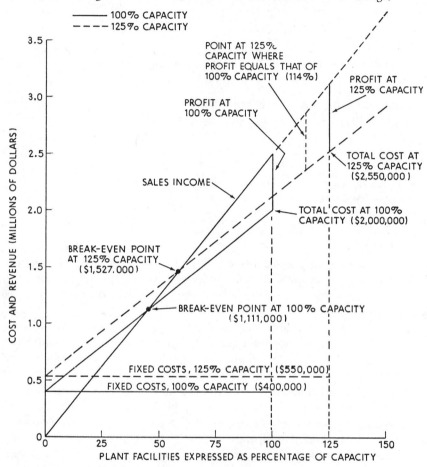

It must be remembered and emphasized that since conditions in manufacturing and distribution are not static in a particular business for any length of time, break-even charts should only be used to project operating results for a short period of time, usually not exceeding one year.

COST-VOLUME-PROFIT ANALYSIS IN EVALUATING SELLING PRICE CHANGES

In the next two illustrations, the following basic information is assumed as having been budgeted for the next 12 months and is used in projecting the probable cost-volume-profit relationships should certain changes in prices, volume of sales, variable costs, and/or fixed costs take place:

Estimated sales volume, 1,000,000 units at $8.00		$8,000,000
Less: Variable costs, 1,000,000 units at 4.80		4,800,000
Marginal income or contribution margin		$3,200,000
Less: Fixed costs		2,500,000
Net Income		$ 700,000

On the basis of these figures, the following ratios and figures may be computed:

Marginal income ratio ($3,200,000) ÷ $8,000,000 = 40%.
Net income ratio ($700,000 ÷ $8,000,000) 8.75%
Break-even sales point ($2,500,000 ÷ 40%) $6,250,000

In order to present the effect of selling price changes on net income and the break-even point, it is assumed that management wishes to examine the probable effect of the various price and volume conditions raised in the following questions:

1. If prices were increased 15 percent and there was no change in the physical volume of sales, what would be the effect on profit and the break-even point?
2. If prices were increased 15 percent and the volume of sales decreased 10 percent, what would be the effect on profit and the break-even point?
3. If prices were decreased 20 percent and there was no change in the physical volume of sales, what would be the effect on income and the break-even point?
4. If prices were decreased 25 percent and the volume of sales increased 20 percent, what would be the effect on income and the break-even point?

The comparative analysis presented in statement form in Illustration 21–8 and graphically in Illustration 21–9 shows the results of the several volume and price alternatives.

The analysis assumes that variable cost per unit remains constant, that total fixed costs will not change, and that there is no change in the sales mix. Should any of these assumptions have to be modified to conform more closely to expected conditions, then different analyses would have to be prepared. Should any of these assumed conditions not remain the same, then further adjustments of the figures will be necessary. Interpreting this statement on the basis of the foregoing assumptions, it should be noted that:

Illustration 21-8

COST-VOLUME-PROFIT ANALYSIS FOR CERTAIN VOLUME AND SALES PRICE CHANGES

	On Chart, See Line Indicated	Budgeted Figures Sales of 1,000,000 Units @ $8.00	No Change in Volume — Prices Increased 15%	No Change in Volume — Prices Decreased 20%	Prices Decreased 25% Volume Increased 20%	Prices Increased 15% Volume Decreased 10%
Sales:						
1,000,000 units @ $8.00	A	$8,000,000				
1,000,000 units @ 9.20	B		$9,200,000			
1,000,000 units @ 6.40	C			$6,400,000		
1,200,000 units @ 6.00	D				$7,200,000	
900,000 units @ 9.20	E					$8,280,000
Sales as projected		$8,000,000	$9,200,000	$6,400,000	$7,200,000	$8,280,000
Variable costs:						
1,000,000 units @ $4.80		$4,800,000	4,800,000	4,800,000		
1,200,000 units @ 4.80					5,760,000	
900,000 units @ 4.80						4,320,000
Marginal income or contribution margin		$3,200,000	$4,400,000	$1,600,000	$1,440,000	$3,960,000
Fixed costs		2,500,000	2,500,000	2,500,000	2,500,000	2,500,000
Net Income		$ 700,000	$1,900,000			$1,460,000
Net Loss				($ 900,000)	($ 1,060,000)	
Management's analysis:						
Net income ratio (net income ÷ sales)		8.75%	20.65%	(14.06%)	(14.72%)	17.63%
Percentage change in net income (budgeted figures equals 100%)		.....	+271%	−229%	−251%	+209%
Marginal income ratio (marginal income ÷ sales)		40%	47.8%	25%	20%	47.8%
Break-even sales point (fixed costs ÷ P/V ratio)		$6,250,000	$5,230,000*	$10,000,000	$12,500,000	$5,230,000*

* Approximate computation.
( ) Loss.

Illustration 21–9
**PROFIT/VOLUME RELATIONSHIPS IF VOLUME AND
SALES PRICES CHANGE**
(Statement shown in Illustration 21–8)
Intersection of Sales Line with Horizontal (Zero) Line Is the
Break-Even Point of Sales

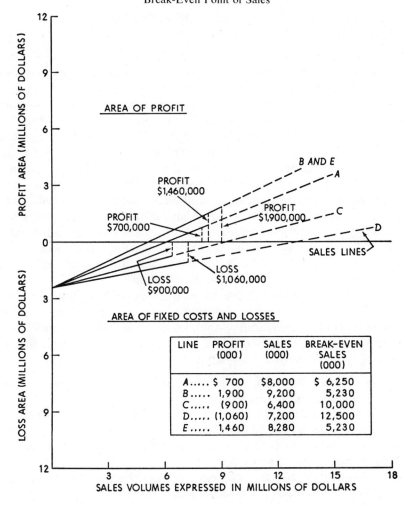

LINE	PROFIT (000)	SALES (000)	BREAK-EVEN SALES (000)
A.....	$ 700	$8,000	$ 6,250
B.....	1,900	9,200	5,230
C.....	(900)	6,400	10,000
D.....	(1,060)	7,200	12,500
E.....	1,460	8,280	5,230

1. *Increasing* prices 15 percent, with no change in volume, will result in a 271 percent increase in the total amount of profit, with a return of 20.65 percent net profit on the sales instead of the budgeted figure of 8.75 percent. On the other hand, if it is necessary to *reduce* prices 20 percent to meet competition and still maintain the present sales volume, then the firm will suffer a loss of 14.06 percent on sales. To *break even* when prices are increased 15 percent, sales total will

have to be only $5,230,000. But if prices are decreased 20 percent, the firm will not break even unless the total sales equal $10,000,000.

2. As the marginal income ratio increases, the break-even point of sales decreases, and vice versa.

COST-VOLUME-PROFIT ANALYSIS IN EVALUATING A COMBINATION OF CHANGES

Increases in variable cost per unit may be anticipated because of new wage agreements or because the price of materials is increasing; decreases in variable costs may occur because of expected gains in labor efficiency or lower unit prices of materials. Gains in labor efficiency may be expected due to methods study and improvement, increased mechanization, employee training programs, or the effect of incentive systems. Lower material prices may be made possible by changing market conditions or purchasing in more economical lots. Selling price reductions may be initiated by a firm when decreased variable costs per unit permit such an adjustment or to secure additional volume which will utilize available capacity more effectively. Also, selling price reductions may be forced by competitors, even though the variable costs of an individual firm may be rising. Substantial decreases in selling price will usually result in expanded sales both for the individual firm and throughout the particular industry in which the firm is operating.

The effect on income and the break-even point of a firm of various combinations of the foregoing conditions may be shown in statement and chart form. The comparative analysis statement (Illustration 21–10) and the related chart (Illustration 21–11) depict the results if the following sets of conditions are anticipated:

1. Variable costs decrease 10 percent, selling price per unit remains the same, and volume increases 20 percent;
2. Variable costs decrease 10 percent, selling price reduced 8 percent, and volume increases 20 percent;
3. Variable costs increase 5 percent, selling price remains the same, and volume increases 20 percent;
4. Variable costs increase 5 percent, selling price reduced 15 percent, and volume increases 20 percent; and
5. Variable costs increase 10 percent, selling price raised 10 percent per unit with a volume decrease of 25 percent.

The results of these various sets of conditions may be summarized as follows:

1. (See Sales Line B.) If it is possible to decrease variable unit costs by 10 percent and volume will expand 20 percent without added marketing effort or price concessions, the net profit rate will jump to

Illustration 21–10

COST-VOLUME-PROFIT RELATIONSHIPS RESULTING IF VOLUMES, SALES PRICES, AND VARIABLE COSTS ARE CHANGED

	Budgeted Figures of Sales of 1,000,000 Units @ $8.00	SALES VOLUME INCREASES OF 20%				VOLUME DOWN 25%
		Variable Costs Decreased 10%		Variable Costs Increased 5%		Variable Costs Increased 10%
		No Change in Sales Price per Unit	Sales Price per Unit Decreased 8%	No Change in Sales Price per Unit	Sales Price per Unit Decreased 15%	Sales Price per Unit Increased 10%
Sales:						
1,000,000 @ $8.00	$8,000,000					
1,200,000 @ 8.00		$9,600,000		$9,600,000		
1,200,000 @ 7.36			$8,832,000			
1,200,000 @ 6.80					$8,160,000	
750,000 @ 8.80						$6,600,000
Sales income as projected	$8,000,000	$9,600,000	$8,832,000	$9,600,000	$8,160,000	$6,600,000
Variable costs:						
1,000,000 @ $4.80	$4,800,000					
1,200,000 @ 4.32		5,184,000	5,184,000			
1,200,000 @ 5.04				6,048,000	6,048,000	
750,000 @ 5.28						3,960,000
Marginal income or contribution margin	$3,200,000	$4,416,000	$3,648,000	$3,552,000	$2,112,000	$2,640,000
Fixed Costs	2,500,000	2,500,000	2,500,000	2,500,000	2,500,000	2,500,000
Net Income	$ 700,000	$1,916,000	$1,148,000	$1,052,000	($ 388,000)	$ 140,000
Management's analysis:						
Net income ratio (net income ÷ sales)	8.75%	19.96%	13.00%	10.96%	(4.75%)	2.1%
Percentage change in net income (budgeted figure equals 100%)	….	+274%	+164%	+150%	−155%	−80%
Marginal income ratio (marginal income ÷ sales)	40%	46%	41.3%	37%	25.9%	40%
Break-even sales amount (fixed cost ÷ P/V ratio)	$6,250,000	$5,435,000*	$6,053,000*	$6,756,000*	$9,652,000*	$6,250,000

* Approximate computation.
( )Loss.

Illustration 21–11

COST-VOLUME-PROFIT RELATIONSHIPS SHOWN GRAPHICALLY WITH
VARIOUS COMBINATIONS OF VOLUME, SELLING PRICES, AND
VARIABLE COSTS

Intersection of the Sales Line with the Horizontal (Zero) Line
Is the Break-Even Point of Sales

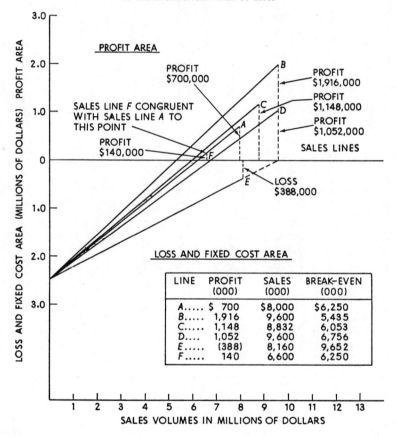

LINE	PROFIT (000)	SALES (000)	BREAK-EVEN (000)
A.....	$ 700	$8,000	$6,250
B.....	1,916	9,600	5,435
C.....	1,148	8,832	6,053
D....	1,052	9,600	6,756
E.....	(388)	8,160	9,652
F.....	140	6,600	6,250

19.96 percent on sales. The decrease in variable costs combines with
better utilization of existing facilities to make this possible.

2. (See Sales Line C.) A decrease in variable unit costs of 10 percent
makes possible a price reduction of 8 percent. With this price reduction the firm will be able to secure more readily a volume increase of
20 percent. This will produce a profit of $1,148,000, at a rate of 13
percent on sales.

3. If it is possible to increase sales volume 20 percent without any
change in selling price or shifts in promotional effort, it will be possible to increase the rate of net profit to 10.96 percent despite a variable
cost increase perhaps due to overtime or other causes.

4. If competitive pressures are likely to force a decline in unit selling price of 15 percent, the additional volume will result in a net loss. This firm with its present cost structure needs to secure a price of about $7.20 to cover variable cost per unit and the approximate fixed cost per unit at the anticipated level. Certain increases in variable costs incurred to produce the additional volume cause the loss to be $388,000.

5. If variable costs per unit will increase 10 percent due to new wage agreements or rising material prices, management may consider a price increase. If study shows that this will reduce volume by 25 percent, a profit of only $140,000, 2.1 percent of sales, will result.

If substantial changes in fixed costs are involved in any alternatives, then additional cost analysis would be necessary and separate charts would have to be prepared.

The trend of sales for individual products or the review of marketing plans by management may make a change in product mix likely. With cost of production data classified by types of product and shown on a direct costing basis, it is possible to determine those products which contribute most to the recovery of overhead and to the total profit of the business. Additional analyses and charts can be prepared to show the effect of planned shifts in product mix and volume with the related changes in variable unit costs and some fixed costs.

C-V-P ANALYSIS IN EVALUATING FEASIBLE PROFIT PLANS

In order to present an analysis involving a large number of changes, the following basic facts and circumstances are assumed for a hypothetical firm:

Estimated sales volume, 800,000 units at $10............	$8,000,000	100%
Less: Variable costs, 800,000 units at 4..............	3,200,000	40
Marginal income...	$4,800,000	60%
Less: Fixed costs	3,800,000	47½
Net Income..	$1,000,000	12½%

The firm has been experiencing a gradual increase in sales and is now operating at almost full capacity. The trend in sales volume is expected to continue. Management also recognizes the fact that the total demand for the type of product being sold is only partially satisfied and that several of its competitors also have substantial shares of the market. Management is trying to decide whether to continue its present policy of gradual growth and maintenance of its share of the market or to take a course involving more risk, that is, try to seize competitive leadership in price and volume.

In determining its objective for the coming year, the basic budget is used to assist in projecting the two plans which seem most feasible.

Alternative No. 1: This involves the following modifications of the budgeted facts:

Volume would increase 5 percent as it has in recent years with prices maintained at present levels.

Variable costs per unit would increase 5 percent.

Fixed costs would increase 2 percent.

In order to meet the normal growth in demand, the company expects to operate a half-day overtime on Saturday during part of the year. This will cause certain increases in variable labor and service costs and a slight increase in fixed costs.

Alternative No. 2: This involves the following modifications of the budgeted facts:

Prices would be decreased 10 percent.

Volume would increase 20 percent.

Variable costs per unit would decrease 5 percent.

Fixed costs would increase 8 percent.

In order to seize competitive leadership, the company would decrease prices 10 percent. The expectation is that this will result primarily in expanding total demand for the type of product, since competitors will probably react with their own price concessions. Yet management also expects to achieve good customer relations by initiating the price reductions and to obtain a small share of volume from its competitors by being the first to reduce prices. Some improvements to existing facilities and some additions of modern equipment are planned to meet the substantial increase in volume. These changes will increase fixed costs. Small savings from larger purchases of materials and from increased processing efficiency are expected to decrease variable costs per unit.

The cost-volume-profit analysis comparing the probable results of these two alternatives is shown in Illustration 21–12.

From a cost and income standpoint the first alternative produces more favorable results for the year ahead. Since its assumed conditions involve less departure from experienced sales trends and from known cost patterns, the projected figures should be very reliable. The second alternative, involving some expansion, raises the break-even point, but with the assumed volume still provides a fairly good profit. However, if there should be only a 10 percent increase in volume instead of the 20 percent shown in the analysis, the firm would find its profits reduced almost one half, to $472,000.

Before accepting the first alternative as the basis for its profit plan for

Illustration 21–12

COST-VOLUME-PROFIT RELATIONSHIPS RESULTING FROM POSSIBLE CHANGES IN
SALES VOLUMES, SALES PRICES, VARIABLE COSTS, AND FIXED COSTS

	Budgeted Figures	Situation No. 1	Situation No. 2
Sales:			
800,000 @ $10.00............................	$8,000,000		$8,640,000
960,000 @ 9.00............................			
840,000 @ 10.00............................		$8,400,000	
Variable costs:			
800,000 @ $4.00............................	3,200,000		
960,000 @ 3.80............................			3,648,000
840,000 @ 4.20............................		3,528,000	
Marginal income............................	$4,800,000	$4,872,000	$4,992,000
Fixed costs................................	3,800,000		
Plus 8%.................................			4,104,000
Plus 2%.................................		3,876,000	
Net Income...............................	$1,000,000	$ 996,000	$ 888,000
Net income ratio (sales ÷ profit).............	12½%	11.9%	10.3%
Percentage change in net income (budget equals 100%).................................		−0.4%	−11.2%
Marginal income ratio (marginal income ÷ sales).	60%	58.0%	57.8%
Break-even sales (fixed costs ÷ P/V ratio).......	$6,333,000	$6,683,000	$7,100,000

the coming year, management needs to examine all relevant circumstances. This is especially important since the firm and industry expect substantial steady growth. Questions such as the following need to be studied and their answers evaluated:

1. How soon would expansion be advisable if it is not undertaken this year?
2. Could a small amount of expansion for the coming year be done economically and be coordinated with the basic long-range plans for expansion?
3. Can competitive leadership be maintained, or will the reactions of competitors leave the firm in approximately the same relative position?
4. Are there any indications that competitors are making plans to grab the initiative?

When these and possibly other significant noncost factors have been reviewed, then management must make the decision which it believes will produce satisfactory profits in the year ahead and be most beneficial in the long run.

QUESTIONS FOR REVIEW

1. Why is it necessary to study the cost-volume-profit relationships? In estimating the overall volume objective of a firm, what factors must be considered? Why is the preparation of the cost-volume-profit considered a cooperative managerial project?

2. What relationship exists, if any, between an income statement prepared under direct costing and the break-even chart?

3. A break-even chart, as illustrated below, is a useful technique for showing the relationships between costs, volume, and profit. Identify the numbered components of the break-even chart. Discuss the significance of the concept *relevant range* to the break-even analysis.

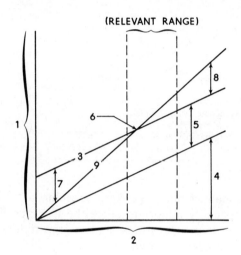

(RELEVANT RANGE)

(AICPA)

4. Under what conditions would a single break-even analysis be adequate for management guidance? When may management need a series of break-even analyses to assist in profit planning?

5. What will be the effect on the break-even point and margin of safety ratio if (a) there is a decrease in selling prices but no change in volume of sales, and (b) if there is an increase in the selling prices but no change in the volume of sales?

6. What is the effect on the break-even point when there is an increase in fixed costs? In variable costs?

7. The fixed costs of a firm are $60,000. When sales increased from $250,000 to $400,000, profits increased $90,000. How much would the profit increase if the sales were to increase to $600,000 from $250,000?

8. On sales of $3,000,000 the P-V ratio is 40 percent. If the sales prices were to decrease 15 percent, what must the sales volume be to earn the same dollar income?

9. Depreciation may be either a fixed cost or a variable cost. Do you agree? Explain.

10. The accounting records of the Wall-Ford Manufacturing Company indicated that the firm operated on a margin of safety ratio of 35 percent and a marginal income ratio of 45 percent. Fixed costs for the year were $450,000. What was the break-even sales volume? The total variable expenses for the year? The profit for the year?

PROBLEMS – GROUP A

Problem 21–1.   Purpose: *Cost-Volume-Profit Relationships*

The Allen Manufacturing Company has made the following information available for your analysis:

	1972	1973	1974
Sales..	$450,000	$500,000	$530,000
Cost of sales..	300,000	330,000	350,000
Gross margin	$150,000	$170,000	$180,000
Selling and administrative expenses.................	60,000	68,000	72,000
Operating Margin...	$ 90,000	$102,000	$108,000

There were no increases or decreases in prices or unit costs.

Required:
a) Compute the fixed costs for the firm.
b) Compute the break-even point for the company for each year.
c) If the federal and state corporation income taxes are 50 percent, what sales volume will realize a profit of $60,000 after taxes in 1973?
d) If sales prices increase 10 percent for 1974, what will the break-even point of sales be if other factors remain unchanged?

Problem 21–2.   Purpose: *Cost-Volume-Profit Relationships and Direct Costing*

The following data for the Ardenol Manufacturing Company are available:

Operating capacities:
Maximum productive capacity .... 200,000 units per year
Normal capacity...................................... 180,000 units per year
Standard variable costs:
Manufacturing costs...............................$ 12 per unit
Selling and administrative costs................   4 per unit
Fixed costs:
Manufacturing overhead 380,000
Selling and administrative costs................. 250,000
Sales price per unit   25
Operating results for the year:
Inventory at the beginning .... 16,000 units
Production for year................................. 160,000 units
Sales for year.. 150,000 units

Required:

a) What is the break-even amount of sales?
b) How many units must be sold to produce a net income of $90,000 before taxes?
c) How many units must be sold to earn a net income of 20% on sales before taxes?
d) If there were a net unfavorable variance from standard costs for the variable manufacturing costs of $35,000 and this variation is closed into the Cost of Sales account, prepare income statements for the year under conventional absorption costing and also for direct costing.

(Adapted from AICPA Uniform Examination)

Problem 21–3. Purpose: *Computation of Profit-Volume Relationships When There Are Changes in Prices and Volumes*

The normal operations of the Anoflex Corporation were as follows for the current year:

ANOFLEX CORPORATION
INCOME STATEMENT
For Year Ended December 31, 19—

Sales (300,000 Units at $3.00)	$900,000
Variable Cost of Sales, $1.50 Each	450,000
Marginal Income	$450,000
Fixed Costs of Sales	160,000
Net Income for the Year	$290,000

In planning for the operations for the coming year, management is desirous of learning the effect of various pricing and manufacturing changes on the net income for the period.

The plant is operating at 60 percent of capacity, so that it could use an increase in the volume of production with only these minor changes in the fixed costs:

1. An increase of 40,000 units of production would result in a $10,000 increase in fixed costs.
2. An increase of 80,000 units would increase the fixed costs by $12,000.
3. An increase of 100,000 or more units would increase the fixed costs by $15,000.

It is assumed that the following results would occur if prices were changed:

1. A 10 percent decrease in prices would result in a 15 percent increase in the volume of sales.
2. A 20 percent increase in price will result in a 40 percent decrease in the volume of sales.
3. A 25 percent decrease in prices would result in a 50 percent increase in volume of sales.
4. A 15 percent increase in price would result in a 15 percent decrease in the sales volume.

Required:

a) Prepare a comparative statement showing the effect on the net profit of each of the four situations.
b) Indicate the break-even point of sales for each situation.
c) Indicate the percentage change of net income from the current position.
d) Which situation is recommended for management use?

Problem 21–4.   Purpose: *Managerial Decisions Based upon Cost-Volume-Profit Relationships*

The management of the Allison Chemical Company has asked your help in arriving at certain managerial decisions affecting its sales and manufacturing operations of its newly developed cottonseed processing unit.

The company has facilities to process 26,000 tons of cottonseed per year. On the basis of scientific studies and test runs, it has ascertained that one ton of cottonseed will produce on average the following products:

	Average Yield per Ton of Cottonseed	Average Selling Prices per Trade Unit
Oil	350 lbs.	$ 0.22 per lb.
Meal.........................	600	60.00 per ton
Hulls	850	25.00 per ton
Lint..........................	100	3.00 per cwt.
Waste	100	0
	2,000 lbs.	

Under present market conditions, the firm feels that it can sell the entire output at current prices.

You have determined that the operating costs for the plant would be as follows:

```
Processing costs:
    Fixed ....................$120,000
    Variable.................     10 per ton of
                                    cottonseed processed
Marketing, all variable..      18 per ton sold
Administrative costs,
    all fixed .................  84,000 per year
```

Required:

a) Prepare a break-even statement for the firm if material costs are $70 per ton.
b) Compute the average maximum amount the company can afford to pay for a ton of cottonseed, so that the company will not have losses in excess of the operating costs if the plant were shut down, if the fixed costs would continue even if the plant is not operating.
c) Compute the maximum amount the company can pay for a ton of cottonseed if it is planned to have a profit of $250,000 before taxes.

(Adapted from AICPA Uniform Examination)

Problem 21–5. Purpose: *Income Statement; Computation of Break-Even Point Break-Even Chart*

The Ameur Manufacturing Company submits the following information concerning its operations for the six-month period ended December 31, 19—:

Inventory of finished goods, 7/1/—	$280,000
Stores inventory, 7/1/—	125,000
Stores purchased	920,000
Direct labor costs	800,000
Variable manufacturing overhead costs	150,000
Fixed manufacturing overhead costs	350,000
Variable selling and administrative costs	120,000
Fixed selling and administrative costs	200,000
Stores inventory, December 31	100,000
Indirect materials used included in the fixed and variable manufacturing overhead costs given above	15,000

There was no work-in-process at the beginning nor at the end of the period.
The finished goods inventory, December 31, 19—, was $500,000.
Sales for the six months totaled $2,660,000.
Federal and state corporation income taxes are calculated at 52 percent of net profit before taxes.
It is assumed that the profit and costs for materials and labor and manufacturing overhead will remain at the same rates as for the past six months, and that the initial finished goods inventory is representative of the costs that prevailed during the past six months and will continue on this basis in the future.

Required:
a) A statement showing the computation of the break-even point.
b) A break-even chart showing the break-even point based upon the six-month data.

PROBLEMS—GROUP B

Problem 21–6. Purpose: *Break-Even Computation; Direct Costing*

The Alear Manufacturing Company is interested in the computation of the break-even point of sales under varying conditions and the effect of direct costing on its income statements.

The following summarize the production data and costs for the year 1972:

Volume of production:
   Maximum productive capacity, 140,000 units
   Normal capacity, 120,000 units
   Production during 1972, 110,000 units
   Initial inventory, 5,000 units
Production cost data:
   Standard variable manufacturing costs, $8 per unit
   Fixed factory overhead, $240,000 per year
   Variable selling expenses, $2 per unit
   Fixed selling and administrative expenses, $168,000

Net unfavorable variances from manufacturing
costs are $26,000. These variances are
written off as an addition to the Cost of Sales.
Unit sales price, $30
Sales during 1972, 100,000 units.

Required:

*a)   What is the break-even point of sales in dollars?
*b)   What must the sales be to earn $40,000 before taxes?
*c)   How many *units* must be sold to earn 10% on sales?
 d)   Prepare income statements for 1972 —
        (1)   Under absorption costing.
        (2)   Under direct or variable costing.
 e)   Explain the reason for the difference in the income in the two income state-
        ments.

   * Omit consideration of variances from standard for (*a*), (*b*), and (*c*).

Problem 21–7.   Purpose: *Computation of Profit-Volume Relationships If Prices,
Volume of Sales, Fixed and Variable Costs All Were to Change; Computation of
Break-Even Point of Sales*

The Algeria Manufacturing Company is presently operating at 80 percent
capacity; and at such a level, it is producing and selling 160,000 units at $10 each.
It wants to make a study of the effect profitwise of a change in prices with the
resulting effects on profit — fixed and variable costs as indicated.

The income statement at 80 percent capacity is as follows:

ALGERIA MANUFACTURING COMPANY
INCOME STATEMENT
For Year Ended December 31, 19 —

	Fixed	Variable	
Sales, 160,000 Units at $10............................			$1,600,000
Cost of Sales:			
Direct Materials..		$240,000	
Direct Labor		320,000	
Variable Manufacturing Overhead.................		160,000	
Fixed Manufacturing Overhead.....................$400,000			
Totals..$400,000		$720,000	1,120,000
Gross Profit on Sales			$ 480,000
Selling and Administrative Costs:			
Fixed		$130,000	
Variable..		80,000	210,000
Net Income..			$ 270,000

If there is a decrease of 20 percent in the unit price, sales volume will increase
to 175,000 units, variable costs will increase *in total* only 5 percent with the increased production, and fixed costs, both manufacturing and selling and administrative, will increase 2 percent.

If there is an increase in the price of 15 percent, sales volume will drop to 145,000 units, variable costs will increase 2 percent *per unit for each element of variable cost,* but fixed costs will remain the same.

Selling expenses are expected to be 15 percent of sales, and profit is to amount to $1.02 per unit.

Required:

a) Compute the selling price per unit.

b) Project an income statement for the year.

c) Compute a break-even point expressed in dollars and in units assuming that overhead and administrative expenses are fixed but that other costs are fully variable.

(Adapted from AICPA Uniform Examination)

Problem 21–8. Purpose: *CPA Problem Involving the Analysis of Operating Results Using Principles of Cost-Volume-Profit Relationships*

Management of the Atterbury Manufacturing Company is concerned because its gross profit has decreased from $130,000 in 1972 to $87,960 in 1973.

An investigation discloses the following information:

| | Plant No. 1 (Makes a Variety of Products) | | Plant No. 2 (Makes Only One Product) | | | |
| | | | 1973 | | 1972 | |
	1973	1972	Amount	Per Unit	Amount	Per Unit
Sales	$200,000	$300,000	$112,200	$10.20	$100,000	$10.00
Cost of Sales	160,000	210,000	64,240	5.84	60,000	6.00
Gross Profit.........	$ 40,000	$ 90,000	$ 47,960	$ 4.36	$ 40,000	$ 4.00

Each of the two plants are operated as separate units.

Required:

Prepare a detailed analysis of the causes for change in gross profit for each of the plants to the extent that the above data permits such an analysis.

(Adapted from AICPA Uniform Examination)

Problem 21–9. Purpose: *Determining Unit Sales Prices Assuming a Change in Profitability Factors*

The Avenida Manufacturing Company produces a domestic automatic humidifier. The costs for each unit were:

```
        Materials .....................................................$50
        Direct labor ................................................  30
        Overhead 100 percent of direct labor.................  30
        Interest on bank loans equivalent to a
           per unit charge of........................................   1
        Federal income tax estimated on a per
           unit basis ................................................  15
```

Effective in the new year starting July 1, material costs decreased 5 percent and direct labor costs increased 20 percent. Interest on the bank loan increased from 4 percent to 5 percent starting with July 1.

Required:

a) Assuming no change in the rate of overhead in relation to direct labor costs, compute the sales price per unit. Present sales price is $200 per unit on sales of 50 units.
b) Assuming that $10 of the overhead costs are fixed costs, compute the sales price per unit that will produce the same ratio of gross profit.

(Adapted from AICPA Uniform Examination)

Problem 21–10.   Purpose: *Computation of the Profit-Volume Relationship If Prices Decrease and the Volume Increases; Computation of the Break-Even Point of Sales*

The Ahone Manufacturing Company is presently operating at 60 percent of capacity and producing 120,000 units of a single product it sells for $6 each. For the current year, the results have been as follows:

AHONE MANUFACTURING COMPANY
INCOME STATEMENT
For Year Ended December 31, 19—

	Fixed	Variable	
Sales, 120,000 units at $6.............................			$720,000
Cost of Sales:			
Direct materials..		$120,000	
Direct labor		240,000	
Variable manufacturing overhead..................		60,000	
Fixed manufacturing overhead $90,000			
Totals..$90,000	$90,000	$420,000	510,000
Gross Profit on Sales....................................			$210,000
Selling and Administrative Expenses:			
Fixed...		$ 48,000	
Variable..		24,000	
Total			72,000
Net Income			$138,000

If sales price per unit could be reduced by 20 percent, the volume of sales would increase to 185,000 units with only a $3,000 increase in the fixed overhead costs.

If prices could be reduced as much as 25 percent, sales volume would reach 195,000 units with an increase in the fixed overhead costs of only $4,000.

Required:

a) Prepare comparative income statements showing the net income under the new profit-volume relationships.
b) Indicate the break-even sales point in each of the above illustrations.

chapter 22

Cost Analyses for
Special Purposes

MANAGEMENT NEEDS COST INFORMATION FOR DIFFERENT PURPOSES

The numerous responsibilities of management require frequent reference to detailed quantitative information, much of which can be provided by an effective cost accounting system. Thus, from the viewpoint of management, a cost system becomes one of the chief facilitating devices in the direction and control of the enterprise. It is unfortunate that much too frequently costs are designed primarily for financial statement presentation and are woefully inadequate when used as the basis for deciding alternative courses of action. Fortunately, this has been changing in recent years.

In preceding chapters it has been shown that historical cost information can provide certain types of usefulness — support for financial and operating statements, measurement of cost performance for each functional subunit of the firm, and data to assist in cost control. Through proper functionalization and detailed classification it has been shown that each type of cost can be studied in relation to a productivity measure appropriate to its function in order to derive a reasonably accurate pattern of behavior for the cost. This serves as the point of departure for establishing the probable amount of this type of cost in the year ahead, taking into account internal as well as external factors which might modify the amount of cost to be incurred. Following this type of approach, expected future or replacement costs are estimated for each cost element in order to prepare flexible budgets and standard costs. Through the use of these "should be" costs, as expressed in flexible budgets and standards, it has been possible to determine more timely and valid measurements of performance, more timely cost information to serve many purposes, and more effective cost control. In addition, the techniques have been described for deriving and presenting the probable future costs for alternative production and marketing plans for the firm as a whole. In providing the foregoing types of usefulness, the preceding chapters have dealt primarily with certain classifications of past costs and their counterparts in future costs.

Assuming several general plans of action had been selected by management as feasible, Chapter 21 dealt with the derivation and presentation of costs in cost-volume-profit analyses so that management could make informed decisions as to the best profit plan for the firm in the year ahead. This chapter deals with the use of costs in making *specific* operating decisions related to production or marketing and in the preparation of special studies which will provide the type of quantitative information which will help management select, from alternative ways of accomplishing some specific production or distribution objective, the one which is most economical or makes the most satisfactory profit contribution.

In operating the modern multiple-product enterprise, the alternatives available are so varied that different concepts of cost are needed for significant comparison and evaluation. Book figures usually do not measure these alternatives correctly, but they do provide the basic data (types of cost elements involved, rough indication of magnitude, and pattern of cost behavior) for building the cost estimates to fit the management need. The better the records available, the more time can be spent by the cost accountant in constructive interpretation and projection. The ability to arrive at proper conclusions depends very much on the reliability of the source data, subject to the degree of care exercised in the establishment of cost centers and flexibility to change cost centers and costs in line with changes in activity in the cost center.

Cost information for decision making requires an understanding of some additional cost concepts and combinations of cost data. Cost has meaning only in terms of specific objectives and specific problems. Cost as a generic term has substantially different meanings in accounting and in economics. Each of these areas of knowledge deals with more than one cost concept. This means that the type of cost concept or concepts being used in facilitating the achievement of any management goal must be carefully identified by appropriate descriptive adjectives. The management use that is to be made of cost data governs the kind and combination of costs which are to be included. It is the responsibility of the cost accountant to determine clearly the use to be made of his reports. He may then proceed with the selection of the type of cost data which will be most reliable and helpful to management in making a particular decision.

SPECIAL DECISION-MAKING COST ANALYSES

Some additional concepts of cost useful for decision-making purposes are described in this chapter. How they are designed to guide management in making specific decisions is illustrated later.

Differential Costs. Differential costs can be helpful in determining the effect on profits of changing sales volume; changing product mix; in making pricing decisions; in deciding whether to make or buy equipment, parts, or materials; and in comparing production methods. The usual meaning is that these are the costs which change from one level of activity to another, or it might refer to the combined *effect* of these individual cost changes, that is, the difference in total cost at one volume and total cost at another volume. If an increase in activity is being studied, they may be referred to as incremental costs; if a decrease in activity is being studied, they may be referred to as avoidable costs. This term sometimes is used to embrace those changes in cost occurring from one point in time to another (commonly from present period to the coming year) because of the changes in prices of the firm's productive factors and with, or without, a change in volume or product mix. Another use of the term is to refer to the differences in the cost of employing one specific method as opposed to another method to accomplish some productive or distributive objective. Distributive and general administrative costs, as well as productive costs, are often involved as differential costs. Mostly variable, semivariable, and semifixed costs are included in a differential cost analysis; but fixed costs may also be involved in certain changes in activity, changes from one time to another, or one method to another.

Traceable Costs. Those costs which are traceable directly to a job or product, a cost center, department, or operating division of a firm are referred to as traceable costs. It is obviously necessary to know whether a product or an operating division is involved as the objective of the tracing since the traceable costs of product will be different from the traceable costs of an operating division. It is not necessary that *all* costs be completely traceable for this distinction to be useful to management. For accurate costing and measurement of performance on jobs, products, cost centers, departments, or divisions, the more costs that are traceable, the more valid and useful the measurement. For example, a multiproduct firm may incur some common manufacturing costs on the various products, but the costs may differ considerably from product to product in other manufacturing and marketing processes. Information on traceable costs is significant in such decisions as adding or subtracting from a product line, product pricing, or modifying product merchandising effort.

Replacement Cost. The cost which attaches here may be selected from a contemporary market or from some anticipated future market. The contemporary market concept is widely used in financial accounting through the application of the "lower of cost or market" principle to obtain the valuation of certain current assets. It may also be used in certain interpretive statements to obtain a restatement of expenses in "real cost" terms. The cost of replacement in the coming year's market is widely used in cost accounting for budget preparation and setting standards. The cost of replacement projected two or more years into the future may become important for certain management purposes, especially capital budgeting (the planning of plant and equipment improvements, additions, replacements, and retirements).

Opportunity Cost. This represents the measurable advantage (some opportunity to obtain a differential or marginal income) foregone in the past or that may be sacrificed as a result of the rejection of alternative uses of material, labor, or facilities. Opportunity cost is often included as an imputed cost in comparing certain proposals for improving profits. It is used in cost accounting systems where decentralization of operations and authority have taken place and measurement of profit performance is made by operating divisions within the company. Its use in this situation places each individual organizational unit in the same position that it would occupy if it were an independent business rather than an operating component of an integrated enterprise.

Imputed Cost. An imputed cost is the dollar amount assigned for the use of any productive service which has not been the subject of an independent transaction between supplier and user to establish a liability or cause a cash outlay. Therefore it is not precisely measurable. It can be inferred or estimated from similar situations outside the firm. Opportunity costs are often imputed in certain comparisons to give a proper presentation of the costs of alternatives.

Sunk Cost. This is the amount invested in a tangible productive asset, an intangible right, or some extended contract for service which can only be recovered by use of the asset over its service life, or the use of a service over the term of the contract. Sunk cost is an invested cost or recorded cost. Future costs are subject to the decision of management and are controllable, whether basically of a fixed or variable nature, until a firm financial investment or commitment is made.

Out-of-Pocket Cost. Those elements of cost which have required, or will require, cash disbursement in the period under consideration are designated as out-of-pocket costs. Many fixed costs, such as taxes, insurance, supervisory salaries, as well as most variable, semivariable, and semifixed costs, are out-of-pocket costs.

Planning and decision-making costs involve primarily traceable, differential costs priced on a replacement dollar basis. In addition, certain imputed costs, or opportunity costs, must often be included to make proper cost constructions for guiding management. These will be illustrated in the section entitled "Different Analyses for Different Purposes."

IMPORTANCE OF DEFINING THE PROBLEM

Before any reliable cost or income information can be developed, the several proposed courses of action which management believes are feasible must be clearly defined. A searching examination of each proposal must be made to determine its impact on the firm in terms of functions affected, time commitment, and its relationship to other management plans. For example, many firms are faced with the problem of more complete utilization of facilities when sales drop. The management alternatives in this instance probably include:

1. To work on quality and design improvement of present product and on improving the efficiency of certain operations.
2. To make, rather than buy, certain component parts for production of present product.
3. To begin the production of new product which has favorable marketing prospects.
4. To solicit special order work where the skilled labor and equipment facilities are such that they will be able to satisfy the expected custom demands.

To explore the effect of any of the foregoing proposals, a number of questions must be answered. Which departments will be affected directly and which indirectly? Will changes in cost type or cost level occur in affected departments? Even without careful definition, out-of-pocket costs such as material, labor, certain utilities, and operating supplies would be included in the cost analysis for each alternative. However, investigation may reveal other costs that need to be recognized in preparing a complete analysis. In order to clearly picture the impact of a proposal, questions such as the following should be asked: What will be the effect on material unloading and handling costs? On inspection costs? On maintenance and repair costs? On engineering costs? On setup costs? On costs of maintaining payroll and labor cost records? On production planning costs? On supervisory costs?

In order to reap cost-saving or income advantages, certain proposals may have to be adopted for a trial period. If any substantial investment in modification of existing equipment or acquisition of new equipment is contemplated, the time commitment is important and would have to be known before the analysis for that alternative could be completed. A specific trial period is frequently assigned to production of new product.

The relationship of each proposal to other management plans must be examined because it may be found that certain proposals either fit rather closely to tentative future plans or will keep the firm in a more flexible position for future change. The estimated costs of discontinuance or reconversion in certain instances may be small, while for other proposals they may be substantial enough to include in the analysis. For example, the alternative to make parts may conflict with the alternative to begin production of new product which is part of the long-range planning program. Therefore, in connection with the second alternative we may have to take into account the prospect of early discontinuance or the fact that after a few years facilities would have to be expanded to continue production of the parts.

When each individual proposal is thus examined and more clearly understood, it can be clearly defined. Cost and income analyses may then be properly prepared.

DIFFERENT ANALYSES FOR DIFFERENT PURPOSES

It has been emphasized that there is no one concept or combination of cost data that will satisfy all the requirements of management. To determine what items should be included in a specific cost analysis, the cost accountant must be familiar with the present and probable future operating conditions of the firm and the purpose for which a particular cost measurement is to be made. Examples which illustrate typical situations in which specific managerial problems require cost data will now be discussed. These analyses will involve *comparisons* of one set of cost figures with another set of cost figures for an alternative solution or the *comparison* of the marginal income − additional income derived less additional cost incurred in deriving that income − of one proposal with that of an alternative proposal. In comparing alternatives it is usually neither necessary nor advisable to present an analysis showing full cost for each alternative. Only those elements of cost which are expected to be different for the one alternative as compared to the other should be included, i.e., *relevant costs*. Costs which will not be affected by the decision to be made are irrelevant and are preferably excluded from the analysis so that the significant cost data may be highlighted. Consequently, *differential costs* may be the most useful in preparing suitable comparative cost analyses for management. The following illustrations describe how differential and comparative cost analyses may be prepared to assist management in selecting those proposals that will contribute most effectively to the profit plan of the firm.

ACCEPTANCE OF ADDITIONAL VOLUME

To demonstrate the nature of differential costs, several illustrations are given; and the results will be shown under both the traditional cost procedure and the differential cost procedure. In the first illustration, it is assumed that:

The plant is not operating at full capacity. In this instance, 80 percent capacity is used and volume of production is 240,000 units. The *fixed* overhead cost is $180,000 under present operating conditions. The *variable* costs per unit are:

Direct materials	$1.50
Direct labor	2.00
Variable overhead costs	0.50
Total variable costs	$4.00
Fixed overhead per unit, ($180,000 ÷ 240,000 units)	0.75
Total Cost per Unit	$4.75

An offer is received from a foreign importer to buy 60,000 units at $4.30 per unit. Management hesitates to accept this offer because this price is less than the total cost per unit as computed under the usual costing method, and also because the current selling price is $5.25.

In solving this problem, it is assumed that the fixed overhead costs will not increase because with this order the production of the firm will be expanded to, but not beyond, 100 percent capacity. Fixed selling and administrative costs under present scheduled production total $82,000, and this figure will not be affected by the additional production.

It is immediately apparent that if management were to make a decision based upon traditional cost accounting, the order would be rejected because the per unit cost of manufacturing is $4.75, and any sale at $4.30 would result in a *per unit loss of 45 cents*. Using differential cost analysis, an income statement in comparative form—with and without the foreign order—would be prepared as shown in Illustration 22–1.

The results in this statement indicate that under the assumed conditions the foreign order should be accepted because:

1. The differential income derived from the additional volume will increase total net income by $18,000.
2. The total average cost, including selling and administrative costs, will be reduced from $5.09 to $4.87. This permits an adequate profit margin since the average sales price of the entire production is $5.06.

Illustration 22–1

ANY COMPANY

COMPARATIVE INCOME STATEMENT
SHOWING DIFFERENTIAL INCOME AND DIFFERENTIAL COSTS

For Period Ended June 30, 19—

	Current Business	Additional Sales	Total
Sales:			
240,000 units @ $5.25..................	$1,260,000		
60,000 units @ 4.30..................		$258,000*	$1,518,000
Variable costs:			
240,000 units @ $4.00..................	960,000		
60,000 units @ 4.00..................		240,000†	1,200,000
Marginal income or contribution margin....	$ 300,000	$ 18,000	$ 318,000
Fixed costs.............................	180,000		180,000
Gross profit on sales.....................	$ 120,000	$ 18,000	$ 138,000
Selling and administrative costs...........	82,000		82,000
Net Income for Period....................	$ 38,000	$ 18,000	$ 56,000

* Differential sales.
† Differential cost (considers only the variable costs).

It should be indicated at this point that the reason for the differential profit is that the *regular* sales price was not affected by the foreign order. If *all* prices had to be reduced to $4.30 per unit because of the acceptance of the foreign order, the result would be a loss of $172,000 for the firm as a whole. It is only when two separate markets exist for the product or where price discriminations can be made between buyers that the differential cost approach is important in pricing. In the long run, the total average selling price must be higher than the total average cost. Assuming acceptance of the foreign order, note that the total average selling price in the comparative income statement, $5.06, is higher than the total average cost, $4.87 ($1,462,000 divided by 300,000 units). The total average cost will be reduced by acceptance of the foreign order from $5.09 to $4.87 because of better utilization of the fixed production, selling, and administrative facilities. Where plants are operating at less than full capacity and the market is not completely and freely competitive, *differential,* not average, costs should be used to determine whether or not a particular order should be accepted.

A second type of differential cost analysis projects operating business conditions at various stepped-up production levels. The rate of change in variable costs will not remain the same as production increases or decreases. As has been stated previously, increased production may change the per unit variable costs because of lower material prices due to large-scale purchases; higher or lower direct labor costs due to incentive systems, overtime, spoilage; lower variable indirect costs such as power because of increased volume of consumption; and so on. The differential cost analysis can be projected at various levels. Many decisions can be reached by merely inspecting the variable costs and comparing them with the differential sales, assuming the rate of change for incurring variable cost does not increase or decrease substantially. However, it is possible that a substantial increase in the rate of incurring variable costs may occur when production reaches such a level that it may require overtime or it may result in greater waste and spoilage.

In this illustration the following is assumed:

A company is operating at 60 percent capacity, with production at this level of 24,000 units and fixed overhead of $12,000. Fixed selling and administrative costs amount to $14,000. Present selling prices per unit are $4.

A customer offers to purchase increasing quantities during the current year at the following prices:

> First 6,000 additional units at $3.00
> Next 6,000 additional units at   2.50
> Next 6,000 additional units at   2.00

Should the orders be accepted? The variable costs under present production schedules show a per unit cost of $2, viz:

> Direct materials $1.00
> Direct labor.......................... 0.60
> Variable overhead................. 0.40
> $2.00

A comparison of these figures and the offered selling prices indicates that the first two lots could be accepted profitably if the anticipated sales did not interfere with the present market. For the first two lots the customer offers $3 and $2.50, respectively, while the differential unit cost is only $2. But these decisions are based upon the fact that the variable costs will not change with the increased production. Let us assume further, however, that conditions are not static and that the changes in the variable costs due to the aforementioned labor, materials, and overhead factors are as follows:

First order of 6,000, no change in rate of incurring variable costs; additional variable costs, $12,000.

Next order of 6,000, some variable costs incurred at reduced rates; additional variable costs, $10,800.

And the third order of 6,000 units involves some overtime and additional costs so that additional variable costs for this order would be $15,060.

Information on the changing pattern of differential costs as the firm approaches its 40,000-unit (100 percent) capacity will make it possible for management to see at a glance that the third lot of 6,000 would not be profitable. For the third lot the differential income is $12,000, while the differential costs have risen to $15,060.

For management consideration the relevant cost and income information could be presented effectively in a comparative and cumulative statement as shown in Illustration 22–2.

Illustration 22–2
STATEMENT OF DIFFERENTIAL COST ANALYSIS

Quantity of Output	Cost of Output		Cumulative Average Cost Per Unit	Selling Prices		Net Income	
	Total	Per Unit		Total	Per Unit	Per Lot	Cumulative
24,000.......	$60,000.00	$2.50*	$2.50	$ 96,000.00	$4.00	$36,000.00	$36,000.00
6,000.......	12,000.00	2.00†	2.40	18,000.00	3.00	6,000.00	42,000.00
6,000.......	10,800.00	1.80†	2.30	15,000.00	2.50	4,200.00	46,200.00
6,000.......	15,060.00	2.51†	2.33	12,000.00	2.00	(3,060.00)‡	43,140.00
42,000.......	$97,860.00		$2.33	$141,000.00	$3.36§		$43,140.00

* Includes variable plus fixed costs.
† Includes only variable costs.
‡ Loss.
§ Approximate figure.

STATEMENT OF DIFFERENTIAL COSTS OF ADDED PRODUCTION

Variable Costs	Volume of Production (in Units)			
	24,000	6,000 Added	12,000 Added	18,000 Added
Direct Material..............	$24,000.00	$ 6,000.00	$11,760.00	$17,600.00
Direct Labor.................	14,400.00	3,600.00	7,100.00	11,500.00
Direct Variable Overhead......	9,600.00	2,400.00	3,940.00	8,760.00
	$48,000.00	$12,000.00	$22,800.00	$37,860.00
Fixed Overhead Costs.........	12,000.00			
Totals.....................	$60,000.00	$12,000.00	$22,800.00	$37,860.00
Number of Units..............	24,000	6,000	12,000	18,000
Differential Costs per Unit......		$2.00	$1.90	$2.10

Interpreting this statement, it should be noted that:

1. If production were to be increased 6,000 over the present 24,000, any sales over the differential cost figure of $2 per unit would be profitable; but if computed on the average or traditional cost basis, it would appear that the sales price of the entire production in a competitive market would have to be above $2.40 to be profitable.
2. If production were to be increased 12,000 over the present production of 24,000, the unit sales price of this additional production would have to be more than $1.90. On the average or traditional cost basis it would appear that the sales price would have to be above $2.30 for the entire lot to be profitable.
3. If production were to be increased 18,000 units over the present volume of 24,000 units, the unit sales price of this additional production on a *differential* cost basis would have to be above $2.10 per unit to be profitable. On the average cost basis it would appear that the entire lot would have to be sold at a price above $2.33 to be profitable.
4. On a differential cost basis, it would not be profitable to accept the order for the last 6,000 because it would result in a loss of $3,060, decreasing the cumulative profit from $46,200 to $43,140.

A serious limitation of cost analysis is that management may go overboard in using differential costing and a company could find itself in financial difficulty. Profits will be increased or losses minimized in the short run if differential costs are covered and something is left over to contribute to fixed costs. The assumption generally made is that differential costing applies to the increment only. For example, assume a company manufactures and sells one product with the following cost:

Materials, 1 unit at $5.00	$ 5.00
Labor, 2 hours at $3.50	7.00
Overhead:	
Variable, 2 hours at $2.00	4.00
Fixed, 2 hours at $1.75	3.50
	$19.50

The fixed costs for the period are expected to amount to $35,000 at a normal capacity of 10,000 units. The normal sales price is $27, and the company expects to sell 7,000 during the period. A special order for 2,000 units could be obtained at a sales price of $17. If the company accepts the order, $2,000 ($1 per unit × 2,000 units) will be the amount contributed to fixed costs and profit. However, if *all* of the business is accepted at $17 per unit, *all* of the costs would not be covered; and although a company might minimize losses in the short run, the full $19.50 must be covered in the long run. Management must be sure to keep this in mind. Differential cost analysis is useful for increments only; the thing to avoid is calling all of the sales "incremental," i.e., every salesman brings in every order at $17!

OPERATION VERSUS PLANT SHUTDOWN

Many executives might feel that a plant shutdown is better than operating continuously at a loss, but a differential cost analysis will prove that often this is not so. For example, assume that the American Sewing Machine Company for many years has had a successful product but in recent years competition with foreign products manufactured at lower labor costs has caused it to operate at a loss. The firm has been trying to diversify its manufacturing operations and is seeking new products since it foresees no change in the competitive market. The firm is now faced with the problem of shutting down completely until new products and plant facilities can be developed or of continuing to operate at a loss, thus keeping together its skilled labor force. The primary information needed to solve this problem involves a comparison between the probable loss at the anticipated low level of operations and the loss that would be suffered if the plant shut down temporarily. Data obtained from the records and from management estimates are:

Normal capacity of plant	120,000 machines per year
Fixed costs when plant is operating	$150,000
Fixed costs when plant is shut down	100,000
Variable costs per machine (direct labor, direct material, and variable overhead)	40
Estimated selling price to meet foreign competition	46
Estimated sales volume at new selling price	10,000 machines

Using this information a brief statement can be prepared to show the *differential costs* and the probable net loss if the firm continues to operate:

Fixed costs if plant is operating		$150,000
Less:		
Differential income: 10,000 × $46	$460,000	
Differential costs: 10,000 × $40	400,000	
Differential income		60,000
Loss If Plant Is Operated at 8⅓% Capacity		$ 90,000

If the plant closed down, the loss due to fixed charges would be $100,000; whereas if it operated at a small capacity, the loss would only be $90,000. The plant operating at this small capacity would suffer a smaller loss and would be able to retain most of its skilled labor force and management personnel.

The Grand Department Store has been maintaining, among others, a silverware department and a luggage department. A well-known company which retails television sets wishes to lease space in the department store to display and sell its line. It has offered an annual rental of $3,600 for the space now occupied by the luggage and/or $4,500 for the space now used by the silverware department on a lease agreement which is to run for five years. The department store is undecided whether to accept or reject the offer in view of last year's profits, which are representative of the usual results of the two departments in question. The silverware department has shown a net income, after distributing all actual expenses, of $6,000; while the luggage department shows a net income of $4,500. Should the Grand Department Store lease the space of either of these two departments and if so which one?

The profitability of these departments has been determined after proper tracing of all actual costs for which a reliable measure of assignment has been established. It would seem at first glance that neither of the present departments should be discontinued so as to lease the space, but in this case the "actual" costs do not reflect the alternative involved. In order to get a clear picture of what is involved, it is necessary to "impute" charges to these two departments. First, consider the rental income which might be obtained as against the present net income of the departments:

	Silverware	Luggage
Profits, per books	$6,000	$4,500
Imputed rent expense	4,500	3,600
Net Income	$1,500	$ 900

In addition to the rent, consider also the fact that the Grand Department Store has capital invested in the inventories and fixtures of these departments which would be available for other uses if the departments were closed. A fair estimate of current values of inventory and fixtures in the two departments reveals:

	Silverware	Luggage
Inventory (average for year)	$20,000	$6,000
Fixtures (present values)	8,500	2,000
Total Invested Capital	$28,500	$8,000

Computing imputed interest at 6 percent on the investment changes the basis of comparison to:

	Silverware	Luggage
Profits, per books	$6,000	$4,500
Imputed rent	4,500	3,600
	$1,500	$ 900
Interest on investment	1,710	480
Net	($ 210) Loss	$ 420 Profit

The Grand Department Store should on this basis discontinue the silverware department, for it will be better off by $210 per year to lease the space than to operate the department. The luggage department, however, should not be closed, for the potential rental income and funds released for other purposes are not sufficient by $420 to offset the present profits. The luggage department is producing $420 a year *more* income by not leasing the space.

Imputed costs may be continuously charged to cost accounts if for purposes of efficiency measurement it becomes advisable to do so. Such procedure need not affect the general books of account. Department charges for interest on investment may be credited to a special income account—Imputed Interest on Investment—which can be used to offset the overstatement of cost from a financial point of view.

EQUIPMENT REPLACEMENT PROBLEMS

Comparative cost analyses may also be used in connection with equipment replacement decisions. Company E has been using a machine for five years. It was estimated that the machine, purchased for $45,000, could be used for 10 years. The annual costs of operation of this machine are as follows:

Direct labor	$ 4,800
Taxes	800
Repairs	200
Supplies	550
Depreciation	4,500
Power	1,810
Apportioned charges:	
Indirect labor	520
Building expense, 100 square feet	300
Total	$13,480

A new semiautomatic machine is now on the market, priced at $45,000 and with the same potential output, 10,000 units per year. However, certain cost savings are claimed for the new machine. Its estimated operating costs are:

Direct labor	$ 500
Taxes	1,200
Repairs (estimated)	250
Supplies	600
Depreciation	4,500
Power	1,600
Apportioned charges:	
Indirect labor	430
Building expense, 150 square feet	450
Total	$9,530

Although the old machine will still function for another five years, the question arises as to whether the company should dispose of the old machine (which can be disposed of *now* for $1,500) and buy the new one.

The alternative in this situation is not adequately depicted by the foregoing cost schedules. We have the alternative not of *buying* one machine *or* the other but rather that of *keeping* the old machine or *acquiring* the new one.

This situation is more adequately portrayed if we recognize that the value of the old machine is a "sunk" or irrecoverable cost and consider only the "out-of-pocket" costs, i.e., the future costs of the two alternatives. A more nearly accurate comparison of relative cost is obtained by:

	Keep *Old Machine*	*Acquire* *New Machine*
Direct labor	$4,800	$ 500
Taxes	800	1,200
Repairs	200	250
Supplies	550	600
Depreciation	300	4,500*
Power	1,810	1,600
Indirect labor	520	430
Building expense	300	450
Total	$9,280	$9,530

* Many firms would use either a sum-of-years'-digits method or a fixed-percent-of-diminishing-value method. This would result in a much larger charge for depreciation the first year.

These schedules of cost result in an entirely different picture. The depreciation charge on the old machine does not enter into the computations of cost in this case, except for the amortization over five years of the $1,500 sacrificed by keeping the old machine. The $300 per year is an *opportunity cost,* the cost of rejecting the opportunity to realize $1,500 on replacement.

However, the foregoing is not yet a completely accurate comparison, for there is another factor which has not yet been considered in these schedules—the investment involved in the purchase of the new machine. This would require a net outlay of $43,500 ($45,000 − $1,500, value of old machine). Regardless of where these funds are obtained, the investment of $43,500 involves an important factor. If we have the cash on hand, we can invest it in securities or other income-producing assets rather than buy the new machine; the income that might be received is *sacrificed* in purchasing the new machine. If we borrow the money to buy the new machine, we shall have to sacrifice cash to pay interest for the use of it. Therefore, we should add to the annual operating costs of the new machine an *imputed cost* for using $43,500 in this way. This cost is often imputed at the going rate, e.g., 4 percent, to recognize this aspect of the situation. This amounts to $1,740 ($43,500 × 0.04). However, if the present earning power of the firm's assets is higher, e.g., 10 percent, this rate should be used:

	4%	10%
Annual cost, new machine, including imputed interest	$11,270	$13,880
Annual cost, old machine	9,280	9,280
Annual saving by *keeping* old machine	$ 1,990	$ 4,600

Obviously, we should *not* buy the new machine under the present circumstances.

Suppose that additional alternatives were available to Company E. The company can continue to buy its power from the local utility or it may build a power plant to manufacture its own. Each year the company spends $260,000 on light and power.

The cost of building a power plant would be $1,000,000, and engineers estimate the plant could be used for 25 years before it became obsolete. Operating costs, including interest costs on expected borrowings to finance the $1,000,000, are expected to average $100,000 per year before depreciation. The combined federal and state tax is 50 percent.

The acquisition of the power plant should result in the following *annual* savings:

Cost of purchased power	$260,000
Operating expenses of power plant	$100,000
Depreciation of power plant	40,000
Savings before tax	$120,000
Tax	60,000
Savings after Tax (Operating Advantage)	$ 60,000

The *payback period* is Investment/Savings + Depreciation:

$$\frac{\$1,000,000}{\$60,000 + \$40,000} = 10 \text{ years.}$$

The *time adjusted rate of return* is computed with the use of the table on page 455. The $1,000,000 investment will return $100,000 in new cash ($40,000 depreciation plus $60,000 savings) in each of 25 years. To reduce to $1 so that the table may be used, $10 of investment is needed for each $1 received annually for 25 years. The table shows that 10.675 is equal to 8 percent and 9.077 is equal to 10 percent. Ten dollars would be equal to approximately 9 percent.

If management of Company E can earn more than 9 percent on alternate investments with comparable risk, the power plant should not be built. If, however, alternatives yield less, the power plant proposal might be accepted.

Another use of comparative costs is found in those firms that manufacture materials or parts which are subsequently used in the production of other products. The materials thus used to make the final finished products might profitably be purchased from other suppliers at less than it would cost to produce the materials or parts in the manufacturer's own plant. This lower cost may be due to the greater specialization or larger volume of the potential supplier of the materials to be used in manufacturing the finished salable products. The manufacturer is faced with the problem of how to determine whether to produce the materials or parts in his own plant or to buy them from outside suppliers. Again, profitability of business operations is the major determining factor.

To illustrate *one method* of solving this problem and answering the question, a woolen company is used and its procedures discussed.

The Woolen-Worsted Company buys raw wool fleeces and processes this material by washing, drying, carding, spinning, and dyeing before knitting the wool into sweaters, gloves, and other finished products. These operations (except the various knitting and finishing operations) result in a series of products which could be sold at the completion of each of several processes. Washed and carded wool and spun yarn and dyed yarn are "products" in their own right.

The company wishes to make certain that the product of no process be allowed to cost more than the amount at which the goods could be purchased at that stage. In fact, it expects that a process justify its continued operation by showing total costs at the completion of the process less than the amount at which similar goods could be purchased. How can this control be achieved in the cost accounts?

The procedure used is known as "*opportunity*" *cost* procedure. Goods are charged to the first process at market price; and transfers made to the next process are valued at market price of similar goods, the difference being credited to a Departmental Profit account. It is true that for income measurement purposes such profits are not realized and therefore adjustments will have to be made; but, nevertheless, control is achieved by using this method, which is effective and inexpensive. The departmental profits or losses will have to be eliminated against inventories and cost of goods sold when financial statements are prepared for publication.

The procedure may be made clearer by exhibiting the Spinning and Dyeing Process accounts in skeleton form:

Spinning

Carded wool (at market price)	10,000	To Spinning Department,	
Labor costs (actual)	2,000	Revenue and Expense	20,000
Factory overhead (actual)	8,000	(Profit and Loss)	
	20,000		20,000

Spinning Department, Revenue and Expense

From Spinning account	20,000	Spun yarn transferred to Dyeing at market price	24,000

Dyeing

Spun yarn (at market price)	24,000	Transferred to Dyeing,	
Labor costs (actual)	3,000	Revenue and Expense	38,000
Factory overhead (actual)	11,000	(Profit and Loss)	
	38,000		38,000

Dyeing Department, Revenue and Expense

From Dyeing	38,000	Transferred to Between-Process Inventory accounts	36,000

Note that the spinning department operated efficiently enough to save the company $4,000 of the "opportunity" cost of spun yarn; the dyeing department "lost" $2,000, in the sense that the product of that department could have been purchased for $2,000 *less* than it cost to produce it. Before making a decision to buy any dyed wool, this $2,000 "loss" should be further analyzed by determining how much of the accumulated cost of $38,000 represents fixed cost, that is, capacity cost which is inescapable and would not have any alternative use if spun wool was sent out to be dyed or if some dyed wool was purchased outright. There may still be a saving (or "profit") if more than $2,000 of the $11,000 of dyeing factory overhead, or of any prior factory overhead, is fixed and inescapable.

Opportunity costs have not been put to so wide a use as they might have been had standard cost techniques been less developed, but the concept is useful for some purposes even though it may not be as generally employed as are other methods. Note that the purpose of opportunity costs is to focus attention on the fact that goods might be sold at the end of a given process rather than processed to a greater degree; the sacrifice of the profit which might be made at this point is considered to be a cost of the succeeding process.

A *second* illustration of whether *to make* or *to buy* component parts used in manufacturing involves the principles of *differential costs* previously discussed. Since fixed costs are assumed not to change regardless of the production volume, they will not be considered, since *it is assumed that the present plant facilities are available* for all necessary manufacturing of parts.

A manufacturer of washing machines at the present time is purchasing a substantial quantity of parts used in assembling the finished product. He wishes to know whether he should continue to purchase these parts or attempt to manufacture them. There are five main parts involved in these machines which could be manufactured, or could still be purchased from the suppliers. Without much additional expense, the firm has facilities available to produce these parts either because they are *idle* or because the facilities are used for assembling the machines and can also be used for manufacturing. The following figures have been compiled to help you in advising management what to do:

<table>
<tr><td colspan="7" align="center">*Estimated Costs to Make*
per Thousand</td></tr>
<tr><td>*Part*
Number</td><td>*Direct*
Materials</td><td>*Direct*
Labor</td><td>*Additional*
Variable
Overhead</td><td>*Total*
Differential
Costs</td><td>*Cost*
to Buy</td><td>*Difference*</td></tr>
<tr><td>1 ....</td><td>$1,000</td><td>$1,500</td><td>$ 500</td><td>$3,000</td><td>$2,400</td><td>$600*</td></tr>
<tr><td>2 ....</td><td>600</td><td>600</td><td>200</td><td>1,400</td><td>1,600</td><td>200†</td></tr>
<tr><td>3 ....</td><td>380</td><td>420</td><td>200</td><td>1,000</td><td>1,200</td><td>200†</td></tr>
<tr><td>4 ....</td><td>840</td><td>160</td><td>200</td><td>1,200</td><td>960</td><td>240*</td></tr>
<tr><td>5 ....</td><td>500</td><td>300</td><td>100</td><td>900</td><td>1,000</td><td>100†</td></tr>
<tr><td>Total.........</td><td>$3,320</td><td>$2,980</td><td>$1,200</td><td>$7,500</td><td>$7,160</td><td>$340*</td></tr>
</table>

* Purchase price is lower.
† Cost to make is lower.

An examination of these figures suggests the following conclusions relating to the question of whether or not to buy or to make any or all of the parts:

1.   To buy all the parts and not make any would be $340 cheaper.

2. If some of the parts were purchased and some manufactured, it would be possible to reduce the total cost of 1,000 units even further, namely, to $6,660, viz:

> Purchase Part No. 1, cost $2,400
> Purchase Part No. 4, cost   960
> Manufacture Part No. 2, cost.................. 1,400
> Manufacture Part No. 3, cost.................. 1,000
> Manufacture Part No. 5, cost..................   900
> Total Cost of 1,000 Parts of Each...$6,660

The saving by purchasing some of the parts and making others over the plan of buying all of the parts is $500 ($7,160 − $6,660). The saving by purchasing some of the parts and making others over the plan of making all the parts is $840 ($7,500 − $6,660).

Of course it should not be overlooked that there may be other factors which might influence the final decision, such as the cash required to obtain a plant large enough to carry on the manufacturing operations or the lack of skilled labor to work in the manufacturing operations.

SELL OR PROCESS FURTHER

The problem of sell or process further is particularly prevalent in the chemical and the oil refining industries. This problem also uses *differential cost* analysis. The following data are used to illustrate this type of situation:

The Acme Chemical Company produces Product A, which is used in manufacturing Product B and Product C. It is possible to sell Product A, or to retain it in the plant to produce B and C. Presently the plant is operating at 75 percent capacity. The firm has 100,000 tons of Product A which it could sell without further processing, or it could be kept and used in manufacturing Products B and C.

Product A costs $7 a ton to produce and can be sold for $9.50 a ton.

To use this 100,000 tons of Product A in the manufacture of Products B and C will result in salable production, through added materials, of 120,000 tons of Product B and 40,000 tons of Product C. Product B sells for $25 a ton, and Product C sells for $18 a ton.

The *differential costs* of processing this 100,000 tons into Products B and C, reduced to a per-ton basis, are:

	Product B	Product C
Materials:		
Product A	$ 7.00	$ 7.00
Other material	5.00	2.00
Direct labor	10.00	4.50
Direct overhead	2.00	2.50
Total Variable or Differential Costs per Ton	$24.00	$16.00

Differential income if 100,000 tons of Product A are sold at $9.50 per ton:

Income from sale of 100,000 tons at $9.50............................$950,000
Less: Cost of Product A, 100,000 tons at $7.00 700,000
Differential Income...$250,000

Differential income if Products B and C are sold:

Income if Product A is used to produce B and C:
120,000 tons of Product B at $25...............................$3,000,000
40,000 tons of Product C at 18.............................. 720,000
Total estimated income....................................... $3,720,000
Less: Cost per ton of Products B and C (exclusive of
Product A cost):
120,000 tons of Product B at $17.00 ($5.00 + $10.00
+ $2.00)..$2,040,000
40,000 tons of Product C at $9.00 ($2.00 + $4.50
+ $2.50)... 360,000
100,000* tons of Product A at $7.00 .... 700,000 3,100,000
Differential Income.. $ 620,000

* As indicated above, 100,000 of A in the manufacture of B and C will result in salable production, through added materials, of 120,000 tons of B and 40,000 tons of C.

On the basis of these figures and the assumptions made, it is apparent that if the 100,000 tons of Product A were further processed to produce Products B and C, it would be more desirable than to sell Product A at $9.50 per ton. By additional processing, there is an advantage of $370,000.

PRICING PROBLEMS

Frequently, replacement values are much more important than actual costs. It is entirely logical, for certain purposes, to consider the "cost" of materials to be the cost of *replacing* the materials consumed at *present* prices. The *sacrifice* of materials to one particular production order may sometimes be more accurately measured by the cost of replenishing the stock in the materials storeroom than by historical cost. For this reason, cost accounting systems sometimes provide for charging costs on a replacement price basis (last-in, first-out inventory pricing).

For example, Company D has been in business for many years manufacturing a product that has no competition. Prices have been set at average cost plus 10 percent. The income statement shows a profit for last year of $20,000 (10 percent of the cost of sales), but the company's Cash account always seems to show a precariously low balance, despite the fact that the physical size of plant, inventories, etc., has not changed. Prices of materials and equipment are constantly rising, but the president thinks that since prices are set at 10 percent above cost, the price increases can be ignored.

Cost plus 10 percent may not be an adequate price if material prices have risen greatly and if material costs constitute a substantial part of the total. For example, a cost sheet may show the following (actual) costs for a given order:

Materials	$ 8,500
Direct labor........................	1,200
Factory expense...................	900
Total......................	$10,600

A selling price of cost plus 10 percent would, in such case, be $11,-660. This amount would be collected from the buyer, resulting in an increase in cash of $11,660. But if, meanwhile, prices of materials had advanced from $85 a unit to $100 a unit, the purchase of materials to replace those used in the order just sold would mean an outlay of $10,000 instead of $8,500. Since the money profit on the sale transaction was only $1,060, the $1,500 additional outlay to replace the materials results in an *economic* loss of $440 ($1,500 − $1,060) on the order. This result may be obscured by the fact that materials inventories, valued at cost, would show the $1,500 as additional inventory value, causing the books to show a profit of $1,060; but the profit would be represented only as part of the higher valuation of an inventory of the same kind and size as the original one. Thus, profits may be swallowed up in inventory values in periods of rapidly rising prices and the cash position of the firm becomes dangerously weak. The tricks which our unstable monetary unit can play upon our judgment are subtle but nonetheless real.

In order to avoid such a condition, a firm might decide to show on the cost sheets not the actual but the replacement costs of materials. This can be done by changing the pricing of requisitions, showing *replacement* costs to be charged to specific orders or cost sheets and *actual* costs to be credited to the Materials account. The difference is carried to a Variation account such as was described in the chapter on standard costs. The cost sheet for the order we have been discussing would then appear as follows:

Materials	$10,000
Direct labor	1,200
Factory expense	900
Total	$12,100

A selling price of cost plus 10 percent would be computed at $13,-310, which would protect the company from the effect of price increases in materials which had occurred at the time of sale or shortly thereafter.

Similar provision might be made to handle other costs on replacement bases. Depreciation of fixed assets should, theoretically at least, be so handled if costs are used as the basis for determining selling prices. The consumption of fixed assets can be measured accurately for this purpose only by considering the depreciation charge as the expense of replacing service units consumed in production at *current* price levels. Space limitations prohibit an extended discussion of this point, but there is no justification for *setting selling prices* on the basis of costs incurred at low price levels which may have no relation to current or future considerations.

LIMITATIONS OF COST ANALYSES

The illustrations given in the foregoing discussion may have tended to overemphasize the importance of cost and income data in solving business problems. Cost computations and income estimates are one means of "attacking" such problems; in many cases, this information is conclusive in making the decision. Many projects and proposals have been shelved simply because the costs involved were too high or the relative income contribution was lower than that of an alternative. *Perhaps this is the very reason why the cost accountant needs to be extremely careful in the translation of the data with which he works lest the use of an inappropriate cost concept preclude the adoption of a proposal which might be beneficial to the enterprise or result in losses that might have been avoided by the use of a proper concept of cost.*

The cost accountant must at all times maintain the proper perspective about the usefulness of cost data. He must recognize that management must give consideration to factors other than cost to ensure the long-run progress of the firm. The pressure of competition, the maintenance of sources of supply and of certain marketing outlets, and the maintenance of existing personnel, organization, and morale may often be the real determinants of business decisions. While costs are important, they do not in themselves provide the key to the solution of all business problems; other factors must be considered and may sometimes outweigh the cost factors.

The cost of deriving information for management usefulness should not exceed the potential benefits to be obtained. Methods must be devised to accumulate and distribute timely cost information for management control and planning at the least possible expense. Efficiency in processing and analyzing cost data has not yet reached its potential maximum, and much can be done to increase the usefulness of cost data by reducing the cost of obtaining it.

Modern integrated data processing applications can provide better service to management at no extra cost and in many cases at substantial savings if there is a large volume of data to be processed to meet daily, weekly, and monthly needs for information regarding sales, production, labor, etc. In most applications, the equipment is used only a portion of the time for other needs, thus leaving some time to make special analyses. While the financial executive must still do the creative thinking that is necessary in a proper program of comparative cost analyses, certain elements of each analysis can be secured more quickly, more accurately, and at less cost. Furthermore, he will be able to devote more time to anticipating management needs for information and to preparing studies which would have been impossible under the time and cost limitations of prior methods.

QUESTIONS FOR REVIEW

1. What are the various objectives, obtainable either directly or indirectly, from a cost accounting system and supplementary analyses? List three types of managerial problems which will require a comparative cost analysis.

2. Define briefly the following terms: (*a*) differential costs, (*b*) traceable costs, (*c*) opportunity costs, and (*d*) imputed costs.

3. Distinguish between average, marginal, and differential costs. List four types of situations in which differential cost analysis may be helpful in formulating managerial decisions.

4. Distinguish between *sunk* and *out-of-pocket* costs. Which of these is more useful for planning and decision-making purposes?

5. Define *payback, simple rate of return,* and *time-adjusted-rate-of-return* in capital budgeting. Which do you feel is the more useful? Why?

6. The Baldwin Products Company's three-story factory building with railroad siding and freight elevator, heated and properly lighted, is presently used for manufacturing in the first two floors. The third floor is available either for manufacturing a new product or for rental for a five-year lease to other manufacturers. Using the third floor for manufacturing will require additional machinery and factory labor but no additional supervision or indirect labor costs. How would you determine whether to rent this space or develop new products?

7. How would you analyze or solve the problem of plant operations at a loss or plant shutdown?

8. What factors should be considered in making a managerial decision of "manufacture" or "purchase" certain component parts?

9. How are differential and opportunity costs useful in helping management decide whether to make or purchase certain materials or parts?

10. "We can ignore fixed costs for purposes of decision making. Therefore fixed costs are not as important for management as variable costs." Do you agree with this statement? Explain.

PROBLEMS – GROUP A

Problem 22–1.   Purpose: *Differential Costs to Purchase or Manufacture Parts*

The Yawley Manufacturing Company has a branch factory located in Courtney, Alabama, in which certain television set parts are made. The factory was erected on leased land at a cost including machinery of $500,000. The lease is for 20 more years. The funds for this plant and machinery were provided in part by a $100,000 issue of debenture bonds at a 6 percent interest rate. These were sold at a discount, which required discount amortization of $4,000 a year. At the end of the year, the balance in the Unamortized Bond Discount account was $24,000. Accumulated depreciation on plant and machinery at the end of the year was $200,000.

The factory ledger trial balance at the end of the year was as follows, and the operating results indicated in this may be considered typical of the plant's operations:

Stores purchased	$ 40,000	
Direct materials issued from stores		$ 80,000
Stores inventory at beginning of year	60,000	
Factory labor, direct	75,000	
Rent	20,000	
Bond interest (6% on $100,000)	6,000	
Amortization of bond discount	4,000	
Fire insurance	5,000	
Repairs	3,000	
Depreciation	25,000	
Work-in-process inventory, beginning of year	52,000	
Transfers from direct materials stores	80,000	
Transfers to main factory (1,000,000 units of finished parts)		240,000
Main factory control		50,000
	$370,000	$370,000

It has been proposed to the board of directors of the firm that the parts be purchased from a reliable parts manufacturer at a price guaranteed by him over a long term at a unit cost of 21 cents each. This manufacturer will take over the lease and purchase the plant and machinery for $200,000 and the inventories at 75 percent of the factory book values.

Required:

Prepare a schedule for the board of directors which will indicate to them whether the company would be better off financially if it continued at the present plan of operations or if it should accept the proposed offer.

(Adapted from NYS CPA Examination)

Problem 22–2. Purpose: *Cost Analysis to Determine Whether or Not to Replace Existing Machines*

The controller of the Yurley Manufacturing Company has been faced with the problem of replacing certain currently used machines (called Machine X) with newer, more advanced models (called Machine AD) doing the same kind of work. The newer models can double the present annual capacity of the X machines, which is 3,000,000 good units. Current market conditions indicate that the 6,000,000 units could be sold at the same profitable price.

The X machines cover the following accounting data:

> Original cost and installation...$250,000
> Straight-line depreciation at rate of 15 percent per
>   annum ....
> Estimated scrap value.. 10,000

Operating conditions with the X machine:
    There is a 20 percent waste factor in the use of raw materials.
    Raw materials costs are $60 per 1,000 units before considering the waste factor.
    Direct labor costs equal 60 percent of the prime costs (prime costs is the sum of
      direct materials and direct labor).
    Factory overhead exclusive of depreciation is applied at the rate of 20 percent
      of direct labor costs.

Operating data for the AD machines:
    Material costs will decrease 20 percent because the company will be able to buy
      in larger quantities.
    The newer machines will reduce the waste factor by 50 percent.
    Direct labor costs in operating this machine will increase 20 percent.
    Direct labor will continue to be 60 percent of the prime costs before the 20 per-
      cent increase in direct labor cost is applied.
    Factory overhead rate will be increased by 10 percent of itself.
    The life of the new machine will be eight years with a scrap value in the ratio as
      the present machine.
    The cost of the new machine including installation will be $600,000.
    The seller of the new machine has agreed to absorb the cost of dismantling the
      old machine.

Required:

a) A statement of the estimated cost comparisons on an annual basis, to the nearest dollar.
b) List additional factors that should be considered in deciding upon the replacement.
c) Comment briefly on the usefulness and validity of the comparisons made in (a) above.

(Adapted from AICPA Uniform Examination)

Problem 22–3. Purpose: *Differential Costs in Ascertaining Whether or Not to Accept Orders at Less Than Cost to Manufacture*

The Your-Comfort Shoe Company manufactures ladies' and men's shoes. Owing to foreign competition, this firm has been operating at 60 percent capacity for the past three years with sales and production remaining more or less constant.

The firm has been offered a contract to sell 60,000 pairs of men's shoes to an Australian importer at a price of $4 a pair, which is $1 less than the selling price in this country. This sale will not affect the normal sales in this country and will not compete with other exports.

The present operating and cost accounting data as taken from the books for the past year indicated the following:

	Ladies' Shoes	Men's Shoes
Sales	$400,000	$400,000
Number of pairs sold	80,000 pairs	80,000 pairs
No finished goods inventory at the beginning or end of the year.		
Direct costs of manufacturing:		
Direct materials	$ 80,000	$ 96,000
Direct labor	96,000	88,000
Direct or variable overhead	16,000	16,000
Other manufacturing costs:		
Indirect labor and superintendence	$ 48,000	
Depreciation:		
Women's shoe department	10,000	
Men's shoe department	16,000	
Other fixed factory overhead	100,000	
Selling and administrative costs:		
Fixed	72,000	
Variable	64,000	

If this order is accepted, fixed factory overhead costs would increase $1,200. Salesmen's commissions would not have to be paid. The commission is 30 cents a pair.

Required:

a) Prepare statements indicating whether or not you would recommend the acceptance of this order.

b) Indicate the reasons for and against your decision.

Problem 22–4. Purpose: *Differential or Comparative Costs If Plant Is Shut Down or Operated at a Loss*

The Youngstown Machine Works, a manufacturer of certain cutting machines, has had increasing competition from foreign producers which has resulted in severe curtailment of production, with an average operating loss of about $95,000 a year at 15 percent capacity.

At present the firm is attempting to reorganize its manufacturing plants and operations by (a) selling some of its obsolete plants, (b) importing a number of parts from low-cost foreign producers and assembling their machines from these, and (c) seeking new products to manufacture. To complete the details of this reorganization will require at least two years.

Meanwhile the firm is faced with these questions: Shall it continue to operate at a loss, or shall it close down the plants completely until such time as the reorganization can be completed?

The following represents the operating data for the latest year, and these seem likely to continue during the next two years:

Sales (1,200 machines at $450 each).................................		$540,000
Cost of sales:		
Direct materials	$ 80,000	
Direct labor...	110,000	
Direct variable overhead costs.......................................	70,000	
Fixed manufacturing overhead.......................................	240,000	
Total Cost of Sales..		500,000
Gross profit on sales..		$ 40,000
Variable selling and administrative costs............................	$ 10,000	
Fixed selling and administrative costs	170,000	
Total...		180,000
Net Loss for Year...		$140,000

If the firm ceased operations, certain fixed costs related to the factory work could be reduced by $40,000; and certain fixed selling and administrative costs could be reduced by $15,000.

Selling prices cannot be raised because of competitive conditions.

Required:

a) Prepare statements to indicate whether the firm should close down operations or continue to operate at a loss for the next two years. It is assumed that over the past 10 years, the capital and retained earnings have been built up to $760,000.

b) Indicate the result if the price remains the same but the sales volume decreases to 420 and 840 units respectively.

c) Indicate the favorable and unfavorable aspects of your decision.

Problem 22–5. Purpose: *Managerial Cost Accounting Involving Cost Reduction through Redesigning the Product*

The Yaggerman Manufacturing Company produces one principal product. The sales for the year 1972 are budgeted at $250,000. The budgeted cost of goods manufactured and sold are:

Direct material costs	$50,000
Direct labor costs	75,000
Variable manufacturing overhead..................	37,500
Fixed manufacturing overhead	25,000

In December, the firm's actual operation approximated those budgeted at the beginning of the year. However, the outlook for 1973 seems to indicate that costs will increase and certain managerial decisions must be made.

For 1973, it is expected that material costs will average 10 percent higher;

labor costs with fringe benefits will be 10 percent higher; and variable manufacturing overhead will also increase 10 percent. If the sales price is to be increased to produce the same *rate* of gross profit as in 1972, there will be a 10 percent decrease in the number of units sold in 1972.

If the product is redesigned according to the suggestions offered by the marketing division, it is felt that a 10 percent increase can be obtained in the number of units sold, with a 15 percent increase in the sales price per unit. However, this redesigning of the product would involve certain changes in the manufacturing costs, as follows:

A different grade of material will be used but it will require 10 percent more material, but the price of the material will be 8 percent less than the currently used materials. Less skilled workmen would be required to process this material, resulting in 10 percent lower labor costs; but 20 percent more hours would be required per unit of production. Variable overhead is incurred directly in relation to production. It is expected that the variable overhead will increase 10 percent due to price changes and an additional 20 percent due to changes in labor hours.

Required:

a) A statement showing the budgeted gross profit if the same product is continued for 1973, and

b) If redesigned product is manufactured in 1973.

(Adapted from AICPA Uniform Examination)

PROBLEMS – GROUP B

Problem 22–6.   Purpose: *To Make or Buy Decision Costing*

The Yuma Manufacturing Company's management has asked you for help in deciding whether it should continue to manufacture an important part in its factory or to purchase it from an outside supplier.

During the year 10,000 of these parts were manufactured. The *total costs* of the precision machinery department in which these were produced were:

Materials	$135,000	
Direct labor	100,000	
Indirect labor	40,000	
Light and heat	11,000	
Power	6,000	
Depreciation	20,000	
Property taxes and insurance	16,000	
Payroll taxes and other benefits	19,600	
Other costs	10,000	$357,600

In the precision machinery department, the following costs apply to the manufacture of this part:

Material	$ 35,000
Direct labor	56,000
Indirect labor	12,000
Power	600
Other	1,000

The sale of equipment used in making this important part would reduce these costs as follows:

Depreciation	$ 4,000
Property taxes and insurance	2,000

The annual requirements for this firm would continue to be 10,000 of these parts. If they were purchased, the following additional costs would be incurred:

Freight	$ 5,000
Indirect labor for receiving, handling, and inspection	10,000

An outside supplier has agreed to furnish this part in the 10,000 quantity needed at a cost of $8.20 each, FOB the supplier's factory.

The cost of the purchased parts would be considered a precision machinery department cost. If the parts are purchased, certain machinery would be sold at the book value.

Required:

a) Prepare comparative schedules showing a comparison of the total costs of the precision machinery department (1) when the parts are manufactured, and (2) when the parts are purchased from an outside supplier.

b) Comment on the factors which should be considered, in addition to cost factors, in arriving at a decision of whether to make or purchase these parts from an outside supplier.

(Adapted from AICPA Uniform Examination)

Problem 22–7. Purpose: *Differential Cost Analysis to Accept Orders at Special Price Concessions*

The Yarker Manufacturing Company produces a special electronic instrument which sells for $15, which is a long-established price. Under present business conditions, the firm is operating at 40 percent capacity with sales of 6,250 a month.

An analysis of the costs for a recent month, during which 5,000 were produced and 6,250 sold, showed the following:

Direct labor	$12,375
Superintendent's salary	2,200
Depreciation of building	2,020
Power purchased	700
Direct materials	8,000
Heat and light	435
Indirect labor	2,800
Miscellaneous supplies	1,000
Depreciation of machinery	4,550
Machinery repairs	600
Property taxes	750
Fire insurance	100
Payroll taxes	570
Miscellaneous	1,400
	$37,500

The total selling expenses amounted to $30,000, which included $1,875 for packing and shipping. The sales on special order would require a similar unit cost for packing and shipping.

Total administrative and general costs were $4,200.

An offer has been received from a large chain store to purchase 75,000 units during the coming year, shipped in equal amounts each month. These would be manufactured with slight immaterial modifications under the store's label. The price offered was $8.50 per unit.

The management does not expect any improvement in business conditions and feels that the chain stores' sales will not affect the firm's sales.

The firm does not feel that it can afford to accept this offer feeling that it would increase the present losses sustained by the firm.

Required:

a) Prepare an analysis in comparative form which will show the operating results if the order is accepted and if the order is not accepted. In this analysis, assume that the various items are either completely fixed or completely variable, depending upon the dominant characteristic of each item and the data given.

b) Comment on desirability of accepting this order.

Problem 22–8. Purpose: *Cost Analysis to Determine Whether or Not to Replace Existing Machines*

The Yorby Manufacturing Company is contemplating the replacement of an existing machine by a new and more efficient model because of the high variable costs incurred in the use of the present machine.

The present machine operates under these conditions:

```
Production.............................................60,000 units per year
Annual depreciation ..............................$ 7,200
Variable cost of manufacturing:
    Material per unit.................................. $1.23
    Labor ...............................................  1.35
    Manufacturing overhead ......................  0.48   $3.06
```

The new replacement machine would cost $150,000, and is capable of producing 75,000 units each year for 10 years. Because of the increased purchase requirements, the variable material costs would be $1.18; direct labor costs, $1.10; and manufacturing overhead, $0.42.

At present time, the earning power of the investments in the company is estimated at 10 percent before taxes. If the company does not purchase the new machine, it could invest the funds in securities with a yield $5\frac{1}{2}$ percent in interest.

Required:

a) Should the new machine be purchased if it is assumed that the present machine has no scrap value?

b) Should the new machine be purchased if it is assumed that the present machine could be disposed of for $30,000? The remaining useful life of the present machine is six years. Prepare schedules to support each of the above.

Problem 22–9.   Purpose: *Cost Analysis in Decision Making*

The Yengler Corporation has its home office in Chicago and leases factories for manufacturing in Rhode Island, Georgia, and California. The same single product is manufactured in each of these three plants covering the 1972 operations.

	Total	Rhode Island	Georgia	California
Sales	$1,200,000	$300,000	$500,000	$400,000
Fixed costs:				
Factory	$ 210,000	$ 60,000	$ 65,000	$ 85,000
Selling and administration	74,000	21,000	26,000	27,000
Variable costs	550,000	110,000	242,000	198,000
Allocated home office costs	65,000	15,000	28,000	22,000
Totals	$ 899,000	$206,000	$361,000	$332,000
Net Income from Operations	$ 301,000	$ 94,000	$139,000	$ 68,000

Home office expenses are allocated to the various plants as shown. The sales price per unit is $10.

Management is undecided whether to renew the lease on the California factory, which expires December 31, 1973, which will require an increase of rent of $24,000 if renewed. If the California plant is closed down, the sale of the equipment will cover the book value of the equipment plus all termination expenses.

If the California factory is shut down, the company can continue to service its customers in California from its Georgia plant by one of the following methods:

1. Expanding the Georgia factory which would increase the fixed costs by 20 percent. Additional shipping costs will be incurred of $3 per unit on the increased production. The Georgia factory would be assigned the California factory's allocated home office costs.
2. Entering into a long-term contract with a California competitor who will serve the California factory customers and who will pay the Yengler Corporation a commission of $2 per unit.

The Yengler Corporation is also planning to establish a subsidiary corporation in Canada to produce the same product. Estimated annual sales of the Canadian corporation will be 50,000 units, on which the costs estimated are:

	Total Annual Costs	Percent of Total Annual Costs That Is Variable
Material	$196,000	100
Labor	90,000	80
Manufacturing overhead	75,000	60
Administration	40,000	20

The Canadian production will be sold by manufacturer's representatives who will receive a commission of 10 percent of the sales price. No portion of the United States home office expenses will be allocated to the Canadian subsidiary.

Required:

a) Prepare a schedule computing the Yengler Corporation's estimated net income from the United States operations under each of the following procedures:

   (1)   Expansion of the Georgia factory.

   (2)   Negotiation of the long-term contract on a commission basis.

b) Management wants to price its Canadian product to realize a 10 percent profit on sales price. Compute the sales price per unit that would result in an estimated 10 percent profit on sales.

c) Assume that your answer in (b) is a sales price of $12 per unit. Compute the break-even point of sales dollars for the Canadian subsidiary.

(Adapted from AICPA Uniform Examination)

chapter 23

Nonmanufacturing Cost Applications and Analyses

INTRODUCTION

In recent years, the principles of cost accounting and control have been extended to other fields. The use of computers has made it possible for additional data to become available with the result that applications of cost accounting techniques to nonmanufacturing situations have become more feasible. In addition, managers of nonmanufacturing activities have become more cost conscious and thus desire more cost data to aid them in the decision-making process. The following nonmanufacturing costs should be considered:

1. Costs for retail and department stores.
2. Costs for financial institutions.
3. Costs of office work as applicable to some of the larger service establishments, such as insurance companies and public utilities.
4. Costs for governmental bodies and other entities not organized for profit.
5. Research and development expenditures.

COSTS FOR RETAIL AND DEPARTMENT STORES

The objective of cost accounting in a retail or department store is to present to management *an analysis of the cost of selling certain classes of goods,* either on a total basis or on some unit basis, such as per dollar of sales or per ton of material. A department store is, in reality, an aggregate of a number of units corresponding to retail outlets. Therefore the problem of the department store is that of segregating for each department its sales and its direct costs and of securing an equitable apportionment of the general and administrative expenses of the entire store among the several departments. Since each department usually specializes in a single type of merchandise, costs can then be reduced for that department to a percentage of sales. In the retail organization where such segregation of costs and expenses by departments is not always practical because of small size, an analysis can be made of sales and costs by products or groups of products.

Cost analysis in a department store or retail organization may be grouped under the following six headings:

1. Administration.
2. Occupancy.
3. Sales promotion and advertising.
4. Purchasing.
5. Selling.
6. Delivery.

Under each of these headings there is a group of expenses which must be allocated to the various departments, such as (1) men's clothing, (2) women's coats and dresses, (3) sporting goods, (4) furniture, and others. The basis of allocation, together with the expenses, might be tabulated as shown in Illustration 23–1.

Items such as bad debts and losses from theft are generally treated as financial items and kept separate from the departmental cost analysis; or they may be placed in the administrative expense section and then prorated.

The tremendous number of transactions involved in some of the department stores sales activities made cost analysis on a detailed statistical basis well-nigh impractical until the computer came along. Today, many stores have, in addition to summary entries, main office accounting records kept by departments and departmental records kept by lines of merchandise and by salesmen. The latter records are statistical, while the former are accounting records entered in the books.

Entries for sales, purchases, and direct expenses are placed in accounts for each department. The entries would be equivalent to:

(1)

Purchases—Men's Clothing Department	20,000	
Purchases—Women's Coats and Dresses	40,000	
Purchases—Sporting Goods	10,000	
Purchases—Furniture	90,000	
Accounts Payable		160,000
To record purchases by departments for the period.		

(2)

```
Cash or Accounts Receivable ...............................220,000
        Sales — Men's Clothing Department..................     50,000
        Sales — Women's Coats and Dresses.................     75,000
        Sales — Sporting Goods ...............................     15,000
        Sales — Furniture..........................................     80,000
    To record sales by departments for the period.
```

Illustration 23–1

Functional Cost Element	Basis of Distribution to Departments
Administration:	
Executive office expense...................	Sales in each department
Accounts receivable......................	No. of charge sales
Credit department expense................	No. of charge sales
Accounts payable........................	No. of invoices
Auditing................................	No. of transactions
Adjustment office........................	No. of adjustments
Training, welfare, and employee relationship................................	No. of employees weighted by number of days' service
Insurance on merchandise................	Average merchandise inventory
Occupancy:	
Alterations and repairs to building.........	To department in which made (direct) or on area basis
Rent and taxes...........................	Area or investment basis
Insurance on building and fixtures..........	Area or investment basis
Light, heat, and power...................	Area
Depreciation on building..................	Area
Depreciation and repairs on fixtures........	Investment in fixtures
Sales promotion and advertising:	
Departmental promotion and advertising....	Direct charge to department
Direct mail and circularization.............	Direct or on basis of sales
Window displays.........................	Direct
Administration of sales promotion.........	Sales basis
Purchasing:	
Management and supervision..............	Sales
Departmental buyers, etc..................	Direct
Receiving and checking...................	Direct, or on basis of volume or number of items
Inventory control........................	Average investment in inventory or number of items
Selling:	
Salaries.................................	Direct
Wrapping and packing....................	Direct or number of packages
Supplies.................................	Direct
Compensation insurance..................	Direct on salaries
Delivery.................................	No. of packages, perhaps weighted according to size

Under this method of accounting and control, it will be necessary to maintain an inventory for each department; it is then possible to determine from the foregoing entries the *gross* profit for each department and for the store as a whole.

In working toward a net profit for each department the expenses may in part be entered in departmental expense accounts, such as Salaries – Men's Clothing Department, etc. Not all of them, however, can be thus recorded; some must be apportioned on appropriate bases. It will therefore be necessary to prepare a schedule of the departmental expenses, both direct and apportioned; then a departmentalized income statement can be prepared, using percentages to indicate the relation between sales and each class of expense and between the net profit and sales. These ratios or percentages are used in marketing cost analysis and also in cost analysis for department stores and retail stores. To illustrate this type of expense analysis, the following schedules are prepared, using the bases for distribution indicated in Illustration 23–1.

This tabulation of expenses, as given in Illustration 23–2, may be analyzed on a *percentage of sales* basis for each expense; but in Illustration 23–3 such costs are shown only for *groups* of expenses. In smaller retail organizations this comparative income statement by departments is prepared on the basis of sales groups, since functional departmentalization is not always so clear cut as in the larger organizations.

COST ANALYSES FOR COMMERCIAL BANKS

As indicative of the method, results, and procedure followed in cost analyses for financial institutions, the application to commercial banks is used. In recent years, greater emphasis has been placed by banks upon the cost of the various services rendered. In most banking organizations today, management knows approximately how much net income is realized on the checking accounts, on the loan service, and on trust work. Charges no longer have to be a guess or a matter of "what the traffic will bear" but can be based upon the cost of performing the services.

The functional organization of a bank must be studied in the same manner as the departments in a large store. Bank functions usually include: (1) a commercial deposit division; (2) a savings deposit division; (3) a trust division; (4) a safe deposit vaults division; (5) a foreign exchange division; (6) a capital funds (capital stock, etc.) division; (7) a loans and investments division; (8) service departments – accounting, duplication, auditing, correspondence, filing, credit, mailing, messenger, personnel, photostat, stenographic, telephone, translation, and wires and cables; and (9) indirect expenses – advertising, administration officers' expenses, directors' fees, library, new business, and pensions.

A bank derives its income from investment of funds and from render-

Illustration 23–2

DEPARTMENTAL APPORTIONMENT OF EXPENSES FOR THE PERIOD

Expenses	Total	Men's Clothing	Women's Coats and Dresses	Sporting Goods	Furniture
Administrative					
Executive Offices......	$ 2,200.00	$ 500.00	$ 750.00	$ 150.00	$ 800.00
Accounts Receivable....	1,200.00	300.00	450.00	225.00	225.00
Credit Dept. Expenses...	800.00	200.00	300.00	150.00	150.00
Adjustment Office......	500.00	100.00	250.00	50.00	100.00
Personnel............	2,000.00	400.00	800.00	300.00	500.00
	$ 6,700.00	$ 1,500.00	$ 2,550.00	$ 875.00	$ 1,775.00
Occupancy					
Alterations (Specific)....	$ 800.00	$ 300.00	$ 500.00	....	....
Rent...............	2,400.00	500.00	800.00	$ 100.00	$ 1,000.00
Light, Heat and Power..	600.00	125.00	200.00	25.00	250.00
	$ 3,800.00	$ 925.00	$ 1,500.00	$ 125.00	$ 1,250.00
Sales Promotion and Advertising					
Direct Advertising......	$ 1,000.00	$ 200.00	$ 450.00	$ 50.00	$ 300.00
Window Displays, direct	500.00	100.00	300.00	....	100.00
Administration........	1,100.00	250.00	375.00	75.00	400.00
	$ 2,600.00	$ 550.00	$ 1,125.00	$ 125.00	$ 800.00
Purchasing					
Supervision..........	$ 640.00	$ 80.00	$ 160.00	$ 40.00	$ 360.00
Departmental Buyers....	6,000.00	1,500.00	3,000.00	500.00	1,000.00
Receiving............	480.00	60.00	120.00	30.00	270.00
Inventory Control......	600.00	100.00	40.00	60.00	400.00
	$ 7,720.00	$ 1,740.00	$ 3,320.00	$ 630.00	$ 2,030.00
Selling					
Salaries..............	$ 20,000.00	$ 5,000.00	$ 6,500.00	$ 1,500.00	$ 7,000.00
Wrapping............	220.00	50.00	75.00	15.00	80.00
Insurance, Compensation	200.00	50.00	65.00	15.00	70.00
	$ 20,420.00	$ 5,100.00	$ 6,640.00	$ 1,530.00	$ 7,150.00
Delivery					
Departmental Expense...	$ 5,000.00	$ 1,250.00	$ 1,625.00	$ 375.00	$ 1,750.00
Total..........	$ 46,240.00	$11,065.00	$16,760.00	$ 3,660.00	$14,755.00
Sales.................	$220,000.00	$50,000.00	$75,000.00	$15,000.00	$80,000.00
Number of Charge Sales...	24,000	6,000	9,000	4,500	4,500
Adjustments...........	500	100	250	50	100
Area, square feet........	240,000	50,000	80,000	10,000	100,000
Employees.............	20	4	8	3	5
Inventory..............	$ 30,000.00	$ 5,000.00	$ 2,000.00	$ 3,000.00	$20,000.00

Illustration 23-3

VICTORY DEPARTMENT STORE
Income Statement by Departments
For Period Ending March 31, 19—

	TOTAL	%	Men's Clothing	%	Women's Coats and Dresses	%	Sporting Goods	%	Furniture	%
Sales.............	$220,000.00	100	$50,000.00	100	$75,000.00	100	$15,000.00	100	$80,000.00	100
Cost of Sales......	130,000.00	59.09	15,000.00	30	38,000.00	50.67	7,000.00	46.67	70,000.00	87.5
Gross Profit on Sales.....	$ 90,000.00	40.91	$35,000.00	70	$37,000.00	49.33	$ 8,000.00	53.33	$10,000.00	12.5
Expenses:										
Administrative.........	6,700.00	3.05	1,500.00	3.00	2,550.00	3.40	875.00	5.83	1,775.00	2.22
Occupancy...........	3,800.00	1.73	925.00	1.85	1,500.00	2.00	125.00	0.83	1,250.00	1.56
Sales Promotion.......	2,600.00	1.18	550.00	1.10	1,125.00	1.50	125.00	0.83	800.00	1.00
Purchasing..........	7,720.00	3.51	1,740.00	3.48	3,320.00	4.42	630.00	4.20	2,030.00	2.54
Selling............	20,420.00	9.28	5,100.00	10.20	6,640.00	8.85	1,530.00	10.20	7,150.00	8.94
Delivery...........	5,000.00	2.27	1,250.00	2.50	1,625.00	2.17	375.00	2.50	1,750.00	2.18
Total Expenses......	$ 46,240.00	21.02	$11,065.00	22.13	$16,760.00	22.34	$ 3,660.00	24.39	$14,755.00	18.44
Net Operating Profit.....	$ 43,760.00	19.89	$23,935.00	47.87	$20,240.00	26.99	$ 4,340.00	28.94	$ 4,755.00 (loss)*	5,944 (loss)*

ing services such as safe deposit, trust, etc. By far the greater income comes from the loan and investment of funds. These funds cannot be segregated in their investments but are usually grouped. It therefore becomes necessary to allocate a certain amount of the investment income to each type of fund. This allocation can be made quite accurately by observing a definite pattern of analysis. The funds are all merged into one large reservoir of funds, since there is no way to pick specific investments for each. This fund is called a *conversion fund*.

The following illustration indicates how these funds, with the necessary deductions, are merged into the conversion fund to compute the income for each by an appropriate allocation.[1] These total funds are then analyzed by types of investments and the income received therefrom during the past six months. This income is reduced to an average annual rate. This rate is used in computing the allocation of the income to each type of fund.

ANALYSIS OF FUNDS AVAILABLE FOR CONVERSION

Six-Month Averages

Capital fund:
Capital		$ 250,000
Surplus		750,000
Undivided profits		178,000
Surplus reserves		192,000
Total		$1,370,000

Disposition of funds:
Bank building	$ 174,000	
Furniture and equipment	27,000	
Accounts receivable, etc.	2,000	203,000
Capital funds available for conversion		$1,167,000

Commercial deposits—demand:
Due to banks		$ 863,000
Cashier's and certified checks		52,000
Individual deposits		7,394,000
Demand certificates of deposit		11,000
United States deposits		126,000
Total		$8,446,000

Disposition of deposits—demand:
Customers' deposits uncollected	$ 375,000	
Federal Reserve requirement	1,211,000	
Cash requirement	404,000	1,990,000
Commercial deposits—demand, available for conversion		6,456,000

Commercial deposits—time:
Time deposits		$ 165,000
Time certificates of deposit		140,000
Total		$ 305,000

---

[1] Adapted, with permission, from the article "Cost Accounting in Commercial Banks," by Harold Randall, in the *National Association of Accountants Bulletin*.

Disposition deposits — time:

Federal Reserve bank requirement ....$	15,000	
Cash requirement	5,000	20,000

Commercial deposits — demand,
    available for conversion..................................   285,000

Savings deposits:

Savings..	$1,055,000
Employees' savings.................................	2,000
Total	$1,057,000

Disposition of deposit:

Federal Reserve requirement...................$	53,000	
Cash requirement	16,000	$ 69,000

Savings deposits available for conversion.............. $ 988,000

Foreign division deposits:

Individual accounts.................................$	3,000
Foreign bank accounts	169,000
Sundry dollar accounts	8,000
Other accounts.....................................	12,000
Total .... $	192,000

Disposition of foreign deposits:

Federal Reserve requirement...................$	26,000	
Cash requirement	10,000	36,000

Foreign funds available for conversion	156,000
Total Funds Available for Conversion	$9,052,000

ALLOCATION OF EXPENSES

In calculating the *departmental* costs, it is usually necessary to allocate expenses. The matter of proration is similar to that found in factories and department stores. Those expenses which can be charged directly to a department, such as salaries, compensation insurance, or depreciation on equipment, can be computed from the records. The building expenses are apportioned on the basis of floor space or area. The service department costs must be redistributed over the income-producing functions on appropriate bases. A list of the expenses and the methods of allocation that might be used follows:

Service Department	*Method of Reallocation*
Accounting	Survey of work done for each income department. May be reduced to percentage basis
Auditing	Same as accounting — by survey
Filing	Survey of work done for each department
Credit	Number of applications and investigations
Mailing	Volume of mail handled
Messengers	Survey of use or number of calls
Personnel	Number of employees
Photostat	Per page of copy
Stenographic	Survey or per page of production
Telephone	Number of telephones in each department plus direct charge for toll calls
Translation	Direct charge

| Indirect expenses | These may be known as *general bank overhead* and apportioned on basis of income produced or in proportion to total expenses for each department |
| Legal | Survey of work actually done |

To this point the bank management has been able to ascertain the income and expenses for each department. To reduce this to cost accounting requires the establishment and compilation of a *unit*. The units are of two kinds: (1) the cost unit for the type of work to be done; and (2) the charge unit—the combination of several cost units. The former might be illustrated by the computation of the cost of handling a number of cash deposits, check deposits, payrolls, and handling sight drafts, documentary drafts, or security drafts; and by machine posting in bookkeeping departments. These are really *work cost units*. Compiling statistics for these work units may be quite an elaborate job, but with an accurate system of internal check and audit they can be secured with little extra effort. Translating these work units or standards into the analysis of an account or charge unit is another problem. However, sufficient progress has been made toward its solution that the cost and profitableness of handling an account can be readily computed. The formula used for a checking account is shown in Illustration 23–4.

A similar analysis can be worked out for computing the cost of trust work or for the foreign deposits. The extent to which a bank may wish to make such an analysis depends upon its general business operating results. Some banks study their accounts continuously. Others accept the standards arrived at by other banks and use them. In any event, every

Illustration 23–4

MONTHLY COST OR SERVICE CHARGE ANALYSIS FOR A CHECKING ACCOUNT

Balance:
1. Average daily ledger balance...................................$600.00
2. Less uncollected funds.. 120.00
3. Average daily collected balance................................$480.00

Income:
4. Earnings at ⅓% (4% a year)....................................$ 1.60

Expense:
5. Checks paid and debit items handled.....................$1.50
6. Deposits received....................................... 0.10
7. Deposited items... 0.30
8. Collections handled..................................... 0.30
9. Checks certified.. 0.30
10. Other expenses and charges incurred...................... 0.10
11. Account cost (per account)............................... 0.50

     Total expense... 3.10

Loss on Account for Month (Service Charge).........................$ 1.50

bank organization should make an effort to study statistically the costs of rendering the service.

Banks should develop standards and standard costs in a manner similar to what has been done in the case of manufacturing operations. Once established and instituted, proper comparisons between actual and standard costs become possible. Variances may be isolated, and appropriate action taken to correct the reasons for the variances. Banks may thus achieve the same degree of control over costs as found in manufacturing situations.

COST ANALYSES FOR GENERAL AND ADMINISTRATIVE OFFICE FUNCTIONS

Cost analysis of office work in the organization of a manufacturer or a department store or bank has already been treated either under the heading of "Distribution Costs" or under special headings of "Department Store Accounting" or "Bank Cost Accounting." The cost analysis referred to in this section, while following the same pattern of procedure as the others, refers to those concerns whose main activity is rendering a service, such as an insurance company or a public utility.

The problem resolves itself into three parts: (1) determination of units for computing the costs of the various office activities; (2) determination of bases for allocation of the office costs, which are really a form of service, to the other departments of the firm; and (3) achieving control over the costs.

To determine the units for computing costs in office work, it is necessary to indicate the types of work that take place in the office. These and the corresponding units for allocation of costs are:

Type of Office Work	Cost Analysis Units
Correspondence work	Per letter or per page of letter
Dictation and transcription	Per line, per page, per stroke
Filing	Per hundred names, or papers handled
Mailing	Number of pieces
Billing	Per invoice or per item
Duplication	Number of copies
Personnel	Number of employees

One of the first tasks facing the office manager is the determination and, if possible, the reduction of the unit costs for each of the departments listed above. An examination of these departments should indicate that they are primarily service departments. In a life insurance company, they render service to the policy division, the claim division, or the investment division. Once the unit costs have been determined, then it becomes a simple job to allocate the costs of these departments to the operating divisions of the firm. To illustrate this more specifically, the costs in the life insurance company would follow the analysis pattern shown in Illustration 23–5. Thereafter, the policy division will reduce its total costs to a *per policy basis;* the investment division to a cost of *per dollar of net income;* and the claim division to the cost *per claim handled.* The functional operating departments really "absorb" the service department expenses, much in the same manner that the producing departments absorb the costs of the service departments in a manufacturing business.

As was the case with banks, standards and standard costs should be established whenever possible so that adequate cost control may be achieved. The standards that are established should be built around a series of work steps. The definition of the work step is important as the beginning and the conclusion of the step must be easily determinable. For example, the billing operation would make up a series of work steps and standards could be set for the performance of this function.

Illustration 23–5

Service Department	Costs	Functional Operating Division		
		Policy Division	Investment Division	Claim Division
Correspondence............	$ 5,000.00	$ 2,000.00	$ 800.00	$ 2,200.00
Dictation and Transcription....	4,000.00	1,500.00	1,000.00	1,500.00
Filing....................	2,000.00	650.00	500.00	850.00
Mailing.................	1,000.00	400.00	300.00	300.00
Billing...................	200.00	200.00	....	....
Duplication..............	3,000.00	1,800.00	200.00	1,000.00
Personnel................	3,500.00	2,000.00	500.00	1,000.00
Total Service..........	$18,700.00	$ 8,550.00	$ 3,300.00	$ 6,850.00
Building Maintenance........	$ 8,000.00	3,500.00	1,500.00	3,000.00
Direct Functional Dept. Charges	10,000.00	5,000.00	2,000.00	3,000.00
Total Costs for Period....	$36,700.00	$17,050.00	$ 6,800.00	$12,850.00

COST ANALYSES FOR GOVERNMENTAL AGENCIES

There are about 176,000 governmental units in the United States engaged in rendering some kind of public service as well as thousands of hospitals, schools, and colleges. Sometimes there is only one type of service, as in the case of a small school district; or there may be multiple services, as in the case of a large city or state. This government service is distinctive in that in most instances it is supported by taxation. The ever-increasing tax burdens have emphasized the need for a more efficient method of studying and recording the costs of governmental services.

In industry and commerce, the use of a cost accounting system should result in greater efficiency, reflected in increased profits. Therefore, the businessman will compute the material, labor, and manufacturing overhead costs for each unit manufactured. He will then study these unit costs continuously, so that, if possible, they may be reduced. He may also use these data to set up standards so that future results can be compared regularly with the standards of operating efficiency. But behind all such cost analysis is the profit objective.

In a governmental unit the use of the cost accounting system is stimulated not by the profit motive but by the need for greater efficiency, so that the taxpayers' or donors' burdens will be less. More specifically, the purposes to which governmental cost accounting may be applied are:

1. To provide data that indicate whether or not certain activities are being performed efficiently.
2. To provide a basis for determining whether certain work should be performed by a governmental unit or by a private contractor.
3. To provide data to be used in preparing the budget.
4. To compute the cost of fixed assets which have been constructed by the government unit.
5. To provide the best service at the lowest cost.

It should be understood, of course, that *all* accounting *tends* toward these objectives. However, it is only when the data are carefully studied and analyzed by means of what is termed *cost accounting* that the *maximum* results can be obtained, since cost accounting breaks down the total figures into detailed operations, thus localizing discrepancies or high costs.

Governmental costs may be computed on either a *specific job basis* or on a *continuous basis*. Where a certain nonrecurring task is to be performed, such as the construction of a bridge or school, the use of a specific job cost system is necessary. In computing the costs of education, police, and fire protection and the other services rendered continuously from year to year, the use of the continuous cost method is necessary. Under this continuous method the total cost of a particular service is computed and then divided by the number of units of that service rendered, to obtain the unit costs.

Certain nonprofit activities are more readily adaptable to cost accounting than others. Cost accounting may be most readily used (1) in those activities where there is some physical output, such as in the construction of a building or of a highway or in the rebuilding of a street; and (2) in those services in which the use of time, materials, and equipment is fairly constant and uniform throughout successive operations. In many instances, it will not be possible to compute the departmental unit cost because there are so many different types of work being performed under one administrative head that there is no common unit. For example, the department of public works in a large city covers the following activities, many of which must be measured with different units:

Activity	Unit of Cost Analysis
Maintenance of sewers	Per mile
Maintenance of incinerator	Per ton of refuse
Collection of ashes and garbage	Per ton
Maintenance of highways and lighting	Per mile
Maintenance of garages and vehicles	Per garage and per vehicle
Bureau of parks	Per acre

It is because cost accounting necessitates the analysis of expenditures for various types of work within a large department that it is most effective in administrative control. In addition to the activities of the department of public works, the following is a list of governmental activities which can be measured by means of cost accounting:

Activity	Unit of Cost Analysis
Police	Per capita
Education	Per pupil
Welfare and relief	Per case
Trucking	Per ton-mile
Garage service	Per vehicle, or per capita
Recreation	Per capita
Hospital care	Per patient, or per capita
Electric light plant	Per kilowatt-hour*
Water plant	Per thousand gallons*
Street-cleaning	Per mile
Construction of streets	Per mile
Repair of streets	Per square yard
Library	Per capita

*Cost accounting for activities such as the water department and the light plant is very similar to that for a private enterprise except that some expenses, such as taxes and insurance, may not be included; frequently a sinking fund cost is included instead of depreciation.

But the foregoing activities and units refer to the departments as a whole. That is probably the best that can be expected in *small* units. In the larger units, however, it becomes necessary to subdivide the activity expenses within a department and to select more accurate units for some of these activities. To use the police and fire departments and the departments of health and hospitals as illustrations, the accompanying tables[2] (see Illustrations 23–6 to 23–8) indicate how a more detailed analysis of costs may be made.

[2]Taken, with special permission, from *Governmental Cost Accounting,* by the Municipal Finance Officers' Association of United States and Canada (Chicago, Illinois), pp. 46, 56, and 59.

Illustration 23-6

Illustration 23-6

TABLE OF ACCOUNTS FOR
COST ACCOUNTING FOR POLICE AND FIRE DEPARTMENTS

General Classification (For All Accounting)	Activity or Service (For Cost Accounting)	Performance Units (For Work Measurement)
Police departments are sometimes classified as to squads; detective, vice, morals, control, foot patrol, motorcycle, auto patrol, and so forth	Administrative and auxiliary services	(An indirect cost which must be prorated over other services)
	Traffic regulation	Intersectional—hours patrolled; curb-mile-hours patrolled (parking), Cars examined (traffic lanes) Man-hours (on duty, not reporting to calls)
	Crime prevention	Calls answered (squad cars) Active cases (detective)
	Criminal apprehension	Man-days (custody of prisoner)
	Special police services	Examinations made (laboratories) Missing persons reported Man-hours special duties (parades) $1,000 property value (recovery of property)
Fire-fighting forces may also be classified according to squads: engine companies, hook and ladder, salvage squads, rescue squads, fireboats, and so forth	Fire prevention	Inspections made Investigations made
	Fire protection	Drills supervised Talks given, etc. Man-hours (on duty, not answering calls)
	Fire fighting	Fire alarms answered
	Other fire department services	Resuscitation cases Man-hours special duty (parades), etc.

METHODS OF RECORDING AND COMPUTING GOVERNMENTAL COSTS

Costs for governmental units may be computed on two bases: (1) statistical, and (2) accounting. In many places, governmental officers are content to have some statistical analyses made of the costs of various activities whenever time permits. This method has two vital weaknesses: (1) there is no compulsion in the matter of ascertaining costs; and (2) there is no method of verifying the accuracy of the figures. In business concerns, at least some relation can be established between the results of statistical cost accounting and the results shown on the financial statements. But such a condition does not exist in governmental units. The recording of governmental costs on the books as supplementary to the general accounting but integrated with it seems to be the more desirable

Illustration 23-7

TABLE OF ACCOUNTS FOR COST ACCOUNTING FOR A HEALTH DEPARTMENT

General Classification (For All Accounting)	Activity or Service (For Cost Accounting)	Performance Units (For Work Measurement)
According to subfunction	Administrative and auxiliary services	An indirect cost
Vital statistics	Recording and registration	Births and deaths registered Morbidity cases recorded
Control of communicable diseases	Field professional services	Nursing visits Physicians' visits
Maternity and child health service	Clinical services	Patient visits
Adult health service	Laboratories	Examinations made
Crippled children service	Distribution of drugs	Ampoules distributed Pamphlets, talks, etc.
Food and milk control Sanitation	Instruction and education Inspectional services	License applications received Inspections made Orders issued Arrests made Violations prosecuted

Illustration 23-8

TABLE OF ACCOUNTS FOR COST ACCOUNTING FOR HOSPITALS

General Classification (For All Accounting)	Activity or Service (For Cost Accounting)	Performance Units* (For Work Measurement)
Separate records for each hospital	Administrative and auxiliary services	(An indirect cost)
	Dietary services	Meals served
	Activities dealing with home and property	Pounds of laundry washed Sq. feet of plant maintained and operated Ambulance miles driven (repairs according to job orders)
	Professional services	Patient days (medical, surgical, and nursing services) X-rays taken Laboratory examinations made Pharmaceutical orders filled, etc.
	Other services	Pupil days (nursing education) Patient hours (recreational services), etc.

* "Patient days" for measurement of total hospital services.

method. The general ledger accounts will control the subsidiary cost accounts and thus ensure accurate cost data. Furthermore, the general accounts will be supported by detailed information so necessary for proper understanding and control. An integrated system of general and cost accounts with a minimum of duplication of records and entries can be accomplished by the use of controlling accounts on the general ledger and cost accounts as subsidiary records. Where it is not possible to integrate the cost accounts with the general accounts, it should be possible *periodically* to reconcile the cost accounts with the figures shown on the general accounting records.

Where cost and general accounts are to be integrated, the original installation of the system should be simple; and as its use becomes recognized, greater detail may be added. The system should be prepared so that the costs will be accurate and will be available promptly. The method of handling funds and expenditures and the allocation between departments and within departments should be fairly consistent from year to year. In order to arrive at such a plan, it might be wise to have the cost accounting concentrated in a central finance office, instead of having each department take care of its own cost accounting, with or without outside supervision.

ACCOUNTING RECORDS AND PROCEDURES FOR GOVERNMENTAL COSTS

Activities may be broadly grouped into (1) administration, (2) construction, (3) equipment service, (4) education, (5) protection, (6) health, (7) law, (8) libraries, (9) parks and recreation, and (10) public enterprises. A careful analysis of these will indicate that certain activities are similar to those performed by profit-seeking enterprises — such as construction, operating public utilities — and therefore their costs usually include the use of materials, labor, and a group of expenses. The other services are in themselves rather exclusively social and public. The costs for this group will cover primarily salaries or wages, supplies (as contrasted with materials used in construction projects or a public utility), and some expenses. To explain the cost accounting for each of these activities would involve an amount of needless repetition. Therefore, only certain types of activity will be discussed.

Cost accounting requires adequate records, which for a governmental unit will include:

1. *Original documents* — evidence of work performed, such as work orders, performance reports, time reports, stores requisitions, equipment reports, and charge tickets.

2. *Registers or journals* — used as an intermediate record for the summation of the original documents. Included here are a material req-

uisition journal, a register of work orders, and others. These journals and original documents are usually supported by subsidiary ledgers. The two most frequently found are: (*a*) the stores ledger or perpetual inventory, on which is recorded the kinds and quantities of materials on hand, received, and issued; and (*b*) the equipment ledger, in which is maintained a detailed record for each piece of equipment owned and used.

3. *Work and cost ledger* – the final basic record in any integrated cost system. In this are recorded the accounts pertaining to each work order issued.

The cost accounting procedure for governmental units must include reference to the accounting for labor, materials, indirect costs, standard costs, and cost reports. In accounting for *labor,* several factors must be considered. If the labor is on several public works jobs in the course of a day, labor reports should be made daily by the workman and checked by his supervisor. In other activities, where the same work is performed more or less continuously, such reports need not be made so frequently. In such cases, however, it might be desirable to divide the labor costs into (1) *effective,* which represents the time actually at work; and (2) *noneffective,* which includes the time spent on vacations and sick leave. Noneffective work is not included in computing the labor costs of a particular work order but will be included with the indirect expenses. Supervisory costs which apply to several activities should be prorated. Bonuses paid for overtime should be included in the expenses to be apportioned to all jobs rather than to the jobs on which they were paid, thus permitting the comparison of costs of one job with those of another. This procedure is similar to that used in industrial cost accounting.

In accounting for *materials,* there are a few principles not already discussed in the early part of this text. Adequate stores control and inventory records must be set up either on a departmental basis or on a *centralized* basis. All issues and receipts must be properly evidenced by vouchers. Pricing may be either on the first-in, first-out method or on the moving-average method.

In accounting for *indirect* costs, there are three types of expenses which require attention. One of the first relates to *equipment* used on a work order. The cost of equipment can be most effectively controlled by the use of a centralized equipment department and an individual perpetual record for each piece of equipment. Thus it becomes easier to charge each job with the proper cost for the use of equipment. This cost may be on the hourly basis or on the per mile of use basis. The cost of equipment is made up of the (1) acquisition cost and (2) the maintenance cost – repairs and operations. Usually in governmental accounting, except in the case of enterprises such as the utilities and waterworks, it is not customary to record depreciation as an expense. However, in computing rental charges for equipment, it is desirable to consider depreciation, since the equipment will wear out in the course of time and must be replaced. Other than governmental units should consider depreciation as an item of cost.

The other two types of indirect costs are (1) expenses of administration and supervision and (2) nonadministrative expenses which cannot practically be charged directly to specific activities or jobs when they are incurred. Such items as travel, telephone, and postage come under the heading of nonadministrative expenses. The use of a *predetermined* indirect cost rate, calculated on estimated direct labor cost, is an accepted procedure. The actual expenses and indirect costs are collected in the Overhead Cost account, and the charges made to various departments are credited regularly to the Overhead Applied account.

Merely to compile costs for a certain activity is not to control it or measure its effectiveness. There must be some measuring base or *standard*. The ideal standard and the one commonly used is the *minimum unit cost* at which the services or work should be done. Such standards may be computed either (1) by comparison with past experience of the governmental unit under consideration, (2) by comparison with other units of similar size and location, or (3) by engineering studies. Usually standards are not used until the cost system has been in operation for a few years, because comparisons with costs in the past are probably the most satisfactory unless the greatest care is used in comparing costs with other communities to be sure that the conditions in each case are comparable. A good illustration of such faulty comparisons is evident in the per capita educational costs in cities of similar sizes. Costs vary widely; but little consideration is given to costs of living, varied types of curricula, and quality of equipment, all of which make for variations.

To complete the picture of cost accounting for nonprofit entities, it is necessary to discuss the proper use of the system installed and the standards set. Cost summaries and reports are the essential link between the cost accounting and the managerial use of the data. To be most effective, these reports should be prepared periodically. Unless this is done, much of the effort and expense incurred in the cost accounting will be wasted. The reports most commonly presented would include the following:

1. *Monthly summary of unit costs,* showing for each activity the total costs, the units of work accomplished or completed, and the resulting unit cost.
2. *Monthly summary of labor costs,* indicating for each activity the various processes involved, the kinds of work performed, the man-hours of work, labor costs, and work units.
3. *Summary of equipment rentals,* showing for each class of equipment and for each piece of equipment, the place of use, the activities involved, the rentals charged, and the costs associated with them.

4. *Summary of materials used,* showing for each activity the type, the quantity, and the cost of materials used.

In addition to the regular reports indicated, it is possible to prepare, from time to time, special reports. Reports on idle and noneffective labor costs, reports on variations from standard costs, and departmental efficiency reports are only a few of those which might be used to study out-of-line conditions. Adequate use of graphic presentation of data is desirable.

COST ACCOUNTING FOR RESEARCH AND DEVELOPMENT ACTIVITIES

Substantial increases in expenditures for research and development activities in recent years has resulted in managements becoming more interested in the costs of these activities. No longer is research and development an unimportant function in many firms. In fact, many an enterprise would be out of business before very long if it were not for the constant development of new products or processes that grow out of the research activities.

Although companies distinguish between research and development activities, the financial executive usually considers the two-in-one category as they are similar for cost accounting purposes.

An important consideration facing management in companies engaged in research and development activities is how much to spend on these activities. For most items other than research and development, the amount allotted by management for costs and expenses varies with the level of operations, i.e., with expected benefits. In fact, flexible budgets based on levels of activity are often established, and these point out that expenditures rise as activities rise. In the case of research and development, however, there is a special problem. A given sum may be spent on a project with the result being a new product of substantial value or the project may result in failure. Thus, although it is possible that people working on a project may be *efficient* and even cost conscious, the *benefits* from the project may be *nil*. To make things more difficult, benefits from a project may not be known until costs have been incurred.

Control over the effectiveness of research and development activities may become a serious problem. A competent manager should head this activity. He should be an individual who might be able to select projects with high probabilities of success. He should also be an individual who is cost conscious and control minded, but he should not be afraid to spend more if he feels adequate results may be obtained.

The research and development activities of a company may be carried on in a centralized research center, or the activities may be carried on by each division at a number of locations. Obviously, cost data need to be accumulated for each location and for the research and development activity as a whole. More important, however, is the necessity for accumulating cost data, both actual and budget, by *project*. In this way management may compare the cost of a project with its expected cost.

The techniques of cost accumulation by projects is similar to accumulating costs by jobs in the factory. A cost sheet is prepared for each project showing actual and budgeted costs. For projects-in-process, status reports should be prepared periodically comparing expenditures and commitments to date with the budgeted amount. A status report is shown in Illustration 23–9.

Illustration 23–9
ABC MANUFACTURING COMPANY
RESEARCH AND DEVELOPMENT ACTIVITY—STATUS REPORT
August 31, 19—

Project No. 843 Date Started January 15, 19—
Purpose Improve liquifying process Expected Completion Date October 15, 19—
In Charge G. T. Jasper

Expenses	Budget	Expenditures to Date	Commitments to Date	Total Expenditures and Commitments	Unexpended
Personnel costs...............	$48,500	$32,000		$32,000	$16,500
Supplies....................	6,000	4,000	$ 500	4,500	1,500
Consultants and consulting services..................	15,000	8,000	3,000	11,000	4,000
Traveling expenses...........	6,000	4,000		4,000	2,000
Administrative..............	7,000	3,000		3,000	4,000
	$82,500	$51,000	$ 3,500	$54,500	$28,000

QUESTIONS FOR REVIEW

1. What basis would you use for allocating the following costs if your firm was a department store?

Salesmen's salaries	Personnel department expenses
Property taxes	Protective service costs
Salesmen's commissions	Delivery expenses
Credit department costs	Advertising expenses
Fire insurance	Unemployment insurance taxes
Rent	Accounting department costs

2. What areas of business activity outside of manufacturing and selling should use cost accounting procedures? Why?

3. "The use of cost accounting is necessary for private enterprises, but there seems to be no need for cost accounting for municipal operations." Do you agree? Explain your reasons.

4. "Analysis of the cost of governmental activities is the simplest of nonmanufacturing cost accounting because the budget requirements for tax purposes makes cost analysis a simple statistical auxiliary study." Is this true? Explain.

5. The Second National Bank is interested in allocating certain general operating costs to the various functional departments. How would you suggest that the following be allocated:

Administrative salaries	Rent
Advertising	Legal expenses
Auditing	Personnel management
Employee fidelity bonds	Stenographic services
Clerical salaries	Property taxes
Accounting	

6. The computation of office costs is not an accounting function but an administrative management responsibility. Do you agree? Explain.

7. How might cost accounting become a cost control device for a commercial bank? How would the bank income be allocated to the various departments?

8. Nonmanufacturing costs are closely associated with budgetary control. Therefore, these need not be incorporated in the accounting records of the firm. Explain. How then are these costs handled, computed, and used?

9. What cost units are applicable to department stores? To commercial banks? To municipalities?

10. How might cost accounting help a savings and loan association desirous of opening a new branch?

PROBLEMS—GROUP A

Problem 23–1. Purpose: *Cost Analysis for Municipal Organization—A School District*

The board of education of the Victoria School District is developing a budget for the school year ending June 30, 1972. The budgeted expenditures follow:

VICTORIA SCHOOL DISTRICT
BUDGETED EXPENDITURES
For the Year Ending June 30, 1972

Current Operating Expenditures:
Instruction:

General	$1,401,600		
Vocational Training	112,000	$1,513,600	
Pupil Service:			
Bus Transportation	$ 36,300		
School Lunches	51,700	88,000	
Attendance and Health Service		14,000	
Administration		46,000	
Operation and Maintenance of School		208,000	
Pensions, Insurance, etc.		154,000	
Total Current Operating Expenditures			$2,023,600
Other Expenditures:			
Capital Outlays from Revenues		$ 75,000	
Debt Service (Annual Installment and Interest on Long-Term Debt)		150,000	
Total Other Expenditures			225,000
Total Budgeted Expenditures			$2,248,600

The following data are available:

1. The estimated average daily school enrollment of the school district is 5,000 pupils including 200 pupils enrolled in a vocational training program.
2. Estimated revenues include equalizing grants-in-aid from the state of $150 per pupil. The grants were established by state law under a plan intended to encourage raising the level of education.
3. The federal government matches 60 percent of state grants-in-aid for pupils enrolled in a vocational training program. In addition the federal government contributes toward the cost of bus transportation and school lunches a maximum of $12 per pupil based on total enrollment within the school district but not to exceed $6\frac{2}{3}$ percent of the state per-pupil equalization grants-in-aid.
4. Interest on temporary investment of school tax receipts and rents of school facilities are expected to be $75,000 and are earmarked for special equipment acquisitions listed as "Capital outlays from revenues" in the budgeted expenditures. Cost of the special equipment acquisitions will be limited to the amount derived from these miscellaneous receipts.
5. The remaining funds needed to finance the budgeted expenditures of the school district are to be raised from local taxation. An allowance of 9 percent of the local tax levy is necessary for possible tax abatements and losses. The assessed valuation of the property located within the school district is $80,000,000.

Required:

a) Prepare a schedule computing the estimated total funds to be obtained from local taxation for the ensuing school year, ending June, 1972, for the Victoria School District.

b) Prepare a schedule computing the estimated current operating cost per regular pupil and per vocational pupil to be met by local tax funds. It is assumed that costs other than instructional costs are assignable on a per capita basis to regular and vocational students.

c) Without prejudice to your solution in part (a), assume that the estimated total tax levy for the ensuing school year ending June 30, 1972, is $1,100,000. Prepare a schedule computing the estimated tax rate per $100 of the assessed valuation of the property within the Victoria School District.

Problem 23-2. Purpose: *Computation of Royalty Cost*

The North-Slope Mining Company started mining in the current year on certain land leased from the Canadian Pacific Railroad Realty Corporation.

The royalty contract provided the following lease stipulations:

1. Minimum annual royalty: $10,000 minimum; $2,500 payable quarterly. Unearned minimum royalties may be recovered in any subsequent period from the earned royalties in excess of the minimum royalties. Minimum royalties of $30,000 were paid for the three years prior to the current year.

2. Earned royalty: $0.15 per ton shipped from the mine plus a per ton amount equal to 2 percent of the amount that the market value of the ore at the mine exceeds $4.20 per ton.

3. Operations in the current year were as follows:

| | | Per Ton | |
| | | | |
Quarterly Period	Tons Shipped	Market Value at Destination	Freight from Mine to Destination
First quarter.......................	None		
Second quarter...................	110,000	$11.00	$4.00
Third quarter.....................	190,000	10.00	4.20
Fourth quarter...................	20,000	9.50	4.00
	320,000		

Required:

Compute the amount of royalty to be paid to the Canadian Pacific Railroad Realty Corporation for the year and the amount of the unearned minimum royalty at the end of the year, if any.

(Adapted from AICPA Uniform Examination)

Problem 23-3. Purpose: *Analysis of Bank Costs*

The Knowlton National Bank of Chicago, Illinois, has an organization of five income-producing departments and five service departments. These income departments are: savings, commercial, safe deposit, trust and estate, and taxation. The service departments are: accounting, advertising, legal, stenographic, and building maintenance.

The trial balance for the month of June, 19—, showed the following account balances:

TRIAL BALANCE
June 30, 19—

Account	Dr.	Cr.
Cash..$	500,000	
Bonds and investments	850,000	
Loans receivable	718,000	
Overdrafts..	500	
Stock in Federal Reserve Bank.....................................	6,000	
Building (depreciated on 20-year basis)........................	50,000	
Allowance for depreciation—building............................		$ 20,000*
Safe deposit vault and fixtures (20 years).......................	5,000	
Allowance for depreciation—vault		2,000*
Deposits		1,600,000
Capital stock..		100,000
Paid-in surplus		100,000
Undistributed profits		300,000
Interest earned..		15,000
Service charges on checking accounts		1,000
Safe deposit box rentals..		1,500
Trustees' fees and commissions....................................		1,500
Taxation service income		300
Taxes on real estate	300	
Interest paid	1,200	
Officers' salaries...	3,000	
Salaries of office workers	5,000	
Salaries of other employees (building maintenance)...........	200	
Office supplies..	500	
Insurance expense	600	
Telephone and telegraph	100	
Repairs to building and maintenance	200	
Traveling expenses	300	
Advertising...	400	
	$2,141,300	$2,141,300

* Depreciation has not yet been recorded for June.

The various expenses are allocated to the income and service departments as follows:

Department	Travel Expenses and Officers' Salaries	Office Supplies and Office Salaries	Building Maintenance	Interest Earned	Interest Expense	Insurance
Accounting......................	4%	4%	500 sq. ft.			
Advertising	3	3	200			
Legal............................	3	3	300			
Stenographic...................	3	5	2,000			
Building maintenance	2	—	—			80%
Savings.........................	20	20	20,000	$1/3$	100%	—
Commercial....................	40	45	25,000	$2/3$	—	—
Safe deposit....................	10	5	12,000	—	—	20
Trust............................	10	12	10,000	—	—	—
Taxation	5	3	5,000	—	—	—
	100%	100%	75,000 sq. ft.			

Department	Telephone and Telegraph	Adver- tising	Account- ing	Legal	Steno- graphic
Accounting.........................$	8			5%	5%
Advertising.........................	5			5	5
Legal.................................	15	On basis		–	10
Stenographic......................	5	of gross		–	–
Building maintenance	5	income		–	–
Savings..............................	5	in each	15%	10	15
Commercial........................	25	department	70	45	50
Safe deposit........................	5		3	5	2
Trust.................................	12		10	20	10
Taxation	15		2	10	3
	$100		100%	100%	100%

Required:

On the basis of the foregoing data prepare:

a) A comparative income and expense statement for the month of June, by departments.

b) Compute the unit costs in the commercial department on the basis of the following data:

(1) There were 3,750 checks deposited, of which one third are on the Knowlton National Bank, one third are on other banks in the city, and one third are on out-of-town banks. There is no charge for checks on this bank and double the charge for out-of-town checks, as compared with checks on local banks.

(2) There were 91,005 checks drawn on this bank by depositors of the commercial department. These are three times as costly to handle as checks deposited in this bank but drawn on local banks.

(3) Drafts and cashier checks cost five times as much to handle as the checks drawn on this bank by depositors. There were 5,000 of these.

PROBLEMS—GROUP B

Problem 23–4.   Purpose: *Municipal Cost Accounting—A Water Company Contract*

The Conscience Water Company furnishes water to the ABC municipality. The adjoining municipality, XYZ, is anxious to obtain a supplementary supply of water for its increasing population and opens negotiations for a long-term contract at a fixed price per million gallons.

The operating costs of the waterworks for the year 1972 were as follows:

Water collecting system costs ....$	25,000
Water purification department costs	50,000
Water pumping station operating costs.................	70,000
Maintenance of distribution system......................	48,000
Commercial office expenses..............................	52,000
General administration expenses	18,000
Debt service requirements.................................	200,000
	$463,000

The income for 1972 was as follows:

> Metered water revenues.....................................$400,000
> Fire hydrant rentals.. 100,000
> $500,000

The proposed contract calls for the installation of meters for the purpose of measuring the water delivery to the XYZ residents and business firms. The cost of these meters will be paid for by the user, plus an installation cost. The contract for the water will be for not less than 20 years.

The engineering department furnishes you with the following data:

	Gallons
Water pumped during year 1972...	1,350,000,000
Water billed to consumers	1,000,000,000
Water used for fire service..	200,000,000
Water not accounted for—leakage, accidents, etc...................	150,000,000
Estimated water to be delivered to XYZ municipality per year..	300,000,000

Additional facilities and costs to be incurred if the proposed contract is accepted:

> Additional pumping equipment...$100,000
> To be acquired by issuance of 20-year bonds, at 5 percent interest.
> Water collecting system expenses and the maintenance of distribution system will be increased 10 percent each.
> The purification and pumping expenses will be increased in direct proportion to the water pumped.
> The commercial office and general administration expenses will not be increased.
> The present facilities are being used 60 percent of capacity.

Required:

Prepare a statement showing the computation of the unit cost per million gallons of water delivered that would be fair to both municipalities.

Problem 23–5.   Purpose: *Administrative Office Cost Analysis*

The Burkhardt Supply Company has a centralized correspondence department. The administrative office manager prepares a budget at the end of each year on a departmental basis. One of the important departments whose costs have come under scrutiny because of its increasing prominence is that of the correspondence division.

The budget of the variable and apportioned costs for the correspondence department of this firm for the three months ending March 31, 19—, were:

	January	February	March
Salaries of correspondents	$10,000	$10,000	$10,000
Stenographic costs	4,800	5,000	5,200
Postage	4,000	4,200	4,500
Telephone and telegraph	3,200	3,200	3,500
Supplies	1,000	1,100	1,200
Maintenance and repairs	300	200	100
Miscellaneous expenses	100	120	130
Share of administrative expenses	500	500	500
Share of personnel department costs	200	200	200
Rent	300	300	300
Light and heat	300	260	200
Depreciation of equipment	300	300	300
Insurance	100	100	100
Payroll taxes	600	600	600

The actual costs for the three-month period were:

	January	February	March
Salaries of correspondents	$ 9,800	$10,000	$10,300
Stenographic costs	4,500	4,500	4,800
Postage	3,800	4,000	4,250
Telephone and telegraph	3,000	3,300	3,500
Supplies	1,200	1,000	1,400
Maintenance and repairs	200	150	150
Miscellaneous expenses	120	100	100
Share of administrative expenses	500	500	500
Share of personnel department expenses	200	200	200
Rent	300	300	300
Light and heat	330	280	250
Depreciation of equipment	300	300	300
Insurance	100	100	100
Payroll taxes	580	630	630

Required:

a) Prepare a three-month comparison of the budgeted and actual. On each month's statement show the cumulative total of the budgeted and actual figures to date.

b) Indicate the possible causes of variation of actual from budgeted figures.

c) Compute the cost of each letter for each month if the volume of production for the department after making allowance for form letters, fill-in letters, and interdepartmental communications was equivalent to: January, 80,000 letters; February, 84,000 letters; and March, 82,000 letters.

d) Indicate your managerial reaction to the results of these figures.

Problem 23–6.   Purpose: *Municipal Cost Accounting; Analysis of Centralized Trucking Department Costs*

The City of Bayoud has organized a centralized trucking service for all of the municipal departments except sanitation (garbage) and street cleaning. These two departments maintain their own trucks.

The cost of operating this service for six months ending June 30, 19—, was as follows:

January 1: Investment in six trucks, costing new $60,000: estimated life, five years; scrap value of each truck, $1,000. Tools and parts, new, cost $8,000; estimated life five years; no scrap value. A municipally owned garage is used for these, on which there is no rental or tax charge.

The costs of operating the service for the six months was:

Gas and oil	$ 3,000
Insurance	3,200
Repairs, outside	2,000
Salaries of drivers with fringe benefits	12,000
Telephone and office expenses	800
	$21,000

The budgeted costs for this six-month period for operating this centralized trucking department was $25,000, and the estimated ton-miles was budgeted at 62,500.

The trucking service was rendered to the various municipal departments according to the predetermined rate as follows:

	Ton-Miles
School and educational department	9,000
Health department	6,000
Printing department	8,000
Road and engineering service	8,800
Street-cleaning department, extra	7,000
Snow removal, extra	10,200
Sanitation and sewer service, extra	5,000
Relief service	6,000
Total Service Rendered	60,000

Required:

a) Prepare a schedule showing the estimated cost per ton-mile.
b) Prepare a schedule showing the actual per ton-mile costs.
c) Prepare schedule showing allocations to the various departments.

part IV

APPLIED COST
DETERMINATION
PROCEDURES

chapter 24

Special Applied Cost Determination Procedures

INTRODUCTION

Mainly for reference when a particular assignment requires a knowledge of peculiar cost determination procedures and for preparation for professional examinations, a few applied cost procedures are discussed. These refer to two groups of procedures:

1. Applied process cost determination procedures.
2. Illustrative standard cost determination situations.

APPLIED PROCESS COST DETERMINATION PROCEDURES

Process cost accounting may be a very simple and easy-to-determine statistical or accounting procedure, or it may become very complex and involved. The basic principles, nevertheless, are the same. The complexity is due to the nature of the manufacturing operations or to some inherent problem of shrinkage, waste, spoilage, or apportionment of costs. In order to show the application of process cost accounting, this chapter will present a brief statement of the methods and problems of process cost accounting of the following:

1. Cement manufacturers
2. Brick manufacturers
3. Foundries
4. Lumber mills
5. Flour mills

COST PROCEDURE FOR CEMENT MANUFACTURERS[1]

Cement is usually made from such materials as limestone, clay, shale, or blast-furnace slag. The manufacture of cement usually involves taking definite proportions of such raw materials, grinding them to extreme fineness, burning them at a high temperature, and then regrinding the resulting clinker. It is a continuous operation. There are two methods of manufacturing cement—the dry process and the wet process. In the dry process the materials are kept dry throughout the entire operations, but in the wet process water is added to the raw materials. Since the latter will cover all phases of the former, the wet process will be described in this section. As an illustration, it is assumed that limestone and shale are used as raw materials and are obtained from the firm's own quarries. Natural gas is used as fuel (although coal or fuel oil could also be used). The manufacturing operations cover the following:

A. *Quarrying* of limestone and shale, which covers:
    1. *Stripping*—removing top refuse material.
    2. *Production*—loading material into quarry cars.
    3. *Crushing* and storing of limestone and shale.
B. *Clinker department,* which covers:
    1. *Raw grinding* of limestone and shale.
    2. *Slurring*—adding water to mixture (only in wet process).
    3. *Blending*—mixing proper proportions of materials (this is done in large tanks of 1,000- or 2,000-barrel capacity).
    4. *Burning* in kilns, to which slurry mixture is passed.
    5. *Clinker grinding*—of the material cooled and stored.
C. *Packing and loading,* which refers to taking the cement from the large silos. The cement is not packed until it is to be shipped either in barrels, cloth bags, paper bags, or in bulk.

The operating accounts represent the cost centers or departments. These departments or centers, as will be shown in cost of production report which follows, are: (1) Raw Material No. 1 (limestone); (2) Raw Material No. 2 (shale); (3) Clinker; and (4) Cement. Incidental or auxiliary departments, such as machine shop, carpenter shop, hospital, hotel, and clubhouse, are included under the general heading of Mill Overhead. The mill overhead may be allocated to the various producing departments or, as is more commonly the case, applied to production as one lump sum in the last—the cement department.

Illustration 24–1 represents the cost summary which may be prepared from the departmental cost of production reports or analyses. A more

---

[1] Adapted, with permission, from Leon E. Smith, "Accounting in the Cement Industry," *N.A.A. Bulletin,* Vol. XXIII, No. 3.

Illustration 24-1

THE BEST CEMENT COMPANY
COST SUMMARY
For the Month Ending March 19—

	Rock Costs	Shale Costs	Raw Grinding	Clinker Burning	Clinker Grinding	Power, Light, and Water	Machine Shop	Packing and Loading	Mill Overhead	Coal Costs	Total
Supplies...............	3,000.00	450.00	1,300.00	1,800.00	1,200.00	1,500.00	150.00	100.00	100.00	1,200.00	10,800.00
Payroll for Labor......	5,000.00	2,000.00	8,700.00	5,200.00	2,400.00	3,000.00	7,850.00	900.00	800.00	800.00	36,650.00
Fuel...................	1,200.00	950.00	400.00			11,500.00	200.00			16,000.00	30,250.00
Depreciation:											
Machinery...........	100.00	50.00	1,500.00	2,500.00	2,400.00					180.00	6,730.00
Buildings...........			300.00	500.00	200.00					20.00	1,020.00
Taxes.................	300.00	100.00									400.00
Depletion.............	50.00	20.00									70.00
Insurance.............	250.00	80.00	300.00	100.00	200.00	150.00	120.00		50.00	20.00	1,270.00
Total.............	9,900.00	3,650.00	12,500.00	10,100.00	6,400.00	16,150.00	8,320.00	1,000.00	950.00	18,220.00	87,190.00
Machine Shop..........	2,000.00	200.00	2,000.00	2,000.00	1,000.00	720.00	8,320.00			400.00	8,320.00
Power, Light, and Water...	100.00		6,000.00	4,100.00	4,600.00	16,870.00				2,070.00	16,870.00
Coal Costs............				20,690.00						20,690.00	20,690.00
Total.............	12,000.00	3,850.00	20,500.00	36,890.00	12,000.00			1,000.00	950.00		87,190.00
Production............	30,000 tons	19,250 tons	64,050 bbls.	64,050 bbls.	60,000 bbls.						
Unit Cost.............	0.40	0.20	0.32	0.5759	0.20						
Transfers:											
Rock, 22,000 Tons.....			8,800.00								
Shale, 13,200 Tons....			2,640.00								
Raw Grinding, 64,050 Bbls...				31,940.00							
Clinker Burning, 60,000 Bbls....					64,477.20						
Gypsum Added..........					4,132.80						
Mill Overhead to Finished Cement Only..........					950.00						
Cumulative Cost Grinding.....			31,940.00								
Cumulative Cost Burning.....				68,830.00 (1.07462)							
Cumulative Cost Cement.......					81,560.00 (1.3593)			81,560.00			
Packing, Loading........								1,000.00			
Final Cost Ready for Shipment...								82,560.00			

Illustration 24–2
COST OF PRODUCTION REPORT
For Month Ending March 31, 19—

	Tons or Barrels	Amount	Average per Ton or Barrel
RAW MATERIAL NO. 1—ROCK:			
Production (Tons).....................	30,000		
Stripping...........................		$ 3,000.00	
Production..........................		7,000.00	
Crushing, Receiving, and Storing.........		2,000.00	
Total Cost of Raw Material No. 1....		$12,000.00	
Add: Inventory at Beginning of Period.....		0	
Total..............................		$12,000.00	$0.40
Less: Inventory at End of Period..........	8,000	3,200.00	
Less: Used in Stone Dust Operations......		0	
Used in Manufacture...;..........	22,000	$ 8,800.00	$0.40
RAW MATERIAL NO. 2—SHALE:			
Production (Tons).....................	19,250	$ 3,850.00	$0.20
Stripping...........................		$ 1,000.00	
Production..........................		2,350.00	
Crushing, Receiving, and Storing.........		500.00	
Total Cost of Raw Material No. 2....		$ 3,850.00	
Add: Inventory at Beginning of Period.....		0	
Total..............................		$ 3,850.00	
Less: Inventory at End of Period..........	6,050	1,210.00	
Used in Manufacture..............	13,200	$ 2,640.00	$0.20
CLINKER:			
Production (Barrels)..................	64,050	$68,830.00	$1.07462
Raw Material No. 1—Rock.............		$ 8,800.00	
Raw Material No. 2—Shale.............		2,640.00	
Grinding, Mixing, and Storing...........		20,500.00	
Burning, Cooling, and Storing...........		36,890.00	
Total Cost of Clinker...............		$68,830.00	
Add: Inventory at Beginning of Period.....		0	
Total..............................		$68,830.00	
Less: Inventory at End of Period..........	4,050	4,352.80	
Used in Manufacture..............	60,000	$64,477.20	$1.07462
CEMENT:			
Production (Barrels)..................	60,000	$81,560.00	$1.3593
Cost of Clinker......................		$64,477.20	
Clinker Grinding.....................		12,000.00	
Mill Overhead.......................		4,132.80	
Reserves...........................		950.00	
Total Cost of Cement..............		$81,560.00	1.3593
Add: Inventory at Beginning of Period.....		0	
	60,000	$81,560.00	$1.3593
Less: Inventory at End of Period..........	0	0	
Less: Cement Used...................	0	0	
Bin Cost of Cement Shipped........	60,000	$81,560.00	$1.3593

condensed summary or statement may also be prepared. For an example of such a statement, see Illustration 24–2.

There are a few special problems in the costing of cement. One refers to *containers*. Materials are shipped principally in cloth sacks, paper bags, and in bulk. Each bag or sack contains 94 pounds, and four sacks make one barrel of cement. Cement is sold on a delivered basis—FOB destination. A charge of 10 cents per cloth sack and 15 cents per barrel is made to the customer. This charge is refundable to the customer if the containers are returned within 90 days. (There is no charge or refund for paper bags.) The company must therefore set up an account for returnable containers in the hands of customers. A second problem refers to *depletion* and *depreciation*. Depletion and depreciation are the same as for most mining companies. However, to have comparable costs from month to month, the unit or production method should be used.

A third problem should be noted. The unit of costing is per ton for raw material, and this is changed to per barrel in the burning department. This transition is accomplished merely by dividing the new quantity unit into the total cumulative cost up to that stage of production.

COST PROCEDURE FOR BRICK MANUFACTURERS

The manufacture of bricks is similar to that of cement. The variety of bricks which one manufacturer can produce is fairly large, the principal difference being in the materials used. In the main, there are usually six operating departments or cost centers, and these represent the work-in-process accounts. That is, the work-in-process is kept by cost centers, which are:

1. *Quarrying*—in which clay and sand are dug.
2. *Pans and machines*—in which the mixture of raw materials is prepared and placed in the pans. The resulting product is known as *wet bricks*.
3. *Drying*—in which the bricks are allowed to dry, making green bricks.
4. *Setting*—in which the green bricks are placed in the kilns for firing and burning.
5. *Burning*—baking the bricks in kilns.
6. *Unloading*—removing the bricks, which have been burned, from the kilns.

Before examining a pro forma cost of production statement, it is necessary to discuss various problems of cost accounting for the brick industry. These are: (1) the handling of spoiled bricks in the pans and machine center, in the process of drying, and in the kilns; (2) the equivalent production of the bricks in the kilns; and (3) plant overhead.

In most problems in the manufacture of bricks the principle laid down is that *no spoilage costs* are to be charged against the bricks still in the process of manufacture in the driers or in the kilns. This means that the bricks spoiled in the drier or in the kilns should be included in the equivalent production; that is, the equivalent production represents both good and spoiled bricks produced. This results in a lower unit cost for the work-in-process, but the total cumulative costs that are transferred from department to department include the cost of the spoiled bricks. In other words, the spoiled bricks are used to compute unit costs for valuing the work-in-process; but this unit cost is a departmental figure only, since for each succeeding department a new unit cost is computed, based on the total cumulative costs divided by the good production (without the spoiled bricks).

The second problem refers to the work-in-process inventory in the kilns. This is usually divided into *fully burned bricks* (completed for that department); *half-burned bricks* (estimated to be one-half complete); and *green bricks,* which are costed at the unit cost of all work up to the kiln.

The third problem is one of *plant overhead.* As in the case of cement production, the plant overhead is added to production primarily in the final (unloading) department. A portion of this overhead, however, may be allocated to those bricks still in the kilns which have been completed but not unloaded.

Illustration 24–3 demonstrates the computation of the quantities of

Illustration 24–3
QUANTITY STATEMENT OF BRICKS MANUFACTURED
For the Year 19—

Wet bricks placed in pans during year		17,450,000
Less: Bricks spoiled in pans and machines		350,000
Good bricks carried to driers during year		17,100,000
Add: Inventory of bricks in driers at beginning of year		100,000
Total bricks in driers during year		17,200,000
Less: Bricks spoiled in drying		700,000
Good bricks dried and in process of drying		16,500,000
Less: Inventory of bricks in driers at end of year		600,000
Bricks set in the kilns		15,900,000
Add: Bricks in kilns at start of year:		
Burned	180,000	
Half-burned	100,000	
Green	80,000	360,000
Total bricks in kilns during year		16,260,000
Less: Bricks spoiled in burning		660,000
Total bricks—green, half-burned, and burned in kiln during the year		15,600,000
Less: Inventory of bricks in kilns at end of year:		
Burned	150,000	
Half-burned	100,000	
Green	90,000	340,000
Good bricks taken from kilns during year		15,260,000
Add: Burned bricks in yard at beginning of year		40,000
Total Bricks Available for Sale		15,300,000

bricks placed in production in the various departments and the resulting good production.

The cost of production for the year, taken from the cost production reports of the various departments, is shown in Illustrations 24–4 and 24–5.

Illustration 24–4

COST OF PRODUCTION STATEMENT

Expenses	Quarrying	Pans and Machines	Drying	Setting	Burning	Unloading
Materials and supplies....$ 2,800		$14,800	$ 1,208	$ 630	$ 3,562	$ 4,000
Labor............... 12,200		35,200	7,800	26,400	64,000	26,000
Coal................. 1,800		...	6,000	...	60,000	...
Powerhouse costs....... ...		15,000	...	...	2,000	...
Depreciation........... 1,200		5,000	800	...	21,000	...
Total Costs........$18,000		$70,000	$15,808	$27,030	$150,562	$30,000

COST ACCOUNTING PROCEDURE FOR FOUNDRIES

Castings of gray iron, steel, brass, aluminum, or other metals constitute the basic materials for numerous products manufactured by such companies as the automobile manufacturers, machine manufacturers, engine producers, and many others. Some of the larger companies operate their own foundries; others have this work done by independent foundries. Except for very small foundries manufacturing expensive castings on special order, most of this work is costed on a process basis; that is, *the costs are averaged by departments even though several different orders are involved.* The unit of costing is the pound. The fact that foundry operations are required in so many industries makes it imperative that the student of industrial accounting be familiar with the *nature of the operations* and the cost procedures that can be followed.

From the accounting manual of one manufacturer of a variety of engines the following nontechnical description of foundry operations is quoted:

The first step in the manufacture of a casting is the making of a *pattern,* usually of wood, from a drawing of the part required. The pattern must be the exact shape as the part to be made and slightly larger to allow for the metal shrinkage. Patterns are made from a variety of woods, some of which are the harder woods, such as mahogany. An accurate record and careful storage is made of each pattern so that it is available for use on subsequent orders for the part.

The *molding operation* is the next step in making the casting. The pattern is placed in a box called a flask, and sand rammed tightly around it. The pattern is then withdrawn, leaving a hollow space in the sand which will shape the molten metal to be poured into it. There are a great variety of shapes and sizes of parts so that different methods of molding have been developed. Some molds are made by hand while machines are used for others. The art of molding includes the

Illustration 24–5

COST OF PRODUCTION REPORT
NATIONAL BRICK COMPANY
For the Year Ended December 31, 19—

	Quantity in Thousands	Total Costs	Unit Cost per Thousand
QUARRYING COSTS:			
Material, Labor, Coal, etc............................	17,450	$ 18,000.00	$ 1.032
PANS AND MACHINES:			
Costs of Pans and Machines........................		$ 70,000.00	
Quantity Placed in Pans and Machines.................	17,450		
Deduct: Spoiled in Pans and Machines................	350		
Good Production in Pans and Machines...............	17,100		
Total Cumulative Cost.........................	17,100	$ 88,000.00	$ 5.1462
DRYING COSTS:			
Costs of Drying...............................		$ 15,808.00	
Inventory of Bricks in Driers at Beginning of Year (½ Complete).................................	100	520.00	
Total Cumulative Costs...........................	17,200	$104,328.00	
Deduct: Bricks Spoiled in Drying.......................	700	....	
Total.................................	16,500	$104,328.00	
*Less: Cost of Bricks in Drier at End of Year (½ Complete)**	600	3,369.18	
Total Transferred...............................	15,900	$100,958.82	$ 6.3496
SETTING COSTS:			
Costs of Setting Bricks............................	15,900	$ 27,030.00	
Total Cost of Bricks Set in Kilns.....................	15,900	$127,988.82	$ 8.0496
BURNING COSTS:			
Cost of Bricks Burned during Year...................		$150,562.00	
Inventory in Kilns at Beginning of Year:			
Burned (@ $18.00)............................	180	3,240.00	
Half-Burned.................................	100	1,300.00	
Green (@ $8.00).............................	80	640.00	
Total Bricks Set in Kilns...........................	16,260	$283,730.82	
Deduct: Bricks Spoiled in Burning....................	660		
Total Bricks to Be Accounted for...................	15,600	$283,730.82	
*Deduct: Bricks in Kilns at End of Year:**			
Burned (150 X $17.5249)........................	150	2,628.74	
Half-Burned.................................	100	1,278.73	
Green (90 X $8.0496)...........................	90	724.46	
Cumulative Cost of Burned Bricks...................	15,260	$279,098.89	$18.2896
UNLOADING COSTS:			
Cost of Bricks Unloaded..........................		$279,098.89	
Unloading Costs................................		30,000.00	
Overhead for Entire Plant.........................		2,305.11	
Total Cost of Good Bricks Produced..............	15,260	$311,404.00	$20.4066

*Computation of inventory:

Bricks in Drier at End of Year:
Transfer Cost (600 @ $5.1462).. $3,087.72
Unit within the Department Cost:
Effective Production...16,850M
Unit Cost ($15,808.00 ÷ 16,850M)............................. $0.9382
Cost in Ending Inventory (600 X ½ X $0.9382) 281.46
Inventory of Bricks in Driers..................................... $3,369.18

Bricks in Kilns at End of Year:
Green Bricks (90 @ $8.0496).. $ 724.46
Half-Burned Bricks:
Transfer Cost (100 @ $8.0496)................................... $804.96
Effective Production...15,890M
Unit within the Department Cost ($150,562.00 ÷ 15,890M)........... $9.4753
Cost in Ending Inventory (100 X ½ X $9.4753)........................   473.77   1,278.73
Burned Bricks [150 X ($8.0496 + $9.4753)] 2,628.74
Total Inventory of Bricks in Kilns................................. $4,631.93

selection of the proper sand, which must be fine enough to give a smooth finish to the casting, porous enough to allow gases to escape and capable of standing up under extreme heat. Provision must be made in the mold for the inpouring of metal and for the escape of gases.

Molds can only control the outer surface of the casting. Inner surfaces such as in holes or hollows are formed by *cores*. These are made of a special sand and baked. Placed in the mold, the metal flows around them, so that when they are cleaned out the desired cavity is left in the casting. It is by the use of cores that an intricate casting can be made. The placing of the cores, called coring-up, is in itself a difficult operation.

Iron is melted in a *cupola*, which consists of a vertical cylindrical steel shell, lined with fire brick. Into this pig iron, scrap and coke are charged in alternate layers. When air is blown into the cupola the coke burns at high temperature and the iron, steel and other ingredients melt. The melt is taken off at the bottom of the cupola into ladles, and thence poured into the waiting molds.

After solidification the casting is taken out of the mold and cleaned. The cleaning, which may be chipping, grinding or sand-blasting, removes the projections and irregularities left on the casting. After cleaning the casting is weighed and reported complete.[2]

As previously indicated, the entire foundry operations may be operated on a process cost procedure. However, for independent jobbing foundries the procedure may be varied, if desired, as follows:

Melting department—process cost accounting procedure
Molding department—job order cost procedure
Core-making department—job order costing
Cleaning department—process cost accounting procedure
Special treatment of castings such as annealing—process cost procedure

The American Foundrymen's Association has prepared a manual on accounting for foundries. For detailed procedure, reference may be made to *Accounting for Foundries*. However, a few outstanding characteristics may be pointed out here.

The control accounts for manufacturing operations may be set up in either of two ways. There may be *one* work-in-process account, known as the *Foundry Work-in-Process account;* or there may be set up work-in-process accounts on a departmental basis, one for each department, such as the *Melting Department, Molding Department, Core-Making Department, Cleaning and Chipping Department*, etc.

There are certain accessory departments, the costs of which must be allocated or charged directly to the four operating departments listed in the preceding paragraph. These departments are the pattern shop, where the patterns are made for the molds, the carpenter shop, and the blacksmith shop.

---

[2]Taken, with permission, from *Accounting and Control Manual of Cooper Bessemer Corporation, Mount Vernon, Ohio*, prepared by James E. Brown, Plant Accountant.

The forms sometimes used are: (1) the *daily melting or cupola report,* on which is recorded the costs of materials, supplies, and labor used in the melting department; (2) the *flask card,* on which is recorded the time or labor used in molding the casting; (3) *core tickets,* on which is recorded the time and labor costs and the material costs for making the cores; and (4) a *summary cost report* showing the costs of the melting, molding, core-making, and finishing departments applicable to the various jobs or orders completed.

There are three bases on which costs are assembled in the foundry: *tonnage costs, class costs,* or *individual job order costs. Tonnage costs* are determined by dividing the various expenses, both direct and indirect, by the entire output of the foundry during a given accounting period. Unless the product is quite uniform in size and complexity, this method is of little use for costing or control, since not all castings have uniform costs per pound because they vary not only in size but in the nature and number of cores. Therefore, the cost per pound, per hundred pounds, or per ton, as determined by dividing the total costs by the total weight of the good castings produced, may be erroneous.

Under *class costs,* castings are grouped (1) by *size* (weight of castings, such as 1–10 pounds, 11–25 pounds, 26–50 pounds, and on up to 401–500 pounds); and (2) by *shape* and *complexity* arising from use of cores. By weighting the size of the castings by the complexity factor (based upon the estimated additional labor required because of size or use of cores), and thus obtaining a weighted average cost per pound, a more reliable cost figure is obtained for control purposes than under the tonnage method. This method has a greater acceptance today than the tonnage method.

The *individual job order cost method* can be used by those foundries manufacturing on order only. For higher-priced castings, such as those of brass, aluminum, or other alloys, this method should be used, even though it involves greater clerical expense than either of the other two methods.

It should be noted that in most foundries not more than 25 percent of the costs are direct costs that can be charged directly to a job; the rest are indirect and must be prorated. This proration is usually done on an estimated basis. This estimated basis depends upon the yield from the tonnage of melted metal poured, which sometimes may be as low as 30 percent and may be as high as 70 percent. Such variables make costing quite difficult except on an estimated basis predicted upon experience with various types of castings.

COST PROCEDURE FOR LUMBER MILLS

The operations of the average lumber mill are divided for cost accounting purposes into (1) cost of logging operations and (2) cost of sawmill operations.

Logging and Lumbering Operations.[3]   *Logging operations* costs are made up of three major items plus a share of the general administrative expenses. Logging costs are joint costs covering all kinds of timber, since it is quite impossible to cut separately each kind of standing trees. The three cost items are:

1. *Stumpage costs,* which represent the cost of the standing timber. Stumpage costs correspond to the material costs of the average manufacturer. These costs may be computed in several ways, depending upon the method of acquiring the standing timber. These methods are: (1) the ownership of the land and the timber, in which case the value of the land and the standing timber must be amortized over the quantity produced, as compared with the estimated footage in the property; (2) the purchase of the standing timber only, in which case the purchase price will be apportioned over the production on the basis of the estimated footage; and (3) the acquisition of the lumber on a royalty basis, in which case the royalty paid becomes the cost of the stumpage.

Stumpage costs may be considered as part of the logging costs or may be included only in the statement of the cost of sales.

2, 3. *Cutting and transportation costs,* which represent the labor and material costs of felling the trees and removing them to the sawmills. The labor costs thus incurred are termed "swamping"—removing the underbrush; "felling and bucking," which refers to the cutting of the trees; "skidding and loading," which refers to the removal of the logs to the transporting medium either by floating the logs, removing by sleds or tractors, or just dragging by horsepower to railroad cars. In large operations the cost of the railroad equipment and spurs are considered as part of the transportation costs. For this work, materials and supplies, such as saws, wire rope, and cutting tools, are required. Charges for depreciation of equipment, repairs to equipment, fire insurance, fire loss, maintenance of transportation equipment, amortization of rail and spur equipment costs, and operating supplies must also be added to the cost of the labor for cutting and transporting the logs.

A share of the administrative salaries, fire-patrol costs, and taxes, including the severance tax imposed by most states, should be included, together with the costs of operating camps where the workmen live during the cutting and transportation operations.

In the logging operations, the quantity of production is measured in feet according to *log scale* measurements. These measurements and expressions of quantity are not accurate, since good timber will overrun the log measurements and defective timber will fall below this quantity when finally put through the sawmill. As lumber comes from the saws, it is *tallied* according to actual measurements. The log scale measurements are then corrected to the lumber tally sheets by adding or deducting the difference. The resulting costs of the production from the saws is expressed on the basis of the board feet units.

Sawmill Operations.   Sawmill operations follow a similar pattern in cost finding. The logs may be cut into *boards,* which are pieces of lumber 1 inch in thickness; *dimensions,* which are 2 inches thick; *planks,*

---

[3] Adapted, with permission, from *Pathfinder Bulletin* (Charles R. Hadley Co.), No. 137 (by Burton N. Smith); and from *N.A.A. Bulletin,* Vol. XXIII, No. 9 (by Edward S. Rittler).

which are 3 inches thick; and *timbers,* which are 4 inches or more in thickness. The operating costs of the sawmill are composed essentially of the following: labor costs, supplies, maintenance charges, power costs, and amortization of the sawmill. The work of the sawmill is grouped under four headings: sawmill, yards, dry kilns, and planing mills. If the operations are not too extensive, the costs of the logging and transportation and the sawmill may be combined into a single statement.

The main cost accounting problem in this division is one of computing the costs of the inventories and of the quantity produced. At the sawmill there will usually be a supply of logs on hand. The number of logs and their footage are usually based on an *estimate.* The margin of error in this estimate is usually too small to affect the accuracy of the figures to any extent. The log inventory is generally valued at average logging cost, plus the stumpage cost if it has not already been included in the logging cost. In computing the quantity of production at the sawmill, the inventory method may be used, as shown in Illustration 24–6.

Illustration 24–6

| | Grades of Lumber (M Board Feet) | | | | |
	A	B	C	D	Total
Inventory at end of month......................	400	500	300	100	1,300
Sales..	400	100	300	200	1,000
Used by mill................................	1,000	800	700	1,500	4,000
Total....................................	1,800	1,400	1,300	1,800	6,300
Less: Inventory at beginning of month...........	500	300	200	300	1,300
Monthly Production......................	1,300	1,100	1,100	1,500	5,000

Shown on pages 785–87 are: a pro forma statement of the cost of logging operations (Illustration 24–7); a pro forma statement of the cost of sawmill operations (Illustration 24–8); and a summary statement of operations (Illustration 24–9).

COST PROCEDURE FOR FLOUR MILLS

Nature of Operations. The operations of a flour mill consist essentially of converting wheat into flour. A bushel of wheat weighs 60 pounds, and a barrel of flour weighs 196 pounds. Flour is the main product of the mill; but there are several grades of flour, some of which are considered in the nature of by-products. Also as a result of milling, a by-product called *offal* is produced, which is sold as feed. Under the cost procedure usually followed, the total cost of manufacturing (milling) is charged to the high-grade flour produced, from which is deducted the sales value of the lower grades and the offal. The lower grades of flour are known as *first*

Illustration 24–7
NORTHWESTERN LUMBER MILLS, INC.
STATEMENT OF LOGGING OPERATIONS
For the Month of October, 19—

	Amount	Per Thousand
STUMPAGE COSTS...............................	$ 2,000.00	$0.40
LOGGING COSTS:		
Rigging Ahead....................................	$ 200.00	
Felling and Bucking................................	5,000.00	
Skidding and Loading..............................	2,000.00	
Equipment Repairs................................	300.00	
Supplies (Saws, Wire Rope, etc.)...................	300.00	
Depreciation.....................................	200.00	
Total Logging Costs...........................	$ 8,000.00	$1.60
TRANSPORTATION COSTS:		
Operating Labor.................................	$ 1,100.00	
Track and Road Maintenance.......................	300.00	
Operating Repairs................................	400.00	
Operating Supplies...............................	500.00	
Depreciation of Equipment.........................	300.00	
Amortization of Tracks and Spurs..................	400.00	
Total Transportation Costs......................	$ 3,000.00	$0.60
OTHER CHARGES:		
Camp Expenses...................................	$ 800.00	
Cruising Expenses for Surveying Stumpage...........	100.00	
Fire Patrol......................................	100.00	
Taxes, Including Severance Tax.....................	300.00	
Insurance.......................................	350.00	
Salaries, Direct and Apportioned...................	2,350.00	
Total Other Expenses..........................	$ 4,000.00	$0.80
Total Cost of Logs Produced..........................	$17,000.00	$3.40
Accounted for as Follows:		
Logs Sold, F.O.B. Log Pond........................	$ 3,400.00	
Logs Kept for the Sawmills.........................	13,600.00	
Total Cost of Logs Produced....................	$17,000.00	
QUANTITY STATEMENT PER LOG SCALE		
Total Logs Produced...............................	5,000,000	
Quantity of Logs Sold to Paper Mills, etc..............	1,000,000	
Quantity of Logs Kept for Sawmills....................	4,000,000	
Total Production for Month......................	5,000,000	

Illustration 24–8
NORTHWESTERN LUMBER MILLS, INC.
STATEMENT OF SAWMILL OPERATIONS
For the Month of October, 19—

	Amount	Per Thousand*
SAWMILL:		
Mill Labor	$ 6,200.00	
Power	800.00	
Supplies	1,050.00	
Repairs	900.00	
General Expense	1,000.00	
Depreciation, and/or Amortization	1,100.00	
Total	$11,050.00	$2.60
YARDS:		
Labor	$ 3,000.00	
Repairs	475.00	
General Expense	500.00	
Depreciation	700.00	
Total	$ 4,675.00	$1.10
DRY KILNS:		
Labor	$ 5,000.00	
Power	1,000.00	
Repairs	500.00	
General Expense	850.00	
Depreciation	2,000.00	
Total	$ 9,350.00	$2.20
PLANING MILL:		
Labor	$ 7,200.00	
Power	3,000.00	
Repairs	800.00	
General Expense	750.00	
Depreciation	1,000.00	
Total	$12,750.00	$3.00
GENERAL OPERATING EXPENSES:		
Salaries	$ 3,000.00	
Taxes	1,200.00	
Miscellaneous	50.00	
Total	$ 4,250.00	$1.00
Total Sawmill Costs	$42,075.00	$9.90

* This statement assumes the averaging of the costs for all types of lumber. If costs are desired by grades, the use of additional columns for each grade may be used. A quantity of production statement is prepared from the sawmill tally sheets. These costs are based upon 4,250,000 board feet production.

Illustration 24-9

NORTHWESTERN LUMBER MILLS, INC.
SUMMARY OF OPERATIONS
For the Month of October, 19—

	Scale	Amount	Per Thousand
LOGS:			
Sales....................................	1,000	$ 8,000.00	$ 8.00
Cost of Sales per Schedule................	1,000	3,400.00	3.40
Gross Profit on Sale of Logs............		$ 4,600.00	$ 4.60
Logs at Mill at Beginning.................	1,000	$ 3,200.00	
Received from Woods per Statement of Logging Costs.........................	4,000	13,600.00	
Total................................	5,000	$16,800.00	$ 3.36
Inventory at End of Month................	750	2,520.00	
Cost of Logs........................	4,250	$14,280.00	
Log Pond Labor and Expenses..............		4,420.00	
Cost of Logs Sent to Sawmill...........	4,250	$18,700.00	$ 4.40

	Board Feet per Thousand	Amount	Per Thousand
LUMBER PRODUCTION:			
Sales.................................	4,500	$99,000.00	$22.00
Cost of Sales:			
Inventory at Beginning of Month..........	350	$ 4,729.00	
Logs Used Above.......................	4,250	18,700.00	
Sawmill Costs per Statement..............		42,075.00	
Total...........................	4,600	$65,504.00	
Inventory at End of Month...............	100	1,424.00	
Cost of Sales.........................	4,500	$64,080.00	$14.24
Gross Profit on Lumber..............		$34,920.00	$ 7.76

	Units (Cords)	Amount	Per Unit
FUEL PRODUCTION:			
Sales.................................	2,000	$10,000.00	$ 5.00
Cost of Sales:			
Inventory at Beginning of Month..........	250	$ 1,000.00	
Labor................................	} 2,100	3,000.00	
Expenses.............................		2,000.00	
Total.............................	2,350	$ 6,000.00	
Inventory at End of Month..............	350	500.00	
Cost of Sales........................	2,000	$ 5,500.00	$ 2.75
Gross Profit on Fuel*..............		$ 4,500.00	$ 2.25

*The gross profit on each type of production is carried forward to an income statement.

clear and *second clear*. Daily production statements are prepared for each grade of flour, based upon the market price of wheat and upon the market value of offal and the lower grades of flour.

Cost Accounting Procedure.[4]   Cost cards showing the gross recovery from milling operations are prepared daily for the various grades of flour and are based upon the market value of offal and of clear and low-grade flour and upon the market price of wheat.

To illustrate the method of preparing cost cards for the various grades of flour, the following information is assumed:

Market value of wheat .... $ 0.70 per bu.
Market value of offal — average run .... 11.00 per ton
Market value of first clear .... 2.20 per bbl.
Market value of second clear .... 1.70 per bbl.
    (4.5 bu. of grain mixture will produce 1 bbl. of flour of all grades and
    74 lbs. of offal.)
Primary grades of flour are....................................... 100% straight grade
                                                                  85% short patent grade
                                                                  10% first clear
                                                                   5% second clear
Average total expense per barrel is ....$ 1.00

To compute the cost of 85 percent short patent flour with the foregoing information, the following outline is given:

4.5 bu. of wheat at $0.70 ....$3.15
Add: Expense, including selling expenses 1.00
        Total wheat expense $4.15
Deduct: Feed at market: 74 lbs. of offal at $9 ($11 − $2 discount)............. 0.333
Cost of barrel of 100% straight flour..$3.817
Deduct: Clears (lower grade) at market:
    10% first clear at $2.00 ($2.20 − $0.20) $0.20
     5% clear at $1.50 ($1.70 − $0.20) 0.075   0.275
85% of 1 bbl. of short patent flour...$3.542

As indicated, the value of the clears has been discounted 20 cents per barrel in computing the cost of patents.

If 85 percent of a barrel of short patent flour costs $3.542, the cost of producing a full barrel of 85 percent short patent flour will be $4.167 ($3.542 ÷ 85 percent). A cost card is then prepared to get an analysis of the items entering into the material cost of a barrel of flour (see Illustration 24–10). Similar formulas and cost cards are prepared for other primary grades of flour.

Cost of Secondary Grades.   Secondary grades of flour are those made of a combination of parts from primary grades. First, it must be determined which of the primary grades are to be used in making the secondary

---

[4]Taken, with permission from Robert R. McCreight, "Flour Milling Costs," *N.A.A. Bulletin,* Vol. XXIII, No. 3.

Illustration 24–10.   Cost Card

	Pounds	Market Price Less Discount	Price	Amount
5.294 bu. of wheat (4.5 bu. ÷ 85% = 5.294)..	317.64		$0.70	$3.7058
Deduct: Low grades and offal:				
10% first clear..........	23.05*	$2.00 bbl.	$1.02 cwt. $0.2351	
5% second clear........	11.52	1.50 bbl.	0.7653 cwt. 0.0882	
27.41% offal............	87.07	9.00 ton	0.45 cwt. 0.3918	
Total deductions.....	121.64			0.7151

1 bbl. of short patent, 196 lbs..$2.9907
Expense per barrel ($1.00÷85).. 1.1764

Cost per barrel of 85% flour..$4.1671

*(317.64 × 27.41%) =87.07 lbs.   (317.64 − 87.07) =230.57 × 10% =23.05.

grades. Then apply the percentage of the cost of the primary grades to be used. Assume that Grade C flour is to be made by combining 80 percent of Grade A flour and 20 percent of Grade X—first clear flour. The costs of each of these component parts are:

Material cost of Grade A flour ....$2.82 bulk
Market value of Grade X flour .... 2.20 bulk

The computation for the Grade C would be as follows:

80% of $2.817 equals ($3.817 − $1.00 selling expense) $2.2536
20% of $2.20 equals... 0.4400
      Total (the material cost of 1 bbl. of Grade C flour)......................$2.6936

In order to get the details of this cost, the percentage of the quantities is calculated as follows:

80% of 4.5 bu. equals 3.6 bu. of wheat at $0.70.....................................$2.52
Plus: 20% of Grade X equals 39.2 lbs. of flour at $2.20 bbl. 0.44
      Total $2.9600
Less: 80% of 74 lbs. of offal equals 59.2 lbs. wheat at $0.45 cwt. 0.2664
Material cost of 1 bbl. of Grade C flour...$2.6936

Part of a good cost system in the milling business involves a budget of manufacturing costs for the year, which should be controlled for variations on a monthly basis. Some of these variations are due to incorrect estimates of the costs, and some are due to value of production. Part of this budget relates to the manufacturing overhead and to the over- or underabsorbed overhead.

Special Items of Cost. Because of errors in estimated income or discount, or due to certain manufacturing operations, the cost figures shown on the cost cards are not always realized. Since the differences involved are not too great, most of these items appear on the income statement as adjustments to the net profit or loss on flour. These items are: (1) offal sales in excess of the cost card values; (2) realization of discount on offal sales due to rise or fall of offal values between dates of booking the order and actual milling dates; (3) realization of discount on clear flour sales, which is similar to the offal sales discount realization; (4) temper gains due to increase of weight by added moisture used to temper or heat the wheat to improve the milling operations; and (5) variances in freight costs, package costs, and ingredient costs.

ILLUSTRATIVE STANDARD COST DETERMINATION SITUATIONS

ILLUSTRATIONS OF STANDARD COSTS USED AS OPERATING DATA

To indicate how the principles of standard costs used as operating data can be applied by business firms to their accounting work, four illustrations have been given. These have been prepared by the cost accountants in the respective firms and describe the procedures used by these firms.

Illustration 1. The standard cost accounting procedure used by a prominent manufacturer of filing supplies is as follows:

There is carried in stock at all times about 5,500 different finished articles. This comprises about 60 percent of our business; the other 40 percent being made special-to-order.

It is necessary to have a complete stores system to handle all of these products, otherwise it would be easy to lose many thousands of dollars in inventory differences.

We use the order cost system for so-called "special work" where products are made to customers' specifications. Standard costs are used for standard products made for our own warehouse. This means that the standard cost is established for the finished product and for each part used in the finished product and any differences between the standard and actual costs are analyzed and recorded according to the cause of this difference.

Standard costs are established for each kind of raw material purchased, and when material is received it is charged to inventory at the standard cost and any difference between this amount and actual purchase price is charged or credited to Loss or Gain on Purchase Variance. From this point on all movements of raw material are handled at standard cost.

Before a product is released for production the engineering department prepares an operation sheet which shows complete description of the article to be made, kind and quantity of material used, a list of each operation to be performed according to departments and operation numbers, together with machine and tool numbers required to perform the work. The operation sheet also shows time allowance for each operation and standard costs per hundred are computed according to material, labor, and manufacturing burden. The operation sheets are typed on ditto master paper so that copies can be duplicated. Ditto copies of the operation sheets are used for production orders, stores issues, cost sheets, etc. This eliminates the necessity of preparing production orders and stores issues by hand or on a typewriter each time an order is issued to the factory.

Raw material withdrawn from stores against production orders is charged to the Process account at standard costs for the quantity actually issued. At the time the order is closed, material costs as charged to the order are compared with standard for the quantity completed and any difference written off to Loss or Gain on Materials Used.

At the same time that the production department releases the order to the factory they also release prewritten timecards for each operation which are prepared from the ditto master copy of the operation sheet. Timecards are sent to the factory and used by operators for reporting their time and production. Operators are unable to report time against stock production orders without these prewritten timecards. Differences between the standard labor cost and actual earnings of the operator are picked up through payroll distribution of timecards and charged or credited to Loss or Gain on Labor.

All indirect expenses which cannot be applied directly to a production order are charged to a Manufacturing Burden account. The standard hours worked in each department as reported on the timecards are accumulated on the payroll distribution, and at the end of the month an entry is made charging Process account and crediting Manufacturing Burden with the number of standard hours multiplied by standard burden rates for each department. The difference remaining in the Manufacturing Burden account is written off to Loss or Gain on Manufacturing Burden. The standard manufacturing burden rate is established at the beginning of each fiscal year and continued throughout the year unless some radical change occurs which would make it necessary to revise the rate.

Illustration 2.   Standard costs as used by a prominent manufacturer of tags and crepe paper:

We have several main products—that is, Tags, Crepe, Gummed Paper, etc., each requiring a slightly different method of accounting. I will, however, give you a brief description of some of the features of our system.

1.   RAW MATERIALS:

We carry all of our book inventories of materials at a standard cost. These costs are made up in October or November for the following year. When the material is received, we charge the inventory accounts at the standard cost and charge or credit any variation between this standard and the actual cost to a Price Variation account. This Price Variation account shows the efficiency of our purchasing department in purchasing materials at or near the standard which they forecast.

2. Materials in Process:

When these materials are requisitioned by the producing departments, we charge a Commodity-in-Process account at standard. Wherever possible, we set up standards of quantity necessary for any given job. We then measure the materials and deliver only that quantity. Should departments need more materials, the additional amount is charged to their Loss or Gain account. If the department is able to produce more from this quantity, we credit any overrun to this Loss or Gain account. This Loss or Gain account represents the operating efficiency of the department in utilizing materials.

Whenever it is impractical to measure materials precisely, we use a statistical checking basis of determining variations between actual and standard usage. Detailed studies are made at regular intervals by waste study men, which studies are used as a basis for accounting entries as well as a basis for a material usage improvement program.

3. Labor and Manufacturing Expense:

In common with most other standard cost systems, we make up a standard manufacturing expense rate for each of our operating centers. This manufacturing expense rate is based on the budgeted expenses for the year. Each department is charged with its actual expenses. These expense accounts are credited at the budget rate. The difference between the charge and the credit represents a loss or gain due to the efficiency of utilizing indirect labor or indirect materials. The offsetting charge to the budget credit is to a Manufacturing Expense Variation account. We credit this Manufacturing Expense Variation account with the earned burden. This earned manufacturing expense is obtained by multiplying the predetermined manufacturing expense rate by the number of hours each center operates. The difference between the charge and the credit in this case represents a loss or gain due to volume. The offsetting charge to the credit to the Manufacturing Expense Variation account is made to a Labor-in-Process-and-Overhead account. This Labor-and-Overhead account is likewise charged with the direct labor payroll. The Labor-and-Overhead account is credited at standard. This credit is obtained by multiplying a predetermined standard rate by the number of pieces produced. The offsetting charge is against the Commodity-in-Process account.

4. Manufacturing Expense Development:

We classify our expenses into two general headings:

a) General Service Expenses.
b) Producing Departmental Expenses.

We list under General Expenses those general administrative and plant maintenance charges which cannot definitely be allocated to any individual producing department foreman. These expenses are outlined on a chart which shows the bases that we use in distributing these expenses to our operating centers. Producing department expenses are those expenses which are directly controlled by a foreman. They will include such things as sweeping, shipping, moving, repairs, experimental, etc.

5. METHOD OF PAYMENT:

Our company has a modified form of piecework payment. We use a punched card system in accumulating our payroll and our statistics for cost control.

Illustration 3. Standard cost accounting procedure used by a prominent shoe manufacturer:

At the beginning of each season or six-month period we prepare a cost catalog of standard costs which is to be used on all shoes made during that season. As these catalogs include hundreds of different prices for the upper leather items, sole leather items, lining and finding items, used on the many styles and types of shoes, we make well over 150,000 different piece rates.

The cost catalog is made up as follows—a standard price per foot for each kind of leather we plan to use during the season is established by the purchasing department. The standard cutting allowance in feet for each style of shoe on each type of leather is determined from analysis of the various patterns to be cut and from past experience. From these figures, the cost of each of the items of upper stock is determined for the catalog. The same general plan is used in determining the cost of various items of linings, trimmings, bottom stock and findings special.

Labor piece rates are determined from time studies and from negotiations with the Shoe Workers' Union, and from these the piece labor allowance for each style of shoe made from the various leathers and on the various lasts is computed.

A small percentage of daywork for each shoe is determined by analysis and from previous experience.

A variable manufacturing expense or overhead budget is determined from past experience and from adjustments in these expenses which we have made or propose to make. The total budget for the season is compared with a moving average of shipments for the previous five years, and a per pair cost for variable manufacturing expense determined for the cost catalog. All of the styles within each grade of shoes are assigned the same variable manufacturing expense charge, but the charge per pair varies between the grades of shoes in approximately the same ratio as the average labor per pair within each grade. In other words, grades of shoes calling for a higher labor cost are assigned a higher overhead.

The factory costs for production purposes are determined as outlined above. For pricing purposes, an allowance for fixed overhead is then calculated with the higher priced lines being assigned a larger amount of fixed overhead.

At the end of each month, the total of the standard costs for the pairs produced that month is compared with the actual material used and payroll spent. Variations from the standards are then shown on the monthly financial statements.

Most of our labor is paid by the piece. Each operator as he completes the work on a case of shoes, clips off a small coupon, and at the end of the week's work, he places all the coupons he has clipped off for the week in an envelope, which he drops in a box at the pay office. Most of our shoes are made in 12-pair cases, but if a case contains a greater or smaller number than the 12 pairs, this change is indicated by a different color coupon, one color for each different number of pairs.

Dayworkers are paid by the hour on timecards. All of our operators are paid by check, and at the end of each week the earnings are determined by the addition of the piecework coupons turned in during the week, or in the case of dayworkers by the number of days worked as indicated by the timecards. The pay checks for each department are written at one time, and carboned through on to journal sheets for that department. At the end of the month, the necessary journal entries are prepared and delivered to the accounting department for posting to the proper accounts.

APPLICATION OF BASIC STANDARD COSTS IN A STEEL MILL

Illustration 4.   The dual or memorandum standard cost procedure used by a large steel manufacturer is described below. Because this procedure represents in detail and in excellent form the dual or memorandum method of recording standard costs, a more complete description of the procedure is given.[5]

The strip mill in which this system (standard costs) has been applied receives steel in the form of billets, which are generally rectangular in cross section and are of various lengths, weighing from 150 pounds to 2,000 pounds each. These billets are first hot rolled into hot rolled strips in any of three hot mills, depending upon the size of the finished product.

The next operation on all material that is to be further processed is a pickling or cleaning operation. The steel is then successively cold rolled, annealed, and finally slit into a finished size. It may also be leveled, or flattened, and it may be copper plated in this particular plant.

The product of the mill is sold in various stages of manufacture, such as rolled, hot rolled, pickled and oiled, cold rolled, and polished. The steel itself may be of any of approximately 125 individual analyses, falling within the following general classifications:

Carbon Steels	*Electrical (Silicon) Steels*
Low carbon	Field Grade
High carbon	Armature Grade
Stainless Steels	Dynamo
Chrome	Transformer
Chrome Nickel	*Magnetic and Other Special Alloys*

PREPARING THE STANDARD COST PLAN

As the first step in the installation of the plan, the important sales-billed classes were determined, and finally about twenty-five product groups or lines were chosen as being sufficiently important for separate treatment in the inventory accounts.

Next the departmentalization of the plant was studied, and finally some twenty-nine direct production centers were established and some twenty-six indirect or nonproductive centers.

---

[5]Taken, with permission, from a report by E. J. Hanley, Secretary and Treasurer, Allegheny Ludlum Steel Corporation, printed in the *N.A.A. Bulletin*, Vol. XXII, No. 21.

The distribution of overhead was carefully analyzed, and new bases were determined wherever this was thought advisable. Then after a satisfactory distribution to production centers had been arranged, and after extended study of activity in these centers, in consultation with the management, normal activity of each center was agreed upon and a normal burden [manufacturing expense] rate in terms of dollars per hour of operation was established. . . .

Production records for several years were reviewed and time standards were established for any size and any type of product in each center, based upon statistics. The standard times so determined were then extended at the average earned rate for the crew and factored for the normal burden rate to determine, finally, a dollar standard for any size or grade of material in each operation. In only one operation, slitting, was any allowance for losses included in the standard. The raw materials in use were also analyzed and standard costs established for each of them. All mill routines were thoroughly studied and checked, and a scrap routine was devised to make sure that all scrap would be properly classified and carefully weighed.

When the job was completed, there had been established about 50,000 standards for labor and burden and about 2,000 standards for material.

OPERATION OF THE STANDARD COST PROCEDURE

When an order is received at the mill, it is scheduled and routed. The order is then passed on to the cost clerk, who really "job costs" it—that is to say, he calculates a standard cost based on the route previously established. A copy of a typical cost card is shown in Exhibit 1 [see Illustration 24–11]. This card is placed in the active standard file and is used daily to cost the production reports and finally to cost sales for the particular order.

Actual expenditures for a given product line or inventory account, including overhead at normal rates, are charged to the proper inventory accounts. In the illustrated case Account No. 281, high carbon, cold rolled annealed material is used. These inventory accounts are further subdivided between labor and burden on the one hand, and material on the other. Similar accounts are maintained at standard and are charged for the actual quantities involved at the standard costs appearing on the cost card, Exhibit 1.

When material is scrapped in any operation, the labor and burden cost to that point, known as "prior labor and burden," is removed from the standard labor and burden account, a contra entry being made to the standard cost control. (The standard cost books carry a standard cost control account, to which contra entries are made in order that these accounts may be self-balancing.) Simultaneously, the standard cost of material is removed from the standard material inventory with appropriate contra entries to the control account. Only the scrap value of material scrapped is removed from the actual inventory account, however, and as a consequence at the end of any period when the ratio to be applied to the standard cost of sales is determined, this ratio picks up the material loss. As an example, assume that the actual cost of material on a particular order to a certain point is $100.00. Assume also that the standard cost of this material is $100.00. At this point there is a $100.00 debit balance in both the standard material and in the actual material account. Assume further that 20 percent of the material is scrapped and that the scrap value is $5.00. The standard value of the material

Illustration 24–11

ALLEGHENY LUDLUM STEEL CORPORATION
Standard Cost per Thousand Pounds

Exhibit 1

Customer __The Blank Company__
Order No. __64321 Z__
Prod. Class __281—12C440__
Weight __75000#__

__Dead Soft Setting Pass Sheared Coils__

H.R. Width __6"__ H.R. Ga. __.078__ Fin. Width __1.4385__ Fin. Ga. __.014__
Date __10/31/__

Kind __6 x 3 x 20'__

Steel Carbon Weight __1000#__

Memo	Center	Size	Mtl.	L. & Br.	P. L. & Br.	Repl.
	6110	078	$14 10	$3 92	$	
	6150			2 01	3 92	
Acid	42		14 52			
	6303	014		7 20	5 93	
	6241			5 20	13 13	
($3.52)	22#Cu		17 65		12 84	
	6180			1 41	18 04	
Total						

Memo	Center	Size	Mtl.	L. & Br.	P. L. & Br.	Repl.
	6242		$	$	$	
				3 01	19 45	
	6212			4 10	22 46	
	Shear Loss	15#	17 92		22 80	
	6250			1 01	26 90	
					27 91	
Total			$17 92		$27 91	

scrapped would be $20.00, which would be removed from the standard inventory account, leaving a balance of $80.00. The scrap value of the material is $5.00 and that removed from the actual inventory account leaves a balance of $95.00. When the material is shipped, there is a ratio of $95.00 to $80.00, or 118 percent plus. The cost of sales of $80.00 is factored by this percentage so that the actual account would be relieved of the amount $95.00. This illustrates how losses are picked up by the variance percentages.

THE PLAN AT WORK

Now for an actual example of the workings of the cost plan. Exhibit 1 is a cost card of 75,000 pounds of copper plated material for the Blank Company —our order 64321Z. The symbol 12C440 notifies the cost department or the schedule that is to be followed in processing this order. Material falls into product class No. 281; widths and gauges are indicated, and also the kind of material and the size of billet. In this instance, we have a compound material, of which the steel accounts for 978 pounds, and plating material 22 pounds. (All figures on this card are fictitious and are shown for illustrative purposes only.)

The operations involved on this order are:

Code	Operation	Department	Code	Operation	Department
6110	Hot rolling	12″ Mill	6180	Annealing	Box Anneal
6150	Pickling	12″ Pickle	6242	Wiping	Wipers
6303	Cold rolling	7½″ Steckel Mill	6212	Slitting	Slitters
6241	Plating	Plating Dept.	6250	Wholesale and shipping	

From our file of standards the cost clerk prepares this cost card showing (1) the material cost at each operation during which the material cost changes, (2) the cumulative material cost, (3) the labor and burden for each operation, and (4) the labor and burden accumulated to the prior operation, called "prior labor and burden." It is to be noted that up to center 6241 the cost is based on 1,000 pounds of steel. At center 6241 the material is combined with plating material, and from there on the cost is based upon 978 pounds of steel and 22 pounds of plating material. At center 6212 where material is slit, a definite allowance is included for the loss, and as a result the standard cost per 1,000 pounds of both material and labor and burden are increased from there on to compensate for this allowance.

In Exhibit 2 [Illustration 24–12] the whole plan is outlined and tied in with the cost card appearing as Figure A. Figure I shows two parallel accounts, in one of which appears the actual cost of material purchased and in the other the standard cost of the same material. As material is purchased and the account "Billets and Bands Purchased" debited at standard, a corresponding entry is made to Standard Cost Control—Figure K, entry N. Then, as material is transferred into process, the weight so transferred is shown on production reports and an entry is made to the proper work-in-process account, No. 281—Figure F, for actual pounds at standard cost. Simultaneously, the actual cost of material is transferred from the raw material accounts to the actual work-in-process account, Figure F, the raw material account being relieved on the basis of the standard cost of material

Illustration 24–12

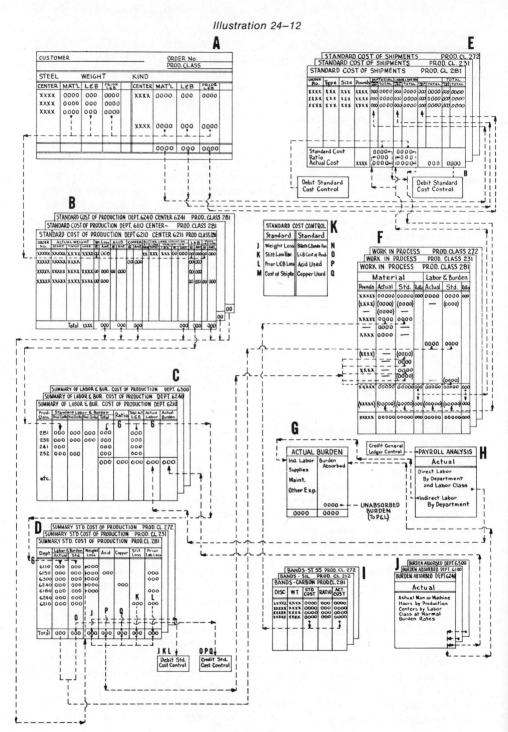

EXHIBIT 2

transferred factored by the ratio obtained at the close of the period between the balance in the actual raw material account and the balance in the standard raw material account. For whatever actual material may be scrapped an appropriate credit is made to the proper work-in-process material account, Figure F, at scrap value.

Actual payroll, Figure H, is reported separately as direct labor and indirect labor. Further direct labor is also reported directly against major product groups departmentally and is allocated to product lines departmentally on the basis of relative standard labor costs for the individual lines within the product group. It is then accumulated by lines for all departments, Figure D, and is thereafter charged to the proper work-in-process account, Figure F. Expenditures for indirect labor, together with other items of expense, are collected departmentally and summarized as burden, Figure G. Burden absorbed, Figure J, is then determined by multiplying actual man or machine hours by the normal burden rate and the burden absorbed is accumulated by product classes in each production center, Figure C. It is then summarized by material classes from all departments, Figure D, and is charged to the appropriate work-in-process account, Figure F.

The difference between the normal burden or burden absorbed, Figure J, and actual burden, Figure G, is transferred directly to profit and loss and does not enter the cost picture further.

All entries to the standard cost accounts, except the entry to account "Billets and Bands Purchased," originate with the production reports from the mill. Each department reports by order number, beginning and ending weights of material, Figure B, and reference is made to cost cards to price these reports at standard.

On operations where material is introduced into process, actual material weight is extended at standard, and likewise the weight of acid and copper, as has already been mentioned. The standard labor and burden information developed from the order is summarized within the departments for the product class, Figure C, and then further summarized by product classes from all departments, Figure D. The weight loss on each item is extended at the standard material cost and also at the prior labor and burden loss. Standard slit loss, where involved, is calculated, and variations from standard slit loss in dollars determined. Appropriate entries are then made to the standard work-in-process account, Figure F. A corresponding credit for the standard labor and burden charge is made to the standard cost control. A credit is made to standard material for the standard value of the material loss and another credit to standard labor and burden for the prior labor and burden loss at standard, with a corresponding entry in each case to standard cost control. Variation from standard slit loss is treated similarly. All this information, except standard labor and burden, is summarized directly by product lines, Figure D, and is entered into work-in-process account, Figure F.

The work-in-process accounts now consist of total actual cost, including burden at normal, while the standard cost accounts include only the standard cost of material and standard labor and burden covering the material actually in the inventory with no allowance for loss material, with the exception of the slitting loss referred to heretofore. The ratios of the balances in the actual accounts and in the standard accounts represent variations for all reasons, that is to say, on account of performance and on account of material scrapped or removed from process for any reason.

Illustration 24–13

A   Exhibit 3

ALLEGHENY LUDLUM STEEL CORPORATION
West Leechburg Division

PRODUCTIVE LABOR REPORT   Period: Nov. 17–30, 19—

Center	Department and Product Group	Actual	Standard	Ratio	Variation		
					Total	Time	Rates
6100	9" Hot Mill						
	Carbon	$0,000	$0,000	000	$ 000	$000	$ 000
6110	12" Hot Mill						
	Carbon	0,000	0,000	00	0,000	000	0,000
	Silicon	0,000	0,000	000	00	00	0
	Chrome	0,000	0,000	000	000	00	000
		0,000		000	000	000	00

B

ALLEGHENY LUDLUM STEEL CORPORATION
West Leechburg Division

MATERIAL LOSSES   Month of November, 19—

Center	Department and Product Group	Pounds Lost	Yield %	Losses in Dollars				
				Material	Prior Labor & Burden	Total	Recovered	Net Loss
6100	9" Hot Mill							
	Carbon Steel	00,000	00.00	$0,000	–	$0,000	$0,000	$0,000
6110	12" Hot Mill							
	Carbon Steel	0,000	00.00	000	–	000	000	000
	Silicon Steel	000	00.00		–	000	000	000

C

ALLEGHENY LUDLUM STEEL CORPORATION
West Leechburg Division

GROSS PROFIT—BY CLASSES OF PRODUCT   Month of November, 19—

Class	Product	Net Sales		$ Price per 1,000#	Gross Profit	
		Pounds	Dollars		Dollars	% to S.B.
231	Plain H.R.—Low Car. Strip	0,000,000	000,000	00.00	00,000	00
232	Plain H.R.—High Car. Strip	0,000,000	000,000	00.00	0,000	00
241		000,000	00,000	00.00	0,000	00
242	P & O—Low Car. Strip	00,000	0,000	00.00	000	00
243	P & O—High Car. Strip					00

During the accounting period, in this case a month, invoices have been priced at standard material cost and standard labor and burden cost, as summarized on the cost cards, and in this manner the standard cost of sales has been determined. At the close of the month "actual versus standard" ratios are computed, based on the beginning balance plus the various charges in the work-in-process accounts, Figure F. Actual cost of sales accounts are then charged on the basis of standard cost factored by these ratios with appropriate credits to actual work-in-process accounts. The corresponding standard entries are again made to standard cost control.

Perhaps the matter of parallel accounts has been unduly emphasized in this paper in order to make clear the mechanics of this cost plan. The facts are that control accounts only are duplicated and the accounting for dual values does not involve duplication of accounting computations. In any standard cost plan, the detail work involves the accumulation of standard cost information. The accumulation of so-called "actuals" in this particular application is extremely simple, as the units for which such costs are accumulated are not jobs, as in job costs, but rather some larger unit, such as the product line.

AVAILABLE REPORTS

With respect to the reports that are available, Exhibit 3 [Illustration 24–13] indicates the three that are regularly issued. Figure A, a report of productive labor, is issued at the close of each pay period, in this case every two weeks. It compares actual labor with standard labor by major product lines in each department. The ratio of actual to standard is shown, the dollar variance occasioned by more time being used than the standard contemplated or higher than standard rates per hour being paid. The calculation of the variance analysis is made as follows: Actual labor cost and actual man-hours are obtained from the payroll by departments for major product classes; standard labor and burden combined are similarly summarized from the standard cost detail; standard labor cost is then obtained by departments by factoring standard labor and burden to remove burden. Actual hours, then, times the difference between actual labor rates per hour and standard labor rates per hour is the variation due to rates. The difference between total variance and this amount is the variance due to time.

Figure B on Exhibit 3 shows the report of material losses by departments and by major product lines. This report is made monthly and is really a summary of all losses at standard and is obtained from the standard cost detail. Figure C of Exhibit 3 is a classified income statement showing the gross profit for each product.

QUESTIONS FOR REVIEW

1. Outline the procedure in manufacturing cement.
2. When is the transition in units made from tons to barrels, and how is this transition taken up in the cost accounting?
3. Brick production goes through four major operations. What happens in each one?
4. How are manufacturing expenses usually applied to production in the brick manufacturing industry? Why is this so?

5. What different types of castings can be produced? Are these produced by hand (manual) or machine labor?

6. What are the producing departments in a foundry, and what kind of work is done in each? What is meant by *auxiliary departments?*

7. What three different bases can be used in computing foundry costs? Explain each one.

8. What factors complicate cost accounting for foundries?

9. What is meant by the *log scale measurements* in lumbering? What other unit is used in determining the quantity of lumber produced?

10. Outline the cost procedure in producing flour. What special factors of cost must be considered in flour cost accounting?

PROBLEMS—GROUP A

Problem 24–1. Purpose: *Cost of Production Report and Quantity Statement for a Cement Manufacturer*

The Inland Portland Cement Company presents you with the following data for the year ended December 31, 19—, and requests you to prepare a statement of the cost of production, showing the average cost per barrel of cement produced. This should be supplemented by a quantity statement showing production by operating departments: raw materials (rock), clinker, and cement.

The inventories on hand at the beginning and end of the year were:

	January 1, 19—		December 31, 19—	
	Quantity	Value	Quantity	Value
Rock and shale, in tons 25,000*	$ 1,150	15,000*	$650
Clinker department, barrels...............50,000*	2,705	0	....
Cement, barrels..............................75,000*	73,400	85,000*	?

*Complete as to labor and materials.

The production costs for the year were as follows: 350,000 tons of rock and shale were mined and used during the year at a cost, including depletion and depreciation of $64,000. Each ton of rock is estimated to produce $3\frac{1}{2}$ barrels of cement on the basis of past experience. Sales for the year were 1,300,000 barrels of cement. The costs of grinding, mixing, and storing in the clinker department were $180,000; and of burning, cooling, grinding, and storing, also in the clinker department, $860,000. The mill overhead for the year is $40,000, and miscellaneous reserves charged against the current production amount to $8,000.

Problem 24–2. Purpose: *Computation of Quantity of Production in the Production of Bricks*

The operations of the International Brick Company consist of (1) blasting, digging, and conveying the shale to the machines, called *quarrying;* (2) grinding, mixing, and molding the wet bricks, called *pans and machines;* (3) drying; (4) building the bricks in the kiln and preparing the kilns for firing, called *setting;*

(5) *burning* or kiln firing; and (6) opening the kiln and unloading and stocking the burned bricks, called *unloading*.

From the following statistics of production and inventories you are to prepare a schedule, by departments or operations indicated above, showing the quantity in process at the beginning, put into process, spoilage, in process at the end, the transfers to other departments, and, finally, the quantity of finished bricks unloaded in the yards:

	Bricks
Wet bricks produced in the quarries	16,000,000
Good bricks carried to the driers	15,500,000
Spoiled in drying	450,000
Spoiled in burning	300,000
Green bricks in kilns not yet fired	100,000
Bricks in kilns completely burned but not yet unloaded	85,000
Bricks in kilns in process of burning	210,000
Bricks set in kilns during year	?

Inventories on hand at the beginning of the year:

	Bricks
Bricks burned in the yard	50,000
Burned bricks still in kilns	180,000
Bricks burning in the kilns	90,000
Green bricks in the kilns	70,000
Green bricks in the dryers	50,000

(Adapted from AICPA Examination)

Problem 24–3.   Purpose: *Preparation of Manufacturing Account for Foundry*

Prepare a ledger Pig Iron Stock account for the Indiana Foundry Company, January 1, 19—, to December 31, 19—, showing balance December 31, 19—.

Administrative and general expense	$ 19,500
Advances on contracts	50,000
Blowing	10,000
Capital stock	1,000,000
Coke (211,400 tons)	687,050
Current assets (net)	908,110
Current liabilities	660,000
Electric current	9,500
Expenditures for blast furnace relining	38,500
Exploration and development expenses	17,500
Fixed assets—sundry (net)	585,000
Fixed liabilities	600,000
Furnace labor	138,750
Furnace plant and equipment	1,400,000
Furnace relining fund	45,000
General works expense	19,750
Handling and delivering coke to coke stock	10,570
Handling and delivering limestone to limestone stock	2,245
Handling and delivering ore to ore stock	24,862
Interest expense	37,000
Insurance	7,800
Laboratory expenses	4,000

Limestone (45,900 tons)	45,900
Ore (248,620 tons)	621,550
Pig iron beginning inventory (6,500 tons)	97,500
Pig iron sales (109,500 tons)	1,916,500
Profit on sales of all purchased pig iron	25,500
Repairs and maintenance	15,500
Selling expenses	53,400
Sundry income	17,500
Supply stores ending inventory	25,000
Surplus beginning of year	583,887
Taxes	5,200
Yard and switching expenses	14,200

Utilize whatever is necessary of the following information:

Production of pig iron for the year was 105,000 tons. Materials consumed in this production were: coke, 210,000 tons; limestone, 40,000 tons; ore, 240,000 tons.

Accrued expenses not recorded: interest, $5,000; furnace labor, $3,600; taxes, $300.

Items paid in advance, not adjusted: interest, $4,000; insurance, $1,800.

A provision of 15 cents per ton of production is to be made for relining the furnace.

Depreciation not recorded was $43,730.

Exploration and development expenses to be written off 20%.

(New York State CPA Examination)

Problem 24–4. Purpose: *Computing Costs for a Lumber and Logging Company on a Departmental Basis*

The Indred Lumber Company submits the following data, taken from its accounting records, from which it asks you to prepare a statement of the cost of goods sold, supported by a schedule showing the cost per thousand feet of production in each department. Use a period of six months ended June 30, 19—.

The cost of the timbering rights for the period was $900.

Logging costs	$600.00
Transportation costs (of logs)	450.00
Camp expenses ($\frac{1}{2}$ logs, $\frac{1}{2}$ sawmill)	150.00
Miscellaneous charges (all logs)	54.00
Sawmill costs	502.00
Planing mill costs	204.20

The production figures for the period were:

Logs produced at the woods, per log scale	550,000 feet
Logs hauled to sawmill	410,000 feet
Sawmill production, rough lumber	290,000 feet
Dressed lumber from planing mill	58,000 feet
Slabs, and other by-products, valued at sales price	$150.00

Sales for the period were:

Rough lumber (at $9 per M)	134,000 feet
Dressed lumber (at $12 per M)	50,000 feet
Sales of slabs and by-products	$100.00

The estimated inventories on hand on June 30, 19—, were:

Logs in the woods	140,000 feet
Logs at the mill	120,000 feet
Rough lumber	98,000 feet
Dressed lumber	8,000 feet

Problem 24-5.   Purpose: *Joint Product Costs; Lumbering Concern Statements*

The Ipathan Logging Company completed its first year of logging operations on December 31, 19—. A list of balances from the company's ledger (before closing) at December 31, 19—, was as follows:

Capital stock		$4,200,000
First mortgage 7% bonds		700,000
Timber	$4,000,600	
Booming ground	9,000	
Main railroad	$309,641	
Subsidiary railroad	235,000	544,641
Logging engines, machinery, and camp equipment	703,000	
Cash in bank and on hand	23,250	
Notes in accounts receivable	113,700	
Notes and accounts payable		40,737
Furniture and fixtures — city office	2,137	
Unexpired insurance premiums	4,134	
Allowance — depreciation		72,210
Wages accrued		23,780
Property taxes accrued		59,575
Labor and expenses:		
Felling and sawing	$ 96,075	
Yarding and loading	102,460	
Scalers	8,837	
Rigging	33,273	
Hauling	135,040	
Booming and rafting	13,577	389,262
Sales		974,500
Maintenance — railroads	$ 32,015	
Maintenance — camp	4,710	36,725
Depreciation — logging engines, machinery, and camp equipment	$ 71,997	
Depreciation — city office furniture and fixtures	213	72,210
Insurance — industrial	$ 13,403	
Insurance — on equipment (fire)	8,075	21,478
Property taxes		59,575
Superintendence		11,970
Administrative salaries		19,415
Interest — on bonds	$ 49,000	
Interest — on notes payable	1,647	50,647
Fire-patrol expense		4,733
City office expense		4,325
	$6,070,802	$6,070,802

In arriving at the results of its operations for the year 19—, the company's officers had not considered depletion of timber cut for the year or the amount which should be charged to cost of operations in respect of amortization of railway construction.

The trustees for the bondholders require a statement of income for the year 19—, showing the average cost of logs cut and of logs sold; also a balance sheet as of December 31, 19—.

The following information is obtained from the records of the company. The total standing timber acquired at the inception of the company was:

	Feet	Cost per Thousand Feet	Total Cost
Yellow fir......................	700,450,000	$4.00	$2,801,800
Hemlock........................	300,200,000	1.20	360,240
Cedar...........................	48,600,000	4.00	194,400
Spruce..........................	113,915,000	4.00	455,660
Red fir..........................	75,400,000	2.50	188,500
	1,238,565,000		$4,000,600

Logs cut during the year 19—:

	Feet
Yellow fir	51,000,000
Hemlock	14,000,000
Cedar	1,800,000
Spruce	6,810,000
Red fir	2,250,000

Logs sold during the year 19—:

Yellow fir	45,400,000 ft. at $15.00 per M ft.
Hemlock	12,500,000 ft. at 12.50 per M ft.
Cedar	1,800,000 ft. at 15.00 per M ft.
Spruce	4,250,000 ft. at 18.00 per M ft.
Red fir	2,250,000 ft. at 15.00 per M ft.

During the year, the company used 100,500 feet of yellow fir for the construction of donkey sleds, which is included in the foregoing figures representing the timber cut during 19—. The cost of logs so used for construction purposes is to be added to capital expenditures at the average cost of production of all logs cut for the year, the construction labor cost thereon having been already included in the Equipment account.

The inventory of logs "in pond" as scaled (i.e., ready for sale) at December 31, 19—, was as follows:

	Feet
Yellow fir	5,499,500
Hemlock	1,500,000
Spruce	2,560,000
	9,559,500

The inventory is to be valued at the average cost of all logs cut during the year, no segregation of costs being made on the various kinds of timber cut.

In addition to the foregoing recorded cut logs, there were 500,000 feet of yellow fir logs and 500,000 feet of spruce logs lying in the woods, felled and sawed; the cost of felling and sawing such logs is included on the company's books as part of the operating expenses for the year 19—. These logs are to be valued at stumpage cost plus felling and sawing cost only, since no other costs are applicable thereto.

The railway construction is described in the accounts as *main railroad* and *subsidiary railroad*. The main railroad is a completed unit, and all the company's standing timber has to be hauled over that road as it is cut. The subsidiary railroad is not a completed unit. Its total cost is estimated to be $540,000. When completed, the standing timber to be hauled over the subsidiary railroad is 600,-000,000 feet. When the timber is all cut, both railroads are to be considered as of no further use and as having no salvage value. Of the total timber cut for the year 19—, 40,000,000 feet were cut from the standing timber adjacent to and hauled over the subsidiary railroad.

Depreciation has been provided on all plant and equipment and is to be considered adequate.

An examination of the accounts receivable disclosed worthless accounts amounting to $5,500.

From the foregoing list of balances and supplementary information prepare the statements desired by the trustees.

(AICPA Uniform Examination)

Problem 24–6.   Purpose: *Cost Cards for Flour Milling Company*

You are given the following data, taken from the records of the Illinois Milling Company:

Wheat costs (60 pounds per bushel) $1.10 per bushel. To make 1 barrel of flour, all grades requires 4.6 bushels of wheat. From this is produced:

Patent flour 70%
First clear flour 20%
Second clear flour..10%
Feed (offal)...80 pounds

One barrel of flour weighs 196 pounds.

Milling costs and selling expenses averaged $1.20 per barrel. Selling prices are:

First clear flour ....$3.00 per barrel
Second clear flour .... 1.40 per barrel
Feed...averages $14.00 per ton

Required:

a) Prepare in good form a statement showing the cost of producing a barrel of 70 percent short patent flour.

b) Prepare a cost card for 1 full barrel of 70 percent short patent flour.

c) Compute the cost of making 1 barrel of flour marketed as Grade C patent flour if it is made of 75 percent of 70 percent patent flour and 25 percent of second clear flour.

PROBLEMS—GROUP B

Problem 24–7.   Purpose: *Process Cost Problem, Brick Industry; Factory Ledger Principle*

The following information is submitted to you, showing the comparative costs of the Tower Brickyards Inc. As sometimes happens, the company used some of its own production in the building of a capital asset, namely, the additional kiln. In order to ascertain how much should be chargeable to this Kiln account, it is necessary to compute the cost of bricks manufactured. The treatment of spoiled bricks is important. It is assumed that the cost of the lost bricks must be absorbed by the good production, since spoiled bricks have no value. This firm maintains a manufacturing account known as Brickyard Operating account, in which are accumulated the costs for the period. You are asked to determine the amount that must be transferred from this account to the Kiln account as a capital expenditure. At the same time, reconstruct the Brickyard Operating account for the current year.

The costs and other information for the two years 1971 and 1972 were as follows:

	1971	1972
Inventory, January 1	$ 3,000	$ 1,000
Wages paid	9,060	15,000
Salaries	2,500	3,000
Plant expenses	4,000	14,000
Head office expenses (allocated)	1,500	2,000
Sales	20,000	10,500

The quantity production statistics for these two years were as follows:

	1971	1972
Inventory, January 1	300,000	150,000
Sales	1,600,000	900,000
Inventory, December 31	150,000	100,000
Bricks spoiled after unloading from kilns	60,000	40,000
Bricks used in building new kiln		700,000

In 1972 work was started on a new kiln by the company's own employees. The expenditures are included in the foregoing accounts. No separate payrolls or analyses were kept for the construction project. Men were put to work at various times and for part shifts. The foundations were dug in clay, and this clay was used in the brick making in the existing kilns. The wage costs per 1,000 bricks, including bricks spoiled after unloading from kilns, were assumed to be 2 percent higher in 1972 than in 1971. The following expenses should be capitalized (against Kiln account):

Salaries	$1,500
Plant expenses	9,500
Head office expenses	600

Head office expenses are assumed to be attributable to the sales.

Required:

Compute the cost per thousand bricks to the nearest cent and the cost to capitalize in the Kiln account to the nearest dollar.

Problem 24–8. Purpose: *Process Costs—Foundries; Journal Entries Ledger Accounts*

The Trafalgar Foundry and Machine Company began operations June 1 with an inventory as follows:

1. Material sufficient to manufacture 120,000 pounds of castings.
2. Steel valued at $60,000.

During the month of June, the following transactions occurred:

Foundry:

Castings to the amount of 120,000 pounds were made at an average cost of 12 cents a pound. This total quantity was disposed of as follows:
To machine shop, 50 percent, at 15 cents a pound.
To customers direct, 40 percent, at 18 cents a pound.
Defective, 10 percent—valued at 50 percent of average cost. Loss on defective work is distributed over good production in department.

Machine Shop:

Steel requisitioned during June amounted to $60,000. Direct labor and manufacturing overhead were applied here as follows:
1. Direct labor at 120 percent of total material cost, which includes cost of production transferred from foundry.
2. Manufacturing overhead at 140 percent of direct labor in machine department.

Product quantities were disposed of at cost plus 12 percent, as follows; exceptions are noted below:
1. To assembly department, 63 percent.
2. To shipping department to meet sales orders, 12 percent.
3. To storeroom, 15 percent.
4. Remaining in process, 10 percent (considered as 50 percent complete as to material, labor, and overhead).

Assembly Department:

The assembly cost of direct labor and manufacturing overhead combined equaled 22 percent of the cost of the product at this point.
Of the product received, 85 percent was completed, delivered to the shipping department, and sent out to customers. (Balance, 100 percent complete as to material, 50 percent complete as to labor and overhead.)

Shipping Department:

The expense of this department was calculated at 6 percent of the total cost up to and through the crating of the product.

Miscellaneous Expense:

Selling expenses were computed as 10 percent of the total cost to make and ship.

Profit was calculated to be 15 percent of sales price.

Required:

a)   Schedule of journal entries with complete explanations.
b)   Ledger accounts with postings keyed for ready tracing.
c)   Summary showing inventories on hand June 30.

(Adapted from New York State CPA Examination)

Problem 24–9.   Purpose: *Computation of Unit Costs; Preparation of Cost and Production Reports; Weighted Average—Foundry Cost*

The Transither Hammer Company produces an expensive line of hammers. It operates its own handle department and a foundry department to produce the hammer heads. Assembly and finishing is a separate department.

In the foundry department, equal parts, by weight, of pig iron and coke, together with special alloy materials, are introduced into a furnace where the materials are reduced to molten metal which is poured into molds. The day's work in the foundry is as follows:

1.   Remove and clean the heads cast on the previous day.
2.   Set the molds for the current day's melt.
3.   Load and "burn" the melt for the day.
4.   Pour the metal into the molds.

One fourth of the labor cost is estimated to be applicable to step number 1.

In the assembly and finishing department, the hammer heads are finished and the handles inserted. Handles are frequently spoiled in the process. Finished hammers are transferred to the stock room immediately.

On October 1, 19—, there was no inventory of any kind in the foundry department. During October, 20,000 heads were completed and transferred to the assembly and finishing department. At the end of the month 1,500 good cleaned heads were on hand in the foundry and 1,000 heads had been poured on the last day. A total of 22 tons of pig iron, coke, and alloy materials costing $1,248 were placed in production. Direct labor costs for the month amounted to $4,380. Indirect costs were applied at 30 percent of direct labor cost. A hammer head weighs one pound. An average of 10 percent of the heads poured are not perfect and are remelted.

On October 1 there were 400 hammer heads in the assembly and finishing department on which no work had been done. Their cost was $128.24. There were no handles on hand. During October 20,000 handles costing $9,876 were received in this department. All of the handles were used in completing 19,800 finished hammers. Labor cost amounted to $1,834, and indirect costs to $1,252.

Required:

Prepare departmental cost and production reports showing unit production costs and the assignment of these costs to interdepartmental transfers or inventories for the month of October, 19—, for the foundry department and the assembly and finishing department. The company uses weighted average cost in its accounts. Unit cost computations should be carried to five decimal places.

(Uniform AICPA Examination)

Problem 24–10.   Purpose: *Cost Accounting for a Lumbering Company; Treatment of Joint Costs*

The Theodore Lumber Company purchases hardwood logs from a logging company and manufactures these into certain kinds of lumber. The products are classified into three grades: Superior, Supreme, and Special. The raw material is in the form of logs which are purchased at flat prices for large lots. These lots may include logs from which two or more grades of lumber are produced. Inventories of each grade of finished lumber are carried at cost. Cost of sales for each grade is computed on the basis of the *average* cost of the opening inventories and the monthly production costs. Costs of production are apportioned to the three grades of lumber on the basis of sales value.

The cost and accounting data taken from the records showed the following:

Item	Inventory 1/1/— Quantity (feet)	Inventory 1/1/— Value	Sales Quantity (feet)	Sales Value	Inventory 12/31/— Quantity (feet)	Inventory 12/31/— Value
Superior grade 250,000	250,000	$5,000	130,000	$4,160	150,000	
Supreme grade.............300,000	300,000	5,100	250,000	6,500	180,000	
Special grade 380,000	380,000	5,700	210,000	4,200	200,000	
Raw material—logs.......		9,000				$18,000
Supplies.....................		2,000				1,800

Other transactions for the year were:

Logs purchased, cost $12,000; supplies purchased, $800; mill salaries and wages, $2,000; other mill expenses, $650; sales department salaries and expenses, $1,200; general and administrative expenses, $500. All work put into process was completed during the period.

Required:

You are asked to prepare a statement of the sales, cost of sales, and gross profit by each of the three grades of lumber. Compute the cost per thousand feet of lumber, correct to two decimal places. Also prepare a condensed statement of income and expenses.

(Adapted from New York State CPA Examination)

Problem 24–11.   Purpose: *Lumbering Costs*

The following trial balance of the Tricontinental Lumber Company, dated December 31, 19—, is submitted.

	Debit	Credit
Cash in banks and on hand ....$	45,900	
Accounts receivable – customers................................	75,650	
Reserve for freight allowances....................................		$ 4,300
Allowance for doubtful accounts		3,500
Standing timber – Tract 1...	1,200,000	
Standing timber – Tract 2...	500,000	
Allowance for depletion – Tract 1...............................		70,500
Lumber inventory, December 31, 19 –	80,000	
Logs in pond, December 31, 19 –	1,250	
Material and stores inventory, December 31, 19 –	7,500	
Land..	5,000	
Buildings and structures...	47,000	
Machinery and equipment...	140,000	
Transportation equipment	175,000	
Allowance for depreciation...		28,710
Prepaid insurance and taxes	4,310	
Accounts payable..		11,850
Accrued wages..		4,750
Capital stock – 6 percent preferred, noncumulative, $100 par..		1,200,000
Capital stock – common, $5 par		900,000
Sales of lumber		565,000
Manufacturing cost of lumber sold..............................	398,000	
Shipping expenses of finished lumber	50,000	
Selling expenses..	30,500	
General and administrative expenses	28,500	
	$2,788,610	$2,788,610

The company began business on January 1, 19 –, with a capital of $2,100,-000, representing cash received for 12,000 preferred shares of $100 each and 180,000 common shares of $5 each. Two uncut timber tracts and the necessary land, buildings, and equipment to carry on a lumber business were purchased. An independent cruise showed an estimate of 400,000,000 and 250,000,000 board feet (log scale) on Tracts 1 and 2, respectively, as available for cutting.

The company valued its closing inventories of finished lumber and logs in pond at average cost per thousand feet produced during the year, irrespective of grades. These inventories, the production for the year, and the selling prices per 1,000 feet prevailing during the year are shown in Illustration 24–14.

Material and stores were correctly valued at the lower of cost or market.

The company used 100,000 feet of its Grade D lumber in the building of a storehouse and charged $2,000 to the Building and Structures account.

The cost data covering the year's operations were extracted from the records as shown in Illustration 24–15.

The reserves for freight allowances and doubtful accounts appear adequate. The fixed asset accounts have been verified, adequate depreciation has been provided, and all ascertainable liabilities outstanding at December 31, 19 –, had been brought upon the books as of that date.

Prepaid insurance and taxes include a charge of $2,500 representing the year's real estate taxes applicable to Tract No. 2. Logging operations will not commence on this tract until several years hence.

Illustration 24—14

Grade	M Feet Board Measure		Selling Price per M Feet
	Inventory	Production	
A................................	600	7,200	$35
B................................	500	6,000	30
C................................	400	4,800	25
D................................	1,600	3,600	20
E................................	600	1,800	15
F................................	300	600	10
	4,000	24,000	
	M Feet Log Scale		
Logs in pond......................	100	23,500	

Illustration 24—15

	Amount	Per M Feet Log Scale	M Feet
Logging operations:			23,500 log scale
Stumpage....................	$ 70,500.00	$ 3.00	
Cutting.....................	47,000.00	2.00	
Skidding....................	23,500.00	1.00	
Spur tracks.................	23,500.00	1.00	
Railroad operation...........	47,000.00	2.00	
	$211,500.00	$ 9.00	
Loading operations:			
Loading to lighters..........	$ 23,500.00	$ 1.00	
Towing to mill..............	58,750.00	2.50	
	$ 82,250.00	$ 3.50	
	$293,750.00	$12.50	
Less: Logs in pond 12/31/—.....	1,250.00		100 log scale
	$292,500.00		23,400 log scale
Over-run on basis of actual board measure......................	....		600
Cost of logs to sawmill..........	$292,500.00	$12.1875	24,000 board measure
Mill operations:			
Unloading at mill.............	$ 31,500.00	$ 1.3125	
Sawmill.....................	96,000.00	4.00	
Sorting shed.................	24,000.00	1.00	
Lumber yard.................	36,000.00	1.50	
	$187,500.00	$ 7.8125	
Total cost of production...	$480,000.00	$20.0000	24,000 board measure

Required:

a) A balance sheet as at December 31, 19—, showing the closing inventory of finished lumber valued by apportioning the production costs to the several grades on the basis of their sales values.

b) A statement of income for the year ended on that date.

State briefly why the aforestated method of inventory valuation should be used. Income tax features in connection with this problem are to be ignored.

(Uniform AICPA Examination)

Problem 24–12.   Purpose: *Cost Cards and Production for a Flour Milling Company*

From the books of the Transton Mills, Inc., the following information is taken as of the end of the first year of operations:

Sales:

Grade A patent flour (90%) ....   300,000 sacks, 98 lbs. each, at $5.00 each
Clear flour (10%) ....   30,000 sacks, 98 lbs. each, at $1.25 each
Feed...120,000 sacks, 98 lbs. each, at $18.00 a ton

Purchases of wheat, including commission, freight, etc., 1,200,000 bushels at $1.30 per bushel (60 pounds per bushel).

Milling costs, including sacks, were $90,000, for which 1,000,000 bushels of wheat were ground. Four and one-half bushels of wheat make 1 barrel of flour, all grades, and 74 pounds of feed (offal). One barrel contains 2 sacks.

The closing market prices of the various products at the end of the year were:

Wheat delivered at mill ....$ 1.40 per bu.
Clear flour (10%) .... 1.25 per sack
Feed...averaged 20.00 per ton

Required:

Using this information you are asked to prepare:

a) Cost card per barrel of 90 percent Grade A patent flour.

b) Cost card per barrel for special patent Grade B flour if it is composed of 75 percent Grade A patent flour and 25 percent clear flour.

c) Statement showing gross profit on sale of Grade A patent flour.

Problem 24–13.   Purpose: *Process Costs—Milling Flour Concern; Inventories; Statements*

The Tionto Milling Company, located at Mill Bury, shows the following data for a fiscal year:

Wheat bought from farmers at the elevator door, 1,050,000 bushels at an average of $1.35 per bushel.

Wheat purchased on option amounted to 150,000 bushels at $1.50 FOB Hamilton, from which point freight to Mill Bury is 18 cents per bushel.

Sales:

Patent flour	149,000 bbls., average $10,		$1,490,000
Clear flour	49,700 bbls., average	6,	298,200
Middlings	3,730 tons, average	22,	82,060
Bran	4,970 tons, average	12,	59,640
Screenings	1,500 tons, average	6,	9,000

All, except screenings, sold FOB at port of export, through brokers who received commissions on:

Flour .... $0.50 per bbl.
Middlings .... 1.00 per ton
Bran .... 0.50 per ton

Screenings are sold in bulk at mill door; all other products are sacked. Sacks for the year are purchased or contracted for at:

Flour .... all 98 lb. at $150 per M, 500,000 sacks
Middlings .... all 100 lb. at 120 per M, 100,000 sacks
Bran .... all 100 lb. at   98 per M, 125,000 sacks

Freight to the port at 70 cents per barrel on flour and $3 per ton on feed. The mill record shows production:

Wheat ground .... 1,000,000 bu.
Patent flour .... 150,000 bbls.
Clear flour .... 50,000 bbls.
Middlings .... 3,750 tons
Bran .... 5,000 tons
Screenings .... 1,500 tons
Millings expense $90,000

The appurtenant elevator shows an expense account of $41,500, which is divided in the proportion of 3 cents per bushel for wheat stored and 1 cent per bushel for transfer to mill.

There is no opening inventory to consider, but the closing market prices are:

Wheat .... FOB Mill Bury, elevator siding, $1.40
Clear flour .... FOB port, $5.50 per barrel, sacked
Middlings .... FOB port, $21.00 per ton, sacked
Bran .... FOB port, $11.00 per ton, sacked

All wheat is 60 pounds per bushel.

Flour is 196 pounds per barrel. Each barrel contains 2 sacks.

The grind is at an average of 5 bushels per barrel, and the flour produced is 75 percent patent and 25 percent clear.

Loss in grinding is one half of 1 percent.

The company has unfilled sales orders for 31,000 barrels of patent flour at an average price of $9.50 FOB port, sacked, subject to brokerage charge hereinbefore stated.

Required:

a) Set up closing inventory from data given.
b) Prepare trading and manufacturing statement, assuming all storage costs are treated as a current period manufacturing overhead cost.
c) Prepare statement showing profit and loss in futures.
   Carry computations to the nearest correct seventh decimal.

(New York State CPA Examination)

appendix

appendix

Program of Cost
Reports for Control

The following pages illustrate the reports used by a large textile manufacturing company and supplement the discussion given in the chapter
on managerial reports (pages 617–39). This plan is so comprehensive
and practical that it is given in detail for its instructional value.

Report No. 1

STATEMENT OF OPERATIONS

SALES DIVISION		
	Amounts	Detailed Rept. No.
Sales:		
Gross sales.................................	$334,326.00	2
Less: Returns and allowances	2,275.00*	3
Net sales......................................	$332,051.00	
Cost of sales:		
Standard cost of net sales......................	289,237.00*	
Gross profit	$ 42,814.00	4
Selling expenses...............................	32,044.00*	5 and 6
Trading profit.................................	$ 10,770.00	
MANUFACTURING DIVISION		
Variations from standard costs:		
Price variations:		
Raw materials.......................$6,859.00		
Manufacturing materials.............. 1,384.00	$ 8,243.00	7
Usage variations—raw materials.........$1,408.00*	1,408.00*	8
Cost variations:		
Labor............................$ 981.00		
Manufacturing materials.............. 1,331.00*		
Burden 6,415.00	6,065.00	9 and 10
Damages:		
Finished damages produced $8,654.00*		
Less: Damages sold.................. 5,909.00	2,745.00*	11
Operating profit.................................	$ 20,925.00	

*Denotes red figures.

THE A. B. C. MANUFACTURING COMPANY
OPERATING REPORTS—MAY, 19—

Report No. 2

SALES ANALYSIS

Product No.	Quota	Sales	Per Cent of Quota
1............................	$ 60,000.00	$ 67,324.00	112
2............................	30,000.00	25,833.00	86
3............................	30,000.00	36,325.00	121
4............................	40,000.00	39,823.00	99½
5............................	10,000.00	7,039.00	70
6............................	120,000.00	144,012.00	120
7............................	10,000.00	13,970.00	140
Total.....................	$300,000.00	$334,326.00	111 (av.)

Report No. 3

RETURNS AND ALLOWANCES ANALYSIS

Reason	No. of Credits	Amount
Damaged...................................	97	$ 273.00
Mismated................................	3	37.00
Off color................................	18	339.00
Short Length	7	229.00
Error in shipping...........................	8	394.00
Order duplicated	2	167.00
Returned by permission.....................	8	162.00
Error in billing...........................	3	64.00
Freight allowances.........................	13	98.00
Price allowances	8	27.00
C.O.D.'s returned.........................	2	125.00
Late delivery	9	360.00
Total...............................	178	$2,275.00

Report No. 4

THE A. B. C. MANUFACTURING COMPANY
OPERATING REPORTS—MAY, 19—
GROSS PROFIT ANALYSIS

	Net Sales		Gross Profit	
	Amount	% of Total	Amount	% of Sales
Retail:				
Product No. 1	$ 30,090.00	9.1	$ 5,872.00	19.5
Product No. 2	11,546.00	3.5	2,364.00	20.4
Product No. 3	16,235.00	4.9	2,967.00	18.3
Product No. 4	17,798.00	5.4	3,298.00	18.5
Product No. 5	3,146.00	0.9	600.00	19.1
Product No. 6	64,365.00	19.4	12,167.00	18.9
Product No. 7	6,244.00	1.9	525.00	8.4
	$149,424.00	45.1	$27,793.00	18.6
Wholesale:				
Product No. 1	23,403.00	7.0	2,162.00	9.2
Product No. 2	8,980.00	2.7	843.00	9.4
Product No. 3	12,627.00	3.8	1,205.00	9.5
Product No. 4	13,843.00	4.2	1,162.00	8.4
Product No. 5	2,447.00	0.7	264.00	10.8
Product No. 6	50,062.00	15.1	4,867.00	9.7
Product No. 7	4,856.00	1.5	305.00	6.3
	$116,218.00	35.0	$10,808.00	9.3
Catalogue and chain stores:				
Product No. 1	13,373.00	4.0	864.00	6.5
Product No. 2	5,130.00	1.5	303.00	5.9
Product No. 3	7,216.00	2.2	450.00	6.2
Product No. 4	7,910.00	2.4	488.00	6.2
Product No. 5	1,398.00	0.4	118.00	8.4
Product No. 6	28,607.00	8.6	1,843.00	6.4
Product No. 7	2,775.00	0.8	147.00	5.3
	$ 66,409.00	19.9	$ 4,213.00	6.3
Total	$332,051.00	100.0 (av.)	$42,814.00	12.9 (av.)

THE A. B. C. MANUFACTURING COMPANY
OPERATING REPORTS—MAY, 19—

Report No. 5

SELLING EXPENSE ANALYSIS

Item	Summary			
	Budget	Actual	Over	Under
Salesmen:				
Travel expenses............	$ 5,000.00	$ 4,664.00		$ 336.00
Salaries and commissions.....	10,843.00	10,557.00		286.00
Social security tax..........	284.00	278.00		6.00
Sales offices:				
New York*	2,367.00	2,451.00	$ 84.00	
Chicago.................	308.00	278.00		30.00
Los Angeles..............	1,173.00	1,263.00	90.00	
General:				
Advertising..............	5,000.00	5,000.00		
Samples.................	973.00	1,065.00	92.00	
Conventions.............	2,373.00	1,992.00		381.00
Management:				
Travel expenses...........	300.00	282.00		18.00
Salaries.................	4,167.00	4,214.00	47.00	
Total..............	$32,788.00	$32,044.00	$313.00	$1,057.00

*See sample departmental report No. 6.

Report No. 6

SELLING EXPENSE ANALYSIS—NEW YORK OFFICE

Item	Budget	Actual	Over	Under
Salaries:				
Floor salesmen............	$ 605.00	$ 600.00		$ 5.00
Office....................	750.00	750.00		
Social security tax.........	39.00	37.00		2.00
Rent......................	677.00	677.00		
Light.....................	55.00	50.00		5.00
Repairs...................	25.00	36.00	$11.00	
Stationery.................	20.00	15.00		5.00
Entertaining...............	100.00	190.00	90.00	
Depreciation..............	80.00	80.00		
Insurance.................	10.00	10.00		
Taxes.....................	6.00	6.00		
Total.................	$2,367.00	$2,451.00	$101.00	$17.00

THE A. B. C. MANUFACTURING COMPANY
OPERATING REPORTS—MAY, 19—

Report No. 7

PRICE VARIATIONS—MATERIALS

	Standard Price	Actual Price	Quantity Purchased	Total Value at Standard	Total Value at Actual	Price Variations
Raw Material:						
Warp yarn:						
10/2 carded............	$0.28	$0.248	54,136	$15,158.00	$13,426.00	$1,732.00
20/2 carded............	0.31	0.30	10,051	3,116.00	3,015.00	101.00
30/2 carded............	0.36	0.355	25,628	9,226.00	9,098.00	128.00
40/2 combed...........	0.50	0.41	2,107	1,054.00	864.00	190.00
Spool yarn:						
20/2 carded............	0.31	0.245	39,371	12,205.00	9,646.00	2,559.00
30/2 carded............	0.36	0.355	60,033	21,612.00	21,312.00	300.00
40/2 combed...........	0.50	0.41	5,003	2,502.00	2,051.00	451.00
50/2 combed...........	0.55	0.46	3,531	1,942.00	1,624.00	318.00
60/2 combed...........	0.60	0.52	5,362	3,217.00	2,788.00	429.00
70/2 combed...........	0.72	0.64	893	621.00	572.00	49.00
Bobbin yarn:						
80/2 combed...........	0.95	0.92	14,780	14,041.00	13,598.00	443.00
90/2 combed...........	1.06	1.03	1,891	2,004.00	1,948.00	56.00
100/2 combed...........	1.19	1.16	1,849	2,200.00	2,145.00	55.00
110/2 combed...........	1.45	1.40	974	1,412.00	1,364.00	48.00
Manufacturing materials:						
Boxes................	0.039	0.033	38,901	1,551.00	1,284.00	267.00
Cartons...............	0.203	0.181	4,927	1,001.00	891.00	110.00
Cellophane............	0.01	0.0077	16,000	160.00	123.00	37.00
Cord and twine........	0.38	0.305	205	78.00	63.00	15.00
Dyes.................	0.20	0.167	14,445	2,889.00	2,412.00	477.00
Envelopes.............	0.0056	0.0052	171,200	959.00	890.00	69.00
Paper.................	0.091	0.043	208	19.00	9.00	10.00
Soap.................	0.08	0.056	13,320	1,066.00	746.00	320.00
Tape.................	1.64	1.48	118	193.00	175.00	18.00
Thread...............	0.565	0.501	953	539.00	478.00	61.00
Total..............	....	....	....	$98,765.00	$90,522.00	$8,243.00

THE A. B. C. MANUFACTURING COMPANY
OPERATING REPORTS—MAY, 19—

Report No. 8

USAGE VARIATIONS—RAW MATERIALS

Loom No.	Standard Cost Allowance, Including Waste	Actual Usage at Standard Prices	Usage Variation	Per Cent of Standard
1...........	$ 4,006.00	$ 3,993.00	$ 13.00	99.7
2...........	4,137.00	4,298.00	161.00*	103.9
3...........	4,692.00	4,623.00	69.00	98.5
4...........	3,675.00	3,856.00	181.00*	104.9
5...........	4,322.00	4,592.00	270.00*	106.2
6...........	3,684.00	3,713.00	29.00*	100.7
7...........	5,003.00	4,967.00	36.00	99.3
8...........	4,751.00	4,683.00	68.00	98.5
9...........	3,573.00	3,693.00	120.00*	103.4
10...........	3,798.00	3,903.00	105.00*	102.8
11...........	3,674.00	3,715.00	41.00*	101.1
12...........	3,916.00	4,003.00	87.00*	102.2
13...........	4,875.00	4,822.00	53.00	98.9
14...........	5,163.00	5,101.00	62.00	98.8
15...........	4,572.00	4,730.00	158.00*	103.5
16...........	4,564.00	4,673.00	109.00*	102.3
17...........	5,003.00	5,180.00	177.00*	103.5
18...........	4,738.00	4,862.00	124.00*	102.6
19...........	3,786.00	3,973.00	187.00*	104.9
20...........	4,803.00	4,763.00	40.00	99.1
Total.....	$86,735.00	$88,143.00	$1,408.00*	101.6 (av.)

*Denotes red figures.

THE A. B. C. MANUFACTURING COMPANY
OPERATING REPORTS—MAY, 19—

ANALYSIS OF COST VARIATIONS BY COST CENTERS

	Standard Cost	Actual Cost	Cost Variations	Cause of Variations			Foremen's Budget	
				Level of Operations	Management Changes	Foremen's Efficiency	Budget Allowance	% of Actual of Budget
Service cost centers:								
Boiler	$ 6,196.00	$ 5,550.00	$ 646.00	$ 302.00	$ 60.00*	$ 404.00	$ 5,954.00	93.2
Power	2,343.00	2,144.00	199.00	152.00	40.00*	87.00	2,231.00	96.1
Plant and building	2,649.00	2,231.00	418.00	164.00	47.00*	301.00	2,532.00	88.1
Machine	2,097.00	1,326.00	771.00	132.00	52.00*	691.00	2,017.00	65.7
Trucking	587.00	687.00	100.00*	40.00	....	140.00*	547.00	125.6
Design	5,260.00	5,099.00	161.00	203.00	123.00*	81.00	5,180.00	98.4
Pattern	4,660.00	3,958.00	702.00	286.00	140.00*	556.00	4,514.00	87.7
General adminis-tration	28,305.00	27,206.00	1,099.00	447.00	240.00*	892.00	28,098.00	96.8
Total	$ 52,097.00	$ 48,201.00	$3,896.00	$1,726.00	$ 702.00*	$2,872.00	$ 51,073.00	94.4 (av.)
Transferred to productive cost centers	52,097.00*	48,201.00*	3,896.00*					
Productive cost centers:								
Yarn preparation†	4,440.00	4,250.00	190.00	220.00	64.00*	34.00	4,284.00	99.2
Bobbin	7,760.00	7,409.00	351.00	308.00	101.00*	144.00	7,553.00	98.1
Warp	1,594.00	1,395.00	199.00	137.00	45.00*	107.00	1,502.00	92.9
Weaving	55,509.00	50,875.00	4,634.00	2,300.00	300.00*	2,634.00	53,509.00	95.1
Mending	3,375.00	3,331.00	44.00	228.00	15.00*	169.00*	3,162.00	105.3
Bleach	4,733.00	4,541.00	192.00	270.00	....	78.00*	4,463.00	101.7
Dress	16,876.00	17,546.00	670.00*	320.00	200.00*	790.00*	16,756.00	104.7
Cutting and splitting	17,056.00	16,891.00	165.00	350.00	226.00*	41.00	16,932.00	99.8
Finishing	17,835.00	17,597.00	238.00	393.00	37.00*	118.00*	17,479.00	100.7
Wrap and label	9,675.00	9,594.00	81.00	364.00	122.00*	161.00*	9,433.00	101.7
Stockroom	6,011.00	5,370.00	641.00	260.00	....	381.00	5,751.00	93.3
Grand total	$144,864.00	$138,799.00	$6,065.00	$5,150.00	$1,110.00*	$2,025.00	$140,824.00	98.6 (av.)

*Denotes red figures.
†See departmental report No. 10.

THE A. B. C. MANUFACTURING COMPANY
OPERATING REPORTS—MAY, 19—

FOREMEN'S BUDGET
Report No. 10   YARN PREPARATION COST CENTER

	Budget Allowance	Actual Cost	Over Budget	Under Budget
Labor:				
Winding spool yarn............	$1,307.00	$1,241.00		$ 66.00
Winding warp yarn............	172.00	139.00		33.00
Winding bobbin yarn...........	125.00	125.00		
Backwinding...................	85.00	85.00		
Stripping.....................	50.00	50.00		
Materials:				
Paper........................	4.00	2.00		2.00
Sizing.......................	35.00	40.00	$ 5.00	
Burden:				
Supervision..................	290.00	364.00	74.00	
Handling.....................	331.00	229.00		102.00
Repairs......................	42.00	21.00		21.00
Depreciation.................	470.00	429.00		41.00
Insurance....................	25.00	23.00		2.00
Taxes........................	228.00	229.00	1.00	
Share of boiler..............	132.00	124.00		8.00
Share of power...............	117.00	116.00		1.00
Share of plant and building.......	209.00	186.00		23.00
Share of general administration	818.00	847.00	29.00	
Total.....................	$4,440.00	$4,250.00	$109.00	$299.00

A. B. C. MANUFACTURING COMPANY
OPERATING REPORTS—MAY, 19—

Report No. 11

ANALYSIS OF FINISHED PRODUCTS
DAMAGED IN COURSE OF MANUFACTURING OPERATIONS

Loom No.	Standard Cost Value of Production	Weaving Damages		Finish Damages		Total Damages
		Value	% of Production	Value	% of Production	% of Production
1......	$ 13,700.00	$ 300.00*	2.2			2.2
2......	13,963.00	315.00*	2.3			2.3
3......	14,573.00	573.00*	3.9	$ 200.00*	1.4	5.3
4......	13,273.00	402.00*	3.0	168.00*	1.3	4.3
5......	14,007.00	296.00*	2.1	28.00*	0.2	2.3
6......	13,566.00	250.00*	1.8	96.00*	0.7	2.5
7......	14,500.00	266.00*	1.8			1.8
8......	14,473.00	403.00*	2.8			2.8
9......	13,109.00	294.00*	2.2	72.00*	0.5	2.7
10......	13,342.00	180.00*	1.3	156.00*	1.2	2.5
11......	12,973.00	216.00*	1.7	307.00*	2.4	4.1
12......	13,496.00	223.00*	1.7	62.00*	0.5	2.2
13......	14,750.00	329.00*	2.2	218.00*	1.5	3.7
14......	14,896.00	287.00*	1.9	162.00*	1.1	3.0
15......	13,921.00	104.00*	0.7	107.00*	0.7	1.4
16......	14,377.00	502.00*	3.5	204.00*	1.4	4.9
17......	14,502.00	490.00*	3.4	152.00*	1.0	4.4
18......	14,042.00	360.00*	2.6	117.00*	0.8	3.4
19......	13,462.00	200.00*	1.5			1.5
20......	13,723.00	510.00*	3.7	105.00*	0.8	4.5
Total..	$278,648.00	$6,500.00*	2.3 (av.)	$2,154.00*	0.8 (av.)	3.1 (av.)
Total damages...						$8,654.00

*Denotes red figures.

IDLE MACHINE REPORT
DEPARTMENT #106 CUTTING

For month ending July 31, 19—
Foreman: A. B. Howard

Machine No.	Standard Hours	Actual Hours			Idle Hours							% of Standard	Burden Rate for Idle Time	Cost of Idle Time	Remarks
		Regular	Overtime	Total	No Operator	No Materials	Repairs	Awaiting Setup	Awaiting Tools	Awaiting Instructions	Total				
C-102	160	160		160											O.K.
C-103	160	150		150		10					10	6.25	$3.10	$31.00	Material held up in drilling dept.
C-104	160	160		160											
F-110	160	140		140				20			20	12.5	1.80	36.00	Improper scheduling.
F-111	130	160	15	175									1.80	27.00*	To make up loss of Mach. #110.
F-112	130	125		130					3	2	5	3.85	1.80	9.00	Job instructions not on hand.
Total	900	895	15	915		10		20	3	2	35	2.77		49.00	

* Credit for overtime.

index

index

M

Machine hours method of applying
  overhead, 305
  with supplementary rate, 305
Maintenance costs, computerized, 429
Management decisions
  additional volumes, 716
  cost accounting systems, 616, 710
  equipment replacement, 723
  make-or-buy, 728
  sell or process further, 729
  shutdown of plant, 721
  spoilage, 238
Management reports
  illustrated, 622
  importance, 617
  integrated data processing, 635
  objectives, 619
  scope of, 620
  types, 623
Managerial control, 10
  controllable overhead reports, 362
  flexible budgets, 323, 447
  idle machinery report, 363
  inventories, 241, 422
  labor costs, 252
  manufacturing overhead, 359–62
  material accounting, 205
  payroll costs, 257
  of production, 213
  spoilage, 238
Managerial implications
  in cost accounting, 4
  in estimated costs, 479
  in problems, 710
Manufacturing overhead, actual, 336
  classification, 337
  departmentalization of, 341–47
  diagrammatic summary of accounting,
    360
  recording of, 337–41
  special problems of, 350–53
  subsidiary ledger of, 339–41
Manufacturing overhead, applied, 316
Manufacturing overhead, budget, 459–65
Manufacturing overhead rates
  departmentalization, 308
  interim change of, 307
  using more than one, 306
Manufacturing overhead, variations
  budget, 562
  capacity, 560
  efficiency, 560
  interpretation, 560
  recording, 586–88
Margin of safety, 688
Marginal income, 688

Market value basis of prorating costs,
  169–71
Matching costs and revenues, 649
Material cost control
  forms used, 189
  functional cycle of, 187
  nature of, 186
  organization chart of, 188
  personnel of, 189
Material cost standards, 528
  illustrated, 529
  quantity, 526
Material cost variations, 530–31
Material costs
  debatable, 239
  tabulated summary of, 242–44
Material mix variations, 532
Material price variations, 583
Material quantity variations, 584
Materials handling charges, 199
Materials issued
  accounting for, 217
  cost accounting for, 213
  costs, 32
  departmentally, 111
  diagram of, 219
  forms for, 22–25, 214
  procedural analysis, 216
Materials purchased, 189–91
Materials used
  accounting for, 217
  costing, 218–26
  diagrammed, 219
  forms of, 214
  procedural analysis, 216
  standards of, 584
Mechanizing cost accounting work, 279
Memorandum standard costs, 581
Moving average inventory pricing, 224
Multiple piece rates, effect on standards,
  538
Multiple products
  classification of, 167
  costs, 171
  federal income tax regulations, 176
  initial department, 98
  one raw material, 98, 99–103
  prorating costs, 168–69
Municipal costs, 753–60

N

Nature of cost accounting, 3
Nonmanufacturing costs, 743–61
Normal operating conditions, 298
Normal standards, 523

O

Office costs, 752
Obsolete inventory valuation, 226